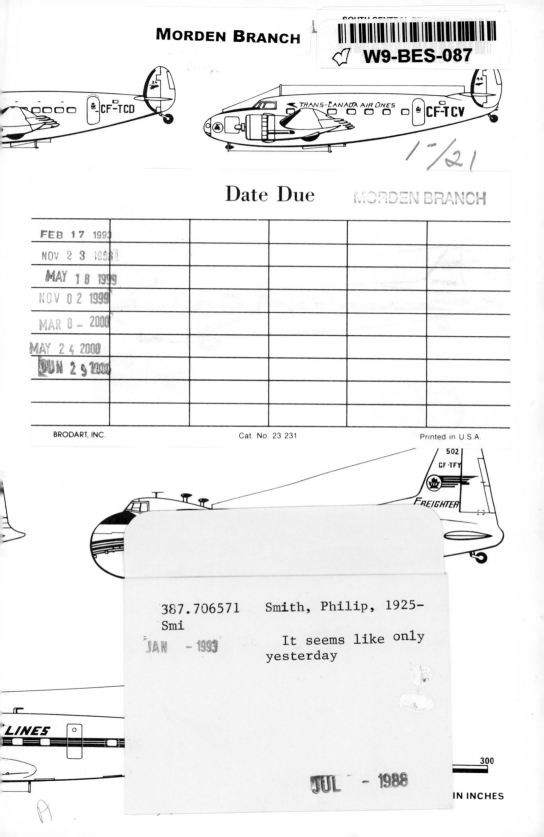

CF-TCD

TRANS-CANADA AIR LINES   CF-TCV

1 - /21

Date Due

MORDEN BRANCH

FEB 17 1993				
NOV 2 3 1998				
MAY 1 8 1999				
NOV 0 2 1999				
MAR 8 - 2000				
MAY 2 4 2000				
JUN 2 9 2000				

502
CF-TFY

FREIGHTER

LINES

300

IN INCHES

IT SEEMS
LIKE ONLY
YESTERDAY

IT SEEMS LIKE ONLY YESTERDAY

PHILIP SMITH

AIR CANADA
THE FIRST 50 YEARS

McCLELLAND AND STEWART

McClelland and Stewart Limited
The Canadian Publishers
25 Hollinger Road
Toronto, Ontario
M4B 3G2

Unless otherwise indicated, photographs are from the Air Canada Historical collection.

CANADIAN CATALOGUING IN PUBLICATION DATA

Smith, Philip, 1925–
  It seems like only yesterday

Includes index
ISBN 0-7710-8211-8 (bound). – ISBN 0-7710-8212-6 (pbk.)

1. Air Canada – History. I. Title.

HE9815.A95S54 1986   387.7′065′71   C85-099840-9

Endpapers by Peter Mossman

Printed and bound in Canada by Friesen Printers

IT SEEMS
LIKE ONLY
YESTERDAY

INTRODUCTION

As a youngster in the mid-thirties I used to take off from Winnipeg bright and early in the morning and fly to Norway House, the old Hudson's Bay post about 300 miles away at the north end of Lake Winnipeg. Unload, refuel and return to Winnipeg, where we had to be safely down before dark. It made for a pretty long day. In 1960, I flew the DC-8 making TCA's first trans-continental jet flight from Montreal to Vancouver. We crossed Winnipeg at about 35,000 feet – and I could see the north end of Lake Winnipeg out of the window.

 HE WORDS ARE THOSE of H.W. "Herb" Seagrim, a bush pilot who rose through the ranks to become executive vice-president of Air Canada. They illustrate an experience shared in some way by all the enthusiastic young men and women who joined Canada's national airline in its formative years and spent their working lives caught up in a technological revolution that changed the whole world.

On land, the origin of the wheel is lost in antiquity, and centuries of experiment and discovery separated the chariots of Rome from the first clanking "horseless carriage." On sea, the same slow acquisition of knowledge governed the progression from rafts and dug-out canoes, through the galleys and galleons of later years, to the *Queen Mary* and the mammoth super-tankers that followed in her wake.

In contrast, the aeroplane came of age in a mere puff of time. The great leap forward and upward from the Wright brothers to today's Jumbo jets was accomplished within a normal life span: an eight-year-old boy in knickerbockers, had there been one lucky enough to have watched that first heavier-than-air flight at Kitty Hawk in 1903, could have cheered the achievement of Charles Lindbergh in his early manhood and celebrated his retirement by flying to Europe himself in a mere six hours.

Air Canada was in the forefront of that revolution – the novelist John Masters once called it "the shrinkage of the earth, the inescapable, irreversible compression of all people into one world." And the evolution was just beginning to gather momentum in 1937, when the Canadian government set up what it originally called Trans-Canada Air Lines. By then, the aeroplane had already demonstrated its worth in Canada: bush pilots employed by the largest flying company in the country at the time, Canadian Airways, flew 5.7 million pounds of freight in 1934 – almost as much as all the United States airlines and Britain's Imperial Airways combined. But there were only a few scattered and unconnected passenger services, and the train was still the only way people and mail could cross the country clear from one side to the other.

Transportation has always been central to a people's prosperity, and even to the spread of civilization itself. So it was this yawning gap in the Canadian communications system that the government of the day set out to fill – with some urgency, since there were moves afoot in both the United States and Britain to jostle Canada aside into the role of junior partner in the coming air age. Since the country had not yet freed itself from the cold grip of the Depression, and since the establishment of a national airline was after all a government incursion into what had hitherto been the preserve of private, and particularly adventurous, enterprisers, considerable political controversy might have been expected to attend its birth. But the expected muttering about the criminal folly of "socialist experiments" was far outweighed by a sense of excitement and national pride: aviation was the wave of the future and Canada was entering the Big Leagues.

Nor was there much grumbling when the government chose a small group of Americans to launch the new company: after all, the United States had at least a ten-year lead on this country in civil aviation, and the men who came to TCA were acknowledged to be among the best in the business. They were welcomed and admired by the eager young Canadians who lined up to join the infant corporation, some of whom came back from good jobs in Europe and the United States to be sure of getting in on the ground floor. Proud to be in the vanguard of something really big, the young Canadians took the best their American bosses had to offer – and in future years improved on it. From the start, only the best was good enough for TCA, and those early recruits, Americans and Canadians alike, set standards of service, performance, and above all safety, that remain among the highest in the world.

The pioneers started out with a "fleet" consisting of two ten-passenger "airliners" and a tiny single-engined biplane fresh from a tour of crop-dusting, purchased for the grand total of $169,176 and 72 cents. (A Jumbo jet today costs more than $70 million.) Starting an airline from scratch, they were in a sense learning on the job. Many of the problems they faced were technical ones common to all airlines at that stage in the development of aviation, but TCA also had some problems unique to Canada and imposed by our geography: our huge distances; the sparsity of population in the great spaces between the major cities; the barrier of the Rockies; and some of the worst flying weather in the world. One by one, as the science of aviation evolved everywhere, these problems were overcome; indeed, TCA pioneered in the solution of many of them, and in so doing forged a pride and team spirit that became the envy of many a less fortunate organization.

The upward path to success, of course, is always strewn with obstacles. And looking back over the years it is clear that some of the obstacles in the airline's path were placed there, unwittingly perhaps, by its owners – the successive governments, and hence ultimately the people, of Canada. Gradually, the company seemed to become the victim of its own success. As it grew, and its place in the national scheme of things became more and more important, it inevitably attracted critics. TCA was, they said, an arrogant monopoly – though in fact it was not a monopoly for very long. Its government backing gave it an unfair advantage and it should be faced with competition – when in fact it had been faced with strenuous competition on many of its routes from the start. Then, when it did set out to compete, with normal commercial practices and promotions, it was "wasting the taxpayers' money" – when in fact for all but a few early years it more than paid its own way.

The original design, clearly stated on many occasions, was that only TCA would carry Canada's flag on main routes in this country and internationally. That principle was soon broached, and later abandoned entirely. And since the relationship between the government and its Crown corporations has never been defined to the full satisfaction of both sides, various governments or individual ministers sometimes tried to make or enforce decisions that the airline resisted as an unwarranted encroachment on its essential managerial independence. Great battles were fought, usually behind the scenes but sometimes in public, and the repercussions of some of them linger still.

All in all, it could be said that Air Canada succeeded despite its government ownership, not by virtue of any advantage this conferred. But succeed it did, and it has long been considered one of the world's leading airlines.

In any work such as this, the spotlight inevitably focuses on the leading players, those "captains and kings" who occupy the top positions and make the decisions that affect the organization's destiny. But those men at the top well know that the decisions they make are the fruit of the talent and knowledge and experience of countless members of the teams they lead who do not share the limelight. Air Canada owes its success to the dedicated work of thousands of ordinary, and often extraordinary, Canadians who inherited the mantle of the handful of adventurous TCA pioneers. All of them, no matter how anonymous, are entitled to a feeling of pride as the organization they helped to build heads into its golden anniversary year.

CHAPTER ONE

RANS-CANADA AIR LINES was established to carry the mail. Passengers, it was hoped, would be forthcoming, but there was some question about that. "Air-mindedness," as a member of Parliament said during the debate on the matter, "is a state of mind brought about through dismissal of fear." There were still plenty of people around in 1937 who would no more have set foot on an aeroplane than they would willingly have stepped into a bear trap. And there were those on both sides of the Atlantic who felt that no matter how intrepid the potential airline passenger might be, he had no place aboard a machine designed to speed the mail. "Mails may be lost but must never be delayed," wrote C.G. Grey, the influential editor of the British aviation journal *The Aeroplane*, to a friend in Ottawa, "and passengers may be delayed but must never be lost."

John Armistead Wilson, the recipient of this letter, was a Scotsborn engineer-turned-civil servant who, almost alone in the official Ottawa of his early days, recognized the possibilities of the aeroplane. He understood how it could shrink the vast distances separating the populated parts of his adopted country, more even than the railroads had done, and how, untrammelled by the need for rails and bridges, it could carry development into faraway regions beyond the reach of any transportation system more advanced than canoes and dog-teams.

Born in Broughty Ferry in 1879, John Wilson was apprenticed to an engineering company in nearby Dundee at the age of 16. A few years after winning his coveted "papers" he came to Canada, and worked on the construction of cement plants in Alberta and Quebec until 1910, when he was appointed director of stores and contracts in the new Department of the Naval Service. A succession of government appointments followed, in one of which he helped to frame the country's first air regulations; and in 1927, the year of Lindbergh's historic 33-hour solo flight across the Atlantic, he became Controller of Civil Aviation.

To Wilson's regret, there was not much to control at that time,

11

and his infant organization was no more than a backwater of the Department of National Defence. But his imposing title gave him a vantage point from which he now set out to prod the government into repairing an omission that had troubled him ever since the end of the First World War: its failure to grasp the great opportunity that war had presented to nurture the development of aviation – and hence, the development of the whole country.

The contribution made by Canadian airmen to the 1914-18 war was a remarkable one, not least because it was achieved with virtually no organized direction or assistance from the government. More than three thousand young Canadians were trained in this country for the aerial dogfights in Europe, and so anxious were they to get into action in this new element that at first they paid for their own flying lessons; when recruiting offices and military flying schools were set up later they were run by the British – the Royal Canadian Air Force was not formed until after the war.

Joined by Canadian soldiers and sailors who transferred to the British air services while already overseas, those "magnificent young men in their flying machines" established a record out of all proportion to the size and relative power of their homeland, and produced from among their number some of the most illustrious "aces" of the war: Bill Barker, Billy Bishop, Raymond Collishaw, Don MacLaren – the names inspired generations of boys on both sides of the Atlantic. Canadian industry – none too flourishing a plant in those early days – was also inspired to distinguish itself in the European conflict; among other things it turned out three thousand training planes for the war effort.

Wilson believed something should be done to harness all this energy for the bright new world that was supposed to ensue. Only a month after the armistice, he suggested to the cabinet minister entrusted with the portfolio of "Reconstruction" that the government should interest itself in the potential contribution of aviation to the development of the North. "I don't think," that worthy replied, "that Canada will ever have need for an air service."

In fairness, it should be said that Wilson was pushing the claims of what few people anywhere yet recognized as a new mode of transportation at a time when the government had trouble enough with the old. It had lately begun the painful process of bailing out bankrupt railroads built not long before with liberal allotments of public funds – a process that would soon culminate in the formation of the Canadian National Railways. With a postwar recession on the horizon, even a politician as enthusiastic about aviation as Wilson was himself could hardly have risked advocating more public expenditure to support the cause of the rickety machines which had so far proved useful only in a particularly dreadful war everyone now wanted to forget.

To be fair again, the Canadian government was not alone in its attitude. Across the Atlantic, no less a personage than Winston Churchill delivered himself of the celebrated dictum, "Civil aviation must fly by itself." Ottawa agreed: there would be no subsidies for airlines as there had been for railroads. If private companies or individual entrepreneurs wished to put the aeroplane tọ work, fine: the government would, and did, co-operate to the extent of laying down regulations designed to ensure safe and orderly flying and controlling the granting of pilots' licences; but there were to be no handouts.

So for the first decade after the war civil aviation in Canada flew, and grew, by itself. Those returning airmen able to raise a few thousand dollars to buy an aeroplane set about earning their living with it as best they could. Some went barnstorming, selling sightseeing flights from farmers' fields and performing "death-defying stunts" wherever they could assemble an audience large enough to make it pay. Others hired themselves out on charter to anyone who would employ them in more businesslike endeavours. Among the first commercial enterprises to appreciate the value of aeroplanes to their operations were the big pulp and paper companies, which began to use them on forestry patrol, spotting fires, photographing and mapping timber limits and ferrying foresters into inaccessible areas. They were so obviously useful in this role that before long, in 1924, the Ontario government set up its own Ontario Provincial Air Service, a fleet of thirteen World War One HS-2L flying boats.

The HS-2L was a huge machine for its day, with a graceful wooden hull containing two open cockpits, suspended beneath two 75-foot-wide fabric-covered wings mounted one on top of the other. Its rearward-facing engine drove a massive four-bladed propeller which pushed the aircraft along instead of pulling it, at something over 60 miles an hour. Primitive though it may have been, the HS-2L was the early workhorse of Canadian aviation. It shared with the float-planes that followed it—which had the added advantage of being readily convertible to skis when the snow came—the essential attribute of being able to land on rivers and lakes at a time when aerodromes were few and far between.

Next to realize the value of the aeroplane to their activities were the mining companies that proliferated in Ontario and Quebec in the twenties, and individual prospectors seeking their fortunes on the wide expanse of the Precambrian Shield. In fact, the first acknowledged regular airmail, passenger and freight service in Canada operated not between any of its cities but between Haileybury, in northern Ontario, and Rouyn, a mining town across the border in Quebec. It was launched in 1924 by Laurentide Air Services Limited, a company formed originally to do forestry work. (A much better-known transportation company, the Canadian Pacific Railway, obtained a charter permitting it to own and operate aircraft as early as 1919, but chose not to activate it until twenty years later.)

Some early flights, particularly those into isolated areas, carried mail, but on an irregular and informal basis. Adhering to the government's no-subsidy policy, the Post Office permitted these flights rather than encouraged them, and operators were allowed to recompense themselves by placing 25-cent "stickers" on the letters they carried. It was not until 1927 that the Post Office included in its estimates an appropriation designed to inaugurate a regular airmail service – the princely sum of $75,000. And it seemed hardly a coincidence that 1927 was the year in which John Wilson became Controller of Civil Aviation.

Certainly Wilson had a hand that year in initiating an experiment whose ultimate success in speeding the mail we can only regard now with a certain rueful nostalgia. In those days, of course, the only way for passengers or mail to cross the Atlantic was by ocean liner. Much of the journey between England and Montreal was spent in Canadian waters: in the Gulf and the St. Lawrence River. So in 1927 an RCAF seaplane piloted by Squadron Leader J.H. Tudhope flew to meet an incoming liner at Rimouski, about three hundred miles downstream from Montreal, to relieve it of its mailbags and hurry them on to Montreal. Sadly, on that first attempt, high waves wrecked the seaplane as it tried to take off after loading the mail. Its crew and contents were rescued, but the ship reached Montreal before its mail.

Undeterred, the authorities levelled a field to make an aerodrome at Rimouski and for the next few years the mail was ferried to and from the liners by fast launch and carried by wheeled aircraft between Montreal and Rimouski. This accelerated the incoming mail service by as much as forty-eight hours, and on outgoing trips sometimes by as much as three days.

And Wilson did not rest there. In 1932, to mark the holding in Ottawa of the Empire Prime Ministers' economic conference which adopted the controversial policy of imperial preference, incoming liners were met in the Strait of Belle Isle, some nine hundred miles from Montreal, and by this means – half a century ago! – letters from London, Cologne, Basle, Brussels and Paris bearing the date stamp June 24 were delivered to their delighted recipients in Montreal, Ottawa and New York on the evening of June 28, a mere four days later.

Writing proudly about this experiment to another friend in England, George Woods Humphery, managing director of Imperial Airways, Wilson predicted that "the final outcome will be a trans-Atlantic all-air service via Newfoundland and Ireland, but the time is not yet ripe for this."

Neither, back in 1927, was the time yet ripe for a service which involved a similarly daunting distance – from coast to coast across Canada. But things were at last beginning to move the way Wilson wanted them to.

As he was continually reminding anyone in Ottawa who would listen, Canada was in danger of being left behind in the world of aviation. Airmail had been carried between London and Paris since 1919, and by 1925 there was a full-fledged regular transcontinental mail service across the United States, with radio beacons to keep the planes on course, airports with lights to permit night flying, and a national weather service for the information of the pilots. None of these things yet existed in Canada; but from 1927 on, the Post Office began to dispense official contracts for carrying airmail. At first the service was confined to outlying areas such as the Magdalen Islands and some northern mining settlements, but soon afterward it was extended to a few intercity routes. By the end of 1929, Wilson was able to tell Air Vice-Marshal Sir Sefton Brancker, Britain's Director of Civil Aviation, that flying companies under contract to move Canadian airmail were carrying more than a ton of it every day. And describing a new 1,600-mile service along the Mackenzie River into the Arctic, he wrote: "Companies like the Northern Traders Limited, a very big outfit who used to do a tremendous amount of dog team work, have now sold all their dogs and are putting all their winter traffic in the air."

He was also able to report gratifying progress with his own department's chief project – construction of the trans-Canada "airway." For all the yeoman service now being performed by flying boats and float-planes, it was realized that aircraft on wheels were essential to a regular and reliable year-round mail service linking Canada's major cities. And with the limited range of contemporary aircraft it was deemed necessary to serve them with a string of aerodromes at one-hundred-mile intervals across the country. Faced with this tremendous construction project, the obvious place to begin was on the flat terrain of the prairies. In his letter to Brancker, Wilson wrote:

We hope to start our night service from Winnipeg to Calgary, 850 miles across the prairie, on the first of February. . . . We are now busy with a survey across the mountains and the Post Office are already talking about a link across northern Ontario, which would give us the full trans-continental.

The optimism voiced in that last sentence was sadly premature. But Wilson's missionary work was clearly beginning to win converts, and in a memorandum he had lately written for the greater enlightenment of the government he had advanced an idea which was to have far-reaching consequences. "So far as the success of the airways depends on their construction and flying," he wrote, "there are many reasons for confidence. It is when the broader aspects of air transportation . . . are considered that there appears need for concern. . . ."

Up to that time, he went on to explain, most of the commercial flying in Canada had been done in the north country, where, "given a good aircraft, the efficient, careful pilot needs little else but a good mechanic, a spare engine, gas and oil to operate successfully." This had provided good opportunities to small operators, of whom there were now dozens in existence across the country, but "airway operation, on the other hand, cannot be efficient without good aerodromes, hangars, workshops, reserve aircraft and personnel, and all the overhead, accounting, storekeeping etc. which inevitably accompany a large organization."

Experience in other countries had shown that small organizations could not sustain operations on such a scale: "In Great Britain, Germany, and France, the governments have forced the amalgamation of competing companies and in the United States control of airway operations has been centralized in the hands of three or four very large corporations."

Perhaps understandably, Wilson did not add that, notwithstanding the brave words of Winston Churchill, Britain had first found it necessary to bail out one of its embryo airline companies with government assistance as early as 1921; and when four struggling companies were merged into the fledgling Imperial Airways* in 1924 it was with an assured subsidy of one million pounds over the next ten years, which later had to be increased. And in the United States, those "three or four very large corporations" of which he spoke – which already included such mod-

---

*Forerunner of the later British Overseas Airways Corporation and today's British Airways.

ern giants as United Airlines and Pan American Airways – were founded on airmail contracts: in 1929, 95 per cent of U.S. airline revenue came from the Post Office.

Wilson's memorandum said economic pressure would probably lead eventually to amalgamations of the many small flying companies in Canada, and he suggested that the Post Office should encourage this by a selective policy of letting airmail contracts: "Price-cutting competition between rival organizations . . . can only end in poor operating efficiency and financial ruin." Then, and later, the Post Office tended to drive some hard bargains in its letting of mail contracts. Wilson proposed that instead it should pay a price which would give substantial operators a fair margin with which to improve their services and buy new and better aeroplanes as they came on the market. This in turn would enable them to go after other traffic, which was essential if the Post Office did not wish to "continue indefinitely carrying the whole cost of operating the airways."

And here Wilson made his most interesting suggestion:

One of the weaknesses of the operating firms is that they are run almost entirely by men whose experience is limited to flying. They have no experience in transportation as a business and its many ramifications. The two Canadian railway companies have this experience on a wider scale than, perhaps, any transport organization in the world. . . . It would be most unfortunate if both the CNR and the CPR entered the operating field, either as principals or through subsidiaries, as rivals. Our aim ought to be to secure their cooperation and assistance to a common flying organization or group of companies. . . .

If such a combination could be formed it . . . would save the continual struggle between rival companies all competing for business and the pressure on the government which accompanies this. It would bring through the railways a wider outlook on air traffic and give the government at all times a strong experienced organization with whom could be discussed the questions now arising as to foreign connections. These may seem remote today but in ten years' time, or even in five, they will be urgent practical matters of great import to the trade of this country. . . . The close association of the Great Railway systems with our aviation would strengthen it enormously. . . .

Wilson's memorandum was dated November 25, 1929 – just one day after the calamitous first day of the Wall Street crash, whose repercussions were to defer the rosy future he foresaw. The extent of that disaster could not have been imagined when, either in response to Wilson's suggestion or because great minds were thinking alike, the president of the CNR, Sir Henry Thornton, paid a visit to a man who has been called "the father of Canadian aviation."

James Armstrong Richardson carried considerable weight, both physically (he was over six feet tall and tended to paunchiness) and by virtue of his position as one of the country's leading grain merchants. He was born in 1885 in Kingston, Ontario, where the family firm, James Richardson & Sons, had been founded ten years before Confederation. He took a BA degree at Queen's University there and in 1912 was sent to Winnipeg to take charge of the company's western branches. By 1918 he was its president, and he expanded its activities into a variety of new enterprises, forming a separate securities division to deal in stocks and bonds, buying a string of radio stations, and investing in mining ventures. It was his interest in this field that directed his attention to the aeroplane and the way it permitted mineral exploration and development in remote areas; and in 1926 he put up $200,000 of his own money to form Western Canada Airways Limited.

The new company flourished under Richardson's capable direction, flying geologists, prospectors and supplies into the northern mining camps and developing a return trade in cargoes of furs and fish. From time to time, Richardson would rescue smaller operators who were continually teetering on the brink of bankruptcy and absorb them into his own organization. One such was Major Don MacLaren, the war ace who had run a general air service on the west coast named Pacific Airways Limited – rather grandiloquently, since it consisted of a lone Curtiss HS-2L. This MacLaren tried to keep busy with any work that came his way, specializing in fishery patrols and from time to time flying the lumber baron H.R. MacMillan around his extensive preserves.

By the time Western Canada absorbed MacLaren in 1928, it had become one of the biggest aviation companies in the country, doing most of the flying from the Ontario border west to the Pacific. And Richardson, his enthusiasm aroused, had begun to invest in other aviation companies in the east – where he soon heard rumours that disturbed him. Like John Wilson, he believed that flying in Canada should be done by Canadians, working for Canadian-owned companies. But it now appeared that several eastern operators, unable to withstand the cutthroat competition, were about to go to the wall; and there was no shortage of potential buyers for them south of the border, where the forerunners of today's major airlines, in their fervour for expansion, were casting covetous glances at the near-vacuum in Canada. Richardson himself received at least one U.S. offer for Western Canada, but refused to sell. And later, when the Aviation Corporation of Canada was formed in Montreal to buy up the four leading companies in the east and keep them out of American hands, he bought shares and became one of its directors.

James Richardson now owned one of the two largest aviation companies in the country and part of the other, and by the time Sir Henry Thornton called on him in Winnipeg he had concluded the time was ripe to put them together to form one strong national organization. Sir Henry explained his visit by saying he recognized that the CNR should keep up with the times and offer its customers service by air, but he had no illusions about the difficulties of setting up an airline from scratch. He had heard great things about Western Canada, so could he acquire an interest in it for the CNR?

Richardson, as a director of the CPR, said he ought to consult his friend Edward Beatty, its president. So he took a train for Montreal and there told Beatty it would be unfortunate if any initiative by the CNR were to force the CPR to spend money in aviation, since there was no possible room for two large aviation companies in Canada. Would it not be better if he carried through with his plan to merge Western Canada and Aviation Corporation into one strong organization operating from coast to coast, with both railroads as minority partners?

Sir Edward Beatty, as he was soon to become, has sometimes been unjustly accused of missing the boat in the field of aviation. But he was already at the head of the CPR when it acquired its airline charter in 1919, and in 1928 he had secretly, using Richardson as his nominee, bought shares for the CPR in one of the companies later merged into Aviation Corporation. He now saw the wisdom of Richardson's proposal, confirmed that he had no desire to enter into wasteful competition, and said he would support the merger plan if it proved acceptable to Thornton. It did, and in 1930 Richardson combined Western Canada and Aviation Corporation into a new company called Canadian Airways Limited (CAL). His initiative had the blessing of both the country's major political parties: it had been agreed to by Mackenzie King's Liberals but was formally approved and consummated after the Conservatives, under R.B. Bennett, came to power in September that year.

The CNR and CPR each put up $250,000 for 10,000 shares of the new company. Richardson received almost 73,000 shares for his interest, more than enough to give him control of what his agreement with the CNR described as "one operating company designed to serve the requirements of the entire Dominion of Canada." His investment in CAL was estimated at $1.3 million, and he became its president, with Thornton and Beatty as vice-presidents.

From the various companies amalgamated into it, CAL inherited almost all the airmail routes and contracts then in existence. True, the Post Office had recently reduced the rates paid to the eastern companies from $1.25 a mile to 90 cents, but this was more than the 75 cents a mile Western Canada had been receiving for its pioneering work on the Prairie Airmail Service it had recently launched. With 1.2 million airmail miles to be flown every year, CAL stood to receive almost one million dollars in annual revenue from the Post Office. Richardson knew this would only barely cover the costs of operating the service, but with the security offered by the four-year contract he received, he could plan for the future and buy new and better equipment than the bush planes he had been using. This would attract new business to supplement the Post Office revenue and he could press on with the development of what all concerned now seemed to welcome as the one strong trans-Canada airline the country needed.

CHAPTER TWO

ECAUSE CONSTRUCTION OF THE government "airway" was more advanced in the West than elsewhere, the Prairie Airmail Service launched by Western Canada Airways early in 1930 was the forerunner of the regularly scheduled, seven-days-a-week, around-the-clock flying operations we now take for granted. Given the conditions under which it operated, the passengers who were occasionally induced to accompany the mail deserve as much admiration as the pilots who flew them.

Initially there were two routes, an overnight service between Winnipeg and Calgary, and a daylight run linking Regina and Edmonton via Saskatoon and North Battleford. On the night run, westbound flights left Winnipeg at 9 p.m. and arrived in Calgary at 5 a.m. next day, after 20-minute stops at Regina, Moose Jaw and Medicine Hat. Eastbound flights left Calgary at 2.15 a.m. and reached Winnipeg soon after noon. Paved runways, radio beacons and control towers were still luxuries of the future, but a network of simple grass airfields had been developed, some by municipalities anxious to share in the benefits of the new form of transportation and others by the civilian flying clubs the government had supported to create a pool of aviation expertise: they received a grant of $100 for each bright-eyed young adventurer they turned into a pilot. But the intermediate strips the government had built along the way were sometimes in poor condition or inadequately lit; the meteorological service available to the pilots was still rudimentary; and the only navigational aids were revolving acetylene lanterns on squat steel towers placed every fifteen miles along the route. These inevitably went out from time to time, a particular hazard when the access roads used by the maintenance crews to reach them were blocked by snow. Even when the lanterns were functioning properly the pilots often found them difficult to pick up or completely blotted out by snowstorms, in which case they tried to navigate by following the street lamps of the towns below. When they became lost, their only recourse was to take a chance and land on some farmer's field, praying they would not tear up too many barbed-wire fences.

The first planes used on the service were lumbering, single-engined, eight-passenger Fokker F-14s and the more advanced Boeing 40B mail planes, which carried only four passengers but proved faster and more efficient. In both models, the pilot sat in an open cockpit above and behind the passenger cabins, which was considered to increase his field of view – and his chance of survival in an accident. The Post Office decreed that the mail must be carried in a closed compartment so that passengers would not be tempted to commit the cardinal sin of tampering with it. At first it was locked up in the toilet at the rear of the passenger cabin; later, separate mail compartments were installed beneath the pilot's cockpit.

Many years later, Don MacLaren, the war ace who was one of the pilots who pioneered the run, recalled the atmosphere:

Passengers sometimes wanted to fly with us – I could never see why they did – and why they wanted to pay for the ride. Some of them fortified themselves with the stuff people use to fortify themselves with and you wondered whether they flew because they had been drinking or drank because they wanted to fly. After watching one passenger trying to open the cabin door to climb out on to the wing at 5,000 feet one night, we decided to look the passengers over more carefully before boarding.

He did not add that the passenger's attempted wing-walking was only foiled when MacLaren threw the aircraft into a steep bank and thus caused the cabin door to slam shut on him.

At one time, the Post Office tried to bar passengers from the flights, complaining that they slowed the mail schedule and that pilots, conscious of their responsibility for their human loads, might cancel flights in uncertain conditions when they would have flown them had they been carrying only mail. Still well aware of the need to build up more business, Western Canada replied that good pilots never took chances, with or without passengers aboard; and that the company had completed 92.8 per cent of its scheduled flights to that date, a record not far behind that of the best American carrier, which had a 94 per cent completion rate after eight years of operating experience. It was a record of which Richardson could well be proud, and consolidating the earnings of all the companies merged into it, CAL had a total revenue in 1930 of $1,140,127. In the following year airmail revenue alone amounted to $941,468 of the company's total.

Then, in 1932, came disaster: the Conservative government

cancelled virtually all the inter-city mail contracts. The country had by now suffered two years of the depression and no end to the misery appeared to be in sight. The Prime Minister, R.B. Bennett, justified his unilateral abrogation of the contracts as an essential economy measure. Explaining it some years later, during the House debate on the establishment of Trans-Canada Air Lines, he said that "with 300,000 of the population receiving some form of relief, there was very little gratification in seeing an aeroplane passing by day after day when the unfortunate owner of the soil could hardly see the aeroplane because his own crop had gone up in dust."

Richardson protested in vain that a contract was a contract. He pointed out that the Post Office recouped from airmail users more than half the money it paid out to the carriers; that the backers of CAL, including himself, had provided almost $3 million in cash in good faith to develop an all-Canadian air service; that on the basis of the four-year contract heavy capital expenditures had been undertaken to buy radio-equipped mail planes, build hangars and lease offices right across the country; and that unless the government changed its mind CAL would have to close down, throwing even more people out of work.

In the event, he kept the company afloat, and the men who worked for him thought he did so partly out of loyalty to them and partly because of his undiminished faith in the future of aviation. He estimated the revenue lost by the cancellation of the last two years of his contract at $2.5 million.

CAL was not the only organization to suffer from Bennett's 1932 economy measures; the government's overall spending on aviation for the year, including that on the infant RCAF, was reduced by 70 per cent. But somehow the indefatigable John Wilson managed to lay his hands on a portion of the funds set aside to build work camps for the unemployed. Thus armed, he put hundreds of single, homeless young men to work clearing bush and levelling the intermediate landing strips along his cherished airway. The men slept in dormitories, were fed army rations, given clothes where necessary, and paid the princely sum of 20 cents a day. Nevertheless, they worked to such effect that in July 1933, Richardson received a welcome letter from Wilson's department. "It seems," this informed him, "that the entire airway from Halifax to Vancouver will be ready for operation by about September, 1934." As it turned out, that forecast was unduly optimistic, but the letter looked like an encouraging sign that CAL had not been completely abandoned by the government. It said an interdepartmental committee had held several meetings and concluded that when the airway was finished the government should continue to be responsible for its maintenance, lighting, the installation of radio aids to navigation when they became available, meteorological services and communications. But carriage of His Majesty's Mail, air express and passengers should be entrusted to one strong private company. "Would it be the wish of Canadian Airways," the letter went on, "to be considered for selection as the operating company?"

Such was, of course, Canadian Airways' fervent wish, and a few days later Richardson appeared before the committee in Ottawa. Its chairman was Major-General A.G.L. McNaughton, by virtue of his position as Chief of the General Staff, and its members included Wilson and Peter Coolican, the assistant deputy postmaster general. Much of the discussion concerned Coolican's opinion, to which he had apparently converted the general, that running the trans-Canada airline was a big enough job for any one company, and if Richardson wanted the contract he must divest himself of what Coolican referred to as his "bush" operations.

This was hardly a flattering reference to CAL, the biggest carrier in the country by far, and the only one remotely warranting consideration as a national enterprise, and naturally, Richardson opposed Coolican's stipulation. He was proud of CAL's contribution to the burgeoning mining industry, one of the few bright spots in the battered Canadian economy in those dark days, and he told the committee no other company could provide such a service to the community. "There are certain operations in this country," he said, "which should be carried on but which are not entirely self-supporting. They must get help, either directly or indirectly, and of course airmail is one of the most satisfactory ways to meet that situation." If the committee feared the interests of the trans-Canada service might be subordinated to those of any larger organization of which it were a part, it would be a perfectly simple matter to hive off the "bush" service into a subsidiary company, with its own separate organization and management.

This, responded Coolican, would not solve the problem. The bush operations should be given to some other company altogether; otherwise there was the danger of creating a monopoly. "As far as the Post Office department is concerned," he said, "there must be competition in the bush operations. . . . The smaller companies play an effective role in this regard and should not be deprived of an opportunity to compete locally."

In view of the curiously inexplicable way the Post Office sometimes disbursed its mail contracts at that time, and for some years thereafter, this attitude was not quite so high-minded as it might sound. "Divide and rule" is an old maxim and the Post Office often applied it. On at least one occasion a contract was taken away from CAL and bestowed upon a neophyte competitor without any apparent tender or explanation. The company sometimes lost long-standing contracts when another operator quite obviously unable to provide equal service submitted an only marginally lower bid. George Herring, Coolican's lieutenant as chief superintendent of the airmail service, was recognized by all the operators as a tough customer determined to have the mail carried at rock-bottom prices. Not unnaturally, this led some of the struggling small operators to make bids at prices which could not conceivably cover their costs, in the hope that once assigned a mail route they would pick up enough other business along the way to make it pay. Some of the more ingenious padded their loads by taking out batches of newspaper subscriptions in the names of long-dead residents of remote settlements, and persuading all their friends and relatives to send for the Eaton's catalogue.

The competition between operators desperate to make a profit also led to the virtually universal practice of overloading planes; this was officially blamed for at least one crash, in which seven people were killed, and was probably responsible for others. Richardson, conscious of the need to establish a reputation for reliability, issued strict instructions against this practice in 1932. In any case, his pilots had long grumbled that they couldn't get away with it, since the government's inspectors found it easier to police their disciplined operation, with its detailed records and meticulously kept logbooks, than to supervise the activities of one-man outfits operating over thousands of miles of wilderness.

As the committee's deliberations proceeded, General McNaughton added his weight to Coolican's argument. The government was thinking in terms of operating the trans-Canada route with "high-speed planes" – he mentioned 160 miles an hour as the objective – and these would obviously not be suitable for bush operations. Nor did he see much place for passengers on "the highly specialized operations" of the trans-Canada airway.

The discussions ended without any firm decisions but with an invitation to Richardson to submit his proposals for operating the new service. It is a pity that John Wilson did not attend the meeting, for the minutes give no indication of his opinions on the views expressed, most of which clearly ran counter to his own. Wilson was, in fact, away in Newfoundland representing

Canada at a conference summoned to discuss a matter that was beginning to arouse some interest in both Europe and North America: how, when and by whom would the first transatlantic airmail service be launched?

Back in 1930, when the British press reported that the CNR and CPR had taken an interest in Canadian Airways, Sir Eric Geddes, chairman of Imperial Airways, had written identical letters to Sir Henry Thornton and Edward Beatty offering them the co-operation of his organization. Imperial Airways, he explained, was "the child of the British government" but was not controlled by it. (The government in fact subsidized the airline from its start and had two nominees on its board of directors, all of whom, without any prompting from the government, considered their organization something of an extension of the diplomatic service, furthering British interests around the world.) Geddes explained that Imperial had been operating a weekly service between London and Karachi for a year and a half and would soon be flying regularly between London and South Africa. "All the Empire governments" on these routes, as well as the British government, were financially supporting them, and he thought Imperial's experience might be useful to the new Canadian company. "While I realise the great strides which Canada has made in aviation," Geddes wrote, "and the great future of aviation in Canada, it seems a pity that my company, Imperial Airways, which is attaining a unique position in the Empire, should be out of touch with your great Dominion, and should, in fact, be closer to the great American Civil Aviation concerns, than with Canada."

Both Thornton and Beatty, busy enough with railway problems, wrote noncommittal replies, explaining that the press reports Geddes had seen seemed to have exaggerated their roles in CAL. Beatty added that he had passed on his letter to James Richardson, but Richardson seems to have done nothing to follow it up.

A few weeks later, Imperial's managing director, Woods Humphery, visited New York to discuss plans for a reciprocal service across the Atlantic with the far-sighted president of Pan American Airways, Juan Trippe. He invited John Wilson to meet him in New York, but Wilson did not go; his correspondence suggests he thought Woods Humphery should have visited Ottawa.

The British concluded from these responses that Canada had little or no interest in Atlantic flying. This was undoubtedly true of the government, struggling with the twin problems of the

Depression and the mountainous deficits of the country's existing transportation system. But it was certainly not true of Wilson. And for the next couple of years the Controller of Civil Aviation fretted that Imperial Airways and Pan American were plotting to go ahead with their plans for the Atlantic without giving due consideration to Canada's interests.

At that time, of course, there were no aeroplanes with ranges permitting them to cross the Atlantic non-stop with a load of mail and passengers, and three possible routes with landing places along the way were being considered: a southern route, via Bermuda and the Azores; the so-called direct route, via Newfoundland and Ireland; and the northern route, via Labrador, Greenland and Iceland. Climatically, the southern route was clearly the easiest; but it was about 2,000 miles longer than the direct route between New York and London and it called for one over-sea stage of 2,125 miles, which was well beyond the contemporary state of the art. The northern route involved four over-sea stages, but the longest was only 795 miles; the Arctic weather along most of the way, however, was intimidating – though Pan Am did commission Charles Lindbergh to survey it. The direct route was the shortest – 3,270 miles between London and Montreal and 3,475 miles from London to New York. But it, too, involved a long over-sea crossing of 1,990 miles, and weather conditions perhaps even more daunting, because of fog, than the northern route.

Some of the methods proposed for spanning these long over-sea stages had a strong flavour of Jules Verne about them. The strangest was actually tried out by the German airline Lufthansa on the South Atlantic. An ocean liner, the *Westphalen*, was stationed midway between the West African and Brazilian coasts as a floating refuelling base. It was equipped with a huge canvas apron which it towed along just below the surface of the water. This was supposed to ensure a smooth landing path for seaplanes, which were then hoisted aboard by derrick, refuelled, and catapulted away again. Various other experiments were carried out with ship-borne catapults, such as winging planes aloft as soon as they came within range of their destinations; the problem then became how to get them home again.

Other early plans for an Atlantic service envisaged the use of flying boats. They were considered safer than land planes with all that water to cross, and at that stage of aviation development they tended to be bigger, and thus able to carry more fuel. Wilson, however, well aware of the scarcity of open water during a

Canadian winter, believed no practical service could be mounted until a land plane came along with sufficient range. He was also a strong advocate of the direct route, because this would involve the use of Canadian territory and admit Canada into the big league of world aviation.

Pan Am, too, was clearly intrigued by the possibilities of the direct route. In 1931 it obtained permission from the Canadian government – and not only permission but a $2-per-mile subsidy from the U.S. government – to fly an airmail service from Boston through Saint John, New Brunswick, to Halifax. The route had no commercial value but it was an obvious toehold for further expansion, as became apparent after two months' operation, when the airline decided to extend it to Newfoundland, the western springboard for the Atlantic. It approached the Newfoundland government – Britain's oldest colony was not yet part of Canada – for exclusive operating rights, in return for which it offered to build the necessary bases and navigational aids.*

This move at last won Wilson a hearing at higher levels for his view that Canada was again in danger of being left at the post in the field of aviation. Thus among the many government committees set up to prepare for the Empire economic conference in Ottawa in 1932 was one to examine the prospects for a transatlantic air service. Wilson was its secretary, and it prefaced its report to the government with the statement that "Canada, the United Kingdom, the Irish Free State and Newfoundland control the approaches to the most direct trans-Atlantic crossing. . . . It is imperative that steps should be taken to safeguard their position."

At the economic conference itself, the governments concerned accepted this view and agreed to continue their exploration of the problem in a series of meetings that extended over the next three years. During the one Wilson attended in Newfoundland in 1933, Pan Am, faced with an apparently united coalition of governments, dropped its request for exclusive privileges in Newfoundland and gave up its original idea of controlling the bases there and their navigational aids. But Imperial Airways had always

---

*This kind of direct dealing with foreign governments was not unusual for Pan American Airways, which was unique among the American airlines. It flew no domestic routes but was encouraged by the government to carry the U.S. flag around the world. Washington ensured that it received all foreign mail contracts, with a subsidy of up to $2 a mile, and Trippe expanded around the world by buying into foreign airlines and negotiating agreements privately with foreign governments. By 1934, his airline was a 40,000-mile transportation system operating into thirty-nine countries and piling up an annual revenue of $13 million.

believed Pan Am's participation in any Atlantic service was essential, since 80 per cent of transatlantic mail was destined for or originated in the United States. So it was agreed to give Pan Am operating rights over the eventual route but retain the bases and aids to navigation "in British hands."

Then, in 1935, Britain, Ireland and Canada signed an agreement to establish a "joint operating company" to run the transatlantic service, with Britain to hold 51 per cent of the stock and Canada and Ireland 24½ per cent each. In fact, the company was never set up—it was soon overtaken by events—but the agreement envisaged each country providing and controlling the ground services needed on its territory, Imperial Airways doing the flying over the Atlantic, and "a company nominated by Canada" flying the mail across to Vancouver. Then, once it became possible to fly the Pacific to Australia and the Far East, there would be an "all-red" route girdling the globe, linking the huge areas still coloured pink on the map of the world, and directed and controlled by the mother country.

But first, a question arose to which there still seemed no answer: which "company nominated by Canada" would be chosen to do the job? James Richardson had continued to meet with government officials from time to time and submit proposals for the operation of the trans-Canada service, but the government had made no move to give out a contract and he was as much in the dark about its plans as everyone else.

The Post Office, displaying an unexpected expertise in advanced aeronautical engineering, had by now come up with a new set of specifications for the aircraft that must be used on the run: they should be capable of flying at 200 miles an hour "in still air at sea level" and have a range of 800 miles with a load of 600 lbs. of mail. But the Post Office officials still showed a puzzling antipathy to the idea of Richardson landing the contract. In a letter to Colonel H. Burchall, assistant general manager of Imperial Airways, George Herring complained that Canadian Airways "seems to have the idea that they have a divine right in the matter." And with a noticeable lack of nationalist fervour, he asked: "Has Imperial Airways no aspirations to get into the picture as a direct participant?"

The sophisticated management of Imperial Airways had no appetite for such a hot potato. As Sir Eric Geddes assured Sir Edward Beatty in a letter in July 1935: "The policy of the board of Imperial Airways has been one of desire to cooperate with Canada along lines desired by Canada, rather than to lay down hard and fast ideas of our own." Beatty, evidently thinking something would have to be done to ginger up Ottawa, had written to Geddes asking "if you are disposed to have any interest in the development of our inland operations." And in the same letter he added: "I must confess that Canada as yet has no definite air service policy, and probably one will not be announced until the new government takes office."

CHAPTER THREE

S THE TIME APPROACHED for the general election of 1935 it was obvious that R.B. Bennett's Conservative government, its head bloodied by five years of intractable depression and the drought that turned the fertile prairies to dust, was doomed to defeat. On October 14, Mackenzie King's Liberals swept back into office with 173 seats, by far the largest number won by any party since Confederation, and more than double the 65 seats that went to the four opposition parties.

It was a stirring mandate for change, and the country looked forward to beginning the task of lifting itself up by its boot straps. In aviation circles particularly, there was a feeling that at last there would be an end to all the shilly-shallying over a national air policy. As Charles Grey wrote from London to his friend Wilson in Ottawa: "I hear that the new government is considerably more air-minded than were Bennett and Co."

James Richardson certainly thought so, and amid the general optimism he approved the wording of a memorandum that went out to all CAL pilots a few days after the election: "As the possibility of the inauguration of the trans-Canada Air Mail looks more favorable at the present time, would you please advise whether you wish to be transferred from bush operations to mail operations in the event of Canadian Airways being awarded this contract. Would you also please advise, with dates, if you have taken the instrument-flying course at Camp Borden."

The technique of "flying blind," which was now recognized as essential to regular airline operation, had been pioneered only a few years earlier by the famous American flyer Jimmy Doolittle. Among the things that made it possible was the invention of instruments such as the gyroscope-controlled bank-and-turn indicator and the artificial horizon, which enabled the pilot to keep his craft on an even keel when he could not see the natural horizon outside his cockpit. The blind-flying course offered by the RCAF at Camp Borden, Ontario, was the only one available in Canada in 1935; strangely enough, it was not considered adequate qualification for the newly introduced Canadian Transport pilot's licence. So Richardson dispatched one of his senior pilots, Zebulon Lewis Leigh, to the Boeing School of Aeronautics in Oakland, California, where he reported that the instrument-flying instruction was much superior to that offered by the RCAF. When he returned to Canada, Leigh was given an aircraft equipped with all the necessary blind-flying instruments and assigned to train those CAL pilots who had chosen to transfer to the trans-Canada service.

Confident now that his men would be ready when the call came, Richardson took the first opportunity that offered to assure the new government that he was waiting in the wings. Just two weeks after the election he called on the Prime Minister in his capacity as Chancellor of Queen's University, to discuss a pending appointment to the faculty for which he had in mind O.D. Skelton, a distinguished civil servant who stood at King's right hand and was the prototype of the generation of Ottawa mandarins to come. He did not get Skelton, but in his diary that night King noted: "He then spoke to me about the airways, and said that during the last year or two there was nothing he wanted that Bennett would have anything to do with; that he did not wish to speak to me about the airways at present, but would like, later on, to have a chance to talk over the project with me."

Richardson knew it was too soon to try to pin the new administration down to any specific course of action; he probably did not yet know that Mackenzie King had already decided that a prerequisite to the solution of the country's many transportation problems was the merging of the various government departments concerned with them into one strong Department of Transport. He had taken the first step toward this as yet unannounced move a few days before, when he had appointed a political unknown to preside over both the Department of Railways and Canals and the Department of Marine.

Clarence Decatur Howe had been born of good New England yeoman stock in Waltham, Massachusetts, forty-nine years before his footsteps led him to this eminence in Ottawa – a sudden and unexpected eminence, since he had never shown any interest in party politics until friends had persuaded him to stand for the Liberals in the northwest Ontario riding of Port Arthur, at the head of the Lakes. After graduating in engineering from the Massachusetts Institute of Technology in 1908, Howe had gone straight to a professorship at Dalhousie University in Halifax, Nova Scotia. Five years later, at the age of 27, he made two decisions that changed his life: he took out British citizenship, and he moved to Fort William, Port Arthur's twin city, to set up his own engineering company. For the next twenty years he designed and built grain elevators all over the country. By the time the call came to enter politics he had made himself financially independent; his fortune was estimated at $500,000 and when he was elected he sold his business to one of his employees and entered the cabinet as probably its wealthiest member and certainly its only self-made entrepreneur.

Henceforth Clarence D. Howe's hard-driving business skills would be at the disposal of his adopted country, and in his customary straightforward manner he wasted no time taking firm hold of his new responsibilities. At the first cabinet meeting of the new government, he told King bluntly that the local commissions which administered the business of the nation's harbours were "sink holes" of wasted public money and should be dispensed with immediately. Howe had not needed to spend much time poking about in the files of the Department of Marine to reach this conclusion: throughout his business life he had worked around harbours and had seen for himself the patronage and worse abuses that flourished there. As for his other department, he told King, the board of trustees established by the previous government to administer the affairs of the sorely troubled CNR was "a miserably poor affair"; his recommendation, once again, was typically forthright: "We should get rid of it right away."

Howe's immediate priorities thus became the creation of a new National Harbours Board and the appointment of a strong new board of business-oriented directors to implement the far-reaching changes he wanted at the CNR. But by early in the new year the signal had apparently gone out to James Richardson that the government was now ready to consider the place of aviation in its transportation plans.

On February 6, 1936, Richardson addressed similar letters to the Prime Minister and Howe, reminding them that Canadian Airways had been set up with the encouragement of the earlier Liberal administration and the participation of both the national railway companies to "establish one strong company that would be able to cope with the needs of the country." It had suffered great hardship when the mail contracts were summarily cancelled through no fault of its own and this entitled it to "every consideration" when the new service was being contemplated. "Our company," he wrote to King, "is the only company in Canada that has the experience and personnel which enable us to deal with this problem . . . and I understand that when the Trans-Canada Air Mail is proceeded with [the railway] companies will greatly increase their interest in the Canadian Airways, and may possibly provide all the new money needed. . . ."

Howe's reply, dated February 12, disclosed that Sir Edward Beatty and S.J. Hungerford, who had by now replaced Thornton at the head of the CNR, had also written to him (no doubt by arrangement) on Richardson's behalf.

Every consideration [Howe assured Richardson] will be given to the past experience of Canadian Airways when plans for new services are being developed. I consider it important that our two national railways be represented on the directorate of whatever Company will dominate the aviation future of Canada, and I feel you are fortunately situated in that regard. . . . I will be glad to go into this matter with you further when civic aviation is definitely taken over by the new Department of Transport.

It was an encouraging response, all the more so since J.O. Apps, the CPR's lawyer and lobbyist in Ottawa, had just reported a talk he had recently had with Howe in which the minister had "expressed the thought that he did not believe in uncontrolled competition with respect to the air operations as he had seen too many instances of operators going broke through competition and irresponsible management."

A month later, the government announced it was going ahead with completion of the national airway, after a cabinet meeting of which King noted in his diary: "We also decided . . . to approve the Trans-Atlantic Air Route agreement reached tentatively last fall, and to develop our flying bases across Canada." There was still, however, no announcement of the government's support for CAL in this endeavour, and by now Richardson more than ever suspected he should not count on the Post Office for its support.

One of the few mail routes maintained by the Bennett government after 1932 was a short hop between Winnipeg and Pembina, North Dakota, which permitted Canadian mail to be fed into the U.S. airmail system. It was an unprofitable route but CAL had operated it until 1935, when the Post Office transferred it to a U.S. company, Northwest Airlines, and gave CAL as compensation a similar mail feeder-route between Vancouver and Seattle, stipulating that it must be operated with a de Havilland Dragon Rapide, a twin-engined, fabric-covered, wooden biplane. No sooner had CAL bought the plane and put it on the route, on October 1, 1935, than the Post Office began to grumble that with its top speed of 157 miles per hour, it was no match for the equipment United Airlines was using – the Boeing 247, introduced a couple of years earlier as America's first all-metal monoplane transport, using supercharged engines hitherto reserved for military aircraft.

A few months later, in February 1936, came more evidence that all was not well between CAL and the Post Office. CAL's general manager, G.A. "Tommy" Thompson, passed on to Richardson a letter he had received from J.A. Glen, a lawyer who represented the Manitoba federal riding of Marquette. Glen, whose son was a CAL pilot, had been discussing the proposed national airmail service with an official of the Post Office, who said his department figured the cost of the service to the operator would be 37 cents a mile, and the Post Office would probably try to negotiate a contract price of 45 cents a mile. These figures were considerably below CAL's estimate; but more serious in Thompson's eyes was a separate note enclosed by Glen with the notation: "Destroy this after reading." It said: "The official (Mr. Herring) is I think and am fairly well convinced, for some reason, not very favourable to your Co. I suggest you should get your friends working. . . ."

Passing this on to Richardson (who also ignored the injunction to burn it), Thompson wrote: "I do not entirely agree with Mr. Glen in connection with Mr. Herring. I do know that there is antagonism on the part of the Post Office Department but I am inclined to believe this comes more from Mr. Coolican."

Whoever was responsible for the antagonism, Richardson knew it existed and that he had better do something to counteract it. He decided to send Don MacLaren to Ottawa to find out as much as he could about the situation and do what he could to rectify it. Not that MacLaren, who was now assistant general manager of CAL, had any particular political contacts, but as a distinguished war ace he knew all the major figures in the aviation field and was liked and respected by them. Also, Richardson decided to buy the most-up-to-date American airliner he could lay his hands on for the Vancouver-Seattle run: a Lockheed 10A Electra, with room for ten passengers and a maximum speed of 190 miles per hour. This, he trusted, would go some way toward mollifying the Post Office, and into the bargain it would give his pilots training on the aircraft that might well be used to inaugurate the trans-Canada service.

Finally, since he felt the need of a sure-footed guide through the unfamiliar political thickets he seemed to be entering, Richardson wrote to an old friend in Ottawa, Norman Lambert. Born in Ontario, Lambert began his working life as a newspaperman–he represented the influential Toronto *Globe* in Ottawa for some years–and then gravitated to the West, where he founded his own grain business. Perhaps because of his newspaper background, or because of an innate talent for making friends in high places, when the grain trade collapsed in the Dirty Thirties he was invited to join the National Liberal Federation with the official title of national secretary, though his position could have been described just as accurately, if less felicitously, as "national bagman."

Richardson knew Lambert was a good friend of Howe's, and on April 18, 1936, he wrote to him complaining about the "disparaging" way George Herring had been talking about CAL in Ottawa. His letter reflected the distrust that had grown up within CAL over the way mail contracts were being awarded:

Herring, I am quite sure, is trying to grind an axe for somebody else. I have had reason to believe that he is very susceptible to influence, and I am quite sure that had our attitude on some of these matters been different, he could easily have been converted into an ardent supporter.

He also raised with Lambert a matter that was giving him even greater concern: disturbing evidence he kept receiving that he was not the only supplicant for the government's boon. For some time now he had been hearing about the existence in Toronto of a company named British North American Airways Limited. Since it had no aeroplanes, and no discernible corporate organization other than its board of directors, this could best be called a "shadow airline"–except that its directors were men of considerable substance. And it was said they were confident they were about to land the contract to run the airmail across Canada.

When Thompson first reported this to Richardson in 1935, he said he thought the company's president, a man named Taylor, was "a retired brewer from London, Ontario." This was at least partly true. E.P. Taylor was indeed the young president of the Brewing Corporation of Canada Limited, but he was far from retired; he was, in fact, only beginning his remarkable career. As he told the author in his engaging fashion many years later: "They asked me to be president [of BNA] but I really wasn't very involved in it. I had no money to put up and I left it to the capitalists – I wasn't a capitalist in those days. I was involved in trying to put together the breweries."

The genesis of British North American Airways was recalled for the author by Charles Burns, who in 1932 founded the investment firm that bears his name with $500 borrowed from his father and a desk rented from another broker for $10 a month. (By the time he died fifty years later, his firm had $33 million in capital and offices all over Canada, in London, New York and Boston.) Burns and his brother Latham were ardent Liberals and in 1935 they joined with a hundred or so like-minded Torontonians to form a loose political group they called the Centurion Club. As their first speaker, at a lunch in the King

Edward Hotel, they acquired C.D. Howe, who, waging his first election campaign, was glad of the platform.

During that first campaign, and later, Howe earned a reputation for sometimes permitting his affability to overcome his circumspection. Relieved to be done with his speech – he was never noted for his oratorical spell-binding – he was in a relaxed mood when he joined a select group of Centurions afterward for a celebratory drink. Informally reviewing the Liberals' plans, he mentioned the country's airways as one of the pressing problems the party was resolved to do something about. Centurions could scent an opportunity as well as the next man, and rightly or wrongly his listeners gained the impression that if a group of congenial souls were to form an airline, only the sky would be the limit.

Among the first to put up their money for the new venture were J.H. "Harry" Gundy, co-founder and guiding genius of the investment house of Wood Gundy, and Percy Parker, a lawyer and prominent Liberal party worker. Both were regular contributors to Liberal party funds and always welcome in Ottawa. Parker, in particular, had been to college with Mackenzie King, though it seems the Prime Minister disapproved somewhat of his later career.* To join them on the board they recruited some of the best-known financiers of the day, including George McCullagh, who was shortly to engineer the purchase of the Toronto *Globe* and merge it with the *Mail and Empire*; the Honourable W.D. Ross, a banker whose achievements were rewarded with the lieutenant-governorship of Ontario; Ray Lawson, of London, Ontario, whose stint as campaign manager for J.C. Elliott, the postmaster general in King's 1935 government, was presumably considered no handicap to the BNA cause; Frank Common, a prominent Montreal lawyer; the Honourable Gordon Scott, a former provincial treasurer of Quebec; and at various times several others with names of equal eminence, good Liberals all.

---

*Latham Burns contracted pneumonia on a visit to Bermuda in 1936, and in those pre-penicillin days died forty-eight hours later. Percy Parker, a pallbearer at his funeral on a cold April day in Toronto, caught a chill and he, too, died from pneumonia within a few days. Mackenzie King attended his funeral, plucked a flower from the casket, and that night wrote two pages about his old friend in his diary. "I felt a deep sorrow," he recorded, "that one whose life had had such great possibilities should have failed of their full and highest realization. . . . Had he accepted the suggestion I made to him a couple of years ago, he would have been the leader of the Liberal Party in Ontario and the Premier of the Province. . . . He will be with his father and mother again, and will through God's grace, I pray, find again his own self and become the man he ought to have been." Parker was successful and well liked, and apart from his lamentable failure to become premier it seems that the only reason for his old friend's disappointment with him was his unabashed fondness for wine, women and song.

They were a powerful group, and Jim Richardson's first solid information on their aspirations came in March 1936, when E.P. Taylor dropped in to see Woods Humphery at Imperial Airways in London. Woods Humphery was away, so Taylor was received by a member of his staff, Lieutenant-Commander Galpin, whose memorandum of their conversation was later passed on to Richardson.

He stated [Galpin reported] that his firm has, to all intents and purposes, obtained from the Canadian Government the contract to run the trans-Continental service from Montreal to Vancouver. . . . He made it quite clear that the awarding of the contract would be influenced to a large extent by political considerations and thought that British North American Airways was in a good position to obtain it for that reason, although he said that there is Canadian Government money invested in Canadian Airways. He is a pleasant-spoken and fairly young man of good type.

Richardson was already worried about another potential competitor, a recently formed eastern company named Dominion Skyways, in which the Molson family of Montreal was known to have an interest and whose vice-president, the formidable Lieutenant-Colonel William A. "Billy" Bishop, V.C., seemed to have been putting in a lot of time in Ottawa. "I hope," he said in his letter to Norman Lambert, "that no promises or commitments of any kind will be given to Percy Parker or Skyways, the results of which would be simply to dilute the equity in our company. . . . Percy Parker, of course, has not the remotest right to cut in in any way that I can see, and Skyway's only right is that they started a local company with the idea that this would prove an entry into a national picture."

Lambert replied to Richardson's letter promptly, promising to make some inquiries in the appropriate quarters, and passing on the news he had just received of Parker's death. This did not, as it turned out, put an end to BNA's lobbying in Ottawa, but when he wrote to Woods Humphery thanking him for Galpin's memorandum Richardson said C.D. Howe had "advised me personally that he had told Mr. Parker he would not discuss the matter with them at all and recommended that if he had anything of interest to discuss in connection with the matter he should take it up with me."

A few weeks later, despite this assurance to Richardson, Howe had lunch with Harry Gundy and William Zimmerman, secretary-treasurer of British North American Airways, and while there is no record of their conversation, the BNA group continued to believe it was in the running for the mail contract. In fact, Gundy told Sir Edward Beatty a few weeks later that "the Toronto group," as it had become known, had strong political support and the airmail contract was "in the bag."

Early in June, however, Richardson had "a very satisfactory chat" with Howe. He was planning a visit to Britain and Howe assured him that he "need not let any possible airways developments at Ottawa interfere, and that nothing adverse to the Canadian Airways' interests would develop."

There are so many gaps in the documentation of this period that it is not possible to reconstruct Howe's thinking. Perhaps as a newcomer he was finding the art of politics far less straightforward than he had imagined. His own plan at this time seems to have been to form a Crown corporation, with the government holding 40 per cent of the equity and the rest being divided among all the other aviation interests in the country. But which share would go to whom? Peter Coolican, of the Post Office, told Tommy Thompson of CAL he "felt Mr. Howe was inclined to under-estimate the question of political expediency . . . and might have difficulty in organizing it just as he would like." Don MacLaren reported to headquarters that Norman Lambert had told him that "Howe would like to deal with us [CAL] direct but he still does not fully comprehend the political ramifications. . . ." Howe himself admitted several times that the issue was "a highly contentious one" within the cabinet. Certainly Ian Mackenzie, the Minister of Defence, was a staunch friend of the Centurions and pushed the BNA cause in the inner councils; so, it seems certain, did the Postmaster General, J.C. Elliott. Charles A. Dunning, the Minister of Finance, supported Richardson and told him at one stage that he was "in line to run the civil aviation set-up." As usual, it was not yet possible to tell where Mackenzie King stood.

At any rate, further evidence that CAL was still in the picture emerged soon after Richardson sailed for Europe. Howe, Lambert and John Wilson flew from Ottawa to Winnipeg in a government aircraft inspecting progress at the airports along the government airway, which Wilson was pushing ahead with that year's $500,000 appropriation for civil aviation. In Winnipeg, Howe sent Wilson along to Tommy Thompson to ask if CAL would buy a second Lockheed Electra and charter it to the government for three months for "experimental radio work between Lethbridge and Vancouver" designed to complete the western section of the airway. Perceiving this as a happy augury of more co-operation to come, Richardson approved the purchase by cable from London. And in his letter acknowledging the cable Thompson said Howe had asked him to meet Richardson in Montreal on his return from Europe "so that we could then go to Ottawa and discuss the operation of the trans-Canada air mail with a special government committee."

No doubt Richardson's decision to approve the purchase of a second Electra–an expenditure of about $60,000, almost as much as CAL's entire revenue for the month of June 1936–was influenced by a cable he had received a few days earlier from his friend Frank M. Ross, an engineer who collected company directorships like philatelists collect stamps. Ross told him:

Returned from fishing trip with Howe who stated arrangements would be made your company for service from Winnipeg to west this fall and next spring arrangements would be again completed with you for service from Halifax Winnipeg stop states definitely nobody else will be considered as has no intention of creating another railway competitor in addition states government under obligation to you which has to be recognized this for your confidential information regards.

Richardson returned to Canada in mid-August, and if he was in an optimistic mood it was soon shattered. Howe was away in the Maritimes, and there was no more talk of a meeting with any government committee. He had to be content with a letter from Howe saying he expected civil aviation would be transferred to his new Department of Transport within the next two weeks, and that the cabinet would then determine its policy on the trans-Canada airways; until then he did not think there was any point in Richardson visiting Ottawa.

Norman Lambert played golf with Howe on Sunday, August 23, and the minister "assured me he wanted to ask Richardson here when he had a definite proposition to put to him" on his idea for a Crown corporation with a 40 per cent government interest. But on September 11 the cabinet rejected this plan. As Mackenzie King recorded in his diary: "We settled broad lines of a policy of trans-Canada air service, ruling out idea of Government having a minority interest in the same beyond shares which the Canadian National might hold."

The long silence deepened Richardson's gloom, and he thought he knew the reason for it. At the end of September he received a visit in Winnipeg from Norman Lambert, and told him he believed Howe "was definitely in league with the Post Office" against him. The allegation puzzled Lambert but he soon received evidence that Richardson's suspicion was well founded.

Norman Lambert's diaries in the archives at Queen's University are remarkably frank, with entries meticulously recording who gave what and when–and quite often even why. On October 2, 1936, he noted that he saw Howe in the evening and "he criticized JR in connection with aviation scheme and said Beatty was now dealing with it. He claimed that R. had given P.O. figures of costs equalling 40 cents [per mile flown], but in his memo to him mentioned 80 to 90 cents; that his word was no good; and that he was doubtful if he wanted him at all.''

This "change of front," as he put it, shocked Lambert, and he told Howe so. He had never before heard Richardson's probity questioned; nor could he believe he would have been foolish enough to have given the Post Office one cost estimate and Howe another. Howe must have been misinformed, and it is fairly clear in retrospect that the misinformation came from someone in the Post Office, since Howe mentioned in the same conversation the complaints Coolican had long been levelling against CAL's operation of the Vancouver-Seattle service. Lambert, well aware of the friction between the Post Office and CAL, "cast considerable doubt" on the information Howe had been given, and a few days later caught up with Richardson in Kingston and told him about the conversation. Richardson "made it quite clear he had not given any figures mentioning 40 cents" and thought they might have been given to the Post Office by Canadian Vickers, another early aspirant for the mail contract. Lambert's diary entry continued: "When he [Richardson] left for England, C.D. Howe was going to make JR the Imperial Airways of Canada–and then quite without any warning he turned against him."

Lambert and Howe remained friends for the rest of their lives– long after the war they used to be seen walking their dogs together in Rockcliffe on Sunday afternoons–but Lambert was quite unable to understand Howe's sudden antipathy toward Richardson. On October 24, he noted in his diary that Howe had been heard in Vancouver "berating Richardson and saying he wouldn't be in the picture because he couldn't work with him." Later that day, he went to Edward Pickering, Mackenzie King's assistant private secretary, and warned him that "the PM should be told about the injurious political implications of Howe's free remarks about Richardson, and his proposed air policy." And on the next page of his diary, the one for Sunday, October 25, he scribbled an entry under the heading, which he himself underlined: "CD's breaches of faith." There were five complaints, one of them concerning his own disappointment at not being given the chairmanship of the National Harbours Board, which Howe had promised him. (In fact, his appointment was vetoed by Mackenzie King, who recognized his value as the party's national secretary and rewarded him for his forbearance three years later by making him a senator.)

The third complaint read: "Up to July 10 or 15, his assurances to JR becoming Imp. Airways of Canada [his own underlining] and in September without explanation becoming violently opposed to him."

Throughout the long career in politics he was only just beginning, C.D. Howe aroused strong opinions, both pro and con, but few of his enemies accused him of double dealing. During the war that was just around the corner some of the most successful and forceful men in the Canadian business world worked hard and long under his direction and emerged from the fire his devoted admirers. The qualities that won their admiration – his direct, no-nonsense approach, the clarity with which his glittering eyes beneath their beetling brows quickly discerned the elements of a problem, and the incisive way he would go about solving it – appeared to some others to be unpleasantly autocratic. But while they might consider him overbearing or mistaken, and frequently both, even his opponents recognized his scorn for the pusillanimous or dishonest.

So Lambert's term "breach of faith" may have been overly censorious; certainly, diaries are highly subjective documents. But that there was a sudden and marked breach in the relations between Howe and Richardson is undeniable. Howe henceforth dealt almost entirely with Sir Edward Beatty, and the most likely explanation for his disillusionment with Richardson is that he was misled by the Post Office department.

Take the question of the price at which it thought the mail should be carried. At this time, the government's interdepartmental committee on civil aviation had accepted the Post Office's proposed contract figure of 50 cents a mile flown, which it based on the going rate in the United States. (This was then around 39 cents, though for some reason Canadian Colonial Airways, a subsidiary of a U.S. company, was receiving 90 cents a mile from the Canadian authorities for the Montreal-Albany run.) But, as CAL pointed out, aviation gasoline and oil cost from 75 to 100 per cent more in Canada than in the United States, and whichever aeroplanes were selected for the trans-Canada service would have to be imported from the United States, raising their cost by a third, because of import duty and taxes. Even more important, the U.S. airlines by now, with ten years' flying behind them, were receiving about 75 per cent of their revenue from passengers, and there was no assurance that Canadians were yet air-minded enough to patronize a new service to that extent. Finally, the greater density of population south of the border enabled the U.S. lines to make more economical use of their aircraft; they could exact more passenger-miles per day from each of their machines than any new Canadian company could expect to do – in other words, the old problem of economies of scale.

Certainly, Richardson's figure of "80 to 90 cents" that had annoyed Howe was higher than it should have been, but he had apparently based it on the early stages of a study that CAL was making for the government. He had been told by his executives that they estimated the costs on the Winnipeg-Vancouver segment of the route at 84 cents a mile; but when the rest of the costs were worked out and the overhead distributed over the whole trans-Canada route the estimate came down to 70 cents a mile.

This was the final figure formally quoted in the proposal to the government – it was transmitted by Sir Edward Beatty – at the end of September 1936. Thompson and the other executives of CAL had been refining and developing their studies ever since the first CAL proposal was presented to the Bennett government and what they now submitted was in effect a complete blueprint for a national airmail service. They had worked out a complete coast-to-coast schedule, based on a fleet of twelve Lockheed Electras with twenty-one pilots and twenty-one co-pilots and covering 3,445 route miles; specified the equipment and personnel required for maintenance and other functions; prepared complete organizational charts; and estimated capital and operating costs. The proposal envisaged CAL hiving off its existing operations into a new subsidiary, to be called Airways Limited. The new company to operate the trunk line across the country would retain the name Canadian Airways, and the new investment required in it was estimated at $3.4 million: $1.65 million for new equipment and terminal facilities, $1.25 million for its participation in the transatlantic service with Imperial Airways, and $500,000 in working capital. This, it was suggested, should be contributed by CAL and the two railroads, with CAL eventually holding 25 per cent of the equity and the CNR and CPR 37.5 per cent each – thus, in Richardson's view, effectively excluding competitors he felt had no right to muscle in.

It appeared for a time that Howe would accept this plan. He wrote to Richardson on October 29 saying: "I had a long talk about aviation with Sir Edward Beatty, and there is little difference of opinion between us regarding the development of the national service. . . ." But whatever past promises he had made to the Centurions – perhaps they had drawn too much encouragement from the easy affability of his campaigning days – seemed to be coming back to haunt him. Certainly, the Toronto group's lobbying continued. Mackenzie King noted in his diary after a talk with Howe on November 19: "He is terribly annoyed at the pressure of private interests, and from friends of the party. . . . I advised caution in making any commitments until Cabinet had a chance of going over the matter very fully. Howe is inclined to go much too far in committing the administration himself. The question is one which will require great care. . . ."

To exercise that "great care," and no doubt to contribute to the political education of his impetuous new transport minister, King forthwith set up a cabinet subcommittee which met to consider the matter on November 26. King noted afterwards:

We were agreed on inadvisability of it being publicly owned, and as between giving it to a private corporation, particularly one in which Members of Parliament would be directly or indirectly connected, and having it placed under a Company representative of the two Railways, we were all agreed on the ultimate advantage of the latter alternative. Clearly, an Air Service will be a competitor with the Railways. To have it left as a purely private concern means a duplication of all sorts of facilities for connecting with railways, ticket agencies, etc., etc., and also possibly make the railways an even greater liability, as was the case with the truck lines, privately owned, which should have been captured at the outset by the Transcontinental systems. . . . This means neither Government ownership outright, nor private ownership outright, but part private, part public, with Government control, the right of the Government to take over the whole project at any time, if thought advisable, and undertaking to have service at cost at the beginning, while the project is getting under way. . . .

The full cabinet met on December 21 and as King noted in his diary afterwards: "We devoted some time to the consideration of the air mail service; to its underlying policy, namely, that of public control with the right of public ownership within time. Meanwhile, ownership to be divided between the two main railway companies and private interests. . . ."

Howe then sent Beatty a memorandum summarizing the cabinet's views on the form the new company should take. Headed "Trans-Canada Airlines Co.," this began: "A private Company formed to operate an aviation service between Montreal and Vancouver, Montreal and Halifax, and such other interurban routes as may be designated to it by the Department of Transport. Stock of Company to be owned 50% by Canadian Pacific Railway and such private Aviation interests as it may nominate, and 50% by Canadian National Railways and such private Aviation interests as it may nominate."

Richardson's first reaction to this was that if both railroads chose CAL as their nominated private interest "this would give entire approval to the proposals we have made." But Beatty soon set him straight. In view of Richardson's directorship of the CPR and his close association with Beatty, the government had changed the proposal "to prevent your company holding the balance of power in the new Company, the Government apparently being persuaded that this was tantamount to Canadian Pacific control." And in fact the government intended that the CNR should offer participation to the Toronto group. "The gentlemen whom the Government desire to have an opportunity to subscribe for stock," Beatty wrote, "are: Mr. J.H. Gundy of Toronto, Mr. Ray Lawson of Winnipeg, Mr. C.G. McCullagh of the Toronto *Mail and Globe* [sic], General Victor Odlum of Vancouver, Mr. Frank Common of Montreal, Mr. Charles Burns of Toronto and the Hon. J.L. Ralston of Montreal. . . . Their pressure has been exerted through the Minister of Defence and the Postmaster General, and their representatives were present in Ottawa on the day the matter received Cabinet consideration." On the other hand, Howe seemed to have left the railways a loophole: "His view was that we should say to these gentlemen that they would have an opportunity of subscribing for a small block of stock (not more than 10 percent in the aggregate) for cash, and he did not anticipate that many of them would take advantage of the offer."

In his letter to Richardson enclosing a copy of the memorandum, Beatty noted without comment that the government undertook to pay all the company's operating losses for the first two years, and that a return of 5 per cent was guaranteed on the capital employed, which was projected as $5 million. He did not object to a provision that the Minister of Transport must approve the initial allocation of stock and any transfers of it later. Nor, at that time, did he comment on the provision that each railway should appoint four directors to the board, with the Minister of Transport nominating one more. But when Howe sent him a draft copy of the proposed bill in February 1937, and invited his comments, Beatty drew attention to this feature of it and said that since he considered the directors of the CNR to be to all intents and purposes representatives of the government, the CPR, while it was expected to put up half the capital for the new company, would be in a minority position on the board. This, he thought, could be solved by including a new subsection in the draft to provide that any matter coming before the directors should require the agreement of a majority of the CNR and CPR directors.

The draft also contained a provision that the government could take over the company at any time at its book value, and Beatty protested that this would ignore any goodwill the company might have built up in the interim. He suggested an amendment to provide that the government could take over the company's stock "on payment to the shareholders of the fair value thereof, which shall not be less than the book value." Another clause in the bill reserved to the Minister of Transport the right to determine what property the company could acquire for stock and on what terms. Beatty sensed that this might have some bearing on the original plan to fold CAL into the new company in return for a 25 per cent share in the equity and complained to Howe that it presupposed a lack of responsibility on the part of the directors and should be deleted from the bill entirely.

He also suggested a few other minor changes in wording and added: "With these changes the bill may be considered satisfactory to this Company, though, of course, I do not know what Mr. Richardson feels about it. In fairness to him I think you should receive any representations he cares to make because, while his Company is not mentioned in the Act, it is understood by all of us that it will be a participant."

In his reply, Howe rejected Beatty's argument that the government ought to pay for the company's goodwill in the event of a takeover, since "any goodwill the Company may have built up is due to the action of the Government in assigning exclusive routes and in guaranteeing the Company against operating deficits." He also insisted on retaining the right to oversee the issuance of stock for property or services, since the government "is entitled to protect itself against the issue of capital other than for a bona fide investment."

Worst of all, in Beatty's view, the minister left his position on control of the new company vague, merely saying he felt it could be provided for in the company's by-laws. He did not want to refer to it in the bill because "it seems unnecessary to introduce this clause into parliamentary debate, particularly as a suggestion is expected that the railways will use control of the company to throttle competition."

And as for Richardson, Howe had only the chilliest of comfort: "Mr. Richardson has seen an earlier draft of the bill. Now that the bill is ready for submission to Parliament I can see no purpose in delaying matters to enable him to examine it in its final form. If he is dissatisfied with the bill he will probably be in the same position as all other companies now engaged in aviation."

Throughout its history, the men at the head of the CPR have been formidable figures, forces to be reckoned with by governments of whatever political stripe. Sir Edward Beatty was as imperious as any man who has held the post. And the letter he forthwith fired back to Howe fairly dripped with his reproach. "Will you permit me to point out," he said, "that if the Government constitutes a company in part with private capital and presumably composed of men of equal integrity to those constituting the Government itself, it is improper to assume that they would act otherwise than in accordance with strict ethics, and would not issue the stock of the Company for inadequate consideration. This is the reason why your proposed Section is, I think, inappropriate. . . ." Furthermore: "May I correct a misapprehension which apparently you are under. The goodwill of the Company will not be built up because the Government has given it a mail subsidy and allocated a route to it; it will be built up through other business which will be secured in consequence of the efficiency and safety of its operations." And as to the question of the company's control: "I would not be agreeable to control of the Company's directorate being in the hands of four directors from the Canadian National and one from the Government. That would put the Canadian Pacific, with a fifty percent interest in the stock, in a minority of the Board, which, of course, is unthinkable."

In short, the sections of the bill to which he objected were "unfair and unacceptable," and: "May I point out, too, that Mr. Richardson can scarcely be considered as in the same position as any other air service company in Canada, and any attempt to put him in that category will, I feel sure, be resented strongly by anyone who has a knowledge of the history of civil aviation in this country."

By this time, Richardson was reduced to the plaintive confession that "there does not appear to be anything further I can do at present." He was, he wrote, "entirely in accord" with Beatty's criticism of the bill, and: "Howe's idea that all important matters concerning the policy and operations of the company should centre on his desk is all wrong. . . ." The minister had assured him that CAL would be treated fairly, but "experience has convinced me that Mr. Howe's word provides nothing very substantial to depend on."

Beatty and Richardson, it seems, were not alone in their reservations about the bill, because when Howe presented it to cabinet it was held up for further consideration. In later years, Howe would make much of the fact that the CPR and CAL had been invited to participate in the establishment of the national airline and had declined to do so. But a reading of the revised version of the bill he now sent to Beatty suggests that, perhaps if not Howe himself, certainly someone in the government had decided to make Beatty an offer he had to refuse. The major change was in the composition of the new company's board of directors: instead of the two railways appointing four directors each and the government one, the bill now proposed that the two railways and the government appoint three directors each. Familiar as he was with business practice, Howe must surely have realized that Beatty's objection to being outvoted five to four could not be met by a suggestion that he be outvoted six to three.

Minutes of cabinet meetings were not kept in those days, and it seems unlikely that the mystery will ever be resolved. But perhaps there are a few clues to the prevailing philosophy in Mackenzie King's diary. The Prime Minister and the chairman of the CPR were both bachelors, and each described the other as his friend – though it seemed to Jack Pickersgill, King's private secretary for so long, that they were "not very friendly friends." Both were proud men, and as such protective of their prerogatives. By virtue of their positions, they were probably the two most powerful men in the land; some degree of rivalry between them must therefore be counted as natural. And in Pickersgill's view, King, "while he wasn't hostile in a niggling way," felt at times that the CPR was "trying to take over the country."

At an early stage of the cabinet's consideration of the plans for a national airways company, King noted in his diary: "I think our ministers talk too much to Beatty, especially Howe." And later: "It seemed to me the bill was drafted to put air transportation too completely in the hands of the two railways; that it did not recognize sufficiently the need for Government ownership and control."

The question of the need, or otherwise, for government ownership, control, or even involvement in private business has always been a controversial one, and it would often bring the hornets buzzing around Howe's head in the years to come. Indeed, he had lately been embroiled in a controversy that had exercised the media (though that term had yet to become fashionable) far more than the problem of the airways, and that was the problem of the airwaves. Howe, since his new department had inherited responsibility for the country's radio communications, had borne the full fury of a campaign by the private broadcasters, and those newspapers which owned or hoped to acquire radio stations, against the government's heinous plan to set up something called the Canadian Broadcasting Corporation under government ownership, which, the broadcasters had been assured, did not automatically mean government control.

One can only assume that Beatty shared the broadcasters'

doubts about this assurance. But by expressing his willingness to enter an equal partnership with the CNR he was in effect accepting it. The problem was, as he saw it, that he was not being offered an equal partnership with the government. He warned Howe again that his Board would probably not accept the government's proposal and was not mollified by the minister's reply: "It is the intention of the Government to appoint directors who are substantial businessmen interested in an efficient aviation service. . . . I cannot agree with your suggestion that Canadian National Railways is to all intents and purposes a department of Government. On the contrary, the Government maintains only a very slight contact with the railway."

A few years later, directing the country's war production, Howe did in fact earn a reputation for appointing men to jobs and then leaving them to get on with them without interference, unless they incurred his displeasure by doing them badly, when retribution tended to be swift and irreversible. But Beatty was not to be persuaded. After all, what could one make of a man who had lately told the House of Commons: "A minister is careful to see that he does not allow himself to get mixed up with politics."

On March 17, 1937, after a meeting of the CPR's executive committee, Sir Edward Beatty wrote Howe a short letter expressing regret that the government's latest assurances had not changed his directors' opinion and adding: "It is not, in the circumstances, necessary to continue our correspondence, and I should appreciate it if, in the Bill as introduced, you would omit any reference to this company."

CHAPTER FOUR

O HIS SURPRISE, and no doubt relief, Howe had a much easier time piloting Bill 74 through Parliament than he had had determining its outline with his cabinet colleagues. Introduced for first reading on March 22, it went through all its stages with only reservations, rather than real objections, being voiced, and received royal assent three weeks later, on April 10.

With the CPR out of the picture, the bill was hastily redrafted to place control of the new airline in the hands of the CNR. It was this feature of it that attracted most criticism, not because the government was trespassing on the preserve of private enterprise by establishing a national airline, but because it was using the debt-ridden and universally derided CNR as its intermediary. The provision that the government could take over the company at any time at book value remained, but the Conservative leader, R.B. Bennett, and J.S. Woodsworth, the socialist founder of the CCF, both urged Howe to go the whole hog and entrust the operation of the new airline right from the start to a separate government commission along the lines of the recently approved CBC. "As we are creating it, let us hold it," said Bennett. "As we are making it, let us keep it."

About the general desirability of Canada having its own airline there was no argument. Introducing the bill, Howe told the House that during 1936 more than a million passengers had travelled on U.S. airlines, and they included many Canadians journeying between points in Canada. Honourable members on all sides appeared to agree that it was high time Canada had its own service. And, as the minister pointed out, added urgency was given to the matter by Canada's commitment to carry the mails from the Atlantic to the Pacific as part of the joint British-Irish-Canadian transatlantic venture about to get under way.

The new company, he explained, would be given an exclusive contract to fly mail, passengers and express "on the main artery of traffic across the country, and such other arteries of traffic as are designated by the government as being of national importance."* The company would not undertake anything other than inter-urban services and there was no intention to interfere with any already existing operations. As to the cost of all this, the capital requirements were estimated at $5 million, and the cost of operations at $1 million a year. "It is thought," the minister said, "that from the start the mail contract and such passenger and express business as is immediately available should cover the cost of the service. We have made provision, however, for a subsidy to protect the service in that period."

The mechanism selected for paying the subsidy became a sore point in the Post Office in later years. For the first two years – what was defined as the "initial period" – the government proposed to make up any deficit the corporation incurred by a direct payment. Thereafter, the rate charged the Post Office would be set at a level high enough to cover the cost of operation plus any deficit incurred during the preceding year. But if the airline had made a profit during the preceding year the cost to the Post Office would be reduced by only half the amount of the profit. "The set-up," Howe explained, "is such that the company will be protected against loss, but its profits will be very strictly limited. In other words, it is organized to perform a certain national service, and it is expected that that service will be performed at or near cost."

On the bill's second reading, Howe confessed that setting up and operating the new service was "a very difficult problem." And here he displayed the tactics that became his hallmark in the years ahead, so admirable to some, so irksome to others: he, personally, had looked into it; he would see that it was done.

I have ridden in every type of equipment used on the mail routes in the United States; I have discussed the problem with the heads of all the successful trans-American companies; I have had the privilege of discussing the problem with the general manager of Imperial Airways and with officers of the British air ministry, and I have read every report in this connection that I have been able to lay my hands on. As a result of all this, I have come to certain conclusions.

---

*These routes were designated from time to time in a separate Trans-Canada Contract between the government and the airline, provided for in the act establishing the corporation. The first contract, negotiated in June 1937, designated TCA to fly "A transcontinental line of aircraft from Moncton, in the Province of New Brunswick, to Vancouver, in the Province of British Columbia, via such route as may be designated by the Governor in Council; a line of aircraft from Lethbridge to Edmonton, via such route as may be designated by the Governor in Council; lines of aircraft that may be designated from time to time while this contract is in force by the Governor in Council."

Those conclusions were that, since the CNR was already in the transportation business, and the new airline would have a parallel requirement for such things as ticket offices, ways of soliciting passenger and express business, and legal services, the CNR "should be the means of organizing this company, just as it was used as the means for operating such shipping as the government has owned, and the means of operating other government transportation facilities." And in turning the problem over to the CNR the minister was "turning it over to seven able business men who have a certain responsibility to the government. . . ."

The question had been asked whether the government had invited private aviation companies to participate in the new venture. "May I say we did not need to invite them," Howe told the House. "They came from every part of Canada and the United States, and put on the most persistent lobby in Ottawa that I have ever seen. The only way we could make progress was to absolutely refuse to talk to them. We said, 'Go back home. We will write our bill, and when we get it written and bring it down you will see it. If you then want any part in it we will give you the chance to discuss the matter'."

The Centurions apparently did not want any part of it, since even though the Trans-Canada Air Lines Act authorized the CNR to sell up to 49.8 per cent of the airline's 50,000 shares to "such persons engaged or interested in aviation as are approved by the Minister," no more was heard of any participation by British North American Airways. As Howe had predicted, merely taking a minority interest in an enterprise whose potential profit was pegged by the government evidently failed to appeal to the Toronto group.*

Nor did the role he was offered, when the offer came, appeal to Jim Richardson. Perhaps Howe, having founded an airline at the stroke of a pen, without the participation of a single representative from the Canadian aviation world, felt himself in an exposed position. At any rate, he seems to have had a change of heart toward the man he had said he could not work with. As

---

*At some stage during the lobbying – whether in exasperation or encouragement is not clear – Howe told the BNA group that their case would be stronger if they owned some aeroplanes. The group had hired as their operations manager W. Roy Maxwell, a flamboyant World War I pilot who had organized the Ontario Provincial Air Service, and so the directors now put up $17,500 each and sent him out shopping. But BNA's first aircraft, a Dragon Rapide, did not go into service until June 1937, after TCA had been established. (On its maiden flight it carried the hockey heroes Charlie and Lionel Conacher to a fishing holiday on Rice Lake, an hour's drive from Toronto today.) BNA eventually had a small fleet of bush aircraft but was wound up a couple of years later. "All I ever got out of it," Burns recalled to the author, "was a sleeping bag."

soon as his bill was through the House, he sent Richardson a copy of it and invited him east to discuss it. "The legislation," he wrote, "has been very difficult to work out, due to conflicting views in the Government itself and pressure from outside, but I think we have finally arrived at a set-up that will permit an efficient operation under conditions that are reasonably workable. I hope you share my view."

Richardson didn't, but he agreed to discuss the matter with Howe and they met in Montreal on April 16. Howe suggested that Canadian Airways buy some of the shares in TCA that the CNR was authorized to sell, and that Richardson take one of the seats on the board of directors (which had now been reduced to seven members, four to be appointed by the "shareholders" – that is, the CNR – and three by the government). Richardson saw no place in that arrangement for the organization he had been preparing and the pilots he had been training, so he countered with an offer to organize and operate the Winnipeg-Vancouver segment of the mail service, in return for "an adequate management fee."

Howe rejected this offer; he said he did not think the legislation would permit it. So after consulting his own board, Richardson decided to take no part in the new company. As he wrote to a friend, he did not want to be "put into the position of taking responsibility without authority, and have to take blame without credit." He prepared a sharp letter of rebuke for Howe, accusing him in effect of misleading Parliament about the strength and experience of the CAL organization and adding: "On the basis of assurances given to me by you many times that Canadian Airways were to be the keystone of the transcontinental service it is very difficult for me to understand the conclusions finally arrived at. . . . I am sorry that you have seen fit to eliminate us." Sir Edward Beatty persuaded him to moderate his rather intemperate tone and in a milder letter written the same day, April 26, he declined Howe's invitation to sit on the board and said CAL would not be buying shares in TCA, though it would like to turn over to the new airline, at cost, its two Electras – one bought at Howe's express request – and the little Stearman biplane used as a back-up on the Vancouver-Seattle mail run.*

*Canadian Airways continued in business and Richardson continued to have his troubles with the Post Office. Eventually, in a private talk with Mackenzie King, he accused Coolican and Herring of demanding a kickback on one of CAL's mail contracts. King had both men on the carpet but was apparently satisfied with their denial of the allegation, since neither was fired. Richardson died suddenly in 1939, at the age of 53, and three years later CAL, with nine smaller companies acquired by the CPR, became Canadian Pacific Airlines.

This offer was eventually accepted, and indeed Howe had placed orders with the Lockheed company for three more Electras even before he had chosen the airline's directors. To represent the interests of the government, which it was agreed would continue to operate and maintain the landing fields, lights, radio beacons, and meteorological services, these were: Commander C.P. Edwards, one of Marconi's original engineers in England, who had come to Canada in 1906 and after a long career at the head of the Marine Department's radio branch had recently been appointed Chief of Air Services in the new Department of Transport; George Herring, of the Post Office; and John Wilson, who as Controller of Civil Aviation had been transferred from Defence to the new department.

The CNR directors Howe placed on the airline's board amply justified his assertion in the House that they would be "able business men." The one destined to play the most important role in the airline's success was Herbert J. Symington, whose mild, round face and pince-nez belied his strength and astuteness. A corporate lawyer in Winnipeg, where he had been a friend of Howe's, Symington had attracted the admiring attention of Izaak Walton Killam, one of Canada's most anonymous multi-millionaires, who had invited him east to become his right-hand man, as vice-president and general counsel of Royal Securities, the company at the apex of Killam's world-wide holdings in power utilities, paper companies and a variety of other profitable enterprises. Symington had become a director of several Killam companies by the time Howe appointed him to the "strong board" he set up to run the CNR after the abolition of the board of trustees.

Of the other three CNR appointments to the airline's directorate, two were men Howe had conscripted into running the railroad—Wilfrid Gagnon, a lively little Quebecker who used his family's shoe firm as a springboard to a remarkable business career during which, among other things, he became chairman of Dow Brewery, the Banque Canadienne Nationale and Canadian Aviation Electronics; and James Y. Murdoch, a tall, tough Bay Street lawyer who had set up, and become the guiding genius of, Noranda Mines.

By virtue of his presidency of the CNR, S.J. Hungerford inherited the presidency of TCA. A lifelong railroader, Sam Hungerford began work as a machinist's apprentice at Farnham, Quebec, at the age of 13, in the days when wood-burning locomotives still rode the rails. During his long career, he invented several mechanical devices used in railroading and became an authority on all phases of the business. But he was now 64, his health was none too robust, and he was bedevilled by problems at the CNR. So quite contentedly – and wisely, as it turned out – he left the operation of the airline almost entirely to the man Howe had chosen to launch it and pilot it through its infant years.

Howe had not been simply posturing when he told the House he had thoroughly investigated the airline business: it had become one of the great enthusiasms of his life. He had flown across the United States from coast to coast, sampling airlines, airports and aeroplanes, casting his engineer's eye over such details as runway lighting, communications and weather services.* He had also made it his business to cultivate such acknowledged titans of the airline industry as Eddie Rickenbacker of Eastern Airlines, Juan Trippe of Pan Am, and C.R. Smith of American Airlines.

His investigations rapidly confirmed his opinion that to overcome the U.S. airlines' ten-year lead he would need to import some American know-how; or perhaps he had had this conviction all along, which might help to explain his reluctance to deal with Richardson. It may have been Trippe who first suggested to him the name of Philip G. Johnson; another school of thought is that it was C.R. Smith. Either way, everyone he consulted agreed that he could do no better – a verdict that is enthusiastically seconded in retrospect by the Canadians who joined the airline while Johnson was at the helm.

The son of Swedish immigrants, Philip Gustav Johnson was an engineer who joined the Boeing Airplane Company in Seattle straight from university and became its president nine years later, at the age of 31. He was acknowledged to be one of the foremost business executives in the United States, and he was available to Howe only because he had become the innocent victim of one of those politically motivated "scandals" that periodically convulse official Washington.

As the airline industry burgeoned in the United States, the Boeing company expanded into a conglomerate that included United Airlines and the engine-manufacturing company Pratt & Whitney, with Phil Johnson at the head of the pyramid. In 1930, Johnson was among a group of airline executives summoned to a conference by the Republican postmaster general, Walter Folger Brown. Brown wanted to make the airmail a paying proposition for the Post Office and believed – like John Wilson – that this could best be achieved by encouraging mergers of most of

---

*Once, hearing that Sir Edward Beatty was going to be in New York, Howe arranged to take him out to Newark, then that city's main airport, showed him around, and ever thereafter quoted him as saying: "It's been one of the most interesting days I've ever spent, Clarence – but it will never become a popular form of *transportation*."

the small, uneconomic companies into a few large, efficient organizations, able to supplement their airmail revenue with a reliable, safe and profitable passenger business. And, he told the assembled executives, he proposed to award mail contracts in a way that would encourage this, and not simply to the lowest bidder. For instance, he specified that bidders for contracts must have at least six months of night-flying experience over routes of at least 250 miles. Since most of the small companies flew only in daylight this favoured the larger, better-established lines such as United.

The small companies naturally resented Brown's policy, but he made it stick. The airline business grew and prospered – until 1933, when Roosevelt's New Deal administration replaced the Republicans and an Alabama senator with a keen nose for publicity, Hugo L. Black, convened an inquiry into the awarding of airmail contracts. Black's investigators raided airline offices, seized files, subpoenaed witnesses, and Black made headlines with a series of charges designed to substantiate his contention that the previous government had shown undue favouritism toward certain large companies which had profited illegally thereby.

Most of the charges were proved unfounded years later, and Phil Johnson was cleared of any transgression more sinister than that of having responded to his government's summons to a meeting. But the Roosevelt administration took drastic action on Black's report; in 1934, it cancelled all mail contracts and called upon the Army Air Corps to fly the mail. The tragic results demonstrated for all time the difference between efficient airline operation and other forms of flying. The military aircraft were unsuitable for the job and their pilots lacked the rigorous training that would have enabled them to fly across the country day and night whatever the weather. Before the experiment was called off no fewer than twelve army pilots had been killed and many others injured in crashes.

When the administration returned the task of flying the mail to the airlines it also imposed a set of stipulations that caused a wholesale shake-up of the industry. Airlines were required to divest themselves of any connection with manufacturing companies, so the organization over which Johnson had presided, United Aircraft and Transport, lost its Pratt & Whitney and Boeing components and United Airlines henceforth had to fly by itself – and without Phil Johnson. For another stipulation was that no mail contract would be awarded to any company headed by an executive who had attended the 1930 conference. Johnson was among a group of airline executives barred by presidential decree from any connection with the airline industry for five years because of their attendance at the conference.

Johnson was shocked and hurt by this decree, but he was already a rich man – from the early days he had taken part of his salary in Boeing stock, a course he also urged on others who worked for him, to their ultimate enrichment – so he retired to his large house on Puget Sound and, in his own words, "just loafed." But loafing soon proved uncongenial to a man accustomed to working as hard as he habitually did, and in 1936 he bought the Kenworth truck plant in Seattle. Even running this was not enough to exhaust his considerable energy and when Howe's offer came he jumped at the chance to return to the industry he loved and to confront the challenge of building a transcontinental airline from scratch.

On June 24, 1937, the board of directors of Trans-Canada Air Lines appointed him vice-president of operations at an annual salary of $17,500, a handsome sum at that time but not one of particular concern to Johnson who, when he installed his family in Montreal, brought his own chauffeur and housekeeper with him. He was given a small office suite in the CN Express building at 355 McGill Street and Maynard Metcalf, Hungerford's assistant, was deputed to ask him if the CNR could supply him with some staff. "Just give me a couple of good clerks," Johnson replied. Metcalf sent him two intelligent and hard-working men whose climb up the ladder of the railway's administrative ranks was temporarily blocked by well-entrenched incumbents in the executive positions above them: W.F. "Bill" English and F.T. "Fred" Wood. Don MacLaren had already been hired as the airline's first employee, on May 15. His lobbying for Jim Richardson in Ottawa had not succeeded, but he had attracted the attention of Howe: he had airline experience and was a "name" in the aviation world, which perhaps Howe still felt he needed. At any rate, with Richardson's rather grudging permission, MacLaren switched over to the new airline, with no clearly defined role, though it was widely assumed he was being groomed for the top job.

Two weeks after Johnson's appointment, he took off with MacLaren as his guide on a 2,550-mile ground and air survey of the proposed TCA route between Montreal and Vancouver. They flew in a Department of Transport Lockheed piloted by Squadron Leader Tudhope, who would be at the controls a few weeks later on a flight that earned Johnson's displeasure.

Back in Montreal, Johnson quickly drew up a "plan of organization" for the new airline for submission to the board. Six of the departments whose establishment he recommended, he explained, "will obviously not be initiated immediately as they would be unable to function." These were: traffic and advertising, engineering, communications, dispatching, accounting, and purchasing. During the organization period, he suggested, some of the functions of those departments could be performed by the CNR; the rest could be carried out by his own department.

"Our first problem," he wrote, "will be to enter a period of training for pilots and ground personnel . . . radio operators, dispatchers, weather observers and mechanics. This training will be carried out on a section of the route over which we can first expect to have in operation radio and weather facilities. In all probability this will be the Winnipeg-Lethbridge run and the Vancouver-Seattle run [which was still being flown by Canadian Airways], if same is absorbed by Trans-Canada Air Lines."

It had been thought selected personnel could be sent to an existing aviation school, but Johnson recommended that TCA do all its own training, with the type of aircraft that would ultimately be used in regular operations – and he had a sufficiently commanding presence to make sure his recommendation was accepted, despite the added expense it entailed. The Vancouver-Seattle run could be used for training, he said, so TCA should buy the two Lockheed Electras and the Stearman biplane Richardson had offered, and take over that route. He also recommended the purchase, for $10,000, of one of the recently developed Link trainers, mock-up cockpits which simulated real flight conditions and were used to train pilots in flying on instruments.

The "general plan of operation" was to divide the airline into two divisions: an eastern division from Montreal to Winnipeg and a western division from Winnipeg to Vancouver. "Logically then," Johnson wrote, "the operations headquarters should be in Winnipeg. The preliminary training program will also be carried out from Winnipeg west, and it also seems proper to predict that the first scheduled operations will be from the same point to Vancouver." Accordingly, he recommended the construction of a 200-foot-square hangar at Winnipeg airport, with a lean-to office and stores building 30 feet wide along one side, at an estimated cost of $200,000, "contingent on the City of Winnipeg carrying out its present airport plans, with immediate commencement of such airport improvements as are called for thereunder." Thus were sown, so innocently, the seeds of much future discord.

Having sketched in a few pages the future shape of one of the world's leading airlines, Johnson now put forward his immediate requirements: he requested authority to employ four instructors, "bearing in mind that they will have to be secured in all probability from the United States." It is worth quoting those requirements in his own words: "One detail operation man capable of supervision and instruction in all matters of operation; one flying supervisor capable of organizing a training program for instrument flying and to select and pass on flying personnel; one specialist in radio engineering, including both voice and beam; one specialist in meteorology as applied to scheduled transport operation." These men, he recommended, should be employed on a temporary basis for two years, during which they would develop Canadians able to take over from them.

The board speedily approved Johnson's plan, and three of the four instructors he brought in had been his trusted lieutenants at United, and had benefited from his advice to take up Boeing shares. D.B. Colyer, his "detail operation man," had been superintendent of the U.S. Air Mail Service before joining United as operations manager and, later, vice-president. H.T. "Slim" Lewis, who became superintendent of flying, was a tall, lean-faced westerner with a ranch in Wyoming; before becoming chief pilot of United he had been one of the elite breed of open-cockpit pilots who pioneered the early U.S. airmail. The meteorological specialist, O.T. "Ted" Larson, was so highly regarded in his field that later, during World War II, he took a leave of absence from TCA at the request of General "Hap" Arnold, chief of the U.S. Army Air Corps, to undertake the hush-hush assignment of planning and installing the meteorological service for the famous "Hump" route between Burma and China. Only the man chosen to supervise TCA's communications had no United background: S.S. "Steve" Stevens came from Eastern Airlines, though he had been born in Canada. Later, Johnson brought in another United Airlines expert, Oliver West, to organize and head the maintenance and engineering branch.

This handful of men, tough and at the top of their field, quickly set the pattern for the new TCA and established standards of performance and reliability that within a comparatively few years made it a leader among the world's airlines. From the start, their emphasis was on discipline and the over-riding importance of safety – a lesson they drilled into everyone down the line, not merely the pilots. Steve Stevens used to tell the radio technicians he hired: "If you ever make a mistake and cause an accident, you'll be blackballed for life." And in imposing their own strict standards on the new organization, the American instructors created a solid esprit de corps, a mystique almost, that persisted long past the era when everyone in TCA knew everyone else.

Soon after Johnson's appointment there was a headline-making flight of the kind that neither Johnson nor Slim Lewis intended to tolerate at TCA. Apparently resolved to imbue the rest of the country with his own enthusiasm for the future of aviation–and no doubt to drum up business for his new airline – C.D. Howe decided to make the first-ever flight from Montreal to Vancouver between dawn and dusk on the same day. On July 30, with Herb Symington and his good friend Commander Edwards, he took off from St. Hubert airport early in the morning in the Department of Transport's Lockheed 12A piloted by Squadron Leader Tudhope. A South African with a distinguished flying record during World War I, "Tuddy" (who would later join TCA) emigrated to Canada after the armistice, tried his hand briefly at farming, then joined the RCAF. Seconded to the Civil Aviation branch, he flew many of the survey flights for John Wilson's airway, and it was fortunate for Howe and his party that he was a meticulous and skilful navigator as well as pilot.

Soon after they climbed off over Montreal on their way to Ottawa, they ran into a heavy thunderstorm, and unable to find a way round it or under it Tudhope turned back for St. Hubert. In a letter describing the flight to Sir Edward Beatty, Jim Richardson said he then put the aeroplane in the hangar with no intention of taking it out again that day, but Howe insisted on making another attempt to get through. Jack Hunter, the co-pilot on the flight, told the author years later he did not know whether the decision to try again was Tudhope's or Howe's, but at any rate it almost proved disastrous.

The Lockheed had been fitted with an extra fuel tank to give it a range of about 500 miles, plus the usual 45-minute reserve, and when Tudhope heard on his radio that there was dirty weather ahead he landed at the emergency field at Gillies, 80 miles north of North Bay, to fill up his tanks–fortunately, because for the rest of the way across northern Ontario they were flying above an unbroken layer of thick fog and their radio reports told them it extended right down to the ground. They were unable to land at either of two future TCA stops, Kapuskasing and Wagaming (now Armstrong), so headed on west toward Sioux Lookout without a glimpse of the ground. Heavy static on the radio now prevented them from communicating with any ground station by voice, but providentially Commander Edwards's early training paid off: as the only man aboard who knew the Morse Code, he manned the key and raised the operator at Sioux Lookout, who told them the sky there was clear. The radio beacons which could have given them their position had not yet been installed on this rugged section of the airway, but thanks to Tudhope's accurate dead reckoning across almost 600 miles of inhospitable bush they cleared the murk about 30 miles from the airport and landed with their tanks nearly empty. "If their gas had given out just before they got to Sioux Lookout," Richardson wrote to Beatty, "they would all have been written off. . . . It was altogether just a fool piece of business and something that could only be gotten away with the odd time. . . ."

From Sioux Lookout on to Vancouver the weather was better, though they had to climb to 14,000 feet to get above the clouds over the Rockies, and soon after they touched down at Vancouver another thunderstorm broke. They arrived 17 hours and 10 minutes after their departure from St. Hubert, and they had been in the air for 14 hours and 10 minutes of that time. Howe stepped off the aircraft beaming, told the assembled reporters how much he had enjoyed the trip, and a good deal of free publicity resulted for the infant airline.

But Philip Johnson had been in Winnipeg when the flight came through and he was not amused. Short and tubby, Johnson had a pink, cherubic face and twinkling blue eyes that almost disappeared into his dimpled cheeks when he laughed at the Swedish-dialect stories he liked to tell. Behind the jovial exterior, though, was a tough, decisive man, and those blue eyes could turn suddenly very cool when he was faced with anything he viewed as tomfoolery or inefficiency. He told Howe disgustedly that he considered the flight nothing but a dangerous stunt. And he privately resolved that there would be no stunting on *his* airline.

CHAPTER FIVE

B Y THE END OF 1937, the new airline had seventy-one employees and the training programs were well under way. They would continue for almost a year and a half before the first transcontinental passenger service was launched, but mail and passengers were already being carried between Vancouver and Seattle. Phil Johnson had quickly come to terms with Jim Richardson and TCA bought his two Electras and the Stearman for the prices he quoted: $55,234 for one of the Electras and $63,618 for the other, which had fewer flying hours and was equipped with skis (which the airline never used); plus $5,000 for the Stearman. The three new Electras ordered by Howe were delivered in the fall, bringing the airline's total spending on equipment for the year up to $492,000. The operating deficit, paid by the government as arranged, was $111,005.07.

One of the Electras bought from CAL was based in Winnipeg for pilot training. With the other, on September 1, TCA took over the Vancouver-Seattle mail run, which thus became its first commercial service. At the controls for the inaugural flight were two of the CAL pilots who had been flying the route, Captains E.P. "Billy" Wells and Maurice F. McGregor. Their instrument-training instructor, Lewis Leigh, had preceded them into TCA as chief pilot ten days earlier, becoming the first pilot hired, at captain's pay of $400 a month; in the months and years that followed many more CAL employees gravitated to the new line.

Johnson had told the board that the Stearman could be used for instrument training but it never was. A few of the pilots were checked out on it in case it was ever needed as back-up for the mail flights, but it was soon parked in a corner of the Winnipeg hangar and the only use made of it was by the hangar cat, which gave birth to kittens on the pilot's seat. It gathered dust until 1939, when it was sold to a bush operator for $1,000 cash.

Slim Lewis – "Old High Pockets" to the pilots, because of his long legs – established his flying school in a former CAL hangar at Stevenson Field, the Winnipeg airport. His first instructors were

Lewis Leigh and Bill Straith, a Canadian who had built one of the first aeroplanes seen in Winnipeg and gone on to become a senior pilot with Northwest Airlines in the United States. All the pilots hired, however extensive their experience, were required to take Leigh's course in instrument flying, night flying and use of the radio ranges, or marker beacons, which were being set up across the country as fast as the Department of Transport could install them. These consisted of four radio towers placed in a square with a fifth, a transmitter used to broadcast an hourly weather report and communicate with the aircraft, sited in the centre. On each side of the square, one of the outer towers continuously emitted the one-short, one-long signal of the Morse Code *A*, and the other the Morse *N* – the opposite sequence, one long, one short.*When a pilot came within earshot of a beacon he would hear these signals in his earphones and steer a path between them until, because of their opposite sounds, they merged into a continuous hum, and he knew he was exactly on course. Shortly thereafter the signals would disappear and he would be in the "cone of silence" – in other words, directly above the beacon. Those beacons placed near airports guided the pilots in to land, though if because of bad visibility they could not see the runway by the time they had passed over the cone of silence at 1,000 feet and then descended to 300 feet, they had to climb away again and either go round for another attempted landing or fly to an alternate airport where conditions were better. Other beacons sited at intervals across the continent kept the pilots on course during their flights – when they could hear them, which was not always in those early days, before the era of VHF, or very high frequency, transmission.

The pilots found that flying on their earphones demanded more practice and skill than flying by sight, and "flying blind," depending on their instruments alone, proved an unnerving experience for some of the old-timers attending Slim Lewis's school, who were accustomed to navigating their way across country by reference to well-memorized landmarks or following the railroads, "the good old iron compasses." But instrument flying had to be mastered, because of a quirk of human physiology. One's sense of balance and orientation derives from a combination of messages to the brain from the eye and a delicate mechanism in the

*On these early ranges, pilots could only track in accurately from four directions. A later and much-improved system, the VOR (Visual Omni-directional Range), introduced after World War II and still in use, gives pilots their bearings when coming in from any direction.

inner ear. Deprived of his visual orientation with the horizon, a pilot suddenly entering a cloud or bank of fog can no longer rely on the signals from his inner ear to tell him whether his aircraft is flying straight and level, going into a steep turn, or even into a dive. Before instrument flying was developed, unsuspecting pilots occasionally emerged from a cloud screaming straight down toward the ground. Some were unable to recover from these involuntary dives; others broke off their wings in the attempt.

So day after day, Lewis, Leigh and Straith took the new pilots up in the Electras, walled off from all contact with the outside world by a canopy over their half of the cockpit and curtains drawn around them. Within this canvas cave, they would have to fly a precise course, on an even keel, solely by scanning their instruments: their artificial horizon, airspeed indicator, compass, turn-and-bank, rate-of-climb, altimeter – the instrument panels of today's automated world, though immensely more complex, differ little in their essentials from those of 1937. And to add spice to the hapless students' lives, the instructor would as often as not cut one of their two engines on take-off, to accustom them to handling their aircraft in emergencies.

Some veterans never mastered this art and could not be "checked out." But if a pilot showed signs of making progress there was no limit to the hours of training he would be given. And always there would be Slim Lewis, with his stress on *safety*, first, last and always. One of his former students recalls that Lewis looked like a cowboy even in his business suit, rolling a cigarette in one hand – he never adapted to Canadian brands – and delivering himself of such terse nuggets of advice as "Always have an ace in the hole." Meaning, of course, that a pilot should never get himself into a situation he did not know how to get out of. He also instilled in his charges the strict principle that airline captains are as much masters of their craft as their predecessors on the world's oceans. "Never take out a flight under duress," he would instruct them, "from management, company personnel, or the public."

The first practice flights were made over the flat terrain of the prairies, but everyone knew there was a greater challenge ahead: launching the first regular air service across the formidable barrier of the Rockies. Those great mountain ranges had already been crossed by a few intrepid pioneers, notably Captain E.C. Hoy, who accomplished the feat as early as 1919, flying from Vancouver (with refuelling stops at Vernon, Grand Forks and Cranbrook) to Lethbridge in an already outmoded JN4 biplane

A 1938 promotional photograph, taken at Winnipeg, suggests the irresistible appeal of air travel to youth.

Relief project. Construction of intermediate landing field in 1934.
— (Public Archives of Canada)

One of the hundreds of radio range stations built at one-hundred-mile intervals across Canada in the 1930s.

James A. Richardson, second from right, was considered to be the father of Canadian civil aviation. He is seen here with Ben Smith, a New York financier, the Honourable J.S. McDiarmid, Lieutenant-Governor of Manitoba, Mitchell Hepburn, Premier of Ontario, and J.P. Bickell, owner of the Grumman G-21 plane in the background. –
(Richardson Archives – Canadian Airways Ltd. collection, Provincial Archives of Manitoba)

P.G. Johnson and D.B. Colyer used a Department of Transport aircraft on an inspection trip from Vancouver, here seen at Winnipeg on July 10, 1937.

Members of C.D. Howe's party and the airways officials who saw them off from St. Hubert airport, Montreal, on Friday, July 30, 1937. From left to right: *D.W. Saunders, L. Parmenter, engineer; F.I. Banghart, airport manager; W.H. Hobbs, secretary, TCA and CNR; H.J. Symington, member of the board of directors, TCA and CNR; Mr. Howe; Squadron Leader J.H. Tudhope, chief pilot; Commander C.P. Edwards, chief of air service, Department of Transport; J.D. Hunter, co-pilot; J.A. Wilson, controller of civil aviation; George Wakeman, divisional inspector of air services; and D.R. MacLaren, TCA.*

Vancouver 1938. Communication from the roof of the Administration Building as plane approaches the airport. TCA radio operator Dunc E. Matheson "on remote."

With the left half of the cockpit curtained off, Captain Dave Imrie demonstrates his ability on instrument flying to J.H. Sandgathe, one of TCA's check pilots, 1938.

Loading mail into the nose compartment of a Lockheed 10A at Winnipeg, May 1938.

Lewis Leigh and H.T. Lewis, right, instructor pilot and technical adviser of flying for TCA, who flew two new Lockheed 14s to Vancouver from the factory, May 10, 1938.

For some time after TCA's first familiarization flight to Toronto airport in 1938 this farmhouse was used as a terminal building.

Loading first express shipments at Montreal, October 17, 1938.

The first two stewardesses thrilled to be hired in July 1938, Lucile Garner and Pat Eccleston, beside a Lockheed 14 at Vancouver.

An hour before scheduled take-off, D.B. Kennedy of the Department of Transport meteorological service discusses weather maps with Captain Herb Seagrim, First Officer William Barnes and dispatcher Irving Thomas to draw up the plan for their flight.

Stewardess practising on a fellow employee how to apply an oxygen mask.

bolstered by an extra 12-gallon fuel tank.* But those early flights had threaded their way *through* the mountains in good weather, rather than soared above them day and night whatever the conditions, as a regularly scheduled airline must do.

So, soon after the training school opened, Bill Straith took a group of the more experienced graduates to Vancouver and they began a series of test flights to explore the still unknown problems they were going to have to overcome to fly the mountains: the sometimes fierce sustained winds and the unpredictable gusts and gaps in them that could toss their little Lockheeds around like corks on a stormy ocean; the towering cloud masses; the often erratic performance of the radio ranges sited in the valleys along the route, where the rough terrain sometimes caused so much distortion of signals that when there was static the pilots could not decipher them; and above all, the pilot's worst enemy at that time – icing.

In certain weather conditions, ice can build up on an unprotected aircraft at the rate of an inch a minute. If enough of it forms on the wings it can disrupt the smooth flow of air over them and destroy their lifting capacity, causing the aircraft to drop off in a stall even though it is flying much faster than its normal stalling speed. And on the piston-engined Lockheeds, ice clinging to the propellers could impair their efficiency, thus reducing the effectiveness of the engines to a dangerous level.

The icing problem is not confined to Canada, though it is worse here than in more temperate climates, and not much was known about the problem when Straith's group began their pioneering flights over the Rockies, where it can occur all year round, as the warm, moisture-laden winds from the Pacific roil around among the ice-covered peaks and finally roll down on to the prairies, which may be basking in the summer sun or gripped by their paralysing below-zero winters.

A pilot encountering icing had to make a critical decision quickly. What was the weather like ahead? Could he climb out of the icing layer into a free zone? Should he turn back for home right away? Or could he descend into a warmer layer of air and melt the ice off? Over the Rockies, this latter course was seldom possible: Slim Lewis had studied the route and decreed that TCA pilots must maintain a minimum altitude of 11,000 feet over the

---

*The Vancouver-Lethbridge crossing was chosen as the easiest route from the beginning, so that Lethbridge was an important station in the early days of TCA, and the route north from there to Calgary and Edmonton was operated as a spur line.

mountains, to give them at least a thousand feet of clearance over the highest peaks.

Eventually, manufacturers in the United States developed de-icing "boots" for wings and propellers: flexible rubberized tubes installed along their leading edges which could be inflated pneumatically to break the ice as it formed. Much later, when the jets came along, systems were developed to funnel warm exhaust emissions from the engines through the leading edges of the wings to heat them and prevent the ice from forming at all. Before these developments, the pioneer TCA pilots faced many anxious moments and some only narrowly averted catastrophe.

After three months of trail-blazing by Straith's group – during which, miraculously, no one came to grief – the time was judged ripe to introduce a daily "ghost service" for training purposes between Winnipeg and Vancouver. It began on February 1, 1938, and of course it provided training not only for the pilots but for all those other specialists essential to the operation of a scheduled airline, such as the maintenance and overhaul mechanics, instrument technicians, radio operators and flight dispatchers at stations along the route.

Most of the early mechanics were recruited from Canadian Airways and some of the other smaller private operations, and some joined from the RCAF and the Ontario Provincial Air Service. Some had been licensed "air engineers," the unsung heroes of bush flying, who travelled with the pilots but trailed far behind them in the glamour stakes. Upon the air engineer had devolved myriad responsibilities, which all boiled down to keeping the machine flying whatever the conditions: he repaired and maintained the engine, not only at home base but on any remote lake where fate might deposit it; he was the one who drained the engine oil as soon as the plane landed in some northern winter, and lit the blowpot to thaw it out again next morning; he was the one who stood waist deep in near-freezing water repairing a float damaged by a collision with a submerged log; and not least, in the words of Emile "Pat" Patrault, one of the breed who later rose through the ranks to become TCA's maintenance supervisor in Toronto, "you passed the rum bottle to the pilot on the way home."

Later, as the various support shops were established at the Winnipeg base to deal with the overhaul of engines, propellers, instruments, airframes and so on, the demand for skilled tradesmen with aviation experience outgrew the supply. It was met by the transfer from the CNR of men who had graduated from its rigorous apprenticeship system with a variety of specialist skills which they were quickly able to adapt to the airline's requirements.

The man in charge of maintenance and overhaul, Oliver West, was a tough taskmaster; perhaps the nagging pain of the arthritis which had badly twisted up his hands contributed to West's fierce temper. But to a man the mechanics – after an initial period of consternation – became proud of the rigid shop standards he applied. You could, as the saying goes, eat your lunch off a TCA hangar floor.

The first employees in the other ground trades came from a wide variety of backgrounds: some had swept hangar floors in return for flying lessons; others had been at sea or worked for the railroads. They were united only by their enthusiasm and their willingness to turn their hands to anything just so long as it would give them a toehold in the exciting new world of aviation. Some were entering trades that were only then beginning to evolve, as aviation itself was evolving. There was not much a man could do, for instance, to prepare himself to be a flight dispatcher, except learn the job as he went along. Actually, the term "dispatcher" was something of a misnomer, since he did not send out a flight: only the pilot decided whether or not he would take off. But the dispatchers played an important and responsible role; they were, in a sense, the pilot's eyes and ears on the ground. The era of airport control towers and specialized air traffic controllers was still in the future, and their function was performed by the dispatcher. In essence, he gathered all the weather reports together – from the Department of Transport's embryo weather service, from "de-briefing" incoming pilots and by telephoning any other sources he could cultivate – and then briefed the pilots before take-off on what they could expect along their route. He also plotted the aircraft's course as the flight proceeded and kept a check on the times at which the pilot was due to report in by radio. If no report came, he would get on the radio and jog the pilot's memory or find out why he was late at his checkpoint. And as a plane came in to land the dispatcher, or sometimes the radio operator, would "go remote" – that is, take his microphone on to the roof of the airport shed and talk to the pilot, advising him about ceiling, visibility, wind direction and velocity, and if necessary, warning him of the presence of livestock on the runway.

Everyone, then, was learning on the job. But the "ghost service" proved so reliable that a little over a month after it was instituted the Post Office began to use it for experimental shipments of first class mail, to the puzzlement of occasional recipients who would note from the postmark that their letter had been delivered long before any train that could possibly have carried it was due in at the station downtown.

Throughout 1938, the training schedules were expanded and night flying became routine. First the Vancouver-Seattle service and then the Winnipeg-Vancouver "ghost" flights were increased to two a day. A similar training service was launched eastward from Winnipeg to Toronto, and on October 1 the Post Office inaugurated regular airmail service on overnight flights between Winnipeg and Vancouver.

By now the pilots on that run had been equipped with an improved version of the Electra, the Lockheed 14H, with which the full-fledged operational service would eventually be launched: ten of them were delivered during the year. The 14 was what the pilots called a "hot" aeroplane, much less forgiving of mistakes than most other aircraft of that era. It flew higher than the Electra, could carry almost three times as much payload, and was 40 miles an hour faster. But its top speed of 244 miles per hour was achieved at the expense of a much higher wing loading – in other words, the wing was small in relation to the aircraft's weight – and this at first presented the pilots with potentially dangerous handling problems.

When the 14 was first introduced in the United States, there were several fatal crashes when pilots banking into turns immediately after take-off lost their lift and stalled or side-slipped into the ground. The prevailing take-off technique at the time – a hangover from the days of bumpy grass airstrips – was to get into the air as quickly as possible and fly close to the ground until the aircraft picked up speed. This posed an obvious danger in the event of an engine failure just after take-off. Slim Lewis anticipated this problem and decreed that TCA pilots should use all their runway, by holding their aircraft on the ground until they had reached the speed at which they could fly on one engine and retain control. He also insisted that pilots climb straight out from the runway for at least a thousand feet before attempting a turn, and make no last-minute turns before landing. "A thousand feet straight in and out" became a TCA maxim that persisted long after improvements in aircraft design outmoded it, but it undoubtedly prevented accidents in the early days.

The TCA pilots also had to learn a new technique for landing the 14s. At that time, most aircraft made three-point landings – that is, the pilots tried to put both main wheels and the tail wheel down on the ground at the same time. But the 14 had to be landed on its main undercarriage alone, with its tail still up in flying position. There was much kangaroo-hopping along runways until the new technique was mastered; and since the 14 was the first transport aircraft with an "integral" fuel tank – the wing itself *was* the fuel tank – on occasion a bumpy landing would spring some wing rivets and cause a dangerous leakage of gasoline along the runway.

Worst of all, the first 14s off the assembly line had a characteristic which would not pass today's more rigorous testing procedures: their vicious behaviour in a stall. Slim Lewis and Lewis Leigh were warned about this when they went down to Burbank, California, to pick up TCA's first two 14s. And one day they were standing on the tarmac at Winnipeg watching Howard "Sandy" Sandgathe, a recent recruit to the instructional ranks, putting one of his students, Jim Storie, through his paces. Sandgathe had shut down one engine and Storie was performing a routine training manoeuvre that required him to put the fully-loaded aircraft – it was ballasted with sandbags – into a 45-degree bank turn. They were flying at about 150 miles an hour, and the inclusion of this manoeuvre in the training manual illustrates the stringency of the standards the TCA pilots were expected to attain: at that speed, even though it was double the 14's normal stalling speed, the aircraft could barely maintain its altitude on one engine even if conditions were well-nigh perfect.

Suddenly, instructor and pilot found themselves flipped over on their backs in a ferocious stall; the aircraft headed nose-down in a tight spin, as if one wing had been shot off. Sandgathe, with the outside world whirling around him as though he were on some particularly diabolical carnival ride, immediately restarted the idled engine and stood on the rudder pedal to try to reassert control. The 14 continued its sickening spiral toward the ground, so he took the power off the engine they had been running on and gunned the one he had just restarted. This threw them into a spin in the opposite direction, and his full weight on the rudder pedal still seemed to have no effect. The horrified watchers below felt certain they were going to crash, but by alternating power to the engines Sandgathe eventually managed to regain control and pull out of the spin – as he recalled it years later, "frighteningly close to the ground."

After he had landed, Sandgathe reported to Lewis that his airspeed indicator on the way down had shown him they were diving at well above the aircraft's maximum permissible speed. And the immense stress exerted on the plane's structure was plainly evident: one wing tip was bent upward at a grotesque angle and when the mechanics took the machine into the hangar for inspection the whole wing was found to be warped and had to be completely rebuilt.

The 45-degree bank turn on one engine was promptly taken

out of the training manual, but clearly something had to be done about the 14's stalling problem before the airline began to carry passengers in it. The solution was eventually discovered by Jack Dyment, TCA's chief engineer. Another of the kids who were "nuts about aeroplanes," Dyment studied mechanical engineering at the University of Toronto "because they didn't have an aeronautical course." In his summers, he learned to fly with the reserve air force and won the Sword of Honour as top cadet at Camp Borden in his final year. He graduated from university in 1929 and joined the aviation division of the Ford Motor Company in Detroit, which was still building the famous Ford Trimotor, one of the workhorses of early aviation. When Ford showed signs of getting out of the aircraft industry he returned to Canada and joined the civil aviation branch of the Department of National Defence, where Oliver West recognized him as a logical recruit when he was setting up the engineering department for TCA.

Dyment had received an A for his applied science thesis on "Stability and Control in Aircraft at Low Speeds," and when he began to study the 14's stalling problem he suspected that it could be cured by a new development called "slots" he had come across in England when he had signed on aboard a cattle ship and worked his way over there to further his education. These were holes cut in the wings out near their tips which acted to smooth the flow of air over them and restore their lifting capacity as they neared the stalling point. He suggested this solution to the Lockheed company and, after due experiment, it was accepted and incorporated into a subsequent production of the 14s.

TCA modified its own 14s (hundreds of modifications were routinely made on production aircraft in those days) and the slots seemed to solve the problem. Then one early fall night George Lothian, one of the first Canadian Airways pilots to switch to TCA, took the eastbound flight out of Vancouver to Winnipeg. A warm front was moving in off the ocean and it was raining as the 14 lifted off and began its climb toward the mountains. A thin layer of ice formed on the windshield as Lothian pushed up through the clouds, but by the time he reached his cruising altitude of 13,000 feet he was in the clear and he handed the controls to his co-pilot, S.G. "Stu" Foley, who later became one of the airline's most experienced Jumbo jet captains. As Lothian turned his attention to the log sheet on his lap, Foley noticed heavy cumulus cloud ahead and began to climb to get above it.

Suddenly, without any warning, the 14 shuddered, stalled and fell off on one wing. Foley recovered control and handed the aircraft back to Lothian, who set about regaining their lost altitude. Equally suddenly, the same thing happened to him. Opening the engines to their limit, he began a long diving turn to the left to regain control and begin heading back to Vancouver. But each time he tried to slow the descent and attempt to resume his normal level flight the aircraft would shudder again in the beginning of a stall. As they sank toward 11,000 feet, below which they knew they could not safely go, Lothian told Foley to stand by to dump one of the fuel tanks – an unpopular procedure with the engines roaring full out and long streaks of exhaust flame trailing past the fuselage.

Both men watched apprehensively as one of their fuel gauges dropped to zero, but with the plane lightened by more than a hundred gallons of gasoline Lothian was able to hold it at 11,000 feet, though only by pushing the engines to a point he knew was unwise. Slowly, battling a 50-mile-an-hour headwind, they headed for the safety of the coast. Outside their windows, they could see that the leading edge of the wing was covered by a half-inch layer of ice, but the puzzled Lothian did not think this was enough to explain its strange performance.

In those days, radio communications with the aircraft could be heard at all stations between Winnipeg and Vancouver, and whenever a flight was in trouble, supervisors and technicians flocked to the various airports anxious to offer whatever help they could. But no amount of advice from the ground could help Lothian and Foley: they could only try to climb back to the safer level of 13,000 feet and hope to clear the clouds across their path to Vancouver.

Lothian knew that when they had to enter the clouds his radio communications would probably be blotted out by static. So before he lost contact he asked Noel Humphrys, the dispatcher on duty in Vancouver, to telephone the police in Hope, on the Fraser River. If the Hope police would listen for the sound of their engines and report in promptly when they heard them, Humphrys might be able to give them their position later. And if he could reach Hope, Lothian would have a chance to descend into ice-free air over the Fraser valley, guided by the Vancouver beacon.

Eventually, with their fingers crossed, they headed into the clouds, their engines shrieking as Lothian held them wide open to maintain his altitude. As expected, a hail of static immediately cut off their voice communication. But they could dimly pick up the range signal from Vancouver – until Humphrys, realizing they could not hear him on the voice channel, interrupted the range's normally constant signal long enough to tell them in Morse Code that the police had reported them safely past Hope.

Now they were able to start down. When they reached 6,000 feet the air was warm enough to melt the ice from the aircraft's surfaces and they landed safely, as puzzled as they were shaken. A week later, by chance, the mystery was solved. Lothian was in the flight dispatch office in Winnipeg waiting to take out a westbound flight when his fellow captain, Frank Young, arrived from Toronto. What he saw through the window sent Lothian racing downstairs and out onto the tarmac: solid slabs of ice jutted down beneath the wing behind each slot. And sure enough, Young reported that he had been making a normal approach, not too concerned about the ice build-up, when suddenly, five or six feet above the runway, the plane simply stopped flying and dropped onto the tarmac like a stone.

It was concluded that the air changing course to flow through the slots deposited so much ice on the underside of the wing that it could completely destroy its lift. Lothian, who recalled this episode vividly in his autobiography,* described it as "equivalent to having a two-by-four nailed under the first three feet of each wingtip."

At Jack Dyment's suggestion, pneumatic de-icing boots were installed in the slots, but they failed to rectify the situation: test flights showed that if they inflated at the wrong time in a stall the aircraft became more unmanageable than ever. So TCA called off its experiment. The slots continued to work well for airlines in milder climates, but TCA panelled them over. Dyment also initiated another attempt to cure the 14's stalling problem. He had noted that its navigation lights projected forward several inches from the wings near their curved tips. Perhaps, he thought, this was what was disrupting the airflow and causing all the trouble. So the lights were moved back 6 inches, an apparently small change but one that made a big improvement in the aircraft's performance. Modifications such as this earned the TCA engineering staff a world-wide reputation for innovation and efficiency.

Another problem encountered in flying the mountains was only beginning to be recognized by the aviation world generally in 1938. This was the anoxia, or oxygen starvation, that pilots suffered in the rarefied upper atmosphere before the introduction of pressurized aeroplanes after World War II. The billions of cells in the human brain require for their proper functioning a constant supply of oxygen, which is carried to them by the blood; if

---

Flight Deck (Toronto: McGraw-Hill Ryerson, 1979).

the oxygen supply is cut off completely, the result is unconscious-ness, and ultimately death. In its early stages, oxygen depriva-tion has the same insidious effects as being drunk: lack of co-ordination, a feeling of over-confidence, impaired judgment, and above all the conviction that one is quite all right, thank you.

As aircraft began to reach higher altitudes, there were several unexplained crashes in which experienced pilots seemed to have done stupid things, and gradually it was realized that anoxia was the culprit. United Airlines was the first to equip its pilots with oxygen, which they were supposed to suck through a pipe; this was both unpleasant and ineffective, because pure oxygen irri-tates the mucous membranes and pilots were reluctant to puff on their pipes throughout a trip. Later, scientists at the Mayo Clinic in Minnesota, developed an oxygen mask that fitted over the nose, leaving the pilot's mouth free and enabling him to breathe a mixture of oxygen and his own exhaled breath, which proved less irritating. Jack Dyment visited the Mayo Clinic to investigate their work and TCA became one of the first airlines to adopt the masks, at first for the pilots on the ghost service and later for passengers as well.

But before the masks were developed, pilots Lewis Leigh and Maurice McGregor and a group of Department of Transport offi-cials they were carrying had a narrow escape that vividly dem-onstrated the potential danger of anoxia. As Leigh recalled it years later, he was "checking out" McGregor on a night flight to Win-nipeg from Vancouver. By the time they crossed the Princeton range, about 150 miles inland, they were flying blind through clouds and rain and encountering fairly heavy icing. They were forced to climb above their 13,000-foot cruising altitude as they headed southeast toward their next range, Grand Forks, on the U.S. border about 200 miles from Vancouver. At 15,000 feet they were still in the icing layer and having difficulty picking up the Grand Forks range signals because of static. Suddenly, as McGregor was trying to tune the main radio receiver, the handle of which was on the ceiling of the cockpit above him, their air-craft encountered a severe jolt of turbulence. They did not know it at the time, but the radio technicians discovered later that the bump had broken the gear train on the tuner, rendering it use-less for the rest of the trip.

Puzzled by their inability to pick up their range signals, they decided to turn back to Vancouver. By now, the icing had forced them up to 17,000 feet – well above the 6,000-foot altitude at which oxygen later became mandatory for pilots – and co-pilot

W.D. "Don" Brady, who was travelling in the passenger cabin, came forward to tell Leigh the Transport officials had all turned blue and passed out. Leigh and McGregor had turned blue themselves, and when they realized they were lost they adopted the emergency procedure, turned south for the United States, where there were more radio ranges, and began to broadcast distress calls on their battery-powered transmitter.

Although they did not know it, their calls were received – and their slurred mumbling told those listening on the ground the gravity of their situation. The air was cleared of all other radio traffic and a message was broadcast asking people on both sides of the border to listen for the sound of their engines.

After they had been in the air for three and a half hours, Leigh and McGregor knew their fuel must soon run out, and they decided all they could do was continue on their southward course until only twenty minutes' supply remained, when they would have to begin to descend. Among the mountains this could mean certain death, but they fervently hoped they might have travelled far enough west to break out over the U.S. coast and find an airport.

At last they began to pick up faint radio range signals on their emergency set, and to their astonishment they seemed to be "VR," the code for Vancouver. Relieved, they followed the signals down and landed, unable to understand why, while they thought they had been flying south for what seemed hours, they had approached Vancouver from the north – as listeners on the ground who had heard them pass over had confirmed by telephone. They had been in the air for four hours and five minutes, in the grip of a powerful mountain weather front with southeast winds that were measured by U.S. mountain-top weather stations at between 150 and 200 miles an hour. Leigh and McGregor concluded that while they had been trying to fly south their ground speed had been slower than the winds, because of the ice build-up, and they had been driven backwards to the northwest. Their colleagues on the ground, who had heard their tipsy-sounding radio messages, suspected another explanation: despite their best efforts, their minds had been clouded by anoxia and they had not been steering the course they thought they were on.

Luck was with Leigh and McGregor that night, but soon afterwards it ran out for two other ghost service pilots. Just before midnight on November 17, 1938, Dave Imrie and Jack Herald left Winnipeg heading for Vancouver with a load of mail but no passengers. When they took off from Regina in the middle of the night there were some fog patches west of the airport. Soon after take-off they crashed, the aircraft burned and they were both killed.

It is difficult to exaggerate the shock and the sense of loss that grips an airline's employees when one of their aircraft crashes. In this case it was magnified: it was TCA's first crash, and the organization was still comparatively small and close-knit – a little over three hundred employees in all.

There seemed at first to be no explanation for the tragedy. The Department of Transport investigators concluded that immediately after take-off Imrie had seen the fog patches and tried to fly under them. Lewis Leigh, who flew to the scene immediately with Slim Lewis, had taught Imrie his instrument-flying and thought this unlikely; in his view, he would have maintained his prescribed rate of climb. Also, he had noticed a fire extinguisher lying beside the bodies, and some distance ahead of the wreckage he had found the wooden lid from a small control box located on the floor between the pilots' seats, bearing burn marks only on its underside.

The mystery remained for some months, until Northwest Airlines suffered a similar fatal accident to a Lockheed 14 during a night take-off at Billings, Montana. In this case, too, the control-box lid was thrown clear of the wreckage and was burned only on its underside. This similarity to the TCA crash prompted Lockheed to investigate the box, which contained the controls for the engine fire extinguishers and the main fuel cross-over valve. When the lid of the box was lifted it automatically switched on an electric light and if – as the investigators surmised – there were gasoline fumes in the box this was enough to cause an explosion and fire. So Imrie and Herald had probably been fighting a fire in the cockpit when they crashed.

Lockheed removed the fuel lines and control valve from the box, which seemed to solve the problem, and Dave Imrie was posthumously absolved from the dreaded charge of "pilot error."

CHAPTER SIX

O N APRIL 17, 1939, Philip Johnson was the dinner speaker at a meeting of the Canadian Railway Club in Montreal. TCA had inaugurated its first transcontinental passenger flights between that city and Vancouver on April 1, and Johnson told his audience the new airline, just two years after its formation, was now flying 6,500 miles a day, or 200,000 miles a month.

He contrasted its development with that of the U.S. transcontinental airlines, which had grown piecemeal over a period of years, and said: "It represents perhaps the largest undertaking of its type in the world." Yet in organization it was quite simple: "We have an operating department, a traffic department, a repair department, an overhaul department and a maintenance department. Such functions as advertising, accounting, purchasing and legal are turned over to the corresponding departments of the railway . . . for reasons of economy and to prevent needless duplication."

He was, he said, well satisfied with the equipment being flown, the calibre of the employees recruited, and the "most modern" repair shop which had been established in Winnipeg:

We can do anything that anybody else can do with an airplane. We can practically build one or assemble one if we have to, and all of our propeller and engine overhauls are conducted in Winnipeg. We think we have the best type of engine, we know we have the best type of propeller, and the navigation instruments are as modern as money can buy. The same is true with the radio equipment. However, tomorrow may bring out something better than we have today, and we will have to get it to carry out our work.

Johnson did not believe in wasting words, and it was a short speech, after which he volunteered to answer questions. The response gives an idea of the uphill task still facing the latest of the TCA departments he had enumerated in his speech, the traffic, or sales, department. Members of the Railway Club, clearly, were not yet particularly air-minded. One of the first questioners was nervous about icing; another wanted to know "What do you do for parachutes?" Johnson, who no doubt would have preferred it if that question had not come up, replied: "We don't use them in transport flying. Experience has proven that a parachute does not do you very much good. . . . " There was also a reference to an unusual malady that diligent research among contemporary medical sources has failed to elucidate: "Will you tell us something about altitudes?" one member asked. "Some of us may have an air heart, and wonder what you have done to take care of that." Johnson could only reply that normally, east of Lethbridge, TCA planes flew from 5,000 to 8,000 feet up; over the mountains it was necessary to climb to 11,000 or 12,000 feet; and the whole fleet was being equipped with oxygen masks, for both passengers and crew.

The parting shot was aimed by the member deputed to thank Johnson for his speech, Mr. W.L. Bayer. It is to be hoped it was delivered in a bantering tone, since it reads somewhat less than graciously in the minutes: "It has been an extreme pleasure to have you come and speak to us on airplanes, and I compliment you, considering the fact that this is a Railway Club. However, there is one thing you omitted in your speech, and I think it is important, and that is: it is always advisable to be close to a railway line when flying in an airplane because, on four different occasions I have found it necessary to complete my trip that way, when it had started in the air . . . ."

The traffic department's job in the beginning was thus not simply to sell tickets but to sell the whole *idea* of air travel. The first passenger agents hired were chosen for their ability to deal with local bigwigs: with the return fare from Montreal to Vancouver set at $255 (three or four months' pay for a starting passenger agent), their clientele was the Pullman-car set. Most of the rookie agents had a background in transportation; some had worked for other airlines, and some for shipping lines or travel agents. W. Gordon Wood, who went on to become senior vice-president, sales and traffic, had been a diesel engineer and accountant for a gold-mining company in Alaska before switching to a subsidiary of Pan Am there. He joined TCA in Ottawa in 1939 and years later recalled his job as "being out all day long handing out timetables to people and trying to get them to fly."

This was no easy task at a time when the reservations proce-

dure was time-consuming and cumbersome,* delays caused by
weather were common, and flights often encountered so much
turbulence that their passengers were subjected to miserable
attacks of air-sickness. The passenger agent's ace in the hole, of
course, was the time saved in air travel. A good example of this
was recalled by W.J. "Jack" Dalby, who had worked for shipping lines, the world-wide Thomas Cook travel agency and United
Airlines before becoming TCA's first traffic manager in Vancouver. Among the local business leaders Dalby used to visit in his
sales effort was a lumberman who had become resigned to spending five months of every year on a sales trip in eastern Canada
and the United States; when Dalby talked him into flying with
TCA he was able to reduce his time away from home to five *weeks*
in the year.

In their missionary zeal, the passenger agents drew up lists of
influential businessmen who might be lured aboard their flights
by personal visits; called on them after their trips to make sure
they had no complaints, or if they had, to assure them that steps
would be taken to prevent any recurrence of whatever unfortunate episode had provoked their displeasure; belaboured service
clubs with speeches extolling the new form of travel; and acted
as official greeters on any convenient special occasion.

The other great missionaries for air travel, of course, were the
early stewardesses. United had been the first airline to introduce
stewardesses to its flight crews, back in 1930, and Lucile Garner, the nurse hired to set up TCA's stewardess department in
1938, drew heavily on the United manual in devising her training course. TCA followed United's lead by stipulating that all its
stewardesses should be registered nurses. This qualification,
which was not dropped until 1957, was a reassurance to potential passengers that if they suffered from "air hearts," or even
less exotic ailments, they would be properly cared for in flight;
it also ensured that the young women who served the spartan
box lunches and paper cups of coffee or lemonade were competent, resourceful and disciplined professionals accustomed to
dealing with a sometimes fractious public.

That they considered themselves to be, and were accepted as,

---

*Reservations were originally passed between stations by the TCA radio operators, using
the five-letter code groups that were standard for Morse transmissions. It could take up
to 24 hours for a seat sale to be confirmed, and if Lethbridge, say, sold a seat to Regina
and the message reporting this failed to reach Vancouver before a flight left it could
result in a through passenger from Vancouver to Toronto having no space for one stage
of his journey. Such situations called for all the tact a passenger agent could muster;
however, they were not often encountered in the early days since most flights were
only half full.

full members of the flight crew was perhaps demonstrated by the selection of their first uniforms. Lucile Garner had commissioned an exclusive Vancouver tailor to design an attractive uniform in beige English gaberdine, with matching blouses in a delicate shade of brick-red. Instead, her recruits expressed their preference for the same dignified navy blue worn by the pilots. Their uniforms cost them $30 each – a hefty slice out of their $140-a-month pay cheques – but they paid up cheerfully, proud to be chosen for this glamorous new career.

Official policy, of course, frowned on frivolity. In the words of a 1939 "memo to all stations":

All contacts between stewardesses and other personnel are to be thoroughly business-like and of a nature to engender the respect of passengers. Stewardesses will address flight officers as "Captain" or "Mr.," other employees as "Mr." or "Miss." Stewardesses will be addressed as "Miss." It is to be appreciated that the stewardesses have had practically no aviation experience and will have to rely on other personnel for assistance from time to time, particularly with respect to the answering of passengers' inquiries, etc. We ask that there be no practical joking on the part of personnel in this connection but that such questions be given serious handling. Passengers are guests of the Company. While on duty there is to be maintained a refined reserve among our personnel. There is no room for "foolishness" while on the job.

Notwithstanding this stern admonition, rookie stewardesses were routinely dispatched to the hangars for a bucket of "prop wash" or a can of "slipstream." But their intensive training course soon initiated them into the mysteries of aviation. Since they were required to attend the "met" briefings with the pilots, they were taught to read weather maps and given instruction in how to answer anxious passengers' questions intelligently. An early recruit, Rose Crispin, was reduced to blushes after one bumpy flight, during which she had been reassuring what she thought to be a nervous passenger with a calm recital of all she had lately learned about aeronautics, only to discover on landing that he was Walter Gilbert, one of the legendary figures of bush-flying and a pioneer of Arctic exploration by air.

The "girls" (they did not mind being called that in those far-off days) also took lectures in communications procedures and were trained to cope with emergencies. One ill-mannered passenger who chided a stewardess for being nothing but a "glorified waitress" received the cool reply: "Sir, I am part of the safety equipment aboard this aeroplane." And there were many occasions, before the era of pressurized aircraft, when passengers who collapsed for one reason or another owed their lives to the stewardess's ability to make a medical diagnosis and administer prompt treatment. Also, while doctors advised women not to fly in the later stages of pregnancy, more than one premature baby was safely delivered by a TCA stewardess.

The first stewardesses used to joke among themselves that their presence aboard the planes was designed to allay the fears of businessmen's wives: if a mere slip of a girl could fly then surely it was a safe enough venture for their husbands. And it is true that they did symbolize the kind of personal service the airline was trying to sell. With the small loads of those days, the stewardesses stood at the counter greeting the passengers and helping them to check in. This enabled them to memorize their names and address them personally during the flight. Air travel was a much more chummy affair then than it is on today's big jets. Many of the passengers were regulars who became well known to the crews. On those not infrequent occasions when a flight was delayed by weather en route, the stewardesses would arrange for their charges to be booked in to the local hotel and would sometimes join them for a game of cards or songs around the piano after dinner. When the news came that the flight could continue, they often had to ferret their passengers out of the local movie house, where they had taken refuge from their boredom.

In such circumstances, romance sometimes beckoned. The girls were warned on their training courses to beware of the occasional idiosyncrasies of married men on business trips, and advised that if they accepted an invitation to a party it should be in someone else's room rather than their own, so that they could leave gracefully if events appeared to be taking an untoward turn. The advice was probably unnecessary: the stewardesses were every bit as accomplished as their fellow-nurses at rejecting unwelcome advances.*

In flight, the stewardesses' duties were not confined to serving sandwiches and coping with such things as chocolate marshmallows and cans of tomato juice which would from time to time explode at high altitudes. At first, for instance, they operated the aircraft's heating system, and were subjected to ceaseless grumbling by the pilots, who complained that they only

---

*Welcome advances, of course, were a girl's own business and romance did sometimes bloom – so often, in fact, that the attrition rate among the early stewardesses was high. Pat Eccleston, the second stewardess hired, married John Maxwell, an early passenger agent who rose through various managerial appointments to become European sales manager in London; and Rose Crispin, her colleague on the Seattle service, married one of the captains on the run, George Lothian, who later became the airline's director of flight standards.

knew two settings: "too hot" and "too cold." Only when the pilots insisted on the heater controls being moved into the cockpit did they realize that this was a deficiency of the equipment rather than the stewardesses, and the matter was passed to the engineering department for its attention. The girls were also responsible for assisting passengers with their oxygen masks and making sure that reluctant ones wore them. This was one duty that sometimes overcame their resilience, since the designers of the oxygen equipment had neglected to provide them with extension hoses for their own masks. More than one girl passed out on the job and had to be revived by her passengers.

The girls took all such contretemps in their stride, and there were occasions through the years when stewardesses displayed great bravery in emergencies. One such occurred at Sydney, Nova Scotia, in 1948, when a four-engined TCA North Star coming in for a night landing hit an unlighted pile of excavated earth just short of the runway and crash-landed in flames. Stewardess Rita Meyer remained in the blazing plane until she had led all eleven passengers to the emergency exit, where Purser Jack Triggs helped them to safety down the ladder. Rita earned headlines across the country as "Stewardess Heroine," and both later received gold watches from their grateful company.

Pursers, the male counterparts of the stewardesses (both designations were borrowed from the shipping lines), first appeared on the scene during World War II, when the rigours of the early transatlantic flights were considered too much for "the gentle sex." And two of them shared the glory when stewardess Mary Dohey was awarded Canada's highest decoration for courage, the Cross of Valour, in 1976. Miss Dohey, a nurse from Newfoundland, had been working for the airline for seventeen years when she took off from Calgary one afternoon in 1971 as part of the crew of a DC-8 bound for Toronto and Montreal. Soon after take-off, a passenger in the first-class section pointed a sawed-off shotgun at Purser John Arpin and ordered him to deliver a rambling note to the pilot, Captain Vern Ehman. The note instructed Ehman to fly to Grand Falls, Montana, pick up $1.5 million (to be supplied by the airline) and take off again immediately, for a destination which would be given to him in due course.

Mary Dohey spent much of the next six hours with the gun pointed at her head, holding two wires that the hijacker said were connected to a bundle of dynamite in his flight bag, which would be detonated if his instructions were not followed to the letter. At one stage, the hijacker fired a blast from the shotgun which miraculously did not penetrate the skin of the aircraft and cause a disastrous loss of pressurization. With incredible calmness, stewardess Dohey talked the man into permitting the 115 passengers to disembark at Grand Falls, and calmed him down to the point at which, when he was proposing to leave the aircraft with a parachute he had carried aboard with the dynamite, Captain Ehman and pursers Arpin and Philippe Bonny were able to overpower him and truss him up for delivery to the police in Calgary. At the same ceremony at which Miss Dohey became the first living recipient of the Cross of Valour, Arpin received the Star of Courage and Bonny and Ehman the Medal of Bravery.

The world was mercifully free of the hijacking nightmare in 1939, but a greater horror lay just around the corner: within months of the opening of TCA's Montreal-Vancouver service, and before the completion of the government airway permitted the extension of the system eastward (to Moncton in 1940 and Halifax in 1941), the country found itself embroiled in World War II.

CHAPTER SEVEN

S THEY DID TO THE whole Canadian economy, the wartime years brought tremendous expansion to the airline. There was an eightfold increase in traffic, from 21,569 fare-paying passengers carried in 1939 to 183,121 in 1945; an increase in miles flown from just over three million in 1939 to 11.5 million in 1945; and a sixfold increase in staff, from 497 employees in 1939 to 3,272 by the end of 1945. Just as important as this swift growth was the experience gained by TCA pilots on the Atlantic, thousands of hours of flying in the most gruelling conditions, which laid the foundations for the international airline that would come into being soon after the war, ending forever any idea that Canada would be a mere junior partner in Imperial Airways' grand design for the "all-red route."

The outbreak of war coincided with the expiry of Philip Johnson's blacklisting from the U.S. airline industry and he resigned his post of vice-president with genuine regret* to return to Seattle as president of the Boeing company, where he took charge of the huge program in which several manufacturing companies combined to build the fleets of B-17 "Flying Fortress" bombers used in the Allied high-level bombing raids. His last act before leaving was to persuade C.D. Howe that the arrangement under which the government was to pick up TCA's operating deficit until the beginning of 1940 should be extended by at least a year. The deficit for 1938, while the training program was at its height and before the transcontinental passenger service had been launched, had been $818,026; the 1939 picture was somewhat better–the deficit was almost halved, to $411,656. But as Johnson pointed out to Howe, the passenger service had not been in

---

*He was asked to stay on as a consultant and offered to do so without pay. The TCA board insisted he accept $10,000 a year but on several occasions thereafter he expressed his willingness to forgo any fee and work for just his travel expenses, an offer that was accepted at the beginning of 1943. At the height of his wartime responsibilities he continued to be consulted by his successors and gave much valuable advice. In 1944, while visiting a Boeing plant in Kansas, he collapsed and died of a stroke at the age of 50.

operation for the full year, and no one could accurately predict the financial results for 1940, when new services were due to be introduced and heavy demands would no doubt be made on the airline by the war effort. Howe, delighted by the efficient way Johnson had launched his cherished airline, readily arranged the requisite amendment to the TCA Act. But in the event, 1940, during which a second daily transcontinental flight was introduced, as well as the extension of service to Moncton, was the year in which the airline recorded its first surplus – $539,263; and for the next five years it "flew by itself," without any government subsidy.

When Johnson returned to the United States, neither Don MacLaren nor any of the other Canadians who had attained supervisory positions were judged ready to replace him, so the vice-president's post devolved upon D.B. Colyer, whose title up to that time had been chief technical adviser. But when in due course Oliver West and Slim Lewis followed their former boss to Seattle – West to supervise the production of the Flying Fortress and Lewis to become chief test pilot for Boeing – it was considered unnecessary to replace them with Americans.

West was succeeded as superintendent of engineering and maintenance by a peppery little Scots immigrant, James T. Bain, who had left school at the age of 14 in 1920 and enlisted in the Royal Air Force, where he trained as a mechanic at the famous cadet school, Cranwell. After eleven years in the air force, he was working for a private airline, British Airways Limited, when it bought some Lockheed Electras and he was sent to the factory at Burbank, California, to observe their manufacture. While there, he wrote an operating manual for the Electra which was adopted by Lockheed, so that he was well versed in TCA's equipment when he was hired by West early in 1938.

When Slim Lewis left, Howard Sandgathe became chief pilot, succeeding Ronald F. George, a CAL bush pilot who had held that post under Lewis before stepping up to become operations manager. A New Brunswicker, Ron George was well over six feet tall and as strong in his opinions as he was physically. He had a superhuman capacity for work and his colleagues were amazed at his ability to fly overnight checking out a crew between Vancouver and Winnipeg, put in a full day at his desk, then join another crew as check pilot on the overnight flight from Winnipeg to Toronto. His problem was that he expected others to be able to work as hard as he could and was not at all reticent about expressing his displeasure if they failed to meet his own high standards. In the jockeying for position inevitable in a fast-growing organization he eventually made some powerful enemies. At one time, the pilots were close to mutiny and there was talk of a mass resignation. Then a group of his rivals for promotion got together and delivered a similar ultimatum. So George–to the lasting regret of some who recognized his brilliance – moved to the United States, where a string of entrepreneurial triumphs in the aviation and plastics fields ushered him into the ranks of the multi-millionaires.

In those days–and for much too long into the postwar era, in the eyes of some subsequent critics–the operations department, the men who flew and looked after the aircraft, overshadowed the traffic, or sales, department, which was charged with recruiting and cosseting the customers. This was not a situation unique to TCA at that stage in the evolution of both airlines and aeroplanes, which, not having reached their current sophistication, needed constant modification and tinkering. Flight schedules, for instance, were commonly dictated more by the exigencies of a maintenance stop than by the convenience of passengers with meetings to attend.

As the pace of the war mounted, TCA's embryo traffic department was almost completely eclipsed, becoming more of a service organization than the company's marketing arm, because of the priority system instituted by the government. There was no need for imaginative advertising campaigns or individual sales calls: the seats were all but filled by "must ride" passengers – government officials and senior armed forces officers, businessmen on missions deemed essential to the war effort, ferry pilots returning to their stations after delivering aircraft to wartime bases on either coast or the flying schools set up under the British Commonwealth Air Training Plan. Ordinary passengers buying a TCA ticket were warned that they could be "de-planed" right up to the moment the flight left by any passenger with the government's "must ride" priority.

De-planing or "bumping" a passenger was, of course, not the best kind of public relations, and it called for all the tact a passenger agent could muster–C.D. Howe never knew how many personal friends he had across the country who were going to write him immediately to protest against this unconscionable disruption of their travel plans–and the company evolved its own system of priorities to guide agents when the unfortunate choice had to be made. There was NEEPLA, or Non-Essential Pleasure Travel; FURLO, for servicemen on leave; NEEBUS, or Non-Essential Business; and so on.

By 1941, when Sam Hungerford retired from the CNR at the

then mandatory age of 70, it was clear that the airline needed more than a figurehead president. But no one had yet emerged from the ranks to claim that position.* So C.D. Howe turned to his old friend Herb Symington, one of the most active directors since the beginning. Symington was already putting in a lot of his time in Ottawa as federal Power Controller, but he agreed to take on the new responsibility. In theory, he was one of Howe's "dollar-a-year men," an elite company of executives who had proved themselves in business and so established themselves financially that they could afford to donate their services to the war effort. In fact, Symington did not bother to collect the dollar due him for either job: although he remained president of TCA until 1947 he never accepted a salary or submitted an expense account. But although he continued to operate from his Royal Securities office and retained his other posts, he was not simply a paper president. Howe trusted his judgment completely, and Howe was still "Mr. Airline": while he had now left the Transport portfolio and been put in charge of the country's war effort as Minister of Munitions and Supply, he had somehow justified retaining the airline under his personal jurisdiction, which he was to continue to do in the three postwar portfolios he held before his defeat and retirement from politics in 1957.

The airline entered the war with a fleet of fifteen Lockheed 14s, and with the rapid build-up of air travel they soon proved inadequate. There were those who wanted to switch equipment and move up to the extremely reliable Douglas DC-3, which carried twenty-one passengers against the 14's ten. But wartime shortages had resulted in the U.S. authorities ruling that airlines must stick to their original equipment; buying a new type necessitated the purchase of a large stock of spare parts, as well as the aircraft themselves. The situation improved a little when Lockheed put out a larger and more powerful version of the 14, the 18, or Lodestar, which carried fourteen passengers, and the airline bought fifteen of them during the war.

The Lockheed 14 was equipped with two 850-horsepower Pratt & Whitney Hornet engines, which were plagued among other things with cylinder-head failures. They gave the pilots

---

*There was no question, of course, of the post going to one of the Americans. In fact Colyer, a handsome and personable westerner who was well liked within the company and filled the vice-president's post competently, if without the drive and brilliance of Johnson, resigned and returned to the United States in 1941 because he felt that if he stayed in Canada he ought to take out Canadian citizenship, which he did not want to do. He was succeeded by Ted Larson, the last of the Americans brought in by Johnson, until he, too, returned to the United States in 1944 and Bill English became the first Canadian to hold the top operating post.

and maintenance branch so much trouble that early in the war it was decided to replace them with the more powerful and reliable 1,200-horsepower twin-row Pratt & Whitney 1830, or Wasp. A modification on this scale entailed an extensive redesign of the aircraft, including a complex technical procedure known as a full stress analysis. But the infant airline had done its recruiting so well that a team from the engineering department under Fred Ades was able to do all the necessary feasibility studies and design work, and supervise the whole conversion job, which was farmed out to the Boeing of Canada plant in Vancouver.

Projects such as these, and contract maintenance work undertaken for the air force, led to tremendous expansion of the maintenance and overhaul branch. New hangars and workshops were built and existing ones expanded, and for much of the war three shifts worked around the clock. And as in other industries, when the men went off to war it was suddenly discovered that jobs which had hitherto been considered exclusively in their domain could be done just as well by women: by 1943, 35 per cent of TCA's employees were female.

Soon after the war broke out the government passed an order-in-council decreeing that TCA employees could join the armed services only with the company's permission. Employees of the traffic department and others not directly concerned with flying operations naturally found this permission easier to obtain than the pilots. Gordon Wood, for instance, took leave of absence from his post as eastern division traffic manager in Toronto, joined the army and qualified as pilot of an artillery spotting plane in Europe. Others, such as Howard Cotterell, an early recruit to the traffic department, put their specialized knowledge to use in the RCAF.

Before the order-in-council was passed, some of the pilots managed to resign and join the air force reserve units they had belonged to while working for TCA. Lewis Leigh, for instance, quit after a disagreement with Ron George and in due course became Group Captain Z.L. Leigh, commanding officer of the RCAF's Air Transport Command. The pilots "frozen" in their civilian jobs nevertheless did much valuable war work, often on their days off: testing, delivering and ferrying military aircraft, and instructing service pilots in the disciplines of transport flying.

The airline also played a supporting but not insignificant role in one of the great Allied achievements of the war, the ferry service across the Atlantic. Both Britain and France had ordered large numbers of bombers from the United States, and when France fell in 1940 Britain took over the French order, thus assuring itself of a supply of machines for the battles ahead–provided they could be safely delivered to Britain before, as at one time seemed likely, she was overrun by the Germans. The U-boat war was at its height and shipping them by sea was considered both too slow and too risky. So Britain's Minister of Aircraft Production, the maverick Canadian millionaire who had emigrated in reverse and become the British press baron Lord Beaverbrook, took the bold decision to fly them over. There were gloomy predictions, fortunately unfulfilled, that losses in the operation would amount to fifty per cent.

Beaverbrook might have been expected to contact C.D. Howe and seek to enlist the experience of Canada's national airline in this endeavour. Instead, the CPR was asked to set up an organization to take delivery of the planes and fly them across the Atlantic. Attracted by the prospect of lucrative adventure, with the pay set at $1,000 a month, a polyglot force of civilian pilots, a sort of free-swinging French Foreign Legion of the air, assembled in Montreal and, with the aid of young air force navigators hastily turned out by the air training plan, flights across the Atlantic, which not long before had been headline-making dramas, soon became routine–dangerous sometimes, and certainly cold and uncomfortable at the best of times, but nevertheless routine. Almost three hundred bombers (mostly Lockheed Hudsons, the military version of TCA's 14s) had successfully made the crossing by the time the service was taken over by the RAF's Ferry Command in July 1941, and thousands more followed.

In the early days, the flights travelled from Montreal to Gander, Newfoundland,* where the supplementary fuel tanks with which the aircraft had to be equipped were filled for the long non-stop journey across the Atlantic. Later, with the construction of the airport at Goose Bay, Labrador, and the opening of the U.S. bases in Greenland, aircraft with shorter ranges than the big bombers could be ferried across by stages.

---

*The airport at Gander had been built by the British government for Imperial Airways' contemplated round-the-world service. Sir Francis Shelmerdine, an Indian Army cavalry officer who had somehow become director general of civil aviation in Britain, sent a party across to find a square mile of flat land in Newfoundland, which could be turned into an airport–no easy task on "the Rock." The choice fell on Gander, and the party's financial man submitted an estimate for clearing the numerous trees and levelling the ground which the government accepted. When it was discovered that he had omitted to take into consideration the cost of grubbing out the trees' roots–an arduous procedure which doubled the estimate – he adopted an expedient that would no doubt be considered drastic in this modern age of almost universal over-runs: he committed suicide.

From the start, of course, there was the problem of returning the crews from Britain to pick up another plane. Transport by sea was slow and uncertain, and there was the danger that legions of trained men would be playing darts in English pubs or tossing about on the Atlantic dodging submarines while the badly needed bombers piled up in Montreal. So in May 1941, BOAC* established the Return Ferry Service, using four-engined American Liberator bombers which carried the crews westbound and VIP traffic eastbound. The journeys were made in something less than comfort: the aircraft were unheated, and the passengers sat facing each other on benches, shivering in the below-zero temperature, or curled up in sleeping bags on the floor for as much as twenty hours. TCA was still opening new services within Canada and had just negotiated with the British authorities to begin flying to Newfoundland; it therefore agreed to supply the repair and maintenance facilities for the ferry aircraft there and at Dorval, the new airport in Montreal built to take the pressure off the overcrowded field at St. Hubert, which was then handed over to the RCAF.

Like every other organization in those days, BOAC suffered from a shortage of trained personnel, and the lot of a young pilot carrying a score of grizzled and exceedingly cold Atlantic experts back the way they had just come was not an enviable one. Also, there were three tragedies in the early days of the service: two of the Liberators crashed soon after take-off from Prestwick, Scotland, the eastern terminus of the service, with the loss of all twenty-two people aboard each, and another was mistaken for a German bomber by an Allied fighter pilot and shot down. Faced with these losses, BOAC appealed to TCA for help, and three complete TCA crews were seconded to the return service. They were headed by three of the airline's most experienced captains: George Lothian and M.B. "Jock" Barclay, a native Scot, were already blooded on the Atlantic, having been seconded to the ferry service in response to an earlier appeal, and J.L. "Lindy" Rood had flown for British Airways in Europe before joining TCA in 1937.

The way these men could read the sky – their ability, born of flying the mountains, to thread a skilful path round or through the boiling weather fronts that bedevil the Atlantic – their precision flying on instruments and the calm with which they faced

---

*British Overseas Airways Corporation was formed in 1939 by a government merger of Imperial Airways and the privately owned British Airways, which had hitherto been its formidable competitor.

that old enemy, icing, made them valuable members of the return service team. And the added experience they gained proved just as valuable to TCA in the years ahead, for it soon became clear that the Return Ferry Service was, to all intents and purposes, the real beginning of BOAC's long-awaited commercial service across the Atlantic. And Canada had by now resolved not to take a back seat in postwar international aviation.

CHAPTER EIGHT

N DECEMBER 6, 1941, Vincent Massey, whose services to the Liberal party had been rewarded by the coveted post of Canadian High Commissioner in London, penned a letter to Ottawa. As C.D. Howe developed Canada into an important arsenal for the beleaguered mother country, the volume of official business between Canada and Britain was constantly increasing. So, too, was the number of Canadian troops gathering in England. Swift and reliable communication between the two countries was thus more important than ever before. But British traffic to and from the United States, of which there was a great deal, was naturally given priority on BOAC's Return Ferry Service, and apart from a summer service by Pan Am there was little other air traffic across the Atlantic.

"Sea passage, with all its attendant delays and difficulties," Massey wrote, "has become the quicker and more dependable means of communication." So, "to meet the situation created by the slow transportation of officials and despatches of urgent national importance," he recommended the creation of a Canadian transatlantic air service.

He may not have been the first to advance this idea officially, and it had certainly been discussed within TCA. In a memo a few months earlier Jock Barclay, from his vantage point as a ferry pilot, had written: "Do not confuse the service run by BOAC and the actual ferrying of bombers. . . . BOAC are operating an Atlantic service and run regular trips back and forth. . . ." The trouble was, of course, that if it started its own service Canada would in effect be repudiating the 1935 agreement with Britain and Ireland, under which it had undertaken the role of junior partner, operating only the Canadian segment of the all-red route.

Nevertheless, it seems that C.D. Howe might already have been contemplating taking that risk, for when he passed on Massey's letter to Herb Symington he suggested that TCA's Lockheeds could be used as far as Newfoundland, with the actual Atlantic crossing being made by the PBY, or Catalina, flying boats then being built by the Canadian branch of the Boeing company in Vancouver. Ted Larson discussed this suggestion with his technical staff and reported to Symington that with a maximum range of 1,500 miles the Catalina was not suitable for the job.

In a later memorandum discussing the impending extension of TCA's service to Newfoundand, Larson wrote: "It had been my understanding that our service to Newfoundland would be considered essentially as a war measure with respect to hemisspheric defence. At the same time, I think we have all had in the back of our minds the thought that ultimately, with the advent of more peaceful times, Newfoundland would serve as a springboard in relation to the trans-Atlantic operation."

In June 1942, before the final decision to go it alone was taken, Symington suggested a joint operation to BOAC, with the British company turning over two of its Liberators to TCA, to be flown by TCA crews, under TCA markings, and with the traffic between Canada and Britain being "pooled," or shared. Larson demurred at this suggestion, saying in a memo to Symington: "I am inclined to feel that if we accept these two aircraft, we will again introduce ourselves into a technical partnership with the BOAC and conceivably jeopardize the full Canadian operation which is now being considered. . . . I guess that BOAC, as a corporation, would like to see TCA wedded to the [return ferry] operation by some manner or means to strengthen their hand in the north Atlantic picture."

In the event, despite the personal intercession of Howe on one of his wartime visits to London, BOAC decided it could not spare any of its aircraft and turned down Symington's proposal. In the meantime, the Canadian troops in England were near mutiny in their anger at their poor mail service: in October 1942, for instance, Symington told Ted Larson there was a two-ton mountain of forces' mail piled up at Shediac, one of the stops on the transatlantic service, unable to find passage with either BOAC or Pan Am.

So in December 1942, Canada officially notified the British authorities that it intended to abrogate the 1935 agreement and launch its own Atlantic service. Already, even at that dark stage of the war, the question of the control and organization of postwar international aviation was recognized as an important one; there had been Commonwealth discussions on the subject in June that year, and a full-scale conference was held the following year, with the Canadian delegation headed by Howe himself. Ottawa was persuaded by the British to defer its abrogation of the treaty until the whole question of civil aviation could be discussed after the war. (Ireland formally withdrew from the agreement in 1945, but Canada seems never to have actually gone through with the abrogation: the joint operating company simply withered on the vine.)

Because of this international complication, when Canada's first transatlantic service was launched in July 1943, it was in the guise of a purely governmental wartime emergency measure. High Commissioner Massey was instructed to assure the British government that:

The planes will be owned by the Crown. They will carry no cargo or passengers for hire or reward. They will carry members of the Canadian armed forces and Canadian government officials engaged on urgent war business and other persons certified by a department of the government as being engaged on urgent war business. . . . The mail which will be carried will be diplomatic mail and mail to and from the Canadian armed forces in the British Isles. The planes will be operated by Trans-Canada Air Lines under contract to the Canadian government and neither the personnel nor the planes will bear Trans-Canada Air Lines insignia....

Massey was asked to negotiate landing rights at Prestwick, Scotland, the eastern terminus of the service, and arrange such matters as servicing and customs facilities; he was told that Ottawa did not anticipate any difficulty in securing the necessary rights "for the duration of the war and six months thereafter." But he was cautioned: "The main thing is to keep the discussions of this wartime government service entirely distinct from any discussions of post-war arrangements."

Actually, of course, the Canadian Government Trans-Atlantic Service, as it was called, was the beginning of TCA as an international airline,* and the three crews who had been on the Return Ferry Service were recalled as the nucleus of its personnel. They launched the service with only one aeroplane, a converted Lancaster bomber. Howe had tried to buy three Liberators from the United States but had been turned down. Then a British Lancaster was brought over as a pattern for the engineers setting up a production run at Victory Aircraft Limited, the government-owned factory at Malton, near Toronto. Howe decided to retain it on this side of the Atlantic. A ship carrying urgently needed construction supplies to Labrador for the air base being built at Goose Bay had been torpedoed and sunk, so the crews led by

---

*No fares were charged until after the war, when the price of a one-way ticket between Montreal and London was set at $572, plus 15 per cent transportation tax; this was soon reduced, on the basis of experience, to $375. In May 1947, CGTAS became a subsidiary of TCA, Trans-Canada Air Lines (Atlantic) Limited, and it was operated separately until January 1, 1952, when it was merged into its parent company.

Lindy Rood and Jock Barclay used the Lancaster to ferry huge steel beams to the site.

Then, to prepare it for its role in the CGTAS, it was extensively modified, partly in Montreal and partly in Britain. Extra fuel tanks were installed in the bomb bay to give it the range required for the Atlantic, the front gun turret was removed to make room for an extra cargo compartment, and new radio equipment and instruments were added. The finished aircraft was dubbed the Lancastrian, somewhat confusingly, since an entirely different plane was later given the same name in Britain. The Canadian Lancastrian inaugurated the Atlantic service in July 1943, with a non-stop flight from Montreal to Britain carrying 2,600 lbs. of forces' mail and three official passengers. The 3,000-mile trip was accomplished in 12 hours and 25 minutes, breaking the existing speed record by 25 minutes.

Howe originally intended to supplement the first Lancastrian with three York aircraft which he had heard about when visiting England. The York was a troop transport version of the Lancaster, with a claimed range of 5,000 miles and room for thirty passengers, and plans were made to build three of them at Victory Aircraft. But when the TCA engineers examined the plane and its specifications they decided it was totally unsuited to the airline's requirements and the project was abandoned. Howe then approached the United States for four Douglas C-54's – the military version of the successful DC-4 airliner. The official application certified that they were to be used entirely for carrying forces' mail and as hospital aircraft to evacuate serious casualties from the fighting then raging in Italy; but once again the U.S. service authorities ruled that the planes could not be spared. So more Lancasters, now emerging from the Malton assembly line in a steady stream, were converted into Lancastrians – later versions being equipped with ten seats, a luxury lacking in the first model. In all, CGTAS took delivery of nine of them. One vanished after sending out a brief distress call over the Atlantic and another was destroyed by fire after crash-landing on a training flight. The surviving seven operated a successful and much-appreciated Atlantic service; but they presented the airline with horrendous maintenance problems, and the pilots, to put it mildly, disliked them.

The problem was that their four Rolls-Royce Merlin engines had been designed for military use in fighter aircraft such as Spitfires and Hurricanes. They had great power for their weight but were intended to operate at full output for short periods; it was a rare military aircraft that flew for more than three hundred hours before it was shot down. Airline flying was, of course, quite different – hour after hour of continuous operation – and this imposed unexpected wear and tear on engine parts, which constantly had to be replaced at overhaul, at tremendous expense.

Worst of all, the Merlin proved frighteningly susceptible to mid-air failure. There were endless difficulties with both the engine itself and its various accessories, which did not always function properly in the extreme conditions encountered on the Atlantic. A peculiarly nagging problem plagued the spark plugs. An aircraft's cruising speed, for obvious reasons, is set considerably lower than the top speed its engines can attain in a short burst of maximum power. Firing for hour after hour across the Atlantic, without the intense heat generated by all-out bursts of power, the Merlin's plugs had a tendency to become coated with lead, sometimes so badly that the build-up formed a solid bridge across the gap and the plug was, to use a modern phrase, "rendered inoperative." To have one or more engines splutter to a stop half-way across the Atlantic was a severe test of a pilot's equanimity, and after several of them had experienced uncomfortably narrow escapes – George Lothian completed one crossing by limping into Montreal on just one properly functioning engine – rebellion began to brew in the ranks. At one stage, Lindy Rood, who by now had been appointed chief pilot, recommended that the service should be suspended until better equipment could be obtained; and in 1945, soon after the end of the war in Europe, the pilots held an angry protest meeting at which they aired their discontent before representatives of the engineering and maintenance department, including its boss, Jim Bain. Bain, who clung to the traditional British admiration for Rolls-Royce, contended that the problems were not as serious as the pilots were making out, and in any case the Rolls-Royce engineers would soon have them licked. The pilots remained unconvinced, and to resolve the impasse Dave Tennant, a promising young engineer, suggested that since TCA did the maintenance and overhaul work on both the CGTAS Merlins and the Pratt & Whitney engines used by BOAC's Return Ferry Service Liberators (which the pilots favoured) the shop records should be examined to see how the two engines compared. To management's discomfiture, the Merlin was found to be having four times as many failures as the Pratt & Whitney.

Eventually, but only after the intercession of the president, Herb Symington, the pilots agreed to continue flying the Lancastrians provided, among other things, that maintenance schedules were amended to shorten the interval between engine changes and permit more time for maintenance checks at Dorval and Prestwick. "None of the above will eliminate our troubles," Rood wrote in a memorandum afterwards, "but they may decrease their number."

Against this background, those pilots with experience of the Lancastrian's idiosyncrasies were incensed when they discovered that the new, made-in-Canada fleet that TCA proposed to introduce after the war would fly on Merlin engines. C.D. Howe's decision that the postwar fleet should be built, if not designed, in Canada may have been influenced by his difficulties in securing U.S. aircraft during the war. He was certainly influenced by the knowledge that thousands of Canadians employed in aircraft manufacturing plants would be thrown out of work when their wartime contracts to build British and American military aircraft came to an end. By now it had become clear that the postwar airline would need a modern, long-range, four-engined transport not only for its transcontinental route but for the Atlantic. TCA engineers, through their wartime connections, were familiar with the four-engined airliners Britain planned to produce, which, because of that country's concentration on military production during the war, were going to be largely civil adaptations of the Lancaster and Halifax bombers. So in 1943 they visited U.S. manufacturing plants to examine their plans, and after intensive comparison studies their choice fell on the Douglas DC-4.

The DC-4, which was designed to specifications drawn up by the five leading U.S. airlines, first flew in 1936. Major improvements had been made to it in the intervening years and its manufacturer had acquired further valuable experience building the military version, the C-54, so the postwar DC-4 was expected to be a well-proved, efficient aircraft likely to be in great demand by the U.S. airlines. The C-54 was being built under licence at Canadian Vickers Limited (later Canadair) in Montreal when Howe heard that the DC-4 was TCA's choice for its postwar fleet, and he decided to approach the Douglas company for the manufacturing rights to build it in Canada. He put the idea to the cabinet on February 1, 1944, and as usual the cabinet gave him the go-ahead.

He had decided that the initial production run of what was later christened the North Star should be fifty aircraft, and only three plants in Canada were considered capable of taking on an order of that size. Victory Aircraft was fully occupied with its contract to build Lancasters for the RAF. The Boeing plant in Vancouver was nearing the end of its wartime contracts but Ralph Bell, the head of a Halifax fishing company Howe had pressed into service as his dollar-a-year Director-General of Aircraft Production, considered Boeing inferior to Canadian Vickers "from the standpoint of relative efficiency and possible cost."

Bell, in fact, did not believe the plane should be built in Canada at all – and he was incautious enough to tell Howe so. "I feel that the decision to manufacture this plane in Canada is wrong," he wrote. "I thoroughly recognize that it is none of my business what plane you choose for Trans-Canada service, but so long as I am charged with responsibility in connection with Aircraft Production, it is certainly incumbent on me to frankly express my opinions. . . ." The planes could be bought in the United States "at a saving of several million dollars as compared with building them in Canada," and since the Douglas company had not yet completed its engineering design for the postwar version of the DC-4 there was a grave danger of costly delays in the production programs.

Howe liked the men he appointed to demonstrate initiative and get on with the job without detailed supervision. He could take advice, but he was not accustomed, having once made a decision, to having it challenged. He fired back a memorandum which began, "I suggest that the policy in question as discussed in your memo is hardly one for the Aircraft Branch," and cooled as it went along: "I wish to confirm your suggestion that you are entitled to no views in Canada's air policy." In short, TCA wanted the DC-4, and what TCA wanted it should have. The government had decided TCA should operate with planes of Canadian manufacture. Therefore the DC-4 would be built at Canadian Vickers. Bell could only summon Jim Bain and ask him to get along to Canadian Vickers as soon as possible to look the situation over. Bain did so, and came away sharing the view that Canadian Vickers was the best place to build the North Star.

That view was emphatically not shared by a man with a prominent forum in which to voice his objections to it, which he promptly proceeded to do. Lieutenant-Colonel George Alexander Drew had commanded an artillery battery in World War I and written several books about military matters afterwards, and he spoke from the further vantage point of being Premier of Ontario. As such, of course, the age-old rivalry between Montreal and Toronto was never far from his mind. As soon as the government's decision was announced he rose in the legislature at Queen's Park and took after Howe with his broadsword. The government, he alleged, had originally intended to build the North Star at Victory Aircraft in Malton, which he obviously felt was meet, just and proper, but it had changed its mind and awarded the contract to Canadian Vickers at the behest of Herb

Symington, who besides being president of TCA was an officer of the Royal Securities Corporation; furthermore – and he did not bother to imply any coincidence here – Royal Securities had been "heavily interested in the financing of Canadian Vickers Limited."

Howe was furious, but he was easily able to demolish Drew's charges. As he told the House, the contract to build the North Star, which was worth only $15 million, had gone to Canadian Vickers because Victory Aircraft was fully occupied with the highest-priority contract, the production of Lancasters for the war effort, which was worth $200 million. Furthermore, both companies were owned by the government: Canadian Vickers merely managed the plant in Montreal. And as for Herb Symington, who had known nothing about the decision until after it was made, he had rendered distinguished service to Canada and was one of his most valuable advisers – and the only connection Royal Securities had ever had with Canadian Vickers was that it had been one of several financial houses which had distributed Canadian Vickers bonds when they were first offered to the public back in 1927. All in all, Howe concluded, "irresponsible statements of this kind are most damaging to Canada's war effort."

When Howe gave out the contract to Canadian Vickers in March 1944, it was anticipated that the first plane would be delivered to the airline in July 1945. In fact, the first North Star did not make its test flight until a year after that, in July 1946, and even then it was not the aircraft the TCA engineers had thought they were going to get back in 1944.

The experience of the CGTAS had shown that to maintain a regular and reliable passenger service across the Atlantic the aircraft used should be capable of flying at any altitude up to 25,000 feet – a considerable height in those days. In the thinner air at that altitude, an aircraft could fly 15 per cent faster than it could at sea level for the same expenditure of power, and the ability to climb to 25,000 feet enabled the pilot to get above icing, take advantage of prevailing tail winds, and choose the levels at which his passengers would be least troubled by turbulence. At that time, civil aviation regulations required that passengers flying above 10,000 feet be provided with oxygen, but postwar airliners, including the DC-4, were expected to be provided instead with pressurized, or especially strengthened, fuselages, enabling the air inside the cabin to be maintained at a pressure equivalent to 8,000 feet even at 25,000 feet, thus eliminating the need for oxygen masks and greatly increasing the passengers' comfort.

The TCA engineers had long since decided that whatever aircraft was chosen for the postwar fleet must be pressurized. But when they visited the Douglas factory to examine its plans in June 1944, they found that the hectic demands of the wartime production program were holding up the design work on the postwar DC-4, and the engineering for a pressurized version was not yet available – indeed, it now seemed that the first pressurized Douglas might be a larger and more advanced version of the DC-4 which was then in its preliminary planning phase, the DC-6. With the engineering of the plane Canada planned to build not yet "set," Jim Bain and Jack Dyment felt free as they framed the North Star's specifications to include those features of both Douglas versions that seemed best suited to TCA's needs. And as long as they were not going to build the stock model, so to speak, they began to cast around for other ways to improve it. Eventually, they decided they could steal a march on the American airlines that would be using the DC-4 (and launch the infant Canadian civil aviation industry on to a bright sea of prosperity) by combining what seemed to be the best available features of American and British technology.

At that time, Douglas proposed to equip the postwar DC-4 with four Pratt & Whitney R-2000 engines developing 1,100 horsepower each. Bain and Dyment believed the North Star would have a greater range and better economy than the straight DC-4 if each of its four engines could develop an extra 200 horsepower. And on his frequent visits to Rolls-Royce in England as the engineers tried to refine the Lancastrians' Merlins, Jim Bain learned that after the war there would be an updated and improved model of the Merlin, the Merlin 620, which was expected to develop 1,370 horsepower at a much lower fuel consumption than the R-2000. Once again the engineers buckled down to their calculations. Although the preliminary engine "curves" appeared to favour another British engine, the Bristol Hercules, it never seems to have been seriously considered for the North Star, perhaps because of Bain's favourable impression of the Rolls-Royce engineers' efficiency and their obliging willingness to consider any modifications TCA suggested. Rolls-Royce was anxious to break into the postwar civil aviation market and since the CGTAS at that time was the only airline-type operation using their engines, Bain was in a strong position with Britain's leading aircraft-engine manufacturer.

At any rate, it was decided that Canadair – as Canadian Vickers had now become – would build a hybrid aircraft, incorporating the best features of the DC-4 and DC-6 airframes and Rolls-Royce engines. But still the engineering from Douglas remained unavailable. With the end of the war, all building of the C-54 came to a sudden halt, in both the United States and Canada, and Benjamin Franklin, president of Canadair, sensed an opportunity. He knew that Howe intended the RCAF to take some of the North Stars when they became available, and figured that service aircraft did not have the same need for pressurization as commercial airlines. How would it be, he suggested to Howe, if he started the production run with half a dozen unpressurized North Stars destined eventually for the air force, which could be lent to TCA until the pressurized version it wanted could be built? These first six planes could be built with war-surplus C-54 parts—and it just so happened that he knew where he could lay his hands on them. The idea appealed to Howe (though not to the airline, which tried to resist it), and Franklin, a shrewd entrepreneur, bought the parts for the first six North Stars in the United States (some said for ten cents a pound, in other words as scrap), trucked them to the Canadair plant in Montreal, and began work.

So when TCA put its first North Star—dubbed the DC-4M1—into service on the Atlantic in April 1947, its pride was tempered by the fact that it was not the up-to-date, pressurized version its engineers had wanted. That version, the M2, did not begin to roll off the assembly line until six months later, and there were dark suspicions within TCA that Douglas had held up the drawings and technical information for its pressurization engineering because the U.S. airlines were afraid the M2 would put their own equipment in the shade. Even when the M2 did go into service, in 1948, the North Star's problems were not yet over.

Notwithstanding these early teething troubles—perhaps, in fact, because of their determination to rise above them—the TCA crews rapidly acquired an international reputation for their expertise in Atlantic flying. Back in those days, before aircraft began to be navigated by radio and then computers, each crew included a navigator using techniques not far removed from those on the bridge of an ocean liner. The TCA navigators, under their supervisors Pete Powell and Ron Peel, led the way in the development of new air navigation methods and procedures. Navigation in the high latitudes, where proximity to the Pole does funny things to compasses, became their specialty. And when their veteran colleague Captain Lindy Rood conceived an idea for using North Atlantic weather patterns to improve the speed and efficiency of the flights, Powell and Peel developed the charts that made its application possible. Rood's idea, a forerunner of the "pressure pattern" flying that is universally accepted today, involved deviating from the simple Great Circle route. This increased a flight's mileage, but by taking advantage of the anti-clockwise wind circulation of Atlantic storms it saved flying time, and thus fuel. There was a northern limit beyond which a flight coud not go and still save time. Thanks to the pioneering work of Powell and Peel it became known as the "Lindy line"and it can still be found on Atlantic charts today.

CHAPTER NINE

T THE HEIGHT OF THE WAR, on April 2, 1943, Prime Minister Mackenzie King made an important policy statement in the House of Commons. He spoke of the "remarkable expansion" that had taken place in Canadian aviation, "in the training of air and ground personnel, in the construction of airports and air navigation facilities, in the manufacture of aircraft, and in the extension of air transport services." Full details of all this could not be disclosed for security reasons, but "Canada today is the fourth greatest military power among the united nations." The great expansion of which the Prime Minister spoke had so far been confined largely to military flying, but "When war necessities permit and suitable equipment can be obtained, the government will encourage the further development within Canada of air transportation services, to supplement and form part of an up-to-date transportation system for Canada by land, water and air."

But let interlopers beware: "Trans-Canada Air Lines will continue to be the instrument of the government in maintaining all trans-continental air transport services and in operating services across international boundary lines and outside Canada." TCA's operations would continue to be limited to "important services of a mainline character" and the development of "supplementary routes" would be left to private enterprise. But, the Prime Minister repeated, "The government sees no good reason for changing its policy that Trans-Canada Air Lines is the sole Canadian agency which may operate international air services. Within Canada, Trans-Canada Air Lines will continue to operate all trans-continental systems, and such other services of a mainline character as may from time to time be designated by the government. Competition between air services over the same route will not be permitted whether between a publicly-owned service and a privately-owned service or between two privately-owned services."

This message, and it could hardly have been clearer, was aimed squarely at an influential target: the Moguls of Windsor Station in Montreal. If there had ever been any doubts within the Canadian Pacific Railway about the desirability of its entering the air transportation field they were dispelled by the formation of CP Air Services to run the Atlantic ferry operation, and its successful performance under the guidance of C.H. "Punch" Dickins, the distinguished World War I and bush-flying veteran recruited from Canadian Airways. Having thus dipped its toe into the water, the CPR found it inviting and plunged in wholeheartedly. The dozen or so bush-flying companies that operated alongside or in competition with Canadian Airways had found their wings severely clipped by the war: mines and other operations closed to conserve manpower and planes were grounded for lack of parts; camps were abandoned all over the North and the adventurous young men who populated them flocked to the colours. Faced with disastrously dwindling traffic, the bush operators were only too glad to sell out to the CPR when that company began to pick them up, eventually folding in Canadian Airways itself in 1941 to form what Howe later described as "a monopoly in the field of transportation by air except for Trans-Canada Air Lines."

The new monopoly, Canadian Pacific Airlines, got off to a flying start. Long before Pearl Harbor, U.S. defence strategists had been growing alarmed about the exposed position of Alaska, sitting up there at the top of the world, isolated from the United States proper by hundreds of miles of ocean and Canadian wilderness, and all but connected to Japan by the island bridge formed by the Aleutians and Kuriles. Japanese naval and air forces operating from bases hidden somewhere in those remote island chains could cut off Alaska from its seaborne routes of supply to the south, so attention turned to the inland route pioneered by the bush flyers from Edmonton northwest across the mountainous wastes of northern British Columbia and into the Yukon. In 1940, on the recommendation of the Canada-U.S. Joint Defence Board, the Department of Transport began to upgrade its primitive airway between Edmonton and Whitehorse, in the Yukon, bulldozing airstrips and building radio range stations in areas previously inhabited only by grizzly bears. Later, after the United States had been drawn into the war, came the Alaska Highway, that mammoth construction project in which thousands of tenderfeet from the south punched a 1,500-mile gravel road through the virgin forests between Dawson Creek, British Columbia, and Fairbanks, Alaska. Later still came Canol, a similarly heroic project involving the construction of a 600-mile pipeline between Norman Wells in the Northwest Territories, where oil had been discovered in 1920, and Whitehorse, where a stripped-down Texas refinery had been reassembled to fuel the U.S. aerial armada based in Alaska.

This frenzy of activity, made feasible only by the aeroplane, was clearly not of a "mainline character" – no one had ever set foot where most of it was going on. But it did take place right in the bailiwick of some of the bush-flying companies that had been merged into Canadian Pacific Airlines, and it made profitable work for every transport aircraft that could be coaxed into the air. So the new airline grew quickly; and with its sponsor, the U.S. military, governing wartime priorities, it was able to expand by buying up-to-date equipment denied to the country's national airline. By the time Mackenzie King made his declaration of policy CPA was a flourishing new growth on the Canadian aviation scene, with ambitions that Howe, and TCA, considered far above its station: its advertising theme of "Wings Around the World" indicated clearly enough its plans for the future.

As might have been expected, CPA did not take the Prime Minister's statement lying down. It immediately mounted a vigorous propaganda campaign aimed at a public which still largely favoured private over government enterprise. A fighting brief pointed out that the CPR had already invested $8 million in its northern air services, which was probably more than the government had put into TCA, and said CPA must have access to the passenger traffic originating in the large population centres to subsidize its vital, though thinly travelled, northern routes. "Today," the brief said, "CPA is virtually as large as TCA in most respects and is rendering far more vital air transportation service than that provided by the publicly-owned airline, which essentially parallels existing surface transport." And as for TCA being the "chosen instrument" for international flying, "by not using the experience, facilities and world-wide organization of Canadian Pacific, which has carried a great part of Canada's transocean traffic for the past 60 years, it would seem that the country as a whole will suffer materially. . . . If equity and justice have any place in the Canadian government's plan, Canadian Pacific should be allowed to carry traffic in the air to supplement its long-established sea routes."

On March 17, 1944, C.D. Howe rose in the House determined to put a stop to all this nonsense. When the government set up TCA, he said – and he reminded all and sundry that the CPR had had its chance to buy into the national airline then – "it had been contemplated that Trans-Canada Air Lines would be a non-competitive, non-profit system of transportation by air, planned to avoid duplication of services that were the outgrowth of competitive building for profit in the field of surface transportation." The Prime Minister only last year had set out the government's views "with great clarity," but this had not stopped the CPR from reaching out for new air franchises. In the past, competition between railways had developed "pressure methods for obtaining new franchises," and this must not be allowed to happen in aviation: "Accordingly . . . steps will be taken to require our railways to divest themselves of ownership of air lines, to the end that, within a period of one year from the ending of the European war, transport by air will be entirely separate from surface transportation. . . ."

Howe had been even more specific in a letter to Herb Symington, who had been consulted before the announcement of the government's decision and had written a long letter to the minister arguing against it. "Council is determined," Howe replied, "to stop a CPR monopoly of secondary aviation in this country, and is insisting that I terminate the relationship of the Railway and its subsidiary Air Lines. We are all satisfied that as long as the relationship continues, there will be interference in every move that the Government may make in the international field, and in fact, in the domestic field. You will agree that this is an intolerable situation."

The CPR's claim to a place in aviation was founded on the fact that its rival, the CNR, had an airline; hence TCA must be separated from the CNR, Howe told Symington, admitting that he regretted what could only be called "an unfortunate business."

Howe's renewed expression of the government's policy caused intense gloom among CPA employees, who saw it as the end of the road, and intense resentment in Windsor Station. But it was Herb Symington's opposition to the government's decision that eventually caused Howe to change his mind, so that the separation was never enforced. In arguing against it, Symington was partly influenced by his own sentimental attachment to the CNR and partly by the practical consideration that it would involve the airline in considerable extra expense. As he pointed out to Howe, it would require the appointment of a new president (who, unlike himself, would have to be paid), a new board of directors, and six new departments to handle the legal, accounting, publicity, medical, insurance, and investment and purchasing work that the CNR carried out for the airline. He couldn't begin to estimate the extra cost, but was sure it would be "a good deal more than $100,000 a year."

In these inflationary times, that sounds a paltry sum to be worried about. But TCA's profit in 1943 had been only $147,889, and when the results for 1944 were in, that figure had slumped alarmingly, to $7,409. Furthermore, Symington knew that the airline would soon face heavy expenditures to upgrade its fleet: in his speech to the House, Howe had said, "If we could double our equipment, indications are that we would have every seat occupied." In other words, there was a whole new travel market out there waiting to be tapped; and Symington was building up his organization to go after it.

The end of the war freed the airline from its dependence on the Lockheeds, which had long been considered outmoded and too small. The urgent need for a new two-engined aircraft for the domestic routes was recognized, but the new postwar designs had not yet emerged. So as a stop-gap measure the airline bought three Douglas DC-3s and twenty-seven war-surplus Dakotas, their military equivalent, which Canadair undertook to convert into 21-passenger airliners, using TCA's specifications. The first "Daks" to arrive were sadly dilapidated – some even had birds' nests in their innards. Converting them to civil use was a major operation, involving such important details as designing new instrumentation, heating and oxygen systems, electrical and radio installations and a host of other modifications. Many had been built to tow troop-carrying gliders and they had huge, unwieldy propellers weighing almost 500 lbs. which were inefficient at airline cruising speeds and vibrated too much for civilian use; they were replaced with new models weighing 113 lbs. less, giving a weight saving of 226 lbs. per aircraft.

To supervise all this work, a team of TCA engineers and technicians headed by Jim Bain moved in to the Canadair plant, which was also busy with the North Star program; but despite the scale of the job, the first three converted Dakotas were delivered to the airline and put in service before the end of 1945.

With the 21-passenger DC-3s just around the corner, and the 40-passenger North Stars expected to follow them into service almost immediately, it was clear that the airline faced a hectic period of expansion. So when the fighting men began to return from Europe they were given preference in the hiring program, which was under way before the war had actually ended. On February 19, 1945, for instance, Herb Symington wrote a long letter about postwar civil aviation policy to Sir Arthur Street, Permanent Under Secretary at the Air Ministry in London. At the end he tacked on a more informal paragraph: "By the way, when you get time, if ever you reach that happy state, I would appreciate your appraisal of various RCAF men who might in future be useful in TCA."

There thus arrived, before the end of the year, "the three group captains," much-decorated combat pilots who had gone on to higher rank by virtue of their administrative abilities and were now parachuted into the executive ranks at TCA – not without some hard feelings on the part of longer-serving men who had moved up in the ranks since 1937. Two of these high-level recruits, Ernest Moncrieff and Paul Y. Davoud, moved on to other things within a few years;* the third, Gordon R. McGregor, was to have an immeasurable influence on the airline in the quarter-century of expansion that lay ahead.

The company's operations at the end of the war were directed by Bill English, who took over as vice-president when Ted Larson returned to United Airlines. One of the two "clerks" Phil Johnson had requested right at the beginning, English was a burly, florid man who to the end of his life boasted a shock of white, curly hair. He had gone to work for the Canadian Northern Railway as a boy of 17 in 1908, and by 1945 his popularity with everyone had made him something of a father figure around TCA. In the early days, he knew all the employees and many of their wives by their first names, and he liked them to call him Bill. Even after he became vice-president he enjoyed touring the airline partying informally with the station employees until long after midnight, and much younger men marvelled when they arrived at the office a few hours later to find "good old Bill" already hard at work. Much as they admired his stamina, and his fairness and geniality, the headquarters staff hated to have to visit English in his office during the winter: they would find him at his desk in his shirt sleeves, tieless, mopping perspiration from his brow – and with his windows wide open to the bitter Winnipeg winds. It was this large, expansive man who was credited with establishing the "family atmosphere" that bound TCA together during its early years.

When the group captains arrived, Davoud was made operations assistant to English and Moncrieff became director of personnel. Both Symington and English knew that one of the most urgent postwar tasks would be to build up the traffic department, which had been something of a Cinderella during the war, with little more than a handful of sales staff. This task was entrusted to Gordon McGregor, possibly because before the war he had been with the Bell Telephone Company and good communi-

---

*Moncrieff became president of Standard Aero Engine Limited in his native Winnipeg, and director of a long list of companies; Davoud went on to a variety of jobs in aviation, including a stint as chairman of the government regulatory agency, the Air Transport Board.

cations were recognized as the life-blood of the reservations system, whose efficiency was essential to the success of the impending sales effort.

Gordon Roy McGregor was born in Montreal in 1901, the only son of a dentist and grandson of a piano-maker whose ivory-handled tools he lovingly preserved in his later years: he was himself an amateur woodworker of better-than-average skill. Like so many other boys of his generation, he was early gripped by flying fever. When he was 8 the first aviation meet in Canada was held near his family's summer home in Quebec and before long he was building model aircraft and tinkering with engines. It was natural therefore that after his early schooling in Montreal and at St. Andrew's College in Toronto he should enrol in the applied science course at McGill University in Montreal.

For some reason, he left before graduating and joined Bell Telephone's engineering department. He retained his keen interest in flying and when he became Bell's district manager at Kingston in 1932 he began to take private flying lessons, to such good effect that in 1935, 1936 and 1938 he won the Webster Trophy, awarded to the best amateur pilot in Canada. Posted by Bell to head office in Montreal in 1938, he joined No. 115 Auxiliary Squadron of the RCAF and when the war broke out he was given leave of absence to go on active service. McGregor had a habit of taking words literally, and to him the "active" part of that phrase was the most important: he immediately went overseas with No. 1 RCAF Squadron and as a flight-lieutenant in a Hurricane fighter became the oldest pilot to take part in the Battle of Britain. He was credited with shooting down five and a half enemy aircraft and awarded the Distinguished Flying Cross. The "half-plane" was probably one of his most daring exploits. He was stationed at Northolt, near London, when a German bomber was detected flying over southern England protected by pea-soup weather in which, with the cloud ceiling almost down to the ground, fighter pilots would ordinarily have been in bed. McGregor and his Montreal stockbroker friend Deane Nesbitt roared off in their Hurricanes and, guided by radar, found the German intruder and shot it down.

McGregor was not an unduly retiring man: he held strong opinions about most things and was not afraid to express them with whatever force the occasion seemed to demand. But he was always reluctant in later years to discuss his wartime achievements, even with close friends. Despite his own reticence, his stature was such that legends inevitably grew up around him. The combination of intrepid fighter pilot and experienced business executive was a rare one, and his promotion was rapid: from squadron leader to wing commander – in which capacity he took part in sweeps over occupied France – to director of air staff at the RCAF's overseas headquarters, and from there to the command of a Canadian wing in Alaska when the Aleutians invasion scare was at its height.

One of the anecdotes his friends and service associates like to recall concerns his days in Alaska. It seems that a young pilot managed to get himself into a spin, and perhaps panicking too soon, departed his aircraft by parachute. The loss of an aircraft was never an experience to Gordon McGregor's taste, and having listened to the pilot's explanation with growing exasperation, the aging wing commander grabbed a parachute, stalked out to an aircraft on the ramp, took it aloft and deliberately placed it into the kind of spin the young man had encountered. Then he performed all the right manoeuvres to bring it back under control, landed, strode over to the shamefaced youngster who had been watching from the ground and coolly told him: "Get packed and be off this base within the hour."

Since the invasion of Alaska never did happen, service in that remote outpost could not long hold McGregor's enthusiasm. Somehow he managed to talk his way back to Europe as commanding officer of No. 126 Wing, part of the group charged with the responsibility of providing air cover for the British Second Army in the coming invasion of Normandy. It was here that he demonstrated the administrative capacity that probably brought him to Symington's attention. No. 126 Wing was assigned to be the first Allied fighter unit to operate from Normandy after D-Day, so McGregor was faced with the task of planning the transfer of planes, ground crews and even a mobile hospital to airfields he had seen only in aerial reconnaissance photographs. By now, in recognition perhaps of McGregor's efficient command, his men were equipped with the latest version of the legendary Spitfire. On the day appointed he led his fighters and all their support apparatus across the Channel, and continued to fly with them as they leap-frogged from one captured airfield to another across Europe.

McGregor had intended to return to his promising career at Bell after the war – in fact he felt an obligation so to do. But when Symington invited him to join TCA he was attracted: after all, he had been mixed up with aeroplanes for the past few exciting years and more. In fact, back in 1937, when he was simply an amateur pilot, he had heard that the CNR was going to have an airline and had written to Sam Hungerford applying for a job.

"My work and my hobby," he wrote, "have combined to make me of more value to an organization engaged in air transportation than in any other field of endeavour, and being firmly convinced that Canada will experience great development during the next decade in commercial aviation, I wish to associate myself with it." Even though by then he held a commercial pilot's licence, he never received more than a formal acknowledgment of his letter. Now, better late than never, his opportunity had come. He told his bosses at Bell he wanted to take advantage of it and they, sharing the prevailing view around the CNR that nothing very much would ever come of this business of carrying people around in aeroplanes, extended his leave of absence by six months to give him time, as McGregor recalled it years later, "to come to my senses."

Having decided to take the plunge, he was hired by TCA at the end of 1945 as special representative in the traffic department, which at that time was without an official head. The first general traffic manager, George Wakeman, a hard-working but abrasive recruit from the Department of Transport, had left in 1941 after a disagreement with Ted Larson. His replacement, Jack Dalby, the United Airlines traffic manager in Vancouver who switched to TCA in 1938, was given only acting status and never confirmed in the senior post, perhaps because Symington or English did not want to freeze all the top positions in the airline while some of the men who might later be judged suitable for them were still away at the war.

McGregor spent his first two months touring the system, familiarizing himself with its employees and their jobs. It was perhaps an unnerving experience for some junior reservations clerk to have this immaculately dressed and obviously authoritative stranger sitting beside her as she worked, observing every procedure with his penetrating brown eyes and occasionally asking a question to which she might or might not know the answer. But after this familiarization period, when he was appointed general traffic manager and began to institute the changes some of the people in the department had been privately thinking were long overdue, everyone realized that this rather stern newcomer, Group Captain McGregor, had not been wasting their time with his searching questions.

Partly because the preoccupation of everyone at TCA in the early days was flying and maintaining the aircraft, and partly because the airline had barely opened for business when the war began and the sales function had been overshadowed by the emergency, the new general traffic manager was confronted by a set of what he called "corporate organizational horrors." His first surprise, as befitted a Bell Telephone man, was that customers calling the airline to book a seat could get an answer only during regular business hours. It was a simple matter to institute 24-hour telephone answering services in at least the main traffic centres, though Herb Symington thought this something of an extravagance.

Some of the other failings McGregor found were more deep-rooted and their solution called for major administrative changes which, as they took place, exposed him to charges of empire-building. Their logic was unchallengeable, however. Many of the functions that should properly have been carried out by the traffic department, whose chief concern was the tender loving care of passengers, had grown up under the aegis of the operations department, which understandably gave more priority to moving the aeroplanes around from place to place safely and as close to schedule as possible. For instance, a passenger, having been sold his ticket by the solicitous traffic department, would be greeted at the check-in counter by an agent under the authority of the operations department, who was perhaps not fully aware of, or attentive to, the aims and objectives of the traffic department.

Similarly, McGregor found that the booking of reservations came under the communications branch, which was also part of the operations department. This was a hangover from the early days, when bookings were made by the radio operators; but by 1945 the reservations clerks were using teletypes, which do not require a knowledge of the Morse Code. The swift, courteous and efficient booking of seats is vital to a sales department trying to attract customers: inefficiency can lead not only to frustrated and angry passengers but unfilled seats, which do not contribute to an airline's revenue. So within a few months of McGregor's appointment the airport passenger agents and reservations personnel were transferred to the jurisdiction of the traffic department. New training programs were developed and new staff hired. In one crash program alone thirty men considered to have management potential were hired and trained as sales agents.

McGregor's next move was to decentralize his department. The operations department was at that time organized into three regions, with an operations manager in charge of each. McGregor followed this precedent and Jack Dalby, a confirmed Vancouverite, was delighted to turn his back on those Winnipeg winters and take over the western region, based in his home town. W.R. Campbell became traffic manager, central region, based in Toronto, and John Maxwell took over the eastern region in Montreal. This system of divided responsibility was adopted at all the different stations on the system, with one man in charge of operations and another in charge of traffic, a situation that would lead to some problems in the years ahead.

CHAPTER TEN

ATE IN 1945 Parliament passed some amendments to the Trans-Canada Air Lines Act which freed the corporation's hands for the expansion ahead, but which also backfired and cost it two million dollars in lost revenue during the following year.

The rate paid by the Post Office to the airline was originally set at 60 cents for each mile flown "in the conveyance of mails by air." (George Herring, wearing his postie's cap rather than his TCA director's homburg, had held out for 50 cents.) In 1940, its first full year of operation, the airline managed to reduce its operating costs by a satisfying 11½ cents a mile – from 88.4 to 76.9 cents. And in October of that year, D.B. Colyer wrote a memo to the CNR's legal department pointing out that at the 60-cent mail rate the airline, which had registered a loss of $411,656 in 1939, stood to make a profit of about $550,000 in 1940, largely because of the extra miles it was flying with the inauguration of new routes and the introduction of its second daily transcontinental flight. "Further service extensions," he wrote, "are proposed in 1941, including a third transcontinental schedule, the Toronto–New York run and additional trips on schedules in eastern Canada. Unless the mail rate is reduced to somewhere near the cost of handling (i.e., operating expenses plus interest less passenger revenues), say 40 cents a mile, the indications are that a very substantial surplus will be built up during the year – in fact a figure of $2,000,000 would, under present conditions, appear probable."

The Post Office, already unhappy in its role of fairy godmother, would no doubt be infuriated if the organization it saw itself as subsidizing made such an inordinate profit.* So, at the airline's

---

*At that stage, the Post Office would not even have shared in the anticipated profit, since the government twice extended the "initial period" during which it undertook to meet any airline deficit, from the originally intended 1940 to 1942. From then on, had the airline incurred a deficit, the Post Office's payment per mile would have been raised the following year to cover it; in fact, for the next few years, the airline registered a profit, which was reflected by a decline in the mail rate from 45 cents per mile flown in 1941 to 42 cents in 1945.

initiative, the mail rate for 1941 was lowered to 45 cents per mile flown.

The quantity of mail shipped by air increased spectacularly in the early years of the war, partly because more flights were available to carry it but even more because of the general increase in economic activity and the wartime separation of servicemen from their families. Airmail volume virtually tripled between 1939 and 1941, from 425,000 to 1.3 million lbs.; and it almost tripled again between 1941 and 1943, from 1.3. million to 3.7 million lbs. But much of this mushrooming growth was accommodated by carrying larger loads of mail on each aircraft, so that the increase in the number of miles flown, while substantial, did not match the tremendous burgeoning of the mail. The rise in the airline's mail revenue thus did not keep pace with the increased amount of mail carried: in 1939, the airline flew 2.7 million miles and received $1.6 million from the Post Office – 70 per cent of its total revenue; in 1943, it flew three times as many miles, 8.9 million, with almost nine times as much mail as it carried in 1939, but received only slightly more than double the revenue from the Post Office – $3.5 million, a sum which was now down to only 37 per cent of its total takings.

Each year, in its annual report, the corporation drew plaintive attention to this proportionate dwindling in its receipts from the Post Office. Even more galling was that under the arrangement the government had devised, the Post Office, since it was paying the piper, naturally expected to call the tune. The Post Office's Coolican and Herring claimed the right to veto any new service proposed by TCA if it did not suit their convenience. The airline challenged this. With more and more "must ride" passengers clamouring for accommodation, it was anxious to increase its services as fast as it could secure aircraft and train crews. But if it wanted to put on an extra daily flight between two cities, this faced the Post Office with added expenditures for the extra miles flown: a new daily transcontinental flight, for instance, would cost the Post Office perhaps $1 million a year. And the Post Office, having spent all day emptying mail boxes, would want the flight carrying its mailbags to leave as late at night as possible. TCA's traffic department, solicitous of its customers' convenience, might want it to leave early in the morning.

It was clearly not a businesslike arrangement, and it could not be permitted to continue if the airline was to take advantage of the opportunities ahead. At the end of the war, disturbed by what he had been hearing about the Post Office generally, Mackenzie King sent in one of his principal private secretaries, Walter J.

Turnbull, to clean house. As deputy postmaster general, Turnbull, a tough little man who had worked in the Post Office himself before joining King's staff, promptly banished Coolican to Peru in response to a request for a postal adviser by that country's government. Then he turned his agile mind to the arrangements with TCA, and made the logical suggestion that the Post Office should get out of the business of trying to run an airline and simply pay TCA for the amount of mail it actually carried. Symington told Howe he did not care for this idea, since whatever ton-mile rate was set would seem high by comparison with rates in the United States, where the costs of aircraft and fuel had always been lower than in Canada and the population densities – and thus mail volumes – were higher.

In those palmy days, a letter could be sent by surface mail for 4 cents; an airmail letter cost 7 cents. Symington suggested to Turnbull that the airline would be satisfied with the extra 3 cents, but Turnbull balked at that, and his views finally won the day. Parliament, among its amendments to the TCA Act in 1945, authorized the corporation to negotiate a new contract with the Post Office on a ton-mile basis, which became effective on April 1, 1946. The rate for the first year was set at 1.5 mills per lb. per mile, or $3 per ton-mile, and since the airmail volume was confidently expected to grow steadily, the airline agreed to a volume discount, with the rate falling year by year to an eventual .9 mills.

To the airline's consternation, instead of growing, the mail volume fell off drastically – by 32 per cent in the first year. Part of the decline could be explained by a general drop in business activity and the return of servicemen to their homes. But the Post Office was responsible for part of it, too, since cost-conscious officials began to divert airmail to railway mail cars (which were paid for in advance) when they considered sending it by air would not get it to its destination any faster.*

The result was that the airline's mail revenue slumped by more than $470,000 in 1946, from $4.25 million to $3.78 million. With the addition of new routes and services, the airline flew 15.8 million miles during the year, a huge advance on the 11.5 million miles flown in 1945. And it was calculated, ruefully, that had the old miles-flown mail rate still been in effect, its revenue for the year – $12.8 million – would have been $2 million higher.

---

*At a later stage in the long-running battle between the Post Office and TCA, C.D. Howe wrote to Symington: "It seems to me that Turnbull of the Post Office is out to wreck aviation, under the silly impression that he will thereby put the Post Office on a business basis."

That would have been enough to turn its embarrassing $1.1 million deficit for the year into a comfortable profit.

The decline in mail revenue was not, of course, solely responsible for the deficit. There has always been in Canada a heavy seasonal fluctuation in air travel, the demand for seats approximately doubling in the summer and early fall. In 1946, the airline initially hoped to cash in on this heavy peak traffic with its 21-seat converted DC-3s. New staff was trained and new offices opened to cope with the anticipated rush. But delivery of the aircraft, expected in the spring, was delayed by strikes and production problems. The airline complained that even when the planes were delivered its own technical staff constantly had to correct defects in them caused by poor workmanship and slack inspection procedures at Canadair. As a result, the new, larger aircraft were not available for the peak season, and more potential revenue was lost.

Canadair apologized and explained that it had assigned most of its experienced workers to the North Star program; but this, too, suffered interminable delays. The airline had originally expected to receive delivery of the first six non-pressurized M1 North Stars in time to put them into the Atlantic service in the fall of 1946. In fact it was not able to do so until April 1947, and the first of the pressurized versions, the M2s, was not delivered until six months after that.

Nevertheless, the North Star, even without pressurization, received a rapturous welcome in the press. The first four-engined commercial aircraft built in Canada, it was confidently expected to be the forerunner of a flourishing new Canadian industry. A week before it went into service on the Atlantic it was introduced to the public with a passenger flight between Montreal and Toronto (the production delays prevented its full introduction into the domestic service until June 1948). A correspondent named Stephen S. Brott went along and in a broadcast to Britain and the Caribbean on the CBC's international service made it clear that he was impressed by the cold martinis and hot lunch he was served. "The comforts of the North Star are on the style of a high-class hotel," he said. "For the ladies there's a powder room with a dressing table and seat, a wash basin and dental bowl, mirrors and other accessories and necessaries. . . . the sort of thing you dream of some day having in your own home. . . ."

Some of the paying passengers were pleased, too. Thomas J. Bata, the Czech immigrant who runs his world-wide shoe business from Toronto, flew home from Europe with his wife on an M1 soon after the service opened and wrote to C.D. Howe, saying: "It is my considered opinion, after having had experience with trans-Atlantic flying on almost every airline, that the Trans-Canada service is now second to none.''

True, some of the passengers complained that the North Star was too noisy – a problem that was not solved for several years, and then not completely – but the worst complaints about Canada's proud new entry into the commercial aircraft stakes came from the pilots themselves. For the new civil version of the Merlin proved just as susceptible to mechanical troubles as its wartime predecessor. It had, also, a new feature which horrified the pilots – and Gordon McGregor – when they first saw it. McGregor had spent many hours behind the old Merlins in Hurricanes and Spitfires, and was accustomed to their thunderous roar; indeed, it was a comforting sound to the pilots who depended on its power for their lives. But both those fighter planes were sleek, streamlined machines whose engines were cooled by the flow of air through small and inconspicuous radiators. There was one disadvantage to them: to avoid over-heating, they had to be flown within a few minutes of their engines being started. This was no problem when a fighter squadron had to ''scramble,'' but airline operation sometimes calls for long periods of idling on the ground. To get around this problem the new Merlin had an oil cooler housed in a large circular radiator which greatly increased the engine's frontal area and created a built-in ''drag.'' In the words of Lindy Rood: ''We pushed around a 50-mile-an-hour headwind for years.'' The unexpected addition to the engine not only reduced the North Star's predicted cruising speed from 280 to 230 miles an hour, but the oil cooler often refused to function in the extremes of weather encountered on the Atlantic and in Canada.

This, and a host of other mechanical problems that plagued the Merlin, would lead to alarming maintenance costs when the North Star went into full service. But with its initial popularity, TCA (Atlantic) Limited carried almost 16,000 passengers during the last eight months of 1947 and managed to make a small profit of $136,303. The parent company's situation was less happy. The number of passengers carried on North American routes rose by 40 per cent during the year, but this was not enough to fill the DC-3s – only 58 per cent of the 33.4 million ton-miles flown produced revenue – and TCA's deficit mounted to $1.7 million for the year.

Perhaps this second successive deficit year influenced Herb Symington's decision to retire. He was now 66, and he had worked long and hard throughout the war on Howe's behalf; he had, in fact, talked about retiring when the government announced its intention of divorcing the airline from the railroad, but had been persuaded to stay on. On October 31, 1947, however, he told TCA's board of directors the time had come when the responsibilities of his post should be shifted to other shoulders. Such occasions can expose those present to a good deal of platitudinous humbug, but there was no one around the airline who disagreed with his fellow director Wilfrid Gagnon's summing up that Symington had "guided the corporation safely through a difficult formative period and laid a groundwork which would stand it in good stead for the future."

The retiring president told the board he was not at the moment prepared to recommend anyone to succeed him, but suggested that Bill English should run the company until a new appointment was made. Naturally, there was plenty of speculation within the company about who would inherit the president's mantle – and no doubt a certain amount of jockeying for the job. There were many who thought the popular Bill English not only deserved it but was sure to get it; among them was Howard Cotterell who, when he returned from the air force, had been put in charge of economic research and contacts with the government instead of returning to his old post in the sales department. Cotterell reported directly to English, who in a memo to Symington around that time called him "my chief assistant," and he expected that when English became president he would be named executive vice-president and would in due course succeed him – English was now 56. Others thought English did not want the job; that he felt he was too old for it and did not relish the responsibility. Some of those placed their bets on a newcomer to the corporation, Anson C. McKim, a well-connected Montrealer with an MBA from Harvard. McKim had occupied several senior overseas positions in Howe's department during the war, had later become Canada's representative on the council of the International Civil Aviation Organization, and had just joined TCA as vice-president, administration, which placed him immediately below English in the hierarchy.*

---

*McKim's arrival ruffled a few feathers. As English reported to Symington: "Mr. Cotterell has discussed his views quite freely with me. He is ambitious and I think quite frankly has anticipated stepping into my position when I decide I have had enough or when events decide that for me. He feels that Mr. McKim's appointment, by reason of the title, places him in a preferred position and is unfair to individuals like himself who have served with the Company almost since its inception, have knowledge of its activities and have demonstrated their ability. He is quite satisfied with his assignment but feels that, taking all things into consideration, he is entitled to a title equal to that of Mr. McKim. I do not think Mr. Bain feels as strongly as Mr. Cotterell, but after the meeting in your office he expressed considerable concern about Mr. McKim joining the organization and as to where he himself would fit in, when things get shaken down."

Notwithstanding all the intramural speculation, neither English nor McKim expected to get the president's job. For, along with Symington, they were the only men in the airline privy to one of the best-kept secrets in its history: the man it was intended should succeed Symington was none other than C.D. Howe himself. After the war, Howe had several times told Mackenzie King that he wanted to quit politics, and on January 7, 1946, after a golfing holiday in Cuba, he cabled Symington from Havana: "Quiet reflection has decided me to drop public life immediately. . . . " On his return, he told King he planned to retire the following summer, and they discussed the possibility of his assuming the presidency of TCA several times. King noted in his diary on February 13: "He said there was no salary attached to that position. I said I thought it might be properly made a salaried position; either one or the other he would be glad to have it."

As usual, King managed to appeal to Howe's sense of duty and he remained in his portfolio. But he continued to hanker after the TCA job, and on May 27, 1947, Bill English said in a letter to Symington discussing the impending appointment of McKim: "Mr. Howe made it quite clear that he intends to come over to TCA as soon as he can get clear at Ottawa and establish headquarters at Montreal. . . . Mr. Howe made it quite clear to Mr. McKim and myself that following Mr. McKim's appointment and his own assumption of the Presidency, promotion would be from within the ranks of the company, provided capable material was available."

That Howe never took the job he had coveted for so long was a demonstration of his sense of public responsibility. In 1947, King himself was seriously contemplating retirement, and in the interest of national unity he desperately wanted Louis St. Laurent to succeed him as party leader and prime minister. St. Laurent had distinguished himself as Minister of Justice and Secretary of State for External Affairs, and by 1947 he was already attending to many matters that a healthier King would have handled himself. But he had been a reluctant wartime recruit to politics and for the sake of his family he now wanted to return to his law practice in Quebec City. Among the factors that persuaded him to change his mind and accept his party's draft was that Howe sacrificed his ambition to head TCA and promised to remain in politics as St. Laurent's right-hand man.

Howe's agonizing over this decision presumably accounts for Symington's inability to announce the identity of his successor when he resigned. And that announcement, when it came three months later, surprised almost everyone – including the recipient of the honour, Gordon McGregor – and shocked some of Bill English's supporters, though English himself continued to serve his new boss loyally and well until his retirement nine years later.

In his two years at the head of the traffic department, "G.R.," as he became universally known, had attracted attention with his air of command and his capacity for hard work. He had flown almost 150,000 miles on his supervisory travels since his appointment, and he always seemed to emerge from even an overnight flight as immaculately groomed as a gentleman turning up at his club for a cocktail party. But it is likely that Symington was led to recommend McGregor to Howe as his successor because of his virtuoso performance at the first joint traffic conference of the International Air Transport Association, held in Brazil in the fall of 1947.

As Canada's representative, Symington had played an important role in the founding of IATA,* and the association of world governments of which it was an offshoot, the International Civil Aviation Organization. The Paris Convention of 1919, ratified by thirty-three nations, including Canada, decreed that "every State has complete and exclusive sovereignty over the airspace above its territory." This was, of course, only natural, a mere extension of every country's historic right to defend itself: while the martial arts of bombing and aerial reconnaissance were still in their infancy, they had proved their potency in the lately concluded war to end all wars. In practice, though, as commercial aviation began to take off, it proved fertile ground for international discrimination and friction. Some countries refused to permit foreign airlines to cross their airspace at all; others used air rights as bargaining counters for national advantages entirely unconnected with aviation; yet others negotiated directly with foreign airlines, which led to ruffled diplomatic feathers and some highly irregular dealings.

By 1944, even though the war was still at its height, the minds of the Allied leaders were already turning to the coming peace, and how it could be preserved. Great hopes were abroad for international co-operation and harmony in every field of human activity, and in 1944 the United States invited fifty-five Allied and neutral states to Chicago to discuss aviation in the postwar world. The Soviet representatives turned back half-way when they heard

---

*An earlier organization, the International Air Traffic Association, had been founded in 1919 by airlines from Britain, Germany, Holland, Sweden, Denmark and Norway. It expanded rapidly during the next few years, as commercial aviation blossomed, but fell apart with the outbreak of World War II.

that Switzerland, Portugal and Spain would be at the meeting, but the rest of the delegates sat down to try to formulate some sort of international control over aviation that would be acceptable to all. The United States, traditionally in favour of private enterprise, would have liked a single world-wide agreement under which all nations would give all others unlimited rights to fly over, land in, and deliver and pick up passengers and cargo in their territories. Some other countries, including the United Kingdom, were badly short of civil aircraft as a result of the war and feared that a complete "open skies" policy would give the big American airlines a lead over all other countries which could never be overcome.

Canada, in the person of "Hoibie" Symington (as he was affectionately called by the American delegate, Fiorello LaGuardia, the colourful mayor of New York), became a sort of mediator between the two points of view, suggesting compromises here, breaking deadlocks there. The conference, while it postponed action on reciprocal air rights for further consideration, was a success. The organization it agreed to set up, ICAO – which the Communist countries joined later, bringing its present membership to 150 states – has governed world aviation practices ever since, setting and maintaining uniform standards in such vital fields as flight safety, air traffic rules, airworthiness certification, meteorological and navigational procedures, and the licensing of air crews.

Its companion organization of world airlines, IATA, also had its genesis at the Chicago conference, in a meeting of airline representatives which Symington was invited to chair. The organization was formally established at a conference in Havana in April 1945, and Symington was elected its first president. Briefly, its objective was to provide a forum where members could exchange ideas and co-operate "to promote safe, regular and economical air transport for the benefit of the peoples of the world, to foster air commerce, and to study the problems connected therewith." Committees were set up to consider the financial, legal and technical aspects of aviation – and the all-important question of traffic.

It was evident that efficient and economic international operations, with passengers frequently changing airlines for different legs of their journey, would demand the same sort of standardized procedures ICAO was introducing. At that time, for instance, there were perhaps a hundred different shapes and sizes of passenger tickets in use around the world, and no uniformity in the information each carried. TCA's tickets, following the old

CNR model, were unwieldy strips of coupons for each leg of a flight, like today's fold-out credit card wallets. On a long journey – flight legs were shorter in those days – perhaps twenty of these coupons would have to be laboriously filled out in longhand by the ticket agent, a process that could take hours, and which was further complicated if some of the legs were to be travelled on another airline using a different form of ticket. Obviously, the use of standardized ticket forms by all world airlines would streamline operations, and the conference chaired by Gordon McGregor in 1947 was convened to consider adoption of this and a long list of other standardized procedures.

The founders of IATA believed it could succeed only if its resolutions and regulations were unanimously approved by its members, however large or small. With sixty-nine airlines from forty-two countries represented at the traffic conference, there was grave doubt that unanimous acceptance could be secured for all the dozens of resolutions on the agenda. And it was feared that unless most of them could be pushed through, the embryo organization would suffer an immense loss of prestige and effectiveness. Gordon McGregor pushed through all of them, in a mere few days, with a combination of decisiveness, tact, patience and good humour. One after another the votes were taken and passed: the delegates voted to design and adopt standardized tickets and baggage checks; standardized reservations procedures; uniform baggage allowances; cargo waybills – the list went on and on.

More controversially, the organization had also agreed on the need for standardized international fares, which would lead in the future to allegations that it was nothing more than a vast cartel. One of the resolutions up for consideration recommended an increase in the transatlantic fare from $325 to $350. Most of the smaller airlines wanted the increase, but it was strenuously opposed by the Pan American representative, Willis G. Lipscomb. It looked as though this resolution, a crucial one, was going to founder. McGregor pulled out his pack of Sweet Caporal cigarettes, scribbled a note on it and passed it to Lipscomb. "Will you go up or not?" it read. "I'll let go if you wish." Lipscomb, impressed by McGregor's orchestration of the meetings and reluctant to hazard the future of IATA, decided to abandon his company's stand for at least a trial period. "O.K.," he scribbled on the packet, "for six months only." The resolution swiftly passed, and harmony was restored.

After the conference, the bible of the U.S. airline industry, *American Aviation*, carried a photograph of McGregor on its front page with the caption: "Frank-speaking, action-minded

McGregor became world-renowned overnight when he succeeded in obtaining harmonious action on all traffic problems
on the agenda – an achievement previously believed impossible."
And Sir William Hildred, IATA's director general, tried to persuade McGregor to become his deputy in the organization.

In a note of congratulation to his general traffic manager,
Symington commented on Hildred's approach: "I told Sir William that he of course could approach you because it was a matter which properly should be submitted to you, but that I would
do everything in my power to dissuade you from making the
change, as I felt that I could say to you in your own interests that
you should refuse."

This might have been taken as a broad hint that greater things
lay ahead, but McGregor recalled in his privately printed memoirs his surprise when Symington telephoned his office in Winnipeg and told him the TCA board had just elected him president.
He had not even been consulted to see if he would accept the
post, but he gulped and asked what he was expected to do first.
Symington suggested he should make an appointment to see C.D.
Howe in Ottawa, and McGregor did so. When he was ushered
in, Howe rose from his desk, shook his hand, and asked him what
he wanted. Taken by surprise, McGregor could only reply: "I
expect I need some terms of reference." Howe gazed at him from
beneath his bushy eyebrows and said thoughtfully: "Most people who come here want more than that. But I'll give you one
term of reference: you keep out of the taxpayer's pocket, and
I'll keep out of your hair."

CHAPTER ELEVEN

T THE BEGINNING OF 1948, Gordon McGregor's chances of observing Howe's injunction seemed slim indeed. The airline he had inherited was now ten years old. And in the manner of some adolescents, it seemed to be out-growing its strength. It had gone into the war with five hundred employees and fifteen planes which, if they were all in the air at the same time, could carry a grand total of 150 passengers. It now had more than 4,400 employees and a fleet of fifty aircraft providing twenty times the 1939 seating capacity. In 1939, the airline flew 12 million revenue passenger miles; by 1947 that figure had grown to 230 million. It was now serving every major Canadian centre—and some that were by no means major. It was flying to six United States cities and across the Atlantic to London every day. In every way, the expansion had been phenomenal, and it seemed certain to continue.

But when Gordon McGregor took stock of the situation it was not a comfortable one. Month after month, new traffic records were being set. But during the past two years the company had piled up a deficit approaching $3 million. Obviously, its operating costs were too high. And one reason for this was the number of unprofitable routes it was required to operate as a matter of government policy.

Furthermore, the situation was likely to get worse before it improved: there were those twenty North Stars on the way, each of them needing forty passengers to fill it. In a note to himself assessing the position, McGregor described the North Star at that stage of its development as "notably inefficient," and said that when the fleet was delivered the company would be over-supplied with aircraft "if and when immigrant movement potential diminishes."*

---

*This was a reference to an Ontario government scheme that brought thousands of badly needed skilled immigrants to the province after the war, with the government subsidizing their air fares. In the summer of 1947, Premier George Drew contracted with a

Having made his diagnosis of the airline's ailments, McGregor compiled a list of eight "answers" for them, the corrective actions he thought necessary:

1. *Operating costs must come down or at least not increase with the introduction of the North Star.*
2. *Regularity must be improved.*
3. *Mail revenue must go up substantially.*
4. *Cargo revenue must be developed.*
5. *Landing charges [airport fees] must come down.*
6. *Dead end trans-border flights must be either abandoned, in most cases, or converted into triangles so as to get more efficient use of U.S. offices and bases.*
7. *Pass[enger] revenue must go up substantially.*
8. *Personnel travelling and transfers must decrease.*

It is perhaps too much to say that in the early days of TCA its financial performance was given only casual attention. But certainly making a profit took second place to building a safe, efficient airline. For years there was no attempt to live within a set budget: the accent was on buying the right aircraft, fitting them with the best equipment, and training top-notch crews to fly them, and whatever it cost to do that was cheerfully spent. After all, C.D. Howe had said right at the beginning that the airline would be run "at or near cost," and the CNR old-timers handling its finances, who could see no great future for this upstart mode of transportation anyway, used to tell the TCA youngsters anxious to demonstrate their ability to run a profitable business: "You're performing a public service; you can't expect it to make money."

Providing a public service was obviously paramount during the war, but the airline also managed to make a profit in those years, though not, on one occasion, without a stratagem that came perilously close to cooking the books. C.D. Howe called Bill English on a Christmas Eve toward the end of the war, when it seemed the airline was about to register a deficit for the year. Given the exigencies of politics, Howe was not pleased, and he

---

California charter company, Transocean Air Lines, to bring forty immigrants at a time across from Europe in converted C-54 transport planes. When Ottawa refused to license the operation, Ontario signed a contract with TCA which – because it was still waiting for its M2s – sub-contracted the flights to Transocean until April 1948. Transocean was paid $10,400 in U.S. funds for each flight; TCA was to be paid $9,000 per flight, but when the airline had acquired practical experience of the M2s' operating costs it asked the Ontario government to increase the payments to $11,500 per flight, even though it found that westbound M2s could carry only 29 to 36 passengers, according to weather conditions. The province objected strenuously to Howe, and the episode did nothing to modify George Drew's distaste for TCA and all its works.

wanted something done forthwith. English called in Bill Harvey, a CNR stenographer who had joined the airline in 1937 and become the chief assistant to Percy Baldwin, the CNR man seconded to run TCA's accounting department. "The Minister wants a profit," English told him, "and he wants the figures on Monday morning."

Harvey, a legendary hard worker – in the early days he sometimes slept on a table at the office rather than waste time going home for the night – summoned a group of his fellow members of the accounting department to work some unpaid overtime and one of them, Henry Keil, came up with a solution: since TCA had spent a lot of money on the crews who were now flying for the CGTAS, why not charge that government service for their training? The auditors applauded Keil's ingenuity, there was a hasty revision of the balance sheet, and Mr. Howe got his profit for the year. Bill Harvey, though he was a self-taught accountant and a self-confessed slave driver, had a gift for surrounding himself with able and hard-working assistants. In due course he became the airline's senior vice-president, finance.

The relaxed attitude toward the corporation's finances had begun to change by the time Gordon McGregor took the helm as president. As the airline began to grow after the war, Bill English set about developing a budget system. And McGregor continued to give this work the highest priority. A few weeks after he took over he wrote to Howard Cotterell, director of research and economic control, saying that while the company was enjoying the largest revenues in its history, even the most optimistic forecasts indicated that it was heading for another serious deficit for the year. "It is my intention," he wrote, "not to continue the management policy of attempting to balance revenues against costs as a method of determining policy, but to measure the financial efficiency of our operations by relating the costs incurred to the volume of transportation work performed; and to measure the financial efficiency of traffic activities by relating the volume of revenue realized to the expenditures associated with the development and ground handling of that traffic . . . it is necessary that you devote your activities entirely to the very pressing problem of developing recommendations to me which have as their purpose the maintenance or reduction of all costs and expenses to the irreducible minimum, while maintaining the company's existing standards of safety and service. . . . "

On the same day, he wrote to Bill English acknowledging receipt of an engineering progress report: "Reading it, I get the disquieting impression that we, as I have thought before, do a lot of engineering properly the responsibility of the manufacturer, and that we do engineering and buy equipment to do work ourselves which could be more cheaply a purchased service."

The new man, obviously, was beginning to take control. And he was under no illusions about the dimensions of the task ahead. His first few weeks of digging into the accounts disclosed that, in an attempt to keep the corporation's postwar losses to at least a respectable level, its fleet of Lockheeds and DC-3s, which were becoming outmoded and would soon have to be replaced, had not been sufficiently depreciated, and their sale at far below the valuation at which they were being carried on the books would add to the serious losses anticipated in the next few years. Also, the traffic department still had no idea how it was going to fill the twenty North Stars when they went into service, and hauling empty seats through the skies would not bring in badly needed revenue.

There was, too, the problem of the uneconomic routes, some of which seemed to have been inaugurated for no better reason than the general euphoria occasioned by the dawning of the Air Age. To meet the demands of the Commonwealth Air Training Scheme, new airfields had been opened at all sorts of sparsely populated places, and when the end of the war emptied them, local boosters naturally sought to fill the gap with scheduled air services. One of the most glaring examples of a route that could not pay its way was that between the Lakehead and Duluth, Minnesota. To operate it tied up an aircraft and crew at the Lakehead, to carry an average of one and a quarter passengers a day each way. McGregor knew this was a fatuous extravagance that must be stopped, but there was a snag. So he went to see the minister. Howe, fascinated as always by the activities of his favourite creation, listened courteously to the man he had recently approved to run it. Then his famous eyebrows knitted in a frown. "Do you know," he asked McGregor, "what my constituency is?" That, McGregor explained, was exactly why he had come to see him. There was only a slight pause, and then the Liberal member of Parliament for the Lakehead – the Minister of Almost Everything, as he came to be called – said: "If it's as bad as you say, what are you waiting for?"

The service was soon discontinued, and the relieved new president of TCA joined the ranks of all those other businessmen who to this day believe there has never been another cabinet minister to match C.D. Howe.

At this same meeting, McGregor received welcome confirmation from Howe that the airline was no longer bound by a commitment Symington had made in April 1946, to support an ill-fated project that later became a matter of considerable controversy. On one of his many visits to the Rolls-Royce headquarters in Derby, England, Jim Bain heard that that company was developing a powerful new jet engine, the AJ-65, later named the Avon. The managing director of Rolls-Royce, E.W. (later Lord) Hives, told Bain that the right aeroplane, equipped with just two Avons, could carry about thirty passengers more comfortably, and faster, than any other aircraft then flying.

Back in Canada, Bain had Jack Dyment and his engineering staff examine the figures Hives had given him and they agreed that the engine had tremendous possibilities. Bain then approached Fred T. Smye, who had been Director of Aircraft Production in Ottawa during the war and was now assistant general manager of A.V. Roe (Canada) Limited, a subsidiary of the British Hawker-Siddeley group which had recently taken over the Victory Aircraft plant at Malton from the government. He told Smye Rolls-Royce was prepared to supply the engines and asked if Avro could design an aircraft for them. Smye was enthusiastic and Bain took him along to see C.D. Howe.

It was a project guaranteed to appeal to the adventurous Howe – an all-Canadian aircraft that could easily become the first commercial jet to go into service anywhere in the world – and he gave it his blessing. Smye then drew up a formal proposal for what became known around Avro as "Jim Bain's plane," the C-102, and Symington sent him a letter of intent which, while it did not specify how many aircraft TCA would require, committed the airline to furnish the detailed specifications for it within four months and bound Avro to deliver the first aircraft by October 1948. Smye could not quote a firm cost until he received the specifications and knew the size of his production run, but he estimated it would be a maximum of $350,000.

Dyment and his group drew up specifications for a 36-seat aircraft with a cruising speed of 425 miles per hour and a "still-air" range of 1,200 miles, and a design team which eventually grew to a hundred people was assembled at Malton. The work was well under way when, in the spring of 1947, the blow fell: the Avro designers were told that the Avon engine would not be available for several years. Several explanations have been advanced for this setback, which proved disastrous. One version is that Rolls-Royce ran into production difficulties with the engine, which was the first axial-flow jet. Another is that Sir Roy Dobson, head of A.V. Roe in England, was reluctant to invest heavily in an untried engine. Yet another is that the British government

Montreal, April 1, 1939, Captain B.A. Rawson and D.R. MacLaren, assistant to the vice-president who acted as co-pilot, on the inauguration of scheduled transcontinental passenger service.

Inauguration of scheduled passenger transcontinental service, Montreal, April 1, 1939. P.G. Johnson, vice-president, shakes hands with the district director of postal service while George Wakeman, general traffic manager, stands by.

Seattle, April 1, 1939; Captain George Lothian and stewardess Rose Crispin accept baskets of fruit from Seattle Mayor Langlie and a United Airlines stewardess to carry on the inaugural transcontinental passenger service.

Montreal, July 18, 1939; J.J. Robinson sells to passenger L. Haase the first ticket on the new service Montreal-Ottawa-Toronto direct instead of the required change of aircraft at North Bay as shown on the wall map of the company's entire service.

Meal service in a Lockheed 14, 1939.

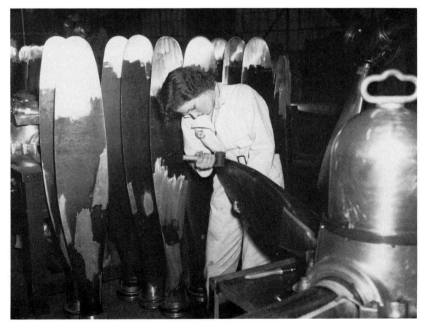

Applying de-icing equipment to RCAF propellers in the TCA shops, Winnipeg, 1943.

A TCA operations meeting at Winnipeg, October 15, 1942. Left to right front row: *P.W. Baldwin, auditor; E.P. Wells, assistant to operations manager; S.S. Stevens, superintendent of communications; R.F. George, operations manager; J.A. Wilson, director of air services, Department of Transport; O.T. Larson, vice-president; Captain B. Rawson, superintendent of flight operations; A.M. Sutherland, assistant of maintenance.* Back row: *D.R. MacLaren, superintendent of passenger service; W.S. Thompson, director of public relations; Walter Fowler, operations superintendent, Moncton; J.T. Bain, superintendent of engineering and maintenance; Maurice McGregor, operations superintendent, Toronto; W.F. English, assistant vice-president; Dr. Emmet Dwyer, medical officer; ''Jock'' Shields, inspector of civil aviation, Department of Transport; Ted Stull, operations superintendent, Lethbridge; Captain J.H. Sandgathe, chief pilot, Lethbridge; J.T. Dyment, assistant superintendent of engineering.*

Engine check on the first Lancastrian flown on the Canadian government transatlantic air service by TCA in 1943.

TCA technician checking Loran navigational equipment at Dorval base, November 1945.

Old-style multi-coupon tickets replaced by coded designations and a hand punch, displayed by T.W. Kirkham, G.T. Featherstone and P.W. Baldwin, March 1945.

Mrs. Clara Adelstone of Chicago (105 years old) going to Montreal to great-granddaughter's wedding. The flight was held half an hour for connection at Toronto but the other passengers cheered her arrival.

Left to right: *C.D. Howe, H.J. Symington, leader of the conference, and J.A. Wilson at the international meeting in Chicago in November 1944 which formulated a convention on world aviation and set up the International Civil Aviation Organization.* – (Public Archives of Canada)

Winnipeg, 1946. A Lodestar makes a quick station stop.

W. Gordon Wood, general traffic manager, with regional managers
W.J. Dalby and W.R. Campbell on his right and J.G. Maxwell on his left.

Sydney, N.S., September 5, 1947. G.R. McGregor, W.F. English and Anson McKim share a joke.

At the Joint Traffic Conference of the International Air Transport Association in Petropolis, Brazil, in 1947, G.R. McGregor (seated centre) *made his reputation as a popular and skilful leader.*

refused to release the Avon from the secret list because it feared Canada would beat it to the punch and fly a jet transport before the Comet, on which so many British industrial hopes depended.

Whatever the reason, the whole aircraft had to be redesigned around four smaller Rolls-Royce Derwent engines, which developed only 3,500 pounds of thrust against the Avon's 6,500 and were much more fuel-hungry. As soon as they saw the new design for what became known as the Avro Jetliner, the TCA engineers concluded it would no longer meet the airline's requirements; the engine change increased the weight of the aircraft from the original 45,000 lbs. to 65,000 lbs., reduced its effective range to 700 miles, and increased its estimated cost to $750,000. TCA immediately pulled out of the project but it was taken over by Howe's department and the work continued.

The only Jetliner ever built made its maiden flight a year later, in August 1949 (the Comet had first flown just two weeks earlier) and its crew waxed ecstatic about its performance. Efforts were made to sell it in the United States, but no one actually placed an order and the prototype was eventually scrapped, foreshadowing the later disappointment with the Avro Arrow. Avro went on trying to persuade TCA to change its mind – McGregor complained several times that Avro publicity releases were giving the false impression that the airline was committed to buy the plane – and to this day the Avro engineers who worked on it claim that the eventual Jetliner met the airline's original specifications. The TCA engineers still insist that it did not, and Gordon McGregor was relieved when Howe assured him the airline would not be forced to accept it.

McGregor's hope that the airline's operating costs would come down or at least not increase with the introduction of the pressurized North Stars was doomed to disappointment. The M2s, which went into service on the domestic routes on June 1, 1948 – by which time the production delays had pushed their price up to $775,000 from the original estimate of $350,000 – were ushered in with a flourish of favourable publicity. They reduced the flight time between Montreal and Vancouver to 13 hours and were generally considered an advance over anything else in the air.

In many ways, they were. As aircraft had become bigger and more complicated, so had the pilot's job increased in complexity. Anything that could be done to simplify it would be an obvious gain in the direction of both safety and efficiency. So the flight operations department, and in particular its chief technical pilot, Herb Hopson, worked closely with the engineering department and the manufacturers to give the North Star what soon became justly celebrated as "the TCA cockpit." A forerunner of the automated marvels in today's jets, this was a two-man cockpit, with the controls arranged so that either man, independently of the other, could perform every function necessary to take off, fly and land the aircraft. A single lever controlled the propellers of all four engines, an aviation "first" which spared the pilot much juggling with the throttles and which, combined with other sophisticated features such as automatic mixture control, greatly simplified his task. The North Star was also the first commercial airliner to be equipped with Loran, the long-range navigational system, and its fire-extinguishing system was well in advance of others in North America: it used the more effective methyl bromide instead of the carbon dioxide used by other airlines and was a "two-bottle" system, meaning that if an engine fire re-ignited after the first shot of extinguisher there was a second shot available as back-up.

The civil version of the Merlin engine was a "universal power plant," with an auxiliary gear-box, housing such accessories as generators, connected to the engine itself by a single shaft. This meant that the TCA maintenance men could change an engine in a fraction of the twenty-four hours required on some other aircraft. Unfortunately, the new engine proved just as susceptible to mid-air failures as the old one used in the Lancastrians, and its maintenance costs were astronomical.

When its failings became apparent, Herb Seagrim, who had been appointed by McGregor to succeed the veteran pilot "Tuddy" Tudhope as general manager, operations, issued a routine bulletin to pilots reminding them of the importance of always having an alternate airport within range in case of trouble. Somehow a copy of this bulletin found its way into the hands of George Drew, and in the middle of a federal election campaign the Leader of the Opposition seized the manna with glee. The North Star, he proclaimed, was "an obsolete white elephant," "a travesty on the laws of aerodynamics," and all manner of other things that gave the impression it was unsafe.

Howe sprang to the North Star's defence. The government had bought it for TCA and the RCAF because it was economic and efficient. It was important also to have a plane made in Canada and geared to Canadian conditions, which required year-round de-icing facilities and other special equipment. McGregor responded too, but he must have done so with misgivings. The North Star, he told reporters, was "an excellent aeroplane" and his company "would not willingly exchange it for any other aeroplane of similar type now in airline service."

He did not add for public consumption what he was beginning to think privately: that if the plane itself could not be
exchanged, at least its engines would have to be. Soon after
Drew's campaign petered out, he wrote a sombre letter to Howe.
Despite the economies he had instituted, the introduction of
budget control, and a 36 per cent increase in revenue, the new
president had ended his first year at the helm with a deficit of
$2.93 million. That was attributed in part to "the over-equipped
condition" resulting from the introduction of the twenty M2s,
and McGregor had assured Howe that as more passengers took to
the air – there was a 27 per cent increase in the number carried
during the year – TCA would begin to show a surplus. Now he
wrote, on July 20, 1949, to warn him that unless the airline's
maintenance costs could be reduced drastically, the 1949 deficit
could approach $5 million:

*It is costing TCA approximately $80 per aircraft hour to maintain its engines,
whereas at higher basic wage scales it is costing the American operator of a
DC-6 approximately $18.40 per aircraft hour to maintain his Pratt & Whit-
ney R-2800 engines. . . . Rolls-Royce have been fully informed of the very
critical nature of the situation and that company knows that as soon as it has
completed its study on our very detailed cost analysis, TCA will request that
Rolls-Royce agree to bear a substantial proportion of this excessive overhaul
and maintenance cost. If Rolls-Royce refuses a proposal of this nature – and I
can see no sufficiently strong reason why that company should agree to pay
$100,000 a month toward TCA's expenses for the privilege of having TCA use
their engines – then I regret to say I will have no alternative but to recommend
to you and the Board of Directors the drastic and expensive step of replacing
the power plants in North Star aircraft.*

Soon after he wrote this letter, McGregor went to Derby to
voice what he described later as his "sustained cry of financial
pain." Armed wth voluminous records demonstrating the high
rate of failure of Merlin parts, and the high cost of their replacement, he read his litany of complaint to Lord Hives. "What are
the Merlins costing you?" he was asked. McGregor gave him the
figure. "How much should they cost you?" asked the managing
director of Rolls-Royce. He was given the comparable figure for
American engines. Accepting both figures without challenge, the
urbane Hives brushed a flicker of cigarette ash from his vest and
said cheerfully: "Rolls-Royce will absorb the difference in the
two costs you have mentioned."

It was an expensive decision, and one that horrified his associates, but Lord Hives believed his company's reputation for
excellence was more important than a temporary financial loss.
"Rolls-Royce engines," he told McGregor later, "should not cost

more to operate than the best produced by any other firm." And to make sure that they didn't, he dispatched some of his best engineers to Montreal where eventually, working with their TCA counterparts, they ironed out the Merlin's problems so that one of its worst pilot critics admitted, if somewhat grudgingly, that it "became more reliable as it went on." The problem of lead deposits building up on the plugs, for instance, was solved when someone discovered that they could be burned off if the pilot opened up his throttles for a few minutes every hour. Later, it was found that the problem disappeared when the size of the gap on the plugs was doubled.

These mechanical bottlenecks, as they were euphemistically called, escaped public notice. But there was one failing of the North Star that TCA's customers could not avoid noticing: the six open exhaust stacks on the inboard side of each engine blasted the cabin with a continuous hail of noise. The Canadair and Rolls-Royce engineers had long given up on this problem before it was solved by a mechanic in TCA's Winnipeg shops. By a strange coincidence, "Mac" MacLeod, as he was universally called, bore the first name of Merlin. He took pains to keep this indignity unknown but in fact it was entirely appropriate: he was a self-taught mechanical wizard whose inventive mind proved invaluable to the airline through the years. The son of a lumber baron in the state of Washington, MacLeod left home young and put his mechanical ingenuity to work devising and installing aerial tramways for mines in the Rockies, to such good effect that a colleague recalls him paying cash for a new Packard limousine in the depths of the Depression. As a welder and machinist he was a true artist, and nothing inspired him more than the chance to tackle a problem that had everyone else stumped. In due course, he designed and built a "cross-over" exhaust manifold that conducted the Merlin's exhaust gases – and much of the noise – over to the outboard side of the engine, while meeting two essential prerequisites that had defeated all the high-powered engineers who had worked on the problem: it successfully withstood the expansion and contraction caused by the intense heat involved, and it altered the engine's frontal resistance hardly at all.

All new aircraft have their teething troubles, and though the North Star had more than its share, it went on to be TCA's workhorse for more than a decade of rapid and uninterrupted growth: the last of its line was not retired until 1961. Its introduction also proved a boon to users of His Majesty's Royal Mail. The airline had been seriously concerned at the decline in its airmail revenue that followed the revised arrangement with the Post

Office negotiated in 1946. Not only did its revenue fall (from $4.2 million in 1945 to $3.7 million in 1946 and $3.8 million in 1947), but the average rate of return it received for each ton-mile ($2.98 in 1947) was – as the airline never ceased to point out – lower than that paid to any other airline in the world. The imminent arrival of the North Stars, with their extra carrying capacity, gave TCA an opportunity in 1947 to suggest a new arrangement to the Post Office: why not use the space to carry *all* first-class mail in the country, at the ordinary surface rate?

The Post Office, predictably, bridled at this suggestion. George Herring protested to McGregor that it would completely disrupt the whole Canadian postal service. Everyone knew that aeroplanes were notorious for being late in bad weather; why, Winnipeg had only recently been cut off for a whole week! How could the Post Office possibly arrange its postal clerks' shifts under such conditions? And more to the point, the Post Office stood to lose its $4 million annual revenue from airmail stamps.

The outcome demonstrated what everybody in the country knew by now: C.D. Howe carried far more clout in the cabinet than any postmaster general. And on June 1, 1948, Canada proudly inaugurated the world's first "all-up" airmail service: any first-class letter weighing up to an ounce mailed at the usual 4-cent surface rate became eligible to go by air if that would speed it to its destination. Airmail volume shot up – fom 1.2 million ton-miles in 1947 to 2.2 million in 1948 and 3.4 million in 1949 – and TCA's mail pay followed suit: from $3.8 million in 1947 to $4.6 million in 1948. (Under the new arrangement, the Post Office agreed to make a fixed annual payment of $5.4 million, which was first paid in 1949, and gradually rose in succeeding years as mail volume increased.)

And as much the gentleman as ever, G.R. McGregor appended a postscript to a letter to TCA's dedicated adversary, the doughty Walter Turnbull, congratulating him on the brilliant publicity campaign with which the Post Office had ushered in its great new service to the Canadian public.

CHAPTER TWELVE

BACK IN 1932, when the spruce new district manager of the Bell Telephone Company, Gordon McGregor, was beginning his flying lessons in Kingston, Ontario, a university drop-out eight years his junior, Grant W.G. McConachie, was staked by his Uncle Harry to a $2,500 Fokker monoplane. Young Grant promptly began his airline career by flying fish from the isolated lakes of northwestern Saskatchewan to the nearest railhead, Bonnyville, Alberta, for onward transmission to the gourmets of Chicago.

Six feet two inches tall, with broad shoulders toughened by a series of boyhood jobs in lumber yards, on farms, and as fireman on a threshing machine, Grant McConachie had grown up in Edmonton. His outstanding assets were a limitless, enthusiastic optimism which he could communicate to everyone he met with his confident, boyish grin—and a bland assumption that rules were made not so much to be bent or broken as to be ignored. He paid for his flying lessons by working in the bush as a fireman on a logging train, and after only twenty hours' instruction—he should have had fifty to qualify for a commercial licence—he incurred official disfavour by renting a plane and selling rides to thrill-seekers at $5 a flip. At the age of 22, he set up his first air company, with his Uncle Harry as president and Grant as pilot and salesman-in-chief. Very soon he established himself as one of the boldest and brightest of the bush pilots, but when another pilot he had hired to share the chores on a barn-storming tour wrote off the Fokker, his first airline venture disappeared into bankruptcy.

In 1934 he tried again, organizing a new company, United Air Transport Limited, with two aircraft provided by Barney Phillips, a prospector he had flown on numerous trips around the north country. For the next few years, he flew fish, made the first commercial flight across the Rockies for a rich Calgary stockbroker with a real-estate deal to close, and landed a contract to fly the airmail from Edmonton 1,200 miles north to Whitehorse in the Yukon (a contract which, to Jim Richardson's disgust, had been taken away from Canadian Airways and awarded to McConachie without tender).

The first scheduled air service to the Yukon made headlines in Edmonton and the mayor of that ambitious city and a flock of accompanying dignitaries turned out to speed the young bush pilot on his way. But to the visionary McConachie, Whitehorse, distant though it was, was by no means the end of the road he meant to travel.

By 1938, like so many other enterprises, United Air Transport was heavily in the red. McConachie had exhausted all the conventional sources of credit – the Royal Bank, for instance, already held $250,000 worth of his notes – and he conceived the audacious idea of hitting up Imperial Oil. After all, he had been buying their products ever since he set up in business. Surely, when they heard his plans, they would give him a $100,000 long-term interest-free credit so that he could go on doing so, rather than lose such a good customer?

Doffing his leather flying gear and dusting off his presidential business suit, he bearded the Imperial Oil directors in their Toronto den. They can hardly have been more astonished by his proposal than by his props: he had provided himself with a piece of string and a $3.95 school-room globe, on which he had traced in red ink (a nice touch that was not unnoticed by his audience) his airmail route from Edmonton to Whitehorse. Planting the globe on the board-room table, he took the string and invited his listeners to follow the extension of that route – across Alaska and the Bering Sea, down over the Aleutians, the Kuriles and Japan, all the way to Shanghai and Hong Kong. An aerial northwest passage to the Orient! And with his marked string, he demonstrated that this Great Circle route from Edmonton to Shanghai was 2,000 miles shorter than the conventional sea route across the Pacific by way of Honolulu. What he called "the logical extension" of his run to Whitehorse could cut the time between Vancouver and Shanghai – ten days at least by the fastest ocean liner – to a mere forty hours.

"It's the short route to China over the top of the world," the salesman-pilot told the oil men. "We intend to fly it in the near future, and it will become one of the great world airways of tomorrow. You are the first to hear about it in detail because your decision today can make it possible. When it does happen it will mean a great deal to your company as well as to ours."

He got his credit, and only a churl could say that the board of directors of Imperial Oil had been strung along. For Grant McConachie was neither the first nor the only aviation man to see the possibilities of the Great Circle route to the Orient. As early as 1933, a paper prepared for the Canadian government by the far-sighted John Wilson had pointed out that Imperial Airways, six months before, had launched a service from Britain to Karachi. That service was about to be extended to Singapore, and soon Imperial planned to extend it to Hong Kong, Shanghai and Tokyo. "Unless some action is taken," Wilson wrote, "the Vancouver merchant, in a few years, wishing to communicate with his customers in China by the fastest route, will send his correspondence across [this] continent in 20 hours by air mail, across the Atlantic by the ship-to-shore route in 3½ days, and from London to the Far East in 4 or 5 days. Allowing for connections, the time of transit will be less than two weeks, as compared with three by the Pacific steamer." Pressure would thus become increasingly great for the establishment of a trans-Pacific airway, and since the Great Circle route was the shortest way to go, "No effort should be spared to ensure that use is made of this route in preference to any other."

The advantages of the Great Circle route had not escaped the men who ran Imperial Airways either. In June 1935, George Woods Humphery approached Canadian Airways – which at that time was still expected to be Canada's "chosen instrument" in the air – seeking its co-operation "to connect our Atlantic service with our Eastern service," which by now terminated at Hong Kong. The connection across Canada, he hastened to add, was regarded as being "a purely domestic affair," and so "the next move in regard to any co-operation with Canada must come from the Canadian government."

The next move was some time in coming, but the idea remained aloft. On May 21, 1937, just days after Parliament passed the legislation establishing TCA, Walter Gilbert, the veteran Canadian Airways pilot on the Mackenzie run, reported to his boss, Punch Dickins: "The Department of Transport has gone on a mad hiring binge – inspectors seem to be appearing from all angles. And Dan McLean [Superintendent of Airways] is enthusiastically setting up maps of a route from Edmonton to Carcross to Siberia to God knows where." Canadian Airways' general manager, Tommy Thompson, was also well aware of the general interest: a couple of months later he wrote to Jim Richardson saying: "It seems to me as though this whole question of an extension to the Orient from the main line through Edmonton and Whitehorse is very much to the fore and there is quite a possibility of some definite action being taken regarding it in the near future. Grant McConnachie [*sic*] has, of course, won the first round." To avoid CAL's losing any subsequent rounds, Thompson suggested enlisting the aid of Imperial Airways in establishing a company "to handle the Oriental mail."

This idea was followed up and Val Patriarche, CAL's general traffic manager, discussed it with Colonel Burchall, of Imperial Airways, who "expressed his interest in continuing the discussion further." By September, Patriarche had done some thinking on the practical operation of the route, and he wrote to Jim Richardson: "Regardless of whether this service is by land machine or seaplane, it appears to me very necessary to obtain a location on one of the islands of the Aleutian chain as a midway base and weather-reporting station." As to how this might be achieved, he advanced a forthright but somewhat startling proposition: "These islands are at present American, but are, I believe, under no strict control, being chiefly inhabited by Orientals. I believe that a suitable island could be selected and simply occupied by a Canadian expedition, in exactly the same manner as Pan American Airways occupied one or two of their base islands in the south Pacific which were formerly British possessions. . . . "

In the event, the mild-mannered Jim Richardson was spared the task of raising a seaborne expeditionary force and trampling all over the Monroe Doctrine: as it became clear that TCA, not CAL, was Ottawa's "chosen instrument," Imperial Airways switched tracks and tried to enlist the government airline's participation in its plan for a globe-girdling Commonwealth air company. The idea was shelved with the outbreak of war, but it surfaced again during the Commonwealth aviation talks in 1943 and 1944. Canada refused to participate directly in the proposed joint company but agreed to operate the Canadian segment of any round-the-world route that resulted, and perhaps part of a route across the Pacific to Australia and New Zealand. Those two countries were more receptive to Imperial's plans and a joint company called British Commonwealth Pacific Airlines was set up, with Australia holding 50 per cent of the capital, New Zealand 30 per cent and the United Kingdom 20 per cent. And in June 1946, Canada and Australia signed an agreement which, as C.D. Howe told the House, provided that "an airline designated by the government of Australia may put down and take up at Vancouver passengers, mail and cargo from Australia, while an airline designated by the government of Canada, which will be Trans-Canada Air Lines, may put down and take up in Australia traffic to and from Canada."

BCPA planned at first to buy North Stars from Canada to operate the route, but when the North Star production program was delayed it bought DC-4s. In September 1946, it launched a fortnightly service between Sydney and Vancouver with stops at Fiji, Canton Island, Honolulu and San Francisco. TCA, it had been agreed, would inaugurate a reciprocal service in the off weeks as soon as the North Stars were available, and Jack Dyment estimated in a memo to Bill English in March 1946 that the new service would require a capital outlay of $2.5 million and a government subsidy of $1.25 million a year.

Canada had still not begun its service when, in September 1947, Sir Alexander Clutterbuck, the British High Commissioner in Ottawa, passed on to C.D. Howe a suggestion that BOAC and TCA co-operate in a joint operation from London to Tokyo via Canada. After consulting Herb Symington, Howe turned down Clutterbuck's proposal. TCA, he said, was committed to a service from Canada to Australia but had not yet decided "whether the service can best be operated by our Northern route to Japan, either from Vancouver or from Edmonton, this service to continue on to Australia." A route study, he added, would be made the following summer.

Before any such study was made, Stanley Knowles, the CCF member for Winnipeg North Centre and a staunch supporter of TCA, began to smell a rat. On four separate occasions in May 1948, he rose in the House to ask Howe whether it was still the government's policy that the Australia service should be run by TCA. Howe could only squirm and stall until, on July 21 (three weeks after the House had risen for the summer recess, which no doubt had something to do with the timing), the Minister of Transport, Lionel Chevrier, made an announcement which revealed that the government had performed a complete about-face. Notwithstanding Mackenzie King's words in 1943, that TCA was "the sole Canadian agency which may operate international air services," and repeated confirmations of that policy in the years since then, Chevrier now announced that Canadian Pacific Airlines would soon be launching two new services: from Vancouver to Australia and New Zealand, and from Vancouver to Asia via the Aleutians.

The moguls of Windsor Station had prevailed after all, and perhaps it was not hard to see why. For they now included among their number the irrepressible Grant McConachie: his company, by then renamed Yukon Southern Air Transport, had been one of the bush airlines bought by the CPR to form CPA, and McConachie had gone along with it, rising rapidly through the hierarchy to be appointed its president in 1947. And Grant McConachie was still as anxious to reach the Orient as any of the early explorers – he would give a pep talk on the topic to any receptive listener at a moment's notice, and to facilitate his presentation he now toted an inflatable globe around in his briefcase.

McConachie was as persuasive a supplicant as ever stalked the corridors of Ottawa, but it is unlikely that he would have achieved his ambition had it not been for a decision by the man whose career inevitably invited comparison with his own: Gordon McGregor. As their names attested, Gordon McGregor and Grant McConachie were both of Scots descent; both were brilliant pilots; both were presidents of airlines – the two biggest airlines in the country. Associates of the two men say their personal relationship was a warm one, though they lived at opposite ends of the country. Fate, however, cast them in the role of rivals, and in the field of business they were very different men. Where McGregor was conservative, McConachie was flamboyant. McGregor was cautious – too cautious sometimes, in the eyes of his critics – and he never made a move without exhaustive thought and analysis beforehand; McConachie was a plunger, an intuitive entrepreneur who when he saw an opportunity would leap at it and let someone else work out the details later. McGregor clung to the old-fashioned virtue of paying cash on the barrel head; he felt there was something irresponsible, if not immoral, about people going into debt for something as frivolous as a vacation and for a long time resisted the introduction of a Fly Now, Pay Later plan to TCA. McConachie, in contrast, was a virtuoso in the delicate art of borrowing, sometimes on no security more tangible than his charming, self-confident smile.

McConachie, in short, was hardly the type of man to be the steward of the nation's interests at the head of a state-owned enterprise, and McGregor certainly saw himself as occupying that position when, soon after his appointment as president, Howe asked him if he was prepared to inaugurate service on the Pacific. The minister's admonition to "keep out of the taxpayer's pocket" was still ringing in his ears, and he was still taking stock of the airline's financial position, with growing dismay. Howe had recently insisted, against McGregor's better judgment, that TCA should open an apparently unprofitable service to Bermuda, and now he wanted it extended to the Caribbean. *

The only record of this crucial conversation with Howe seems to be the one contained in McGregor's memoirs, which parallels his reply to a remarkably clairvoyant letter from Anson McKim, who had lately been named vice-president, traffic. McKim was in France when he wrote on May 31, 1948, to say he had heard rumours that CPA was being awarded the Pacific. "I am loath to see CPA go into such an international route because of possible consequences," he wrote.

CPA have ambitions for a trans-continental route, as you know, and as Grant McConachie has told me, all their actions have this in view plus international expansion. I would expect CPA to move as follows: first, to take on all routes moving east and west, no matter how unprofitable, hoping to make their map look as much like a transcontinental as possible; second, enter a Pacific route with the avowed intention of taking a loss against future development of airline cum shipping; next, with a more sympathetic government point out that TCA is reimbursed for its Atlantic losses (or Bermuda or other international losses) and claim in equity that CPA is entitled to the same assistance. Then point out that they almost have a transcontinental and, by enlisting support from Chambers of Commerce in CPR towns or places not on our through route, try for the remaining missing parts of their route. They would say TCA has an unfair advantage in taking their Pacific traffic as soon as it reaches the coast and complain that the Government hogs all the paying mileage and the more lucrative Atlantic route, while giving CPA the lemons. It could be a very plausible case. . . . Why all the hurry about the Pacific? Can't CPR be held off till we have considered how best and when to fly that route?

In his reply, McGregor admitted that Howe had asked him if he was prepared to inaugurate "the Pacific service," and added, "My reply was in the negative." He had given the minister two

---

*McGregor and a group of his colleagues had made a survey flight to Bermuda and the Caribbean as early as September 1946. Both before and after he assumed the presidency, McGregor had expressed the view that the time was not yet ripe to begin regular service to the area, at least not without permission to carry passengers there from the United States, which could only be obtained by intergovernmental negotiation. In deference to Howe's wishes, however, service to Bermuda began on May 1, 1948. Howe kept pressing for its extension to the Caribbean and in September McGregor wrote warning him that the extension would add half a million dollars to the annual deficit of TCA (Atlantic) Limited. Howe replied: "I have been well aware that profitable business does not exist at the moment, and that the hope for the route is that tourist business from Canada can be built up to a profitable level, particularly during the winter months. Canada desires to offer an outlet for Canadian tourists in sterling areas, and, for that reason, I think that the route should be operated in the national interest. You may be surprised at the amount of business that can be developed by active promotion. In any event, it will take off the pressure for improved boat service between Canada and the Islands. . . . Therefore, please get this service under way as soon as possible." TCA began to fly to the Bahamas, Jamaica and Trinidad on December 1.

reasons for his refusal: that BCPA was operating with consistently light loads, even though it had been given the privilege of picking up and dropping passengers at San Francisco; and that the North Star was "eminently unsuitable if not physically incapable of flying the route, even via San Francisco, with more than a 25 percent payload in a westerly direction." The minister had then stated that "he proposed in view of my expressed opinion to grant the route to CPA, to which I raised no objection." McGregor assured McKim that he "attributed McConachie's desire for the Pacific operation to exactly the same motives which you describe, but I am none the less satisfied that forgoing the right to operate the Pacific at this time is very much the lesser of two evils. . . . If CPA gets the job and uses the Canadair Four, I am inclined to the belief that they will establish an all-time record for operating losses, and I think that this or any succeeding government would receive coldly any suggestion that CPA be subsidized in respect of this operation."

McGregor ignored McKim's rhetorical question as to why the CPR could not be "held off" until TCA was ready to fly the route – no doubt because he did not have an answer for it. Nor does there seem to be any surviving explanation of Howe's thinking at the time. Why did he not simply insist on TCA flying the route, as he had done with Bermuda and would shortly do with the Caribbean? Possibly he thought another million dollars-plus on TCA's deficit might be more of a political liability than even he could stand. At any rate, the matter went before the cabinet on May 20. Lionel Chevrier, as Minister of Transport, had had a background paper prepared which said that not only did Canada lack an air service across the Pacific, but because of the Canadian Pacific's wartime shipping losses it had no steamship service either. "If such an air service were provided," the paper said, "it would tend to protect Canada's trade position in the Pacific to some extent before American air lines operating in this area have become too strongly entrenched."

A letter had been received from CPA seeking permission to operate the Australian service and a service between Vancouver and Hong Kong via Kodiak Island, Shemya, Tokyo and Shanghai. The letter pointed out that the Canadian Pacific had been in the Pacific transportation business since 1886 and still had agents at twenty points in the area, maintained at a cost of $200,000 a year. It was thus in a better position to establish the proposed air services, and at a lower cost, than anyone else – and it was not requesting a subsidy. Furthermore, "with the close co-operation which exists between Canadian Pacific Airlines and Trans-Canada Air Lines, it would be possible to turn over to TCA at Vancouver air passengers for New York and Europe. TCA would thus benefit indirectly from the services of all Canadian Pacific agents throughout the Pacific." Had McGregor been privileged to read cabinet documents, this paragraph might have induced an attack of apoplexy.

The cabinet also had before it a paper prepared by an up-and-coming baseball fan in the Department of External Affairs, one Lester B. Pearson. This reminded the cabinet members of the previous official affirmations that TCA was Canada's "chosen instrument" for all international routes and pointed out that with a private airline operating internationally as well, the government might at some future date find difficulty in "pursuing consistently that policy which it considered to be in the long-run interest of Canada, even though it might not be in our short-run commercial interest."

Howe told his colleagues that TCA was not in a position to proceed immediately with the development of Pacific operations, and would require heavy financial assistance if it did so, and therefore it would be desirable to "modify" the government's previous policy.

Full cabinet minutes were not kept in those days; only the outlines of decisions taken at the meetings were recorded. These reveal that "further discussion" ensued, during which the Prime Minister, Mackenzie King, said that whatever decision was made should be "based on the understanding that no subsidy would be provided to CPA." Apparently there was some reluctance to accept Howe's proposal, since the meeting adjourned without a decision. The issue was considered again on June 26, and this time it was resolved that "designation of CPA to operate the international air services requested in the Pacific be approved." The Prime Minister once again insisted that CPR would receive no subsidy, and Howe, when he communicated the glad news to McConachie, stipulated that the service must be operated with North Stars. McConachie was no admirer of the North Star, but he accepted Howe's stipulation cheerfully enough. The super-salesman knew he had his foot in the door.

The reasons for the government's about-face have never been fully explained, but it seems Howe feared, as he once wrote to McGregor, that if *some* Canadian company did not fly the Pacific the routes would go by default to BOAC or perhaps various American airlines. Also, after the death of Sir Edward Beatty, whose attitude toward governments tended to be one of confrontation, succeeding generations of CPR management adopted a more subtle, conciliatory approach, and it would have been easy for them to reason that since the prevailing mood of the country was by no means favourable toward socialist experiments with nationalization, CPA was here to stay and a place must be found for it. Certainly, since BCPA had been operating the Australian service for almost two years, it would have been politically difficult to defend what the CPR could easily have portrayed as a "dog-in-the-manger" attitude: that if the government airline did not want to fly the route, no other company could, even if that company was prepared to stand whatever losses it occurred without asking the government for a cent.

McGregor always maintained that no one at TCA realized until Chevrier's announcement that the rights to the Orient would go along with the Australia–New Zealand service. This seems strange, since all references to the subject were to "the Pacific service," and McConachie, as McKim's letter showed, had for years been trumpeting his desire to fly to China. "On to Vladivostok!" had become his rallying cry. And a suggestion that McGregor might have already begun to regret his decision (though he never afterwards admitted it to any of his intimates) may lie in his testy reply to a cable from Gordon Wood, his successor as general traffic manager.

TCA's employees had been looking forward to the start of the Pacific service: it would open up new opportunities within the company and offer those fortunates chosen to operate it the chance of adventure in the Mysterious East. Many still regret McGregor's decision and consider it the greatest mistake of his career. Gordon Wood was in Montreal when Chevrier made his announcement and he promptly wired McGregor in Winnipeg: "Re CPA award transpacific since majority TCA employees were keenly interested in our long-range plans for Pacific services I endorse [Jack] Dalby's recommendation that company make immediate release to all employees explaining our position in order offset general disappointment resulting from apparent loss of important route."

McGregor responded: "Retel Pacific stop Recommendation not repeat not concurred in and who's disappointed?" Since he received this curt reply by the none-too-private medium of the teletype, Wood was embarrassed. He wrote to McGregor telling him so, and explaining why he had supported Dalby's suggestion. McGregor wrote apologizing:

The truth of the matter is I suppose, that I was, and am, feeling a little bit crotchety about the whole affair, not because I begrudge CPA the Pacific route, but because I feel there is no justification for any Canadian carrier flying it now, or for some years, and I dislike seeing TCA lose its monopoly as Canada's one international flag carrier as a result of what I consider to be a phoney presentation of the case by CPA. However, I still heartily disagree with the idea of making anything purporting to be an explanation to the employee body. Nothing could be said to our own people that would not sound like a palpable lie, except a factual statement of what led up to the government's action in this case, and if that were publicized, the government would be embarrassed beyond words, particularly the Minister who was not responsible, but over whose name the announcement was made. I see no point in flying in the face of Providence to this extent. I appreciate what you say about TCA people looking toward route expansion as an avenue leading to advancement, and I naturally hope that that will prove to be the case, but at the same time I also hope that there will be few if any TCA employees who would wish to walk into more responsible jobs along a path knee deep in operating deficits.

McGregor was not alone in his belief that McConachie would lose his shirt on the Australian run: the feeling was widespread within the airline industry. And in fact the Australian service, launched in July 1949, did not begin to pay its way for about twenty years. But two months later, CPA began to fly to Japan. And soon after that the Korean War broke out – and every aircraft capable of flying from North America to the Orient staggered into the air under the weight of a full load.

Rod MacInnes, wartime head of public relations for the RCAF, who had been transferred from the CNR to head TCA's public relations department, was the one who told McGregor the war had broken out. "~~Jesus Christ~~," McGregor exploded, "only A McConachie could be that lucky." WE ARE

CHAPTER THIRTEEN

HE AIRLINE'S DEFICIT for 1949 was a record $4.3 million, which exposed Gordon McGregor to four days of grilling in Ottawa by a tribunal he appeared to view as a revival of the Star Chamber: the Sessional Committee on Railways and Shipping Owned, Operated and Controlled by the Government. At that time, this all-party parliamentary committee met annually to consider the accounts submitted by those stewards of the national interest, the directors of the CNR and its affiliate TCA.

Like many other businessmen, McGregor was such a whole-hearted admirer of C.D. Howe that all other politicians suffered by comparison; by the end of his career, he was, in fact, inclined to regard most of them with scorn, if not contempt. In his memoirs he summed up his views on the importance of having the "right types" in both government and the public service to give the country "the clear thinking and decisive action" it needed:

Speaking broadly, I don't think the present system is ever going to attract many – there will be exceptions of course, but not many – really good administrators to serve in parliament. Whatever induces a man of that type, other than one who is making a second career of it, to run for parliament these days, I do not know; it is certainly not the compensation, which in comparison with industry is low. For his pains he is required to work long hours in a city which is not his home, for the most part, and be subjected to a great deal of unkind and even unjust criticism on matters for which he is not personally responsible. I don't think there are enough talented young to middle-aged Canadians around with the necessary dedication to populate the House of Commons. So we find that the small town lawyer who has virtually no industry experience whatever can put his name up as a candidate and find himself in the House, and perhaps even in due course in the Cabinet.

McGregor believed he had been appointed to do a job; that he and his management team knew how to do that job better than any "small town lawyer," and that they should be left to get on with it. He was proud of his management team and asserted often that it was "the best in the industry"; if that boast was hardly susceptible of proof, the respect accorded to TCA within the international aviation organizations, ICAO and IATA, and the number of key committees of those organizations chaired by TCA executives and technical people gave ample support to his claim. Perhaps because of Canada's important role in the formation of these international bodies, and the siting of their headquarters in Montreal, no other world airline applied itself more conscientiously than TCA to making their work a success. McGregor himself succeeded Herb Symington on the executive committee of IATA in October 1949, and remained one of its most influential members until his retirement two decades later. He was president of IATA for the 1953-54 term, and he encouraged his top executives to serve on its various committees concerned with all aspects of world aviation.*

At home, too, the airline was quick to realize the importance of the Air Transport Association of Canada, the national service organization of the aviation industry. Particularly during its formative years, during and immediately after the war, the association received the whole-hearted support and encouragement of TCA's top executives. Among those who guided its destinies as its president or chairman at various times were Howard Cotterell, Fred Wood, Jack Nickson, Gordon Wood's right-hand man in the traffic department for many years, and, more recently, Claude Taylor and his successor as president, Pierre Jeanniot.

Against this background, McGregor could barely conceal his irritation when, during his appearances before the parliamentary committee, some member would shun the great issues of domestic and world aviation in favour of a discussion on mislaid baggage or the inadequacies of TCA sandwiches. Actually, given his private views on politicians, McGregor was surprisingly successful in his dealings with the committee, defending his company's performance with logical explanations and deflecting the worst barbs hurled in its direction with patience and good humour. He and his staff were grateful for the fact that TCA's appearance customarily followed that of Donald Gordon, president of the CNR. Gordon, a giant bear of a man in stature as well as accomplishment, was more easily provoked by politicians than McGregor, and his appearances before the committee in the fif-

---

*The tradition continued through the years. Air Canada's current chairman, Claude Taylor, was elected to the executive committee of IATA in 1977 and the following year he headed a five-man international task force credited with averting the threatened collapse of the organization. He served as president of IATA in 1980, and in 1984 Air Canada was represented on no fewer than forty-four IATA sub-committees and working groups.

ties and sixties seldom failed to provide fireworks for the press. McGregor and his staff used to believe that by the time the committee members got around to the airline's accounts so much blood had been spilt that it was given a relatively easy passage. Another explanation may have been the exhaustive preparations always made for the hearings: Bill Harvey, who by 1950 had become general auditor of TCA, used to whip his staff into a frenzy of overtime for weeks before the meetings, preparing tons of documentation to be shipped to Ottawa so that no one could possibly ask McGregor a question for which Harvey and his boys could not supply the answer on the spot.

The committee hearing scheduled for April 1950 threatened to be more than ever an ordeal for McGregor. He faced the unpleasant task of defending – and he hoped explaining – a $4.3 million deficit to the representatives of the Canadian people who were footing the bill. And three days before the hearing, TCA's old nemesis, George Drew, had himself named to the committee in place of William J. Browne, a Newfoundland lawyer. Scenting battle, C.D. Howe decided McGregor might need reinforcements and on the morning of the first day of the hearing he himself replaced a little-known Quebec Liberal on the committee.

The session opened with McGregor's reading of TCA's annual report, and there followed a long series of questions from Drew about the connection between various TCA directors and senior officers and the CNR, none of which appeared to have much relevance to the airline's accounts, but which led up to his demand for the tabling of the salaries earned by TCA executives. Before McGregor had a chance to field this question, Howe broke in with an abrupt, "It has never been the practice of this committee to give information on salaries." A wrangle about whether this practice should be changed ensued, during which Drew seemed surprised to hear that TCA directors received neither salaries nor expense allowances. His resolution to force disclosure of the executives' salaries was ultimately defeated, and as the hearing ground on another member asked McGregor whether CPA held any government mail contracts. Again, before McGregor could answer, his Minister took over: "Yes," he said, and added: "CPA get a lot more money for carrying the mail than we do."

Similarly, when on the second day of the hearing Drew managed to direct the questioning to the topic he had had himself placed on the committee to air – the alleged shortcomings of the North Star – Howe fielded as many questions as McGregor. McGregor, however, produced figures on engine failures which indicated that the situation was improving: they showed that in two recent months the Merlins had run for more hours between failures than the Pratt & Whitneys in the DC-3s. This evidence, though it surprised some of his own operations men, spiked Drew's guns, and from the Opposition's point of view the hearing may be said to have fizzled.

Drew did, however, manage to force the appearance before the committee of an unscheduled witness, Harold Cooper, joint comptroller of the CNR and TCA. After thirteen years in operation, the airline had an accumulated deficit of $9 million, but Cooper told the committee members this should not be considered a loss. For instance, $3.6 million of it was actually still in the airline's hands, set aside in its self-insurance fund and invested in gilt-edged securities. Similarly, a further $2.5 million of what appeared as the deficit had been spent on training captains, first officers, navigators, radio operators and ground personnel, so it really counted as a continuing company asset. Also, some of the money the government had advanced to the airline had been "turned back to the Post Office for the carriage of mail at less than the rate we think we should get." Howe broke in to Cooper's evidence here to make another point: "While there is only $25 millions invested by the government in the airline,* the actual assets of the airline amount to about $31 millions."

McGregor was also questioned about another matter that had aroused some controversy during 1949: the transfer of the corporation's headquarters staff from Winnipeg to Montreal. Before this move, McGregor used to spend the second week of each month in Montreal, and there was a good deal of travel back and forth between those two cities by other senior executives. This was, of course, costly, and one of the answers to the airline's financial position he had jotted down for himself on his appointment as president was "Personnel travelling and transfers must decrease." The move was a logical one. Montreal had become the terminus of both the Atlantic and Caribbean services and, thanks to a recently concluded agreement with the United States, was about to become the terminus for new services to New York and Tampa, Florida; the headquarters of the CNR, IATA, and ICAO were all in Montreal; and Montreal is much closer than Winnipeg to Ottawa, where the corporation had so many business

---

*The $5 million capital subscribed by the CNR to set up TCA had been increased to $25 million in the 1945 change to the TCA Act, and the original 5 per cent annual interest paid on it was reduced to 3 per cent, the same figure paid by the CNR on its borrowings from the government.

dealings with the Post Office, the Air Transport Board and the Department of Transport.

Some of those who did not relish the idea of uprooting their families and settling in the apparently alien, more costly, and housing-short environment of Montreal suspected the move was inspired less by these considerations than by McGregor's own affection for his native city, but in fact it had been mooted in Symington's day. Indeed, it was not so much a move as a reversion to the status quo: the company's headquarters had originally been established in Montreal, and when in 1940 Vice-President Colyer suggested to the board that his office, and that of the general traffic manager, should be moved to Winnipeg to adjust to wartime conditions, he had used the phrase "transferred temporarily."

Nevertheless, the announcement of the intention to move (even though only 159 of the corporation's 5,137 employees were involved) aroused protests in Manitoba, and efforts were made to have Ottawa reverse the decision. Among those who protested against it was the Winnipeg MP Stanley Knowles, and in response C.D. Howe wrote him saying: "One of my responsibilities toward TCA is to free its operation from political interference. I feel that in refusing to intervene in this matter, I am carrying out that obligation."

Among the organizations that added its voice to the clamour was the Winnipeg Chamber of Commerce, which feared that the headquarters transfer was only the forerunner of a wholesale exodus of TCA shops and services from the city, which would obviously have been a grave blow to its economy. McGregor hastened to reassure those who harboured that fear, and said publicly that Winnipeg, at the mid-point of the continent, was "in a favorable position so far as air service was concerned" and "appeared to be a natural conjunction point for service from New York and Chicago to Alaska and the Orient." Furthermore, as he recorded later, "I could not foresee the transfer of such massive units as the main overhaul base away from Winnipeg."

That statement would return to haunt him in the years ahead, but all in all, the airline emerged from the 1950 hearing, if not unscathed, at least not too badly scarred. Indeed, a closer examination of its 1949 results might have suggested to the committee members that it was about to turn the corner. By far the larger part of the deficit – almost $2.9 million – had been incurred by TCA (Atlantic) Limited, since the aeroplane had not yet replaced the ocean liner as the preferred mode of transatlantic travel, and the traffic between Canada and Europe was even more seasonal than domestic travel. The airline flew fewer transatlantic flights than the year before, but the average load factor for the year was only 64 per cent, which meant that 36 per cent of the seats crossed the ocean empty. Also, the infant Caribbean services, which had been included in the Atlantic company's bailiwick, were registering the heavy losses McGregor had foretold.

The parent company's situation was somewhat better. Its operating revenues actually exceeded its operating expenses by almost $2 million during the year, even though those expenses included an extraordinary $1 million increase in the cost of engine parts – from $890,000 in 1948 to $1.89 million in 1949. The year's operating expenses also included a $2.3 million increase in the corporation's wage bill, caused not by increased hirings (the number of employees rose by only 53 during the year in spite of the greatly increased volume of work performed), but by what the annual report described as "the impact of the rising cost of living." The company also repaid during the year a $1.5 million capital-equipment loan it had received from the CNR. But its operating surplus was more than wiped out by the first full year's depreciation costs on the North Star fleet ($2.8 million) and its $470,000 "fixed charges," the interest paid on its $25 million capital. (McGregor raised with Howe the propriety, if not the dubious legality, of the corporation paying interest on its capital shares when it was in a deficit position. Howe responded acidly that since the CNR had to pay interest on the money it had invested in the airline, it would smack of "sharp practice" for TCA to try to avoid the interest charges.)

On the unwritten side of the ledger at the beginning of 1950 were several items that indicated better times ahead. The Merlin engine problems were being ironed out, as evidenced by the airline's extremely high level of "on time" performance – 84 per cent on average over the year and more than 90 per cent during some months – and the fact that 97 per cent of all its scheduled mileage was completed. Partly responsible for this excellent record, the envy of many other airlines, was the equipping of more and more Canadian airports with improved navigational aids, notably the ILS, or instrument landing system. The forerunner of today's infinitely more sophisticated automatic landing systems, ILS consisted of two radio beams that permitted pilots to guide their aircraft almost down to the runway in the worst weather conditions. Naturally, TCA's flight operations department was anxious to see every airport equipped with the new system as soon as possible, but the Department of Transport initially lacked the specialized personnel capable of handling its installation. So in 1946 the airline supplied the department with one of its DC-3s and the services of Herb Hopson, its chief technical pilot, and Bill Taylor, one of its most experienced radio engineers. For the next five years, Hopson and Taylor toured the country setting up the new system at every major airport between Victoria and St. John's. The experience gained on this assignment stood Hopson in good stead later when, as a TCA representative on IATA and ICAO working groups, he played a major role in establishing world standards for instrument landing approaches and runway lighting systems.

Side by side with all the technical progress being made in those years, the airline was evolving new reservations procedures, refining its traffic forecasting techniques and beginning to experiment with family and other incentive fares. Passenger traffic was compounding at the tremendous annual rate of more than 20 per cent and McGregor was confident that this, together with the economies he was still introducing, would soon pull his operation out of the red. He was elated when the 1950 figures for the domestic company showed a 20 per cent increase in operating revenue, to $31.8 million, and a modest surplus of $201,206. The Atlantic company's deficit was almost halved, to $1.5 million, and only $275,922 of that was contributed by the Atlantic routes, the rest being attributed to the still under-nourished Caribbean routes.

Small though it was, the thrifty McGregor wanted to set aside his surplus in a new fund to provide for the re-equipment of the fleet which he knew lay ahead. But Howe quickly disabused him of the notion that the government would cheerfully pay the overseas company's deficit and permit McGregor to retain $200,000 that could reduce it. In an attempt to enlist the minister's support to defend TCA against "the acquisitiveness of the Treasury," McGregor wrote: "Morale is an intangible thing, but it is, as you know, extremely important. The sight of the admittedly small but very hard-won surplus of the North American company being absorbed by the overseas organization would be a sad one to those 4,000-odd TCA people who will regard each penny of that modest $200,000 as more important and symbolic of achievement than each dollar of their own money."

In more workaday vein, he also argued that if the public saw that any surplus earned on the North American routes was being used to make up the deficits on the Atlantic there would be an outcry that by buying a ticket between, say, Winnipeg and Toronto, a passenger would be subsidizing people better off than himself who could afford to jaunt around Europe on holiday. It was a good point, but neither Howe nor the Treasury was swayed, and the $200,000 vanished into the general deficit.

The minister was more helpful on another matter, when he intervened in the continuing skirmishes between the airline and the Deputy Postmaster General, Walter Turnbull. TCA carried 7 per cent more mail during the year – a total of 3.64 million ton-miles – but in accordance with the agreement reached when the "all-up" service was introduced, its payment from the Post Office remained at the same $5.4 million figure. The airline's return per ton-mile thus fell from $1.59 to $1.48. Throughout 1950 Anson McKim negotiated with the Post Office authorities for a new arrangement. TCA's case was that it was not receiving any compensation for the extra mail carried and for new services inaugurated since the agreement, such as the run to Newfoundland, which was now part of Canada and thus came under the domestic service, and the impending new services to New York and Tampa. The airline wanted to fill the extra space in its North Stars, which could carry 3,600 lbs. of mail, and it wanted to be paid for the amount of work it performed. In return it offered the common commercial concession of a unit rate that declined as the business it was given increased – the customary volume discount. In anticipation of much higher mail loads, and as an inducement to the Post Office to agree to new terms, McGregor offered to carry six million ton-miles of mail at a basic rate of a dollar a mile, with provision for a higher unit rate if that much mail did not materialize, and a correspondingly lower rate for any extra mail carried.

The postmaster general of the day, G. Edouard Rinfret, at first seemed disposed to accept his offer, but his deputy, the peppery Turnbull, still convinced that the airline was reaping in far too much of the Post Office's money already, opposed it. C.D. Howe had little patience for battles between ministers and their deputies, and in those days Howe was seldom bested in cabinet. Thanks to his intercession, the terms the airline wanted, which seem in retrospect to be a perfectly normal commercial arrangement, were incorporated in an amendment to the mail contract at the beginning of 1951.

As it turned out, the victory gave the airline more psychological satisfaction than practical advantage. By 1951, mail revenue had dwindled to 15 per cent of its total receipts (against 70 per cent in 1939) and the volume discount brought in only an extra $341,000 during the year. But the boom in air travel continued, and TCA rose to the occasion. With no new routes or equipment, the airline flew 11 per cent more miles than the year before. A fourth daily transcontinental flight began and by midsummer there were fourteen daily scheduled flights between Toronto and Montreal. At the height of the travel season, 500 more seats were available every day than during the same period in 1950. Air express and cargo loads rose by 13 per cent during the year, and a ten-year progress chart included with the annual report pointed out that the commodity ton-miles flown annually had risen from 217,411 in 1942 to 5.4 million in 1951, an increase of 2,409 per cent. Passenger miles flown rose from 57.5 million to 545 million during the same period. Six hundred new employees were taken on during the year, partly to handle the extra work load but largely because the work week had been shortened from 44 to 40 hours. The statistic that probably pleased McGregor most was the one accepted within the industry as a measure of an airline's efficiency: the unit cost of the "ton-miles of air transportation made available for sale." This was reduced during 1951 from 40.48 to 37.22 cents, an improvement of 8 per cent.

The result of all this activity was a $5.2 million increase in revenue, and to everyone's gratification, the domestic company managed to declare a surplus of $3.8 million for the year. This time, since TCA (Atlantic) Limited had also turned around and managed to register a small surplus of $47,231, the government permitted McGregor to salt his profit away in a reserve for buying new aircraft, which he knew would be vastly more expensive than the North Stars and DC-3s. (The airline contributed to that reserve until 1954, after which it depended on depreciation and additional capital investment for its equipment financing.)

Since both the domestic and overseas companies were now in the black there no longer seemed any reason for them to operate separately, and so they were merged at the beginning of 1952. This simplified the accounting problems of Bill Harvey, who became comptroller of TCA when Harold Cooper retired from the railroad (as part of what might be termed the gradual "patriation" of TCA from the CNR), but in that same year the airline was faced with a new financial problem. An amendment to the Income Tax Act made Crown corporations liable for income tax in exactly the same way as private companies, and the Department of National Revenue ruled that TCA's annual interest payments to the CNR on its $25 million capital stock would not be deductible as an operating expense before calculation of its taxes.

The airline's inflexible capital structure had already become a matter of concern to McGregor and he had raised it with Howe several times. The CNR's investment was treated as a bond, and the interest on it had to be paid regardless of the corporation's financial position from year to year; had part of the corporation's capital been common stock in the normal way, it could have reduced, or even withheld, dividends in a bad year. Furthermore, TCA was deprived by law of the normal advantage of a bond issue – the ability to redeem it if or when it happened to have surplus capital funds.

Airlines are unlike most companies, in that only a small proportion of their total capital is invested in long-lasting assets such as buildings; at that time, 70 per cent of TCA's investment was represented by its fleet of aircraft, their associated spare parts and the tools used to maintain them. To illustrate the problem this presented: to pay for the North Stars and their associated parts and equipment, the airline had had to supplement its $25 million capital with a $1.5 million loan from the CNR. But the economic life of aircraft at that time of impending technological change was so short that the high rate of depreciation universally accepted meant that they were quickly written off on the balance sheet. So by 1951 the airline had repaid the CNR's loan and accumulated $6 million in temporarily surplus cash. Unable to apply the surplus to reducing its $25 million capital – and thus the interest it had to pay on it – the airline had invested it in bonds, but unhappily the bonds were bringing in less interest than the corporation had to pay out to the CNR.

The new income tax legislation in 1952 brought matters to a head and the TCA Act was revised in 1953 – not soon enough to spare the airline a $1.2 million tax payment in 1952. Under the new dispensation, $20 million of the airline's $25 million capital stock was converted into a twenty-year fixed interest-bearing debenture, and the 3 per cent interest payable on it to the CNR became an operating expense before taxation. (The original 50,000 shares of capital stock, representing $5 million, remained in the Treasury, but the CNR received no dividends on them until 1964, when the airline declared a dividend of $3 per share.)

All but unnoticed in this welter of financial detail was another new provision in the revised TCA Act: it authorized Trans-Canada Air Lines to use the alternative name "Air Canada," which was considered by the traffic department to have more promotional punch in Europe. More would be heard about that in future years.

CHAPTER FOURTEEN

NE OF GORDON MCGREGOR'S favourite ways of combining business with pleasure was to attend the annual air show staged by the British aircraft manufacturers at Farnborough, about thirty miles southwest of London, which gave him an opportunity to revisit some of his old haunts and renew friendships made during the war. Farnborough, as well as being familiar to Canadian veterans of World War II because of its proximity to Aldershot, is the home of the Royal Aircraft Establishment, Britain's leading centre of aeronautical research and development. And its annual air show, a de luxe version of the air circus that captured McGregor's imagination as a boy, also served the more serious purpose, as Britain attempted to regain its position as an exporting nation, of displaying British products to the world.

Back in 1949 there were perhaps a dozen old-established aircraft manufacturers in Britain, and with one of them, de Havilland, having lately flown the world's first "pure-jet" airliner, the Comet, and the others competing to stay in the race, there was much to see at Farnborough that year. But McGregor's most interesting experience occurred at nearby Wisley, in Surrey, where the Vickers-Armstrong company was testing the prototype of an aircraft designated the Viscount 630.

The turbine engine did for aeroplanes what the steam engine had done for ships. But the first pure-jet engines were much more voracious consumers of fuel, particularly over short distances and at low altitudes, than the "prop-jets," which used the power generated by the continuous combustion of compressed air and fuel to drive a conventional propeller rather than push the aircraft through the air directly. The Viscount was the first commercial aircraft equipped with turbine-propeller engines, and McGregor was delighted when he was invited by a Vickers salesman to fly in it. And as a potential customer he was given the royal treatment: he was met at the train by Sir Hew Kilner, Vickers' managing director, and driven by limousine to the airfield at Wisley, where he was introduced to the company's chief designer, George Edwards, who would soon be promoted to the managing directorship, be knighted, and, in later life, be awarded one of Britain's highest honours, the Order of Merit.

It was a close, humid day, and as Edwards led McGregor out to the waiting Viscount, where the pilot was running up its engines, they could see the slipstreams rippling out behind its four propellers. Edwards pointed out that they did not overlap, and McGregor could clearly see the gap between them. The propellers of most other aircraft at that time created an overlapping turbulence that contributed to the vibration inherent in piston-engined aircraft, and McGregor congratulated Edwards on a fine piece of design. Edwards, who disguised his formidable intellect with a jaunty, informal manner and a mastery of dialect stories, laughingly professed that it was pure luck.

Whether the design of the Viscount was pure luck or genius, McGregor found it was the smoothest aircraft he had ever encountered. The Vickers salesmen delighted in balancing pennies and pencils on end during flight, and when McGregor was offered the pilot's seat he thought he was back in a Spitfire: instead of the standard system of cables and pulleys, the Viscount's controls were operated by push-rods, so that there was no slack in the response of the ailerons, elevators and rudder to the pilot's operation of his controls. As hundreds of pilots later found, the Viscount was as light to fly as a fighter.

As McGregor cruised placidly above the English countryside he loved, revelling in the Viscount's sweetness, George Edwards surreptitiously reached forward between the two pilots and yanked back both starboard throttles; under such violent treatment any other aircraft would have swerved sharply to the right. But McGregor was easily able to hold his aircraft steady by only a slight pressure on his controls. Back on the ground, he was like a boy confronted with a train set in a store's Christmas display: he just had to have it.

After his return to Canada, he wrote about his "amazing experience" to his friend Sir William Hildred at IATA: "There is a possibility that this aircraft, or one like it, may prove most embarrassing to the industry, as I doubt very much if a passenger, once exposed to that vibration-less and nearly noiseless air travel, will thereafter be easily induced into a piston engine powered machine." And soon afterward, in a letter to Whitney Straight, managing director of BOAC, he said: "I cannot get away from the idea that an airline might be well advised to attain to the condition of operating full jet aircraft by the stepping-stone of turbo-prop power."

The selection of new aircraft is an enormously complex task for all airlines, and a machine that may be ideal for one company may be quite unsuited to another's needs. Such factors as route patterns, the length of their "legs," or stages along a route, the size of the market to be served, terrain, climatic conditions – all these and more must be considered. And at the beginning of the fifties the task was complicated even more by the fact that everyone knew the jets were on the way, although the Americans were slower to accept this as inevitable than the rest of the world. As McGregor wrote to a British aviation writer, John Longhurst, in 1952: "In spite of the fact that the Comet is now in scheduled service and prototype Viscounts have flown revenue flights, you will still hear the opinion expressed by top rank U.S. aircraft people that piston engined commercial aircraft will be leading the field ten years hence. It is by no means to the credit of our neighbors to the south, but I really believe that one of the reasons for this attitude is the fact that the continuous combustion engine was not originally developed in the U.S., and therefore cannot be much good."

When TCA took delivery of its North Stars the traffic department feared there would not be enough passengers to fill them, and it was confidently predicted they would provide adequate capacity until the airline could be re-equipped with jets several years hence. But the growth of traffic so outstripped all forecasts that by 1951 they were being worked between nine and ten hours a day – a record for plane utilization at that time – and the airline had to buy three more from CPA and convert its whole fleet to accommodate 48 passengers instead of 40, which provided the equivalent of 3.4 extra aircraft. Even this was not enough to cope with the traffic offering at peak seasons, and by now it was apparent that the advent of the jets would be delayed by the pressures of military production for the Korean War. So in August 1951, five Lockheed Super Constellations were ordered for delivery in the winter of 1953–54, with the intention of using them on the company's overseas services and releasing more North Stars for the domestic traffic. The 63-passenger "Super-Connie" was equipped with four powerful Wright "compound" engines, in which a turbine driven by the exhaust system returned some energy into the main power train to boost its output by 450 horsepower. (Unfortunately this system gave TCA's maintenance department considerable trouble when the aircraft went into service.)

Traffic forecasting is a complex art, which must take into account such factors as anticipated economic and business conditions, past and current travel trends, and the effect of various fare levels, promotional efforts, competitive services and the possible addition of new routes. It is an art that has been considerably refined since the introduction of the computer, but in those days Gordon Wood, who became vice-president, traffic, when Anson McKim returned to the chemical industry, would ask his regional managers for their best "guesstimates" of the traffic expected in their areas for the following year, and then strike an average of the results. And in 1952, two entirely separate forecasts were drawn up; they differed by less than 1.5 per cent in their conclusions, and both predicted that even with the addition of the Super Constellations to the fleet there would be a serious capacity shortage by the spring of 1955.

Because of the long lead time between the placing of an order and the delivery of aircraft, McGregor knew that whichever type was selected to take up the 1955 slack must be ordered by the fall of 1952. And with the Super Constellations expected to supplement the North Stars adequately on the long-distance TCA routes until the arrival of a long-range jet, the main need was for a replacement for the short-haul DC-3. For eighteen months, study groups made up of representatives of the various departments concerned assessed the merits of the several 40- to 50-passenger aircraft available. The choice eventually narrowed down to two: the American Convair type 340 and the British Viscount.

When McGregor had returned home in 1949 so enthusiastic about the Viscount his colleagues had been inclined to interpret his praise for it as just another manifestation of his affection for all things British. But after several of the TCA pilots had flown it they agreed it was a beautiful aircraft to handle. Most of the technical opinion around the airline, however, strongly favoured American equipment over British, particularly after the troubles encountered with the Merlins. So for a while the betting was on the Convair, which was powered by the pilots' friend, the old reliable Pratt & Whitney R-2800 engine. Unfortunately, it only had two of them, and that was considered an encroachment on safety in an aircraft weighing 60,000 lbs. Also, McGregor cautioned his colleagues that choosing a new fleet of Convairs would commit TCA to exclusively piston-engined operation well into the period during which he foresaw that competing airlines would have re-equipped with jets.

So a study group from the engineering department flew over to England to take a long, hard look at the Viscount. Their first sight of the Vickers factory at Weybridge shocked them. Accustomed to such California plants as Douglas in Santa Monica and Lockheed at Burbank, they expected immaculate modern facilities and equipment. But California had been a long way from the war in Europe. "What we found," wrote Clayton Glenn, one of the group, "were old buildings, old machines, untidy shops and antiquated fabrication techniques."

In response to the study group's report, Jack Dyment and Jim Bain flew over and spent some time going through the Vickers shops. They, too, were dismayed by what they saw and recommended an immediate house-cleaning. The obliging George Edwards saw their point and within a very short time Vickers accomplished the recommended clean-up.

The TCA engineers, when they studied the Viscount's specifications and went over the prototype, were not much more impressed than they were by the Vickers factory. They considered many of the aircraft systems to be poorly designed. For instance, the electric control system for feathering the propellers was unduly complicated, and they proposed a simplified redesign that eliminated twelve relays, or switches. Similarly, the air-conditioning and pressurization systems were so involved that it took two pilots to operate them. An even worse design deficiency showed up in the fuel system: although the Viscount was a four-engined plane its fuel system was designed as if it were a twin, and thus a single failure in it could shut down two engines on the same side.

Jack Dyment drew up a long report recommending that the aircraft not be bought unless these deficiencies were rectified. The fuel system must be redesigned so that all four engines were supplied independently; the cockpit must be modified to TCA's "one-man" standards; the aircraft must be equipped with a system to permit it to be heated on the ground when the engines were not running; and so on. The list seemed endless. But to everyone's astonishment George Edwards put up no argument; he agreed to make all the changes TCA wanted, for an extra $25,000 per aircraft. From the airline's viewpoint, this was an insignificant sum on a machine costing $1 million, but it was obvious that Vickers would be out of pocket on the deal. "My lot," as Edwards told the author years later in his colloquial style, "thought I was crazy. But I told them it was the best chance we had of getting into the American market."

Reassured by this promise, and armed with the same "never-be-sorry" warranty from Rolls-Royce on the Viscount's Dart engines as he had extracted on the Merlin, McGregor recommended to his board of directors in October 1952, that, subject to the results of cold-weather trials the following winter, TCA should buy a fleet of fifteen Vicounts for delivery during the win-

ter of 1954-55. It was quite a leap into the dark for the board –
$15.8 million for an aircraft and a new form of propulsion that
had not yet proved itself in service. But after McGregor had made
his presentation, Herb Symington, who had retained his director's seat, said, "Well, I suppose we're here to make decisions,"
and proposed acceptance of management's recommendation.
C.D. Howe, when McGregor informed him of the decision, wrote:
"While I am not too happy about buying U.K. aircraft, I have
noted the reasons for your recommendation and since your board
of directors have approved, I am not disposed to object. If you
decide to close the agreement, I hope you will keep careful watch
of progress, and make sure that you get your deliveries. U.K.
deliveries are very bad indeed and this purchase will not be good
unless you can get the planes on time."

The Viscount passed its cold-weather trials at Churchill, on
Hudson Bay, if not with flying colours at least satisfactorily, subject to some more modifications to such things as rubber door
seals which froze to the point where the aircraft could not be
pressurized. And during the trials more and more TCA pilots came
to share McGregor's enthusiasm for the plane; furthermore, it
was clear that its smoothness and quietness – and its huge oval
windows – would make it popular with passengers.

The airline took delivery of its first Viscount in November
1954–Howe's forebodings about late deliveries notwithstanding–
and the aircraft went into service in April 1955, making TCA by a
large margin the first North American airline to advance to turbine power. And the predictions about its popularity with the
clientele proved accurate; it was not long before passengers
started grumbling if the trip they planned was not on one of the
Viscount's routes.

George Edwards developed great respect for the professional-
ism of the TCA engineers and freely admitted in later years that
their modifications to the Viscount made it possible for him to
land several big U.S. orders; the company sold a total of 435
around the world, of which TCA ultimately bought 52. But naturally there was some initial friction between the visiting colo-
nials from Canada, with their incessant carping, and the Vickers
engineers, who believed they had a damned good aeroplane to
start with. And the relationship was perhaps not improved by
the strong friendship that developed between McGregor and Sir
George Edwards.

The two men shared a passion for sailing – though Edwards
recalled that McGregor "used to put the fear of God in me when
he sailed a boat because he had everything just about as tight as

it could get." Reminiscing about their relationship, Edwards seemed to feel guilty, certainly regretful, that he had emerged from hospital after one of his "carve-ups," as he termed the long series of operations for internal complaints that plagued his retirement, just the day before McGregor died; it was as though he would otherwise have flown to his bedside. "I worshipped the bloke," he said.

I mean, there was his war record as a base to show what he was, but I didn't need that to see what he was. . . . He was tough, and brave, and kind and considerate – and as straight as a gun barrel, absolutely as straight as anybody I've ever met. . . . When there was a question of a decision that he had got to take, and he wanted my word that certain conditions that his minions were imposing were going to be met, I used to get a summons to go to Montreal and I just used to jump into the next aeroplane and go, and he knew perfectly well that if I looked him straight in the eye and said, "Yes, it will be done like that," or "Yes, they will be delivered like that," he knew that it would be done and that would be the end of it. . . . The other side of the coin, as you can well imagine, was that both sets of minions regarded with a bit of suspicion this arrangement between their two masters, because my lads used to throw their hands up at what I would bring back and say I'd agreed to do, and they had now got to put their heads down and get on with it. McGregor's lads used to regard with considerable suspicion any proposition to buy any more aeroplanes from Vickers, because they were quite certain it was a deal being cooked up between McGregor and me.

On one celebrated occasion, the differences between the two sets of "lads" extended beyond the merits or otherwise of various aircraft systems. After a day of discussions at Weybridge both sides sat down to dinner at a local hotel and an argument developed over whether a baseball pitcher could make a ball curve in flight: the magazine *Life* had recently published photographs purporting to prove that the breaking ball was an optical illusion.

George Edwards was a cricketer of note in his youth – he once bowled out the celebrated West Indian player Leary Constantine for the low score of eleven runs – and later became president of the illustrious Surrey County Cricket Club. And he maintained stoutly that whether or not a baseball pitcher could curve a ball, *he* certainly could. No ball being available at the time, he was unable to prove his point until Dave Tennant, one of the TCA engineers who went on to become vice-president, operations, turned up at lunch next day with a brand-new cricket ball. (To the Englishmen's intense amusement he apologized for what he thought its eccentric colour – the traditional ox-blood red.) And since Tennant had been a hockey goalkeeper in his younger days he volunteered to receive George's bowling and stationed himself at the end of a long hotel corridor. In cricket, unlike baseball, the bowler bounces the ball in front of the batsman. No one could tell afterward whether George Edwards made the ball swing in flight – though he still maintains he did – but it certainly changed direction sharply when it hit the floor and only a nimble sidestep by Tennant saved him an embarrassing injury.

As the acquaintanceship between both sides ripened, and it became obvious that the TCA modifications were improving the Viscount's prospects on the international market, much of the mutual suspicion evaporated, and TCA was well-served by the Viscount. It proved a highly efficient and popular aircraft and was in service for almost twenty years, during which only five were lost. Two crash-landed at Toronto without loss of life; one was hit while taxiing by a jet fighter taking off at Bagotville, Quebec, with the loss of one passenger and one crew member; another was hit by a runaway cargo aircraft on the ramp at New York; and the fifth was destroyed by an electrical fire at Sept-Iles, Quebec, with one passenger being killed during the evacuation. And on another occasion, a propeller came off in flight and sliced through the cabin, killing a passenger.

These tragic incidents apart, the plane McGregor fell in love with at first sight amply justified his faith; and it was widely acknowledged to be the most successful commercial aircraft ever built by a British manufacturer.

CHAPTER FIFTEEN

OME TIME TOWARD the end of 1953, Captain Kent Davis piloted a TCA cargo flight into New York. He was standing beside his aircraft while the ramp attendant struggled to open its cargo doors when an American Airlines pilot strolled by. Raising his eyebrows, the American asked Davis, "Did you fly that thing in here?" Davis admitted that he had, and the American followed up, "Did you make it yourself?"

His witticism was inspired by the ungainly conformation of the aircraft that had the shortest career of any to belong to the TCA fleet except perhaps the original Stearman biplane: the British-designed Bristol 170, Mark 31. The most conspicuous feature of the Bristol Freighter, as it was called, was a huge bulbous nose that opened down the middle and created an entrance large enough to admit a sizeable vehicle and permit easy handling of the six tons of cargo the aircraft could carry. Unfortunately, this feature made it look like a flying pollywog.

Ugly ducklings though they were, the Bristol Freighters had their admirers and they performed to the full satisfaction of some of their specialized purchasers. But they were totally unsuited to TCA's needs, having neither the speed nor the range required and being too expensive to operate. In fact, they lasted in the TCA fleet for only a couple of years, and Gordon McGregor's decision to buy three of them in 1952 seemed inexplicable to most people around the airline. McGregor, however, was by no means a man of frivolous impulses, and he had ordered them for a good reason: he had learned that CPA was about to file an application with the Air Transport Board for a licence to operate a transcontinental all-cargo service. His top aides, Herb Seagrim, Gordie Wood and Bill Harvey, agreed with him that even though there was no time for the kind of intensive comparison studies that preceded the choice of the Viscount, the purchase of an all-cargo aircraft, appropriately publicized, would be one way to fend off the threat represented by the CPA application.

TCA had carried air express traffic from its earliest days, even before it carried its first passengers. But air freight was a more gradual introduction, largely because of the restricted size of the early aircraft. After the war, with the arrival of the larger DC-3s, a special cargo department was set up under Howard Cotterell, the director of research and economic control,* and an attempt was made to drum up freight business. Some early successes were registered: fresh daffodils were flown from Victoria to the rest of the country for the Easter trade, and TCA salesmen persuaded some food stores in Montreal and Toronto to buy consignments of fresh fish and live lobsters from the east coast. This latter initiative was strongly discouraged by the existing frozen-fish packers; there were questions in the House that managed to convey the impression that the vast resources of the state were being improperly used to poach on the livelihoods of struggling fishermen, although the small, independent inshore fishermen who shipped their day's catch by air to the appreciative metropolitan markets presumably saw things from a different perspective.

Unfortunately, the cargo trade tended to be strongly one-directional and often seasonal, and it did not rank high on the airline's scale of priorities. In 1952, for instance, the combined revenue from air express and air freight contributed only $3.3 million to the year's total receipts of $55 million. Also, experience in the United States had shown that all-cargo aircraft were unprofitable unless they were war-surplus machines picked up at knock-down prices or had previously been fully depreciated in the passenger trade. So, with the exception of one all-cargo DC-3, TCA carried whatever cargo loads it was offered on its regular passenger flights; and it set the cargo rate high enough to restrict the business to levels it could comfortably handle.

The impression thus developed around the Air Transport Board, and in the mind of the cabinet minister responsible for it, Lionel Chevrier, that TCA was dragging its feet in the cargo field and not providing the Canadian public with the service to which it was entitled. McGregor's relationship with the ATB, and Chevrier, as Minister of Transport, was complicated by Howe's determination to retain responsibility for the airline whatever his portfolio at the time. In April 1952, McGregor dictated a reminder to himself:

Arrange appointment and call on Lionel Chevrier. R.A.C. Henry [a TCA director who had been one of Howe's most valued colleagues during the war and later become the

---

*As general traffic manager, McGregor thought this somewhat illogical, and as soon as he became president he relieved Cotterell of responsibility for the cargo section and transferred it into the traffic department.

first chairman of the ATB] says that Chevrier feels slighted by me because I have not discussed DOT air problems with him. Chevrier to be told that, rightly or wrongly, I follow the policy that I have only one proper contact with the government, which is through my minister.

The Air Transport Board was established in 1944 and its members, appointed by the government, were charged with advising the Minister of Transport on civil aviation matters and the licensing and economic regulation of commercial air services. Henry's successor as chairman was John R. Baldwin, who had been teaching history at McMaster University when he was recruited in 1942 as assistant secretary to the war committee of the cabinet. Baldwin, who went on to become deputy minister of transport and a leading Ottawa mandarin, was well versed in aviation matters. He had been closely involved in the wartime talks on postwar civil aviation, and later in life he was destined to become, for an unhappy and self-curtailed interlude, president of Air Canada. And he, too, was acutely aware of the "sacred cow" relationship under which the country's national airline reported not to his boss, the Minister of Transport, but to Howe.

So it was to Howe that Baldwin addressed a memorandum on April 15, 1950, saying that the ATB was being subjected to growing pressure from private air carriers wanting permission to fly bulk cargo that TCA either could not or would not carry. The two specific cases he mentioned involved a quantity of fish ten to fifteen times greater than TCA was then carrying, and the movement of bulk ore concentrates from western to eastern Canada.

Howe forwarded the memorandum to McGregor, saying in his covering letter: ". . . it seems to me that, if TCA is not prepared to handle [this] movement, which I understand to be the case, the Board should permit private industry to enter this field." Feeling himself under siege, McGregor replied to Howe saying he did not want to be a dog in the manger, but thought the board was overlooking one aspect of the public interest, in that if TCA was deprived of revenue by any attempt to satisfy the interests of "a comparatively small number of shippers and consignees," then "the interests of all taxpaying Canadians are adversely affected." The airline did not yet have the equipment to operate all-cargo flights, which in any case were not proving rewarding in the United States; but it was carrying an increasing amount of cargo on its passenger flights and "it is obvious that the loss of any cargo business which we are now enjoying would represent a direct loss in revenues and for that reason I most sincerely hope that the ATB will be given every encouragement to stave off the granting of any licences to air cargo operators on existing TCA routes or portions thereof.''

There was little comfort in Howe's reply:

I fully understand the objection to competition on TCA routes for cargo business. I will do what I can to hold off competition for another year, but I think that competition cannot be held off indefinitely, unless TCA wishes to solicit the business. It is certainly in the national interest to move all the fish into consumption by airplane that the market will absorb. . . . I am not enthusiastic about seeing TCA get into the cargo plane business, as I doubt if it is a money maker for the system. On the other hand, a private venture might be able to make a living by concentrating on the development of commodity movements.

In the event, Howe had a word with Baldwin and the threat was staved off for the moment, but the exchange increased the wariness with which McGregor regarded the chairman of the Air Transport Board. He had, in fact, complained about the board's activities in a letter to Howe a year earlier:

During recent months there has been an increasingly noticeable tendency on the part of the Air Transport Board to gradually assume the role of – as it were – a supernumerary management of TCA. TCA is being asked to answer more and more frequent questions as to whether it has considered this route, or that stop, this type of rate structure or that approach to a cost problem. Naturally, as a government company, TCA is ready and willing to supply answers to all such questions, and to abide strictly by all air rulings established by the Board. . . . but I would like you to know first of all, that there appears to me to be a trend toward an attempted split in the direct line of authority from you to TCA, and that secondly, I for one would very much welcome a return to the condition under which the Air Transport Board and at least the air branch of the Department of Transport were answerable to you, rather than another minister. It would seem to me that this arrangement would put the majority of Canada's air interests into one tidy package, under one well-informed and experienced head. It would certainly avoid the present condition of duplication of certain efforts and occasional conflicting interests as among the three units concerned.

Against this background, McGregor was concerned, but not unduly surprised, when Baldwin called him a few days before Christmas in 1951 and told him Grant McConachie had broached a plan for a transcontinental all-cargo service to both Howe and Chevrier, and that they seemed receptive to the idea. McGregor immediately consulted his most accessible board members, Herb Symington and Donald Gordon in Montreal, who required little persuasion to his view that McConachie, backed by the CPR, would regretfully but manfully shoulder any losses CPA sustained on its new service – just long enough to enable him to prepare a case for the ATB demonstrating that unless CPA's unused cargo space could be filled with passengers it would go broke. McGregor's fears were shared by Symington and Gordon – who also perceived a threat to the CNR's express revenue–and he wrote in protest to Howe: "It is perhaps unnecessary for me to say that this complete reversal of previously declared policy with respect to TCA main line operations produced in me a feeling of shock, and gravest concern for the financial future of this company."

Then, like any other well-schooled military commander under siege, he set about preparing his counter-attack: TCA's cargo rate was soon cut by 10 per cent, and shortly thereafter it was announced that the success of this "experiment" had encouraged the airline to follow it up with a further reduction of 30 per cent, bringing the rate down to the 20 cents per ton-mile CPA was proposing (a rate which, McConachie later confessed to a friend, would have cost him his shirt). And, of course, there were the three Bristol freighters on order. When they came into service – the previously valid arguments against all-cargo aircraft now seemingly forgotten – they would continue "the further orderly and steady development of commodity traffic throughout the TCA system."

The Air Transport Board's hearing on CPA's application did not take place until February 1953. In preparation for it, the board proposed to conduct hearings across the country to "assess the public attitude" – which, McGregor grumbled to Howe, was obviously a waste of money: "I can think of no municipality which, confronted with the question of whether it would like two air cargo services or one, would not unanimously vote for the two services."

In a none-too-subtle attempt to avoid the appearance of mounting the directly parallel competition with the national airline outlawed by sucessive governments, McConachie proposed to fly from Vancouver to Montreal and Toronto, with stops at Edmonton and, instead of Winnipeg, The Pas, in northern Manitoba. He magnanimously proposed to refrain from carrying traffic between Montreal and Toronto – which, as McGregor hastened to point out, was a short-haul run well served by rail connections and as such unprofitable for air cargo. In explanation for the stop at The Pas, McConachie claimed there were 21,000 pounds of fresh lake fish there every week around the year clamouring for speedy transmission to the markets of the east – only to have one of his own witnesses confess that the fish trade could not even carry the burden of railway express charges and as a result virtually all the area's fish moved in refrigerated trucks.

The hearing lasted three weeks, during which time Hugh O'Donnell, the lawyer who represented TCA in its intervention, managed to effectively demolish CPA's case. McConachie claimed there was a large untapped market; O'Donnell showed that even after TCA's rate reductions its five daily transcontinental flights carried enough cargo to fill only between 9 and 58 per cent of the space available, thus disposing of CPA's allegation that TCA was short of cargo space. O'Donnell also managed to show that CPA had considerably under-estimated the cost of its proposed service, and considerably over-estimated the amount of cargo available. In other words, CPA was deliberately planning to undertake an un-economic operation in order to get its foot in the transcontinental door. Furthermore, CPA had suggested that it would only encroach on TCA's revenue by at the most one-third of 1 per cent; this, said O'Donnell, was ridiculous, since if the new service took away only half of TCA's transcontinental cargo business it would cost the national airline about $400,000 in lost revenue.

Even though McGregor later claimed to have detected "a strangely partisan [meaning anti-TCA] attitude" attaching to the ATB, the committee of the cabinet which considered the board's recommendations decided it would not be in the public interest to issue the licence to CPA.

The CNR was not directly involved in the hearing, but its burly chairman and president, Donald Gordon, followed its progress with close interest. McGregor records in his memoirs that when he and Gordon first met as fellow members of the TCA board, "We started out regarding each other with the mutual suspicion of two bull mastiffs, but this quickly dissolved into friendship and trust." Their common Scottish ancestry may have forged a bond between the two men, though the more reserved McGregor would hold back on those convivial occasions when Gordon, as he often did, tried to prevail upon any fellow-Scot in his vicinity to join him in spirited renderings of such sentimental ballads of his native land as "My Ain Folk." Whether the alliance was formed around the board-room table or after hours, McGregor came to value Gordon's support and advice, and Gordon, though by vir-tue of his position he might technically have been considered the "owner" of the airline, never pulled rank. Once he had decided that McGregor belonged to his "ain folk," he was con-tent to leave him to run his own show – which he used to refer to around the railroad as "our rich relation."

The CPA application troubled Donald Gordon, not only because of its potential impact on his "rich relation" but also because of its possible effect on his own organization, whose financial plight he was struggling mightily to alleviate. "It seems apparent to me," he wrote to McGregor on February 20, 1953,

that we are now realizing the effects of a settled air policy on behalf of our Canadian Pacific friends aimed specifically at destroying the monopoly position of the TCA respecting trans-continental traffic. Coupled with this I also suspect that they have aimed their feeder airlines with the specific purpose in mind of tapping every point where the Canadian National had a preferred position. . . .

With this preamble I am wondering if TCA and CPR policy has been as farsighted as it might have been. As a general rule the defence of a monopoly position is not good fighting ground and I think the Canadian Pacific have again demonstrated this fact. In the process they have picked up what apparently were regarded as bad bargains by the TCA and have now woven them into an airline system which threatens to blanket Canada far more effectively than anything now possible by TCA. In other words, if the CPA succeeds in getting the trans-continental licence . . . they will produce a main-line plus feeder-line airline service, which will back TCA off the map. . . .

This brings me to another point which affects the relations between our two organizations. It is that I am of the view that our Canadian Pacific friends have a far greater sense of community of interest than exists between the combined organizations of the TCA and CNR. In other words, I believe that airline traffic policy – passenger and freight – and rail traffic policy in the Canadian Pacific orbit is considered solely on the basis of what is best for the community of effort being put forth by the Canadian Pacific family. I am not persuaded that such a clear principle exists between our organizations notwithstanding many discussions and meetings intended to bring that about.

In reply, McGregor readily agreed with Gordon's fears about Canadian Pacific's long-term designs. "I am convinced that at some point in the development of this country," he wrote, "there will be virtually complete airline competition. It seems equally certain that competition, when it does occur, will be uneconomic and will do little to improve the airline service to the public, unless TCA abuses its monopoly. These opinions cause me to hope that east-west competition may be fought off for many years to come, not only in order that the economic deterioration may be deferred as long as possible, but because the longer competition is deferred the better TCA will be able to meet it when it comes." He agreed also with Gordon's thesis that "our defence must by the very nature of things be a rear guard type of action." He protested, however, that

it is not correct to say that Canadian Pacific Air Lines has picked up "what were regarded by the CNR and TCA [Gordon had mentioned only TCA] as bad bargains" in the way of air routes and made a go of them. In the first place, TCA's function was and is, clearly defined, as a main line and international carrier. . . . In other words,

TCA has stuck to the job which it was given, while CPA continues to make passes at that same job.

Furthermore, I am firmly convinced that CPA has not been an economically sound operation in its own right, since its inception. The company shows black figures, but as I think you know, this is only achieved by the Canadian Pacific Railway carrying a very high proportion of the airline's overhead, plus a substantial amount of the airline's direct operating costs. . . . In other words, as you suggest, the railway company is strongly subsidizing its airline. I do not think this is a healthy situation, and I would be the last to suggest that the CNR should behave in a similar manner toward TCA, even if our meticulous accounting procedures and our responsibility to the government would permit it. The fact remains, however, that with one airline required to shun routes which will obviously be uneconomical for at least several years to come in order to maintain a sound financial position, and the other airline at liberty, perhaps even encouraged, to indulge in "brave" experiments of this kind, TCA will always be open to criticism of over-cautiousness in the matter of route development.

The question of the degree of co-operation—or the lack thereof—between the parent railroad and its precocious child had always been a ticklish one. In the earliest days, the friendly links Bill English and Fred Wood retained with their erstwhile colleagues on the railroad eased many of the frictions that were bound to occur in the enforced wedlock of two competing modes of transportation. But the railroad's vice-president in charge of passenger traffic, Alistair Fraser, when it was first suggested to him that TCA should be given a front spot in the railroad's ticket offices, rebelled. "No sir," he is recollected as saying, "my men will sell railroad tickets first, last and *only*." As late as 1947, R.C. Vaughan, Gordon's predecessor at the head of the CNR, wrote to Fraser saying that while it was obvious that the railroad would lose some business to the airline, "We would have no better luck in stopping it than the stage coach proprietors had in their efforts to stifle early steam railroads." In the meantime, Fraser should reflect that besides the somewhat arbitrary fee of $50,000 a year that the airline paid for what were described as "administrative services" rendered by the CNR, "we derive something like $400,000 of freight revenue a year from the movement of gasoline and other supplies for the airline; TCA is paying Canadian National Telegraphs in excess of $250,000 a year; and by and large the annual payment we receive from the airline in freight, express and passenger charges, for departmental services rendered by the Railway and other sundry items, runs to more than $800,000 a year, and I am sure there are indirect revenues which it is difficult to segregate."

By 1952, when the perennial question of the divorce of the

railroad and the airline was being considered again, it was estimated that over and above its $750,000 interest payment the airline bolstered CN revenues by at least $2 million. This figure covered such things as teletype rentals ($429,456), CN's handling of TCA's air express consignments ($279,000), TCA's rent for CNR-owned office space ($124,456) – and $55,000 in commissions to CN passenger agents who went on selling airline tickets notwithstanding their boss's disapproval.

On their part, the early TCA people, gung-ho about the endless horizons of their new form of transportation, tended to write off as old fogies the railroad men with whom they were continually thrown into contact on administrative matters. McGregor himself was dismayed when, having assumed the presidency of the airline, he was introduced to the comptroller he perforce had to share with the railroad, Harold Cooper, who greeted him with a dampening welcome: "I certainly hope you don't have any silly ideas like Mr. Vaughan, that a Canadian transportation enterprise can be operated at a profit."

When the airline was founded, it seemed entirely logical in the interests of economy not to duplicate a number of departments unconnected with the flying of aeroplanes that already existed within the railroad; these included all the various legal, corporate secretarial, financial, insurance and claims and medical services indispensable to a large corporation. As the airline grew it became obvious that if its management was to have effective control over its destiny it would have to take over most, if not all, of these functions. But in the absence of the divorce envisaged by the government during the war, the separation came only gradually.

The airline set up its own architectural department in 1948 – though this was one of the departments whose work McGregor came to think might better be contracted to outside firms. That same year, the experienced public relations man Rod MacInnes switched over from CN. (McGregor had to enlist Howe's aid to prevent him being appropriated by the Defence Minister, Brooke Claxton.) The airline's purchasing remained in the hands of the railroad until 1951, by which time it had become clear that the CN men, however well versed they were in the acquisition of locomotives and steel rail, knew less about the attributes of aircraft than TCA's own staff, and a new TCA purchasing and stores department was set up under Howard Cotterell. A year later, Bill Harvey became comptroller and took over the airline's accounting from the CN.

In later years, as its growth continued, the airline acquired its own legal counsel and gradually took over most of the other services performed for it by the railroad. But as late as 1976 the CN was still performing some of the functions of its corporate secretariat, such as filing the minutes of directors' meetings. And even the changes in the TCA Act in 1977, under which the airline's shares were transferred from the railway to the government, did not complete the divorce: until the end of 1981, Air Canada's flight crews were checked out by an aviation medical specialist who received his pay cheque from the CNR.

CHAPTER SIXTEEN

HE 1950s WERE YEARS OF dizzying development for TCA, years during which the airline came of age and took its place as the seventh largest in the world. Between 1951 and 1960 the number of passengers carried and the operating revenues earned more than tripled. In 1951, the airline carried 973,337 passengers; in 1960 it carried 3.4 million. Operating revenues rose from $47.9 million in 1951 to $148.9 million in 1960, and the number of passenger miles flown sky-rocketed from 545 million to 3.1 billion.

During the same period, the number of employees only doubled –from 5,512 to 11,284–and fares, even though the general cost of living had begun the upward spiral that eventually led into the stratosphere, actually fell. The one-way fare between Montreal and Vancouver, which had stood at $181.40 since 1949, was reduced to $175 in 1958, thanks partly to the economies of scale afforded by the increased traffic and partly to the increasingly streamlined operations of the airline, whose efficiency improved as its experience grew. The reduction in the cost of Canadian air travel (U.S. fares were rising at the time) was furthered by the introduction into what had been an all first-class service of tourist fares; they were introduced on the Atlantic route in 1952, in response to pressure by the U.S. airlines in IATA, and extended to the domestic routes in 1954. The one-way Montreal to Vancouver tourist fare was set at $145 when it was inaugurated; in 1958 it was cut to $123. Family discounts and other incentive fares introduced as experiments to keep the planes filled also contributed to the downward trend, and taking the 1949 cost of living index as 100, average fares in 1960 had dropped to 93, while the general cost of living had mounted to almost 130.

But the most significant development of 1960 was the introduction of the company's first full jet aircraft, the DC-8, each one of which, cruising at 550 miles per hour, could do the work of four Super-Constellations, which cruised at 310 miles per hour. The DC-8 made its maiden transcontinental flight on April 1, which fittingly was the twenty-first anniversary of TCA's first transcontinental passenger flight; it reduced the flight time between Montreal and Vancouver from nine hours, fifteen minutes to just over five hours. Transatlantic service began on June 1, reducing the travel time from Montreal to London from eleven hours, ten minutes to six hours. Thanks to the unrivalled speed and comfort of the new jets, they flew with consistently high loads; and because of their size – the first models carried 127 passengers – and their relatively low maintenance costs, they lived up to the prediction that they would substantially reduce the all-important operating cost per seat-mile.

The decision to buy the DC-8 had been taken years earlier, before the aircraft had even been built, which had made it something of a gamble. Aircraft selection, never a simple matter, confronted all the airlines with some agonizing decisions in the mid-fifties. Piston-engined aircraft were obviously destined to be shouldered out by either turbo-props or full jets, and the first airlines to re-equip with turbine-powered fleets – though at enormous capital expense – would reap an instant competitive advantage, in both operating costs and passenger appeal. But it was not yet clear how many types of turbine aircraft would come on to the market, or what their characteristics would be.

The British had been first in the pure-jet field with the Comet, but TCA had not bought it because its range was thought too short for the Atlantic and Jack Dyment, as chief engineer, considered its metal skin too fragile to withstand the speeds and pressures to which it would be subjected. After two BOAC Comets broke up in the air, later models were considerably strengthened, but neither the Comet nor the French Caravelle, which first flew in 1955, was deemed suited to TCA's long-distance routes. The American builders had been slower to commit themselves to the jet contest, but Boeing flew the prototype of the world's second jet airliner, its 707, in 1954, by which time Douglas had announced its entry into the stakes with the DC-8.

At TCA, the study groups got out their slide rules and set up their blackboards once again. When they were first exposed to the DC-8, in 1954, it amounted to only a set of preliminary drawings. By 1955, plans were more advanced, and Pan Am sent a shudder of apprehension through the executive suites of the other airlines by ordering twenty-one DC-8s and twenty Boeing 707s, at a price of more than $5 million each.

The task of those trying to choose the aircraft best suited to their own requirements was further complicated by the fact that all the engines available to the U.S. manufacturers were in military use and thus shrouded in official secrecy. Douglas could only tell the TCA engineers they had three engines available, and give them an outline of the DC-8's projected performance – such basics as its fuel consumption, cruising speed and range – according to which engine was chosen. In the absence of specific information on the engines' characteristics, the TCA study groups were unable to make the more detailed calculations essential to the selection process.

Faced with buying an unprecedentedly expensive pig in a poke, TCA once again began to investigate the possibilities of a "hybrid" aircraft, and Clayton Glenn was assigned to develop a performance specification for an up-rated version of the existing Rolls-Royce Conway engine which could be used to power the DC-8 or 707. To do so he needed to know the aircraft's basic drag, which the manufacturers refused to reveal in case anyone, working backwards, could deduce the secrecy-shrouded performance details of the various engines. Glenn solved his problem with a little impromptu industrial espionage. He was visiting Douglas's head performance engineer one day and noticed on his desk, not quite tucked out of sight, the drag curves for the DC-8; fortuitously, the engineer stepped out for a moment to talk to a colleague, whereupon Glenn sneaked a look at the curves and with his practised eye for a drawing quickly noted some of the critical points. Later, in his hotel room, he was able to reconstruct the information he needed, from which he went on to estimate the performance characteristics of one of the potential engines, the Pratt & Whitney J75, which Rolls-Royce was eventually able to match in the Conway.

Gordon McGregor knew that if TCA was to have a full jet in operation as soon as one could be delivered, in 1960, he must place his order in the spring of 1956. So early that year a TCA team headed by Herb Seagrim, who had become vice-president, operations, on Bill English's retirement, visited the Douglas and Boeing plants. By now, after exhaustive internal studies embracing everything from passenger traffic forecasts to the state of the Canadian economy and the likelihood of future wage increases, it had been decided that TCA should complete the transition to turbines begun with the acquisition of the short-haul Viscount by adding two other types: for long-distance routes, a full jet aircraft such as the DC-8 or Boeing 707, with at least 120 seats, a cruising speed of 550 miles per hour and a range of 5,500 miles; and an intermediate-range turbine aircraft, either full jet or turbo-prop, seating from 60 to 80 passengers, having a cruising speed of 400 miles an hour and a range of 2,400 miles.

Boeing, which had already built the B-47 and B-52 for the military, had more practical experience than Douglas with the swept-back wing design necessitated aerodynamically by the high speed of the jets. But its last civilian aircraft, the piston-engined Stratocruiser, had not been a spectacular success. Douglas, on the other hand, had an excellent record for civilian transports. On paper, even though the 707 was flying and the DC-8 was still on the drawing board, there was little to choose between them: with the same engines, the two aircraft were forecast to have virtually the same speed, range, payload and seating capacity; they were expected to cost the same price, burn the same amount of fuel and have the same direct operating costs.

In such a close contest, it was perhaps unfortunate for Boeing that when the TCA team visited Seattle its engineering department was in the throes of moving house and the TCA engineers were unable to find the Boeing counterparts able to answer their questions adequately. They left with a jaundiced view of the Boeing operation and went on to Douglas, where they were welcomed by old friends with whom they had worked before. Douglas at that time had an excellent reputation for its follow-up "product support" engineering, and that was one of the factors that influenced TCA's decision in the spring of 1956 to order its first four DC-8s and place an option for two more. Similarly, there was little to choose between the Rolls-Royce and Pratt & Whitney engines, but TCA decided to put the Conway in its DC-8s because it was expected to be somewhat cheaper than the J75, considerably lighter, and probably less noisy.*

The selection of the medium-range aircraft proved to be even more difficult. This would be the backbone of TCA's fleet, plying its highest-density traffic routes, and McGregor did not feel qualified to make the choice when the order was placed for the DC-8. Originally, there were several contenders, including the British Bristol Britannia, a four-engined turbo-prop that was eventually flown by BOAC and CPA, among other airlines; but the Bristol Aircraft Company was at that time three years behind in its deliveries and the Britannia was considered to be too expensive, both to buy and to operate, and too big for TCA's requirements. The TCA engineers were still wary of the Comet, and the two-engined French-built Caravelle was unable to fulfil one of their basic design requirements—the ability to fly non-stop from Toronto to Calgary.

---

*TCA's first eleven DC-8s were all equipped with the Conway, and Alitalia ordered it in their DC-8s, as did BOAC in their 707s; but for its later purchases TCA switched to the new and more powerful Pratt & Whitney JT3D.

The choice had narrowed down to two four-engined turbo-props, the Lockheed Electra and the Vickers Vanguard, when three American companies – Douglas, Convair and Boeing – announced that they were developing full-jet aircraft designed for the medium-range market. McGregor therefore postponed his decision until more information was available about their plans.

The Electra – the name had nostalgic echoes of TCA's early days – was intended to be powered with engines built by the Allison division of General Motors; but on an inspection trip Glenn and his fellow engineer Phil Whittingstall were not impressed by the Allison engine and recommended that if the Electra were to be considered it should be powered by the Rolls-Royce RB-109 engine, later called the Tyne. This was the engine destined for the Vanguard, which could carry 102 passengers in an all-economy version and 92 passengers in mixed first and economy class, against the Electra's 87 in all-economy and 74 in mixed class. The Tyne-powered Electra promised to be slightly faster than the Vanguard, cruising at 430 miles per hour to the Vanguard's 410. And the prices for the two planes were similarly close: $2.7 million for the Vanguard and $2.9 million for the Electra.

The price of the full jets – which included the Convair Skylark, or 880, and a scaled-down version of Douglas's DC-8 called the DC-9, quite different from the DC-9 flying today – promised to be at least $1 million higher. Furthermore, at that stage of their development there were serious doubts about the operating economy of full jets on the kind of routes TCA planned for them. Eventually the renewed comparative studies showed the Vanguard coming out on top of all contenders by a wide margin on purchase price and on lowest direct operating costs. It also had space for a substantial 1,500 cubic feet of cargo under its main deck – a good selling point, since the Post Office had complained that the Viscount sometimes could not carry a full load of mail. There was also the matter of Rolls-Royce's generous warranty terms and George Edwards's demonstrated willingness to go to any lengths to adapt Vickers' products to TCA's requirements. So in November 1956, the airline ordered twenty Vanguards for delivery in late 1960 and early 1961.

With the make-up of his fleet set for years to come, McGregor now had to consider arrangements for its overhaul and maintenance, which was one of the airline's major operating expenses. Obviously, more complex and much larger overhaul facilities would be needed than now existed in Winnipeg: but where should they be built? With the advent of faster equipment able to serve the country's major cities directly without intermediate stops, would it any longer make economic sense to route aircraft to a city that did not generate much traffic merely to have them serviced?

The problem was handed to the Canadian branch of a well-known U.S. consulting firm, Wallace Clark, which was commissioned to study the airline's existing overhaul and maintenance system and make recommendations for its most efficient and economical operation over the next twenty years. In its report, submitted on May 31, 1957, Wallace Clark advised against any attempt to expand the existing plant to cope with the entirely new work expected when the jets took over. One consolidated new base, it said, would offer the most satisfactory industrial layout and the best opportunities for future expansion, and it should be located at "one of the two centres of population and traffic in the East." The Winnipeg base would still be needed until the transition from Constellations and North Stars to the DC-8s and Vanguards was complete. Whether the Viscount work should be moved from Winnipeg to the new base depended on their retirement date; if they were to remain in service until 1963 the Winnipeg base should be closed and the whole fleet serviced at the new base.

That the new base was eventually built at Montreal, rather than Toronto – which some thought should have been the centre of TCA's operations – has sometimes been ascribed, like the headquarters move in 1949, to McGregor's affection for his home town, which had not yet been displaced as the business and financial capital of Canada. But Montreal was recommended by Wallace Clark for several reasons: "The choice between Toronto and Montreal is strongly influenced by the aircraft routing scheme for trans-Atlantic flights. . . . The airport developments at the two cities must be taken into consideration. There has been some discussion of a new airport at Toronto, with Malton being given over to the military. . . . The difficulty is that an early decision may not be made regarding the future use of the airport, and since you cannot risk building at the wrong one, you may delay your decision longer than would be advisable. . . ." Also, during the transitional period from the piston engines to the jets, workers would have to be retrained, supervisors' duties and responsibilities might sometimes overlap, and the inevitable difficulties would be accentuated if the airline's technical staff were dispersed over three bases: "These problems will exist under any circumstances, but will be greatly magnified under a condition requiring establishment of a new facility at a location remote from existing operations." All in all, it was decided, the uncertainties surrounding Toronto were not outweighed by any tangible economic advantages in its favour.

When the report came before TCA's board of directors, W.J. "Bill" Parker, a prominent Winnipeg businessman and World War I pilot, loyally pleaded his home town's cause. The closing of the base would be a grave setback to the city's economy – and after the warning shots heard at the time of the headquarters move, the directors did not need to be reminded that it would create a political furore. To soften the blow, the directors therefore decided to retain the Winnipeg base to maintain the Viscount fleet, even though the report estimated that this would cost an extra $1 million a year.

McGregor broke the news of the company's decision to build its new $20 million "consolidated maintenance and overhaul, engineering and stores facility" at Dorval airport to a mass meeting of all the workers concerned in No. 2 Hangar at Winnipeg's Stevenson Field on October 28, 1957. The overhaul work being done on the DC-3s and North Stars would of course be phased out as those aircraft were retired "in accordance with the overall fleet plan," but the base would continue to do all work on the Viscounts, and the work load would not decrease since the twenty-nine Viscounts then in service would be joined by twenty-two more by the spring of 1959. When the new base was completed late in 1959 some "numerically small specialized functions consisting of Engineering Laboratory, Instrument and ancillary equipment overhaul" would be transferred there from Winnipeg in the interest of efficiency and the avoidance of expensive duplication of effort, but "considerably under 100 workers" would be affected.

"Company plans which are finalized through 1961," McGregor said, "provide for no other transfer of work from the Winnipeg base to the planned Dorval base." Dorval was the logical site for the new base since it would be the terminus of most of the DC-8 and Vanguard flights, and the new plant would be doing only work not at present being carried on by TCA. "It is impossible to foresee what fluctuations may occur in the Maintenance and Overhaul work load from year to year," McGregor concluded, "but it is not expected that there will be any reduction in the personnel requirement at the Winnipeg base over the period covered by the plan."

The assembled workers, who had been disturbed by rumours that their base was going to be closed, were reassured by their boss's statement. It looked as though their jobs were safe. With all those new Viscounts on the way, their ultimate obsolescence seemed a distant prospect, and even then, no doubt they would continue to work on whichever newer aircraft supplanted them. Few seemed to see any particular menace in the last sentence of McGregor's speech, his reference to "the period covered by the plan"; nor did they seem to link it with his earlier reference to the company's plans being "finalized through 1961," which was only four years away.

This point was seized upon, however, by the *Winnipeg Free Press*, which said the decision was "merely another step in what appears to be a long-term policy of the airline eventually to move as much as possible of its ground operations away to Montreal." The loss of jobs and industry was a serious matter for the city and the province as a whole, and the writer wondered why the area's members of Parliament had not raised it with the minister responsible.

By now, that minister was no longer C.D. Howe. On June 10, 1957, Clarence Decatur Howe, who had damaged himself more than he realized when he rammed the trans-Canada gas pipeline legislation through the House, was defeated in the riding he had held for twenty-two years by a then-unknown history teacher named Douglas Fisher, of the CCF. Howe was not the only one in his party to feel the electors' displeasure, and the Progressive Conservatives under John Diefenbaker took office with 112 seats to the Liberals' 105. And within a month, responsibility for Trans-Canada Air Lines was officially transferred from the Minister of Trade and Commerce to the new Minister of Transport, a handsome former Toronto Argonaut football player and British Empire boxing champion, George Hees.

The departure from the scene of "Mr. Airline" was widely regretted within TCA, but the man who had done more to build Canada's industrial capacity than any other was not permitted to leave public life without some press carping. Gordon McGregor was incensed at an editorial in the Toronto *Globe and Mail* which said Howe had shown genius only in "the constant enlargement of his own power." Much more to McGregor's taste was an editorial in the *Montreal Star* which saluted Howe as "a very great figure, a man of vast talent and ability," and complained about the criticism to which he was being subjected by "the little dogs barking at his heels."

McGregor learned from his public relations man, Rod MacInnes, that the *Star*'s tribute had been written by its eminent editor, the former Winnipegger George Ferguson, and wrote to congratulate him on providing an adequate rebuttal to the "revolting and dishonest" attack in the *Globe and Mail*. "The author of that filth," he wrote,

included in the rest of his garbage a statement to the effect that now that they were free to speak, the officers of TCA would reveal the whims of C.D. Howe under which they had been forced to work. It is unnecessary, I think, for me to tell you that the only "whim" of C.D. Howe's with respect to TCA which he ever conveyed to the company through me, was an adominition to keep out of the red, as did every other well-run business. While on occasion he criticized decisions taken, on no occasion during my time as president did he ever attempt to interfere with the selection of aircraft type, the selection of airframe or engine manufacturer, the number of air-craft ordered, the new route applications made, or any other matter which lay within the jurisdiction of the company's officers or its board of directors.

In later years, he would frequently lament the failure of subsequent ministers of transport to live up to his ideal.

CHAPTER SEVENTEEN

SOON AFTER HOWE'S DEFEAT, the board of directors of TCA resolved unanimously that for old times' sake he should be permitted to retain his airline pass, numbered "One," the first ever issued. But when the Air Transport Board, as required, was asked to approve the resolution, it demurred: the airline was asked to spare all concerned possible embarrassment by withdrawing the request, which it was feared would anger the new powers-that-be in Ottawa. McGregor indignantly refused to toe this line and the matter went all the way up to the new Minister of Transport. In due course, McGregor was able to forward the pass – which Howe in his retirement called his proudest possession – and a covering letter saying George Hees had promptly approved its reissue with the comment: "Nobody deserves one more."

From McGregor's point of view, the honeymoon did not last long. The Tories had made much during the election campaign of the old-fashioned virtues of private enterprise and free competition, in the air and elsewhere, with the implication that the dictatorial C.D. Howe and his Liberal colleagues were bent on stifling them in favour of state monopolies. Hees, a comfortably prosperous businessman, certainly shared his party's views on this topic, then and twenty-five years later, when he told the author: "There is nothing that keeps a company straighter than competition: if you own a factory that turns out things nobody wants, or charges prices higher than the guy down the road, you're going to go to the wall."

Hees was a conspicuously public figure, and it seemed to him he couldn't walk through an airport without being button-holed by some traveller with a complaint about the iniquitous treatment he had suffered at the hands of the nation's airline. "Under C.D. Howe," Hees recalled, "TCA got everything it asked for; it was a complete spoiled child. And if the public didn't like their service, the public had no alternative but to take the train. I got a lot of complaints from the public." One of those complaints was that the airline deliberately over-booked flights to keep its aircraft as full as possible, and that its passenger agents displayed a lofty disregard for the plight of anyone "de-planed" as a result. Soon after he took over his portfolio, Hees raised this apparent failing with McGregor.

McGregor replied with a categorical denial that TCA ever deliberately over-booked a flight. True, all airlines were plagued by the problem of "no-shows" – passengers who booked reservations but then failed to take up their seats. In the United States, their numbers had recently reached the "shocking figure" of 125 per thousand. An airline's stock-in-trade, of course, is the seats it sells. But seats are not like widgets, in that they cannot be stock-piled in an inventory until there is a demand for them: whenever an aircraft takes off with an empty seat, the revenue it represents is lost forever. McGregor told Hees it was often suggested that a passenger who didn't claim his seat should be charged for it anyway; but TCA felt it was prohibited by law from charging for a service that had not been rendered. In self-defence many airlines did sell more seats than were available on their flights, confident that the surplus passengers could be accommodated in seats left vacant by no-shows. While TCA was not one of them, "deplanements through oversales do occur, to the extent of approximately 1.5 passengers per thousand bookings." This was considerably better than the industry average in the United States, and only to be expected, since the complex process of making 1.25 million bookings a year afforded so many opportunities for delayed "stop-sale" orders, mislaid teletype messages, and sundry human errors by travel agents or TCA's own staff. As for the complaint of discourtesy by the latter: "TCA as a public utility is more dependent on good customer relations than are most other forms of business. All levels of the company organization are fully alive to this fact, are given special training on the subject of treatment of passengers, and, with their own knowledge, a substantial proportion of the contacts between Sales Department employees and the public are observed and recorded." (This inspection and monitoring system, of which McGregor was very proud, had been adopted as a result of his prewar experience with Bell Telephone.)

The day after McGregor wrote to Hees, Donald Gordon told him he had received a call from John Baldwin, now Hees's deputy minister, saying that the minister was under pressure from his cabinet colleagues to implement a new air policy, including competition; that TCA did not seem to have volunteered any suggestions to this end; and would it be a good idea if they did?

McGregor and Gordon agreed this "might be a method by which it would be made to appear that TCA came up with some suggestions about competition off its own bat." Having no desire to connive in the accomplishment of their own demise, they decided Baldwin's suggestion should be "treated with extreme care, and certainly not complied with unless there was a formal written request."

Baldwin later that day also called McGregor, who noted in a memo recording the call: "I said that TCA's position vis-à-vis competition was as it always had been and was based on the known economics of civil aviation in Canada, that anybody who studied the matter would find that only on the very high density route legs, such as Vancouver-Victoria, and perhaps Montreal-Toronto, could duplicated air services be intelligently considered." In a covering note to Gordon which he forwarded with his memo on August 16, McGregor said: "I felt it might be wise to have a confidential record of this beginning of what might be a very controversial subject. As in your case, Baldwin seemed flustered and under stress over the phone. . . ."

McGregor believed that the demand for air transportation, while it continued to grow pleasingly every year, was nevertheless limited, and that any private airline permitted to compete on one of TCA's profitable routes would be taking money out of his pocket. (He was not naive enough to imagine that a private airline would apply for one of the lightly travelled unprofitable routes social policy compelled the national airline to operate, under the process known as "cross-subsidization.") He had been fighting a rearguard action to protect TCA's revenues ever since CPA slipped its foot in the door on the Pacific. For, despite all his protests, the Liberal government had since 1952 granted McConachie permission to fly from Vancouver to Mexico* and Lima, Peru; then on to Buenos Aires, Argentina, and Santiago,

---

*McConachie had negotiated for this service directly with the Mexican government, observing the local custom of paving the way to an agreement by the judicious distribution to selected recipients of handsome gifts, in this case Cadillac limousines. The Mexican custom of *mordida* was abhorrent to the high-principled McGregor and he refused to countenance it. TCA's negotiations for the Toronto-Mexico service, following agreement between the two governments, thus encountered numerous frustrating delays, and TCA did not begin to fly the route until January 1954. The U.S. government permitted the necessary refuelling stop at Tampa but denied TCA the right to carry passengers from there, and the route was never profitable. In the meantime, the federal government, responding to demands for TCA service by local businessmen, had been pressing McGregor to open a service from Montreal to Quebec City and the North Shore of the St. Lawrence. McGregor protested that this would parallel a long-standing CPA route and invite CPA applications to parallel TCA routes. The problem was solved in November 1955, when TCA exchanged its Toronto-Mexico route for CPA's North Shore route.

Chile; then from Vancouver to Amsterdam – which McGregor regarded much more seriously as an uneconomic route which would nonetheless impinge on both TCA's transcontinental and transatlantic services; and lastly from Toronto and Montreal to Lisbon and Madrid–which he opposed as another route unprofitable in itself but bound to hurt TCA's traffic to Europe. Now, with a new government in power, it seemed he must spend his whole life fighting rearguard actions, all in the misguided interest of what he regarded as the mere shibboleth of "competition."

He had already addressed the question of the alleged TCA monopoly in a memorandum to the Liberal government, and he readily gave Baldwin permission to show it to Hees. Far from being a monopoly, he had said, TCA was exposed to competition on more than 85 per cent of its route mileage. On the transcontinental, for instance, CPA competed between Calgary and Vancouver and Edmonton and Saskatoon, and Canadian passengers also used gateways such as Seattle, Chicago and New York to cross the continent by U.S. carriers, with little difference in fares and the added advantage of stopovers in New York and Chicago if they desired. There was also direct competition between TCA and U.S. carriers on the Toronto–New York and Montreal–New York runs; likewise there was competition on all of TCA's southern routes to Bermuda, the Caribbean and Florida; and on the transatlantic, quite apart from CPA's indirect competition, TCA faced head-on competition into and out of Montreal from BOAC, KLM, and Air France.

In his later years, McGregor expounded his airline philosophy in an interview with the popular Montreal editor and columnist Frank Lowe. Drawing on his only previous business experience, which was in another regulated industry, he likened TCA to Bell:

There is a tendency on the part of people to regard monopoly as a bad thing; they believe if there is competition the service is going to be better and the price lower. And aviation, in my opinion, and telephony, are two industries that disprove this belief. . . . For example, if you have two telephone services, your corner grocer is going to have duplication of phone service in his little shop so his customers can reach him. You'll have two sets of poles up every back alley – great duplication, increase in costs, less convenient service. . . .

Who would think of having a municipality with two sources of lighting supply, or two sources of sewage disposal, or even two sources of garbage collecting? This doesn't make very good sense. . . . Generally speaking, a country's civil aviation needs can be better served by one organization than two or more working against each other. And I can show you examples where duplication of effort and facilities resulting from competitive service all tend to increase the end cost of the product, and therefore increase the cost to the consumer.

He found it strange, McGregor told Lowe, that the many governments around the world that owned airlines were invariably prone to confront them with competition. Lowe interjected at this point to ask "Why?" and McGregor replied:

If you wanted to be terribly cynical you could say that a government organization cannot contribute to war chests, and others can. This may be far too cynical an attitude to take. . . . But I would think that a strictly honest political view should be that a government would move heaven and earth to protect the interests of the airline which is its property, providing of course that the airline is showing that it is doing a satisfactory job of serving the needs of the nationals of the country. . . .

McGregor was by no means the first to voice such sentiments: the merits, or otherwise, of state versus private enterprise can be – and have been – argued ad infinitum in Canada. Herschel Hardin, the west coast writer and broadcaster, saw the criticism of TCA and the perceived need to smarten it up by confronting it with competition as a manifestation of a colonial mentality, a chronic lack of confidence in purely Canadian enterprise: "The hardest flying that TCA ever had to do was through thick ideological fog."[*]

Others besides Hardin attributed the gradual whittling away of TCA's exclusive mandate to a doctrinaire belief in competition for competition's sake. There are frequent references in TCA's files to the alleged pressure Hees was under from "anti-TCA" members of the cabinet, though he himself denies there were any such. And in his memoirs McGregor seems to saddle Hees with more than his share of the blame for what he came to call the "depredations" to which the national airline was subjected; after all, the Pacific and so many other international "give-aways" (another term that gained universal currency within TCA) had been bestowed upon CPA by the Liberal government which had originally established the monopoly, and blessings continued to flow to the private airlines from post-Diefenbaker Liberal administrations. In fact, Canada would have been unique in the western world had it preserved a state monopoly of aviation. Even in Britain, after all its experiments with socialism and nationalization, the state-owned British Airways (successor to BOAC and British European Airways) faces competition from more than forty other airlines.

---

[*]*A Nation Unaware: The Canadian Economic Culture* (Vancouver: J.J. Douglas, 1974).

For whatever reason, the Diefenbaker government appeared intent on clipping the wings of the national airline, though when Hees wrote to McGregor on September 30, 1957, outlining his "tentative decisions" on the proposed new aviation policy and inviting his comments, McGregor felt that "it did not seem unreasonable." (John Baldwin, who as deputy minister presumably contributed much to the new minister's sudden grasp of the intricacies of civil aviation, thought in retrospect that within cabinet Hees often protected the airline against what might have been worse depredations if some of his colleagues had prevailed.)

A week later, in his reply to the minister's letter, McGregor professed to welcome the first item in the new policy, which was that "in the major international field, TCA and CPA should both continue to expand their international operations without, however, engaging in direct competition one with the other. Each should be on equal footing as far as governmental approval of route applications is concerned, and applications from each should be treated on their respective merits without a preferred position being accorded to either of them."

McGregor said he was "delighted" with this:

With the exception of the short extensions of its London service to Dusseldorf and Paris, TCA has had no permanent additions to its international route pattern during the last eight years, while many important routes of this character have been assigned to CPA. The result is that today CPA is operating unduplicated international routes of 33,922 miles, as compared with TCA's 14,682. We in the company had begun to fear that a policy had been adopted but undeclared, which contemplated CPA as the Pan American of Canada. . . . Under these circumstances I cannot tell you how relieved and encouraged we in TCA are to be assured that it is your intention to move toward equalization in the future assignment of international routes as between the two Canadian carriers.

Another point in the new policy was that "In the international field generally, some greater flexibility in our bilateral agreements and in offering concessions may be desirable if we are to achieve the additional rights we wish for TCA and CPA. This could apply in the matter of granting 5th freedom rights and in the matter of designating additional Canadian gateways where necessary (other than Montreal and Vancouver). . . ."

This was a reference to the so-called "five freedoms" adopted by the International Civil Aviation Organization after the early attempt to reach a multilateral international agreement failed. The system of exchanging international routes became a matter for negotiation between the two countries concerned, with each granting the other, subject to mutual agreement:

1. the privilege to fly across its territory without landing;
2. the privilege to land for non-traffic purposes;
3. the privilege to put down passengers, mail and cargo taken on in the territory of the state whose nationality the aircraft possesses;
4. the privilege to take on passengers, mail and cargo destined for the territory of the state whose nationality the aircraft possesses; and
5. the privilege to take on passengers, mail and cargo destined for the territory of any other contracting state and the privilege to put down passengers, mail and cargo coming from any such territory.

The international horse-trading involved in so-called bilateral negotiations often goes on for years, and the fifth freedom, of course, is the most coveted, and most jealously guarded, of all: as an example, a European airline given fifth-freedom rights at Montreal can pick up Canadian passengers there on a flight terminating at, say, Chicago, thus entering into direct competition for domestic traffic with any Canadian airline authorized to fly from Montreal to Chicago. Since the negotiation is between governments, it is handled for Canada by the Department of External Affairs, and McGregor felt that the representatives of that department, bent on preserving Canada's "good guy" image, were often sadly unaware of the commercial value of the rights they were prepared to disburse.

Likewise in the matter of gateways, the airport at which a flight originates or terminates is a key point in bilateral negotiations, and more important to a country the size of Canada than to a small country such as Britain. When all transatlantic flights terminated at Montreal, TCA automatically inherited most of the passengers destined for other Canadian destinations. A foreign airline given rights to land at Toronto or Winnipeg, say, would thus deprive TCA of a considerable amount of internal traffic.

Reminding Hees of these complications, McGregor warned him that there could be occasions when a proposal made in bilateral negotiations might be advantageous to one of Canada's international airlines but highly disadvantageous to the other, in which cases due thought should be given to "the over-all value or lack of value to Canada as a whole." To illustrate his point, he cited bilateral negotiations with Italy which had broken down some years earlier when, in return for admitting TCA to Rome, the Italians had made the "ridiculous" demand for fifth freedom rights between the United Kingdom and Canada on a Rome-Montreal service. Since this would have given a third carrier a share of the Canada–U.K. traffic historically divided between TCA and BOAC, McGregor had advised the government not to agree to the Italian terms. Now, he told Hees, McConachie would probably propose that since his route to Lisbon and Madrid was unprofitable it should be extended to Rome – and "CPA would not have the slightest objection to TCA being confronted with another competitor with traffic rights between Canada and U.K., if by so doing it was granted the route to Rome."

As to the question of gateways, the importance of Toronto, which had by now become by far the largest traffic-generating centre in Canada, could not be over-emphasized: "It is difficult to conceive of any air rights in the gift of any foreign government which would even closely approach the value to that government of obtaining access to the Toronto market."

In the domestic field, the new policy outlined by Hees envisaged "a limited introduction of competition as between scheduled airlines," but only "on a gradual and regional basis rather than by the present introduction of any new trans-continental operations." Here he seemed to be accepting McGregor's advice: "Without directing the Air Transport Board to take any particular action, I would limit my expression of views to suggesting that they might wish to consider from the point of view of competition only the Vancouver-Victoria route and the Montreal-Ottawa-Toronto triangular operation; and that a reasonable trial on these routes might be a logical thing to expect before considering further expansion of the principle."

McGregor was reassured by this point in the minister's program, which he considered no change from existing government policy. So he was horrified when, in November, CPA filed an application with the ATB for three complete and two partial transcontinental routes, each to be operated once daily each way: Vancouver-Calgary-Saskatoon-Ottawa-Montreal; Vancouver-Edmonton-Montreal; Vancouver-Winnipeg-Toronto-Montreal; Edmonton-Regina-Toronto; and Winnipeg-Ottawa-Montreal.

He lost no time in discussing this ominous development with his board, and on November 28 wrote to Hees saying the TCA directors had unanimously concluded that the establishment of the proposed CPA services would constitute a violation of the Trans-Canada contract between the Crown and the corporation. Furthermore, to "fulfill its clear obligations" under the TCA Act the airline had already committed itself to the expenditure by 1961 of $181 million to re-equip its fleet with DC-8s and Vanguards and build a new base to service them, and "the board was certain that any dilution of the company's primary source of revenue [its transcontinental service] could have no other effect than to produce heavy operating deficits." Therefore, "since the granting of CPA's application would constitute a complete departure from the Canadian civil aviation policy approved by parliament," the directors had asked him to convey to Hees "their unanimous and most strong recommendation that there be appointed a Royal Commission to study in detail the whole question of airline competition within Canada, and arising out of that study, to recommend for adoption by the government, a clearly defined policy."

The government rejected the idea of a royal commission and when Hees made his new aviation policy public in a speech at Timmins, Ontario, on February 7, 1958, he announced that instead he had commissioned an eminent British aviation consultant, Stephen Wheatcroft, to study the economic implications of airline competition in Canada. Wheatcroft's report, he said, would be available to the Air Transport Board when, as he had requested, the board held a public hearing on the CPA application and "the general need for additional trans-continental air services."

In his terms of reference to Wheatcroft, the minister showed that his proposed new air policy had changed somewhat since he had outlined it to McGregor a few months earlier. "I am of the view," he wrote, "that the time has come for the introduction of some measure of competition on our trans-continental routes. The rapid growth in airline traffic would seem to indicate that competition can be introduced gradually, without major detrimental effects to existing operations" – a statement that seemed to anticipate whatever findings Wheatcroft might make.

Wheatcroft, a graduate of the London School of Economics and World War II navy pilot, had been an executive of British European Airways and had recently published an authoritative book on the economics of aviation in Europe. He spent the spring of 1958 in Canada interviewing aviation people at all levels within the airlines, the Department of Transport and the ATB, and submitted his exhaustive report in May. It began by accepting the assumption made by Hees in his Timmins speech that competition would be "a valuable stimulus to more efficient operation and to the provision of better service to the public," but warned that: "The presumption that competition will keep costs at the lowest level is considered to be open to doubt." Similarly, there was little doubt that competition would be a stimulus to rapid technological progress, "but this does not necessarily imply that TCA's equipment has been inferior." In fact, he concluded, "the strongest argument in favour of competition is that the travelling public unquestionably wants the right, wherever possible, to have the satisfaction of choosing which airline it will use. In the absence of this right to choose, the passenger often magnifies small complaints against a monopoly carrier."

As to how TCA had carried out its mandate so far, Wheatcroft gave the airline a clean bill of health:

In the field of operating and sales standards, TCA domestic services compare quite favourably with airlines in other parts of the world, including the United States. All airlines make mistakes: but there is no evidence that TCA makes more mistakes than other airlines. After comparing TCA operating costs with those of airlines serving broadly the same type of routes in other parts of the world, it is concluded: firstly, that the higher level of TCA costs compared with U.S. airlines is explained largely by the lower average density of Canadian operations; secondly, that the level of TCA costs compared with those of CPA gives no support to the charge that TCA is inefficient in Canadian conditions; and thirdly, that it is from an intensification of the traffic density that future reductions in Canadian air transport costs will probably be achieved.

All in all, Wheatcroft concluded that the advantages of competition "do not appear so great that they would be worthwhile irrespective of the risk of higher costs." And he found from his study of passenger statistics that there were only three routes in Canada with a traffic volume "adequate to sustain competitive service without danger of an increase in average operating costs." These were: Toronto-Montreal, Vancouver-Victoria and Toronto-Winnipeg.

An examination of the possible effects of competition on TCA's financial position in the immediate future indicates that, unless it were strictly limited in extent, it would almost certainly lead the company to an overall deficit. A competitive operation of five services daily in 1959 can be shown to be much too large a capacity increment for the trans-continental routes without causing serious financial difficulties, probably for both airlines. The maximum competitive capacity which could be permitted in 1959 without leading to a TCA deficit is approximately four daily trans-continental services. This allows no room for any increase in TCA capacity and might therefore be reduced to two daily in order to ease the TCA problem of disposing of aircraft already ordered.

To the dispassionate reader, the Wheatcroft report might have appeared to carry the message, "Competition if necessary but competition doesn't seem to be necessary, at least not yet." It was available to the Air Transport Board when it began its hearings on the CPA application on October 6 under the temporary chairmanship of Clarence D. Shepard, the previous incumbent having died suddenly a few weeks before. Shepard, a Winnipeg lawyer who had battled the CPR in railway freight rate hearings, was at that time chairman of the Board of Transport Commissioners; to initiate him into the mysteries of airline economics Stephen Wheatcroft was appointed a special board witness.

So that regional groups could comment on the CPA application, the first few days were devoted to hearings across the country at which such organizations as the City of Vancouver and local chambers of commerce supported CPA's case, some wholeheartedly and some with the reservation that competition would be desirable if it did not unduly increase costs. The government of Saskatchewan submitted a brief opposing competition, at least for the time being, as did some groups from the Maritimes, which favoured the local regional airline, Maritime Central Airways.

The hearing proper began in Ottawa on October 20 and the rancorous proceedings dragged on until December 3. Legally, the board's function was only to examine the evidence and make recommendations; the actual decision on the application had to be made by the government. Perhaps because McConachie knew this and regarded the government's approval as a foregone conclusion, CPA's witnesses seemed to expect the hearing to be a mere formality, and in later years they admitted their case had not been well prepared. McGregor, on the other hand, had planned his rearguard action with all the determination and attention to detail he had demonstrated in his wartime operations, and to lead his attack he had chosen one of his wartime brothers-in-arms, the Toronto lawyer John Edison.

It was part of CPA's case that most of the passengers it would carry if its application were granted would not be diverted from TCA but would consist of entirely new traffic generated by the new services. Edison was easily able to demonstrate that this was not based on any valid statistical evidence. In fact he extracted the admission that CPA had not even undertaken a full-scale traffic study, based on a market survey and followed by a revenue analysis and detailed cost estimate. Edison argued that the CPA planners had in fact followed an inverse procedure: "That is, they had seven redundant DC-6Bs; how best could these aircraft be used?" Furthermore, they had under-estimated the cost of the new services: depreciation by 15 per cent, fuel oil by $118,000, service and maintenance by $77,000, and passenger supplies and expenses by $204,000.

The CPA witnesses naturally tried to play down the financial effects on TCA of the proposed new services, and said any deficit incurred could be more than made up by a reduction of the $17

Gordon R. McGregor, president, 1948 to 1968.

Minor adjustment to a North Star at Bermuda drew the curious, 1948.

The station manager at Brandon, Manitoba, on TCA's prairie "milk run" awaits the arrival of a DC-3 flight in the winter of 1952.

Bristol Freighter ingests a truck.

The stewardess graduating class, August 17, 1954.

Two of the many two-generation airline families: Captain Al Edwards pins his daughter Janet, a graduate stewardess, and Captain R.M. Smith welcomes his son Rod as first officer in an overseas Super Constellation.

Transatlantic service by Super Constellation out of Toronto was launched with a flourish on May 14, 1954.

Vancouver airport, 1959, with Super Constellation, North Star and DC-3 aircraft.

Passengers enjoying the big windows in a Viscount in the beginning, when the seat rows were suitably aligned, 1955.

The presidents of Canada's two great railways and their respective airlines:
Donald Gordon (CN), <u>*Grant McConachie*</u> *(CP Air); Gordon McGregor (TCA)*
and W. Mather (CPR), on a social occasion. When battle lines were drawn
Mr. Mather had been succeeded by N.R. Crump, here seen below with Ian
Sinclair, his legal adviser. – (CP Rail)

The new base at Dorval under construction, 1959.

TCAS DC-8 attracts attention in Barbados.

Overhauling Dart engines for the Viscount at Winnipeg base.

A busy reservations office in 1954 used telephone lines and entirely manual recording.

million in extra costs which they alleged were attributable to TCA's "inefficiency." Edison quoted other airlines' costs to demonstrate that TCA's were not out of line, and said that if the sum of $17 million were deducted from its 1957 expenses TCA would have so low an operating ratio in relation to other world airlines as to be "ridiculous."

Expanding on the potential financial effects of the new services on the national airline, a TCA witness pointed out that in 1957 the airline's net profit on its transatlantic services had been $4.7 million, and on its transcontinental routes $5.4 million. In contrast, it had lost $9.9 million on its unprofitable social routes. If the CPA application were granted and CPA took over only 20 per cent of TCA's transcontinental traffic in 1959, TCA could look forward to a deficit for the year of $8 million – rising to $12.6 million in 1960 if CPA gained a further 5 per cent of TCA's traffic.

Day after day, primed by nightly briefing sessions with the eager TCA staff, Edison tore the CPA case apart. At one stage he managed to demonstrate that if CPA followed its proposed operating plan all the aircraft it owned would have to be in the air at the same time. From the way CPA had presented its case, he said, it was clear that what it wanted was "not competition in the true sense, but rather regulated substitution of one carrier for another on certain routes."

The hearing was, of course, reported extensively in the press, and among those who read the reports with growing alarm was a British Columbia railroader's son who had taken a labourer's job on the CPR as a boy and worked his way up to the president's office in Windsor Station: Norris R. Crump, known to one and all as "Buck." Buck Crump did not like what he was seeing. One day he picked up his phone, called the railroad's general solicitor, Ian Sinclair, and told him: "We're going to Ottawa tomorrow." They arrived at the hearing unannounced and sat silently watching the proceedings for several hours. And next day Sinclair rose and requested Shepard's permission to take over the CPA case. Thereafter, the TCA witnesses faced much heavier going: Sinclair's skilful retrieval of the CPA cause is widely regarded as one of his most crucial steps up the ladder to the presidency and later chairmanship of the CPR. It did not, however, win CPA all that McConachie had confidently hoped to achieve.

After considering all the evidence, the board found that additional transcontinental services could not be introduced at that time "without major detrimental effect to existing operations" and without economic hardships and possible deficits for both airlines. And it rejected CPA's application because its expense estimates had been computed on an "unreasonable" added-cost basis; its revenues had been estimated without any traffic study; and its proposed schedules appeared to have been based on "optimistic" estimates of aircraft speeds and turn-around times.

However, to McGregor's intense dismay, there was a codicil: "The Board finds that the position of CPA as a Canadian carrier operating international services needs strengthening and for that reason, the Board, subject to the approval of the Minister, proposes to issue to CPA a licence to operate a Class 1 scheduled commercial air service serving Vancouver, Winnipeg, Toronto and Montreal restricted to a frequency of one return flight a day." Hees announced the government's acceptance of this recommendation on January 21, 1959, and CPA began its transcontinental flights the following May.

The new service provided the desired link between CPA's terminals at Montreal and Vancouver, and while covering its overhead with just one flight a day was not an enticing economic prospect, McConachie was elated. Once again the master salesman had got his foot in the door. On his part, McGregor was so disappointed at the recommendation that he could never afterward believe his old friend Clancy Shepard had made it. "I have never been convinced," he wrote in his memoirs, "that the final paragraph emanated from the Board."

In this, he had apparently overlooked the fact that the board's recommendation had been foreshadowed in a section at the end of the Wheatcroft report titled "Incidental Competition." As examples of what this might be, the report cited "the licensing of a carrier on certain domestic routes in order to improve the coverage of its existing international services; or granting a licence for a route between two separate parts of a carrier's existing network; or granting traffic rights on sectors presently flown without local traffic as part of a through route. . . . It would appear that, providing they are strictly limited, there is room on the trans-continental sectors for some new services providing incidental competition to TCA without major adverse consequences."

Shepard and McGregor, who had met overseas during the war, kept up their friendship during McGregor's sojourn in Winnipeg and afterwards. Shepard smiled in recollection as he denied that the government had tried to influence the board's recommendations. "I talked to Gordon a lot after the hearing," he said, "and he didn't have a very objective view. He viewed it so personally, and he viewed me as his friend, and he couldn't *believe* I would be a party to creating a report which would give him the competition that he didn't think he could survive."

At any rate, McGregor did not permit his disgust at the finding to impair either his friendship or his respect for his old friend Clancy: some years later, when he began to wonder who would pilot his cherished airline after his retirement, he asked Shepard to join TCA as executive vice-president, with the idea of eventually succeeding to the presidency. Shepard, who had by then become general counsel for BA Oil (later Gulf Canada), attributed his offer to the exaggerated respect McGregor had acquired for the apparent knowledge of aviation he had displayed as chairman of the CPA hearing. He chuckled as he explained this had been imparted to him by Wheatcroft in daily briefings. And for a variety of reasons he turned down McGregor's offer – without cause for regret, as it turned out, since he went on to become chairman of Gulf.

CHAPTER EIGHTEEN

HE AIR TRANSPORT BOARD'S recommendation was only the first of a series of blows rained on the national airline during the next few years. On January 23, 1959, two days after Hees announced the government's decision, McGregor wrote to him predicting – accurately, as it turned out – that CPA, anxious to make the most of its one flight a day, would fly its transcontinental route with 98-passenger Britannia turbo-props, much larger than the 61-seat piston-engined DC-6Bs its representatives had told the hearing they would be using. The effect on TCA's traffic would thus be even worse than McGregor had feared. The Britannia, he said, would have considerable passenger appeal, since it was a hundred miles an hour faster than the Viscounts and Super-Connies TCA would have to operate on the route until the arrival of its DC-8s at least a year hence.

There will be a natural tendency for the travelling public to try the new service [McGregor wrote], and the market for it will be further strengthened by that large group of the public who have a strong predilection for the support of "private enterprise" in preference to a publicly-owned service. Also I think it is safe to forecast that by over-glorified cabin service, perhaps even with the inclusion of alcoholic beverages, CPA will endeavour to popularize its flight to the greatest possible extent, without regard to economic considerations. It is therefore undoubtedly the case that the CPA flight will operate at a high load factor.

This would result in some passengers being turned away, particularly during the summer, and McGregor predicted that by September CPA would be asking the government to remove the one-flight-a-day frequency limit set by the ATB, despite the board's stipulation that the service should be operated for two years before it was reviewed. He asked for the minister's assurance that no further CPA applications for transcontinental services would be accepted or considered until that two-year period was up, which Hees gave him in a friendly letter dated January 27. Only two days later, however, the minister delivered another body blow: he wrote that he proposed to give BOAC landing rights at Toronto in addition to their existing rights into Montreal.

When TCA first started to fly the Atlantic, aircraft ranges demanded a stop at Prestwick, in Scotland, as well as at London; this entitled BOAC to two destinations in Canada, and in the first U.K.–Canada bilateral arrangement negotiated after the war Britain agreed to take Montreal and The Pas, the latter seeming to be a potentially useful stopping place on the still-contemplated round-the-world Commonwealth air service. When this idea finally died, BOAC turned its attention to the rich Toronto market and by 1959 Britain had been pressing Canada to change the agreement for several years. When the government showed signs of giving in to the British demand, McGregor said he would rather give up Prestwick, to remove the justification for the British claim for two destinations. But in his letter, Hees said this would be interpreted as "evidence of a TCA desire to maintain monopolistic competition even at the expense of reducing its operations," and "I believe there would be a considerable outcry from Toronto which would be directed not just at the government but at TCA as well." So, even though he knew it would be a disappointment to McGregor, he proposed to negotiate with Britain "on the basis of opening up Toronto but to sell the traffic rights in Toronto as dearly as we possibly can."

The horrified McGregor replied that the minister's decision was not simply disappointing, it was "beyond any possibility of doubt disastrous." The airline expected to lose between $2 million and $3 million in transcontinental revenue in 1959, depending on whether CPA used DC-6Bs or Britannias; and one BOAC Britannia flight daily into Toronto would deprive it of a further $2.9 million in domestic and transatlantic revenue in a twelve-month period.

Hees had said in his letter that he agreed with the Department of External Affairs that "the U.K. feeling is so strong on this point that we must take some specific action to deal with the situation rather than run the risk either of notice of termination of the agreement or of a major and bitter difference of opinion which would affect our U.K. relations." McGregor said he appreciated this problem, but of all the solutions open to the government "the one most injurious to the country and having the least popular appeal would be the one placing a drain on the public purse of the magnitude which I have indicated."

McGregor reminded Hees that some time earlier he had been asked to prepare a list of air rights Canada might seek from Britain in return for access to Toronto; these had included: fifth freedom rights to pick up travellers in Britain for points beyond there;

the right to "change gauge" in the U.K. – that is, to operate from there to other points in Europe with aircraft smaller than those required on the Atlantic; and air rights for a second carrier at Hong Kong. The British had rejected his list in its entirety. "The fact is," he wrote, "that anything less than the lion's share of any business transaction is completely unsatisfactory to the British government negotiator. . . . I cannot see how you or any other Canadian could be criticized for denying BOAC Toronto rights, if they so much as quibble at agreeing to this rather pitiful list, which in total represents but a fraction of the value of the invasion of Toronto by BOAC."

Despite McGregor's entreaties, BOAC was given access to Toronto in negotiations conducted later in the year, in return for TCA landing rights at Hong Kong. In an attempt to offset at least part of the expected diversion of revenue, TCA then accepted a proposal it had turned down when BOAC first made it: the "pooling" of transatlantic services. Pooling, while it had already become a common, indeed almost universal, practice in Europe, was opposed by the more dedicated advocates of private competition. When two countries designate airlines of their choice to operate a service between them, the airlines can engage in head-on competition, scheduling flights at virtually the same time and striving all-out to fill them with passengers. The result is likely to be half-empty aeroplanes. In a pool, the two airlines co-operate to schedule as much capacity as they think is needed, at times and frequencies that suit as many passengers as possible, and share the revenue on the basis of the capacity each provides. For instance, if there is only enough traffic to fill one flight a day each way, the airlines can serve the route on alternate days, enhancing the chance that each will have a profitable load. Further economies become possible when the airlines co-operate to perform for each other such functions as reservations, ticketing and passenger handling. Even with the pool, TCA estimated later that $2.6 million in revenue it would have received was diverted to BOAC in 1960, the year it began to fly into Toronto.

In a further attempt to reduce the economic impact of these "depredations," McGregor now asked Hees for permission to fly from Montreal and Toronto to Tokyo, and on to Hong Kong. He claimed that this would not parallel CPA's route to the Orient from Vancouver, any more than CPA's Montreal-Lisbon service was considered to parallel TCA's routes to London and Paris. Japan was only just beginning its remarkable postwar rise to the status of industrial giant, and it did not seem there would be much traffic between eastern Canada and Tokyo. But McGregor pointed out that the requested service would give TCA the shortest and fastest route between the U.S. eastern seaboard and the Orient, and with its Toronto–New York service as a feeder line it could expect to tap the rich U.S. market.

McGregor coupled this request with another: that the Canadian delegates in the forthcoming bilateral negotiations with the Italians should press for fifth-freedom rights permitting TCA to extend its Montreal-Paris service to Rome. The so-called "French half" of those rights, permitting TCA to pick up passengers in Paris for points beyond there, had been won the year before in return for Air France being given fifth freedom rights at Montreal. This agreement enabled Air France to pick up Canadian passengers there and fly them direct to Chicago–a route that the United States had not yet opened up to any Canadian airline.

In support of his requests, McGregor submitted yet another estimate of the harm that would be done to TCA's revenues by the CPA transcontinental service, BOAC's admission to Toronto, and several other recent "give-aways," such as the Montreal-Chicago route to Air France and the admission of two new airlines, SAS and Sabena, to Montreal. The total yearly diversion of revenue, he said, would be $6.5 million. While TCA had managed to record surpluses throughout the 1950s, they were usually modest ones.* In only three years–1951, 1952 and 1956 –did they exceed $1 million, and in 1958 the surplus had been only $547,429. In these circumstances, McGregor wrote, the airline could not absorb a $6.5 million diversion of revenue without suffering "shockingly huge deficits for some years to come." With a fleet of thirty large and extremely expensive turbine aircraft about to be delivered, its only hope of avoiding those deficits lay in its expansion on to new routes.

Hees accepted McGregor's argument for the Tokyo service, though apparently with misgivings, since the letter in which he granted McGregor's request, received by TCA on June 2, 1959, bore no date.

---

*McGregor believed that Crown corporations were "in a cleft stick": if they made too much money, their success would invite attempts by private enterprise to cut itself in for a slice of the pie; if they lost too much, their managements would be vulnerable to political interference because they seemed weak and incompetent. Bill Harvey, his vice-president, finance, was proud of his ability to juggle the airline's few discretionary budget items, such as depreciation and allocations to the airline's self-insurance fund, in a way that would both satisfy the auditors and achieve a presentable balance sheet. This, McGregor recorded in his memoirs, was "a recurring source of amusement at board meetings to Donald Gordon, who quite correctly realized that depreciation was being used as a valve by which net income could be regulated, within reason."

I have considered your comment regarding the urgency of planning in the matter of the Orient service [the minister wrote]. You may take this letter as my approval of the designation of TCA for service from Toronto direct by way of Alaska to Japan and Hong Kong, providing the necessary arrangements can be made under existing bilateral air agreements. . . . You may convey this information to your Board of Directors and to your senior planning staff, but I do not wish, at this time, to make any public announcement, and I would prefer that the public announcement be made through myself if and when the time comes.

Unfortunately for TCA, that time never came. The impending resumption of bilateral talks with Italy, which had broken down over the "ridiculous" Italian demand for fifth-freedom rights between London and Montreal, had been brought about by the continuing entrepreneurial zeal of Grant McConachie. As McGregor had predicted to Hees, McConachie soon decided that CPA's Montreal-Lisbon-Madrid route needed beefing up by the addition of Rome. But instead of going through the prescribed channels – the Air Transport Board and the minister – he approached the Italian airline, Alitalia, directly; and through Alitalia he entered into what McGregor described to Hees as "illegal negotiations" with Italian government officials. In so doing, McGregor alleged, he had managed to convey the impression that Canada must have an Italian bilateral at any price, thereby weakening the Canadian position in any subsequent negotiations.

Once again, McGregor's logic seemed to have swayed Hees. He sent John Baldwin and Paul Davoud, then chairman of the Air Transport Board, to remonstrate with Buck Crump about McConachie's unilateral approach to the Italians. The two men told Crump Canada now proposed to defer the Italian negotiations until it could rectify the damage done by McConachie's unauthorized advances. Ian Sinclair and McConachie shortly thereafter paid a return visit to Davoud and Baldwin and meekly accepted the postponement of the negotiations in apparent repentance for McConachie's sins. But they made it clear that since CPA would not now be getting the rights to Rome it was imperative that, to salvage its financial position, it be given the right to fly from Vancouver to London.

By now, TCA had been operating a through flight between Vancouver and London, via Winnipeg and Gander, for more than a year–the "Hudson Bay Service"–so McGregor viewed this latest CPA ambition as a direct encroachment on one of its routes, in contravention of the minister's declared policy. He wrote to tell Hees so:

It would be an insult for me to think that you would give serious consideration to this most recent CPR demand for the right to wreak further financial damage on a gov-

ernment property. . . . Your experience since taking over the portfolio of Transport has been such that you will not need to be told that granting traffic privileges to CPA is like paying hush money to a blackmailer. Each CPA request carries an implication that its granting will solve that company's problems and satisfy its ambitions indefinitely. In practically every case after a route demand has been met, however, within a few months it is followed by another demand. Even the faintest suggestion that you might consider a Vancouver-London request will not in the slightest reduce CPA's determination to serve Rome exclusively, to the complete disregard of TCA's prior rights.

These prior rights, as McGregor explained, went back to 1951, when TCA had first expressed its interest in serving Rome to the chairman of the ATB. After that, a TCA representative had served on the Canadian delegation in the abortive bilateral talks with Italy in 1955. And finally, TCA had actually been designated as the Canadian carrier to operate to Italy by the previous Liberal government early in 1957.

This time, also, the strength of McGregor's position seemed to impress the minister. Hees had a long meeting and a friendly lunch with Crump on Friday, August 21, during which he told him he could not assign CPA to the Vancouver-London route since it would be contrary to the policy – his and the cabinet's – which he had enunciated in his Timmins speech eighteen months earlier. Crump asked him if that was the only reason, and he assured him it was. In that case, Crump said, amicably enough, he would raise the matter with the Prime Minister.

This placed Hees squarely on the spot, for he now remembered his commitment a couple of months earlier to assign TCA to the Toronto-Tokyo route, which surely could be interpreted by CPA sympathizers as a similar violation of the Timmins policy; furthermore, Hees knew (as McGregor perhaps didn't) that around that time John Diefenbaker was hopping mad at TCA and its president.

The episode that had aroused the Chief's wrath had begun in June, when McGregor wrote Hees a letter which, considering its content, was surprisingly brief. It read, in its entirety:

Dear George:

You will be glad to learn that this company's Board of Directors agreed at the meeting held in Montreal on June 24 to proceed as quickly as circumstances permit with the adoption of the name "Air Canada" as TCA's primary trade name.

Kindest regards,
Yours sincerely
G.R. McGregor.

Hees apparently did not recognize the explosive potential of this brief letter. He merely acknowledged it without comment.

The proposal to change the airline's name had originated within the traffic department, and there were sound commercial reasons for it. First of all, with the expansion of its international routes, the term "Trans-Canada" no longer accurately reflected the full scope of the airline's operations. Also, the company's full name, particularly in French – *Lignes aériennes Trans-Canada* – made an unwieldy mouthful for advertisements and company signs. The new name, in contrast, had many advantages: it was bilingual; it followed the pattern established by such companies as Air France, Air India and several others; it was succinct, easy to remember, and it carried a valuable national identification; and finally, it had been used for some years in Europe as a trade name sanctioned by the 1953 amendment to the Trans-Canada Air Lines Act.

Gordon Wood, as vice-president, sales, easily persuaded McGregor and the board that the change was desirable. But as English Canadians quite at home in the cosmopolitan atmosphere of Montreal, they had perhaps not reckoned with the fear and suspicion aroused by all things French in some other parts of the country. Before the ten thousand letters that were to have announced the change to the employees were circulated, rumours of what was in the air swept across the always efficient airline bush telegraph, and Herb Seagrim, as vice-president, operations, began to receive petitions and letters of protest from all points of the compass. The feeling built up to the point at which Seagrim felt he should draw it to McGregor's attention. "As I expected," he wrote on July 7, 1959, "this decided-upon change is causing considerable resentment, not so much because of the change itself, but because, in the minds of many people, 'Air Canada' is a French designation having little meaning in English."

Inevitably, someone's resentment spilled over into the Toronto press, and when conjectural stories about the change began to appear John Diefenbaker hit the roof. Who, he demanded of Hees, does this fellow McGregor think he is? And what is he up to? No doubt the Chief could sense the kind of controversy that later accompanied the choice of a new Canadian flag. At any rate, he told Hees, McGregor had no right to make such a major decision; it was a political matter and it should have been submitted for the government's approval in advance; after all, it was the government that would have to answer the questions it would undoubtedly provoke.

Hees promptly called McGregor and apologized for not reading his letter about the change more carefully. He had not realized, he said, that the company intended to use the new name in Canada; could it not be confined to overseas use? At least could the airline hold off making the change until he had had a chance to discuss it within cabinet?

McGregor replied that having, as he thought, received the minister's approval of the change, he had proceeded with its implementation, which was now close to the point of no return. However, he agreed to a short delay while the matter was cleared through cabinet – though he presumed that was a mere formality and there was no possibility of the board's decision being overruled. "I formed a strong impression," he wrote later to the directors, "that Mr. Hees was on the verge of instructing me not to proceed with the change of name, but was having difficulty bringing himself to interfere in a matter patently the prerogative of management."

McGregor took his management prerogatives very seriously indeed, and it seems that when he telephoned Donald Gordon to tell him about the minister's call he said he would resign if the government insisted on overturning the board's decision. Gordon left for a holiday in Britain shortly thereafter and on July 18 he wrote from the Ritz Hotel in London offering his customary sage advice. He had not thought, he said, that the matter could become an "issue," and certainly not one with "consequences as suggested by you in regard to your personal position." McGregor, he advised, should not make the issue appear to be a personal fight, but should merely give the reasons and considerations that prompted the board's decision. And in due course the storm would probably die down.

Which is what eventually happened. In a personal interview with McGregor, Hees repeated the government's strong objections, but as McGregor noted afterward:

I got the impression that the Minister felt extremely uncomfortable at having to ask this company to shelve its name plans, and that he was hopeful the matter could die a quiet death, with the acquiescence of TCA directors. I feel reasonably sure that as long as we do not force the issue with respect to the name change, he will feel himself to be under substantial obligation to TCA, and it is naturally my hope that this will translate itself into his continued refusal to accede to the CPA demands, which in terms of this company's future are of far greater importance at this time in history than is the name change.

Hees, and the Prime Minister himself, may have been mollified by a letter strongly supporting the name change from Edward W. Bickle, a Toronto broker and Tory stalwart who had been appointed to the TCA board to fill the vacancy created by the retirement of Herb Symington. At any rate, a head-on confrontation was averted, and while McGregor did not completely back down, he issued instructions that the new name was to be introduced only gradually, beginning in Britain, and only as a trade name, to be used alongside the company's existing corporate name. The matter surfaced in the Commons again once or twice in succeeding years, but without any great controversy developing, and in 1964, after the Liberals had returned to office, the company's corporate name was officially changed to Air Canada, with effect from January 1, 1965.

Against this background, when Crump announced his intention of taking CPA's case for access to London to the Prime Minister, Hees had second thoughts about his designation of TCA to the Tokyo route and asked McGregor to return the letter in which he had promised it. He was sailing from Montreal with his family on August 25 for a European vacation, and he asked McGregor to bring the letter to his suite at the Queen Elizabeth Hotel that morning. When McGregor arrived, Hees told him he had refused Crump's request for the Vancouver-London route because it ran counter to his policy that TCA and CPA should not be put in direct competition with one another on international routes. It would be embarrassing for him if Crump now discovered he had already violated this policy in principle by designating TCA to the Orient. He therefore wished to expunge his promise from the record, and had McGregor brought the letter with him?

McGregor replied that he had not – because not only had he duly acknowledged its receipt but it had been mentioned in other correspondence, so its suppression would not aid the minister's cause and might prove even more embarrassing than its disclosure. He suggested instead that Hees write another letter, saying that on further consideration he had decided the assignment of TCA to the Orient might be considered to conflict with the government's policy on international routes and he was therefore rescinding it, which Hees did after his return from Europe.

By now, the Toronto-Orient route had become a less attractive proposition, since Northwest Airlines had inaugurated a one-stop service from New York to Tokyo, appropriating the market TCA had hoped to tap, and McGregor had decided it would be worth sacrificing any ambitions to fly the Pacific if an end could be put to further "depredations." With the concurrence of his board, he had suggested to Hees that Canada's position in international negotiations would be stronger if the government laid down a firm policy dividing the world between its two international carriers: CPA to have exclusive rights to the Pacific, Mexico and South America, and TCA exclusive rights to the Atlantic and Caribbean. Hees replied that "I am by no means sure it is feasible to consider a complete withdrawal to the rather hard and fast line of geographical separation which you have suggested." McGregor concluded that the minister felt that having denied CPA the Vancouver-London route – Crump's intercession with Diefenbaker having so far borne no fruit – he must compensate by giving it the rights to Rome.

At any rate, McGregor's hope that his forbearance in not forcing a public confrontation on the change of the airline's name would fend off further route awards to CPA was not fulfilled. That fall, Canada signed what he considered a ludicrously one-sided agreement with Italy under which CPA gained access to Rome and Alitalia received fifth-freedom rights from Montreal to Mexico, Chicago and Los Angeles. At that time, the United States had not yet granted any Canadian airline permission to fly to Chicago or Los Angeles, so Alitalia was given access to a sizeable pool of Canadian passengers. And to underline McGregor's oft-voiced objections to the casual way Canada dispensed air rights, the designation of CPA as the only Canadian airline permitted to fly into Rome prevented either Canadian airline from taking advantage of the hard-won "French half" of the Paris-Rome fifth freedom. Henceforth, TCA could not extend its Montreal-Paris service to Rome. And since TCA had the rights to Paris, CPA could not introduce any service between that city and Rome.

Within days of that agreement being announced, McGregor received another blow: the Minister of Finance, Donald Fleming, refused to approve the airline's capital budget for 1960. Because of the tremendous expense of re-equipping the fleet with DC-8s and Vanguards, this was a record $97.5 million – an increase of $27.5 million over the year before – $82.4 million of which the airline proposed to borrow from the CNR (in other words, the government) with the remaining $15.1 million being provided from its own depreciation account. The figures, though small by today's standards, disturbed the economy-minded Fleming. And unlike some of his colleagues, he seemed to appreciate the inevitable effect on TCA's finances of the continual "giveaways" to CPA and other airlines, and the danger that the growing competition would put the national airline in the position of being "over-equipped" – having more seats than it could find passengers to occupy. "The large cash outlay program for 1960," Fleming wrote to his colleague George Hees, "is based upon an aircraft acquisition program of far-reaching proportions. It seems to me before any commitment can be made in relation to such a program the whole question as to the relationship of Trans-Canada Air Lines to trans-Atlantic competition ought to be carefully studied and submitted to decision on the highest policy level by our colleagues.''

Hees asked McGregor to draft him a reply to Fleming's letter, and in it McGregor pointed out that $76.7 million of the $97.5 million had been authorized in previous budgets, partly to pay for six DC-8s which had been on order for three and a half years, four DC-8s on order for more than a year, and twenty Vanguards on order for more than three years. The impending introduction of these aircraft demanded further expenditures for maintenance and overhaul facilities, spare parts and ground handling equipment. New commitments for which authority was being sought amounted to just over $20 million, of which only $6.7 million would be spent in 1960. "I think you will agree," McGregor's draft said on behalf of Hees, "that under the circumstances this is an extremely modest figure, and provides for only four additional aircraft, to meet the growth requirement represented by the traffic to be carried in 1962."

Before he sent the letter to Fleming, Hees added a paragraph saying that failure to approve TCA's budget "would undoubtedly be interpreted by the public as a government decision not so much related to the financial situation as to civil aviation policy pointing in the direction of restriction or elimination of TCA from the aviation field."

TCA's financial future thus looked cloudy indeed when McGregor's troubles were compounded by the defection of one of his own directors. At the beginning of a board meeting on January 7, 1960, Frank M. Ross asked for the floor and then startled his colleagues by announcing that he proposed to resign as soon as the government approved the airline's 1960 budget. Ross, a prominent businessman and Lieutenant-Governor of British Columbia, expressed the friendliest feelings to all his fellow directors, who shared McGregor's impression that he was resigning in protest against the government's route licensing policy.

Instead, Ross soon made it clear that he was seriously concerned about the amount of money TCA was spending and seemed to think it should start phasing itself out of business. He visited Prime Minister Diefenbaker to make his case and followed up his call with a letter in which he said:

My considered opinion is that Canada has no business justification to be in world aviation and if it continues to be, before the second term of the present government is over, it will be faced with an investment of at least $300 million in equipment of a *type which has not yet been stabilized and which could be made obsolete quite quickly [at that time, high hopes were still being held out for the introduction of supersonic aircraft]. . . . My belief over a period of years has been that Trans-Canada Air Lines should be the exclusive main line air carrier from Victoria to Newfoundland, retain its West Indies service, and if possible a prestige run to London, which after all is the centre of the Commonwealth, and no more.*

Ross's defection obviously annoyed McGregor, but in a later letter to another director, R.A.C. Henry, he said he was not sorry to see him go, since "there is little doubt in my mind that Board decisions and planning reached CPA, and/or the CPR, through far western channels." And Ross's criticisms, coming on top of Fleming's refusal to approve TCA's budget, at last brought about the personal interview with Diefenbaker that McGregor had been seeking unavailingly for months. In preparation for this meeting, which took place on January 22, 1960, he drew up a long memorandum describing the airline's past, present and future planning and reiterating the statement that further "depredations" would make all the plans ridiculous and turn TCA into a chronically deficit Crown company.

The airline, this said, had recently added some Viscounts to its fleet to reduce the high load factors for which it had been criticized by passengers unable to make desired bookings. It had also lowered tourist fares. But it had still managed to show a modest surplus in 1958 of $547,429. The decision to permit transcontinental competition, however, had impaired the accuracy of its planning, and hence its economic value, by lopping $4 million off the revenue it had counted on for 1959. The airline carried 3.2 million passengers that year—more than all those carried in its first thirteen years of existence – but the slim profit margin under which it operated meant that the tiny surplus of $152,554 that resulted when all the figures were in would have been a deficit had the flying weather been bad on the last two days of the year. The admission of CPA to transcontinental service and BOAC to Toronto, McGregor told the Prime Minister, would produce a deficit of at least $2.5 million for 1960. (In fact, it turned out to be $2.6 million.)

Diefenbaker went over McGregor's memorandum paragraph by paragraph and asked some searching questions, and McGregor reported in a letter to Herb Symington later that he "gave every evidence of shock and surprise." The meeting took place on a Friday morning, and on the following Monday the cabinet approved TCA's 1960 budget. "The next evidence of a change in the direction of the wind," his letter to Symington continued, "was that CPA, who had applied for the right to operate

Vancouver-Calgary-Amsterdam, in addition to their existing route Vancouver-Edmonton-Amsterdam, and had been told that they would get it, were turned down flatly, together with, I am informed, a gratuitous advice to 'lay off' in future.''

As a further result of what McGregor took to be Diefenbaker's new understanding of the threat to the nation's airline, TCA was asked to collaborate with the Department of Transport and the ATB in an investigation of the government's air policy, both international and domestic. In the course of this study, the airline prepared yet another long memorandum reviewing the history of the various route "give-aways" and the lost revenue they entailed and making the bold suggestion that to rectify the situation TCA and CPA should be merged into one large domestic and international carrier. As justification for this proposal, the memorandum said both airlines stood to lose money in future, and their merger would bring about substantial economies and ensure the most efficient use of aircraft, ground facilities and manpower. It would also ensure the ability of the national flag carrier, through cross-subsidization, to continue to serve smaller communities within Canada, and eliminate the bad bargaining at the international level that resulted when government negotiators had to try to reconcile the needs and wishes of two competing carriers. Furthermore, the proposed merger would protect the national interest by presenting foreign flag carriers with united competition.

That first memorandum did not specify how the merger could be accomplished, but as the idea was explored in succeeding months TCA was invited to submit an expanded version of it to the government committee studying air policy. McGregor must have known there was little chance that CPA would willingly be bought out by TCA, or that a Conservative government would enforce its nationalization, and the updated draft of the memorandum, submitted in August, suggested that the merged company should be owned by the two railroads in proportion to the current size of their respective airlines – which at that time would have meant the CPR owning 20 per cent of the new airline and the CNR 80 per cent.

Advancing this proposal to John Baldwin, the deputy minister of transport, McGregor wrote that if the CPR refused it, "then surely life is made considerably easier for the Minister." The next time he was submitted to pressure for additional CPA routes, Hees could tell Buck Crump:

I am giving you an opportunity to buy into a consolidated airline which internationally would be much stronger than either TCA or CPA, and from which domestically you would share profits rather than the inevitable deficits which both airlines are and will continue experiencing in trans-continental competition. I can only interpret your refusal of this offer to mean that it is not your wish to share to a reasonable extent in the civil air development of Canada, but that it is your objective to damage a valuable government property, and ultimately achieve a position of dominance in Canadian civil aviation. Since I will not be a party to such a plan, I consider myself fully justified in denying any and all future CPA air route licence applications, and will do so.

McGregor had, of course, discussed the memorandum with Donald Gordon before submitting it to the government committee, and Gordon considered it the saddest document he had ever read. It would, he said, result in the CPR taking over Canadian aviation, since the logical case for one merged airline was irrefutable, but the CPR would never accept anything less than 51 per cent, or majority control, of the resulting new company. In the event, even though the cabinet committee which discussed the idea was reported to be in favour of it, the CPR regarded it as neither practical nor necessary and rejected it out of hand. Instead, CPA continued to campaign for more flights on its trans-continental service, the route from Vancouver to London and–a new request – a route from Toronto and Montreal to London, using propeller-driven aircraft only, which under the IATA agreement then in force would have permitted it to charge $30 less than the jet fare charged by TCA. With what McGregor considered appalling effrontery, it sought to justify these requests by claiming that because of competition from TCA and other airlines it was losing its share of the London market. (It had been routing passengers on to London from Amsterdam at no extra charge, which McGregor considered an illegal encroachment on TCA's territory.) All in all, CPA complained, it had suffered four consecutive years of losses, including no less than $4.7 million in 1960 alone.

By now–no doubt to his great relief–George Hees had moved on to another portfolio, Trade and Commerce, and the new Minister of Transport was the member for Trois-Rivières, Leon Balcer. A personable lawyer and wartime naval lieutenant, Balcer led the Quebec Tories but had earned John Diefenbaker's enmity by opposing his election as leader at the 1956 party convention. Soon after his appointment, Balcer managed to arrange another opportunity for McGregor to plead his cause with the Prime Minister, and during their talk Diefenbaker let it be known that he was not at all pleased with TCA's continuing use of the Montreal-based advertising agency Cockfield, Brown, which he considered to be far to cosy with his hated Grits. McGregor had hired Cockfield, Brown to represent the airline soon after he was made president and he was quite satisfied with its performance. In fact, one of its vice-presidents, Murray Turner, whom he had known since his Winnipeg days, had become one of his closest friends. So, since Diefenbaker did not directly order him to switch agencies, he crossed his fingers and let sleeping dogs lie.

It remains a fact of Canadian political life that agencies handling government advertising tend to change whenever the government does. But the Conservative government laid down some guidelines on the matter in October 1959. No agency, it ruled, should receive a total of more than $700,000 a year in advertising from government departments; wherever possible, government advertising should not represent more than 15 per cent of any agency's total billings; and all government advertising should be placed with Canadian-owned agencies. Hees communicated these guidelines to McGregor but added that they were not binding on Crown companies. McGregor expressed his relief that TCA would not have to abide by them: "Our annual expenditure for Canadian media advertising is in the order of $1.25 million, with, as you know, display and associated advertising handled by a second agency. It would be next to impossible, and extremely inefficient, to split the media advertising between different agencies, in an effort to recognize the $700,000 limitation."

He could read writing on the wall as well as the next man, though, so he had the sales department carry out a thorough evaluation of the various leading Canadian advertising agencies. This reported complete satisfaction with the services rendered by Cockfield, Brown, the second largest Canadian agency; but "should it be deemed necessary and desirable" to change agencies, the next best choice would be the largest company in the country, MacLaren, on a split basis with Stanfield, Johnson and Hill, which was already handling the airline's "collateral" advertising – printed matter, direct mail and display.

Thus armed, McGregor was not unduly concerned when Diefenbaker grumbled about his continued use of Cockfield, Brown. But a few months later a study paper on government advertising expenditures somehow turned up on the desk of a Toronto reporter, Judith Robinson. It showed that out of $2.5 million allotted for advertising by TCA, $1 million was to be spent in the United States. The remaining $1.5 million, "the largest single advertising contract given by any department or agency of the government of Canada," was going, "just as it did in old pipeline days," to the people who had supported "ministerial tyranny" by the Liberals – Cockfield, Brown. "Nobody," the article concluded, "can say us Tories are not magnanimous with the country's cash."

Magnanimity in matters such as these was not John Diefenbaker's strong suit, and when McGregor was in Ottawa a few days later Balcer warned him that the Prime Minister was still asking what TCA proposed to do about Cockfield, Brown. McGregor replied that the corporation was still pleased with the agency's work. In fact, the firm had just received two awards for the excellence of its TCA advertising and if TCA dropped it now it would be clear to everyone, including newspaper editors, that the decision had been made not as a result of the quality of its work but because of government intervention. Leaving Balcer's office, he bumped into the Postmaster General, William Hamilton, who had been an advertising man himself before entering politics. Hamilton went even further than Balcer: in the minds of many members of the Conservative party, he said, TCA was deliberately flaunting Cockfield, Brown in the government's face. "I believe he was making a basically friendly effort," McGregor wrote later, "to let me know that TCA was prejudicing its position vis-à-vis the government."

With CPA still campaigning for new routes, McGregor again decided that winning the government's sympathy – or at least reducing what he viewed as its enmity – was more important than provoking a public confrontation on a point of principle. In September 1961, Cockfield, Brown lost the TCA account, which was split among three agencies considered more congenial to the government: Foster Advertising, F.H. Hayhurst, and Stanfield, Johnson and Hill. (The airline's earlier second choice, MacLaren, was rejected because it, too, was deemed to have a Liberal taint.) And all three agencies were warned that the contracts were conditional on them so conducting their affairs "that they do not have any clearly defined affiliation with partisan national groups or any political party."

All these pressures and frustrations were building up on Gordon McGregor. Despite the torrents of paper he rained down on Ottawa, he could not seem to make the bureaucrats and politicians understand the *facts*. He viewed Grant McConachie's expansive business methods as unscrupulous and his enthusiastic determination that private enterprise should prevail at all costs as inimical to the nation's best interests. And the politicians he expected to be the vigilant guardians of those interests he found at best short-sighted, at worst seized by unworthy, even sinister, considerations of self-interest.

He began to suffer from insomnia, and early that summer developed a numb feeling in his left leg; then he had a couple of giddy spells in the office; and on June 18, 1961, he was admitted to hospital with a cerebral thrombosis.

211

CHAPTER NINETEEN

CGREGOR ALWAYS REFERRED in later years to his "slight" stroke, but his doctors considered his condition serious enough to keep him in hospital for thirty-three days. He had delegated his authority for the operation of the airline to Herb Seagrim, vice-president, operations, under the watchful eye of Donald Gordon. But he hated the enforced idleness of a hospital bed and could not bear to be out of touch with his office. Within a week of his admission he insisted on daily visits from Beth Buchanan, the secretary who had worked for him ever since he joined the company and was almost as knowledgeable about its affairs, and certainly as devoted to its welfare, as he was himself. To "Miss Buchanan" – he was never known to call her anything else – he dictated letters and a stream of instructions designed to keep the company on its toes during his absence. And for the last week of his stay in hospital he slipped away every morning to put in the hours between 10 a.m. and 2 p.m. in his office.

It is not possible to say with certainty, of course, that overwork and worry brought on McGregor's stroke, which left him with a slight limp and weakness of his left arm, afflictions that irritated him sometimes in later years, however manfully he tried to conceal them. But even after a course of physiotherapy at home and a month's convalescence in the Bahamas, he continued to fret about the airline's future: he had not even left the hospital when Balcer informed him that the government proposed to grant CPA's request for the Vancouver-London route, though not for Toronto-London.*

The irony of McGregor's position was that all the time he was devoting so much of his mental energy to fending off the competition he thought would prove fatal, his management team was

---

*BOAC was no happier with this route award than TCA, since it opened the way for a second British carrier to cut itself in for a slice of the Atlantic traffic. After some informal exchanges between TCA and BOAC and unofficial representations at the civil servant level, the British government refused to admit CPA to London, so the route was never flown; the Canadian government revoked CPA's designation to it in 1965.

cementing TCA's position as one of the world's leading airlines. By the time he had his stroke, the DC-8 had been introduced on the Atlantic and the Vanguard on the transcontinental routes, and as its North Stars and Super Constellations were being taken out of service and sold, it was well on the way to becoming the first airline in North America with an all-turbine fleet. Much was made of this, naturally, in the airline's publicity. Stories appeared in the press pointing out that one DC-8 could carry as many passengers across the Atlantic in a year as the largest ocean liner,* and contrasting the DC-8's size with the diminutive Lockheeds the airline had been flying not so many years earlier. Passengers loved the comfort and smooth ride of the jets, and so did the pilots. Recalling their conversion training, Jackie Jones, a veteran who started out flying the little Lockheed 10A, said: "We were just like a bunch of kids – we used to go out at dawn and watch 'em take off and say 'Oh boy, wait till we get our hands on that one'. This was the first time you had more power to play with than the aeroplane could stand. In the old days, you'd occasionally wish you had three, five or six engines – hang 'em all over the place."

Before the pilots could get their hands on all this power, of course, they were trained on a flight simulator, which was essentially a computer in a stationary mock-up cockpit that reproduced virtually everything an actual aeroplane would do in the air. The DC-8 simulator cost $1 million, but it was considerably cheaper than training the pilots on the plane itself. The chief difference between flying a jet and the early Lockheeds, of course, was their speed. The pilots had to adjust to everything happening twice as fast. But once they became accustomed to that, they found the DC-8, with all its advanced instrumentation, easier to fly than their old piston-engined planes.

Neither the DC-8 nor the Vanguard, as was to be expected, was introduced to service without the usual teething troubles. The first transcontinental service using DC-8s was introduced on April 1, 1960, but delayed deliveries of later aircraft prevented the introduction of a second daily flight until October, when the peak summer traffic was over. The Vanguard deliveries were also late,

---

*The jets, of course, would rapidly end the era of the ocean liner. In 1962, more than two million people flew across the Atlantic, well over twice the number carried by sea. The jets saved the passengers money; but more than that, their speed opened the prospect of transatlantic travel to millions who had not until then been able to spare the time to go by sea. The subsequent phenomenal increase in the number of tourists of all nationalities – dubbed by an American wit "the herd shot around the world" – had an enormous impact not only on the airline industry, but on the whole of modern life.

and the continued use of North Stars and Super Constellations upset the airline's financial calculations and worsened its deficit by bringing in less revenue at greater cost.

But the worst disappointment of the early DC-8s was that Douglas had under-estimated the aircraft's drag, and its weight had to be considerably increased to carry the additional fuel needed to give it the required range. This failing was corrected in later versions of the plane; when the enlarged "Stretch 8" came along some years later it was able to carry 40 per cent more than its predecessors at only a small increase in its operating costs. It was later estimated, however, that TCA's first eleven DC-8s cost the company between $15 and $20 million in added fuel expenses during their lifetime.

The first Vanguards brought with them a succession of costly maintenance problems that kept the new Dorval base busy. Because Vickers was late in its deliveries to British European Airways, TCA was the first airline to put the Vanguard into scheduled service; it thus bore the brunt of the unavoidable chore of working the bugs out of a completely new airframe, engine and propeller system, an expensive process complicated in this case by delays in securing parts from England. The aircraft's Rolls-Royce Tyne engines needed frequent repair. They did not break down in flight but aircraft were often out of service while their engines were being changed. And the aircraft's hydraulic system gave endless trouble until, after almost a year, the source of it was discovered. It turned out to be annoyingly trivial – in effect, inadequate machining of a milled groove and the resultant wearing away of a washer – but, again, fixing it proved expensive.

From the passengers' point of view also, the Vanguard was not as popular as its Vickers predecessor, the Viscount; it was noisy and plagued by excessive vibration. The cause of this was eventually found by accident when an inboard engine on the right-hand wing was shut down during a test: the slipstream from its propeller was drumming against the fuselage and bouncing off the tail, a feature of the design it was impossible to alter.

On the other hand, the aircraft handled well and was popular with the pilots. It was also as ruggedly built as a tank – a feature credited with averting a major disaster a couple of years after its introduction. It is usual for manufacturers to upgrade aircraft engines as experience is gained with their operation, modifying them to give each new version more power, and one of the few criticisms levelled at the Viscount by the TCA engineers was that its single-spar wing construction was not strong enough to make full use of the bigger engines that came along later in its service life. So while the Vanguard was still on the drawing board, TCA's engineering department asked its designers to be sure its wing could withstand the higher speeds that might be attained with future engines. The wing design was already laid down, and the Vickers designers knew that changing it would cost their company money and make the finished aeroplane heavier than they thought it needed to be. Engineering's request sounded like just one more of those "frills" TCA had insisted on incorporating in the Viscount, and they refused to make the change.

One of those frills, as it happened, had been the cockpit windows. TCA had stipulated in ordering the Viscount that its cockpit windows be built of a strengthened glass which was both proof against collisions with birds and internally heated by electricity to prevent icing. Since that type of glass was not yet being made in England, TCA provided specifications to an American manufacturer, Pittsburgh Plate Glass, and had the cockpit windows built there and shipped to England for installation as "buyer-furnished equipment." When, after the Viscounts proved so successful, the American company Capital Airlines ordered them, it stipulated that they conform to TCA's specifications – including the cockpit windows. Vickers ordered the windows from the Pittsburgh company, and learned that it would have to get a release for the design from TCA. There ensued a bout of the horse-trading that so invigorates business dealings, in the course of which Vickers decided it would be a very good thing to strengthen the Vanguard's wing, and TCA obligingly provided the release Vickers needed for its windows.

The Vanguard thus had a wing structure strengthened in critical areas and 400 lbs. heavier than it needed to be for its original engines. This extra strength may well have saved Flight 502-6, which had just crossed the Rockies in May 1963, carrying sixty-four passengers and five crew from Vancouver to Edmonton. Its pilot, Captain George Smith, ran into light turbulence at 21,000 feet near Rocky Mountain House, and moments later, without warning, his aircraft suddenly plummeted 800 feet in a few seconds. Its fall was so violent that the three flight attendants and several passengers who had not yet had time to fasten their seat belts were injured by being thrown against the ceiling and hat racks, and one passenger died of a heart attack. Damage to the aircraft was confined to loosened and damaged seats and dented hat racks. Such a severe jolt, the engineers thought later, might have torn the wings off a less solidly built plane.

The modernization of the fleet, and the tremendously increased carrying capacity it brought with it, called for modernization and improvements in all the other departments of the airline, and the organization was more than equal to the challenge. In 1961, it introduced an electronic reservations system which put it in the forefront of contemporary technology.

The original cumbersome system of booking seats by radio was superseded early in the war by the introduction of teletypes. This was an undoubted improvement, but still primitive by today's standards. A ticket agent in Montreal needing a seat from there to Winnipeg, say, would send a message requesting it to the central control office in Toronto, where it would come off the machine in a continuous strip like a stock exchange ticker-tape. The reservations clerk would then consult his or her charts to see whether a seat was available; if so, the notation "confirmed" would be added to the original message; if not, the clerk would add "unable" to the request and the ticket agent would have to consult the potential passenger about alternative flights. This lengthy procedure tied up the teletype and agents elsewhere on the system were unable to file their requests for seats until it was completed. The result, naturally, was that the end of every day found stations along the system snowed under with requests for seats the agents had not yet managed to move on the teletype, and hopeful passengers might have to wait twenty-four hours to find out if they could get aboard the flight they wanted.

Later still, this procedure was replaced by what was called the "sell and record" system: the agents were permitted to sell seats aboard any flight and merely report the sale by teletype to the central control office in Toronto, where the reservations clerks sat before a huge board upon which coloured discs were hung to indicate the status of each flight. As soon as a flight was full, a red disc would go up and a "stop sale" order would go out to all ticket offices. Naturally, there were occasions when a ticket agent might sell a seat in the interval between central control realizing a flight was fully booked and the agent's receipt of the "stop sale" order; to compensate for this, a cushion of perhaps ten seats would be withheld from sale at the time the "stop" order was issued.

This, too, was an improvement on the previous system, but it was still unwieldy and imprecise, and it would sometimes result in aircraft leaving with empty seats that might have been sold. Also, as the number of flights increased and the planes became bigger, the amount of paper work entailed in keeping the passenger inventory up to date and making up manifests threatened to overwhelm the system. So in the early fifties C.J. "Cammie" Campbell, an air force communications specialist who had succeeded Steve Stevens, the airline's first director of communications, assigned Lyman Richardson, a radio operator with an active, original mind, to consult the various departments concerned in a thorough-going examination of what must be done to improve the reservations procedures. Computers, or electronic brains as the popular term had it, were still in their infancy, but Richardson realized they held the key to future progress. So he buckled down to learn all he could about them, enlisting the help of manufacturers such as IBM and individual experts, even including Sir Robert Watson-Watt, the British radar pioneer.

After years of study, during which his "far-out" thinking and high-pitched excitable laugh became familiar across the system, Richardson decided he had the answer. Noting that passenger agents used scratch pads to jot down the details of their transactions with prospective passengers, he designed a sort of "scratch pad" card that could be used to communicate with a central computer. The pre-printed card bore a series of little squares corresponding to all the information needed to book a seat on any flight anywhere on the system; all the agent had to do was block out the inappropriate squares with an ordinary lead pencil. Richardson then took his card to Ferranti Electric of Toronto, whose engineers designed a desk-size machine called a "transactor" which could read the marks on the cards when they were inserted in a slot and flash the information over leased telephone lines to the central computer in Toronto. Properly programmed, the computer flashed back the "confirmed" or "unable" signal within a couple of seconds to any station on the system.

The cards were also designed to fulfil other functions, such as asking whether a flight was on time or cancelling a booking, and the system became a valuable aid to the important airline function of scheduling. One of the many factors airline schedulers must take into account is the time of day at which most passengers want to fly. Using the simple method of counting the passengers on, say, a 10 a.m. flight from Toronto to Winnipeg, the schedulers might conclude that there was a popular demand for that flight. Richardson pointed out that it could be a "false demand" – since many of those passengers might have tried to travel on a flight leaving at, say, 8 a.m., but found it fully booked. So the new system was designed to record a passenger's first choice as well as the flight he ultimately travelled on.

The ReserVec* computer was claimed to be the first "real-time" computer system developed in the world. At around the same

---

* A contest was held among the employees to find a name for the new system, and Harry J. Simper, passenger office manager at Lethbridge, won $100 for coming up with the name ReserVec – from Reservations Electrically Controlled.

time, American Airlines was working with IBM to develop its own electronic reservations system, which was named "Sabre." The Sabre system encountered costly teething troubles and affected the airline's balance sheet for several years. ReserVec, which cost $4 million to install across the whole airline, performed beautifully from the start. While it was designed to handle sixty thousand transactions a day, it proved capable of handling more than three times that number before it was superseded by a more modern system, ReserVec II, nine years later.

Even before the DC-8s arrived, McGregor and his management team had realized that the increased pace of the jet age would demand the adoption of the most modern methods and techniques. So, as well as assigning Richardson and the others to modernize the reservations system, in 1957 he hired a brilliant Canadian physicist, Peter Sandiford – who later founded the faculty of management at McGill University – to fill the new post of director of operational research. An exotic new field in Canada at that time, operational research can perhaps best be described as the application of mathematical and scientific techniques to business management. It began in wartime England, when Churchill assembled a group of eminent scientists to examine the most effective way of using the country's scarce resources: how many bombs were needed to pulverize a German factory, for instance, or what was the most economical way of searching the Bay of Biscay for submarines. The technique had been adapted to business use after the war, but it was still so new that Sandiford was astonished to find that an operational research group had already been set up at the Dorval maintenance base by a young quality technician named Pierre Jean Jeanniot.

Cosmopolitan backgrounds, innate or acquired, are not unusual in the airline business, but Pierre Jeanniot had seen more of the world than most people by the time he entered his teens. His French father lived in Ethiopia, running a railroad from Addis Ababa to the port of Djibouti in what was then French Somaliland. With Pierre on the way, his mother, unimpressed by the Ethiopian hospitals of the day, headed for her parents' home in the Jura mountains, on the French side of the Alps across from Switzerland.

She never got there, for Pierre, showing early evidence of the impatient urge to make things happen that characterized his later career, burst into the world on April 9, 1933, at Montpellier, in the south of France, long before she could complete her journey. After a couple of weeks, Mme. Jeanniot returned to Addis Ababa, and Pierre spent the first four years of his life in that troubled capital. After the Italian invasion of Ethiopia, the railroad was sold to the Italians and Jeanniot père took his family back to France, where they lived during the German occupation in World War II.

When Pierre was 13, his mother took him to Montreal to visit his sister, who had married a Mountie. She had hardly arrived when she received word that her husband had died back in France. Alone with her two children, Mme. Jeanniot decided to stay in Canada, and Pierre completed his grammar school and high school in Montreal. There was no money for university so he took a job as an electrical draughtsman with what is now Northern Telecom and began to take night classes at Sir George Williams College (now Concordia University). After a year and a half spent designing a telephone exchange in suburban Montreal, he landed a job with Sperry Gyroscope of Canada, a subsidiary of the American company set up to manufacture instruments for the F-86 Sabre jets then being built at Canadair. There, the chief engineer, recognizing that his new recruit was well into his degree course in physics and mathematics, made him a junior engineer.

All told, Pierre attended night classes for ten years, winter and summer. After earning his B.Sc. at Sir George, he spent three more years in a post-graduate course in business administration at McGill. To obtain a full MBA he would have had to attend day classes for a year. With a wife and three children, and a mortgage to pay, he was unable to do this, but the lack of the formal degree did not hamper his future progress: he went on to lecture at McGill and later took a year's sabbatical from the airline to set up the multi-campus Université du Québec.

Pierre Jeanniot's introduction to TCA came when Sperry undertook to supply instruments for the airline's new Super Constellations. He was taken on at Dorval in 1955, as part of a small group of technicians involved in failure investigation: whenever a new technical difficulty arose, they would try to analyse the reason for it, and then devise a suitable "fix." And once the problem was identified, and classified, steps could be taken to deal with it when it next arose – or better still, prevent it happening again.

In his mathematical courses, Jeanniot had become interested in actuarial studies. If statistics could be used to predict such things as human life expectancy, he reasoned, perhaps mathematical models could be constructed to do the same thing for aircraft parts. And so, as the computer shouldered its way into the business world, he moved from the simple physical examination of failed components into what was essentially the field of operational research. Fortunately, his bosses supported his interest, and he was able to set up his own operational research group. His first recruit was Anne Bodnarchuk, a graduate in mathematics from Queen's University who had worked on one of the first practical computer operations in Canada, at the Manufacturers' Life Insurance Company in Toronto. Together they developed a computer program that was able to simulate an aircraft engine's life cycle and predict when its various components would need replacement. Approximately coinciding with the introduction of the jets, this was a notable step forward in aviation that was quickly copied by other airlines around the world. It led to improved engine reliability – and thus aircraft safety – and cost reductions resulting from increased efficiency, such as better on-time performance and better management of maintenance work.

Engineers in other companies, of course, were pursuing similar studies, and one day Jim Bain asked Jeanniot to evaluate a device that had been invented by a British company. This was an electronic recorder designed to monitor various aspects of an aircraft's engine performance during flight, with the idea that subsequent analysis of the tape would be useful as a maintenance tool. Jeanniot experimented with the device and concluded that the mass of information it gathered was far too unwieldy to be usefully analysed. It was, he thought, rather like taking a man's pulse every five minutes during his lifetime in an attempt to predict when he might have a heart attack.

At the risk of incurring Bain's displeasure, he returned the device to its British manufacturer, along with his verdict that the device was too complex to be of value as a practical maintenance aid. He had, however, been impressed by the recorder's sophistication, and he softened his rejection of it by suggesting that there was one period in an aircraft's life when it might indeed prove invaluable: that period just before it crashed. In such unhappy circumstances, the weeks or months needed to interpret the tape would be well worth while. The British engineers went back to their drawing boards – and came up with the famous "black box" so eagerly sought today by crash investigators.

When Peter Sandiford joined the airline, he naturally tried to incorporate the Dorval operational research group into his new unit at headquarters. Jim Bain, however, recognized the potential importance of Jeanniot's work to the maintenance branch, and refused to let him go. So Sandiford turned to Britain for his first two assistants. Howard Whitton, a Welshman, had done operational research for the National Coal Board, and Roger

Linder, a former Fleet Air Arm pilot, was fresh out of university with a degree in mathematics and statistics. They began work at headquarters in such fields as scheduling, passenger flow, inventory control and fleet planning. And, as evidence of the important place operational research came to occupy within the corporation, thirty years later, Jeanniot was president of the airline, Linder group vice-president, sales and operations, Whitton vice-president, marketing planning and support, and Anne Bodnarchuk vice-president, computer and systems services.

The new sophistication necessitated by the advent of the jets was extended at the beginning of 1961 to the airline's fare structure. In the early days, when transcontinental flights could only be accomplished in a series of short hops of similar lengths, it was natural that fares were set at a fixed rate per mile across the system: it made little difference to the cost whether a passenger was flying between Montreal and Ottawa or between North Bay and Kapuskasing on the way from Montreal to Winnipeg. But as aircraft acquired longer ranges and the old refuelling stops were eliminated in favour of non-stop flights between the country's major population centres, it became apparent that it costs much more proportionately to fly a passenger on a short journey than it does to fly him a couple of thousand miles. There are many reasons for this. Once a plane is airborne, of course, its fuel consumption increases with the distance flown. But it uses considerably more fuel taking off than it does at cruising altitude; on a short flight a modern jet may barely reach its cruising altitude before it begins to descend, so the extra fuel burned on take-off becomes a much larger proportion of the total fuel used than it is on a long flight. Also, there are many fixed costs attached to all flights, regardless of their length: the overhead costs of making a reservation, issuing the ticket, boarding the passenger and handling the aircraft on the ground are the same whether the passenger buys a $100 ticket for a short flight or pays $550 for a long one. Similarly, the landing fee paid to the government for the use of the airport is the same whether the aircraft has flown 2,000 miles or 200; but spread over 2,000 miles the cost of that landing fee per mile is only one-tenth of what it would be on a 200-mile flight.

Much midnight oil was burned in an attempt to break down all the airline's overhead costs and construct a curve on a graph showing the actual operating costs per seat-mile in relation to flight distances. It was calculated that it might cost 10 cents a passenger-mile to operate an aircraft over a 175-mile route but only 5 cents a passenger-mile over a 1,500-mile route. And when the curve was applied to all TCA routes in North America – from the 47-mile segment between Vancouver and Victoria to the 2,161-mile non-stop route between Toronto and Vancouver – it was found that the existing fares were too low on the short-haul routes, about right between 400 and 600 miles, and too high on the long-distance routes. So in January 1961, 2,200 new fares were introduced, some lower than they had been, and some higher. For example, the one-way economy fare from Montreal to Vancouver dropped from $123 to $110, and the one-way economy fare from Montreal to Toronto rose from $24 to $28.

It was not possible to adhere completely to the curve – it would have been prohibitively expensive to make the shortest routes fully pay their way – but the new fare structure, as McGregor said, was "properly and honestly related to carefully calculated operating costs." It reduced the return to the airline per passenger-mile, but it was expected to attract more customers; and as an added inducement to them, the airline simultaneously introduced new excursion rates 25 per cent lower than the normal economy fare, available for eight months of the year. By June, after the new rates had been in effect for six months, TCA's traffic was up by 25 per cent, while the U.S. airlines were experiencing a 4 per cent drop.

While McGregor was entitled to take these developments as gratifying evidence that his people were more than keeping up with the times, the airline, labouring under the cross borne by all Crown corporations, remained a whipping-boy for the more contentious segments of the press. On August 18, 1961, the *Globe and Mail* published an editorial castigating TCA for "gloomily estimating" that because of the assignment of CPA to the Vancouver-London route it would lose $3 to $4 million a year in revenue. "This," the editorial said, "was a sadly typical TCA reaction to any news that it is going to have to face vigorous competition on a service where it had previously enjoyed monopoly. There is never a welcome word for the new competitor and a cheerful promise to fight hard for the business; never even an admission that the new service might be a convenience to the public. All that the tearful TCA can ever find to say is that it is going to lose money."

These shortcomings on the part of the national airline, the editorial suggested, were probably caused by its realization that it was "an over-staffed, high-cost bureaucracy which cannot hope to prosper when faced with efficient, free enterprise competition." As evidence to support this allegation, the newspaper produced figures furnished by CPA to the Air Transport Board purporting to show that TCA's operating expenses, at 36.7 cents per available ton-mile, were higher than those of comparable U.S. airlines: Braniff's 29.5 cents, Delta's 29.6 cents and Northwest's 27.8 cents. The reason for this advanced by the editorial (again on the evidence supplied by CPA) was the low productivity of TCA's employees. Where TCA employed 11,172 people, the newspaper said, Braniff had only 5,589, Delta 7,567 and Northwest 6,636. "TCA may wish to quarrel with these figures," it concluded. "If so, TCA should produce the statistical evidence to prove its points, and to disprove CPA's accusation."

McGregor needed no urging. He responded with a crisp four-page letter to the editor in which he gleefully pointed out that the latest Dominion Bureau of Statistics figures showed that CPA's operating cost per available ton-mile for 1960 was higher than TCA's: 37.8 cents against 36.88 cents. And the discrepancy was even more marked in revenue ton-miles, CPA's cost being 71.48 cents against TCA's 62.35 cents. So much for the alleged superior efficiency of private enterprise. As to the lower costs of the U.S. airlines, he pointed out that many factors made comparisons difficult. One was the wide difference in the price of aviation fuel in the two countries: it had been established at the Air Transport Board hearing on CPA's first transcontinental application in 1958 that had TCA been able to buy all its fuel at the same price as it paid in New York, its annual expenses would have been reduced by $2.25 million. Another was the basic difference in financing between TCA, as a government-owned corporation, and the privately owned U.S. airlines. "TCA is almost entirely financed by fixed interest bearing capital," he wrote. "These interest charges, now amounting to $10,500,000 per year, are an operating charge against the company. On the other hand, most U.S. carriers are financed to a substantial degree by stock issues, the dividends of which are paid out of net earnings, and are not included in the recorded operating cost per available ton-mile. . . ."

Also, the statistics on employee productivity obviously depended on how much of the airline's work was done within the company and how much was contracted outside. Unlike some other companies, TCA did all its own maintenance and overhaul work. CPA, for example, had major overhaul work done in Japan and Holland, and its Britannia aircraft were consistently overhauled by the Bristol company in England. And – a nice crowning touch – CPA also farmed out its DC-8 engines for overhaul to "the allegedly high-cost operator, TCA."

His case, McGregor considered, was iron-clad. But once again, patiently (though no doubt with scant hope of converting the heathen), he reiterated what he had been saying for so long:

The basic facts with respect to Canadian civil aviation are quite simple. The total population of the country represents a potential air traffic market of fixed size, both domestic and international. If that market is divided between two carriers, the gross revenue available to each will obviously be less than the total, and the inevitable duplication of effort will tend to increase total expenses. The result can only be, as is now the case, that both carriers will lose money. Losses by TCA affect every Canadian taxpayer. Losses by CPA affect only the CPR, and indirectly, the owners of CPR stock, only 24 per cent of which is registered as being in Canadian hands.

Soon after he took this satisfying swipe at his critics, McGregor reported to his board of directors that the Minister of Transport, Leon Balcer, was "favourably disposed" toward his plan for a merger of TCA and CPA, and thought the cabinet shared his view. But politics has its own imperatives. Amid much enthusiasm, the city of Trois-Rivières was about to open its new airport, and as its representative in Ottawa, Balcer took the opportunity to ask McGregor to have one of TCA's daily flights between Montreal and Quebec City stop there for the convenience of those local residents who might have business in either of those cities. Since Trois-Rivières is only eighty-five miles from Montreal and even nearer to Quebec City, and since plans were afoot to build a brand-new highway over the route, TCA was not, in McGregor's words, "sanguine with respect to the future development of traffic." In fact, he warned Balcer that making even one stop a day each way at the new airport would cost the airline an estimated $115,000 a year – and the estimated revenue to be gained thereby would amount to only $80,000. However, McGregor wrote to his minister, "I appreciate the undesirability of a newly constructed airport remaining without scheduled service, and the other non-monetary considerations which are involved in this case." He would, therefore, recommend the new service to his board; but he hoped it would be made clear that it could not be launched until the Department of Transport had improved the new airport's navigational facilities, which consisted of but one radio beacon, and its runway lighting and meteorological services.

Expressing his deep appreciation for McGregor's "personal interest in this matter," the minister replied:

This is excellent news for me, and for the population of the Three Rivers region. There is a tremendous interest in aviation at the present time in our area, which has a population of approximately 200,000 people within fifteen miles of the airport. Our Municipal Airport Commission is a very active group which will give you the utmost *cooperation. Also, our Flying School is very progressive and will help in spreading the interest in aviation in the area. John Baldwin has already lined up his people to furnish the airport with the necessary equipment for your intended service.* *

Once again, McGregor's conciliatory attempt to accommodate himself to political pressures, distasteful as he found it, failed to bring about the reciprocal understanding he had hoped for on the part of the government. The new blow was delivered not by the appreciative Balcer, but by the Minister of Finance, Donald Fleming. In its 1961 budget, the airline had won government approval for the purchase of five more Conway-powered DC-8s for delivery early in 1963. Toward the end of the year, as the added competition from CPA took effect, passenger forecasts were revised downward and it was decided only four DC-8s were needed. As an additional hedge against any further drop in passenger forecasts, it was decided to change the order and buy a new version of the DC-8 – the DC-8F Jet Trader, a versatile aircraft with a strengthened floor designed to carry all cargo, all passengers, or any combination of cargo and passengers called for by the traffic demand. When he heard of this change of plan, Fleming refused to sanction it. It would, he told Balcer, require cabinet approval of a full-scale formal amendment to the 1961 capital budget – and it was now November of that year.

Since the government had approved the purchase of five aircraft and the company now wanted to buy only four, this appeared at first sight to be pointless quibbling on Fleming's part. But there was a reason for it, a reason McGregor intensely resented: Geoffrey Notman, president of Canadair, was in the midst of a gloves-off campaign to pressure the government into ordering the national airline to "buy Canadian" – or, more precisely, to buy the Canadair-built four-engined, turbo-prop freighter, the CL-44.

After the North Star production program, Canadair had successfully produced U.S. Sabre jet fighters under licence, and when the RCAF needed a long-range coastal patrol aircraft it had purchased the rights to the Bristol Britannia and modified

---

*As it turned out, it was September 1963 before the airport improvements were completed and TCA began its service. The results, notwithstanding the efforts of the Municipal Airport Commission and the local flying club, justified the pessimism of the TCA analysts: during 1964 an average of six passengers a day flew in and out of Trois-Rivières. In response to local representations, the flight schedule was changed for the next two years, and the number of daily passengers rose to ten. In 1967, the year when everyone was flocking to Expo '67 in Montreal, the daily average was back to six, and the airline was losing not the $35,000 a year it had predicted but $100,000. The service was discontinued soon thereafter.

it to create the CL-28, or Argus, which gave yeoman service for many years. It then approached Bristol again for further rights and produced a "stretch" version of the Britannia, using the more powerful Tyne engine instead of the original Proteus. Twelve of these were sold to the RCAF (which called them Yukons) and Canadair went on to make a civilian version, the CL-44, whose chief novelty was its tail, which swung open to permit the loading of bulky cargo. Several of them had been sold to the U.S. cargo airlines Slick, Seaboard and Flying Tigers before the company mounted its campaign to sell them to TCA.

TCA, whose initial opposition to all-cargo aircraft had not been changed by its experience with the Bristol freighter, was developing its domestic cargo business rapidly and seeking to expand its transatlantic business, but it could not foresee sufficient traffic to warrant all-cargo aircraft between Canada and Europe. The DC-8F looked ideal; if not enough freight materialized, it could be used for passengers. The CL-44 could not; as a turbo-prop it would not have been competitive with the jets on the Atlantic. The DC-8F had another advantage: it was equipped with a new Pratt & Whitney engine, the JT3D-3, which was at once more powerful and more economical than the Conway installed in TCA's first DC-8s. As a further handicap to Notman's ambitions, the CL-44 did not use the standard rigid cargo pallet, which could be handled by fork-lift trucks available at every airport; instead, it had a flexible pallet that slid along a track on the aircraft's floor, necessitating sophisticated devices for loading and unloading. TCA conducted the usual exhaustive analysis of both aircraft, and came down hard in favour of the DC-8F.

The government, however, had invested heavily in the construction of the CL-44, and McGregor found himself embroiled in a classic early manifestation of a dilemma that has become even more marked with the passage of the years: how to reconcile the aims of government departments intent on encouraging Canadian industry and fostering exports with those of businessmen bound by the normal constraints of the marketplace – in other words, the need to make a profit. The issue has often been more hotly contested than many other points of philosophy, and in this case it led to a bitter break between two men who had long been friends.

Geoff Notman was a big man – well over six feet tall – with a well-developed egotism and a justified reputation as a manufacturing engineer: he had been general manager at Dominion Engineering for years before going to Canadair. He and McGregor had been classmates at McGill, and his attachment to Montreal was every bit as deep as McGregor's: his grandfather was the pioneer photographer William Notman, whose early work is a priceless part of the country's heritage. Only a few months earlier, Notman and his wife had sent flowers and a book to McGregor's hospital room. But there was little cordiality between them when Notman called on McGregor in his office on December 1, 1961.

Their conversation was not taped for posterity, but it is obvious they argued their respective cases with vigour. Their views can be summarized quite briefly: Notman believed that McGregor, as president of a government-owned corporation, had a patriotic duty to support Canadian enterprises that created jobs for Canadian workers; McGregor believed that if the CL-44 was not an economic proposition for TCA – as his experts assured him it wasn't – he had a duty to resist any attempt to steam-roller him into buying it.

The heat generated at the meeting can be adduced from the eight-page letter Notman wrote as soon as he returned to his own office that day, a letter one of his own executives later admitted was "unfair." Not only did the letter pull no punches; Notman stoked his old friend's resentment by sending copies of it to Diefenbaker and the members of his cabinet, and to all the directors of TCA.

The letter began by accusing TCA (and by implication McGregor himself) of "a total lack of cooperation" with the Canadian aircraft manufacturing industry, and of thereby being "contemptuous of the national interest." The aforesaid industry provided direct and indirect employment for fifty thousand Canadians, and in these circumstances "it is not unreasonable to expect that those charged with the management of TCA would, in the formation of its policies, give due weight to the broad public interest." Instead, during the past twelve years, TCA had spent more than $200 million on the purchase of aircraft, "not one cent of it" in Canada; TCA had pulled the plug on the Avro Jetliner project, which could have put Canada "in the forefront of the world in the production of the short-range jet passenger aircraft"; it had rejected several Canadair designs for a Canadian-built aircraft to succeed the North Star; it had turned down a Canadair proposal to modify the Britannia to meet the airline's need for a medium-range aircraft and instead decided to buy the Vanguard and thus "launch an aircraft program for the U.K. aircraft industry – the very thing you have been so violently opposed to doing in Canada." Furthermore, "TCA, at a cost of millions of dollars of the Canadian taxpayers' money, has unnecessarily created facilities for the maintenance, overhaul and servicing of engines and equipment which duplicate facilities already in existence in private industry."

The proposal to operate the DC-8F in a combined passenger-cargo configuration, Notman wrote, "constitutes an unjustifiable experiment with a new concept which may be expected to prove calamitous." The answer was an all-cargo aircraft, and "TCA should make up its mind now either to get properly into the business of carrying freight by air or to stay out of it; in the latter event, TCA should be prepared to relinquish its air freight routes to another Canadian operator which has already declared its willingness to acquire such rights and to purchase Canadian-built equipment for the purpose of serving its customers."

In response, McGregor wrote that he could find nothing in Notman's accusations that he had not rebutted in person at their meeting, so he assumed the purpose of the letter was to convey Notman's "unsubstantiated opinions" to the Prime Minister and its other recipients. His reply, he said, was written out of a sense of obligation to provide those other recipients with "the relevant facts"; it is worth quoting at length as what he obviously intended it to be – a warning to all those, whether politicians or civil servants, seized by the seductive idea that they could somehow serve the national interest by intervening in the normal play of business forces.

He began by getting off his chest some complaints of his own about the airline's past business dealings with Canadair. For instance, the TCA engineers had foreseen that the North Star would have a noise problem and the purchase contract obliged Canadair and Rolls-Royce to take steps to reduce the cabin noise to an acceptable level. Rolls-Royce had tried to honour this obligation but Canadair had not, and the airline had had to find the solution itself, with the cross-over exhaust manifold. TCA made this design available to Canadair, which quoted a firm price for manufacturing and installing the systems but tried to persuade the airline the price would be lower if it signed a cost-plus agreement. TCA preferred the firm price, only to have Canadair complain later that it had lost $466,000 on the contract. While it was under no obligation to do so, the airline had agreed to split that loss and pay Canadair $233,000 more than the $759,000 stipulated in the contract.

Nevertheless, TCA had tried to do business with Canadair again in 1957, when it asked for a quotation for a major structural repair to a damaged aircraft. Canadair estimated the job would cost $450,000 and take seven months. So TCA did the repair itself, along with some other work on the aircraft – in two and a half months and at a total cost of less than $160,000.

Furthermore, before TCA ordered its Viscount fleet, McGregor told Notman he foresaw an American market for at least fifty Viscounts and suggested Canadair might explore with his friend Sir George Edwards the possibility of building them under licence. Notman had seen Edwards, and found him receptive to the idea, but had then told McGregor he felt the licensing cost was too high and the North and South American markets for the Viscounts too small to justify Canadair's participation. "Since then," McGregor wrote, "something in the order of 150 Viscounts have been sold to airlines operating in North and South America. . . . In the light of this history, I think it will be generally agreed that it is patently dishonest for you now to allege that TCA has in the past not done its best to place business with Canadair."

The letter went on to remind Notman that the airline had been carrying cargo for twenty years, recalled its unsatisfactory experience with the all-cargo Bristol freighter, and reiterated its belief that combining passengers and cargo was a perfectly sound proposition. It also pointed out that after Notman had decided to build a modified Britannia he had met Grant McConachie in McGregor's office and both airline presidents had told him they were not impressed with the idea. Notman had "as usual" responded that Canadian airlines had an obligation to buy Canadian-built equipment whether or not it met their requirements, and McConachie had ended the conversation by saying: "Go ahead and build it if you want to, but don't expect me to buy it."

McGregor said he had stressed to his staff that TCA's policy was "to purchase Canadian products from Canadian companies in every case except where to do so requires the acceptance of a substantial penalty in either quality or price," and went on:

I find your allegation that TCA's failure to buy the CL-44 is prejudicial to the export market for that aircraft to be unintentionally flattering to the technical standing of TCA in the civil aviation industry, but entirely inaccurate. Airlines do not buy or fail to buy any particular aircraft because some other airline has or has not bought it. While their early delivery date would have been a feature of value to TCA at the time, both the Mark 1 Comet and the Lockheed Electra were not purchased by TCA, on the advice of its technical departments. This seemingly did not prevent other carriers from buying these types, both of which eventually proved to have serious design faults, with resulting accidents, and major financial problems for both the manufacturers and the airlines.

As to Notman's "rather loose" statement that all other national airlines bought equipment built in their own country, McGregor pointed out that BOAC, after its experience with British aeroplanes such as Tudors, Comets and Britannias, had switched to U.S.-built equipment such as Stratocruisers and Boeing 707s, and was disposing of its Britannias. Other airlines operating U.S. equipment included Air France, SAS, KLM, Lufthansa, Alitalia, Air India, Japan Air Lines and Qantas.

He also corrected Notman's assumption that TCA's capital spending came from the taxpayer's pocket: "It must be remembered that the taxpayer of Canada only becomes involved in TCA's finances when the company experiences a deficit. Capital for the purchase of new aircraft and equipment is obtained through interest-bearing public bond issues via the CNR and the government. It is essential that TCA do its utmost to avoid any deficits, by operating as efficiently as possible. . . . In short, and as I told you last Friday morning, TCA, with the full approval of its Board, has decided against the purchase of CL-44 aircraft, at this time or in the foreseeable future."

In the event, the government did not press the issue to a confrontation, and the airline's capital budget, revised to include the four DC-8Fs, eventually received cabinet approval – though not until the last day of the year. Notman lost the contract, an old friend, and his chief salesman for the CL-44, John McGill. McGregor had been much impressed by McGill's sincerity and competence during their negotiations, and after the controversy had died down he called him in and said: "I didn't buy the CL-44 – but I'd like to buy you." McGill, who admitted years later that the decision not to buy the CL-44 had been amply justified by events, entered the airline as its first system sales manager; he was, in fact, the first executive hired at that senior level since the immediate postwar period. And by the time he left the airline in 1983 to become president and chief executive officer of Canadian Liquid Air he was its executive vice-president and chief of group enterprises.

CHAPTER TWENTY

N AN EARLIER AGE, when steam locomotives were beginning to intrude on a slower-paced world, the Duke of Wellington delivered himself of some thoughts on the matter. The Iron Duke was no welcomer of the iron horse. It would, he grumbled, "only encourage the lower classes to move about needlessly."

Something of the same thing happened with TCA's new fare structure: it stimulated traffic to record levels, but there was a much larger swing from first to economy class than the analysts had expected. The prediction had been that the proportion of passengers flying economy would rise from 44 per cent to 69 per cent; instead it shot up to 79 per cent. This brought in a lower yield per passenger-mile than had been anticipated, and the airline ended the year with the biggest deficit it had suffered up to that time: $6.45 million. By the following year, almost 90 per cent of all passengers were choosing to fly economy. The airline reacted by raising economy fares to bring them closer to the first-class rate and modifying its fleet to enlarge the economy sections. These measures, and the continuing appetite for air travel, reduced the 1962 deficit to $3.45 million – the last red ink registered during McGregor's years at the helm.

McGregor, of course, continued to attribute the major part of these losses to the government "give-aways"; he said that had it not been for the competition of CPA on the transcontinental route, the 1962 deficit would have been a profit. But in the early 1960s all airlines were in financial trouble because of the enormous cost of introducing the jets and the huge increase in seating capacity they brought with them; for example, TCA's passenger load factor for the year was only 60 per cent, which meant that on average 40 per cent of the seats on every flight were empty. The crisis in the aviation world became so grave that in the United States the Hartford Insurance Company organized a symposium to try to figure out how (or even whether) the insurance industry could recoup the $2 billion or so it had lent to the U.S. airlines.

TCA turned the corner in 1963 and registered a small but welcome profit: $527,000. Otherwise, the year was one McGregor
would undoubtedly have liked to forget. The airline was seldom
out of the headlines, and few of them were welcome ones. A
continuing controversy, which had its genesis long before and
would persist long afterward, arose from a letter he addressed
to all employees of the Winnipeg maintenance and overhaul base
in November 1962. Back in 1949, when he had reinstated TCA's
headquarters in Montreal, McGregor had assured those Winni-
peggers nervous about the economic future of their city that he
"could not foresee the transfer of such massive units as the main
overhaul base away from Winnipeg." Nor, of course, could the
master shipbuilders of Nova Scotia have foreseen the consequences when one of their neighbours, Samuel Cunard, moved
to England in 1838 and founded the first regular Atlantic steamship line. Likewise, the British shipbuilders who created those
ocean-going marvels the *Queen Mary* and *Queen Elizabeth* for
the company Cunard founded could hardly have foreseen that a
few years later the world's largest ships would be built in Japan.

From the days of the Wright brothers, events in the sky had
moved much faster than those on the ocean, and by the time
McGregor announced the building of the new Montreal base in
1957 he was aware that his crystal ball had been somewhat
clouded eight years earlier, and that the centre of gravity of Canadian aviation had already swung away from Winnipeg just as
surely as the age of steam had doomed the magnificent Nova
Scotia schooners. When he had promised that he did not anticipate any reduction in the work load of the Winnipeg base he
had been careful to specify that he was referring to "company
plans which are finalized through 1961." Only the *Winnipeg
Free Press*, it seemed, had sensed the menace in that qualification. But now, in 1962, the whole city awoke vociferously to
the threat.

McGregor had been in Winnipeg a few days earlier to attend
one of the parties held across the system to celebrate the airline's twenty-fifth anniversary, but he had refrained from making any comments on company planning because a party was
not the place to "talk shop." He had, however, promised an early
statement "to facilitate as far as possible the personal planning
of the base personnel." The decision to build the Montreal base
to service all the company's jets, his letter now said, had "obviously meant that as TCA moved toward an all-jet fleet, the Winnipeg base as an overhaul centre would cease to exist." He had
promised that the Viscounts would continue to be serviced at

Winnipeg, and TCA would be operating a Viscount fleet of not less than forty aircraft until 1965, "but it is quite possible that the Viscount fleet will start to dwindle in numbers, perhaps quite rapidly, early in 1966." TCA's most probable next purchase of a new aircraft type would be a short/medium-range jet and its major maintenance would thus be "engineered into Dorval, not Winnipeg, in conformity with the original planning, and the dictates of economic common sense."

Having assured his employees that the company would treat them "fairly and intelligently," McGregor hoped his statement would remove the doubt about the future that had surrounded their personal decisions in recent years. "I hope, too," he wrote, "for such of you to whom this may apply, that you will not regard the prospect of changing your scene of activity to Montreal with reluctance. I think that those many who have already made the move are actually enjoying living in the Montreal area." *

A few days later, McGregor tabled a copy of the letter before the parliamentary committee on transportation, accompanied by a written statement in which he said there was "a tendency to exaggerate the extent and effect" of decisions like the one he had had to make. In fact, the closing of the base would affect only 860 of the 1,813 permanent and 80 temporary workers in Winnipeg, and by 1966 that number would probably have shrunk to 650 because of transfers to other positions, normal retirements and attrition. The company, he said, had an obligation to make every reasonable effort within its power to provide alternative employment to the workers affected, and there was "an obligation on all parties concerned to place the least troublesome interpretation on the terms of union agreements having to do with the exercise of seniority and the transfer of personnel."

One man who did not think the "extent and effect" of the closing of the base could be exaggerated was the mayor of Winnipeg, Stephen Juba. He promptly summoned a meeting of all Manitoba MPs to discuss this "$15 million death blow to Western Canada" and cabled McGregor to tell him so. McGregor could do no more than wire back correcting the mayor's figures: if every one of the base employees were moved on the morrow, he said, the reduction in the company's payroll would be only $5.8 million.

By January, the controversy was in full swing, and a delega-

---

*Most of the many employees transferred to Montreal through the years settled quite happily in their new surroundings. But some diehards left their families behind in Winnipeg and used their employee transportation passes to commute home for the weekend.

tion representing the province of Manitoba, the city of Winnipeg and an assortment of other interested groups descended on Ottawa to present a brief embodying their howls of outrage at what they saw as TCA's long history of duplicity and expressing the belief that the $1 million a year the airline estimated it would save by closing the base was neither valid nor important when the welfare of a whole community was at stake.

Faced with this kind of organized pressure, Leon Balcer made a statement in the House: no further staff transfers would take place from Winnipeg, he said, pending further investigation by the government and TCA. At this, McGregor was forced to register his own protest; it would mean that Winnipeg employees destined to be displaced four years hence would be denied their rights in the interim to bid for vacancies arising at Dorval, which by union agreement had to be posted on all company notice boards. The minister backed down gracefully. He made another statement in the House explaining that what he had been referring to was "the transfer of positions rather than persons." There was "no thought of preventing Winnipeg employees from exercising their right to bid for positions at Dorval."

With the pressure building and an election in the offing, the government took the predictable course: it shelved the issue at least temporarily by announcing that another investigation would be undertaken by a leading independent engineering consulting firm.

By this time, McGregor had found himself embroiled in another unwelcome rash of headlines. Herb Symington, who had remained on TCA's board of directors until 1958,* formed the habit in his declining years of spending the winter in California. Shortly after the new year in 1963, he was taken seriously ill

---

*In 1958, the Conservative government decreed that TCA directors should serve for only three years unless they were reappointed. The company's board had been remarkably stable until then: Symington, of course, had been on it since the beginning; so had C.P. Edwards, who retired in 1959, and Wilfrid Gagnon, who followed suit in 1961; J.A. Northey, who also retired in 1961, had been a member since 1939. With the exception of Donald Gordon and R.A.C. Henry, whose counsel he greatly valued, McGregor sometimes found himself from 1958 on with – to use his own words – "more recruits than seasoned players." On occasion, he had to look up a newly appointed director in *Who's Who* to find out who he was. And he commented acidly in his memoirs that "one of the first appointees, and I do believe also his government sponsor, learned with complete disbelief that the honour did not carry with it a fat fee." (It did, however, carry a far from intangible benefit, in the form of handsome airline pass privileges.) It is only fair to add that McGregor expressly exonerated from his implied criticism of some of the "recruits" the names of former Ontario premier Leslie Frost, Toronto insurance man Harry Price, Vancouver industrialist Walter Koerner and Ralph Scott Misener, the Winnipeg head of the shipping firm that bears his name.

there, and his son-in-law, the Montreal lawyer and shipping man William R. Eakin, called the airline to try to arrange an itinerary to fly him home that would impose as little stress as possible on a sick 81-year-old (the normal flight at that time involved changing planes twice). When the request was referred to McGregor, he quickly dispatched a DC-8 to Los Angeles to pick up Mr. and Mrs. Symington and a doctor and fly them to Montreal non-stop. And when the plane reached Dorval he was there to greet his old mentor who, before being sped to hospital, asked him to send him the bill for the flight.

McGregor, mindful of the many years of unpaid service Symington had given the airline, had no intention of doing so. But a week later – the airline apparently being as susceptible to "leaks" then as it became in later years – the Toronto *Daily Star* burst out with the piquant news that "a sick man and two companions" had hired "a giant jet liner" for a 5,300-mile flight. The normal charter fee for such a flight, the newspaper said, would be $22,203. But it quoted McGregor as saying the flight had cost TCA "a basic $2,000 to $3,000," and the airline had "certainly not" lost money on it. The day after the story appeared, McGregor reluctantly sent Symington a bill for $3,066, assuring him that it covered "all items of direct out-of-pocket expenses to TCA," including fuel and oil costs of $271.18 per hour, cabin attendants at $13.50 an hour and ground handling expenses in Los Angeles of $89.

Saddened that he had been forced by the headlines to charge for what he had seen as a simple humanitarian gesture – in another context, he said in his memoirs that he was "opposed to management by public clamour" – McGregor signed the letter enclosing the invoice with regret. So he was much cheered a couple of days later when Rod MacInnes, his public relations man, passed on to him a teletype he had received from Bob Kolb, district sales manager in Edmonton, which showed that others in the airline shared his respect and affection for their former president:

We in Edmonton heartily endorse president's humane action towards Mr. Symington proud to be associated with it stop not only out of respect for Mr. Symington but because some individual or organizations may use this incident against us, and for their own private gains, suggest that thousands of other TCA personnel would wish to join us in voluntarily subscribing to a fund to defray all Mr. Symington's illness expenses including charter.

Right away, McGregor wired Kolb that he was delighted to receive this message and found it

Encouraging to know other people in the airline feel the same sense of gratitude toward Mr. Symington for the job he did for the company in his early days.

Encouraging as this evidence of the old TCA esprit de corps may have been, the attendant publicity, and the continuing rumbles from Winnipeg, did nothing to enhance McGregor's popularity in Ottawa, where the disintegrating Diefenbaker government was preoccupied with the election it must face before long. He had continued to complain that the lack of a firm national aviation policy and the resulting uncertainty about the routes it would be flying complicated TCA's fleet planning, and he was still pushing the politically explosive idea of merging TCA and CPA. Personally, he got on well with Leon Balcer – he considered him a reasonable man, open-minded and well-meaning – but he had not been overly optimistic when the minister told him toward the end of 1962 that a committee of the cabinet set up to consider air policy had agreed that CPA would not be given any new routes, including its proposed "propeller-only" service from Toronto and Montreal to Amsterdam, and that the government would withdraw its certification on the Vancouver-London route. By now the Conservative government's procrastinations had become legendary and he knew that Diefenbaker's hostility to Balcer was such that the two were not even on speaking terms. Consequently, though disappointed, he was not surprised that no new air policy was proclaimed before the election that spring, when the Conservatives were defeated and Lester Pearson took over as prime minister. His spirits rose when the Liberal cabinet appointments were announced: the new Minister of Transport was a fellow Scot, George McIlraith, an Ottawa lawyer who had been in the House since 1940 and was, like himself, a devoted C.D. Howe man, having served as the old warrior's parliamentary assistant for eight years. McGregor lost no time in renewing his contact with McIlraith and sent him two long briefs reviewing the airline's history and recapitulating all the complaints about the previous government's policy which he had been voicing unavailingly for years. He came away from his first meeting with the new minister confident that he now had a valuable ally. McIlraith seemed sympathetic to all he had to say; he agreed, for example, that the government should immediately rescind CPA's designation to the Vancouver-London route. (In fact, this was not done until two years later.)

The Liberals had been in office only a couple of months when the Winnipeg base closing returned to the headlines with the visit to Ottawa of a second Manitoba delegation, which claimed that the base could be converted for the maintenance of the expected new jets as economically as the necessary new facilities could be built at Montreal. The delegation's brief complained that TCA's decision rested on "narrow financial considerations only, without regard for the impact on the general provincial and national interests," but went on to admit – contradictorily, in McGregor's view – that TCA "must operate as efficiently as possible." The delegation had to be content with the assurance that nothing would be done pending completion of the study the previous government had ordered, which was then being carried out by the eminent U.S. aviation consultants R. Dixon Speas and Associates.

By now, yet another storm was brewing, not over where the new jet should be serviced but over what its identity should be. It had long been obvious that the turbo-prop Viscounts and Vanguards would in due course have to be replaced by a pure jet, and by early 1963 there were five candidates in the running, two of them American, the Douglas DC-9 and Boeing 727; two British, the de Havilland Trident and BAC 111;* and one French, the Sud Aviation Caravelle.

The evaluation of those five aircraft, which lasted for many months, was the most thorough the airline had conducted up to that time. By now, the computer had been pressed into service to record the full history of all the material and labour costs involved in the maintenance of each DC-8 in the fleet, and the company had developed an ingenious method of extrapolating those costs to other aircraft – even if they had not yet been built – which proved so successful that it was later adopted by both Boeing and Lockheed. The attention to detail that went into the evaluation was unprecedented. For example, Pierre Laforest, who rose through a variety of managerial appointments to become the airline's director of merchandising, devised a method of forecasting the operating costs for an aircraft's brakes and tires, by assessing such factors as its take-off and landing speeds, the size of its wheels and depth of the tire tread, the kinetic energy that had to be absorbed when it landed, and the braking effectiveness of its engines' thrust reversers. Using this technique, the TCA engineers estimated that the future brake costs of the BAC 111 would be only a tenth of the Trident's; and experience proved them right.

This was also the first evaluation in which the traffic, or sales, department played an important role. Until then, the operations

---

*The initials stood for British Aircraft Corporation, a merger of the Vickers company with three other British aircraft builders, Bristol, English Electric and Hunting.

and sales departments had dealt with each other at arm's length, and the operations department had made all the major decisions on equipment. But in the late 1950s a close working relationship had developed between Dave Tennant, the director of operations planning, and Claude Taylor, who had joined the airline as a passenger agent in Moncton in 1949 and worked his way up to the post of general manager, commercial planning. Thanks to this informal relationship, which circumnavigated the sometimes treacherous shoals of "normal channels," the views of the sales department had begun to creep into the airline's equipment planning; the realization was gradually spreading that the company was in business to sell seats and carry passengers and not simply to operate airplanes. So the evaluation team, as well as assessing the technical qualities and operating costs of the candidate aircraft, took into account commercial factors raised by the sales department. For instance, the Boeing 727 carried 101 passengers, the Trident 103; the sales department pointed out that they were too big for the short-to-medium and trans-border routes on which the new jets would be used, and that the choice of a smaller plane with fewer seats would permit the airline to improve its service by operating more frequent flights.

It was no secret to the evaluation team that Gordon McGregor wanted the 66-seat BAC 111, another product of his friend Sir George Edwards. But by this time almost everyone else in the airline was opposed to acquiring any more British equipment: the maintenance department was still having problems with the Vanguard and the purchasing department had dozens of expediters over in England trying to improve the supply of spare parts which, one study showed, were costing two and a half times more than DC-8 parts. The weight of technical opinion thus favoured the 72-seat DC-9, although the flight operations department preferred the 727 because it had three engines, against the DC-9's two. The Caravelle was never viewed as a serious contender, but because it had been flying since 1955, whereas the BAC 111 had not yet gone into service and the DC-9 had not even been built, it was included in the study as a sort of benchmark to measure the other candidates against. In the event, the breakdown of the Caravelle's expenses per seat-mile on TCA's routes showed that both its purchase price and its operating costs were too high.

The evaluation was still months away from completion, however, when a campaign began in Quebec to have the airline buy the Caravelle. Newspapers reported that if it did so the aircraft would be built at Canadair, thus providing much welcome employment in the province. McGregor commented that this would be unlikely, since the version of the aircraft that TCA was considering had Pratt & Whitney engines built in the United States, and the potential market for the Caravelle in North America would not justify the cost of tooling to produce the airframe at Canadair. Also, McGregor knew that Canadair was putting its money on what seemed like a much better bet: Geoff Notman was negotiating with Sir George Edwards, who ultimately agreed that if TCA selected the BAC 111 he would have $400,000 worth of the construction work on each aircraft done in Canada, 70 per cent of it at Canadair and the rest at the Bristol of Canada plant in Winnipeg. Perhaps because this information was not generally available at the time, Quebec premier Jean Lesage entered the fray, asserting that he didn't think the Caravelle should be rejected by TCA "just because it's French."

The study was still in progress on August 13, when the airline received the Dixon Speas report, which recommended that "the Winnipeg base should be closed down at the earliest possible date in the interests of most efficiently and economically operating Trans-Canada Air Lines. The continued operation of that facility would involve the airline in an extremely heavy penalty in unnecessary operating expenses and if Winnipeg were to be equipped to overhaul the new jets an additional heavy burden of capital expenses would be incurred." Keeping the base open until 1966, the report said, would cost the airline an extra $10 million, and if it remained open to service the new jets it would cost an extra $40 million over ten years.

When McGregor took the report to Ottawa a couple of days later to deliver it to the Minister of Transport, McIlraith told him there was concern within the cabinet about the campaign to have the airline buy the Caravelle. It was because of this concern that he had told the House a few days earlier that TCA had been asked not to sign any purchase order until the matter had been discussed with the government. McGregor reassured him that the evaluation process was still far from complete, and said that if the potential Canadian labour content of the jet purchase was of concern to the government it should be remembered that the Douglas company had already agreed that de Havilland of Canada at Malton would manufacture the wings and tails of all DC-9s sold anywhere in the world; and if the BAC 111 was chosen, the work that would be done by Bristol in Winnipeg would help to solve the problem of the base phase-out. Furthermore, he explained to the minister that no Canadian construction work could be done on any of the five candidate aircraft without increasing the costs to the manufacturer, who would inevitably pass them on to the purchaser; in which case, it was "quite ridiculous" to allow the amount of Canadian labour content to exert a serious influence on TCA's choice of aircraft.

McIlraith had arranged an interview with the Prime Minister for McGregor that afternoon, and McGregor noted afterward that it was "extremely useful and conducted in a very friendly and pleasant atmosphere." Pearson reassured him immediately that it was not his intention, or his cabinet's, to interfere in any way with TCA's conduct of its affairs; but McGregor would appreciate that the government had an interest in the implications of TCA's choice of aircraft. He agreed with McGregor that the primary considerations in any choice must be mechanical integrity and economics of operation, in that order. However, if two of the aircraft in consideration seemed to be neck and neck in contention, it would obviously be better for Canada to buy from the United Kingdom than the United States. A British purchase would be a move toward correcting a serious imbalance of trade in Canada's favour, whereas a U.S. order would accentuate a serious imbalance in favour of the United States.

Pearson, according to McGregor's notes, "seemed entirely content" with his assurance that the technical study would not be completed until the first week of October, and any decision TCA's board of directors based on it would be conveyed to him through the Minister of Transport "before anything was said to any manufacturers, or anyone else." The Prime Minister also agreed with him that the conclusions of the Dixon Speas report "seemed to be incontrovertible," and that the least said about the closing of the base for the time being, the better.

There is no indication in McGregor's record of the meeting that Pearson mentioned the Caravelle. But there is no doubt that the campaign mounted on its behalf was very much in the Prime Minister's mind, as were all the other aspects of what was beginning to be described in the press of English Canada as the "restlessness" in Quebec. Harry Price, a stalwart Tory who had been appointed to the TCA board by John Diefenbaker but who also had good connections in the Liberal party, told the author that he warned Pearson in June 1963 to expect trouble on the issue. A well-informed friend of his at Lloyd's of London, he said, had told him the French government was going to put great pressure on Ottawa to order TCA to buy the Caravelle, but that if the government tried to force the airline's hand its directors would resign *en masse*. Pearson pooh-poohed his fears. Drawing on his years of diplomatic experience, he told Price: "That just couldn't happen, Harry. The head of one government would never approach the head of another government to force the sale of anything." Months later, Price recalled, the Prime Minister admitted on several occasions how wrong he had been, and that he had had "direct intervention" on the part of General de Gaulle, which had surprised him. Pearson did not specify whether the "intervention" came through the French ambassador in Ottawa, but the ambassador and members of his staff certainly mounted a strong lobby in favour of the Caravelle, in Ottawa and the province of Quebec.

The government, despite the pressure, did not try to interfere with the evaluation and in October the study team recommended purchase of the DC-9. The BAC 111 came a close second in the evaluation, and the Caravelle a distant last. The recommendation was due to be considered by the board of directors on October 22, and a few days before that date Sir George Edwards flew to Montreal to make one last pitch for his BAC 111. He was not told the result of the evaluation, of course, but he did learn that the decision would be made at the board meeting on the 22nd.

He had just arrived back in England when, on that very morning, the first BAC 111 prototype crashed, killing its five-man test crew. Well aware that this could be fatal to the aircraft's chances, and amid all the turmoil and horror the crash had caused at British Aircraft Corporation's headquarters, Edwards nevertheless found time to telephone his representative in New York and ask him to be sure McGregor was told about the tragedy before he went into the board meeting.* The crash, of course, had no bearing on the result of the evaluation, and after hearing the study team's blackboard presentation the directors unanimously approved the purchase of six DC-9s.

Only now did the government give an indication that it might be thinking of interfering in the choice; McGregor was asked to delay the announcement of the airline's decision. And on November 12 McIlraith called him to say the cabinet had withheld

---

*The cause of the crash was soon found: in a deep stall test, the prototype's nose had come up to such a steep angle that its wing blotted out the flow of air over its tail and the elevators could not be moved to pitch the plane into a dive and enable its pilot to recover control. The wing also cut the flow of air to the plane's rear-mounted engines, so they could not be used to pull it out of its tail-down drop 15,000 feet to the ground. Sir George Edwards knew the DC-9's rear-engine design was similar to the BAC 111's, so he immediately flew to California to alert the Douglas company to the danger. He knew the top people at Douglas; they were "good blokes," and despite competitive considerations he did not want any deaths on his conscience, so he also passed on all BAC's information on the crash to other manufacturers. The problem was, of course, solved by design changes.

approval of the purchase because the French ambassador had passed on to one of its members, Lionel Chevrier, a statement by General Puget, head of Sud Aviation, alleging that TCA had not had sufficient contact with Sud to make a proper assessment of the Caravelle. McGregor promptly prepared a detailed rebuttal of Puget's allegations and had it delivered by hand to the minister's house next evening; he also took the opportunity to tell him the board was becoming restive at the continued delay in announcing the purchase, and that the choice of the DC-9 had already leaked to the press.

McGregor's rebuttal satisfied the cabinet and he was told the Prime Minister would announce the purchase of the six DC-9s a few days hence, on November 22. The day before the announcement was to be made, McIlraith called McGregor after a cabinet meeting and told him Pearson intended to add to his statement a few words on the Winnipeg base. He read the relevant passage over the phone and asked for McGregor's reaction. "I told him I was completely horrified," McGregor said in a memo he dictated immediately after the call, which survives in Air Canada's files with its pink identification tag: "Memo re PM's statement – attempt to abort."

The attempt was unsuccessful, and Pearson went ahead with his statement, in which he stressed the amount of DC-9 work that would be done by de Havilland and added that United Aircraft of Canada Limited in Montreal was expected to receive many millions of dollars' worth of DC-9 engine work from its U.S. parent company, Pratt & Whitney. He also enumerated various military contracts which would ensure that Canadair continued to enjoy "a substantial share of the aircraft production work carried out in Canada."

Then came the passage McGregor dreaded: "TCA's study of the purchase of new aircraft," the Prime Minister said, "was made against the background of the corporation's forward plans for the next ten years. The effect of this planning is to indicate that much the greater part of TCA's fleet of turbo-propeller Viscount aircraft will continue to be needed throughout the ten years. I am therefore now able to announce a change from the previous expectation, which was made known a year ago, that the overhaul and maintenance base in Winnipeg might begin to be phased out early in 1966. For at least as far ahead as planning now extends, that is at least ten years, the Winnipeg facilities will continue to be used."

This was so far counter to the Dixon Speas recommendations, and so different from what he himself had said on the matter before, that McGregor ever afterward seemed to believe the Prime Minister must have been the innocent victim of a misunderstanding. Several years later, when the issue had still not gone away, he explained in a letter to a subsequent Minister of Transport, Paul Hellyer, how he thought the commitment to keep the base open had come about. At the height of the lobbying for the Caravelle, TCA had been summoned to Ottawa to give an explanation of its choice of the DC-9 to a group of senior deputy ministers and Tom Kent, of Pearson's office. The corporation's planning was explained with the aid of large charts showing the relative economic effects of various potential fleet "mixes" over the coming ten years. One of the charts, McGregor said, bore a small overlay tentatively forecasting the effects of the company's continued ownership of Viscounts into 1973, and he had concluded that whoever drafted the Prime Minister's speech had based his commitment on that.

Hellyer was not directly concerned in the decision back in 1963, but he told the author years later that he believed there had been no misunderstanding, and that Pearson had intended quite deliberately to over-rule McGregor. Tom Kent confirmed his belief. Despite the pressure in favour of the Caravelle, Kent told the author, the Prime Minister had agreed that the airline should be permitted to make its own decisions on technical matters such as aircraft purchases; but he also felt McGregor must be prepared, in the time-honoured way, to recognize the government's political imperatives and accept a compromise in the interests of regional economic welfare. In other words, it was the DC-9 in return for slowing down the phase-out of the Winnipeg base.

If McGregor did not recognize that, he nevertheless knew he would be subjected to close questioning about the Prime Minister's statement in his appearance before the parliamentary committee, scheduled for the first week of December. He turned up for that hearing, to use his own words, "haggard and heart-sick." Three days earlier, on the wet and blustery Friday evening of November 29, TCA Flight 831, a DC-8F five minutes out of Dorval on its way to Toronto, dived into the ground near Ste. Thérèse de Blainville, north of Montreal, with the loss of all 111 passengers and crew of seven.

CHAPTER TWENTY-ONE

T HE TRAGEDY AT STE. THÉRÈSE was the worst in TCA's history. Its passenger death toll exactly equalled at one stroke the total killed in all four previous fatal accidents involving passengers. These, of course, became progressively more tragic as the size of aeroplanes increased. The first occurred in February 1941, when a Lockheed 14 was coming in to land for fuel at Armstrong, Ontario, in the middle of the night. For some reason never discovered it flew into the tops of some trees almost a mile short of the runway and all nine passengers and three crew were killed. Twelve passengers and three crew died six years later, when a Lockheed 18 nearing Vancouver received clearance to land, headed out to sea to make its approach turn, and simply disappeared, with no trace of wreckage ever being found.

There was no doubt about the cause of the next crash, in 1954: a young NATO pilot took off from the airport at Moose Jaw, Saskatchewan, and five minutes later his single-engined Harvard trainer, still climbing, flew from beneath into a North Star crossing the city at 6,000 feet on its way from Winnipeg to Calgary. The impact tore off the North Star's outboard motor and half of its left wing split seconds before the Harvard buried itself in its fuselage and both planes erupted in flames. The total death toll was thirty-seven, including the thirty-one passengers, crew of four, the NATO pilot, and the woman occupant of a house demolished by the falling wreckage.

The last fatal crash before Ste. Thérèse was in December 1956. A North Star bound eventually for Montreal took off from Vancouver on a rainy Sunday evening carrying fifty-nine passengers, including several Saskatchewan Roughrider football stars who had played in the East-West Shrine game the day before. There were fierce winds at the higher altitudes and Flight 810 encountered some icing and turbulence on its climb to cross the mountains. Fifty minutes after take-off, Captain Alan Clarke reported that he had reached 19,500 feet and was nearing Princeton. Then he added the dread words: "Looks like we had a fire in

No. 2 engine. Have shut down No. 2 – request descent clearance back to Vancouver via Cultus Lake – Abbotsford.''

With the clearance received, Clarke turned round and headed back into the teeth of the gale. A few minutes later he reported he was having difficulty maintaining 19,000 feet on his three remaining engines and was given clearance to descend to 14,000 feet. The last message received from him, at 7.10 p.m., said he was at 14,000 feet and had passed Hope on his way home. Then silence. By 8.30 p.m. the first of the search planes, a CF-100 jet interceptor from the RCAF base at Comox, was in the air.

It snowed almost every day for the next two weeks in the area where Flight 810 was presumed down, but one of the most intensive air searches ever mounted in Canada continued without a trace of wreckage being sighted. An area of six hundred square miles was photographed from the air and ground parties pushed as far as they could into the mountains, though hindered by snow drifts as deep as twenty-five feet. By February, the search had to be suspended until summer, with still no hint of the wreck's whereabouts. In May, an expert climber named Elfrida Pigou was leading two male companions on a climb up the west side of Mount Slesse, a steep, jagged peak in the Cascade Mountains, when she came across a torn piece of metal about a foot long, with numbers painted on it. She took it back to Vancouver with her, and the mystery of Flight 810's fate was solved: it was identified as a fragment of the missing plane's wing.

At the request of TCA, Paddy Sherman, publisher of the Vancouver *Province* and a well-known mountaineer, flew to the scene of the find by helicopter to pinpoint the wreck. He found that the North Star had flown into a sheer rock face just fifty feet below the summit of the 8,200-foot mountain. Next day, Sherman, Elfrida and a party of climbers from the Mountain Rescue Group were landed by helicopter on the lower slopes of the mountain and climbed to the crash site. Their unanimous conclusion was that the area was far too dangerous to permit any attempt to recover either human remains or wreckage until some of the snow had melted and the risk of avalanches had abated.

In the meantime, Sherman gave a short course in mountaineering to two accident investigators – Ian Macdonald, an engineer then in TCA's flight safety department, and Desmond Murphy, of the Department of Transport – and when conditions were judged safe he escorted them in to study the mangled debris uncovered by the melting snow. The destruction was so complete that many of the metal fragments were unrecognizable, but Macdonald was armed with a complete list of all the North Star's parts and numbers, and with this he was able to identify parts of the wing, tail and fuselage, and units from all four engines. From these he concluded that there had been no mid-air failure or bomb explosion – that the aircraft had been intact when it flew into the mountain. But why it was forty miles south of its allotted course, and so much lower than the pilot had thought, remained a mystery.

Accident investigators, however, are like good detectives: they never give up on an unsolved case. Years later, Macdonald and his colleague in flight safety, Captain Cliff Seddon, evolved a theory that might explain the Mount Slesse crash. During their investigation into the sudden drop of the Vanguard near Rocky Mountain House in 1963, they began to hear about a meteorological phenomenon of mountainous regions known by several terms – Bishop wave, standing wave, or lee wave – which was only then beginning to be understood. This is a strong current of air that rushes almost vertically down the lee side of a mountain range when a rare set of conditions develops: the wind must cross the mountains at a certain angle, there must be a certain mixture of changing air pressures and temperatures, a certain combination of alternate layers of stable and unstable air and so on. After consulting international experts on the phenomenon, Macdonald and Seddon gathered all the weather reports for the area at the time of the Vanguard incident and studied them for days. Eventually, they concluded that all the requisite conditions had existed to form a standing wave, and the Vanguard had flown into what can be described as a waterfall of wind and been sucked down almost to its destruction.

Having reached this conclusion, they both suddenly remembered the unsolved Mount Slesse crash. Accident reports are voluminous documents, zealously preserved; in their files was a Manila folder containing all the weather reports for the day Flight 810 met its fate. They dug it out and began to study it – and sure enough, all the conditions for a standing wave had existed on that day, too.

It can never be known for sure, of course, whether Alan Clarke's North Star was driven down to its doom by a ferocious wave of wind. Nor will it ever be known why Captain John Snider and First Officer Harold Dyck were unable to pull their DC-8 out of its dive to destruction at Ste. Thérèse, despite many months of the most thorough-going accident investigation in aviation history up to that time. Snider had taken off to the east, reported in by radio at 3,000 feet as instructed, and been given clearance to make a left turn and climb to the west on his way to Toronto.

Some time before he was next due to report in, at 7,000 feet, the DC-8 apparently banked off to the right and dived into a wood, exploding on impact.

The scale of the investigation to find out what had gone wrong was staggering: at one stage, more than fifteen hundred people were involved. Computer simulations and test flights were used to reconstruct the possible flight paths the aircraft could have taken, and in case anything had dropped off it and contributed to the crash a ground search was made along them. Five hundred men of the Royal 22nd Regiment covered forty square miles, advancing shoulder to shoulder through the woods and fields, without finding anything. Helicopters duplicated the ground search and an area within a twenty-mile radius from the crash site was photographed from the air, again without result. The plane had buried itself deeply in the ground – the impact was such that some of the wreckage was found almost a mile from the site – and to recover the debris from the boggy site proved difficult. A camp was erected on the spot, cranes and power shovels were brought in, and the digging began. But the ground was like jelly, and the sides of the excavation kept collapsing. So a steel coffer dam was built around an area measuring 140 by 120 feet, and the work of recovery went on for five months. The machines went down 60 feet and removed 26,000 cubic yards of earth, all of which was carefully sifted for debris. As each fragment was recovered it was cleaned and taken to Dorval, where it was laid out on a hangar floor in as close an approximation to its place in the aircraft as the engineers could manage. The aircraft's total weight had been 135,030 lbs.; all but 29,500 lbs. of that total was recovered.

Perhaps twenty "possible causes" for the accident were examined as the work went on, to try to find a "probable cause." For instance, the jacks powering the aircraft's horizontal stabilizer were recovered, badly damaged but locked in a way that suggested the pilot had "trimmed" them to put the aircraft into a nose-down position. This in turn suggested that he had been obtaining a wrong reading from a failed instrument, and relays of pilots were put to work on the DC-8 flight simulator to try to reproduce the various circumstances in which this might have happened, and what effects each might have had. But no conclusive explanation emerged; the cause of the worst disaster in the airline's history remains a mystery today.

The horror of the crash cast a pall over the whole airline. Gordon McGregor told the men who accompanied him to the parliamentary committee hearing the following week they must consider themselves in mourning and govern their public conduct accordingly. The subdued mood of the TCA party did not extend to the hearing itself. French-speaking members, in particular the Créditiste Gilles Grégoire, harried McGregor with questions about the rejection of the Caravelle. Grégoire, after failing in an attempt to have him produce all the confidential reports on the various aircraft considered, went on to complain about the lack of French Canadians in senior positions in the airline and demanded successfully that McGregor produce a list of the most senior French-speaking employees. When he tried to extract a commitment from McGregor that if a vice-president with a French-speaking deputy dropped dead or left his job, the deputy would be promoted, McGregor replied that the airline was interested in "bilingualizing the company to the greatest possible extent, but we are far more interested in obtaining the best man we can for the job." In other words, the job might go to one of the company's nine regional managers, who might or might not be French-speaking.

At one stage, as he became more and more irritated by the grilling about the choice of aircraft, McGregor said bluntly, "The Caravelle is no good for TCA," and in a whispered aside to his colleagues at the table added: "Not that I think it's any great shakes, either." Unfortunately for him, his microphone was still switched on and the intended aside was heard by all. The reaction in the Quebec press was instant and highly vocal: one writer went so far as to accuse McGregor of fostering separatism by his anti-French attitude, in an article so vitriolic that Grégoire publicly dissociated himself from it.

The indignation built up to such an extent that French-speaking students from the Université de Montréal staged a demonstration on the plaza outside the airline's headquarters, which had by now moved into Place Ville Marie, the city's first skyscraper office tower. Wisely, McGregor agreed to receive a delegation of six of the students and an impromptu aircraft-selection presentation was arranged for them. This apparently persuaded them that sound technical reasons and not racial prejudice had governed the choice of the DC-9 and the furore died down without McGregor suffering the indignity visited upon Donald Gordon, who had been burned in effigy in reprisal for the allegedly anti-French bias of the CNR.

The Caravelle uproar overshadowed the closing of the Winnipeg base at the hearing, but that issue continued to make headlines in Manitoba. McGregor had no choice but to confirm before the committee the commitment the Prime Minister had made.

The anticipated life of the base, he said, had been extended to 1973 because a study of the new small jet aircraft had "indicated the desirability of continuing to use a substantial number of Viscounts for a longer period than originally estimated." He added that the Dixon Speas report had originally estimated the cost of maintaining the base beyond 1966 to 1973 at $19.8 million, and that between 1964 and 1973 about two hundred of the base's eight hundred employees would be transferred out of Winnipeg.

A few days after the hearing a third Manitoba delegation descended on Ottawa, led by Premier Duff Roblin, who said the only acceptable solution to the problem was to convert the Winnipeg base to overhaul the new small jets;* anything less would be "a delaying action only," and he asked for a public inquiry into the whole matter. Pearson told the House he would consider this request and repeated that it was government policy to maintain employment at the base and, if possible, to increase it. This once again conflicted with what McGregor had said about the likelihood of transfers from Winnipeg as the work load there was reduced, and McGregor pointed out to McIlraith that he had received no directive from the Liberal government or its predecessor forbidding staff reductions. Somehow this fact reached the ears of the *Winnipeg Free Press*, and when a reporter telephoned him in February McGregor confirmed it. He said no assurances had ever been given by Ottawa or the airline that there would be a freeze on employment at the base, and repeated what he had been saying all along: that the size of the Winnipeg maintenance staff must be related to the work load there, and that some employees would be transferred before 1973.

Outraged at this seeming defiance of the Prime Minister, Premier Roblin fired off a sharp telegram to Pearson, saying:

This confirms our worst fears about the gradual whittling away and dismantling of this base. This is the process that has been going on ever since Mr. McGregor moved to Montreal himself. This situation confirms our worst fears for the future and virtually renders your assurances worthless.

Stung by Roblin's tone, Pearson wired back telling him the government had not issued a directive to TCA because it had no legal power to do so. "Governmental control of TCA is exercised only through general control over the capital budget," he said. "Government policy therefore is expressed in the only possible

---

*McGregor had told McIlraith this was not possible: the Dixon Speas report had said it would cost the company an extra $4 million a year and would make a large proportion of the capacity of the Dorval base redundant.

way, namely TCA concurrence with my statement Nov. 22. This concurrence was given and will be maintained." The future of the Winnipeg base was settled, he went on, exactly in accordance with his November 22 statement: "Base will be maintained in operation at about present level until 1973 at least. This is government policy. I am sure that you will wish to withdraw your completely unfounded suggestion that my assurances are worthless."

A week later, the demand for a public inquiry was renewed in the Manitoba legislature by Industry Minister Gurney Evans, who accused TCA's management of "deliberate deceit and trickery" and an arrogant defiance of the government and the people of Canada. The pot was kept bubbling in March when it was announced that the two International Association of Machinists lodges concerned had reached an amicable agreement covering the terms of members' transfers from Winnipeg to Dorval. And in June Ottawa bowed to the inevitable and appointed a respected Winnipeg lawyer, Donald A. Thompson, as a one-man royal commission to inquire into the future of the base and "the possibility of maintaining and increasing employment at the said base."

By now, McGregor was dealing with a new Minister of Transport: John W. Pickersgill, the Manitoban history professor who joined the public service in 1937 and worked for prime ministers King and St. Laurent until he was elected to the House for the Newfoundland riding of Bonavista-Twillingate in 1953, thereby earning himself the soubriquet "Sailor Jack." In the closing months of George McIlraith's tenure as minister, McGregor had formed the impression that the government was about to proclaim a new aviation policy which would include approval of a merger of TCA and CPA. So he lost no time sending Pickersgill yet another memorandum detailing "the infanticide that the Diefenbaker government was perpetrating on a government-conceived and sponsored enterprise which could have remained, and still could be, financially self-sufficient, if the Canadian government firmly resists the encroachments of existing and potential outside competitors."

Buck Crump, on behalf of CPA, also urged the new minister to declare the government's policy, though naturally his idea of what it should be differed considerably from McGregor's. The indignant McGregor could hardly believe his ears when he heard that one of Crump's proposals was that CPA should swap its Polar service from Vancouver to Amsterdam for TCA's service to Paris.

Pickersgill came to office resolved to try to develop an integrated policy rationalizing all the country's various modes of transportation, but his first few months were largely taken up with framing legislation to implement some of the recommendations of the recent McPherson report on the railroads. In a private meeting, though, he assured McGregor that "as long as he was Minister of Transport no government action would be taken which would be detrimental to TCA's interests with respect to its trans-continental services." He also said that in general he thought some means must be found to end direct competition between the two Canadian carriers on overseas routes. Furthermore, he seemed to agree with McGregor that CPA should not be permitted to charge a lower economy fare than TCA on its trans-continental service, which it had been doing ever since McConachie had refused to follow suit when TCA raised its fares in 1962. Perhaps, the minister said, this and all the other issues between TCA and CPA could be resolved if the presidents of both railroads and both airlines got together at a round-table meeting, at which he would outline his basic views.

The Four Presidents' meeting, as it became known, was held in Pickersgill's office on April 27, 1964, and he began it by distributing copies of three principles on which he proposed to base his civil aviation policy. The first was that services provided by Canadian carriers on international routes "should not be competitive or conflicting, but should represent a single integrated plan, which could be achieved by amalgamation, by partnership or by a clear division of fields of operations." Secondly, while the principle of domestic competition was not rejected, it should not "compromise or seriously injure the economic viability of TCA's mainline domestic operations. . . . In other words, there must not be the kind of competition which would put TCA into the red." And thirdly, there must be a role for general air carriers which would give them "a reasonable chance to operate without government subsidies."*

There followed an hour and a half of not very profitable discussion. The minister repeated that TCA must not be "reduced

---

*An indirect subsidy by TCA to one of the regional airlines, TransAir, had recently been questioned in the Commons. Against its better judgment, TCA had been pressured after the war into linking several small western communities such as Brandon, Swift Current and Yorkton with a service that became known as the Prairie Milk Run. This was uneconomic at the best of times, and because of the small airports it became impossible when the DC-3 was replaced by the Viscount. Two DC-3s were retained long into the Viscount era solely to serve the milk run, and when TransAir claimed that as a smaller organization it could provide a cheaper and more efficient service TCA gladly cut its losses by selling it two DC-3s and a Viscount at bargain prices and handing over the route. TransAir's confidence proved misplaced and there were widespread protests when it began to abandon services.

to a chronic deficit operation," and did not rule out the possibility of small subsidies having to be paid to regional carriers. He added that fares on the transcontinental service must be equalized, and both airlines must feed each other rather than feed foreign carriers.

At one stage in the discussion, Donald Gordon asked Crump: "How much will you take for CPA?" Crump slowly removed his cigar from his mouth, glared at Gordon from beneath his formidable brows, and asked: "How much will you take for TCA?" That ended discussion of a merger for the moment, and Pickersgill assured Crump the government had no intention of legislating CPA out of business. Crump said he was glad to hear it; all he and McConachie wanted was "a chance to make a living." Years later, Pickersgill told the author that while he had thought the idea of some form of amalgamation a good one, he also considered that reversing what had already been done was politically impossible: "The foot was in the door."

Since the meeting was proving far from productive, Pickersgill suggested that the four presidents meet again in private to try to hammer out some agreement. They did so right away, over lunch in the Château Laurier, and while there was little more progress, they did agree to put their staffs to work to assess various ways in which the two companies might co-operate.

Much of the rest of that year was taken up by TCA-CPA meetings at various staff levels to discuss this. It was suggested, for example, that the two airlines might share joint offices in cities to which neither actually flew; that they might co-operate on scheduling to provide the best possible service to the public; that CPA might use TCA's ReserVec system for its bookings; that each airline should incorporate the other's schedule in its timetables; and that both airlines should push the "Fly Canadian" theme in joint advertising. Perhaps unsurprisingly, since they were already in vigorous competition, the hours of meetings yielded few results. Nevertheless, in October the government was able to announce that they had agreed to sell each other's services before any other airline's; in other words, if one carrier could not accommodate a passenger because of inconvenient routing or lack of space it would book him on the other Canadian carrier rather than any foreign carrier with which it might previously have had a reciprocal arrangement. The announcement also said each airline would serve as the other's sales agent in those countries to which it flew.

But as the talks dragged on, Grant McConachie showed no inclination to give up the competitive advantage of his lower transcontinental fares, and even in private talks he and McGregor were unable to agree on the geographical split of the world McGregor kept advancing as the only solution to their problems. Nor, of course, did he drop his opposition to what McGregor kept pushing, euphemistically, as "the one-carrier concept."

At one stage, the Montreal accounting firm of Touche, Ross carried out a detailed financial study of how the two airlines could be merged, and the likely benefits therefrom. And in the fall, the Calgary financier Max Bell, a large shareholder in the CPR, approached Pickersgill with a bold proposal: he and his fellow Calgary millionaire, R.A. Brown, Jr., would buy out both airlines and offer shares in the resultant private company to the public. Brown told McGregor he was prepared to put $40 million into the new company, which he estimated would need a total capitalization of about $400 million, with $160 million of that being equity. The CPR would probably take 25 per cent of that, and he was confident the rest could be sold to the public, unless the CNR wished to take 25 per cent too. This idea was seriously discussed for several months, and at one time McGregor was told that the Prime Minister was in favour of it. But Pickersgill eventually told Bell that under no circumstances would the government permit a private monopoly of air services in Canada and both Bell and Brown lost interest in the idea.

Early in the new year, McGregor took the initiative in an attempt to break the deadlock that had developed in the negotiations on a split of geographical rights. He wrote to Pickersgill suggesting an alternative to the status quo as it then existed and asking whether he should take it up with McConachie. His proposal was that CPA and Air Canada (as it was now officially called) should enter a pool from eastern Canada to Rome and Paris, thus enabling use of the controversial Paris-Rome fifth freedom. In return CPA should abandon its western Canada to Amsterdam route, and Air Canada, in return for sharing the Paris market with CPA, should be given the right to serve eastern Canada to Tokyo. As McGregor pointed out, his proposal would require "substantial bilateral agreement modifications" and it was "not without some element of financial hazard to Air Canada." Pleased to see at least some movement toward an agreement, Pickersgill agreed enthusiastically that he should put the plan to McConachie.

The two men met yet again in Vancouver on March 16, and McConachie accepted McGregor's first proposal, for the Paris-Rome pool. He also agreed at long last to equalization of fares on the transcontinental route. With effect from April CPA raised its economy fares to TCA's level (which had been $10 higher on a

Montreal-Vancouver trip), and TCA raised its first-class fares slightly to bring them up to CPA's level. But further than that McConachie would not go. "Rightly or wrongly," McGregor reported to Pickersgill, "I formed the impression that McConachie was not surprised or disappointed at the breakdown in negotiations. . . . For my part I was disappointed but not surprised. After fifteen years of sparring with McConachie I know perfectly well that his basic philosophy is to win advantages for his company without the slightest consideration being given to the concession of any quid pro quos. . . ."

A few days later, Gordon Wood called on the deputy minister, John Baldwin, and was told that there was "a startling dissimilarity" between McConachie's impression of the meeting and McGregor's, and that McConachie had "expressed considerable optimism about the future possibilities of Air Canada and CPA resolving the competitive problems on the North Atlantic through pooling."

By now, Pickersgill's patience with both men was wearing exceedingly thin, and he summoned them to a meeting in his office. He was pleased, he told them, that the two companies had made some progress in the area of mutually supporting sales efforts, but more was needed: the time had now come to agree on the geographical division of international routes. He was leaving on a transatlantic trip next day and if any bilateral amendments were required he wanted to be able to raise them while he was in Europe. In his opinion, if CPA was to be the sole Canadian carrier designated to the Orient, Air Canada should be the sole Canadian carrier designated to the United Kingdom. Consequently, he intended to reject Air Canada's renewed request to be named to Tokyo, and he thought that "in time" Amsterdam should be taken away from CPA.

What he was anxious to achieve, he said, was a clean geographical separation of the companies' international routes, with Air Canada having all points north of a line through western Europe and CPA having all points south of it. And with that, he excused himself and left his office on the pretext of checking the progress of a debate in the House; actually, he went to the washroom and cooled his heels for a while.

His stratagem worked: in his absence, McGregor and McConachie quickly decided to stay with the devil they knew rather than risk the government's imposing some possibly worse arrangements on them. When the minister returned it was soon agreed that Air Canada would forgo its ambition to get into Rome and CPA would drop its demand for Paris; also, Air Canada would drop its opposition to CPA's desire to serve Amsterdam from Montreal as well as Vancouver, and CPA would agree to Air Canada operating directly from Vancouver to the United Kingdom if this could be arranged with the British authorities.

Pickersgill gladly accepted this new spirit of concord and so when he announced the government's aviation policy to the House on June 1 it varied little from the three principles he had laid down the year before. It was, in fact, largely a preservation and confirmation of the status quo – except for one passage in which McGregor scented the stench of betrayal. Pickersgill repeated his assertion that competition must not be permitted to put Air Canada into the red. But then he added that the government intended to engage an outstanding international aviation consultant "to advise whether the growth of the main line service would now permit some further degree of competition."

To McGregor, that could mean only one thing – the dreaded second transcontinental flight a day for which McConachie had been pushing all along. It looked, he thought grimly, as though he was about to be double-crossed.

A few weeks earlier, when the minister had returned from his trip to Britain and France, McGregor had met him at Dorval and flown with him to Ottawa to hear about his bilateral discussions. Pickersgill had told him then that the Prime Minister was as pleased as he was that he had been able to work out a mutually satisfactory arrangement with McConachie. McGregor felt he had made substantial concessions to reach that agreement, and he took the government's approval to mean that all the issues that had bedevilled his relations with Ottawa for so many years were finally settled.

But it was apparently not to be. Even before the minister announced his new policy in the House, he learned from John Baldwin that the government was considering appointing his old adversary Stephen Wheatcroft to make yet another report on the state of Canadian aviation. "I am extremely worried," he wrote to Pickersgill on May 7, in a letter seeking his assurance that, in the interest of logical and accurate planning, he need not take these "evil rumours" seriously. He pointed out that the first CPA transcontinental had put TCA into the red for three successive years, for a total amount of more than $12.5 million; a second flight would mean a further loss of between $6 million and $7 million annually, and "it would certainly violate your declared principle that government action vis-à-vis CPA would not be taken which would have the effect of putting this company into a deficit position."

In reply, Pickersgill assured him he still intended to keep TCA's domestic operations in the black, but added: "What we have to do is to find some objective method whereby growth can be measured and, if warranted, permitting some measure of participation by CPA in that growth. . . ." Reporting receipt of this letter to his directors, McGregor said he thought it was intended to be reassuring "but in my opinion it falls very far short of the firm declaration of policy against a second CPA trans-continental which we would like to have."

McGregor's growing conviction that a man just couldn't trust anyone in Ottawa perhaps inspired the intemperate tone of a letter he wrote to John Baldwin toward the end of June. Pickersgill had told him on his return from London that the British government authorities were not prepared to grant Air Canada permission to fly direct from Vancouver to London without some major concession on Canada's part. McGregor now told Baldwin he regarded this attitude as "completely dishonest," and since it had been made clear that his agreement with McConachie was conditional on the government's success in obtaining the required bilateral amendments, Air Canada regarded the terms of the agreement as not having been fulfilled, "and it therefore does not regard itself as being bound by the international route divisions announced in the House by the Minister on June 1."

As a properly circumspect civil servant, Baldwin wanted nothing to do with such inflammatory declarations. In what he thought to be McGregor's own interests, he returned the letter forthwith, saying it was not the kind of document that should "be on open file or in the category of unclassified correspondence which might be required for tabling or production as matter of record."

But a few months later, McGregor's forthrightness – in Ottawa they were beginning to look upon it more as obduracy – caused him to couch another letter in terms which this time angered the minister himself. When Baldwin wrote to Wheatcroft in July giving him his terms of reference, he said in part: "The Minister wishes you to make an analysis of the Air Canada network of domestic services, with a view to reporting to him whether you consider that any further development of domestic mainline competition in Canada, at the present time, would compromise or seriously injure the economic viability of the Air Canada mainline domestic operations." But when they began to talk to Wheatcroft, and supply him with the statistics he needed, the Air Canada staff decided uneasily that he had a somewhat differ-

A ReserVec I transaction using a coded card in 1962.

ReserVec II introduced in 1970 is one of the most sophisticated computer networks in the world.

A cargo load for a Vanguard in TCA colours at Calgary.

Her Majesty Queen Elizabeth departing for London from Ottawa in the first aircraft in Air Canada colours on October 13, 1964. – (National Film Board)

Celebrating the introduction of DC-9 aircraft to New York in February 1966 by serving champagne, the stewardesses are wearing black and white "fantasies," an accessory of their new turquoise summer uniforms worn during meal service in the late 1960s.

The sad sight of aircraft tied down at Dorval base during the two-week IAMAW strike in November 1966.

Russian and Canadian inauguration of service between Moscow and Montreal, November 1966.

The new regime: J.R. Baldwin, Y. Pratte and H.W. Seagrim in December 1968.

Stewardesses wearing red, blue or white mini-skirts in 1968.

At Toronto, April 30, 1971. Incoming baggage from the inaugural Boeing 747 service.

The "mix and match" choice of wear for flight attendants introduced in 1973.

Over the Christmas season in 1984 nearly a million pounds of live lobster were flown from Halifax to Europe.

Official opening of Mirabel airport in October 1975: Yves Pratte flanked by Robert Bourassa and Prime Minister Pierre Trudeau.

At the roll-out of the L1011-500 in December 1980: from left to right: *E. Cortright of Lockheed with P. Taschereau and C.I. Taylor of Air Canada and Lockheed's chairman R.A. Anderson. (In the background Pierre Jeanniot takes a closer look.)*

C.I. Taylor, chairman and P. Jeanniot, president.

The "space age" Boeing 767 – off and climbing.

ent impression of his task. Claude Taylor, general manager of marketing services, reported to McGregor after one meeting:

When questioned as to who would gain by additional trans-continental competition (it being accepted that Air Canada would lose), Mr. Wheatcroft stated repeatedly that: "It is not a question of whether or not a competitive service is a good thing–it is accepted government policy that competitive service is a good thing". . . . The impression was gained that Wheatcroft considered his terms of reference to be to decide whether the price to be paid (losses to Air Canada) were such as to prohibit further competition.

McGregor duly complained to Pickersgill that Wheatcroft seemed to think he had been asked to report not on whether more competition was needed or justified, but on whether it would hurt Air Canada–and if so, how badly. Pickersgill assured him this was not what he wanted and promised to see Wheatcroft and tell him so. Around the airline, however, the nervousness persisted. What would the report contain, and what would the government do when it received it?

In January 1966, in one of those expertly noncommittal parliamentary answers for which he was celebrated on his side of the House and reviled on the other, Jack Pickersgill seemed to show a less whole-hearted dedication to the Air Canada cause than its directors deemed appropriate. The board, to use the time-honoured term, "instructed" McGregor to write to him expressing its concern, and McGregor did so in a brief letter the minister considered altogether too brusque. He had, he wrote, been "told to advise you that the directors wished you to assure them that the Wheatcroft report, whatever its import, would not be published or any action taken with respect to it, until after the board had been given an opportunity to comment upon it to the government."

The peremptory tone of this communication to a minister of the crown incensed Pickersgill, and he immediately summoned McGregor to appear on the ministerial carpet in Ottawa for what he recalled years later as "a very bitter exchange." Reporting to his board on the dressing-down he had received, McGregor wrote that the minister had registered his "extreme dissatisfaction" and had said in effect that "he was not taking orders from Air Canada's directors with respect to matters of government air policy, which by statute were his responsibility, and that he therefore regarded my letter as an encroachment on his prerogatives." Pickersgill's recollection of the meeting, as expressed to the author, was somewhat more informal but no less succinct: "I didn't relish the idea of being treated as a rubber stamp," he said. "I made him withdraw a letter, totally, that he had written to me. I said, 'If this isn't withdrawn, one of us will go – either I'll cease to be Minister of Transport or you'll cease to be head of the airline. I'm not trying to run the airline – I know I'm not competent to do that – but you're not going to run the Department of Transport either'."

McGregor immediately accepted the opportunity to retract the letter and said he was sorry it had inadvertently given offence. Neither he nor any other director, he said, had intended "to introduce any element of friction" between the minister and the company. And a few days later, he wrote another letter, making the same point but with a more seemly deference. The minister acknowledged it with a brief note in which he also said he had seen Wheatcroft and "made clear to him precisely what I hoped his report would cover."

The report, when it was delivered later in the year, retraced some of the ground Wheatcroft had gone over in 1958, but also reviewed the effects of the intervening seven years of limited competition. CPA's advent on the transcontinental route, he said, had not produced any major benefits under the first four headings of what he had outlined in 1958 as "the general case for competition" – more adequate service; more efficient service; more rapid technological progress; and more rapid traffic development. Under the fifth heading, as a yardstick of efficiency, the CPA operation had been of some advantage because it had shown that Air Canada was operating "a highly efficient service." The only major gain had been under the sixth and last heading: the public had "derived a considerable satisfaction from being able to choose which airline it will use on the trans-continental route." This had benefited Air Canada, too, because the public attitude toward the national airline was better now that it was no longer a monopoly operator on the route.

As to the cost of this benefit, Wheatcroft made a subtle distinction that others besides McGregor found difficult to grasp: "Although Air Canada cannot be said to have suffered direct financial injury," he wrote, "it undoubtedly has suffered through loss of potential profit." Using a different method of calculation, he estimated this loss of profit at $5.7 million, whereas Air Canada's estimate was closer to $21 million. "From a purely commercial point of view," the report went on, "any loss of potential profit is a misfortune to Air Canada; but only in the same way as it would be to any other enterprise which lost a share of its market to a competitor." Air Canada claimed that had it not been deprived of this profit it would have been able to benefit the public by lowering fares, improving its passenger service and introducing new flights, including a freighter service to the Maritimes. But the implications of all this involved "political judgments . . . outside the terms of reference of this study."

Wheatcroft concluded that undoubtedly there would be a further loss of profit to Air Canada if competition was increased, but "a limited amount of additional competition, such as the amount which would result from a 50-50 sharing of transcontinental traffic growth between Air Canada and CPA would not *directly* compromise or seriously injure Air Canada's economic viability." As to how the increased competition should be regulated, Wheatcroft warned the minister that CPA had said it would operate its transcontinental service with 61-seat DC-6BS but in fact had begun it with 89-seat Britannias. These had been replaced in 1961 with 124-seat DC-8s which were later modified to accommodate 141 seats, so that the capacity of CPA's one-flight-a-day service had been increased by 58 per cent since its inception. The answer to that, he said, was simple: the Air Transport Board could exercise control by limiting the number of seats, rather than flights, that CPA could put on the route each week.

The report elicited the customary blizzard of rebuttal papers from Place Ville Marie, and a full-blown presentation to a cabinet committee. But in March 1967, Pickersgill announced that CPA would be permitted immediately to double its transcontinental capacity. And henceforth, subject to annual review, it would be permitted to grow until it had 25 per cent of the total transcontinental capacity, which it would be allowed to keep permanently.

Grant McConachie did not live to savour this latest triumph; he had collapsed and died of a heart attack on a business trip to California in June 1965. He was 56. Gordon McGregor, his tired and aging rival (he was now past the official age of retirement), was left to reflect gloomily on the second transcontinental. "We can grow as much as we like in any year," he wrote in a memorandum after Pickersgill had given him the unwelcome news, "but in growing we will be increasing what the 25 per cent means."

CHAPTER TWENTY-TWO

HE MID-SIXTIES were boom years for air travel and, notwithstanding the political turmoil detailed in the preceding chapter, for Air Canada, too. In the early years of the decade, passenger traffic had continued to grow, but only modestly – by 4 per cent in 1962, 3 per cent in 1963 – and with the extra capacity of the jets the airline was easily able to handle the increase. Those were slow years for the country economically, but in 1964 a business recovery began and that fall there was an unexpected demand for travel that boosted the traffic increase for the year to 6 per cent.

The airline had based its estimated requirements for aircraft on the modest growth rate it had been experiencing and the sudden surge in demand took it by surprise. It arranged to increase the economy-class seating on some DC-8s from 117 to 123 and ordered two more DC-9s. But because of the two-year time lag between the ordering of an aircraft and its delivery it found itself short of capacity in 1965, when the boom accelerated and the annual rate of traffic increase more than doubled, to 13 per cent. In 1966, the airline took delivery of two more DC-8s and its first six DC-9s and that summer it provided 35 per cent more capacity on the transcontinental service than it had during 1965. But still the boom continued, fuelled partly by a rash of strikes in other forms of transport: shipping in Britain, the railways in Canada, five major airlines in the United States, trucking in Ontario and cargo handling in Quebec ports. In July alone, the airline operated 462 more flights than its regular schedule called for, but the complaints from frustrated passengers continued. Many of them reached the ears of MPs, there were questions in the House, and the general discontent with the nation's airline almost certainly influenced the government's decision to sanction CPA's second transcontinental.

The shortage of capacity extended into Expo year, 1967. Foreseeing the demand for seats by visitors flocking to the World's Fair in Montreal, the airline had ordered five more DC-8s and thirteen DC-9s for delivery in late 1966 and early 1967; but because of production delays and U.S. military priorities, most of them did not arrive until the fair was over and the visitors had gone home. Though the airline managed to carry 22 per cent more passengers during the year, it was deluged with complaints from those turned away or unable to get reservations on the flight of their choice.

The crowded planes, though they irritated the customers, greatly improved the company's financial performance. Having turned the corner from its three deficit years in 1963 with a modest surplus of $500,000, it registered a $1.4 million profit in 1964 and was able, for the first time since 1946, to pay the CNR a dividend of $3 a share on its 50,000 issued shares – in addition to $11.4 million in interest on its loans and debentures. Its profit almost tripled in 1965, to $3.9 million, and the dividend was raised to $4 a share, which the airline continued to pay until its capital structure was changed in 1977. The $2.9 million profit in 1966 would have been even larger had the airline not been closed down for two weeks in November by the first strike in its twenty-nine-year history.

The history of organized labour relations at TCA began with the pilots. Ten of them met in a Winnipeg hotel room on December 13, 1937, and chipped in $1 each to provide the modest capital for "a body able to consolidate pilot views on airline problems and with authority to voice them when necessary." They called it the Canadian Airline Pilots Association (CALPA) and elected Jock Barclay its first president. The dispatchers were next to organize, during World War II, and by 1947 the company had signed collective agreements with seven separate bargaining units.

In its early years, the company was remarkably free of labour troubles. The "one happy family" atmosphere of the Winnipeg days persisted and the team spirit was such that when contracts were being negotiated the company adopted a paternalistic attitude and the thought of a strike was abhorrent to both sides.

By 1960, though, Air Canada had more than eleven thousand employees, and the days when bosses could wander around addressing workers by their first names had long gone. Things were now more remote, more impersonal, and what had been a vocation to be proud of–being part of an elite group of pioneers – became for many of the newcomers just another job. In the early days, for instance, a mechanic poking about the innards of a Lockheed could comprehend the whole scope of the job and he was given a high degree of independence; he made many of the decisions about what had to be done himself and he could see the results of his handiwork. The jets brought with them a more specialized, assembly-line approach; they were so big mechanics found themselves performing isolated tasks which were closely supervised, subject to numerous quality-control checks, and usually just one part of a much larger job whose outline they could only dimly perceive. In other fields, too, it became increasingly difficult for a worker to identify his or her contribution to the whole and enjoy the feeling of being part of the team.

The advent of the jets also stepped up both the volume and the pace of the employees' work, and among those most immediately affected were the flight attendants. Since the jets travelled almost twice as fast as the old aircraft, the stewardesses had to serve more passengers on flights that lasted only half as long. In 1961, their union, the Canadian Air Line Flight Attendants Association, demanded a "jet speed clause" which would have paid them an extra minute an hour for each ten miles by which an aircraft's speed exceeded 300 miles per hour. This would have credited them with an hour and 20 minutes' time for each hour they worked on a DC-8. The company flatly refused the demand, pointing out that it would result in the stewardesses' receiving four hours' pay for each hour worked when the supersonics arrived on the scene, which they were still confidently expected to do. A conciliation board scaled down the union's demand but the company still refused to accept any formula that would provide more than an hour's time for an hour's work, and the union set a strike deadline. The dispute was not resolved until six hours before the strike was due to begin, when the union accepted the company's offer of an 8 per cent pay premium for work on the DC-8s.

That dispute spelt the end of the "happy family" era and the beginning of almost two decades of troubled labour relations. From 1962 to 1965 the company was locked in virtually continuous dispute with its largest union, the International Association of Machinists and Aerospace Workers (IAMAW). The give and take of old days was replaced by dragged-out conciliation hearings and last-minute settlements as the new generation of union leaders became more and more inflexible in their demands, reflecting the militancy of their younger members, who were uninhibited by memories of the hardships of the Depression or the war and considered the old esprit de corps nothing but sentimental hogwash.

By 1966, the atmosphere was such that a strike by one or other of the company's unions seemed inevitable – and because of the different time zones across the country one actually started before yet another last-minute settlement averted its spread across the system. The leadership of the Canadian Air Line Employees Association (CALEA), representing the passenger agents, had twice reached agreement with the company on a new contract, only to have it rejected by the union's members. When the company's third offer was put to them, the members voted to strike; but after federal mediation, and a late-night telephone call from Prime Minister Pearson to Gordon McGregor, the company made an eleventh-hour concession which averted the strike. Employees in Newfoundland and Halifax who had walked off the job at midnight went back to work a few minutes later.

CALEA settled for an annual wage increase of 5.6 per cent, which was less than a conciliation board had recommended. But that same year, striking longshoremen in St. Lawrence ports and workers on the Seaway were given two-year contracts providing for an increase of 15 per cent a year, thanks to the intervention of Prime Minister Pearson, who feared they could disrupt wheat shipments to the Soviet Union and undermine national pride by preventing the completion of Expo '67 construction on time. This was immediately taken by union leaders and the press as evidence that "the Pearson formula" sanctioned 15 per cent annual wage increases for all Canadians, or at least all those working for the government or government-owned bodies.

Pearson's intervention – businessmen considered it a disastrous blunder – had unfortunate repercussions on Air Canada's negotiations with its unions for years. The members of CALEA naturally felt they had been sold down the river: their president and the rest of the negotiators who had reached the settlement resigned, and their successors vowed to catch up in the next round of bargaining. And when the time came for the IAMAW to negotiate a new contract in August, its leaders resolved not to fall into the same traps. Before meeting the company representatives they consulted their members who, as skilled technicians, were furious that they were now making less money than mere longshoremen; the members instructed their leaders to hold out for an annual raise of 20 per cent and fringe benefits which the company claimed would add another 22 per cent to the package. From the beginning, the company said it could not afford such a large increase; the union negotiators, with the fate of CALEA's leadership clearly in mind, said they were powerless to accept anything less than their members, who had been consulted in true democratic fashion, had instructed them to demand.

A conciliation board reported that it seemed unlikely that the union membership would ratify a "sensible" wage increase, because of the mistaken impression that the government had established a guideline approving 15 per cent increases, and its chairman, Richard Geddes, was appointed to mediate the dispute. He suggested an increase of 12 per cent in the first year of the contract, plus adjustments worth an additional 3.5 per cent already approved by the company, and a 6 per cent increase in the second year. When the union negotiators turned down his recommendation, Geddes decided to go over their heads and submit his proposal to the union's rank and file directly, with copies to McGregor, Pearson, the Minister of Labour, Bryce Mackasey, and the press. He said in his letter he was "amazed" that the negotiating committee thought the union members would reject an increase of more than $1,000 in the first year of the contract and go on strike for even more.

For the sake of convenience – the strike deadline set by the union was only two days away – Geddes used Air Canada's facilities to type, duplicate, stamp and mail the letters. This infuriated the union negotiators, who felt the company had engineered the whole scheme in the hope that the rank and file would force their hands, and they told Geddes his services as mediator were no longer required. Their suspicions were magnified when, on the morning of November 14, the day set for the strike, the company made Geddes's proposal its last official offer. At 4 p.m. the 5,200 maintenance men walked off the job and closed down the airline for the first time in its history.

Public opinion across the country almost unanimously condemned the union and editorials appeared under such headlines as "Time for a Showdown" and "Mr. McGregor Takes a Stand." McGregor himself told a press conference the company had accepted Geddes's proposal only with reluctance, to try to avert the strike, since it would add $5.5 million to its wage bill in the first year and $3 million in the second. He regretted the inconvenience to the public but believed the public would put up with it temporarily rather than pay indefinitely for Air Canada deficits caused by the union's "exorbitant and completely unjustified" demands. "What is taking place here," he said, "is not collective bargaining but a bare-faced attempt to coerce a publicly-owned utility, based on the belief that it cannot or will not defend itself against avaricious demands."

Talks resumed on November 19, and when the strike ended after two weeks it was with a settlement only slightly better than the Geddes proposal the union had rejected: the machinists received a 12 per cent increase in the first year and the second period of the contract was extended to 14 months, with a 5 per cent increase for the first eight months and an additional 3 per cent for the last six months. The net cost to the airline while the strike lasted was estimated at more than $300,000 a day.

In the normal course of events, Gordon McGregor would by now have retired and someone else would have had the unpleasant responsibility of coping with the machinists' strike and its aftermath. Both he and Donald Gordon reached the customary retirement age of 65 in 1966, but in March Jack Pickersgill told McGregor he had spoken to the Prime Minister and they wanted him to stay on for at least a year beyond his birthday in September. He advanced two reasons for the request: they did not want the presidency of both the CNR and Air Canada to fall vacant at about the same time, and he had not had the oportunity to get to know McGregor's chosen successor, Herb Seagrim.* Consequently, he did not want anything said or done that would commit the company or the government to Seagrim's appointment as McGregor's successor.

McGregor decided at that point he had to tell the minister that the board had just agreed to promote Seagrim, who was then senior vice-president, operations, to the post of executive vice-president. Pickersgill agreed to this enthusiastically enough, but then sounded what McGregor took to be an ominous note: Seagrim, he said, should be warned that he could only consider the appointment to mean his eventual promotion to the presidency if the vacancy was filled from within the company. McGregor protested that it would be most unwise to import a new president from outside the company, partly because of his belief in Seagrim's ability to handle the job and partly from the point of view of company morale. Pickersgill appeared to agree with this but said he still wanted the stipulation made to Seagrim and included in the minutes of the directors' meeting at which the appointment was confirmed.

---

*In 1962, after McGregor's stroke, he and two fellow directors, Donald Gordon and Harry Price, had been appointed as a sub-committee of the board to consider possible candidates to inherit the presidency, from both inside and outside the company. By 1964, they had agreed on McGregor's own choice, Seagrim, who from then on was being groomed to take over the helm on McGregor's retirement. In 1966, however, Seagrim was still an unknown quantity to Pickersgill, who told the author years later that Donald Gordon, on his visits to Ottawa, had made a point of taking along the CNR's legal counsel, Norman MacMillan, "and it was very clear to me that when Donald retired Norm MacMillan would be his successor." On the other hand, "The management of Air Canada was an autocracy . . . and I practically didn't know Seagrim at all. On the rare occasions when I had met him, I felt he was far too deferential to Gordon McGregor. He didn't give me the impression that he was giving his mind to me at all, and I just felt – well, I just didn't feel he was adequate, and that may have been very unfair to him."

Innocuous though all this may have seemed to an outsider, it was the beginning of what would eventually be the most calamitous upheaval in the airline's history. But in the meantime McGregor and his old team appeared to be riding high, with the airline continuing to expand its routes, its revenue and its profits. Thanks to the conclusion of long and arduous bilateral negotiations with the United States, Pickersgill announced in March 1966 that Air Canada would henceforth be able to fly direct between Montreal and Chicago, from Toronto to Los Angeles, and from Montreal and Toronto to Miami (until then, the southern service had been restricted to Tampa). CPA, to its chagrin, was given only Vancouver to San Francisco.

In 1966, also, Air Canada inaugurated with much fanfare a new international route: from Montreal to Moscow. Permission to establish this service had been a long time coming. McGregor had first approached C.D. Howe about it in 1954, and Howe had Lester Pearson, who was then Secretary of State for External Affairs, explore the idea with the Russians in 1955. Nothing came of this feeler at that stage of East-West relations, but in the spring of 1958 McGregor was invited to join a private delegation of businessmen on a visit to the Soviet Union; he agreed with alacrity and quickly obtained a visa from the Soviet Embassy in Ottawa. But a few days before he was due to leave, Prime Minister Diefenbaker summoned him to Ottawa and asked him to cancel his trip. Even though he was not a civil servant, the Chief said, his visit would imply a relationship between the governments of Canada and the Soviet Union that could well be offensive to Canadian "ethnic groups." Diefenbaker continued to discourage all attempts to pursue the issue for the rest of his administration, but after the Liberals returned to power McGregor was once again invited to join a private delegation to Moscow and this time Pearson raised no objection.

The visit was in May 1964, and as well as touring Soviet factories, including the Ilyushin aircraft plant, McGregor had several talks with General Loginov, head of the Soviet airline Aeroflot. He reported to the Prime Minister on his return that the Russians were enthusiastic about the suggested service, and Pearson agreed with him that a direct link between Canada and the Soviet Union might do much to improve East-West relations. This seems to have been McGregor's main objective in pushing for the service, since he never appeared to think the route would be a moneymaker, at least in its early stages; indeed, at first, he tried to persuade the government the airline should run it as a government-subsidized charter operation. He also hoped to pick up some U.S.

business by operating the only service between North America and the Soviet Union. At that time there seemed no prospect of relations between the United States and the Soviet Union relaxing sufficiently to permit a U.S. airline to fly to Moscow, though a few years later Pan Am and Aeroflot did launch a reciprocal Moscow–New York service.

While Pearson apparently favoured the new service, there was considerable doubt about it within the cabinet – Pickersgill recalls that he predicted McGregor would lose his shirt on it – and it was many months before McGregor's informal approach was followed up by negotiations at the official level. But after much visiting to and fro by representatives of Aeroflot and Air Canada,* an official bilateral agreement was signed in July 1966, and the service began soon afterward. There was never enough traffic to make it profitable for Air Canada, even though the operation was pooled from the start and the airline added a stop at Copenhagen in an attempt to bolster its disastrously low load factors. What had apparently been launched more as an exercise in diplomacy than as a commercial venture was eventually discontinued in 1977.

Late in the year, when the time came to send the government the capital budget for 1967, it contained provision for the preliminary payments on ten aircraft no one around the airline really wanted to buy: four Anglo-French supersonic Concordes and six U.S. supersonics which had not yet been either designed or named.

As with the subsonic jets, Europe was ahead of the United States in the pioneering of supersonic transports. In 1962, with the encouragement and financial support of their respective governments, British Aircraft Corporation and Sud Aviation had pooled their technical and productive resources to design and build the aircraft that was eventually named the Concord in Britain and Concorde in France. (The British added the final "e" later in the interest of international amity.) The Americans at first hung back, because there were so many uncertainties about the economics and practicality of supersonics in commercial use, and the enormous development costs were far beyond the individual resources

---

*On one of these visits, Air Canada's Don McLeod was exchanging cocktail-party pleasantries with a Soviet general who could not understand what he did in his capacity as director of public relations. Through an interpreter, McLeod tried to explain the multifarious ways in which public relations practitioners undertake the judicious enlightenment of press and public. He was having little success until something he said brought an appreciative light to the general's eyes and he beamed and said: "Ah, *now* I understand – propaganda!"

of even the biggest American aircraft manufacturers. But again, as with the jets, it was Pan Am that forced the pace: faced with the prospect of BOAC and Air France competing on the Atlantic with airliners capable of carrying 120 passengers from Paris or London to New York at 1,450 miles per hour, Pan Am ordered six Concordes in 1963. This forced the U.S. government's hand and it announced that it would subsidize the building of an American supersonic; a manufacturers' design competition was held and the Boeing company was awarded the contract to build an even faster competitor to the Concorde, which would fly at 1,800 miles per hour with 250 passengers.

Air Canada was in no hurry to commit itself to the supersonics: both design projects were running into difficulties and delays, and an Air Canada internal study estimated that the Concorde would cost almost twice as much per seat-mile to operate as the DC-8. But with airlines all over the world lining up to buy them – CPA had ordered three of the Boeings months before – McGregor was forced in self-defence to follow suit. At that stage in both projects it was not necessary to make an actual down-payment; a lesser sum sufficed to reserve what is known as a "line position": the right to buy a certain aircraft as it came off the assembly line. So many other airlines had joined the Concorde queue by 1966 that the required payment – $981,000 – reserved only positions far down the line: those numbered 73, 79, 81 and 85. At that time, the Concorde was expected to enter service in 1971, and Air Canada's lowly line position meant it would be more than two years after that before it could begin to meet the supersonic competition of its rivals. The Boeing was not expected to be in service before 1974, and Air Canada found itself even further behind in the line-up: its $1.3 million could only secure line positions 110, 117, 124, 131, 138 and 145.

Perhaps because the 1967 budget was the first for four years in which new capital had been sought, the government approved it without undue qualms. But a year later, McGregor received an unpleasant surprise: the government told him it could not provide all the funds requested in his 1968 capital budget. Counting $125 million to cover projects authorized in previous years, the budget requested a record $200 million. It included provision for more DC-8s and DC-9s, three of the new Jumbo jets – the 366-passenger version of Boeing's huge 747 – the updated ReserVec II computer reservations system, and expanded maintenance facilities at the Dorval base to cope with the growing jet fleet.

No elaborate comparison studies went into the selection of

the 747: there was just no other aircraft like it. When the Air Canada flight operations team went to Seattle to see the prototype for the first time, the men who had cut their teeth on the Lockheeds simply could not imagine that the 747 would fly. It stood as tall as a six-story building and weighed 340 tons at takeoff – more than twice as much as a DC-8 and an incredible sixty-five times as much as the original Lockheed. It could carry 89 tons, almost three times as much as a DC-8. And despite its huge size, it was 50 miles an hour faster than the DC-8, could fly 600 miles further, and could use the same runways. (The press later supplied some less vital statistics, such as the fact that there was room for a tennis court on each side of the wing.)

The Air Canada evaluation team estimated that the 747's operating costs would be 6 per cent lower per seat-mile than the DC-8's, but added that this saving would be cancelled out by the extra costs associated with introducing a new type of aircraft to the fleet. This time, however, the sales department clinched the decision to buy. All Air Canada's competitors planned to equip with the Jumbos, and such was the appeal of their roomy cabins to passengers that the airline would be left behind if it did not follow suit.

By ordering the 747, Air Canada was committing itself to the expenditure of $23 million for each aircraft; the airline was becoming more than ever "big business." Before the government held up the 1968 budget, McGregor had already supplied it with a ten-year forecast of the airline's capital requirements: $2.56 billion from then to the end of 1977. The airline expected to be able to generate $1.45 billion of that huge total internally during the ten years, but this still left $1.1 billion to be raised in new borrowing. As to its immediate requirements, it considered it would be able to generate $65 million of the $200 million in the 1968 budget itself, from profits and depreciation accruals. This left $135 million to be provided through new borrowings. It was a tight-money era and the government had already told its departments and agencies it planned to restrict 1968 financial advances to their 1967 levels. As McGregor pointed out, this was an unrealistic objective for Air Canada, since commitments for its 1968 spending approved in previous budgets already exceeded its 1967 budget. Nevertheless, he was told that the government could provide only $75 million of the $135 million through the customary vehicle of the CNR Financing and Guarantee Act. The airline would have to explore the prospect of borrowing the remaining $60 million itself from outside sources.

The Minister of Transport was now Paul Hellyer, Jack Pickersgill having retired from politics to put his transportation expertise to good use as head of the new Canadian Transport Commission he had decided was essential to the country's welfare. Hellyer, who had made himself financially independent as a Toronto home-builder and developer before entering politics at the early age of 25, had been a controversial figure in his previous portfolio of Defence: Gordon McGregor was only one of countless World War II veterans disgusted by his unification of the three armed services.

The first clash between the new minister and the refractory president of the national airline was not long in coming, and once again the flashpoint was the old, intractable problem of the Winnipeg base. As the government had hoped, the report of the Thompson Royal Commission had taken most of the steam out of the controversy: in essence, it supported the airline's case for the phasing-out of the base and chided Manitobans for continuing to champion a lost cause for unsound economic objectives which, if realized, would be damaging to the country as well as its airline. Some further repair work on the fences was affected by the airline's decision to build the third-largest cargo terminal in the country at Winnipeg airport. But the uneasy truce was shattered by a terse announcement from Place Ville Marie on October 5, 1967.

The airline had told the Thompson Commission two years earlier that it would be operating at least thirty Viscounts for several years into the future, which was taken locally as confirmation that the base would continue in operation at least until 1973, as Prime Minister Pearson had promised. But as more DC-8s and DC-9s were bought to cope with the mid-sixties traffic boom, continuing internal studies showed that only twenty-eight Viscounts would be needed by 1970 – and thirty had been set, perhaps too arbitrarily, as the cut-off point for the Winnipeg base. In accordance with its commitment to keep the machinists informed, management notified the union in a brief letter that "the movement of main base functions to Dorval will begin in the latter half of 1969 and the closing of the Winnipeg base is expected to be completed by the end of 1970."

The outburst of anger this provoked in Winnipeg was matched in Ottawa, for, with the growing intransigence he displayed toward politicians in his later years, McGregor had not warned either Hellyer or Pearson that the announcement was coming. Hellyer had been in office only a little over two weeks, and perhaps he had not yet been fully briefed about the political minefield on the prairies. At any rate, he told the House next day there had been no federal decision to close the base by 1970, and the airline's announcement had been issued without consultation with the government and had come as a complete surprise. He offered to meet with Manitoba officials at any time and added: "We want to find an appropriate means of keeping the facilities at Winnipeg open."

When John Baldwin communicated the minister's displeasure to him, McGregor coolly suggested that he draw Hellyer's attention to the final paragraph of a letter Pickersgill had sent Premier Roblin after they had met to discuss the base phase-out in 1966. Confirming his promise to continue working with the Manitoba government to solve the problem, Pickersgill had added: "At the same time, I have made it clear in our discussions that this statement of broad objectives should not be construed as an indication that the federal government has any intention of issuing directions to Air Canada in areas which are customarily left to company management. . . ."

This did nothing at all to mollify the new Minister of Transport. He considered McGregor guilty of wilful defiance of the government and when he flew to Winnipeg a couple of weeks later for talks with the Manitoba Air Policy Committee he assured Premier Roblin the government would stand by the Prime Minister's commitment that the base would be kept in operation until 1973. And he told a press conference afterward: "I will not permit Air Canada to overrule the Prime Minister."

In a letter to McGregor telling him of his commitment to the premier, Hellyer was a little less definite. "I did not indicate," he wrote, "that this necessarily meant continued operation by Air Canada itself or continued operation solely as a Viscount maintenance base; alternative possibilities would have to be considered . . . which, of course, could involve a cooperative attitude on the part of Air Canada. If these other alternatives do not develop, it will be necessary to have further consultations between the government and Air Canada as to the most satisfactory means of carrying out this commitment." In the meantime, he asked that the board of directors should reconsider the airline's future maintenance plans on a national basis: "I would like the company to keep in mind economic and other factors which bear on any decision involving concentration of all or virtually all maintenance activities in a single location, and the extent to which this may create vulnerability on several fronts. . . ."

In conversation with the author, Hellyer said he was not at that time worried about the possible fate of the Montreal base if Quebec separated from the rest of the country, but he *was* concerned that the Montreal labour scene was "very volatile." Jack Pickersgill had a colourful explanation for his own opposition to the concentration of all the airline's maintenance facilities in Montreal: "It's no use having unnecessary jugular veins." At any rate, Hellyer felt so strongly on the issue that he linked it to the government's approval of the airline's 1968 capital budget. He wrote to McGregor on January 29, 1968, stipulating that the belated approval of the reduced budget – it was still $60 million short of the sum originally requested – was conditional upon the airline's suspending all further expenditures on the Dorval base until the "general question" of the airline's maintenance facilities had been reviewed and approved by the government. In other words, until the Winnipeg base problem was solved. And he imposed another condition: the airline must not commit itself to the purchase of any new aircraft or parts, other than those already covered by firm letters of intent, until he had approved whatever arrangements it was able to make on the financial market to raise the $60 million the government was unable to provide.

The airline had been considerably encouraged by its exploratory approaches to banks and financial institutions in both Canada and the United States. In fact it was so confident that it could borrow the money it needed that it was contemplating raising its capital needs for 1969 in the same bond issue, rather than having to go to the market twice in the same year. But before the negotiations had gone very far the government told McGregor to suspend them, on the grounds that because of its own borrowing needs it might find itself in competition with its national airline on the money market.* This was another blow to McGregor, but by retaining more Vanguards in service than it had intended and cutting its aircraft orders from six DC-9s and five DC-8s to three of each, the airline managed to adjust to its reduced financial circumstances.

The Winnipeg base problem, however, remained as intractable as ever. On one occasion, McGregor suggested to Hellyer that he had the answer to the problem in his own hands. Since he

---

*In effect, the corporation raised its first non-government financing in 1972, when it leased two L-1011s from a United States investment group, Haas-Turner. Under this "pay-as-you-go" arrangement, instead of raising the huge capital sum required to buy the planes outright, the airline rented them for the six summer peak months for an annual payment of $2.3 million, which it met out of their earnings. In subsequent years, it met its capital requirements by borrowings from such sources as the U.S. Export-Import Bank and international financial markets. But leasing remained a convenient way to reduce its capital needs, and at the end of 1984 twenty of its fleet of 112 aircraft were leased from a variety of private investment groups.

had assured McGregor that in his pledge to the Premier of Manitoba he had not specified that the base would continue to be operated by Air Canada, and since as Minister of Transport he was the proprietor of the second-largest aircraft fleet in the country, why didn't he transfer the maintenance of the Department of Transport fleet to Winnipeg? The suggestion did nothing to warm the frosty relationship between the two equally strong-willed men.

But picking up the minister's suggestion that "alternative possibilities" be considered, the airline set out to look for another company prepared to take over the base. Most of those approached shied away from the political complications on sight, but in 1969 the base was purchased by CAE Industries Limited, a Canadian holding company with widely diversified interests that started life in Montreal after the war as a high-technology aviation electronics firm. CAE received a contract to continue to maintain the airline's Viscounts, the last of which was not retired until 1974, and was later able to obtain other aircraft maintenance and manufacturing work for the plant. Three hundred of the almost eight hundred Air Canada employees elected to transfer to the base's new tenant, and almost the same number remained on loan to CAE on a temporary basis; most of the rest took early retirement or were transferred to Dorval.

By the time the changeover occurred, Gordon McGregor had retired, but the issue that had haunted him for so many years persisted long after his death from cancer in 1971. In 1974, with a federal election in the offing and employment dwindling at CAE with the phase-out of the Viscounts, the Winnipeg Liberal James Richardson took his constituents' cause to the cabinet. Air Canada, he suggested, should either buy the Winnipeg base back from CAE, or build a new hangar there to overhaul its Boeing 727s when they came into service.

The airline planners had already decided a new overhaul facility would ultimately be needed for the 727 fleet. A lot of things had changed since the original decision to establish the Dorval base; new technology and new route patterns now made Winnipeg seem the logical place to overhaul it. But the first 727 had not yet arrived, and when the airline was told the government planned to announce the construction of a new overhaul hangar in Winnipeg it protested that it would not be needed for at least three years. While the Liberal sun had not yet been totally eclipsed in the West, Richardson knew it was sinking fast and he badly needed a carrot to dangle before the electors. So the government agreed to finance the construction of the new hangar until the airline needed it, and on a brief stop-over at Winnipeg before the election, Prime Minister Trudeau lifted local spirits – if not the Liberals' fortunes – by announcing that the national airline would be returning to the home of its first maintenance shops.

The airline moved into the new hangar in 1977, and the subsequent growth of the 727 fleet to thirty-nine aircraft eventually necessitated its expansion. By the end of 1984, the airline had a total of 2,051 employees in Winnipeg, 340 of them in the maintenance and engineering branch, and the airline's changed pattern of operations had also led to the building of two new hangars in Toronto and one each in Vancouver and Halifax.

CHAPTER TWENTY-THREE

ORDON MCGREGOR FINALLY RETIRED in May 1968, eighteen months after his sixty-fifth birthday. In the twenty years of his presidency, the airline he lived for had doubled in size every five years and become by all accepted standards of measurement one of the top ten in the world. The achievement, of course, was not exclusively his own: he had far more dedicated and talented lieutenants than it is possible to mention by name in these pages.

By common agreement, the three men upon whom he relied most were Herb Seagrim, executive vice-president; Gordie Wood, senior vice-president, sales; and Bill Harvey, senior vice-president, finance. All had been with the airline since before the war. The other three vice-presidents–Dave Tennant, operations; Bill Sadler, administrative services; and Rod MacInnes, public relations–were only slightly less junior in terms of service, as were the incumbents in the tier of management just below the vice-presidents. Even the up-and-coming youngsters of the next generation, such as Claude Taylor in the sales department, could boast many years of service with the airline.

All these men – the upper levels of management had not yet been thrown open to women anywhere–were linked by admiration for, and loyalty to, their boss, "G.R." And together, under his inspirational leadership, they had developed the systems and procedures which had transformed the puny TCA of prewar years into a huge organization carrying more than six million passengers a year and generating annual revenues of almost $400 million.

The man McGregor had chosen and groomed to succeed him, Herb Seagrim, was, like his boss, a pilot's pilot. Born in Winnipeg, he learned to fly in the early 1930s by swapping a day's labour as mechanic's helper at the local flying club for fifteen minutes' flying instruction. By the time he joined TCA in 1937 he had earned his air engineer's licence and accumulated three thousand hours in his bush pilot's logbook. After six years as a TCA captain, he began the steady ascent through the management ranks that took him to the top operations post: chief pilot in the western region in 1943; assistant superintendent of operations in 1945; director of flight operations in 1946; general manager, operations, in 1950; and vice-president, operations, when Bill English retired in 1956.

Seagrim was a popular executive, noted for his low-key approach and his easy delegation of responsibility to those who won his trust. What Jack Pickersgill saw as his excessive deference toward McGregor was actually a manifestation of his total loyalty to his superiors and to the organization for which he worked. His attitude was: "The boss is the boss, and you can't argue with your boss. You can present your viewpoint or recommendations, but once the decision is made, that's it."

In the closing years of his administration, McGregor entrusted Seagrim with complete responsibility for the day-to-day operation of the airline. His succession to the presidency was taken as a foregone conclusion within the corporation, and it would have been a popular appointment. But circumstances conspired against him. For one thing, in his later years, McGregor had become more and more cantankerous in his dealings with Ottawa, and Seagrim, with his well-known loyalty to his boss, was considered too much the mixture as before.

McGregor had originally stayed on past his normal retirement date at the request of Pickersgill, a request renewed later by Paul Hellyer. In the months leading up to the date upon which it had been agreed he should finally go, May 31, 1968, he repeatedly tried to persuade the airline's directors to name Seagrim as his successor. In the absence of a clear mandate from Ottawa, the directors refused to commit themselves. When May 31 arrived there had still been no decision, so Norman MacMillan, head of the CNR, was elected acting president. This news, of course, left Seagrim in limbo, and there was a rash of press comment demanding that the government make up its mind, preferably in his favour. McGregor himself, combative to the end, told reporters in a farewell interview: "I'm so worried about a political appointment that I can taste it."

In the months that followed, many names were mentioned, both publicly and privately, as candidates for the job. The deputy minister of transport, John Baldwin, had made it clear to his boss, Paul Hellyer, that he felt the presidency of the national airline would be a fitting capstone to his career in the government's service, and Hellyer thought Baldwin's long experience with aviation matters might well qualify him for the job. And among the other names that cropped up were those of politicians, businessmen – both in and outside the field of aviation – and at least two air vice-marshals.

Eventually, the idea developed in Ottawa that there should be a dual appointment, though how the chairman and president envisaged in this arrangement should, or could, divide the executive responsibility does not at first appear to have been thought out. Also, Pierre Elliott Trudeau had just replaced Lester Pearson as leader of the Liberal party and prime minister and, in the climate of the times, it was decided that one of the appointments must go to a French-speaking Canadian.

The issue of bilingualism in the nation's airline had surfaced from time to time long before the official languages policy had become a matter of public controversy. As early as 1947, before he became prime minister, Louis St. Laurent complained to C.D. Howe that only one of the twenty-two TCA employees in the ticket office at the Château Laurier in Ottawa could speak French – and not very well, at that. Howe passed the complaint on to Herb Symington, suggesting that at least one bilingual clerk be on duty on each shift. Symington replied that in Ottawa the civil service was a heavy competitor for the type of bilingual employee required by the airline, a point McGregor repeated when the issue arose again in 1950. The situation had not improved much by that time; only two of the twenty-six TCA employees in Ottawa were bilingual. The picture was somewhat better in Montreal, where 50 out of 109 employees were classified as bilingual, though only nine of them were actually French Canadians. McGregor was also able to assure Howe by this time that public announcements at Montreal airport were being made in both English and French, and "the use of French timetables, primarily for distribution in France, is now under consideration."

There were, of course, exceptions to the general rule that the airline was a bastion of English Canadianism. The fact that one of his best mechanics, Emile Patrault, was a French Canadian did not deter Jim Bain from installing him as regional supervisor of maintenance at Toronto in 1947, to the discomfiture of some of the locals with strong Orange sympathies. * And Romeo Vachon,

---

*An incipient revolt against Patrault was snuffed out by his own larger-than-life qualities: his cordiality, his wit – which was both spontaneous and uproarious – and his ability to be tough when the occasion demanded. Before he was posted to Toronto, while he was in charge of maintenance at Moncton, a mechanic carelessly left a hammer in a North Star exhaust pipe. When the engine was started, the hammer flew out in a shower of sparks, and Patrault fired the culprit. There was a grievance hearing at which the union representatives protested that the man had been guilty only of a simple human error. Patrault, who was never inhibited by his lack of formal education, won his case with the dry comment: "If everybody makes that error, pretty soon we're out of hammers."

a legendary pioneer airmail pilot in Quebec, became TCA's station manager in Montreal when his flying days were over, before moving on to become a member of the Air Transport Board.

In June 1963, after the Quebec government had begun to assert its position on language rights more vociferously, McGregor set up an internal committee on bilingualism to study the company's policies and practices and recommend, among other things, "the degree of bilingualism appropriate to the Company, considering, with other factors, its geographically widespread operations." The committee continued to meet through the years and changes were instituted so that by the time McGregor retired more than 34 per cent of employees across the system, and more than 57 per cent of those in Quebec, were classified as bilingual; and in those positions requiring contact with the public, more than 95 per cent of the employees in Quebec could speak both languages. But there were still no French Canadians at the senior management level; the highest-ranking francophone in the company was Pierre Jeanniot, who had by now become superintendent of maintenance systems at Dorval. The view had therefore formed in Ottawa that the country's national airline was encrusted with the patrician atmosphere of an exclusive men's club. Its circle of top management around Gordon McGregor was seen as too conservative, and too deeply entrenched, for the good of either the company or the country.

From the government's point of view, then, the problem seemed to be not simply to replace McGregor, but to give the airline a thorough shake-up and a whole new sense of direction. As the search for his successor progressed, it seemed that the two-man team most heavily favoured for the task consisted of Lucien Saulnier, Mayor Jean Drapeau's right-hand man as chairman of the executive committee of the city of Montreal, and Rod McIsaac, a Winnipeg businessman and member of the airline's board of directors. Saulnier was offered the post of chairman of the airline and was interested – until he pressed Ottawa on his terms of reference and concluded from the response that he would be little more than a figurehead, a position foreign to his dynamic thinking. He made it plain to the Prime Minister that he would accept the job only if he was the chief executive officer. When Ottawa tried to juggle the job descriptions to re-assign the executive responsibilities McIsaac lost interest in what he foresaw would be a toothless president's job, and both men retired from the fray.

The task of finding McGregor's successor fell originally to Paul Hellyer, as Minister of Transport, and he assigned the preliminary inquiries to his associate minister, James Richardson, son of the Jim Richardson who had so nearly become the proprietor of the national airline thirty years earlier. Richardson had approached several potential candidates even before McGregor finally retired, just a few weeks after Trudeau became prime minister. Trudeau had not previously taken any part in the matter, but Hellyer recalls that when he first discussed the progress of the search with him, the new prime minister casually mentioned the name of Yves Pratte, who was, he explained, a brilliant and much-respected Quebec City lawyer. Hellyer had never heard the name before, and since there were still several other horses in the field he did not pay much attention to it. But months later, after Saulnier and McIsaac had retired from the race at the last minute, the Prime Minister suggested Pratte's name again and he was asked to take on the post of chairman.

The impression grew up in later years that Pratte owed his appointment to his friendship with Trudeau, but in fact until he was approached about the job he had never met him. He did know the minister popularly supposed to have influenced the Prime Minister in his choice, Jean Marchand, but only slightly: he had acted both for and against him in labour negotiations in Quebec. Pratte, born in Quebec City in 1925, graduated from Laval University in 1947. After post-graduate studies at the University of Toronto, he joined Louis St. Laurent's Quebec City law firm, where he soon earned a reputation as an outstanding practitioner of taxation and corporate law. He was dean of the law faculty at Laval from 1962 to 1965, and a special legal adviser to the Quebec government from 1965 until his appointment to Air Canada. He was never associated with any political party – in fact, when the Liberal Jean Lesage, who had appointed him, was defeated by the Union Nationale in 1966, the new premier, Daniel Johnson, asked him to stay on as his legal adviser. Nor had he any administrative experience in industry, though he had become fascinated by the workings of the business world during his practice of law and jumped at the opportunity offered him by Trudeau.

In November 1968, the long hiatus at Air Canada was ended, and it was announced that henceforth the airline's destiny would be in the hands of two outsiders, Yves Pratte as chairman and John Baldwin as president. In the words of the official announcement: "The chairman will be the chief executive officer of the corporation and as such will have complete responsibility before the board of directors for all aspects of company operations. In particular, he will be concerned with financing, long-range planning and development." Baldwin, for his part, would be responsible to the chairman and the board "for the management of current operations and for such other duties as are assigned by the chairman."

The stability that had existed within the corporation for twenty years was now seen as something of a disadvantage: despite the company's tremendous growth, its management structure had remained virtually unchanged. Operationally, the airline had kept well abreast and usually somewhat ahead of the times, and it had come through the transition from the piston-engined era to the jet age with its reputation for safety and technical excellence if anything enhanced. But the men around McGregor realized that the administrative structure that had served in the early days was no longer adequate, and that changes were needed.

The most widely recognized deficiency, one from which almost all early airlines suffered, was a holdover from the days when the pilot owned the plane, sold the ticket, and pocketed the fare. This was the gulf that separated the operations side of the organization from the traffic, or sales side. Divided authority is a potential cause of friction and an obvious cause of inefficiency, and in Air Canada there were two entirely separate streams of authority. In every district and region there was one man in charge of operations and one in charge of sales, with neither being the overall boss: and at the risk of over-simplification, the sales people were concerned with moving passengers and the operations people were concerned with moving aeroplanes, regardless of their contents. This gave daily opportunities for conflict, and the efficiency of the enterprise depended entirely on how well the two men in charge understood each other's needs and were able to work together. In practice, of course, most disagreements were settled by the kind of informal contacts that develop among people working together for the same organization. But if a really fundamental difference arose demanding adjudication at a higher level, there was no formal mechanism by which it could be resolved until the two streams of authority converged – which was not until they reached Gordon McGregor.

Whether by accident or design, McGregor's style of management seemed to be based on what might be called "creative tension," the theory being, as one headquarters manager expressed it, that "if you keep your deputies at each other's throats, you'll keep them on their toes." This is not at all to suggest that the Air Canada executive suite was riven by personal feuds and backbiting. On the contrary, the group around McGregor was so loyal and close-knit that some of those lower down the ladder occasionally felt it was too cliquish, a sort of old-school-tie network they could never penetrate without some magic password they lacked. But in fact McGregor seldom met his closest deputies as a group; he seemed to prefer to deal with them individually, and in a sense each was walled off from the others' activities.

From time to time through the years, there would be a full-scale management conference at some lakeside resort where all would gather to discuss proposals for reorganizing the company's management structure. McGregor would listen amiably enough, but he never seemed sufficiently persuaded by whatever arguments were advanced to make any far-reaching changes; some thought he feared that to do so would hurt some of those who had worked longest and most loyally for him. So the commercial side of the airline and its operational side remained compartmentalized – and it was no secret that by training and inclination McGregor was an operations man. The conviction grew in the sales department that on any major issue demanding a decision between the two sides, McGregor would come down in favour of the operations department. This was not prejudice on his part; in fact he had started out in the sales department and its head, Gordie Wood, was one of his closest friends. But he seemed most at ease making technical decisions, things he could confirm on his slide rule, back up with solid facts. If the operations department opposed something the sales department wanted – say the rescheduling of an existing flight – it could always support its case with the factual detail: the time the sales department wanted the flight to leave was impossible because the maintenance schedule called for the aircraft to be somewhere else at that time, or no pilots would be available, and so on. The sales department, in contrast, often operated on hunches: if the flight left an hour later there were probably fifty extra passengers to be picked up. If McGregor asked why, Wood could only respond by saying, "Well, that's my best guess." And with McGregor, incontrovertible facts beat guesswork any day.

For Herb Seagrim, when he was senior vice-president, operations, this was a comfortable situation about which he could hardly be expected to complain. But in fact he was among those who recognized that changes were needed, and he had already begun to make some, as executive vice-president, before Pratte took over as chairman. The team Pratte inherited, therefore, was ready for change and prepared to accept it. Perhaps Pratte failed to recognize this, or lacked confidence in the ability of those who had shaped the system, or grown up within it, to make the radical changes he thought necessary. Either way, no one could have envisaged the upheavals and carnage that lay ahead.

Pratte began to interview the airline's department heads individually even before the board finally approved his appointment, on December 15, 1968. He asked them to send him memoranda outlining the functions and responsibilities of their departments and suggesting areas of the company's activities they thought could be improved. Predictably, this approach brought a flood of suggestions – and a few cautionary notes. For instance, K.E. "Kitch" Olson, general manager of purchases and stores, wrote: "Our own department – like others – has people who deserve consideration by reason of their past contributions but do not completely meet today's requirements. Their presence is an obstacle to hiring the quality of people needed for today's work. There should be some acceptable method of dealing with these people." On the other hand, Olson pointed out that "at the instigation of the executive vice-president we have compared our labour costs with those of similar departments in other airlines," and the results "have generally shown both inventory and labour costs to be reasonable." His memo ended: "The morale in the Company would be immensely improved by the knowledge that the Chairman and President were actively seeking new responsibilities for the Company. Over the years the impression has grown up that we seldom do more than try to retain – not always successfully – what we already have."

Dave Tennant, who had joined TCA as a young engineer and risen to succeed Herb Seagrim as vice-president, operations, drew his new boss's attention to a vulnerability of the airline which would soon confront him with the longest and costliest strike in its history. This was "the ability of unions to take a service organization, such as Air Canada, right down to the last minute in labour negotiations, lose nothing themselves, and create a great deal of embarrassment and loss of revenue to the company." Tennant, recapitulating his talk with the new chairman, also wrote: "I pointed out to Mr. Pratte that I thought he might be helpful in the area of the Company's approach to the bilingual problem. He expressed a certain reticence, because of the fact that he is basically a French-speaking Canadian, to become a driving force in this area. I suggested, however, that his judgments as to how far the Company needed to go in achieving a result that was acceptable to both the English and French-speaking elements of Canada, would be most helpful."

Gordon Wood submitted a list of ten objectives he thought Air Canada should pursue in its mission of serving the public, and underlined three areas as vitally important: "to become fully customer-oriented, profit-oriented and people-oriented." The last of these was "probably the most important and probably the one to which the least personal attention is given at the senior management level." Air Canada, like other companies, had three major compartments: people, material, and capital. "Of the three," Wood wrote, "only people, and in particular management, has the ability to grow, develop and enrich the enterprise since the material and money are subject to the laws of mechanics and are only as effective as the sum of their parts. People make the difference and are our greatest resource."

Herb Seagrim accompanied his memo with an organizational chart representing the concept "which I had thought to put in effect had I been appointed to the Presidency," and explained:

You will notice a sharp divergence toward Customer Service as the central theme in my approach. In the past, a great deal of effort has been concentrated on technical matters, partly because of the relative strengths of people within the company, and partly because technical considerations do in fact play an especially important role during the formative years of an airline. Now I think it is safe to say that technical excellence has been conceded to Air Canada by the public and the industry at large, and it is my opinion that increased emphasis should now be placed on customer service, which is really the stock in trade of the airline. Accordingly, my proposal visualizes a very strong customer service field organization supported on one hand by a headquarters marketing service group, and by a technical service group on the other.

Seagrim's proposal envisaged a direct line of authority down from the chairman, with the three main branches of the organization he mentioned all reporting directly to the executive vice-president, and with one vice-president in overall charge of each region on the system. He also enclosed with his memo an assessment of five well-known firms of management consultants, three American and two Canadian. The "top-recommended" firm, this said, was McKinsey Company, of New York, whose "noteworthy" airline experience included organizational studies for American Airlines, Eastern Airlines, KLM and Alitalia. McKinsey had recently opened its thirteenth international office, in Toronto – one of its alumnae was James Coutts, who later won fame in the Prime Minister's office – and its Canadian clients included Alcan Aluminium Limited, the Bank of Montreal, MacMillan Bloedel and Massey-Ferguson. It had also, according to its own literature, "played a key role in developing new strategies or establishing new approaches to the management of a wide range of government-owned or controlled enterprises in France and the United Kingdom" – including Air France, British Rail and Britain's General Post Office.

Pratte had decided right at the outset that he would need the help of competent management consultants to reorganize the airline, and by the time McKinsey submitted its formal proposal at his request in March 1969, he had apparently made his own diagnosis of the situation. "Since assuming his new responsibilities," the proposal said, "Mr. Pratte has concluded that the structure and range of management activities in Air Canada are quite inadequate. For example, we understand that the present organization is characterized by loosely defined roles, overlapping responsibilities, insufficient provision for critical activities (e.g., corporate planning and personnel administration), excessive compartmentalization, interdepartmental rivalries, and poor communications. . . . Mr. Pratte also is concerned that Air Canada has not operated with the profit orientation that characterizes many international airlines. Instead, a break-even result has been considered satisfactory."

Pratte confirmed to the author years later that his first impression of the airline was an unfavourable one. "It was quite clear," he said, "that it was an inefficient operation. It was grossly overstaffed and many people were incompetent – they were not properly trained and didn't know anything about management." And he attributed the slackness to the lack of the traditional business discipline of attention to the bottom line: "Money didn't count, and the customers didn't count – the inefficiency came out of not wanting to be profitable."

While they believe he perceived the situation as worse than it really was, many of those who served McGregor loyally and retain great affection for his memory concede the validity of Pratte's criticism of the absence of the profit motive at the airline. After all, C.D. Howe had created it in the expectation that it would be no more than a break-even operation: "The set-up is such," he had said in those long-ago days, "that the company will be protected against loss, but its profits will be very strictly limited. In other words, it is organized to perform a certain national service, and it is expected that that service will be performed at or near cost."

McGregor considered Air Canada to be a public utility and never tired of recalling his terms of reference from Howe: "You keep out of the taxpayer's pocket, and I'll keep out of your hair." Nor did he try to hide his fears that if the airline ever made large profits it would encourage more poaching on its preserves by private interests. If substantial profits were in the offing he preferred to use them to hold the line on fares, and he was several times during his career able to boast that despite the higher costs of doing business in Canada, air fares were lower here than in the United States. The effect of this break-even policy, however, was that the return on the capital invested in the airline was low. In 1967, for instance, the company registered a profit of $3.5 million after taxes, but this translated into a return on investment of only 5.2 per cent. The airline's capital requirements at the time were conservatively estimated at $2.5 billion over the succeeding decade, of which more than a billion would have to be borrowed, and the government was becoming increasingly anxious about its ability to supply such huge sums. But a return on investment of only 5.2 per cent was far too low to attract the needed capital on the money markets of Canada and the United States.

Pratte knew the airline must show far better financial results if it was to prosper under his direction. But by the time he had engaged the McKinsey organization to tell him how he might achieve them, any hopes he may have had of turning things around in 1969 had been dashed: on April 20, the airline was once again closed down by a strike of the 6,350 members of its machinists' union.

Because the terms of settlement that had ended the 1966 IAMAW walkout had been only slightly better than those offered by the company beforehand, a feeling had developed among the rank-and-file members that the union had lost the strike. Their disgruntlement and growing militancy convinced their leaders that they must defeat the company in the next round of negotiations. The issue on which they chose to fight became the achievement of dollar-for-dollar parity with IAMAW members in the United States. In November 1968, the company was confronted with a demand for a wage increase of 20 per cent in a one-year contract.

The horns had thus been locked before Pratte came on the scene, but nevertheless a strike right at the beginning of his administration was an unpleasant prospect. He and John Baldwin had been made aware as soon as they arrived that the prolonged uncertainty about the company's future leadership and all the press speculation about "political appointments" had been churned up by the rumour mill to create a damaging atmosphere of doubt and unrest across the system. They had immediately undertaken a series of "get-acquainted" visits to all stations in an attempt to repair the damage and establish a mood of hopefulness and co-operation for the future. A strike now would undermine whatever they had managed to achieve, and the resultant loss of revenue would end any hope of improving the company's financial performance for 1969.

But equally clearly, the company could not afford to give the largest segment of its labour force a 20 per cent increase in one year. For one thing, the echoes of the Seaway Authority's 1966 settlement were still reverberating across the land; as another Crown corporation, Air Canada had no wish to set a similar inflationary precedent. Also, as a Crown corporation, it had to take into account the policy in Ottawa, which had toughened somewhat as a result of the Seaway debacle. The government, under pressure to curb inflation, had embarked on a campaign to persuade business and labour to restrict wage settlements to 6 or 7 per cent a year, and there were broad hints that if these so-called voluntary guidelines were not observed it would be forced to consider the introduction of wage and price controls. So the company countered the union's demand by offering a two-year contract containing an increase of 7 per cent for the first year and 6 per cent for the second. Predictably, the union refused to consider the offer, and after intervention by a federal mediator the company raised it to 8 per cent in the first year and 6 per cent in the second. The union negotiators still refused to budge from their 20 per cent demand, however, and despite a final offer from the company which amounted to an increase of 23 per cent over three years, the workers walked off the job at one minute before midnight on Sunday, April 20.

The airline was closed for thirty days before the union accepted a new company offer: a 26-month contract with an increase that amounted to 8 per cent a year. As press commentators pointed out at the time, it was a battle lost by both sides.

On each of the thirty days the strike lasted, the airline lost an estimated $1.2 million in revenue, and when the planes began to fly again the empty seats made it obvious that rather than risk disruption of their vacation plans many peak-season travellers had booked with other airlines. All told, the company estimated the total loss of revenue caused by the strike at $40 million. There was also an indirect loss that became apparent only later. Like its predecessor in 1966, the walkout demonstrated the public's vulnerability to an airline strike when most of the country's routes are flown almost exclusively by one carrier. In each of the strikes, the government had permitted the smaller regional airlines to operate on domestic routes normally reserved to Air Canada, and in the circumstances they had provided creditable "fill-in" services. Now the government embarked on a program of strengthening the regional carriers which led in time to more inroads on the national airline's routes.

From the union's point of view, by failing to achieve parity it had lost a crucial test of strength, and to some extent the support of its more far-seeing members. Rod Blaker, a commentator on radio station CJAD in Montreal, did some on-air arithmetic and calculated that the difference between the company's last offer and the deal the union settled for amounted to a total of $208 for the average mechanic. To achieve it, he had sacrificed a month's pay, or $690. "To make up for that loss," Blaker said, "will take each and every mechanic four years—and the contract only runs two years." So, Blaker concluded, the workers had lost, the company had lost, and so had a lot of other people: "All the hotels, cab drivers, stores and restaurants—they all lost money too. The Air Canada pilots, stewardesses, and passenger agents all automatically lost their salaries during the period of the strike. This is almost unbelievable. . . . I'm at a loss for words."

An explanation for the strike was advanced by a former NDP member of Parliament with good sources who was never at a loss for words about the airline—the Ottawa columnist Douglas Fisher, who years before had dislodged C.D. Howe from his parliamentary seat. Fisher attributed the "heightening of tension" between the airline's management and its employees to the "benevolent paternalism" of Gordon McGregor, whose last message to the employees had been "emotional, warm and full of nostalgic pride." The pride, he wrote, was merited, in view of the airline's growth, efficiency and financial record. But McGregor had "seemed to appeal for a concept of the company in its links with the workers that was supra-unions." Indeed, Fisher claimed to have detected in company officials over the years a tendency to be "almost supercilious" about the unions. He quoted an unnamed union official as complaining: "Management's leadership, especially in Montreal, has an enormous conceit which won't recognize that our organizations can play any role in improving efficiency. It is impossible to get senior personnel to take seriously our grievances, particularly about the quality of many of the supervisors. Too many boot-lickers got promoted in the late McGregor years as the airline expanded. The headquarters offices are overloaded with bodies."

The union official, as quoted by Fisher, specifically exempted one Air Canada executive from his criticism. "Most of us," he said, "respect Charlie Eyre, the man who handles labor relations, although he's a hard man. But his bargaining staff is incompetent and he never seems to be sure what some of his vice-presidents will accept or even what they have in mind."

Eyre's talents in the field of labour relations were recognized beyond the confines of the airline,* but one of the weaknesses of the old organizational structure pinpointed by the McKinsey study was that his department, personnel and industrial relations, stood too low in the management hierarchy. It was, in fact, only one segment of administrative services, a kind of grab-bag department which also embraced activities as diverse as operational research, printing and publishing, office services, and the operation of the computer at the Dorval base. As only one of many in the company with the rank of director, Eyre was not part of senior management. Lacking formal entrée to the inner circle of vice-presidents, much less their advantage of direct access to the president, he was severely constrained in his ability to win acceptance for company-wide programs for the improvement of supervisory training, management, development, employee communications and the upgrading of the work environment – all those sophisticated new approaches to personnel relations that should have been introduced as the company grew and the old face-to-face contact and easy camaraderie between worker and boss became impracticable. "Correction of these problems must be one of the major objectives of Air Canada's management over the next five years," said the major report to come out of the McKinsey study. It recommended that personnel and industrial relations should be a separate department, under a vice-president reporting directly to the chairman and chief executive officer and charged with the responsibility of helping to provide "a more stimulating working environment."

The McKinsey experts had begun their examination of the airline's administrative structure in June 1969. A letter from the new chairman urged all key managers to co-operate and "take advantage of this opportunity to express your opinion with total candor."

As part of the study, the McKinsey researchers sent out an "in-depth analytical questionnaire designed to probe the attitudes and opinions of approximately two thousand key managers and supervisors concerning Air Canada's goals, organization and management practices." Some of the replies complained

---

*In March 1970, many of Canada's foremost labour relations experts gathered at McGill University in Montreal for the nineteenth annual conference of its Industrial Relations Centre. They heard the guest speaker, Bryce Mackasey, praised as "the best Minister of Labour this country has had since Mackenzie King in 1909." In his turn, Mackasey regretted the dearth of talent in the labour relations field in Canada but added: "There are some first-class men in the business – men like Charlie Eyre, men who really know their business – but there are not enough of them."

about "empire-building," the allegedly unfair power of "in" groups, and the blighting presence of too many "passengers" in management ranks – the kind of griping that might be elicited in a similar survey of any other large company. But 80 per cent of those who received the questionnaire responded to it, and taken together their comments clearly portrayed an organization in some disarray.

The researchers supplemented the questionnaire by interviewing employees at all levels of the airline and examining all aspects of its administration. They were surprised, among other things, to find so many employees who had never worked in any department other than the one they had first joined; there was not, in other words, the degree of cross-fertilization of ideas and experience they expected to find. Equally surprising, and even more serious, was the fact that, because of the system of divided authority, managers were not simultaneously responsible for both costs and revenue. The field sales units and operations department used different budget and control procedures, and sales territories did not always match operations territories. As a result, in the words of the McKinsey study: "No one below the President is responsible for both the revenues derived and costs incurred in selling and delivering the product."

When all the evidence was in and assessed, and several progress reports had been submitted to Pratte, the McKinsey team made a presentation to the board on January 27, 1970, and Pratte secured the directors' approval for the changes he proposed to make. He disclosed these at a crowded meeting of top managers on January 30 – a day that ever since has been known as "Black Friday."

The airline, he said, faced a challenging future that called for a level of performance far above anything achieved so far. Marketing must become "the competitive cutting edge of the business" and to ensure its primacy a new position was being created, that of vice-president, marketing, reporting directly to the chairman. Another key position would be vice-president of customer service, a new department combining all customer-related activities, from sales to station operations, thus ending the historic division of authority: henceforth there would be a single manager responsible for all activities at each station, and each region would be under the overall control of a vice-president. Three other new departments would be created: strategic planning; schedule planning; and movement control, which would be responsible for coping with deviations from the schedule, mounting extra sections and organizing spot charters.

To underline their importance, all these departments would be headed by vice-presidents, as would the personnel and industrial relations department.

These changes all seemed to bode well for the future, and Pratte's audience listened to his description of the shape the new organization would take with interest. But when he began to announce the appointments to the new posts the nervousness in the room mounted. The key job of vice-president of marketing was left open and it was obvious the chairman intended to go outside the company to fill it. Another key position, vice-president of customer service, went to an operations man, James McLean, who had entered the Winnipeg shops as a boy fresh from school and worked his way up to the post of general manager, maintenance. The vice-presidency of personnel and industrial relations went not to the experienced Charlie Eyre, as everyone had expected, but to Dave Tennant, who had previously been vice-president, operations.

Some of the appointments occasioned less surprise. No one quarrelled, for instance, with the elevation of Lindy Rood to the post of vice-president, flight operations. And it had been obvious to everyone who knew him that the new vice-president of strategic planning, Claude Taylor, was destined for higher things. But there seemed to be no place in the new set-up for Herb Seagrim.* For Gordie Wood, McGregor's other chief lieutenant, the appointment of vice-president, government and industrial affairs, was obviously a step down from heading the whole sales department. And since there was no longer an administrative services department, where did that leave its boss, Bill Sadler?

In fact, all these men knew by now that they had no place in the new organization, and the board of directors had already agreed on the terms for their early retirement. Seagrim and Sadler knew they would be leaving right away; Wood, even though he had long been recommending some of the changes now being made, knew his latest appointment would last only until the end of the year; McGregor's financial man, Bill Harvey, knew he would be staying only until his successor could be recruited from outside the company.

The outgoing team recognized that any new chief executive officer wanting to give an organization a wholly new direction

---

*In fact, though this was not generally known, Seagrim had written to Norman MacMillan seeking early retirement in December 1968, when it became known that Pratte would be taking over. He had stayed on out of loyalty to the corporation only when Pratte came to see him and urged him to do so.

is likely to import his own team to back him up. But by the time the meeting ended, everyone in the room realized in consternation that the axe was going to bite far deeper than that. The stunned executives found it difficult to believe, but the names of all 3,500 managers and supervisors in the company's employ had been thrown into a hat–and no one had a job in future unless he was picked for some slot in the new machinery, which had yet to be designed in detail.

CHAPTER TWENTY-FOUR

VES PRATTE STILL BELIEVES he was resented by the Air Canada people from the first and denied the co-operation he should have received, and that at least part of the reason for the animosity toward him was his French-Canadian background. Those in senior positions at the airline today agree that his appointment certainly aroused some resentment. But they deny that it stemmed—at least at the upper levels of the company— from any anti-French feeling. It was based originally, they say, on the fact that he was not an airline man, and in fact had no experience at all at administering a large business. Much more disastrous to his hopes of winning the trust and support of the airline's employees was the way he chose to implement the reorganization recommended by the McKinsey study in one fell swoop, virtually overnight.

A week after "Black Friday," two task forces made up of a cross-section of company employees seemingly chosen at random, but guided by the advice of McKinsey researchers, set to work to map out the structure of the new organization in detail. Jim McLean, who had been selected by Pratte to head the important new customer service department, was placed in charge of the group that determined the future framework of the line, or field, organization—in effect, the one he would be heading. The other, under H.D. "Dunc" Laing, assistant vice-president of finance, drew up the blueprint for the headquarters staff. By May, the new organizational charts had been approved and posted up in offices at Place Ville Marie, and the incredible process of filling up the boxes from scratch began. The names of all the airline's managers were actually stuck to the walls on magnetic tags and the new heads of departments took their pick of the available candidates to fill the vacant slots on their charts. Those who were not picked, regardless of their seniority, simply had no job any longer. By the end of this tension-filled selection process, about 350 management-level employees remained unplaced; they included some of those who had worked for the company since before the war and had seemed impregnable in their positions. About half that unhappy number left the company for other jobs or were able to negotiate early retirement; the rest managed to find positions three or four levels below those they had held before or went on "unplaced status," in the hope that something might turn up in future. The experience was a traumatic one for the whole company and there were some tragic repercussions in the form of heart attacks and nervous breakdowns among those who could not stand the strain of the uncertainty.

The reorganization, of course, had its positive features. Most important, it ended the system of divided responsibility, the gulf that had hitherto existed between operations and sales. The new regional vice-presidents, wherever they came from within the corporation, were given responsibility for all aspects of the airline's business in their areas. And the creation of a new department, computer and systems services, was generally agreed to be a logical and progressive move.

The airline's first venture into the field of automatic data recording had occurred as early as 1947, when a small IBM tabulating installation was set up in the finance department in Winnipeg. Some time later, the department acquired automatic calculating machines, the forerunners to computers; later still, in the 1960s, it installed its first computer, an IBM 1401. By then, the Dorval base had independently acquired its own computer system, beginning in 1958 with an IBM 650 to handle the stores inventory for the new jets. Meanwhile, of course, the sales department had also acquired its own computer installation for the ReserVec system, and there was yet another computer group engaged on corporate work at the company's headquarters in Place Ville Marie. These four computer centres were to some extent rival groups, reporting to four different vice-presidents. The McKinsey reorganization took the logical step of combining them into one department, computer and systems services, which also took in the telecommunications department and the operational research groups which had hitherto worked separately at Place Ville Marie and Dorval.

The new department was placed under Pierre Jeanniot, who thus became the company's first francophone vice-president, at the age of 37. Jeanniot's first priority was the second generation of the company's electronic reservations system, which was months behind schedule. The planning for ReserVec II had begun years before, under the aegis of Jack Grossman, director of telecommunications, Norm Stoddart, who spearheaded the project in its early stages, and Bill Rathborne, the airline's supervisor of reservations for many years, whose expert knowledge was often sought by IATA.

It had been decided at the outset to switch from the Ferranti computer used in ReserVec I to Univac equipment, but at the time computer and systems services was formed serious consideration was being given at the upper levels of the company to making another switch: the Univac computers had been installed but the system was not working properly. United Airlines had run into similar teething troubles and had switched to IBM equipment, with all the catastrophic costs of changing horses in midstream. Air France was also installing a Univac system and its program was even further behind than Air Canada's.

Jeanniot and two of his key deputies, Anne Bodnarchuk and Jack Maloney, joined Stoddart in several months of intensive study of the problems, and by the end of 1970 they had ironed all the bugs out of the system and ReserVec II was off and running. One of the most sophisticated computer networks in operation even today, within or outside the airline industry, it is a considerable advance over ReserVec I. Basically, the earlier system could only make and count reservations. The state of the art at the time restricted the amount of other information it could handle. The passenger's name, for example, could only be recorded as four letters, and the passenger inventory still had to be compiled by hand and filed in a mammoth card index.

In the new and vastly expanded system – it uses two central computers and cost $35 million to install – each passenger agent has a CRT, or cathode-ray terminal, which displays all the relevant information, including the passenger's name, on a little screen. The computers also record such things as flight schedules and aircraft delays, information that proves invaluable to other departments of the airline, such as scheduling and maintenance.

When ReserVec II came on line in 1970 it was designed to handle 40,000 transactions an hour; today, in peak periods, it handles more than 250,000. It includes reservations systems contracted out to Air Canada by many of the country's regional airlines, Air Jamaica, and the Department of National Defence. In addition, it embraces more than 2,600 travel agencies which, with their own terminals, have the same instant access to the central reservations system as the airline's own passenger agents.

Many of those Air Canada people who survived the McKinsey reorganization, and welcomed its positive features, still regret that it was undertaken so quickly and with so much upheaval. Others, though, believe it could not have been accomplished in any other way – that the weight of inertia and tradition, if not outright obstructionism, would have defeated any attempt to bring in the changes over, say, a period of five years. Pratte himself says he was advised by the McKinsey organization to take quick action. "The choice," he told the author, "was to do it gradually or quickly. I decided – I'm not saying I'd do so again – it was better to be brutal and do it quickly. That way, at least after the dust settled it would be all over. I think it was the right decision."

Pratte realized the anguish his decision was sure to cause, but he is a man of great intellectual toughness and once having made up his mind he did not shrink from what he believed was his responsibility to the company. He was determined, also, to avoid giving any indication that he intended to favour fellow French Canadians for the new appointments called for in the reorganization plan. The first and most important of these were the vice-presidencies of marketing and finance, and when he commissioned an executive placement agency to find top-notch candidates for those two key posts from outside the airline, he stipulated that both could be English Canadians but only one could be a French Canadian.

In the event, the French Canadian he chose as vice-president of marketing, Yves Ménard, proved to be the most popular of the newcomers he brought into the company. Born in Ottawa in 1925, Ménard took a Bachelor of Arts degree at Loyola College in Montreal in the immediate postwar years, before marketing had been refined into a science. A lively young man with an eye to the future, he was early impressed by the swaying power of radio – television had not yet invaded the field – and he joined a small station at Granby, Quebec, writing and selling commercials and producing the programs to go along with them. As the major national companies began to realize the importance, and the special requirements, of the Quebec market, he found his exceptional talents as a salesman in brisk demand and rose through a series of senior appointments in firms like Procter and Gamble and Johnson and Johnson until he was recognized as one of the most knowledgeable and effective marketing men in the country.

With a French Canadian installed in one of the two key positions, Pratte then chose an English-Canadian vice-president of finance: Earl Orser, who was born in Toronto in 1928 and attended Danforth Technical High School in the staunchly British east end before taking his Bachelor of Commerce degree at the University of Toronto. As a chartered accountant, Orser had worked for a variety of commercial companies before joining

Air Canada, but like Ménard he had no airline experience. Nor did the other men Pratte appointed to senior positions: Maurice d'Amours, a Bell Telephone executive who became vice-president of the eastern region based on Montreal; and Philip Chartrand, a management consultant specializing in the technique of change who had been applying his expertise as a government employee at the Post Office and who became vice-president, personnel, when Dave Tennant moved on to become Pratte's personal assistant.

The lack of an airline background undoubtedly affected the reception all these new bosses received when they landed in the executive suite, but Ménard told the author he never encountered any "Anglo bias." On the contrary, he thought his being a francophone was a help to him, because the sales staff he inherited recognized that a good part of the passenger growth they were seeking would have to come from the largely untapped Quebec market. Ménard's initial impression of the Air Canada organization, in fact, was much more favourable than Pratte's. He was aware of the magnitude of the task he had taken on–the airline was being subjected to more competition than ever before, and passenger demand was no longer growing at the tremendous rate of the sixties–but he was able to fill up the slots in his organizational chart to his complete satisfaction from the names available. "The talent was there," he recalled to the author. But he could not fail to see the damage inflicted on the organization by the wholesale reshuffling that had gone on just before his arrival. "It had been shaken to its roots," he said.

In fact, the reorganization left the airline in a state bordering on chaos. Inevitably, some square pegs had been uneasily rammed into round holes, and even some of those who had been deservedly promoted found themselves trying to learn jobs about which they knew little or nothing, with no one to appeal to for help because the previous incumbent who knew which levers to pull had left the company entirely or disappeared to a job in some other branch. For a while it became a joke for managers leaving for lunch to tell their secretaries, "If my boss calls while I'm out, for God's sake get his name."

Survivors of this turbulent period agree that the attempt to make so many revolutionary changes so quickly destroyed the strong informal organization that had arisen over the years to cope with the airline's divided stream of authority. The resultant confusion persuaded Pratte that the problem was really a lack of communication among his top executives. In the spring of 1971, he instituted regular Friday meetings by an executive committee made up of himself, John Baldwin, and all twenty or so vice-presidents. A working paper setting out the rationale for the committee identified its four specific functions as: "Providing a systematic basis for making critical decisions; providing a key vehicle for achieving corporate integration at the top; providing a forum in which the President can regularly solicit corporate viewpoints on major operation problems, and top corporate managers can solicit operating viewpoints on major corporate problems; reviewing branch performance, initially with major concentration on monitoring progress in implementing programmed changes in management method and style." A cautionary note added: "At the outset, it should be clearly understood that the Executive Committee is *not* a substitute for executive management and individual accountability of its members." But that is exactly what it became: action became subordinated to discussion and red tape abounded.

Part of the problem was Pratte's own working style. Behind his desk, or at meetings of the executive committee, he could be an intimidating figure, his challenging, almost pugnacious features dominated by a pair of coal-dark, intense eyes. But behind the formidable exterior he was an almost painfully shy, lonely man, and his innate reserve was interpreted by those who did not get to know him well as aloofness and indifference. He seemed incapable of establishing an easy working relationship with his lieutenants, and perhaps because of this he was unable, or unwilling, to delegate responsibility. "He tried to do everything himself," one not un-admiring aide said, recalling an occasion on which an order for some new plastic knives and forks was delayed until the chairman had approved their design. Pratte's staff attributed his failure to delegate authority to his lack of administrative experience. But it was probably as much a product of his own conscientiousness: he explained to the author that he was not prepared to rubber-stamp decisions submitted to him for approval until he thoroughly understood the facts on which they were based. Unhappily, as a result even senior executives shrank from making quite minor decisions until they had been thrashed over at the Friday meetings of the executive committee – which all too often spilled over into the early hours of Saturday – and had received the chairman's approval. Gradually, the normal work of the airline succumbed to a kind of creeping paralysis.

While his attempt to impose what he saw as a more rational system on the airline's administration seemed to create more problems than it solved, those who worked for Pratte unanimously admire his brilliant intellect and the way he was able to master the intricacies of the airline business by the simple but arduous expedient of putting in eighteen-hour days at his desk. "He was a good learner," one recalls. "I thought he would even learn to fly." Prodigiously though he worked at the task, it was Pratte's misfortune that his attempt to render the fat from Air Canada's corporate structure and transform it into a lean, competitive organization dedicated to profitability coincided with the beginning of a decade of troubling times for the whole airline industry. Throughout that period, costs spiralled steadily upward but the anticipated flood of passengers to fill the Jumbo jets did not materialize.

It was just before Pratte's arrival that the airline had decided to buy its first intermediate-range wide-body jet, the three-engined Lockheed L-1011 Tri-Star, which in its original configuration carried 256 passengers. Once again, as with the DC-8 and the Boeing 707, there was little to choose between the two aircraft assessed in the comparative study, the L-1011 and the Douglas DC-10: they had roughly the same range and payload, basically the same seating, and theoretically equal operating costs (they were both only on paper at the time). But Douglas had some time earlier run into difficulty with its DC-8 production program and the consequent delayed deliveries had forfeited some of the goodwill it had always enjoyed at Air Canada, which was left short of capacity during the important Expo year. Air Canada pilots had tried out both aircraft on the simulator and concluded that the L-1011 would handle better, and since the L-1011 was to use Rolls-Royce engines there was a prospect of attractive British financing terms for part of the deal. So the L-1011 was chosen and the airline ordered ten of them for delivery between 1972 and 1974, thus avoiding the tragic structural failures that made such unwelcome headlines for the DC-10 in later years.

The L-1011, however, was not without its own problems; in fact, for an anxious few months early in 1971 it seemed the aircraft might not be built at all. The engine chosen for it, the RB-211, had to have a thrust of 42,000 lbs., which made it by far the biggest engine Rolls-Royce had ever set out to design—more than twice the size of the Conway installed in the first Air Canada DC-8s. It also contained so many completely new features that its development was plagued by horrendous delays. It had been planned, for instance, to use an unproved carbon-filament material for the fan blades and some other parts. Unfortunately, this material flew apart in bird-impact tests and had to be replaced by titanium, which imposed a heavy penalty in added weight.

The delays increased the estimated development costs by millions of pounds, to a point where 60 per cent of Rolls-Royce's net worth was tied up in the project. As a result, the company was forced to tell Lockheed it would have to increase the price of each engine by at least $240,000; it could also see it would be late in its deliveries and wanted to be absolved from the contractual penalties this entailed.

The Lockheed company itself had recently incurred heavy cost over-runs on military contracts and had only been pulled back from the brink of financial collapse by a last-minute agreement with the U.S. government. The British government, too, had heavily subsidized the RB-211 engine program, and on a visit to London in February 1971, Lockheed's chairman, Dan Haughton, had to tell the Prime Minister, Edward Heath, that his company was in no position to meet Rolls-Royce's new terms. Next day, Britain – and much of the rest of the world – reeled under the staggering news that the great Rolls-Royce company, once the pride of the empire, had been placed in receivership.

If there was to be no RB-211, there would be no L-1011, since Lockheed could not afford to switch engines at that late stage. And if Lockheed went bankrupt, which it would if it had to abandon its investment in the L-1011, it could well drag down with it several major sub-contractors and quite possibly two major airlines, Eastern and TWA, which had invested heavy sums in advance payments for the planes and engines. In Air Canada's case, the collapse of Lockheed and the L-1011 program would have meant the loss of $30 million in advance payments, and for a hectic few weeks Yves Pratte was engaged in high-level meetings on both sides of the Atlantic trying to salvage the project. The continued support of those airlines that had contracted to buy the L-1011 was vital to Lockheed's efforts to persuade the British government to rescue Rolls-Royce and guarantee the continuation of the RB-211 program. Initially there was some wavering among them. Pratte himself was tempted to cut Air Canada's losses and get out of the program altogether, and some aviation insiders attribute the British government's eventual decision to take over Rolls-Royce and salvage the RB-211 program to the fear that Air Canada was going to pull out, which could well have doomed the whole L-1011 project. With the support of the British government assured, Pratte decided to stay in the program, and though the L-1011 was not available for the 1972 season as originally planned, maintenance schedules were juggled and more Viscounts retained in service so that the airline could go on moving its passengers.

Pratte's growing grasp of the airline business and his excellent negotiating skills were demonstrated again in the supersonic transport debacle. Boeing had won the American government's support for its SST with a complicated swing-wing design that involved a hinge arrangement to vary the degree of sweep of the wing for subsonic and supersonic flight. In practice, it proved impossible to engineer this arrangement within the plane's acceptable weight limits, and the Boeing engineers had to confess defeat and switch to a different design. While the project limped through its repeated delays, environmental groups stepped up their campaign against it, objecting among other things to the well-known fact that sonic booms could break windows in towns far below, and the rather more arcane possibility that the speedy Boeing's comings and goings through the stratosphere would so disrupt the earth's ozone layer that Lord knows how many innocent bystanders on the ground would be stricken by skin cancer. Faced with this intimidating prospect, and Boeing's stratospherically ascending costs, Washington dropped out of the supersonic race and left the field to Britain and France.

Fortunately for Yves Pratte's hopes of establishing Air Canada's profitability, the $1.3 million it had advanced for its line positions was returned, though without interest. The terms under which the airline had entered the contract for the European Concorde also provided for the return of its $981,000 advance payment without interest if the BAC/Sud consortium defaulted on its obligations. By 1970, it was obvious that the Concorde development program, too, was in difficulties, and by mutual agreement there were a series of extensions of the contract. Pratte himself was cool toward the idea of buying the Concorde. The passenger forecasts of the late 1960s were turning out to have been far too optimistic, the aircraft's operating costs were clearly going to be astronomical, and there were serious doubts that the federal government would permit its operation on the transcontinental route for which it was intended. But to have withdrawn from the program at that stage would have cost the airline its deposit. So instead, each time BAC/Sud approached him for an extension of the contract, Pratte managed to extract better terms as a quid pro quo for his concessions; as a result, when he officially notified the consortium in June 1972 that Air Canada would not be buying the Concorde, the airline received not only the return of its advance payment but interest on it at the rate of 7 per cent dating from March 1967, when the order was first placed.

By 1972, Pratte could congratulate himself that his plan to turn the airline around seemed to be succeeding. Its profit that year was an encouraging $8.6 million (after a loss of $1.07 million in the recession year of 1970 and a modest profit of $1.6 million in 1971) and its return on investment rose slightly, from 4.6 per cent to 5.7 per cent. The marketing innovations introduced by Yves Ménard seemed to be working, and there was a 23 per cent increase in traffic during the year.

One of Ménard's first initiatives after his appointment had been to institute the most intensive program of market research ever conducted at the airline, to try to discover exactly what its customers wanted – in other words, what it should be trying to sell. Among other things, this disclosed that 67 per cent of passengers on the domestic routes were travelling on business, while 83 per cent of international passengers were pleasure travellers – either vacationers or what became known as VFR passengers: visiting friends and relatives. Ménard realized that those people with enough money to contemplate flying for pleasure might prefer to spend it on other leisure items such as campers, boats or summer cottages, and the advertising designed to attract their custom must therefore be quite different from that aimed at businessmen. So, having identified the passenger "mix," the airline began to reshape its advertising programs and introduce new services designed to appeal to the different market segments.

Typical of the successful ventures in this field was the "Sun Living" program introduced in the winter of 1971-72 for passengers vacationing in Florida, the Bahamas and the Caribbean. Basically, this was a package-tour program under which the airline guaranteed the performance of all the tour people, hotels and other services included in what was called "the total travel experience." The result was impressive: a 14 per cent increase in traffic for the season.

Among the innovations designed to suit the convenience of business travellers was the Rapidair service between Montreal and Toronto, introduced in April 1972. At first, Pratte wanted this to be run like a municipal bus service: frequent flights with the passenger walking straight on without any reservation. Much juggling with possible schedules was done on the computer before he agreed that this would be impracticable. For one thing, 30 per cent of the traffic on the route at the time was "non-local" – passengers who had onward connections to make and therefore needed firm reservations. Also, both Montreal and Toronto host frequent conventions and without advance notice in the form of reservations the airline could not hope to cope with the flood of passengers when a convention broke up. And finally, experience in the United States had shown that an unreserved shuttle service requires about three times as many aircraft to operate satisfactorily as a normal reserved-seat service.

Many other factors had to be considered in planning the service: aircraft and crews had to be specially assigned to it; ticket counters and lounge areas had to be in permanent locations as near as possible to ground transport; ticketing and baggage-handling procedures had to be streamlined. But when the service was introduced, with hourly flights both ways during the day and half-hourly flights at peak periods, it was an instant success. Montreal-Toronto traffic almost doubled in its first two months of operation.

Since neither the DC-8 nor the DC-9 was ideally suited to the Rapidair service – basically, the DC-9 was too small and the stretch DC-8 too big for all but peak periods – it was decided to add a new type to the fleet: the Boeing 727. With 144 seats in its original configuration, this proved to be the ideal aircraft when, in 1974, the airline was awarded a series of new routes to U.S. destinations.

Historically, Canada had complained that U.S. air policy had favoured its own airlines over Canada's, because Canadian companies, with rare exceptions, were permitted access only to cities close to the border, and Canadians bound for destinations further south had to switch to U.S. airlines. After a study by the Canadian-born economist J.K. Galbraith for the U.S. authorities, the balance was redressed somewhat in the 1966 bilateral agreement. Air Canada gained permission to serve Miami as well as Tampa and was also granted the Toronto–Los Angeles route. Galbraith had recommended that new routes between the two countries should henceforth be developed to meet traffic demand, with public convenience as the deciding factor. But when Canada later entered talks with the Nixon administration on new routes it became apparent that competitive advantage had once again begun to outrank concern for the public convenience. The on-and-off negotiations continued without result for three years, until Canada played one of the few trump cards in its hand.

Shortly before his retirement, Gordon McGregor had written to Transport Minister Paul Hellyer about the "pre-clearance" system by which U.S. customs and immigration officers were stationed at Canadian airports. "Apart from being another example of United States encroachment in Canada," he wrote, "pre-clearance is of decreasing value to passengers and in fact is already detrimental to many of them, seriously compromises the competitive ability of the Canadian carriers, and requires unnecessary capital expenditure in Canadian terminal buildings."

Nothing was done about the matter at that time, but just before a resumption of the U.S.–Canada bilateral talks in June 1973, the Canadian government told Washington it wanted the pre-clearance system ended within ninety days.

Even though both Canadian and United States citizens enjoyed the convenience of clearing customs before boarding their flights, the system had always favoured the American airlines, because of their large internal route networks. It enabled an American company with a limited trans-border route – from Montreal to Boston, say – to fly passengers from there to any of its other internal destinations on direct, one-stop flights, sparing them the inconvenience of changing planes. So in effect the U.S. airlines were able to provide passengers booking in Canada with a large number of destinations they were not permitted to serve directly under the bilateral agreement. Air Canada contended that if the pre-clearance system was ended and all passengers had to leave their planes for customs examination at their first destination in the United States, many of them would fly Air Canada on the first leg of their journey – to New York, say – even if they were unable to continue on the same plane to a destination denied to Air Canada by the bilateral agreement.

When the issue was raised in the negotiations, it came close to dominating the proceedings. And in September, a new bilateral agreement was reached under which Canada agreed that pre-clearance could continue and in return received seventeen new "long-penetration" routes into the United States to be launched over the following five years. (The United States was awarded twenty-nine new routes, most of them comparatively unimportant short-haul runs.)

The routes having been obtained for Canada, the question then arose of which airlines should be designated to fly them. CPA, though the redoubtable Grant McConachie had long departed the scene, expected to be awarded what he would have considered a fair share: at least half. But Air Canada considered it had "grandfather" rights; after all, it had for years been promoting the need for the new services among business organizations and city, provincial, state and federal governments in both countries, and it had laboured long and hard to provide ammunition for the Canadian negotiating team. Also, Yves Pratte had proved to be no less untiring than Gordon McGregor in trying to persuade the government that concessions to CPA automatically hurt the national airline. He considered that CPA's increasing presence on the transcontinental route – it was rapidly building up toward the 25 per cent share of the market it had been promised – was a hindrance to his campaign to make Air Canada profitable. Furthermore, the government had recently awarded CPA the potentially lucrative rights to Milan, which Air Canada had tried hard to obtain as a staging post for possible services to Africa and the East. So Pratte brought his undoubted skills as an advocate to bear on the Minister of Transport, Jean Marchand; and in August 1974, much to the disgust of CPA, Air Canada was awarded all but three of the seventeen new routes. They included, in addition to services originating in eastern Canada such as Toronto to Houston/Dallas and Montreal to Boston, several valuable routes from the western cities of Edmonton and Calgary to Los Angeles, San Francisco, Chicago and New York. CPA, which considered this an incursion into its own territory and an abrogation of Jack Pickersgill's "division of the world" policy, had to content itself with two new routes: Vancouver to San Francisco and Vancouver to Los Angeles.

Pratte's dealings with Ottawa were rarely as happy as this. He believed it was important for the airline to have a specific set of agreed objectives against which its performance – and therefore his own – could be measured, and he tried repeatedly through the years to persuade the government to spell out the role it wanted its national airline to play. He was continually frustrated, of course, since the actual, as opposed to theoretical, relationship between the government and its Crown corporations has always varied with the philosophical bent of the cabinet of the day, and the bureaucracy hesitates to commit itself to any exposed position from which it cannot withdraw gracefully without loss.

Nor were Pratte and his vice-president of finance, Earl Orser, any more successful in persuading the government to overhaul the airline's basic capital structure. McGregor had for years complained about the effect on the company's financial performance of its "ridiculous" debt-equity ratio of roughly 96 to 4, and Pratte and Orser continued his campaign. Every annual report drew attention to the handicap it represented, contrasting it with the more normal 60 to 40 ratio of the major U.S. airlines. And in 1974, when Air Canada registered a record deficit of $9.2 million, the annual report pointed out that if its debt-equity ratio had been 60 to 40, its interest expenses would have been reduced by $20 million and it would have shown a profit of $1.4 million.

Several factors beyond Pratte's control had combined to produce the huge 1974 deficit. One was the sudden quadrupling in the price of oil by OPEC at the end of 1973. The average price paid by Air Canada for a gallon of fuel rose from 19.47 cents in 1973 to 33.87 cents in 1974, which pushed the airline's total outlay on fuel up to $138 million, an increase of 81 per cent on the year before. Altogether, 1974 operating expenses amounted to $815 million, a rise of 25 per cent, 33 per cent of which was accounted for by wage increases.

The company had managed to more than keep pace with its rising costs during the 1960s, thanks to the increased productivity of the new jets and the tremendous annual growth in traffic they brought with them. But at the start of the 1970s, as the less productive turbo-props were retired and the fleet settled down with the newer and more efficient jets, gains in productivity became more difficult to attain. To compound the problem, passenger traffic was growing at much slower rates and the airline was being subjected to increasing competition by the regional airlines and charter operators.*

The airline business is so capital-intensive that it is difficult for any company to respond quickly to a sudden fall-off in business: half-empty aircraft cost as much to operate as full ones, and even those temporarily taken out of service and "parked against the fence" go on eating up their share of the company's total depreciation costs. In addition, managements are reluctant to lay off highly trained pilots and skilled technicians lest they lose their services permanently and have to incur the high costs of training their replacements when business conditions improve.

The most obvious answer to Air Canada's financial plight in the early seventies was a fare increase. But when Pratte first told Marchand he proposed to apply for one, the minister forbade him to do so: the voters, he said in effect, would not stand for it. And when the CTC did approve a 10 per cent increase in 1974 it proved too little and too late. The situation became even more serious in 1975, as the worldwide recession gathered momentum and the whole international airline industry suffered. For the first time in history, there was no growth at all on Air Canada's domestic routes, and traffic to Europe actually fell by 20 per cent. The airline responded by seeking another fare increase, once again applying the "Bell curve" formula and trying to make the short-haul routes shoulder more of their fair share of total

---

* Air Canada responded to the growing competition of the non-scheduled charter operators in 1969 by allocating two DC-8s exclusively to charter work and introducing special group fares on ordinary flights, but its charter business grew slowly. Charter revenue in 1972, for instance, amounted to only $22 million out of total passenger revenue of $457.7 million. So, in an attempt to harness more expertise in the charter field, the airline sought to buy an interest in the fast-growing independent operator Wardair. Negotiations extended over many months but the parties were unable to come to terms and Air Canada withdrew its offer in December 1974.

operating costs. Still fearful of the public reaction, the government insisted that the increases on eighteen short-haul routes should be limited to $5. When all the figures were in, the deficit for the year was $12.4 million.

A less tangible, but no less real, reason for the airline's poor financial performance in those years was the havoc wrought by the 1970 reorganization – which might better have been called a total disorganization. The workings of a major airline are so complex that it is difficult to break down the various overlapping functions and responsibilities into neat categories, and the changes did not end with the original purge. For instance, a veteran flight dispatcher, George Goode, was named vice-president of the new movement control department, but before he could see his name in the annual report in that capacity his title had been changed to vice-president, systems operations control. The most powerful post in the new organization – in practice the man who held it ran all the airline's day-to-day operations except actually flying and maintaining the aircraft – belonged to Jim McLean as vice-president, customer service. When he left for Cornell University on a sabbatical in 1972,* two more new appointments were made. Maurice d'Amours, the Bell Telephone vice-president who had taken over the airline's eastern region, became group vice-president, sales and service, and Dave Tennant, who had left personnel to become Pratte's personal assistant, returned to the operations field as group vice-president, technical services. But whereas McLean, like the vice-president of flight operations, Kent Davis, had reported to the president, d'Amours and Tennant now reported directly to the chairman.

Some years earlier, Lucien Saulnier and Rod McIsaac had lost interest in running Air Canada as a team because they had been unable to see how their authority could be successfully divided. Their concern had clearly been justified. As Pratte had gathered more and more of the reins of authority into his own hands, John Baldwin, as president, had found himself with less and less to do. Feeling frozen out, he took early retirement at the end of 1973, to be replaced by Ralph T. Vaughan, an ex-journalist who had gone on to study law and moved over from the CNR to become secretary of Air Canada in 1962. With an old editor's hard-headed realism, Vaughan did not delude himself that he would be anything more than the chairman's chief-of-staff.

Inevitably, all this confusion and turmoil at the top perco-

---

* McLean never returned to Air Canada. Instead, he went on to become president of a newly formed airline, Ontario World Air, in 1975. He had retired before Ontario World Air went into receivership in 1980.

lated down through the whole company, and the destruction of morale was reflected in a general deterioration of performance at all levels of the organization. Airlines are high-technology businesses and it costs millions of dollars to keep them up to date with training programs, quality control measures and the like. These functions began to be neglected, and the quality of service dropped disastrously. Fortunately, the operational side of the airline seemed to escape almost unscathed in the post-McKinsey reorganization, so there was no deterioration in maintenance and safety standards. But elsewhere in the company, the constant switching of lines of authority and men in top jobs sapped the loyalty of even the most conscientious employees and what was left of the old TCA esprit de corps rapidly ebbed away. Employees who don't give a damn can inflict immense damage on any company, particularly a service organization such as Air Canada. Complaints about discourtesy to customers, mislaid baggage and late flights mounted to unprecedented levels. A day seldom went by without some member of Parliament taking a potshot at the national airline, and the press was full of horror stories leaked by disgruntled employees.

The company's fortunes sank to a new low level on March 1, 1975, when the *Gazette* in Montreal published a story that began: "Air Canada vice-president Yves Ménard resigned 'for personal reasons' last night. His resignation follows an investigation by the *Gazette* into his 1973 purchase of a villa in Barbados and his signing 11 months later of a $1 million airline rental contract with the holiday resort where it is located." By itself, this seemed at worst to indicate a technical conflict of interest. But the next paragraph gave the story a more sinister aspect: Ménard admitted that though he had signed the purchase agreement on the $43,800 villa more than a year earlier, he had not yet made any mortgage payments on it. He explained that the villa was part of a resort owned by Sunset Crest Rentals Limited, but not one of the 25 privately owned villas and 104 condominium apartments at the resort leased by Air Canada to accommodate patrons of its "Sun Living" package tours. And, Ménard said, while he had signed the Air Canada agreement with Sunset Crest he had not been involved in negotiating it and had merely approved it in his position as vice-president. "My buying property in Barbados has nothing to do with the other deal," he was quoted as saying. "I would have bought the property regardless. I didn't get any special favor because I didn't ask for one. I've got nothing to hide."

As Ménard and other people at the airline familiar with Barbados knew, there was nothing unusual in the delay in beginning the mortgage payments: life moves at a more casual pace in the Caribbean than it does in Montreal, and the process of gaining title to a house sometimes takes a year. But after the two reporters who wrote the story, Kendal Windeyer and Bill Fox, had come to him to check their facts, Ménard told Pratte he thought that for the sake of the company he ought to resign, even though he had been guilty of no wrong-doing. Pratte at first urged him to hold off his decision, but after telephoning all the company's directors and consulting members of the executive committee, as well as seeking advice from trusted friends and associates outside the airline, he agreed that Ménard's departure would be in the best interests of the company.

Once the news of his resignation was published, an aura of scandal became superimposed on the stories that had been appearing for months alleging disaffection in the ranks and managerial disarray. And there was even worse to come. As Ménard had developed his marketing program and begun to sell the "total travel experience," he had realized how much the airline depended for its business on travel agencies. As he told the author much later: "If you own oil and gas wells and a pipeline, but no system for distributing your product to your customers, the retailers will eventually tell you how much you're going to sell." So he conceived the idea of purchasing an interest in a national travel agency.

Some of the seasoned airline men around him opposed his plan, pointing out that the airline depended upon travel agencies for almost half of its business and its direct incursion into their territory would draw howls of outrage and probably provoke retaliation. There were also grave doubts that such an investment was permitted by the company's charter, but Ménard did not think this a serious matter because he knew there had been talk in Ottawa for some time of revising the Air Canada Act to give the airline more freedom to compete in allied fields. And when he was offered the opportunity to invest $100,000 in a Montreal company, McGregor Travel,* which was at that time planning to link up with companies in Toronto and Vancouver to form a national network of travel agencies, he decided it was a good chance to get in on the ground floor. Unfortunately, since it seemed the airline was not permitted to make an investment in a

---

*The company was named after its president, Bob McGregor. He and Gordon McGregor were not related, and the former president of Air Canada never at any time had any connection with the agency.

retail travel agency, he decided to make the $100,000 payment for suspiciously vaguely worded "consulting services," though it was actually intended to be an option to buy 10 per cent of the shares of the nation-wide chain of agencies McGregor contemplated. Also, fearful that his plan would be strangled by red tape if he submitted it to the executive committee, he decided to cut that corner and went ahead on his own.

The transaction did not come to light until after Ménard's resignation, and for the government it was the last straw. Mr. Justice Willard Z. Estey was commissioned to carry out a judicial inquiry into the airline's financial controls, accounting procedures and fiscal management. In three months of hearings in Montreal, he gathered nine thousand pages of evidence from fifty-five witnesses, and in December 1975 issued his 312-page report. The evidence, he said, "reveals no criminal action on the part of any employees and no attempt by any employee to deprive the airline of any of its assets or revenue; nor is there any evidence of any conspiracy between any employee and anyone outside the airline to do anything which might be contrary to the interests of Air Canada." Ménard was described as an "innocent, if insensitive, victim of circumstances," and Judge Estey added: "The one common element linking all the problems involved in this investigation . . . is a serious lack of communications in the top levels of the corporation's management."

The report made some comparatively minor criticisms about the airline's system of financial controls and procedures, but on the whole gave it a clean bill of health. As the columnist James Stewart wrote in the *Montreal Star*: "Air Canada has just been given a high compliment, in a back-handed sort of way. . . . Either the Estey inquiry failed to get to the bottom of things or we're forced to conclude that Air Canada is a far better organization than most of us, in these disillusioned times, had any reason to expect."

But the years of unrest, and the constant sniping at the national airline in press and Parliament, had taken their toll. By the time the report was published, Otto Lang had become Minister of Transport. Long before that, Pratte suspected he had lost the confidence of Ottawa. "The government," he told the author years later, "has never come to grips with the problem of how to manage a crown corporation."

Before the Estey report was published, Lang summoned Pratte to Ottawa and gave him a copy to read. Having done so, Pratte realized his days were numbered unless he could count on the minister's support. He asked Lang if he was prepared to back him in the House. Lang replied quite bluntly, "No." So Pratte, a lonely and bitterly disappointed man, returned to Montreal and on November 28, 1975, wrote Lang a letter of resignation sharply criticizing the government's failure to defend the airline from all the attacks made on it through the years, and ending: "As I leave I want to offer my successor, whoever he may be, my sincere good wishes. He will soon discover that it is a great privilege to be the leader of the Air Canada team. He will take over a Company that is truly a national asset of which every Canadian has the right to be proud. I know that he will have the support of the employees of Air Canada; I only hope that he will have that of Government."

CHAPTER TWENTY-FIVE

LAUDE TAYLOR, vice-president of public affairs for the beleaguered Air Canada, was in Ottawa one Sunday in January 1976 to appear on the televised presentation of the annual amateur sports awards to the country's foremost spare-time athletes, coaches, managers and sports administrators, an event the airline had sponsored for years. He had to rush away right after the show, having been summoned to a meeting with the Minister of Transport, Otto Lang, at his Rockcliffe home. Once again, the government seemed to be having trouble choosing a new man to head the company, and Taylor was quite flattered that the minister spent three hours or so cross-examining him about its many troubles, and what might be done about them. He did not yet realize they were about to be handed to him. But a few weeks later, he received a Sunday night call at his home in the unpretentious Montreal suburb of Cartierville, and Lang told him the board of directors was going to name him president of Air Canada at its meeting two days hence, on February 16. This time, the government had wisely decided to entrust the direction of the national airline to a man with sound airline experience, and Taylor was assured he would also be chief executive officer.

Claude Ivan Taylor's appointment to one of the most important positions in the country elicited a collective sigh of relief from Air Canada's 20,500 employees, who had feared that another outsider would be parachuted in to guide their destiny. Claude was one of their own, a smiling, unassuming man with glasses and greying hair who had been in the union like themselves and had spent twenty-seven years climbing through the ranks from his first job with TCA, behind a passenger agent's desk in Moncton. A farm boy from nearby Salisbury, Taylor was born in 1925 and ten years later, in the midst of the Depression, his father died. Young Claude began his business career by touring the local countryside on the family horse, selling magazine subscriptions. Having accumulated a modest capital, he bought fifty hens and hitched a ride into town with the milk truck every Saturday morning to sell their eggs at the market.

He supplemented his farm earnings through his high school years with a variety of odd jobs, and studied accounting at a local business school. His first full-time job was as an $8-a-week office boy at Eaton's in Moncton. From there he moved to a firm of chartered accountants in Saint John, and in due course became assistant general manager of a company that operated a drug-store, a restaurant and a small department store. But all the time he was hankering to get into TCA, and after repeated applica-tions over a period of several years he finally landed a job as a passenger agent in 1949. By that time he was married to a fellow accountant, Fran Watters, who kept on working so that Claude could take a pay cut from $160 a month to $125 to get into TCA.

He soon attracted attention in his new job. In 1950, trans-ferred to headquarters in Montreal, he began a steady rise through the sales department, studying industrial accounting on the side in extension classes at McGill University. His varied career at the airline prepared him well for the role of president. He negoti-ated the first traffic pool with BOAC, and many of the others that followed. He became general manager, marketing services, in 1965, and as such dealt with bankers, government officials and businessmen to arrange the 1968 deal with the government of Jamaica by which, in the tradition of Commonwealth aid schemes, Air Canada undertook the financing, organization, and in the early stages operation, of that country's national airline, Air Jamaica.

Soon after he was appointed vice-president, strategic planning, in the McKinsey reorganization, Taylor was moved into the post of vice-president, government and industry affairs, which increased his familiarity with Ottawa and its ways. He became something of a trouble-shooter around the airline and after a cou-ple of years his responsibilities were broadened to embrace the public relations department. As vice-president, public affairs, he prepared the ground with the public on both sides of the border, and officials in Ottawa and Washington, for the important U.S. bilateral agreement in 1973. And by the time the government came to name a new leader for Air Canada he had many support-ers who were impressed by his competence, sincerity, and dedi-cation to his job.

Taylor's first act as president was to ask his predecessor, Ralph Vaughan, to stay on as senior vice-president, corporate services, which Vaughan readily agreed to do. The government wanted the airline to have a full-time French-speaking chairman and among those considered for the job was one of its directors, Pierre Des Marais II. Des Marais was unwilling to give up his other business interests and the mayoralty of the Montreal suburb of Outremont, and the job went to a man Taylor found easy to work with, Pierre Taschereau, chairman of the CNR. Taschereau, who had worked his way up through the railway's law department, had taken over as temporary chief executive officer of the airline after Pratte's departure. He also had valuable experience in Ottawa, having served for four years as vice-president of the Canadian Transport Commission.

Taylor's parents were devout Baptists and with all the pressures of his career he has never wavered in his dedication to the Christian ideal. He remains a deacon of the neighbourhood church he helped to build as a young man, but there is no trace of sanctimoniousness in his relationship with colleagues and associates less ardent in their faith. His feeling for the concerns of others is patently genuine, and he realized that his immediate task was to restore the shattered morale of the organization he had inherited. So he quickly embarked on a series of "show-the-flag" tours, talking to employees in the shops, at the counter, in their cafeterias, with the constant theme that the airline was not as bad as it had been painted, and that they now had one of their own to defend them against criticism. He made it clear he had confidence in the organization, and in turn the employees soon developed confidence in his fairness and honesty. Clearly, Claude Taylor was not going to conduct any purges or wholesale changes that would threaten their jobs.

Equally clearly, and just as important, the employees could see that he was not going to be any pushover, either. One of the problems he inherited was a festering labour dispute with the five hundred or so white-collar employees in the Winnipeg accounting office. One current executive admits that in those days the Winnipeg office was a "sweatshop"; it was certainly a hotbed of discontent and it was blamed for many of the leaks that had given the airline such a bad press. All through the first half of 1976, the office workers conducted a series of rotating strikes and go-slows, and the company's paper work was reduced to a state of utter chaos, with late and lost billings costing thousands of dollars every month.

Prolonged negotiations with the union, the Canadian Air Line Employees Association, proved fruitless, and Taylor knew he must do something drastic to halt the continuing damage to the company. One of his first moves was to bring back the popular Charlie Eyre from his post in Europe and make him vice-president of personnel. Then, with other branches and casual employees organized to handle the work, he issued instructions that the accounting office should be closed on June 17. Two days later, its employees were advised by mail that if they were prepared to end their disruptive tactics and work on the company's terms, they were welcome to return. The first clerks returned to their desks on June 21, and most of the rest were back at work by the end of July. Many of them had not wanted to strike in the first place, and as a result of their dissatisfaction with the union, CALEA lost its certification for the accounting group and was replaced by the machinists' union, the IAMAW.

Claude Taylor's early months in office were also bedevilled by the bitter language controversy that resulted in a nine-day strike by pilots and the grounding of the whole Canadian air transport industry in the summer of 1976. Initially, Air Canada was not directly involved in this dispute over bilingualism in the air. It erupted the previous fall when two air traffic controllers were disciplined by the Department of Transport for using French in directing traffic at Dorval. At that time, an experimental program permitted the use of French for aircraft flying under visual flight rules at five smaller Quebec airports. But the department's policy was that "two-way communication in the English language only" had to be used in the control of aircraft flying on instruments or above 9,000 feet.

There was an immediate wave of protest in Quebec, led by a newly formed organization named l'Association des Gens de l'Air, or the Association of People of the Air, whose members included some commercial pilots and air controllers and others who had no direct involvement with aviation but were extremely concerned about the future of the French language and culture. Liberal MPs in Ottawa joined the fray and Transport Minister Otto Lang reversed the department's policy. Henceforth, he announced, fully bilingual air communications would be progressively introduced at all Quebec airports. This in turn led to angry protests by English-speaking traffic controllers and pilots, who made headlines with their allegations that the use of anything but English in air traffic control would expose the air traveller to horrendous risk.

In the early stages of the dispute, les Gens de l'Air and other defenders of the French language directed their fire at the federal Department of Transport. But Air Canada became the target when the flight operations department, in response to requests for a clarification of the airline's policy, issued a directive saying:

Flight Operations fully supports the Corporate policies on bilingualism as established in 1969. The Corporate Policy specifically defines the technical language to remain English. English only will be used on the Flight Deck, with the exception of passenger announcements.

This was, of course, like trying to fight a fire with gasoline. Headlines in an outraged Quebec press protested against "this insult," and some of the airline's French-speaking pilots were quoted as saying it meant that in future they would have to use English even to ask a French-speaking flight attendant for coffee. This had not, naturally, been the intent of the directive, which was quickly revised. And the airline issued statement after statement trying to spell out what it had been intended to say. A typical example read:

Air Canada does not prohibit the French language from being spoken in the cockpits of its aircraft. However, for reasons of safety, the airline's current policy states that the English language shall be used in the cockpit where technical matters are concerned. This is a corporate policy which was established by the company in 1969. Air Canada's present policy in no way prohibits the use of the French language in private conversations among Francophone crew members.

The ruckus continued, however, with the federal government torn between support for the cause of bilingualism and attempts to mollify the English opposition to it. Before it died down, Jean Marchand had resigned as federal Minister of the Environment because "I could not stay in a government that is prepared to negotiate bilingualism"; several other federal ministers from Quebec had voiced their support for les Gens de l'Air; the air traffic controllers' union had threatened to strike but been headed off by a court injunction; and CALPA, the pilots' union, had walked out on strike in their stead. The uproar did not subside until the government appointed a commission of three judges which, after a three-year investigation, recommended that both languages be used in Quebec skies as soon as the necessary technical changes could be made.

By that time, Air Canada had already made tremendous progress with the bilingual policy it had introduced years before. When the airline became embroiled in the controversy, Pierre Jeanniot had just taken over his newest responsibility, as vice-president of the eastern region, which includes Quebec. He immediately resolved that French should become the language of work in all Quebec operations: at regional headquarters, in reservations, at the airports and cargo terminals. The required retraining programs, translation of manuals and other adjustments took about three years, but the airline's Quebec operations are now conducted almost entirely in French. A sort of affirmative action program also increased the proportion of francophone pilots, only about 7 per cent at the time of the bilingualism dispute, to its present 12 per cent. And if all crew members in the cockpit understand the French language, they are now permitted to use it in flying the aircraft.

For some time before he took over the presidency, Taylor had realized that the decision-making process at the airline had been paralysed by the cumbersome system introduced with the McKinsey reorganization. The day after his appointment he summoned the executive committee and announced that it was no longer going to meet every Friday. "Look," he told his executives, "we're going to have to adopt a more informal style. In future, we'll meet once a month to review the operation against the plan. Bring forward only those things you think need a collective decision. Otherwise I expect you to come one on one to me, if it's something that doesn't involve anyone else. Or if it's something that involves two of you, then the two of you get together and make the decision, and only bring it to me if you can't agree. You know what you're doing, you know what you're supposed to do, so get out there and do it – and if you get me in trouble you're going to hear from me." His staff found this approach to the delegation of authority a refreshing change, and at least one executive who had been planning to quit turned down the job he had been about to accept and stayed on to help his new boss salvage the airline's fortunes.

With his marketing background, Taylor knew that if he was going to succeed in doing that he would have to raise fares to keep pace with the airline's rising costs. At his first press conference, a reporter asked him: "What are you going to do first?" Taylor replied: "I'm going to make sure that our product is priced on the basis of what it costs us to produce it." So he immediately set the various departments to work analysing all the company's costs in detail. As he recalled to the author: "With fuel price increases coming at us every month it was pretty obvious that if we didn't do something quickly we'd have to go for a 40 per cent fare increase or something." It is easy to imagine the uproar this would have caused. Instead, he was able to get permission for two quick smaller increases: 8 per cent in April and 4 per cent in September, which raised the one-way economy fare between Montreal and Vancouver in two stages from $170 to $192.

Having taken steps to increase the company's revenue, the new president now set about instituting economies to cut its costs. Paradoxically, the McKinsey reshuffle had increased the size of the airline's staff rather than reduced it: the switch to a regional system of administration had resulted in much duplication of activities formerly confined to headquarters. The independent managers in charge of each region had been given their own people to handle such things as personnel management, accounting and public relations; and as usual in any organization, what were at first intended to be small, self-contained units had mushroomed, and their activities sometimes conflicted with those of the corresponding units at headquarters. Taylor cut back, with a generous early retirement scheme, but he did it gradually, without the dislocation that had caused so much distress earlier. "He promised he wouldn't change anything," one vice-president told the author, "and then he proceeded to change everything, but gently."

Taylor's thorough understanding of the mechanics of the airline business, and his crisp way of making decisions, both eased the tasks of his lieutenants and increased their effectiveness. The airline's fleet of fifty-three DC-9s, as was customary, contained both first-class and economy seating. For months there had been discussion about whether it would pay to eliminate the first-class seats and, by converting the planes to all-economy seating, increase their capacity by about 10 per cent. "Let's do it," said Taylor. Extra seats were also added to the 747s and L-1011s and the fleet finished up with as much extra capacity as if it had been bolstered by one new 747, one new L-1011, and three new DC-9s.

Similarly, the experienced Taylor understood the many subtleties and the over-riding importance of scheduling. Some lightly used services were suspended, other projected new ones deferred, and schedules juggled to get more use out of the fleet. Even before Pratte left, there had been talk of discontinuing the unprofitable "glamour run" to Moscow, but nothing had been done in case the government objected for reasons of diplomacy. Taylor merely wrote a brief, four-paragraph letter to Lang on December 21, 1976, which began: "This will confirm that Air Canada's Board of Directors has approved the suspension of service between Canada and Shannon, Brussels, Prague and Moscow. The effective date of the suspensions will be February 1, 1977, or the earliest possible date thereafter, depending on commercial agreements with the carriers of the other countries."

A few days before the proposed cut-off date, he called Lang and pointed out that he had not received an acknowledgement of his letter. Lang asked what he would do if he never received one. "Well," said Taylor, "the services will come off." Lang simply replied "Well?", and the man who had inherited Gordon McGregor's mantle was confirmed in his belief that the *fait accompli* was a more effective way of dealing with Ottawa than endless requests for instructions.

Again, with Taylor's marketing experience, he encouraged his staff to make more experiments with "incentive," or discount, fares. There was a slight increase in the total number of passengers carried on the system during 1976: 10.9 million, compared to the 10.7 million of the previous two years. But the Canadian economy was now growing more slowly than in the past, and the airline lost some business on its Atlantic services during the year. This was balanced by an 11 per cent increase in the traffic on its U.S. routes and a smaller increase on its Caribbean services. But domestic passenger traffic – 60 per cent of its total business – fell by 1 per cent. So at the end of his first year at the helm Taylor just had to grin and bear another large deficit: $10.4 million. As the annual report pointed out, the company would have registered "a marginal profit" had it not lost $22.5 million in revenue because of the pilots' strike. And there were other encouraging signs: employee productivity improved by 4 per cent, and the passenger load factor rose from 58 per cent to 61 per cent.

In 1977, the airline marked the fortieth anniversary of its formation, and there was good reason to celebrate, for the old TCA team spirit seemed to be returning, bringing with it a revival of the company's fortunes. Increased flexibility in scheduling and better use of aircraft matched the capacity put in service more closely to the business available. The improved productivity of staff and equipment brought a 6 per cent increase in revenue ton miles per employee. The passenger load factor rose by a further two points, to 63 per cent, and the airline flew 5.5 per cent more passengers during the year with fewer aircraft in service. The restored spirits of the staff – at the ticket counters, around the airports, on the planes – did not go unnoticed by the customers, and the passengers began to come back.

All this increased efficiency, and the continuing campaign for economies, put the airline solidly into the black with its biggest profit ever: $20 million. Since the price of fuel and all the company's other costs were still increasing alarmingly – to the tune of an extra $141 million for the year – this was a gratifying triumph for Taylor and his whole team. But forty years after its formation the airline was still operating under ground rules laid down in an earlier age, when planes carried only ten passengers and no one could have imagined the ramifications of the modern mass travel business.

As the competition for the tourist's dollar developed, it was decided within Air Canada that if the airline was to keep pace with its competitors it must diversify into other fields such as hotel ownership and selling its expertise to other companies. Those who framed its corporate structure in 1937, intent on providing air transportation across the country "at or near cost," could not have foreseen that need. And their failure to provide for it with specific provisions in the TCA Act pinioned the airline's wings as the competitive climate changed through the years. The evidence before the Estey inquiry disclosed several well-meaning attempts to do indirectly what could not be done directly according to the strict letter of the law. In fact, the inquiry would probably never have come about if the airline had been empowered to handle new activities as they seemed to be advisable.

Also, as Gordon McGregor had long complained, the airline's capital structure unfavourably distorted its annual balance sheet. In the early days, when aircraft could be bought for a few thousand dollars, there was no undue discrepancy between the company's equity – the $5 million invested in its shares by the CNR – and its borrowings. But as the infant airline grew, and the cost of aircraft mounted into the millions, the company's need for capital followed suit. A normal commercial company, needing capital to finance its growth, can go to its shareholders for more money with a new stock issue. This avenue was not open to TCA, so the ratio of its borrowings to the original $5 million invested rapidly became top-heavy: by 1975, it had reached 97 to 3. Similarly, if a normal commercial company has a bad year it can withhold payment of a dividend to its shareholders. Air Canada could not; the interest on its huge load of debt had to be paid whatever its temporary financial circumstances. In 1975, for instance, when the airline showed a net loss of $12.4 million, it paid $63.9 million interest on its long-term debt. If its debt-equity ratio had been a more normal 50 to 50, its interest payments would have been reduced by about $30 million and it would have registered a profit of almost $3 million.

Whether the airline should remain a ward of the deficit-ridden CNR had been discussed from time to time during the days of C.D. Howe and Herb Symington. It became even more of a live issue as the company's need for capital mounted to the point where the government began to wonder whether it could continue to supply it. In 1967, when the ten-year forecast indicated a need for new borrowing amounting to more than a billion dollars, Jack Pickersgill initiated yet another study of the basic relationship between the airline and the railway, with the idea of putting the airline's capital structure on a more rational basis. The idea was pursued by Yves Pratte, and during the early 1970s a stream of memoranda and policy papers suggesting how this might be done passed between Place Ville Marie and Ottawa.

The Estey commission, rather than unearthing any dereliction of duty by the men who were trying to make Air Canada competitive and profitable, brought to light the failings of the archaic set of rules under which they had to operate. And in 1977, the government at long last introduced sweeping changes to the Air Canada Act designed, as Transport Minister Lang told the House, to put the country's national airline "on a footing similar to that of the airlines with which it competes."

The Air Canada Act, 1977, which came into force on February 28, 1978, freed the airline from the shackles of the past. It authorized it to set up subsidiary companies to own hotels and carry out all the normal charter and package-tour operations available to its competitors, and to sell its own expertise, in the form of "computer and teleprocessing systems and technical, advisory and consulting services."

The change also gave the company a more conventional debt-equity ratio. The government, as it had been urged to do many times in the past, assumed direct ownership of its airline, removing the CNR as an intermediary. Before the promulgation of the new act, Air Canada owed $344 million to the CNR and $290 million to the government. Under the new legislation, the government took over the debt from the CN and also bought back its 50,000 shares of the airline. Having consolidated the company's debts, it then split them, taking up 329,000 shares at $1,000 each, creating a new equity of $329 million, and issuing a long-term note for the rest, $311 million, which the airline is repaying in semi-annual instalments until 1993.

The wisdom of the new act became apparent within the year. Apart from the upheavals in the Winnipeg accounting office, the airline had enjoyed reasonably tranquil labour relations during Claude Taylor's first years in the pilot's seat. But in the summer of 1978 the company and the IAMAW locked horns again. After the meagre rewards of the 1969 strike, the IAMAW had taken to rotating strikes as a means of imposing the maximum pressure on the company with a minimum of loss to its members: thirteen days of disruption of services in June 1973 infuriated affected passengers but the airline managed to keep flying. Thanks to the government's wage and price controls, there was a strike-free period in the mid-seventies. And when trouble erupted again in 1978 it was not over wages: the larger pay settlements achieved by Canadian unions through the years had gradually won the mechanics and station attendants parity with their U.S. counterparts. This time the issue was a jurisdictional squabble over how long the company could suspend delinquent employees.

The negotiations began in April and dragged on throughout the summer. Twice the company and union negotiators signed a tentative agreement, only to have it rejected by the membership. Then in late July, after a third agreement had been tentatively signed, the employees began a series of wildcat walk-outs in different parts of the country. The company tried to maintain its services by using management and clerical staff, but the disruptions were such that its passengers began to drain away to other airlines. As one executive recalls it: "It got so that you couldn't put an aeroplane up because you didn't know whether there would be anyone to receive it at the other end."

So early in August the airline addressed a letter to all the union's members, saying:

It is now clear that the uncertainty, disruptions and public inconvenience caused by these work stoppages cannot continue. Therefore, the company must inform you that it will consider employees who withdraw their services or participate in work stoppages or rotating strikes after 0001 hours, Sunday, August 6th, 1978, as having placed themselves on strike against the company for the duration of this dispute. During this period, the ability of such employees to return to work will be solely at the company's discretion.

The warning went unheeded. One evening three weeks later, word was received in Montreal that a group of mechanics had walked off the job in Ottawa. Soon afterward, they were followed by a group in Toronto, then another in Vancouver. Charlie Eyre and his assistant Bernie Miller, director of labour relations, figured it was time to enforce the terms of the letter. Claude Taylor was called out of a private dinner for a retiring executive, and when he heard the news he immediately summoned a meeting of the executive committee out at the Dorval base. He had a difficult decision to make, and the debate raged until 3 a.m. Eyre and Miller argued that the terms of the letter must be enforced for the sake of management's future credibility. On the other hand, because of the pattern the previous rotating strikes had taken, Taylor knew that to enforce the letter would be to close down the airline. This would provoke the wrath of thousands of passengers whose travel plans would be wrecked and incur for the airline the opprobrium always attached to an employer who locks out his workers. In the end, there was general agreement that the public safety was paramount, and that safe air travel depended on unvarying routine: unpredictable disruptions of that routine simply could not be countenanced. At the end of the meeting, a weary Claude Taylor issued instructions to close down the whole airline at 5 o'clock that morning, August 24.

The fleet was grounded for ten days, and in previous years the annual report would have bewailed the millions of dollars lost in revenue. Instead, thanks to the new act and the company's improved debt-equity ratio, it was able to report its most successful results ever: after paying $36.6 million in corporation income tax, Air Canada ended 1978 with a profit of $47.5 million and paid a $13.2 million dividend to its shareholders – in effect, the people of Canada.

Elated by this turn-around in the airline's fortunes, Taylor realized that the time had come to remove once and for all any justification for the criticism that it owed its success to its protected position as a ward of the government. Proclamation of the new Air Canada Act was soon followed by an important development in the United States. Until 1978, the Civil Aeronautics Board had administered every aspect of the U.S. airline industry. By its system of licensing, it governed which of the country's many routes a carrier could fly and, perhaps even more important, whether or not it could discontinue an unprofitable service. It approved fares and enforced a myriad of other rules, right down to the type of meals that could be served. But in that year an act of Congress provided for the removal of all restrictions on an airline's business operations and the abolition of the CAB, which disappeared at the end of 1984. Henceforth, any airline could fly any route it wanted, and charge any fare it liked. The rationale for deregulation, of course, was the traditional American belief in the sanctity of free enterprise: if entrepreneurs were as free to launch and run airlines as they were to set up shoe shops, the theory went, market forces would regulate the industry and in the end an equilibrium would emerge that could not fail to benefit the customer.

Because of Canada's different circumstances, Canadians have always been more ready than Americans to accept government intervention in various fields, particularly that of transportation over our immense, sparsely populated distances. But new trends south of the border usually lap over on to the Canadian scene, and Taylor realized that a growing segment of the Canadian public believed some deregulation of the airline industry in this country would bring about a delightful era of bargain air fares. Sooner or later, he knew, the government would have to make concessions to CPA and other Canadian airlines to improve their ability to compete with what was sometimes seen as the Air Canada "octopus."

Through the years, as Gordon McGregor had fought to defend every inch of his territory against CPA incursions, there had been others in the corporation who had welcomed the competition as a stimulus to their own organization's performance. Claude Taylor had been one of them. Now he believed that the national airline, its pinioned wings freed by the new Air Canada Act, could face the changed circumstances that undoubtedly lay ahead with complete confidence. He told Otto Lang that Air Canada was ready and eager to meet any competition CPA could offer. And on March 23, 1979, Lang announced that the 25-per-cent-of-market limitation on CPA's transcontinental service had been removed; henceforth Air Canada's principal competitor was free to put as many seats on the route as it could sell. Thus, at long last, Canada entered the era of "open skies."

CHAPTER TWENTY-SIX

GEORGE HEES, recalling his days as Minister of Transport and the Diefenbaker government's occasional exasperation with Gordon McGregor, expressed a philosophy to which most politicians would probably subscribe. "The relationship between a government and the head of a Crown corporation," he said, "is a very delicate matter. In theory, the president or chairman of a Crown corporation is independent, but all presidents know they must come and get the government's okay for their actions because they are spending the people's money. The government makes the decisions."

McGregor was not the only head of a Crown corporation to interpret his mandate quite differently, and to believe that he was not just empowered but *required* to run his organization as efficiently as it could be run, regardless of the wishes or theories of politicians and civil servants.

Successive governments have wrestled with this problem without ever really resolving it. In 1977, the Liberal government issued a Blue Book, or policy paper, on the accountability, control and direction of Crown corporations. This said a conventional wisdom had grown up to the effect that governments "must avoid all but the most cursory intervention" into the affairs of proprietary, or Schedule D, Crown corporations lest their commercial performance be jeopardized. "This view," the paper said, "ignores the fact that without exception such corporations were established by the Government of Canada to achieve broad policy objectives. . . . The pursuit of commercial goals was never intended to override the broad social, cultural or economic goals that Crown corporations were established to pursue."

On the other hand, undue encroachment by governments on the management responsibilities of Schedule D corporations "would almost inevitably undermine their efficiency and reduce their capability to recruit and retain capable top management. . . . For this reason, the Government proposes that only a directive of a general nature may be issued to Schedule D corporations."

This laudable intention was echoed in section 8 of the new Air Canada Act: "The corporation shall, in the exercise of its capacities and the carrying out of its activities, comply with directions of a general nature given to it by order of the Governor in Council."

In the late seventies, there were two episodes that illustrated the complexities of this problem. In one case Claude Taylor was able to assist government policy, and in the other he felt bound to resist it.

The first of these episodes, in which the country's national airline could have been said to have been acting as the government's "chosen instrument," was its purchase of the successful regional airline Nordair, a pioneer in large-scale air transport operations in the North. Nordair began life in 1947 as Boreal Airways, operating out of Quebec's Lac St. Jean region with one single-engine Norseman bush plane. By the time Air Canada began negotiating to buy it in 1977, it had absorbed several other small companies and had a fleet of six Boeing 737s, one DC-8, three F-227s and two Lockheed Electras. It had 850 employees in Quebec, Ontario and the Northwest Territories. Its operations ranged from the magnetic North Pole south to Pittsburgh, and from Montreal west to Windsor, Ontario. And it had suffered only one loss year in its history.

Air Canada's purchase of Nordair was seen by some as more evidence of the predatory propensities of the country's national airline. But in fact it was undertaken at the request of the government in an attempt to help it to tidy up its regional aviation policy. As laid down in Jack Pickersgill's day, this envisaged only one main regional carrier in each of the five regions into which the country was divided. Nordair was assigned to the Ontario region. But it remained based where it had grown up, in Quebec, operating side by side with that province's approved regional carrier, Quebecair. In the government's view, one way of resolving this competitive anomaly, and rationalizing the regional air transport system in Ontario and Quebec, would have been to merge Nordair and the less successful Quebecair.

Nordair's chairman was James F. Tooley, a Winnipeg-born chartered accountant who, after a long career at Canadair, had bought control of the airline with a group of partners in 1967. Transport Minister Lang called Taylor one day and told him Tooley wanted to sell. Among several potential buyers he had approached was Quebecair, but he had been utterly unable to come to terms with its owner, the Montreal millionaire Howard Webster. The situation was further complicated, the minister said, because another possible buyer was Great Lakes Airways Limited (later

Air Ontario), a company based in London, Ontario, which would no doubt want to move Nordair's operations to that province and thereby cause unemployment in Quebec. Perhaps, Lang suggested, if Taylor would see Tooley he could act as a sort of catalyst in bringing Tooley and Webster together.

Taylor and Tooley met for lunch, and after explaining the situation Tooley suggested that a good solution to the problem would be for Air Canada to buy both Nordair and Quebecair, put them together and resell the resultant larger company. Lang approved of this course and Air Canada began to negotiate a price with Tooley. Quite apart from the fact that it might be furthering government policy, the deal made good commercial sense to Air Canada. The new Air Canada Act was about to free it to make outside investments, and this looked like a good one: Nordair was a successful company with a sound balance sheet and a consistent record of profits. It had a strong presence in the North, where the national airline had none. And it had a flourishing charter operation, which brought in $27 million in revenue in 1976; its acquisition would therefore give the national airline new expertise in an area it was only then beginning to exploit.

Early in January 1978, Air Canada announced that it had reached agreement with the controlling shareholders to purchase all Nordair's shares for $25 million. The deal was subject to the approval of the Canadian Transport Commission, and at an eleven-day hearing that spring it was opposed by the governments of Quebec, Ontario and Manitoba and several other groups, including the Consumers' Association of Canada. The CTC deliberated for three months and then approved the purchase. After the inevitable appeals had been heard, Transport Minister Lang, in November 1978, permitted the purchase to go through but said Nordair would be resold to the private sector within a year.

The deal was completed in January 1979, with Air Canada buying 86.5 per cent of the Nordair shares for $24.1 million. But selling Nordair back to the private sector proved to be a more difficult process than buying it. Within months, Air Canada was involved in discussions with ten or eleven potential buyers, including Quebecair. By now, Webster had sold Quebecair to Alfred Hamel, owner of a chain of Quebec trucking companies. The question then became who would buy out whom, and the Quebec government entered the picture by insisting that control of Quebecair remain in Quebec hands.

In 1981, Nordair made an offer for all Quebecair's shares, with the provision that control of the merged company would remain in Air Canada's hands. The Minister of Transport, now Jean-Luc

Pepin, approved this arrangement provided the deal was acceptable to the governments of Ontario and Quebec. Ontario accepted it, but Quebec turned it down. In response, the federal government announced in February 1982 that Air Canada could retain its 86 per cent holding in Nordair indefinitely and continue to operate it as an autonomous subsidiary. Jean Douville, a chartered accountant from the Montreal investment world who had been brought into Air Canada in 1977 to handle its new acquisitions program and had conducted many of the negotiations leading to the purchase, resigned his post to become Nordair's new president.

But the tussle over its ownership continued. At one time the Quebec government bought the 14 per cent of its shares that had been owned by a Lac St. Jean credit union, Caisse d'Entraide économique. But when it realized its action conflicted with a federal regulation governing provincial government ownership of airlines having interprovincial routes, it quickly sold them to the Société d'Investissement Desjardins, the investment arm of the huge Caisse Populaires Desjardins movement.

Nordair's northern operations make its service vital to the Inuit and Indian populations of the area, and one of the organizations that tried to buy it was the Makivik Corporation, set up in 1976 to administer the $90 million received by five thousand Inuit in the James Bay land settlement. Eventually, the tussle boiled down to two rival bids: one by Air Ontario, this time in partnership with the Grand Council of the Crees of Quebec, also seeking to invest some of the money received in the James Bay settlement; and the other by Innocan Incorporated, of Montreal, a venture-capital company with holdings ranging from a fireworks factory in Lachute, Quebec, to various high-tech companies. Innocan partners include such institutional investors as the pension funds of Air Canada and Canadian National, and the Canadian Development Corporation.

In May 1984, the federal government decided to accept Air Canada's recommendation that Nordair be sold to Innocan for $31 million. The cabinet was thought to have been influenced in its decision by the fact that Innocan offered Nordair's employees the opportunity to acquire a block of the airline's shares, an offer that was enthusiastically taken up when the deal was consummated early in 1985.

While this attempt by the government to use its "chosen instrument" as a vehicle with which to influence developments in the private sector failed in its original intent–to rationalize its regional air policy–at least it did not prove damaging to Air Canada. The second late-seventies episode bearing on the government's relationship with its Crown corporations, on the other hand, caused Claude Taylor deep concern.

The Air Canada planners had realized by early 1978 that their fleet needed modernizing to cope with the increasingly competitive environment that lay ahead. Its aging DC-8s could not meet the more demanding noise standards due to be introduced in both the United States and Canada in the mid-eighties. And they were much too hungry for fuel: the price of a gallon of aviation fuel, 19.5 cents before the OPEC screws were applied, had risen to 58.5 cents by 1978, and it was still on the way up. Squeezed between constantly rising costs and public clamour for lower fares, the airline must obviously go into the 1980s with the most productive and fuel-efficient fleet it could devise.

The anticipated extra competition, and the way route patterns were evolving, were already threatening to make the huge Boeing 747s too big for all but the busiest long-range routes. But along with the Boeing 727s and Lockheed L-1011s, they were reasonably fuel-efficient and able to meet the new noise standards. So it was decided these types should be kept in service but supplemented by two new ones: a medium-range wide-body twin jet with about 200 seats, for use primarily on the transcontinental routes and to the Caribbean; and a long-range tri-jet with about 250 seats able to operate over the airline's longest routes, including western Canada to Europe.

With each new aircraft likely to cost around $50 million, the decision would undoubtedly be the most important the company had ever made, and the analysis of the various types available was the most intensive in its history. The candidate aircraft were subjected to rigorous scrutiny by an evaluation team composed of some of the airline's most experienced technical, operating, passenger and cargo sales and financial experts, led by the veteran lawyer Ralph Vaughan, who had become a master at co-ordinating this kind of complex operation during his long career. Representatives of the major international airframe and engine manufacturers visited Montreal to present their cases and the evaluation team made dozens of visits to plants in the United States and Europe.

The manufacturers were informed early in the process that the government was interested in "industrial offset" programs – the amount of work on whichever planes were chosen that could be done in Canada. But the airline made it clear that its choices would be made solely on the merits of the aircraft and any offsets attached would be a matter for direct negotiation between the government and the manufacturers.

For seven months, the engineers plied their slide rules far into the night, the computers spilled their scroll-like print-outs all over the floor, the binders full of charts and graphs piled up on the shelves. Nineteen possible combinations of airframes and engines were closely examined. And by April 1979, the choices had been made: the intercontinental tri-jet, all departments agreed, should be the Lockheed L-1011-500, a longer-range version of the L-1011 already serving in the fleet; and the North American routes would be ideally served by the Boeing 767, a twin-engined aircraft still on the drawing board but backed by the pre-eminent reputation of the Boeing company for jet production and product support. A presentation explaining the reasons for the two choices was prepared for the company's directors and they were expected to make their decision at a board meeting scheduled for April 30 in London, England.

Early that month, there were disturbing indications that an area of severe turbulence lay ahead: the government seemed to be more than usually interested in the airline's choice of the medium-range aircraft for its domestic routes. The final two candidates in that race had been the B-767 eventually chosen and the A-310, a very similar twin-jet being planned by Airbus Industrie, the largely government-controlled European consortium of manufacturers jointly owned by France, Germany, Britain and Spain.

At around that time, there was considerable support in Ottawa for the idea of a "third option" for Canada: an expansion of trade with the European Common Market countries to lessen Canada's heavy dependence on trade with the United States. It was thought that an Air Canada order for a European aircraft, and whatever offset work resulted from it, would be a powerful shot in the arm for that policy. It was also reported that among the incentives offered in the Airbus Industrie package was sales assistance in Europe for the Dash-7 short take-off and landing aircraft being built by the government-owned de Havilland plant in Toronto.*

A few days before the London board meeting at which the direc-

---

*Had the Dash-7 been available in the mid-seventies it might have been the salvation of the experimental short take-off and landing service launched between Montreal and Ottawa in 1974. The service was run for the government by an Air Canada subsidiary, Airtransit Canada. Operating from the old Expo parking lot in Montreal and Rockcliffe airport in Ottawa, Airtransit's Twin Otters cut the downtown-to-downtown travel time to 90 minutes and proved popular with business travellers. But the Otters could carry only eleven passengers in somewhat cramped comfort. It was originally intended to replace them with the roomier Dash-7, but Dash-7 production delays and a government economy campaign combined to end the service early in 1976.

tors were expected to decide on the two new aircraft types, Claude Taylor received a telephone call from de Montigny Marchand, deputy secretary to the cabinet, asking him to postpone the decision on the B-767. Taylor explained that, as customary, because of the long lead time between the ordering of an aircraft and its delivery, the company had taken "line positions" with the manufacturers and if it was not to lose its B-767 positions – and thus be at a competitive disadvantage with its rivals – the decision had to be made at the end of April. Marchand suggested he extend the options and Taylor agreed to try, though he was not hopeful that Boeing would agree.

While Taylor was pondering his next move, he received a second call from Marchand summoning him to a cabinet committee meeting to consider the matter on April 25. The Air Canada delegation to the meeting consisted of Bryce Mackasey, chairman; Taylor; Lyle M. Raverty, senior vice-president, technical operations; Pierre Jeanniot, senior vice-president, marketing and planning; and W.J. Reid, vice-president, finance.

Mackasey's appointment as chairman of the airline a couple of months earlier had been widely assailed in the press as a political plum for a veteran Liberal war horse. But he soon made it apparent that he did not consider himself to be merely a figurehead. And as events developed it became clear that he supported the school of thought in Ottawa that apparently favoured the European A-310. More ominously, his interpretation of the phrase "directions of a general nature" contained in the Air Canada Act was obviously much broader than Taylor's. In fact, he told several of Taylor's lieutenants that it would be the cabinet that would make the decision on the new aircraft.

As the committee meeting progressed, it turned out that the cabinet was not unanimous about the course it thought the airline should take. There was some fear that the choice of the A-310 might reduce rather than increase employment in Montreal: Canadair had already received a $145 million contract from Boeing for sections of the B-767 fuselage and its president, Fred Kearns, thought his company had an excellent chance of landing further contracts if Boeing's market expanded. The result, he believed, could be between six and nine hundred stable aerospace jobs at Canadair for the next twenty years.

The discussion placed Claude Taylor in an unenviable position. The government's own Blue Book had said that "the Governor in Council may only issue directives cast in broad terms and not of application to any specific managerial decision. . . ." And, like Gordon McGregor during the Caravelle controversy years before, Taylor firmly believed that the choice of future equipment was the most important managerial decision the chief executive officer ever had to make. After all the months of intensive investigation by his staff, he was convinced he had made the right decision: for many reasons, both technical and commercial, the B-767 was considered by far the most suitable aircraft for Air Canada's requirements.

The cabinet committee meeting ended without any conclusive decision, and Taylor was no doubt relieved that he was not ordered to change his recommendation to the board. But as he was having lunch with the Air Canada team he received a call from de Montigny Marchand, who told him the cabinet had decided to set up a working group drawn from several government departments to review the airline's evaluation procedure.

Marchand wrote to Mackasey that afternoon, saying the government had no objection to the decision on the long-range L-1011-500, but asking that the April 30 board meeting should not include consideration of the mid-range domestic aircraft selection. Two days later, in a letter to Taylor, he left no doubt that the government considered the airline's choice of equipment to be a matter of a "general nature." The cabinet, he said, had "found it desirable to delay its final decision on the choice of an airplane which could qualify as a North American type" pending the review by the interdepartmental working group, which would be led by J.M. DesRoches, deputy minister of supply and services.

By the day before the London board meeting it had become clear that the government did not even want the choice of the B-767 discussed by the directors, and Mackasey held out for the view that the management recommendation in its favour should be deleted from the agenda. Taylor considered this highly irregular and refused even to contemplate it. In his view, management had thoroughly researched the question, had made its decision, and its recommendation must be brought before the board, even if the decision was then postponed.

Only hours before the meeting, in his suite at the Inn on the Park, Taylor was heard to say that if the agenda item was deleted it would be "over my dead body." A worried director who was well aware of the gravity of the situation asked him later if that phrase meant that he was tabling his resignation. "Well," said Taylor, more enigmatically than usual, "if you want to take it that way. . . ."

In the event, a direct confrontation – if such there might have been – was averted by the fortunes of the political wars. The board meeting duly approved the purchase of six Lockheed L-1011-500s at a cost, including spares, of $300 million, and the taking out of options on nine more. But, at Taylor's suggestion, it deferred its decision on management's recommendation that it also buy the B-767.

Three days after the meeting, Taylor wrote to Transport Minister Lang strongly protesting against the letter he had received from Marchand and appealing for his support in opposing "what could well develop into an attempt to impose on Air Canada a new and entirely inappropriate decision-making process." He also told DesRoches that, as president of the airline, he had no intention of appearing before his committee, which was made up of senior civil servants from the departments of Supply and Services, Industry, Trade and Commerce, Transport, the Treasury Board and the Privy Council Office. He did agree, however, that Ralph Vaughan's evaluation team would co-operate with the committee, and in several days of meetings beginning in Montreal on May 8 the government representatives were given an exhaustive explanation of the airline's selection procedures and the reasons for its choice of the B-767.

DesRoches also summoned representatives of the Boeing and Airbus companies to put forward the cases they had already put to the airline at great length, which they did separately in Ottawa on May 23 and 24. Air Canada representatives sat in on those sessions to make sure neither company added any last-minute "sweeteners" to its presentation.

After hearing all sides and carefully examining the voluminous documentation, the DesRoches committee submitted its report to the government early in June. It strongly endorsed the airline's selection procedure and agreed that the B-767 was the aircraft best suited to Air Canada's requirements.

By this time, DesRoches and his colleagues were reporting to a different government: on May 22, Joe Clark's Progressive Conservatives defeated Pierre Trudeau's Liberals. The new Minister of Transport, Don Mazankowski, had been the Conservatives' transportation critic and as such he had been raising parliamentary questions about the delay in announcing the airline's choice of domestic aircraft. He questioned Taylor about it at their first meeting and, after receiving the report of the DesRoches committee, announced at the beginning of July that the government felt confident that "the final selection by Air Canada will be a sound commercial decision." The government would therefore "indicate no preference to Air Canada" but would support whatever decision was made by its directors.

The Air Canada board met in Montreal on July 9. After Taylor's appearance before the cabinet committee in April, Boeing had agreed to keep Air Canada's line positions open, and a couple of days after the board meeting Mackasey, as the airline's chairman, announced that it had decided to buy twelve B-767s and spare parts for $556.2 million and taken out options for eighteen more. As with the Lockheed order, Mackasey said, the purchase would be financed entirely from retained earnings and public borrowings, with no federal government financing or guarantees involved.

Mackasey had been in politics long enough to realize that with a new party in power in Ottawa his days at the airline were numbered. And Air Canada's annual report for 1979 included the brief sentence: "Pierre Taschereau, former Chairman of the Board of Directors, returned to the Chair in September when he succeeded the Hon. Bryce Mackasey."

CHAPTER TWENTY-SEVEN

PILOTS HAVE BEEN COMFORTED through the years by the code word CAVU – Ceiling and Visibility Unlimited. And it looked as though clear skies lay ahead for Claude Taylor and his crew as they entered the 1980s. The company that had started out not much more than a generation earlier with a couple of ten-passenger Lockheeds and the $1,000 Stearman crop-duster was now a huge corporation employing almost 23,000 people and generating a billion and a half dollars in revenue every year.

The year-end results for 1979 showed another record profit – $55.4 million – and the company paid its second $13.2 million dividend to its shareholder, the government of Canada. Thus, in two years, it had returned $26.4 million to the taxpayer – more than the total of $23.9 million in government subsidies it had received in its struggling early years. (The last year in which the government provided a subsidy to its airline was in 1962.)

During 1979, Air Canada flew 12.8 million paying passengers, five million more than it had at the beginning of the decade. Its cargo business was expanding rapidly too: it flew 318 million freight ton-miles during the year, a substantial increase on the 185 million figure for 1970.

True, there were a few clouds on the horizon. Its operating costs were increasing as fast as its revenues, at the rate of about 20 per cent a year. Fuel, for instance, had accounted for 10 per cent of the airline's costs before the OPEC crisis. But during 1979 its price rose by another 10 cents a gallon – no small item when the fleet consumed 440 million gallons during the year. Fuel costs, more than $300 million for the year, now constituted 20 per cent of the company's operating expenses, and that proportion seemed likely to go on rising.

Also, the airline would clearly face greater competition during the years ahead, as the U.S. deregulation philosophy lapped over into Canada: after the removal of the capacity restriction on CP Air the Canadian authorities gradually relaxed the regulations governing charter operators and permitted regional carriers to expand on to long-distance trunk routes previously denied them, where they began to compete head-to-head with Air Canada.

But Claude Taylor had confidence in his crew's ability to respond to these challenges. "The company has proven itself to be commercially successful," he said in his annual report, "and there is every reason to believe that it will continue to succeed."

A crucial clause in the new Air Canada Act bade its board of directors have "due regard to sound business principles, and in particular the contemplation of profit." The fundamental business principle underlying the airline industry was defined by the American pioneer Eddie Rickenbacker, simply if somewhat inelegantly, as "putting bums on seats." Flying empty seats around can rapidly become ruinous, and even before the new act freed Air Canada to face competition, Claude Taylor had encouraged his planners to find ways of filling their planes with "incentive" fares.

Initially, their ability to do this was limited by Canadian Transport Commission regulations. Excursion fares, as they were called, were available only on long-distance routes and during the slow winter season. The discounts at which tickets could be sold were restricted, at first to 35 and later to 30 per cent of the full economy fare. And various "fences," such as length-of-stay requirements, limited the number of passengers who could take advantage of them. But in 1977 the CTC began to relax its rules by permitting first "charter class Canada" and later "advance booking charter" fares to individual passengers rather than "affinity groups." Fences were progressively lowered, controls on permitted discounts were eased, "incentive" fares were extended to more routes and seasons, and the bargains proliferated.

The Air Canada planners were assisted in their efforts to take advantage of this gradual, if unstated, deregulation by the ubiquitous computer and the new sophistication it brought to the art of traffic forecasting. Over the years, the airline compiled "profiles" of its various flights. Questionnaires were distributed to passengers and the information they elicited collated; tickets were scrutinized to see how far in advance they had been bought, where their holders were going and why, and how long they stayed. Fed into the computer by knowledgeable hands, this mass of data came out the other end as a series of "probability analyses" predicting with remarkable accuracy the make-up of the passenger load on, say, a Tuesday flight from Toronto to Edmonton in the third week of September.

Once in possession of these analyses, the planners could go about filling the planes with the appropriate pricing. If you know you are going to have a hundred passengers on Flight 543 paying the full fare, it makes sense to sell the remaining fifty seats at whatever price you can, rather than send them off empty, at a nil return. By 1979, the passengers on any one flight might have been charged as many as half a dozen different fares. A passenger who had to book at the last moment and thus pay the full fare might resent sitting next to some carefree vacationer who had booked weeks before at half that price. But the marketing principle involved was simple and unassailable. And it proved so successful that in February 1979 the airline announced the first-ever across-the-board seat sale.

For a seven-week period beginning at the end of March, it placed all its surplus charter-class seats on virtually all its North American flights on sale at unprecedented discounts, varying from 48 to 68 per cent off the regular economy fare. Some "fences" were retained to prevent the high-yield full-fare passengers – mostly those travelling on business – from taking advantage of the sale prices. Passengers had to book thirty days in advance, for instance, and pay for their tickets within seven days of making their reservations. But when the sale was announced, the airline's reservation clerks were snowed under by the telephone bookings. The experiment proved so popular that a similar sale was announced for the fall. And by the end of the year 400,000 passengers had taken advantage of the low prices.

Claude Taylor was well pleased with the success of this innovation, which was soon copied by other airlines; in the United States, a rash of "super" seat sales and "incredible" seat sales filled the advertising pages with bargains. But he was uncomfortably aware that profit margins in the airline industry generally are not large enough to generate the huge amounts of capital needed to renew fleets as they become outmoded and ensure healthy growth. Even Air Canada's record 1979 profit of $55.4 million, for instance, would be almost entirely swallowed up buying one Lockheed and its parts.

Other major international airlines faced with this problem had tried to solve it by diversifying into allied fields, such as ownership of hotel chains. Air Canada's original charter imposed severe restrictions on the kind of outside investments it could make; the new act in 1978 removed many of them. And in August 1980 Taylor reshuffled his organization to take advantage of it and go out after other business. As one of his lieutenants put it: "We can't afford any longer to be just an airline."

The reshuffle, accomplished without the shell-shock that had rocked the company a decade earlier, split the corporate organization into three streams. Financial, legal and other corporate staff functions remained under Taylor, as chief executive. Pierre Jeanniot, as executive vice-president and chief of airline operations, took over all the planning, flight operations, technical and sales activities that make the airline run. John McGill became executive vice-president and chief of group enterprises, responsible, in essence, for the diversification push – for subsidiary and associated companies and the vital computer and systems services.

"This group enterprises organization," Taylor said when he announced the change, "will be marketing outside the things we are good at doing inside, such as advanced computer, communications, maintenance and other high technology services. Rather than diversifying into a side range of unrelated products and markets, top management believes the corporation must concentrate on ventures which will continue to capitalize on proven strengths."

The airline's first rather tentative ventures into diversification had occurred in the early seventies. In 1971, it joined with its parent company, CN, to form CANAC Consultants Limited, a joint venture designed to sell both air and ground transportation expertise around the world. The following year, through CN Realties, it bought an interest in eight hotels on six Caribbean islands by joining a three-way partnership with Commonwealth Holiday Inns of Canada Limited and the Commonwealth Development Corporation, an aid and development organization along the lines of our own CIDA.

Both these arrangements were ended with passage of the new Air Canada Act, but another venture undertaken in 1973 survives in the form of Touram Incorporated, a wholly owned subsidiary operating package tours. Touram began life as Econair Canada Holidays Limited (soon renamed Venturex), a company formed to combat the inroads being made into the airline's business by international charter operators. At first, Venturex concentrated mainly on the development and handling of group and convention traffic, such as European farmers wishing to make inspection tours of Ontario dairy farms. In 1974, it bought a small Quebec company with particular expertise in this field, Touram Group Services. And as Canadian regulations were eased in later years, making it possible to sell charter-class tickets to individuals, the nature of its business changed.

Touram today charters aircraft from Air Canada – and from other carriers such as Nordair and Quebecair – and sets out to fill them with vacationers on package tours, with all transportation and accommodation costs prepaid on the one ticket. The regulations permit it to fly charters to destinations not available to Air Canada, such as Hawaii, Greece and the Mediterranean. It offers its customers holidays on the beaches of the Caribbean, ocean cruises, skiing vacations in Canada and Europe and, in summer, motor-coach tours in Canada. It has 155 permanent staff and thirty temporary employees scattered across Canada and the United States and the so-called sun destinations in the Caribbean. It has four reservations offices – in Halifax, Montreal, Toronto and Vancouver – which deal with the wholesalers and travel agencies through which all its tours are sold, to avoid complaints about unfair competition.

Touram's success can be judged from some recent figures. In the peak winter season of 1982-83 it sold 20,000 "sun" tours; the following winter it doubled that total, to 40,000; and in the 1984-85 season 60,000 vacationers bought its package deals. Air Canada benefits from its ownership of Touram in two ways: the company spends about $35 million a year buying charters and such services as its reservations system from its parent; and at the end of the year its profit – half a million dollars in 1984 – is passed "upstairs" to the airline.

Touram is, of course, a wholly owned subsidiary engaged in essentially the same business as its parent: putting bums on seats. But in its quest for profitable diversification, the airline has also invested in a number of outside companies operating in allied fields. It has a half-share, in partnership with Marathon Realties, in MATAC Cargo Limited, which owns a cargo terminal at Montreal's Mirabel airport. In 1981, it bought a 30 per cent interest in Innotech Aviation Limited, a general aviation company providing a wide variety of services for executive jets, such as engine maintenance and overhauls, hangaring, fuelling and the provision of custom interiors. And in 1984, it acquired a 20 per cent share in Global Travel Computers Limited, a company providing accounting services to Canadian travel agencies.

Global Travel is owned by a group of large Canadian travel agencies who were anxious to gain access to ReserVec II and the airline's technical expertise in the computer field. Pierre Jeanniot knew many of its principals well and he assigned his long-time deputy Anne Bodnarchuk to look into the deal, along with Ray Lindsay, who had been involved in many of the negotiations leading to the acquisition of outside companies and later became the airline's treasurer. After about a year of negotiations, it was agreed that the airline would accept a 20 per cent share in Global Travel in return for the services it supplied.

The most successful of the airline's outside investments turned out to be its purchase of a part-interest in a company named GPA Group Limited, which began life as Guinness Peat Aviation Limited, a small aircraft trading company based at Shannon, Ireland. The guiding genius behind Guinness Peat was Tony Ryan, a former executive of Aer Lingus, a man enviously described by his competitors as "the kind of fellow who can follow you into a revolving door and come out ahead of you." Ryan had set up the company in the mid-seventies with £30,000 contributed equally by Aer Lingus and the Guinness banking interests in London. Essentially, he intended to concentrate on something at which he is an acknowledged expert: the buying and selling of used aeroplanes. But under his aggressive leadership the company expanded rapidly, operating aircraft as well as buying and selling them, leasing them out and financing them.

The idea that Air Canada should take an interest in GPA was first advanced by Lyle Raverty, who was at that time the airline's vice-president, technical services. Born in Sleepy Eye, Minnesota (which owes such international fame as it has to its occasional mention in "Little House on the Prairie"), Raverty served in the air branch of the U.S. navy during World War II and then joined Northwest Airlines. During his 27-year career there he rose to head its maintenance department, until he was wooed away by Air Canada to become vice-president, maintenance, in 1974. Raverty was introduced to Ryan in 1977 by Ted O'Keefe, an Air Canada used aircraft salesman who was born in Ireland, and they spent an afternoon talking shop at the appropriately named Shamrock Motel in Shannon.

On his return to Canada, Raverty told Claude Taylor he thought some sort of link between GPA and Air Canada would benefit both companies: GPA would certainly be a help in marketing the airline's old aircraft as they became surplus, and Air Canada could supply GPA, which had not yet broken into the huge North American market, with its considerable expertise on the Boeing, Lockheed and Douglas aircraft in its fleet. Taylor recognized the possibilities of a deal and Pierre Jeanniot, then senior vice-president, marketing and planning, asked Jean Douville, as director of acquisitions, to look into it. Douville returned from his first visit to Ireland with the impression that Ryan favoured some sort of partnership with Air Canada. But after months of dickering aimed at setting a price on the airline's participation in GPA, the negotiations ground to a halt in the fall of 1979.

Shortly thereafter, Jeanniot and Raverty ran into the president of Aer Lingus, David Kennedy, at an IATA general assembly meeting in Manila. Jeanniot told him that if Air Canada had realized

GPA did not really want a deal it would have dropped the negotiations much sooner. Surprised, Kennedy showed him a memo from Maurice Foley, who had handled the negotiations for GPA, expressing *his* suspicion that Air Canada was not interested in a deal. So the negotiations resumed. But they still proved difficult. The problem was to set a price on an operation that depended essentially on Ryan's prowess as a salesman, but possessed little in the way of concrete assets. Eventually, however, after the groundwork done by their respective staffs, Claude Taylor had lunch with Geoffrey Knight, GPA's chairman. A World War II Royal Marine officer, Knight later became a director of the British Aircraft Corporation, and as such had a hand in the design of the only commercial supersonic transport ever built, the Concorde. He and Taylor quickly reached agreement on a deal which was approved by the Air Canada board in May 1980: Air Canada paid $9 million for 29.3 per cent of GPA's shares, with Aer Lingus and the Guinness interests retaining 29.3 per cent each and Tony Ryan holding the remaining 12.1 per cent. Four years later, GPA's net worth was estimated to be almost $100 million, and Air Canada's share of its 1984 earnings amounted to $2.4 million.

With its diversification program well under way, and its seat sales apparently so successful, Air Canada entered the 1980s in a seemingly impregnable position. It carried more than thirteen million passengers in 1980, yet another new record. In 1979, it had been one of only three major airlines in North America to improve its profit position. In 1980, it improved it again, with a record $57 million after providing for corporate taxes of $48.3 million and once again paying a $13.2 million dividend. But that fall its passenger statistics began to show a mildly disturbing downward trend. No one realized it yet, but as the western world slid into the worst recession since the Depression, Air Canada, together with the rest of the airline industry, was about to enter the most difficult period in its history.

In 1981, the summer peak traffic on which the company's financial performance had always depended just did not appear. As the economic situation worsened and the unemployment figures rose, leisure travellers nervous about their future abandoned plans for holidays and banked their money, fearing even rainier days ahead. Companies cut back on business travel, too. That year, for the first time in its history, Air Canada carried fewer passengers than it had the year before: 12.5 million, a drop from the previous year's 13.1 million, and fewer even than the 12.8 million it had flown in 1979.

The decline in traffic, unhappily for Claude Taylor and his crew, was not accompanied by a decline in the cost of doing business. The airline's operating expenses rose to $2.1 billion during the year, an increase of 15.5 per cent. Fuel costs alone–"pushed by various forms of fuel taxes," as the annual report reprovingly pointed out * – rose by 40 per cent during the year, to $567 million. They now amounted to 26 per cent of the company's total operating costs.

The recession could not have hit the North American airlines at a worse time. During the late 1970s, with the demand for their services still seemingly inexhaustible, they had ordered new aircraft to expand and update their fleets. The sky-rocketing rise in the price of fuel demanded new engines that were not so hungry; new anti-noise regulations had to be met; and every company wanted to be placed to retain or expand its market share in the new deregulated environment. Now, with interest rates sky high, the bills for these new fleets had to be paid, and the passengers needed to fill their seats were deserting in droves. The result was a series of knock-down, drag-out price wars that wreaked further carnage on the airlines' balance sheets.

The fare reductions that emerged from the price wars in the United States were by no means universal. With airlines free to fly anywhere they cared to, they naturally tended to go for the longest and most heavily travelled routes. The competition brought down long-distance fares, but those on many smaller, less popular routes increased, sometimes by as much as 100 per cent. It became possible to fly clear across the continent for less than it cost to cover a few hundred miles. In 1980, for instance, a traveller from New York to Columbus, Ohio, had to pay a coach fare $12 higher than he would have had to pay for a flight five times as long, from New York to Los Angeles.

New airline companies were formed to take advantage of the new environment. The most publicized of these, People Express, prospered with a policy of carefully picking the most profitable routes, "no-frill" flights, and labour costs half those of the established airlines. Some of the new airlines and many of the old eventually went bankrupt, the most notable collapse being that of Braniff, a company that fostered a "life in the fast lane" image

---

* In addition to fuel taxes, the airline pays about $85 million a year to the Canadian and foreign governments for user charges, which includes such things as fees for landings and take-offs and sundry other airport charges – and en route payments to the governments of countries flown over, to cover the cost of providing navigational aids, air traffic control, communications and meteorological services. En route charges on a one-way L-1011 flight from Toronto to Singapore, for example, paid to more than twenty countries, total $6,420 and include a $49 payment to the government of Cyprus.

and had at one time been the fastest growing airline in the United States.

The upheaval in the industry in Canada was less marked, in keeping with Ottawa's more cautious approach toward deregulation. But as well as losing passengers by the thousands, Air Canada also lost some of its market share. Before the "open skies" proclamation took the wraps off CP Air, Air Canada had 77.7 per cent of the domestic traffic carried by the two lines; by 1983 its share had declined to 73.7 per cent. And with the smaller carriers permitted to expand outside their regions, its share of the total traffic within Canada declined also, from 52.7 per cent in 1979 to 48.4 per cent in 1981.

The struggle for market share among the Canadian airlines, and the CTC's gradual relaxation of its controls on the size of the discounts that could be offered, led to an era of price wars in Canada no less fierce than that south of the border. Air Canada's Nighthawk service offered return flights on night-time departures at a dollar above the normal one-way economy fare. CP Air's Skybus service offered discounts varying from 28 to 62 per cent off the economy fare. During one Air Canada seat sale it was possible to fly from Newfoundland to California at an 80 per cent discount. The regional carriers joined the fray, the bargain fares proliferated, and the canny passenger was soon able to buy a seat on sale at any time of the year.

The effect on airline balance sheets was disastrous. Trying to fill the planes at any cost brought down the average yield per passenger, and to prevent the weaker going to the wall the CTC resumed some control over the deep discounts. But more than 60 per cent of the passengers who fly Air Canada today travel on discount fares.

It is impossible to isolate from the mass of statistics how much Air Canada's balance sheet was harmed by the U.S. deregulation. But as a trans-border carrier it must have suffered some damage. For example, US Air (formerly Allegheny Airlines), with a comparatively short trans-border hop from Toronto to Pittsburgh, was able to offer Canadians flights to no fewer than seventy-eight other U.S. cities from its Pittsburgh "hub." Had that convenience not been available, it is reasonable to assume that many passengers bound for those cities would have flown the first leg of their journey on Air Canada and made their connections at one of its traditional gateways to the United States, such as New York or Chicago.

Surprisingly, though the warning signals were beginning to light up all over the control panel, the corporation still managed to record a $40.1 million profit for 1981, and pay its fourth $13.2

million dividend on the previous year's operations. But the trend that company executives referred to delicately as "negative growth" continued. The airline lost well over a million passengers during 1982, and its cargo business declined also, by 15 million revenue ton miles. Overall, it lost 5 per cent of its traffic during the year. And when all the figures were in, it registered its first loss since 1976: $32.6 million.

It was by no means alone in its plight. CP Air, only a third of Air Canada's size, lost even more: $34.7 million. The charter operator Wardair lost $13.5 million and Quebecair $16.3 million. The U.S. airlines were battered also. Continental lost $64.7 million during the year, and after an even larger loss in 1983 followed Braniff into bankruptcy. Eastern Airlines lost $75 million and Republic $40 million. And it was the same on world routes. Pan Am lost an incredible half a billion dollars and Air France $120 million. In all, the International Air Transport Association estimated its member airlines' losses for the year at more than $2 billion.

The crisis facing airline managements everywhere was unprecedented. In the past, government regulations had provided a sort of safety net to protect them against the worst effects of cut-throat competition. Also – and this was probably just as important – their whole experience, virtually since the industry's earliest days and certainly since the introduction of the jets, had been one of almost uninterrupted growth. In any business, handling growth is much easier than coping with decline. Good times can cushion temporary business reverses and compensate for or even conceal the kind of comfortable slackness that can only too easily develop in a corporate body long accustomed to success. Hard times, in contrast, call for hard decisions.

Thanks to its day-to-day monitoring of its operations, Air Canada detected the downward trend in traffic early (though even the most refined forecasting techniques could not have predicted the full depth of the problem) and its management was able to start making the necessary hard decisions before the worst of the crisis. The response began in 1981, and to prepare the airline's employees for its impact the pubic affairs and personnel departments collaborated to produce a dramatic audio-visual presentation called the Air Canada Challenge. Shown across the system, this explained the developing crisis in graphic terms and its obvious message was that solution of the monumental problems ahead would call for the understanding and co-operation of all concerned.

Any company faced with declining revenue must cast around for ways of cutting costs, and austerity became the order of the day. "We didn't quite use pencils down to the eraser," one vice-president said, "but managers were asked to reduce their budgets and all sorts of economies were made." Wages and salaries made up 35.4 per cent of the airline's operating costs, but no one wanted to save money by wholesale firings. A hiring freeze was imposed instead, and employees who retired or left for other jobs were not replaced. With fuel costs consuming a further 25 per cent of the budget, suggestions were invited for ways of economizing. Pilots began to taxi on one engine where possible and some cruising speeds were reduced, saving fuel but adding only a few minutes to the duration of a flight. As one manager said: "Like any other cost-saving, it's the aggregation of little things."

As the crisis deepened, the little things were supplemented by much more fundamental and far-reaching economies. In August 1982, Claude Taylor announced an eight-point restraint program designed to "reduce the scope of our operations in the face of today's declining market, while at the same time retaining the necessary efficiency to take advantage of an economic upturn when it occurs." The program continued the hiring freeze and set an example by postponing the annual raises due to 225 senior executives until July 1, 1983. (In fact, the raises were delayed until November of that year.)

Taylor also announced a voluntary separation program under which managers were offered various incentives to take early retirement. Yves Pratte, who had stirred up so many hornets when he tried to tighten the airline's belt a decade earlier, might have been forgiven a wry smile when it was announced that 650 employees had accepted the offer, trimming the airline's management ranks by almost one-sixth.* Some of the vacated duties, of course, had to be assumed by those who retained their jobs, but other low-priority functions were just permitted to disappear in the struggle for survival. The incentive payments cost more than $32 million, but it was estimated they would reduce future payroll costs by $26 million a year.

Taylor also announced that talks had begun with the company's unions on a voluntary restraint program "which could minimize and perhaps eliminate the need for lay-offs." In subsequent months, agreements reached with three of the four major unions softened the impact on the employees of the airline's reduced level of activity. The pilots accepted a reduction in their flying hours, and thus also a cut in pay. Some flight attendants agreed to work-sharing arrangements, and some took long-term leaves

---

*A further four hundred management jobs disappeared early in 1985, as the airline continued to tighten its belt with a non-voluntary program of retrenchment.

of absence with a guarantee that they could return to their jobs later without loss of benefits. CALEA, the union representing the passenger agents, agreed that when full-time employees took leaves of absence, part-timers could be hired to do their jobs. But the company was unable to reach an agreement with its largest union, the IAMAW, which was thus the one most affected by those lay-offs that proved unavoidable. Several hundred employees across the system were laid off for varying lengths of time, but most had been recalled by the middle of 1984.

Another economy measure in the eight-point program was a continuation of the virtual freeze imposed on all the airline's capital spending, with the exception of money already committed to the renewal of the fleet. While the future options on new aircraft were dropped, the company went ahead and bought all the Lockheeds and B-767s for which it had placed firm orders. But all its other projected capital expenditures – for such things as new cargo terminals and expensive ground equipment – were subjected to rigorous scrutiny and 80 per cent of planned spending was eliminated.

The only expenditures left untouched were those intended to improve the efficiency of the fleet, and here some bold decisions were made. It had been expected that as the B-767s began to arrive they would gradually displace the company's aging and fuel-hungry DC-8s. But even before the first 767s were delivered there was a wholesale juggling of the airline's schedules which enabled the entire DC-8 fleet, the backbone of the airline for years, to be grounded at one stroke. The planes were "parked against the fence" at Marana, Arizona, where the climate is more suitable for storing aircraft in the open than it is at Dorval. Three were later sold and six were given new engines that increased their fuel efficiency by 17 per cent and are still rendering efficient service as freighters.

As the passenger traffic fell away, two of the airline's seven Jumbo 747s, which were becoming difficult to fill, were grounded and later sold. The rest remained in service, though two of them were converted into "combis" designed to carry both cargo and passengers. The thirty-nine B-727s in the fleet, which, along with the DC-9s, took over the work of the DC-8s, were taken into the Dorval shops and given engine modifications that improved their fuel efficiency by almost 6 per cent. Before the fall-off in traffic, discussions were being held about replacing the airline's thirty-seven DC-9s with a more modern, fuel-efficient type. Instead, they were completely refurbished to give them the wide-body interior popular with passengers, and their engines were modified to reduce their fuel consumption by 2 per cent.

It is impossible to say just how much all these changes cost, though it was a substantial amount: the DC-9 refurbishing, for instance, cost about a million dollars per aircraft. Nor is it possible to set an exact figure on the savings they accomplished, except to say that without the airline's quick response to its changed circumstances, its 1982 financial performance would have been far worse than it actually was. For example, when the figures were all totted up at the end of the year it was found that the sales and service branch, making up its budget at the end of 1981, had over-estimated the actual revenue that would be taken in during the year by $250 million. Fortunately, as the branch continued to monitor sales and issue ever more pessimistic reports, the company's budget was several times revised downward and new economies were instituted. Had this prompt remedial action not been taken, the actual $32.6 million deficit could easily have been $200 million or more.

The austerity campaign continued through 1983, which was a year that everyone connected with the company would like to be able to forget. The price wars among Canadian airlines – a process described by one executive as "self-mutilation" – raged on unabated. The number of paying passengers on Air Canada fell again, all the way down to 10.5 million, the lowest total since 1975. Cargo revenue was down, too, if only by $10 million. And that year, for the first time in its history, the airline actually put less money in the till than it had the year before: its operating revenue slipped to $2.3 billion, a drop of $7.4 million from the loss year of 1982.

But the continuation of the slump was not the worst of the year's misfortunes. On May 12, a DC-9 making its second attempt to land at Regina during a freak spring snow storm skidded off the icy runway and two of its fifty-seven passengers received minor injuries. Then, on the evening of June 2, passengers noticed smoke escaping from a washroom at the rear of a DC-9 bound from Dallas to Toronto and Montreal. As the plane filled up with toxic fumes, Captain Don Cameron made an emergency landing at Cincinnati. The cabin staff managed to deploy the emergency exit chutes as soon as the aircraft came to a stop, enabling eighteen passengers and the five crew members to escape to safety.* But twenty-three passengers still trapped aboard were killed and the aircraft was destroyed by the fire.

---

*The Royal Canadian Air Force Association later presented the 1984 Gordon R. McGregor Trophy to the DC-9's crew: Captain Cameron, First Officer Claude Ouimet, and the cabin staff: Sergio Benetti, Laura Kayama and Judy Davidson.

First reports suggested the fire originated in the electrical flush motor on one of the aircraft's toilets, and six weeks after the crash the U.S. National Transportation Safety Board recommended that all airlines make an immediate examination of all flush motors and their wiring. Air Canada had done that within days of the accident. And in fact after a year-long investigation the NTSB was unable to establish whether the flush motor had in fact been the cause of the fire, which remains officially "undetermined." But the board ordered U.S. airlines to equip their fleets with fire-blocking seat covers within three years. Here again, Air Canada had begun to work with manufacturers to evaluate suitable fire-blocking materials soon after the accident. And almost two years before the Cincinnati accident the airline had begun a program, since completed, of replacing its acrylic cabin carpets with a more fire-resistant material containing 90 per cent wool. Within months of the accident it had also installed lavatory smoke detectors and improved fire extinguishers on all the planes in its fleet and instituted a $5 million program to work with manufacturers on the testing and evaluation of materials and technology which the industry had not yet been able to adapt to commercial use.

The horror of the Cincinnati fire was still fresh in everyone's mind when an even worse tragedy was averted by a remarkable feat of airmanship–and a remarkable stroke of good old-fashioned luck. On July 23, a Saturday evening, Air Canada Flight 143, a brand new B-767 bound for Edmonton from Montreal and Ottawa, ran out of fuel high above Red Lake, Ontario. Its captain, Robert Pearson, was a twenty-five-year veteran of the airline who had started out flying Viscounts. And fortunately for the sixty-one passengers and seven other crew members aboard, he was an accomplished glider pilot.

When his instruments first warned him of the impending crisis, Bob Pearson had no chance of keeping his disabled craft aloft long enough to reach the nearest suitable airport, Winnipeg, which was still 120 miles ahead. But by the merest chance, his route led him close to a wartime air training scheme airstrip at Gimli, Manitoba. When all its complex electronic systems are working normally, the B-767 can land itself automatically. But when both its engines fell silent, Flight 143's main power source was cut off. Its computer went dead, the lights on all its electronic gauges vanished, and Captain Pearson was left with only the rudimentary instruments available to that earlier generation of pilots who flew by the seats of their pants: a magnetic compass, an artificial horizon, an airspeed indicator and an altimeter.

With these simple aids, and his skill as a glider pilot, Pearson side-slipped to lose height and speed and guided his 88-ton aircraft safely down to Gimli's 7,200-foot runway. His co-pilot, Maurice Quintal, managed to lower the main landing gear into position manually, but the nose-wheel failed to lock and collapsed as the plane landed. This proved to be fortunate, since the friction created by the aircraft's nose dragging along the ground stopped Flight 143 short of a crowd of campers at the far end of the runway, which was being used that weekend for a drag-racing meet.

An immediate internal investigation disclosed that Flight 143's brush with disaster stemmed from a series of errors by both flight and ground crews. Since the aircraft's fuel gauges were not functioning properly, the amount of fuel in its tanks was measured manually, using the dipsticks provided for that purpose. In line with government policy on metrication, Air Canada had ordered its B-767s with a metric fuel system, so their dipsticks are calibrated in centimetres. Calculating the weight of fuel aboard therefore entails first translating centimetres to litres and then converting litres to kilograms. Various tables and conversion factors are provided to accomplish those calculations, but those involved in refuelling Flight 143 mistakenly used the conversion factor for translating litres into pounds, the one in general use on all the other aircraft in the fleet. To arrive at the correct weight in kilograms, the resulting figure should have been divided by 2.2. Since this was not done, the aircraft took off with only about half the fuel needed to reach its destination. The airline immediately changed its refuelling procedures and retrained all those involved in them, both flight and ground crews.*

Shaken by this string of three incidents occurring in such unwelcome succession, Claude Taylor began to wonder whether the external buffeting the airline had taken at the hands of market forces was beginning to affect its internal standards, the source

---

*In July 1985, the government released the report of a board of inquiry into the Gimli incident conducted by the Manitoba jurist, Mr. Justice George H. Lockwood. Judge Lockwood blamed the accident on a series of errors by both ground and flight crews, defective equipment and inadequate communications within the airline. He made a series of recommendations covering sixteen areas ranging from standardization of the fleet through improved fuelling procedures to reorganized communications, directed not only at Air Canada but also at Transport Canada and the manufacturers. Judge Lockwood acknowledged that "Air Canada, to its credit, has already made significant improvements to its operation and corrected some of the obvious deficiencies which contributed to the Gimli accident." At the time of writing, the rest of the judge's recommendations aimed at improving airline safety were under active consideration by both the government and Air Canada.

of so much pride throughout its history. As he said later in that year's annual report, Air Canada had always been committed to the view that "safety has no margin of tolerance." So he commissioned an independent team of U.S. airline and safety experts to conduct an "in-depth analysis of the airline's operational procedures." The team was headed by Bob Buck, a pilot who flew with Trans World Airlines for thirty-seven years and had undertaken similar investigations for many other international airlines. It included pilots and engineers from the two companies whose aircraft had been involved in the incidents, Boeing and McDonnell Douglas, and two observers from Transport Canada.

The team submitted its report at the end of September, and while it was not made public the corporation's annual report for the year quoted it as saying that Air Canada's operations were "of the highest order and without doubt one of the best of more than 50 airlines, including most of the free world's major carriers, that team members had observed, trained or flown for." Bob Buck went even further when a *Globe and Mail* reporter interviewed him by telephone at his home in Vermont, saying his team members were amazed by the excellence of Air Canada. "We have never seen a better airline," Buck said. Air Canada crews were "among the finest in the world" and "trained more than any of us have ever seen."

The team's report was a great relief to Taylor and his colleagues and a month later, when they moved into new headquarters a couple of short blocks east of the Place Ville Marie complex they had occupied for almost a quarter of a century,* it was with renewed confidence and optimism for the future. There was a feeling that the company had confronted the worst problems in its history and not only surmounted them but come through the fire both toughened and strengthened. The year-end financial results showed that the austerity campaign and all the upheavals of the past couple of years were beginning to bring results. True,

---

*In December 1982, the board of directors approved management's recommendation that the airline should purchase ten floors of a new condominium office building from Trizec Corporation, its landlord in the Place Ville Marie offices it had occupied since 1960. When the decision was announced, press reports quoted rival developers' complaints that they had offered the airline better deals in other new buildings. The headlines became more sensational when it was reported that RCMP investigators had interviewed both Claude Taylor and René Amyot, a Quebec lawyer and company director appointed by the government to the board of directors in March 1981 and named chairman nine months later. Even more embarrassing headlines followed in April 1983, when RCMP investigators searched Amyot's Quebec City home and his offices there and at the airline and were reported to have taken away some of his papers. On November 3, 1983, it was announced in Ottawa that Transport Minister Lloyd Axworthy had accepted Amyot's resignation.

the airline's takings were down, but so were its operating expenses, by a satisfying $61 million. And the previous year's loss had been turned into a profit of $3.8 million. In effect, even though the airline had carried 2.6 million fewer passengers than it had in the peak year of 1980, it had broken even.

The headquarters staff that moved into the new building – Place Air Canada, as it was called–had been trimmed and reshuffled earlier in the year in what the annual report described as a "streamlining of the organizational structure." And it was now accountable to a new "Office of the President," which consisted of Claude Taylor as chief executive officer and Pierre Jeanniot, with the new title of executive vice-president and chief operating officer. It had now become apparent that Jeanniot would one day inherit Taylor's presidential mantle, and the two men worked even more closely under the new arrangement than they had in the past.

The group enterprises division, formed in the palmy days of 1980 when it was thought the company could not afford to be "just an airline," disappeared in the struggle just to stay alive as an airline. Its functions were absorbed into the corporate departments dealing with finance and planning, but the outside investments already undertaken went on contributing to the company's revenue, bringing in $3.6 million during the year. The company also earned $109.8 million from the sale of its technical expertise. The Dorval base, whose establishment had caused so much controversy, is now renowned as one of the most advanced in the industry. Its facilities, such as its pneumatic shop and avionics test centre, put it in the forefront of high technology development.

Computers perform a myriad functions aboard modern aircraft. They do the navigation, manage the flight controls, and can even land the aircraft virtually blind without human assistance. Dorval's avionics test centre for the maintenance and repair of all this electronic equipment is considered to be one of the most sophisticated installations of its kind outside those operated by the manufacturers. It makes Air Canada one of the few airlines in the world able to do all its own maintenance work, and the Dorval base also does contract overhaul work for forty other Canadian and international airlines.

The rich pool of technical skills built up within the airline brings in welcome revenue in a variety of other ways. In recent years, Air Canada has trained pilots and flight crews for more than twenty foreign and domestic airlines. Its ground staff handles aircraft for other airlines in places such as London and Frankfurt. Its enRoute card is the largest of all airline credit cards, honoured by many other major airlines and hotels, car rental firms and other companies serving travellers around the world. Operated as a separate business centre within the company, its billings now exceed half a billion dollars a year.

The sale of its computer services gives the corporation another profitable sideline, one of its major customers being VIA Rail. The country's passenger rail service commissioned Air Canada to design a reservations system based on ReserVec II, and the resultant ReserVIA was introduced in 1980. The first fully automated rail information system in the world, it is now linked with the ReserVec II network, which connects the airline's central computers to thousands of terminals in all parts of Canada, the United States, Europe, the Caribbean and the Far East.

The ReserVec II system was installed in 1970, and such is the pace of obsolescence in this high-tech world that it is nearing the end of its useful life. Work began in 1981 to design its successor, to be called PRISMAC – for Passenger Reservation Information System Management for Air Canada. PRISMAC promises to introduce air travellers to a world they have hitherto encountered only in science fiction. It will store not only the names of frequent travellers but also their preferences. If a passenger likes a window seat in the smoking section, say, this will come up on the screen when he starts to make a reservation. Passengers with personal computers will be able to make their own reservations, not only for flights but for hotels and car rentals, with all the information about available bookings displayed on their screens in clear language, not airline code words. The system will also supply the airline's marketing people with much more information about customers and their preferences. In the words of Pierre Laforest, who is in charge of PRISMAC planning, "What has so far been a servicing tool will be transformed into a selling tool."

Constantly fed with accurate, up-to-date information, PRISMAC will be a considerable improvement on the traditional airline time-tables which, in today's travel world, start becoming obsolete the moment they are published. As the passenger traffic started to fall away, the airline adopted a practice known as the "consolidation" of flights to try to keep its seats filled. Two weeks before the departure of any flight, the reservation lists were examined and if it was not booking up according to pattern, prospective passengers would be telephoned and told apologetically that they were being transferred to another flight leaving later in the day. Or, on routes where there were not enough daily flights to permit consolidation, the schedule would be juggled to replace an under-booked flight with a smaller plane.

In what became known as the "frequency strategy," there was a wholesale juggling with schedules across the entire system to replace large planes with smaller ones wherever possible. When the marketing branch began to push for this strategy, there were grave misgivings in the financial branch. It is obviously cheaper to fill up one 747 with passengers from, say, western Canada to Germany and fly it once a week, than it is to fly a smaller L-1011 two or three times a week. But the marketing branch insisted that to attract and hold the high yield, or business, traffic it was essential to have small aeroplanes flying more frequently, rather than big aeroplanes flying less often.

With all this shuffling of schedules, the unpopular practice of over-booking, so indignantly denied by Gordon McGregor in an earlier, easier, era, became inevitable. The airline has set a sort of "pain threshold" of eight passengers denied boarding out of every thousand, but constant examination of bookings holds that figure down in practice to four or five per thousand. Passengers unable to fly on their chosen flight are, of course, offered compensation–say a half-fare flight on a later plane, and free hotel accommodation if they are delayed overnight. This is often enough to induce a passenger who has already boarded a flight to disembark and make way for a latecomer without a seat.

The first-class seats are, of course, never over-booked. And as the price wars intensified and the number of passengers flying on discount fares mounted, the airline concentrated on measures to attract more high-yield traffic. Its most spectacular and successful innovation was the Intercontinental luxury service inaugurated on its long-distance international flights early in 1983. First-class passengers found themselves reclining in roomy "Sleeperette" seats and eating seven-course gourmet meals at tables, instead of from trays, with fine china and a choice of even finer wines from real glasses. Other business passengers in the Executive class were only slightly less pampered, and those flying in the Hospitality class also received better service than they would on a normal economy flight. Soon after its introduction, the influential *Executive Travel Magazine* pronounced the Intercontinental service the best on the highly competitive North Atlantic routes. And Air Canada's share of the total passenger traffic between Canada and Europe rose from 23.1 per cent in 1983 to 26 per cent in 1984.

Its international traffic is likely to become even more important to Air Canada in the years ahead. As the restrictions were lifted from CP Air and the regional airlines began to expand their operations, it was realized that Air Canada had little opportunity to expand at home and that it must look overseas for the growth that is vital to any healthy company. One of the most ambitious policies to emerge from all the task forces and brainstorming prompted by the hard times was the so-called global expansion strategy. This had its germination in 1980 when, in a series of bilateral negotiations, British Airways was finally granted its long-coveted access to western Canada. The question then became what rights Canada should be awarded in return. Air Canada already had all the landing rights it wanted in Britain, at London, Prestwick and Manchester. So it urged the Canadian government negotiators to press for the most coveted of the international freedoms of the air, the fifth. And Air Canada was granted the right to pick up traffic in the United Kingdom for points in Africa and the Middle and Far East. In negotiations with Germany soon afterward – in which Lufthansa won rights to western Canada also – and with France, Air Canada received valuable fifth-freedom rights from those two countries. It was thus able to extend some of its transatlantic services to additional European destinations, such as Dusseldorf, Geneva and Zurich, and for the first time pick up passengers for them within Europe. And after later negotiations with India and Singapore, it was able early in 1985 to begin a long-range service from Canada to Singapore via London and Bombay, making it a truly international airline.

After the resignation of René Amyot late in 1983, the company carried on under the interim chairmanship of Geno F. Francolini, a much-respected businessman from Tillsonburg, Ontario, who had been on its board of directors for eight years. But on June 1, 1984, the government recognized Claude Taylor's long contribution to the airline by appointing him its chairman, the first to have come up all the way through the ranks. Pierre Jeanniot stepped up to the post of president and chief executive officer, and the two men who had led the team through the worst crisis in the corporation's history thus continued to work closely in tandem on the problems that will undoubtedly face it in the years ahead – chief among them, inescapably, the endless struggle to make profits large enough to finance the renewal and constant updating of its fleet, without which its healthy growth will be impossible.

Taylor assumed his new office at a time when shafts of sunlight were beginning to break through the clouds. The three-year slide in passenger traffic seemed to have been arrested: the fleet carried 11.3 million paying customers during the year, an increase of 800,000. This was still far below the figure for the peak year of 1980, but the year-end results were a considerable improvement on those of 1983, showing a modest profit of $27 million. And the national airline C.D. Howe had launched with $5 million of the taxpayers' money was now revitalized, a tougher, leaner organization than it had ever been in its history. As it headed toward its golden anniversary, it depended still, as it always had, upon the patronage of the travelling public. But Claude Taylor was able to say, with a good deal of relief, and pardonable satisfaction: "The passengers are beginning to come back."

ACKNOWLEDGMENTS

In researching this book, the author depended heavily on extensive interviews with men and women–too numerous to acknowledge individually–who were involved in the events it describes. Among them, of course, were dozens of current and former employees of TCA/Air Canada. The author also offers his thanks to the many others involved in civil aviation and aircraft manufacturing on both sides of the Atlantic, as well as several politicians and public servants concerned with regulation of the industry through the years, who graciously acceded to his requests for interviews. By thanking them collectively, rather than individually, the author hopes to absolve them from responsibility for any errors of commission or omission, which are entirely his own.

The book would not have been possible without the access granted the author to the files and archives of TCA/Air Canada. Thanks are also due to the staffs of the Public Archives of Canada, the Richardson Archives–Canadian Airways Limited Collection in the Provincial Archives of Manitoba, the Library of British Airways in London, and the Royal Air Force Museum at Hendon, Middlesex.

INDEX

London School of Economics, 190
Longhurst, John, 157
Los Angeles, 205, 235, 266, 302, 304, 341
Lothian, George, 70–72, 89, 93
Lowe, Frank, 185–86
Loyola College, 295
Lufthansa airline, 27, 230

Macdonald, Ian, 245–46
MacInnes, Rod, 144, 171, 180, 235, 275
Mackasey, Bryce, 264, 282n, 330, 331, 333
Mackenzie, Ian, 39
MacLaren, Maj. Don, 12, 18, 22, 35, 39, 57, 84
MacLaren agency, 210
MacLeod, Merlin "Mac," 132
MacMillan, H.R., 18
MacMillan, Norman, 265n, 276, 290n
MacMillan Bloedel, 283
Madrid, 185, 189, 200
Magdalen Islands, 15
Mail and Empire, 37
Maloney, Jack, 294
Malton, Ont., 93, 94, 97–98, 128, 178, 239
Manchester, 353
Manila, 339
Manitoba, 35, 149, 167, 232–34, 236–37, 248–50, 270–73, 326
Manitoba Air Policy Committee, 271
Manufacturers' Life Insurance Co., 220
Marana, Arizona, 345
Marathon Realties, 338
Marchand, de Montigny, 330, 331, 332
Marchand, Jean, 279, 304, 305, 315
Marconi, Guglielmo, 54
Maritime Central Airways, 192
Marquette riding, Man., 35
Massachusetts Institute of Technology, 32
Massey, Vincent, 91–94
Massey–Ferguson, 283
Masters, John, 7
MATAC Cargo Ltd., 338
Maxwell, John, 112
Mayo Clinic, 73
Mazankowski, Don, 332
McConachie, Grant W.G., 134–36,
my 1st cousin

137, 139–40, 142, 143, 144, 166, 167–68, 184, 189, 192, 193, 194, 200, 211, 229, 251, 252–55, 259, 303
McConachie, Harry, 134
McCullagh, George, 37, 45
McDonnell Douglas, 349; *see also* Douglas Aircraft Co.
McGill, John, 230, 337
McGill University, 108, 218, 219, 226, 288n, 312
McGregor, Bob, 308n
McGregor, Gordon Roy, 107–11, 117, 120, 121–22, 124–27, 129, 130–32, 133, 134, 139–41, 142–44, 145–51, 152, 153, 155–57, 158, 159–61, 162, 163, 164–67, 168, 169–70, 171, 177, 178, 179–81, 182, 183–87, 188–90, 192, 194, 196, 197–211, 212, 218, 222, 223–25, 226, 227, 228, 229–30, 231, 232–36, 238–43, 244, 247–49, 250–51, 253–59, 263, 264–67, 268, 269–70, 272–73, 275, 276, 277, 278–79, 280–81, 284–85, 287, 290, 302, 303, 304, 308n, 319, 323, 324, 330, 352
McGregor, Maurice F., 62, 73, 74
McIlraith, George, 236, 239, 240, 241–42, 249, 250
McIsaac, Rod, 278, 279, 306
McKim, Anson C., 118–19, 140, 141, 143, 158
McKinsey Co., 283
McKinsey report, 283–89 *passim*, 292, 293, 294–95, 312, 316, 317
McLean, Dan, 136
McLean, James, 290, 292
McLeod, Don, 267n
McMaster University, 165
McNaughton, Maj.-Gen. A.G.L., 24, 25
McPherson report, 251
Medicine Hat, 21
Ménard, Yves, 295, 296, 301, 307–09
Merlin engine, 94–96, 99, 130–32
Merlin 620 engine, 99, 117, 148, 150, 159
Metcalf, Maynard, 57
Mexico, 184, 205
Meyer, Rita, 81
Miami, 266, 302

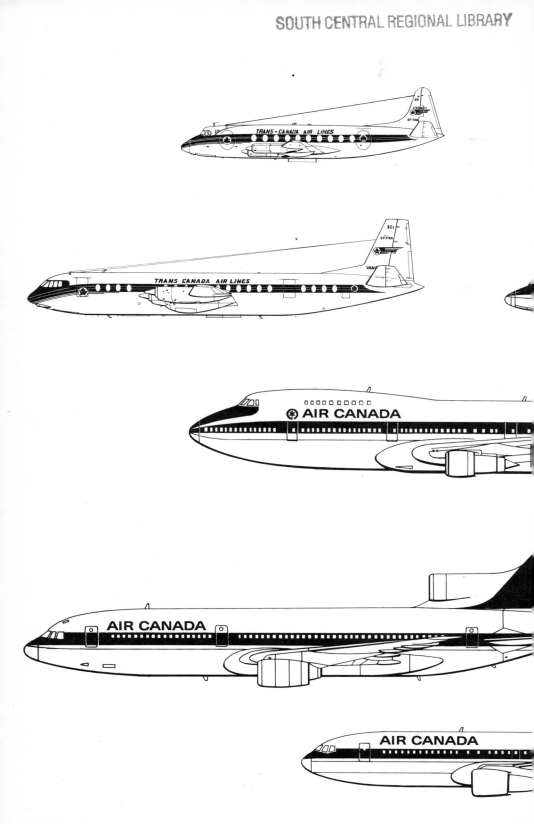

Yale Historical Publications

David Horne, Editor

Studies 22

Between Two Empires

The Ordeal of the Philippines

1929-1946

Theodore Friend

YALE UNIVERSITY PRESS, NEW HAVEN AND LONDON, 1965

To My Parents

Preface

I HAVE ATTEMPTED here to tell the story of an emerging nation caught between two competitive empires. Perhaps I have only achieved, as a friend tells me, an account of stress upon Philippine and American policy in time of danger from Japan. In any case, I have assembled from the Philippines, the United States, and Japan documentary sources and interviews on the question of Philippine independence. To this material, much of it new information, I have tried to bring some insight from the social sciences as well as the ordinary inquiries of an historian.

Several things I have not done. I have not attempted a full treatment of the wartime occupation of the Philippines, intending that for a further study of my own. I have given only secondary attention to the question of agrarian unrest and radicalism, because lengthy examination would have prevented achieving my major purpose in a book of decent size. I have not written a history of Philippine-American relations, but have chosen what seems to me a fascinating transitional phase, beginning with one colonial crisis, caused by the Great Depression, and ending with another, caused by the Second World War. I have somewhat foreshortened my description of events in 1945–46, leaving a detailed account to whoever shall treat that time more as the beginning of an era than as the end of one.

In the final version I have pared down my footnotes considerably. They once included much explanatory material on the documents in question: the language in which they were composed, the degree of secrecy intended, their state of revision, and state of preservation. All this I have stricken, in favor of the blanket explanations that follow.

About two-thirds of the letters and cables by Filipinos are in

English, and about one-third in Spanish. A scattering are in Taga-log, especially those by Generals Aguinaldo and Ricarte. One may assume that all documents cited to Japanese authors are in Japanese unless otherwise stated.

A large proportion of documents in all languages were sent in code, or under injunction of various degrees of secrecy. These in-clude most American military, naval, and diplomatic messages and planning papers; most captured documents of the Japanese Min-istry of Foreign Affairs; some communications of the Bureau of Insular Affairs; and most of the cables exchanged between Filipino missions in Washington with leaders in Manila. I have chosen not to indicate where each document lay on the scale of "confidential" to "super secret," since the context usually suggests the degree of sensitivity and importance of the message.

The Quezon Collection posed a special problem in research be-cause many documents had been damaged by water or white ants; others had interesting histories of revision and duplication. I have cut all explanatory matter of this kind from the footnotes, as being more fully and properly the function of future editors of the Quezon papers.

I have silently corrected some errors of grammar and punctua-tion—again, mostly Quezoniana—because I preferred to convey uncluttered the substance of his thought. On a few occasions, where letters report conversations, I have put indirect discourse into direct quotation.

As I wrote and rewrote, I looked forward to the time when I could thank a few of the many who have helped me with this work. A Fulbright grant provided me with shelter and three square meals a day for fifteen months in the Philippines, in 1957–58. A grant-in-aid from the American Philosophical Society helped to defray the expenses of research in the Philippines and a research trip to Japan. During a leave of absence from my present position in the academic year 1961–62, a Rockefeller Foundation Grant in International Relations provided basic maintenance. Then and after, a grant from the University of Buffalo, now the State University of New York at Buffalo, helped to cover costs of translation, photoduplication, and typing.

Through the courtesy of General Courtney Whitney I was able to read in galley proof the *Reminiscences* of General Douglas

MacArthur. Although my own manuscript was then already being edited, I have made a few changes in the text and have tried to indicate in the notes major instances in which General MacArthur's story differs from, amplifies, or corroborates, the account I have given.

I am deeply grateful to the directors, librarians, and archivists of the following institutions: National Archives, Washington, D.C., especially the Social and Economic and the Legislative Branches, and, above all, Richard Maxwell of the former; the World War II Records Center, Alexandria, Va.; the Office of Naval History, Navy Department Service Center, Arlington, Va.; the Archives of the Department of State, Washington; and the Library of Congress, especially the Manuscripts Division. Also the Sterling Memorial Library of Yale University, the Michigan Historical Collections at the University of Michigan, the New York Public Library, the Buffalo and Erie County Public Library, and the Lockwood Memorial Library, State University of New York at Buffalo. Abroad: The Bureau of Public Libraries, now The National Library, Manila, especially the personnel of the Quezoniana Collection; the University of the Philippines, Filipiniana Collection; the Library of the International House, and the Kokusai Bunka Shinkokei, both in Tokyo; the Library of National Taiwan University and Taipei Provincial Library, Taiwan.

Mrs. Jenifer Louden and Mrs. Marie Coleman conscientiously and carefully typed my manuscript through its several stages. Albert Baggs assisted me in checking references and putting Japanese citations in proper style. Brenda Shelton helped in reading proof.

The late Ishikawa Kin-ichi was immensely generous in his help to my research in Japan, arranging interviews, acting as interpreter and translator, and in general as teacher, counselor, and friend.

Several other people translated documents or secondary materials for me. Above all I depended upon Mikiso Hane, of Knox College, who faithfully and ably supplied me with English versions of important documents in Japanese; I cannot thank him fully enough. Harry Nishio, of the University of Delaware, helped with Japanese books on the Philippines. I am grateful to Mrs. Elisabeth Ponafidine for translations from Russian, David I. J. Wang from Chinese, Derk T. H. Huibers from Dutch. Miss Flordelisa Kasilag and Mrs. Nelson Isada translated from Tagalog. French and Spanish I handled myself, but upon the considerable quantity in the latter language I received some help from Mr. C. del Rosario and the late Don Manuel Bernabe.

Through conversation or correspondence a great many persons contributed to my factual knowledge and the development of my point of view. I have acknowledged only a few in the essay on sources at the end of the book, these chiefly participants in the history of which I write. Others, scholars and friends, are acknowledged in footnotes, or with silent gratitude. Among friends, I must thank especially the family of Tomas B. Lichauco of Pasay City, Philippines, for kindnesses beyond naming or numbering.

Under the guidance and discipline of Samuel Flagg Bemis I first embarked on the study of Philippine-American relations and began to learn the craft of the historian. As the book grew, it benefited from a number of other readers. A. V. H. Hartendorp read the entire manuscript in a very early phase. In semifinal draft, F. A. Terry, Jr., read the Prologue and Epilogue, Julius Pratt and L. P. Curtis, Chapters 7 and 8, Father Horacio de la Costa, S.J., and Jose Lansang, Chapters 1 through 4, and E. D. Hester, Chapter 18. John M. Blum, at a time when he was himself extremely busy, took pains to show me how to cut a bulky manuscript and to straighten winding prose. G. W. Pierson, Harry J. Benda, and Carl Landé all commented helpfully on the final version.

All my translators, informants, and critics deserve credit for the merits of this work, but I lay exclusive claim to its defects.

I wish also to thank Jane Olson for her cheerful, meticulous, and instructive editing, and David Horne for editorial encouragement. Arthur Beckenstein designed the book; Charles Staurovsky provided the maps.

I am deeply grateful to my wife, Elizabeth, who has frequently discussed the book with me, the more tenderly and intelligently for not having read a blessed word of it.

Lastly I am moved to thank, in anticipation, those who, reading the book, will feel moved to write me about it. I will welcome correction of any errors in detail that may have escaped my attention. My larger hope is that others will share with me their opinions on the perspectives I have adopted and judgments I have expressed.

Theodore Friend

Buffalo, New York
1 August 1964

Contents

Illustrations

Frontispiece. Filipino guerrilla returns to his home in Leyte, 1944, attached to an American unit. Courtesy of National Archives (U.S. Office of War Information, 208-AA-289-B-1)

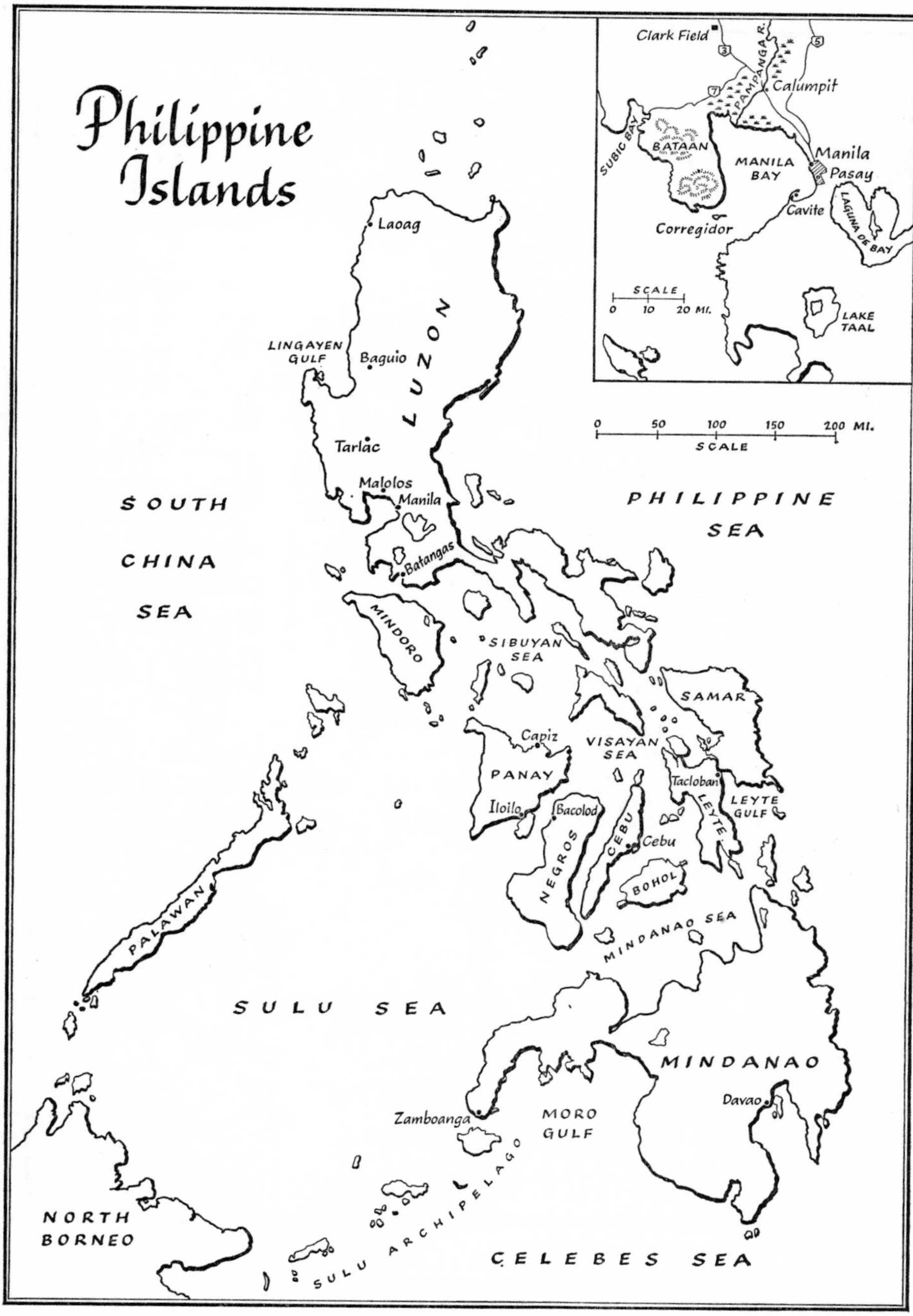

Philippine Islands
Clark Field
PAMPANGA R.
Calumpit
SUBIC BAY
BATAAN
MANILA BAY
Manila
Pasay
Cavite
LAGUNA DE BAY
Corregidor
SCALE
0 10 20 MI.
LAKE TAAL
Laoag
LUZON
LINGAYEN GULF
Baguio
Tarlac
Malolos
Manila
Batangas
0 50 100 150 200 MI.
SCALE
SOUTH CHINA SEA
PHILIPPINE SEA
MINDORO
SIBUYAN SEA
SAMAR
Capiz
VISAYAN SEA
PANAY
Tacloban
LEYTE
LEYTE GULF
Iloilo
Bacolod
NEGROS
CEBU
Cebu
BOHOL
MINDANAO SEA
PALAWAN
SULU SEA
MINDANAO
Davao
Zamboanga
MORO GULF
SULU ARCHIPELAGO
NORTH BORNEO
CELEBES SEA

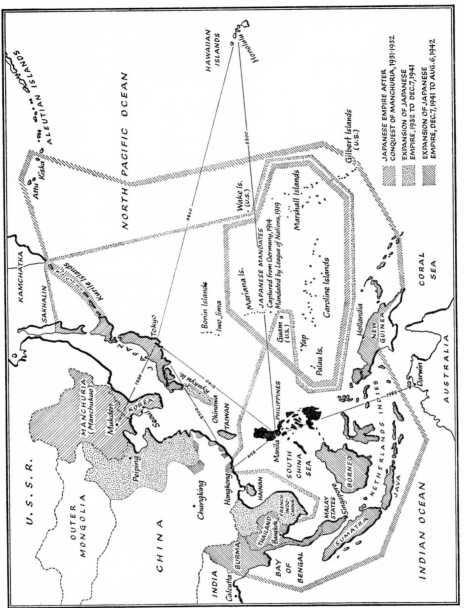

Japanese Expansion in Asia and the Pacific, 1931–42.

Abbreviations

BIA   Files of the Bureau of Insular Affairs, War Department; Social and Economic Branch, National Archives, Washington, D.C.

Cong Rec   *Congressional Record*

FDR   Archives of the Franklin D. Roosevelt Memorial Library, Hyde Park, New York

For Rel   *Papers Relating to the Foreign Relations of the United States* (Washington, United States Government Printing Office)

Gaimushō   Captured Japanese documents; microfilm reel numbers as in Cecil H. Uyehara and Edwin G. Beal, *Checklist of Archives in the Japanese Ministry of Foreign Affairs, Tokyo, Japan, 1868–1945* (Washington, Photoduplication Service, Library of Congress, 1954)

H   Papers of Joseph Ralston Hayden, Michigan Historical Collections, University of Michigan

HC   Records of the Office of the United States High Commissioner to the Philippine Islands; Social and Economic Branch, National Archives, Washington, D.C.

HLS   Papers of Henry L. Stimson, Sterling Memorial Library, Yale University

House Ins   Hearings of the House of Representatives, Committee on Insular Affairs

JPL   Papers of Jose P. Laurel, Laurel Memorial Museum, Lyceum of the Philippines

O/Q   Papers of Sergio Osmeña, 1944–46, in the Quezoniana Collection, National Library, Manila

Q   Papers of Manuel Quezon, Quezoniana Collection, National Library, Manila

SD   Archives of the Department of State, Washington, D.C.

Sen Terr   Hearings of the Senate Committee on Territories and Insular Affairs

WCF   Papers of W. Cameron Forbes, Manuscripts Division, Library of

Congress, Washington, D.C. All journal references are to the "Journals, Second Series"

ABBREVIATIONS of military terms and titles follow those used by the Office of the Chief of Military History, Department of the Army, in its multivolume History of the United States Army in World War II. Some of the most frequent:

CG   Commanding General
CinC Commander-in-Chief
CNO   Chief of Naval Operations
CofS Chief of Staff
GB   General Board, United States Navy
JB   Joint Board of the Army and Navy
JPC   Joint Planning Committee of the Joint Board
WPD   War Plans Division

Prologue

IMPERIALISM tends to be vicious; nationalism, vulgar. The greater the difference in color, culture, and wealth between the ruler and the ruled, the greater tend to be the misunderstandings ensuing from conquest. The afterimage of recent imperial relationships between rich whites and poor colored peoples has been on the one part condescending, on the other sharply resentful, in most cases with the particularly obsessive quality of a parent-child relationship which both know to be a failure.

One of the least disturbed of post-imperial relationships has been that between the United States and the Philippines, despite a normal history of hypocrisy and misunderstanding in both the strong and the weak. In the Philippines the United States had the good fortune to inherit a colony already partly westernized by the Spanish. Having Christianity in common, even though it differed in kind, helped mitigate, for Filipinos, the cultural shock of conquest. Both countries were also fortunate in that the United States did not need the Philippines economically and could govern with some measure of disinterest.

Thus the question of independence, elsewhere a matter of grievous dispute on principle, was for the United States and the Philippines only a question of "when?" Having fought against the Spanish, 1896–98, and against the Americans, 1899–1902, the Philippines had made clear that, unlike Hawaii and Puerto Rico, it preferred to rule itself. At the same time, conquest troubled American conscience, for anti-imperial sentiment in the United States was deeper and more continuous than in other great Western powers.

Lowering the American and raising the Filipino flag would eventually satisfy the sense of national honor of both countries. In the meantime, however, other senses demanded satisfaction. American officials were unwilling to leave the job of developing a self-governing and relatively self-sufficient nation until they thought the task satisfactorily advanced—until trained Filipinos would make sure that independence meant further progress instead of retrogression. The Filipino leaders themselves were, in private and sober moments, unwilling to let America withdraw until it appeared that the islands would continue economically stable and strategically secure.

All these conditions, objective and emotional, helped give to Philippine-American relations a continuity and stability considerably exceeding those of other colonial relationships in Asia. The history of the Philippine-American partnership consists of peaceful steady growth between two traumas—the Spanish-American War and the Second World War. Broken down chronologically, the story takes on seven phases:

1) 1896–1902: The Philippine wars of revolution against Spain and the United States.

2) 1901–13: "Americanization" of government and education under Republican administrations.

3) 1913–21: "Filipinization" of the civil service and encouragement of nationalism under Democratic administration.

4) 1921–29: Gradual achievement of equilibrium between native ambition and imperial restraint.

5) 1929–35: The first colonial crisis: the Great Depression, Japanese expansion, and Philippine nationalism move Congress to set a schedule for independence.

6) 1935–41: The era of the Commonwealth: uncertain and fractionally successful preparation for independence.

7) 1941–46: The second colonial crisis: invasion and partial "Japanization," followed by American liberation and the final achievement of Philippine sovereignty.

These phases may be crudely divided into periods of gestation (the first four phases) and of birth (the last three). This book will confine itself to the birth phases, during which the Philippines suffered most acutely the pangs of struggling through to sovereign independence. But to understand the difficult emergence of the Philippine nation, it is important to look briefly first at the period in which it took nourishment from security: the political, economic, and military patterns of 1901–29 that affected ensuing years.

THE CRITERIA for independence first came under scrutiny during the administration of President Wilson, who had overcome his Anglophile conservatism in the campaign of 1912 and taken the anti-imperial position of the Democratic party. Before that, American officials with Filipino assistance had organized and staffed a modern government, modernized most of the old Spanish legal codes, introduced a modern currency system, and taken a systematic census. They had begun a sweeping system of popular education. They had inaugurated a public health service. They had undertaken a public works program, which included building schoolhouses, developing artesian wells, and providing irrigation facilities; making roads, bridges, and port improvements; erecting markets and various public buildings. They had brought under "sympathetic control" the pagan tribes of Northern Luzon and the Muslims of Mindanao and Sulu. They had separated church from state and had purchased for the public domain church lands, which valuable estates, in the hands of the friars, had been a cause of the revolution against Spain.[1] They had quickly set up local and provincial elective governments, and as early as 1907 conducted elections to the National Assembly.

Apparently believing that the achievements of 1901 to 1913 were enough, Wilson's governor general, Burton Harrison, sought to turn them over to native management. He rapidly Filipinized the civil service, the cabinet, and even his own office, by yielding some of its prerogatives to Sergio Osmeña and Manuel Quezon, the two foremost native leaders. But in 1921, after Harrison's eight years in office, the health and wealth of the islands were both in grave danger: cholera and smallpox epidemics had broken out, and the Philippine National Bank, through corruption and mismanagement, was almost bankrupt.

The policy of Leonard Wood, Harrison's Republican successor (1921–27), was to restore the level of stability, efficiency, and honesty that Harrison's Republican predecessors had achieved. This Wood did, although not always diplomatically. His frequent tactless-

1. As summarized by Joseph Ralston Hayden, "The United States and the Philippines: A Survey of Some Political Aspects of Twenty-Five Years of American Sovereignty," *Annals of the American Academy of Political and Social Science*, 122 (1925), 29–32.

ness contributed to the storm of nationalism Manuel Quezon raised
against him. When Wood declared that the Filipinos not only were
unprepared for, but did not want, independence, Quezon's legislature passed a bill providing for a national plebiscite on the question. Wood's veto only contributed further to his reputation for
delaying the day of Philippine sovereignty.

Although Wood deserved his reputation, the Filipino leaders themselves were secretly afraid of their own slogan, "Immediate, absolute, and complete independence." In 1916 Congress came close to
passing the Clarke amendment, which would have made the Philippines independent in two to four years. Quezon, who had lobbied
for it in Washington, apparently went to bed sick with anxiety,
while Osmeña, who had supported it in Manila, was reportedly
trembling with fear.[2] Catholic prelates, fearing disorder in the
Philippines, rallied Northeastern Democrats against the measure.
The latter, deserting their party, beat the amendment in the House,
and incidentally saved Filipino leaders from the responsibilities of
premature independence.

When next a measure for independence made headway in Congress, the Fairfield Bill of 1924, Quezon and Osmeña themselves
starved it with indifference. Although Washington knew them to
have killed the bill's chances,[3] the Nacionalista party kept its major
issue alive. Quezon could declaim that he would "prefer a government run like hell by Filipinos to one run like heaven by Americans."[4] Frequently, however, he seemed to prefer the popularity
that accrued from criticizing foreign rulers to the responsibility of
replacing them. "Damn the Americans," Quezon exclaimed to a
friend. "Why don't they tyrannize us more?"[5]

2. Concerning Quezon's prostration: Roy Watson Curry, "Woodrow Wilson and
Philippine Policy," *Mississippi Valley Historical Review*, 41 (1954), 435–52, esp.
p. 448; concerning Osmeña's trembling: Quezon to Harrison, 2 July 33 (Q), referring to a conversation of the latter with the former. See also "BIA Confidential
Diary Notes, Jan. 31–May 11, 1916, During Discussion of the Clarke Amendment"
(HC).
3. Positive evidence for this statement, not offered in any of the standard sources on
the period: Gen Frank McIntyre (Chief, BIA) to Wood, 3 June 24 (Q); file on
Independence Mission, 1923–25 (HC); and author's interview with Sen Claro Recto,
4 Sept 58.
4. A provincial speech of 1926, quoted by Teodoro M. Kalaw in his MS autobiography (Collection of Sen Maria Kalaw Katigbak).
5. Interview with Gen Carlos Romulo, 27 Dec 56.

By 1916 the Filipinos had obtained complete control of the legislative branch from the Americans; yet Quezon and Osmeña evaded settlement of the independence question and chose to live on the issue rather than to live with the reality. Although their people were certainly growing in capacity for self-government, other aspects of Philippine development remained flawed and unsure.

WHILE THE PHILIPPINES moved straight ahead toward greater political autonomy, American economic policies worked at cross purposes: some prompted self-reliance and others fostered dependence. The result was an uncertain and unimpressive development of the Philippine economy.

Congress had early passed land and corporation laws that made it difficult for foreign capital, including American, to build large plantations or cartels within the islands. Anti-imperialists interested in protecting Filipinos had joined with sugar, tobacco, and other interests anxious to protect themselves from prospective Philippine competition.

When the Filipinos obtained complete legislative power they jealously guarded these laws, as insurance against powerful homegrown lobbies opposed to independence. American progressivism, with its conservation and trust-busting movements, would continue to affect the Philippines until after independence, when the concern for economic growth began to catch up with the fear of monopoly.

The budget of the insular government, like the land and corporation laws, reflected more concern for native than for foreign interests. Because the insular government intended ultimately to extinguish itself, it spent relatively little money on bureaucratic apparatus; the cost of civil administration in the Philippines, relative to total expenditure, was less than that of any European colony in Southeast Asia, and also less than that of independent Siam.

Concomitantly, the amount of money the Philippine budget allotted for "social services"—for education and health—was higher, as a proportion of total expenditure, than in British Malaya or French Indo-China and nearly three times greater than in the Netherlands East Indies.[6] The Filipinos welcomed these American policies, which put insular taxes more into building up native literacy and

6. Earl B. Schwulst, "Report on the Budget and Financial Policies of French Indo-China, Siam, Federated Malay States, and the Netherlands East Indies," Apr 1931, Philippine Manuscript Reports, 1931 (BIA).

longevity than into supporting a foreign bureaucracy and military establishment.

While promoting Philippine self-reliance with one hand, American policy nevertheless furthered dependence with the other. While calling for an "Open Door" policy in China, the United States followed a "Closed Door" policy in the Philippines. By 1913 colony and mother country were on terms of reciprocal free trade, and tariff barriers thereafter minimized the role of other powers in commerce with the Philippines.

By 1930, 63 per cent of Philippine imports came from the United States and 79 per cent of Philippine exports went there. Reciprocal free trade drastically limited Philippine ability to protect native manufacturing and radically stimulated a taste for American consumer goods. Money which might have gone, in a more austere culture, into capital investment, instead went into luxuries and prestige purchasing. The importing habits of the Filipinos would make economic independence always difficult to obtain, and their exporting habits even weakened the desire for political independence. Concentrating as they did on profitable agricultural exports, especially sugar, coconut oil, and hemp, and relying as they did on American buyers, many Filipino investors began to grow wary of independence unless it could be connected with continued free trade.

In addition to creating these patterns of dependence, American policy was partly responsible for two other weaknesses in the Philippine economy. In comparison with the rest of colonial Southeast Asia, the Philippines was not significantly built up in roads and railroads, in airports and seaports, in all kinds of communication and transportation.[7] This lesser emphasis on public works was partly a function of the greater emphasis on health and education and therefore not seriously disturbing to most Filipinos.

Filipinos were concerned, however, about increasing competition from Oriental minorities. The Chinese community, better protected under American law and policy than under Spanish, grew steadily more numerous and prosperous. Japanese, almost nonexistent in Spanish times, had entered early in the twentieth century by invitation from the American colonial administration and had grown into a significant community by the end of the First World War. To

7. So, at least, Gov Gen Dwight F. Davis reported after a survey tour, in an address 14 Apr 31, Manila Hotel, Philippine Manuscript Reports, 1931 (BIA).

Americans, accustomed to absorbing immigrants, a plural society
was not necessarily incompatible with equal opportunity. To the
Filipinos, however, a plural society meant having to compete at a
disadvantage not only with an Occidental minority, mainly American, but with Orientals as well, both Chinese and Japanese.

AMERICAN MILITARY POLICY concerning the Philippines was in one
sense generous and in another, dangerous. The United States used
no insular taxes for military expenses—whereas all the European
powers did, the Dutch thereby consuming 26 per cent of colonial
revenue.[8] American taxpayers bore the entire cost of military expenses within the Philippines, including the Scouts, a regular army
force of seven thousand highly trained Filipinos. These would be
the nucleus of any independent Philippine army; in addition there
were six thousand in the Constabulary, the native police.[9]

There was no Philippine navy, no air force, and, of course, no
military-industrial complex. "Independence" had barely any military dimension at all, in the Philippine mind or the American. Imperial powers were not in the habit of outnumbering themselves
with large complements of native troops; and, after the last guerrillas
had surrendered early in the century, the Filipinos themselves had
reverted to their normally pacific ways of thinking. Unless the
United States someday launched a program, the Philippines would
become independent with virtually no defensive capacity of its
own.

Less excusable and more ominous, the islands were admittedly
indefensible even under the American flag. Only five thousand American troops were based in the islands, and the Asiatic Fleet consisted
mainly of a few destroyers and submarines. Ever since Japan's victory over Russia in 1905, the United States faced a potential Oriental
foe with increasing power and uncertain designs. Discrimination
against Japanese immigrants in California upset diplomatic relations in 1906 and periodically thereafter.

With only one-third of the Navy in the Pacific and no major base
in the Philippines, Theodore Roosevelt, who had been strongly for
annexing the islands, changed his mind. They had become "our heel
of Achilles . . . all that makes the present situation with Japan dan-

8. Schwulst report, 1931 (BIA).
9. These and subsequent figures are for 1926; W. Cameron Forbes, *The Philippine
Islands, 1* (Boston, Houghton Mifflin, 1928), 192, 227.

gerous." [10] From then on Roosevelt favored independence. Since the United States would not fulfill Admiral Mahan's "large policy" with a bigger navy and more bases, there was no choice but to return to a "small policy" and to recoil from dangerous exposure in the Philippines.

Roosevelt said, "It is at best foolish and at worst criminal not to correlate policy and armament." [11] Yet all the Republican administrations of the 1920s fell into precisely that error. They subscribed to naval limitations in the Washington treaties that left the islands vulnerable; and even after Congress passed exclusion laws, aggravating poor relations with Japan, Coolidge emphasized the indefinite retention of the Philippines rather than ultimate independence.

The danger from Japan might have been eased in either of two ways. Building up troops and armaments might have made the Philippines what Leonard Wood wishfully called it, the "spearhead of the great Christian effort" [12] in the Orient. As an alternative, Filipinization of the government with a program of economic adjustment might have made the Philippines truly a "showcase of democracy." The United States instead hung in between, unwilling yet to free the Philippines, unready still to defend it.

In SUM: while committing some errors of its own in the Philippines, the United States in its first thirty years there had avoided most of the grosser errors of European imperial powers elsewhere. Many latifundia from the Spanish period remained, but new land and corporation laws prevented further development of the public domain in plantation style. American business learned to adjust to the small-plot psychology of the Filipinos and to build profitable sugar and pineapple enterprises without land monopolies. The War Department and the insular administration successfully opposed plans to split off Mindanao and Sulu for rubber plantations like those of Sumatra and Malaya; they also rejected proposals for the massive importation of Chinese laborers.

For such negative accomplishments the Filipinos in general could

10. Roosevelt to Taft, 21 Aug 07; Elting Morison, ed., *The Correspondence of Theodore Roosevelt*, 5 (8 vols. Harvard University Press, 1951), 762.
11. Roosevelt to Cameron Forbes, 23 May 16, ibid., 8, 1044–45.
12. For instance: Wood to Hermann Hagedorn, 8 July 25, Hagedorn, *Leonard Wood, A Biography*, 2 (2 vols. New York, Harper and Bros., 1931), 466. Wood's successor, Henry Stimson, liked the phrase and also used it.

be grateful: no encouragement of great estates, as in Indochina; no assistance to Muslim separatism, as in India; no wave of coolie labor flooding the country, as in Burma and Malaya; no government opium concession, symptom of social decadence and symbol of imperial hypocrisy in Indonesia, Indochina, and the Malay States.

Imperialism has brought many underdeveloped areas in touch with the modern world, but frequently with such attendant repression that little or no gratitude survived the departure of foreign sovereignty. The French in Indochina, for instance, punished nationalist agitation in 1930 with 3,000 arrests, 546 sentences for life, and 699 executions without trial.[13] Even the British, comparatively permissive, in the years 1930–33 convicted perhaps 120,000 Indians for various kinds of civil disobedience. During the same period, Gandhi himself spent two years in jail,[14] while Filipino leaders enjoyed the luxury of wrangling among themselves about the precise terms of independence they would accept.

Barring the years of the Philippine-American War, whose generalized miseries and specialized atrocities compare with anything in the annals of colonialism, American rule was light and relaxed. The worst was over at the beginning, and Filipinos later could accept American rule with a minimum of distrust. That rule brought with it modernization. The Spanish empire had mostly played down or screened out advances in health and education. Under the United States, modern health services contributed to doubling the Philippine population in twenty years. Public education had increased the literacy rate from one-fifth of the population to one-half in thirty-six years. If the Philippines came to suffer from the problems of a dual economy, part traditional, part transitional, both sectors at least reflected change: the rural part became at last partly monetized, the urban part slowly industrialized.

Such progress was bound to affect the established synthesis between Filipino and Spanish culture. Popular values were becoming less familial and more national; the rhythms of Philippine life were growing less liturgical and more commercial. Devotees of the Spanish heritage complained about "merciless materialism." Don Claro Recto,

13. Joseph Buttinger, *The Smaller Dragon, a Political History of Vietnam* (New York, Praeger, 1958), pp. 436–37.
14. B. R. Nanda, *Mahatma Gandhi* (Boston, Beacon Press, 1958), p. 338, and chapters 33–39, passim.

politician-literateur and member of the Spanish Academy, summed
it up: "We have fertilized the soil of our native land with North
American guano and have rendered it unfit for the germination and
florescence of the spirit." [15]

Most Filipinos, however, were more proud of the current association with the United States than the past association with Spain.
Some were worried about their young people aspiring to service in
counting houses instead of in cathedrals, but more took readily to
the roads that Americans helped them pave. They traveled, largely
content, toward a native style of presidential democracy, with free
secular public education, a free and libertarian press, and a business
system with a strong accent on free and private enterprise.

IN THE FIRST THIRTY YEARS of American rule, 1899–1929, the Filipinos
had proceeded fastest with self-government, because that was most
in the American genius to bestow and most in their own appetite to
receive. Toward economic self-sufficiency they had accomplished
far less, because of the mixed aims of American policy and the limitations of a traditional economy. Toward a capacity for self-defense
they had made almost no progress, partly because no imperial power,
not even the United States, armed its colonies and partly because
the Filipinos were least interested in that aspect of nationhood.

Latent economic weaknesses left the Philippines vulnerable to
Japanese enterprise from within the country, and military weakness
left it vulnerable to Japanese aggression from without. In the 1920s,
the Japanese empire appeared liberal and conciliatory and had no
special designs on the Philippines.[16] The next decade, however,
would aggravate already serious issues: the threat to Japan of residual American power in the West Pacific; the insult of American
immigration laws; the frustration, to which America contributed, of
Japanese expansionist designs upon the Asian mainland.

When these questions flared up in war, the Philippines, an innocent party, would be twice ravaged by fighting. Between victory
in 1942 and defeat in 1945, Japan would try to impose upon the
Philippines still another style of life, vastly different from the Span-

15. "The Desertion of Manuel Bernabe," a prologue to Bernabe's Cantos del Tropico;
republished in Recto's Asiatic Monroeism and Other Essays (Manila, 1929), p. 118.
16. As revealed by captured Japanese Foreign Office documents, especially Gaimushō
SP 123, pp. 46–53—Hitō dokuritsu mondai (Problems relating to the independence
of the Philippines), Survey by Bureau of European and American Affairs, 31 Aug 24.

ish or the American. She would attempt to transform the Philippines
into an autocratic satrapy, with an education emphasizing obedience,
with a controlled press, and with an economy subordinated to the
needs of the Greater East Asia Co-Prosperity Sphere. The Philippines
would emerge with immense loss of life and property. Occupation,
misery, and deprivation would have injured private Hispano-Cath-
olic morality and impaired the public governmental morality taught
by Americans. Materially weakened and wounded in spirit, the
Philippines, under its own flag and in peace, would resume pursuit
of an independence that it would repeatedly redefine.

Part 1: The Philippine Context

"Onhoorbar groeit de padie"
"Silently grows the paddy"

MOTTO OF A
JAVANESE NATIONALIST

1

Division and Coherence in Philippine Society

IF A PEOPLE may be known by their statuary, perhaps the two key icons in Manila were the Rizal Monument and the Black Nazarene of Quiapo Church; they stood for other monuments, other crucifixes, all over the islands. The life-size Black Nazarene, said to have healing power, had been a special object of devotion among the poor for two centuries, perhaps because it was dark mahogany, and hence not obviously the god of fair-skinned conquerors.

The statue of Jose Rizal stood in tribute to a brilliant oculist, linguist, novelist, and nationalist. Although he had opposed violence, his books helped prepare the way for the revolution against the Spanish, who executed him in 1896. A cult of Rizal soon grew up. William Howard Taft, with other American colonial officials and some conservative Filipinos, chose him as a model hero over other contestants—Aguinaldo too militant, Bonifacio too radical, Mabini unregenerate.[1] In so doing, had the officials launched a movement or merely assisted one? In either case Rizal statuary multiplied; he appeared in scores of municipalities and became the symbol of an emerging state—moderate and constitutional. Erect and proud, the martyred hero gazed, book in hand, at an ideal future, while across the square in the church the martyred god's head hung in perpetual

1. As related to me, 7 Nov 57, by Dr Thomas McHale, who had seen the original document in the archives of Prof H. Otley Beyer, Manila.

suffering. Between them dust blew across the plaza, and boys played basketball.

Although the Black Nazarene and the Rizal Monument may have suggested things liturgical and secular which most Filipinos held in common, the tendency of American observers before independence was to make more of the divisions in Philippine society than of its inner coherence. For those divisions, however, Americans could or would not supply basic remedies; and for the tensions their own presence created they could hardly provide solutions. American imperialism was more self-critical than most, but still it tended to neglect its own deficiencies while projecting on the Philippines an exaggerated picture of that society's defects—its inability, for instance, to develop and absorb its native minorities, and its inability to compete with foreign minorities.

The leading indigenous minorities were the pagans, largely concentrated in Northern Luzon, and the Muslims of Mindanao and Sulu, whom the Spanish had labeled Moros. Both pagans and Muslims were relatively satisfied with their own ways of life and somewhat apprehensive of the Christian Filipino. The American policy of educating and integrating them was modestly successful; it established some basic contact between minorities and majority, but it could not establish trust. "We are like a calf," Moro leaders declared, "who once abandon [ed by] its mother would be devoured by a merciless lion." [2] Native minorities were fearful of America's withdrawing her sovereignty and wary of how the Christian Filipinos might then wield power. The latter, in turn, were embarrassed before the outside world at the lesser developed peoples among their own and unenthusiastic about carrying on the work of uplift where the Americans left off.

Although the Christian Filipino was content to ignore the indigenous minorities, he found it impossible to ignore the East Asian minorities who joined him by immigration. Of the pagans and Muslims he tended to be ashamed, but of the far less numerous Chinese and Japanese, he was actually afraid. Certainly these two foreign communities, often cited as threats to an independent Philippines,

2. Letter of 120 Datus (chiefs) of Lanao Province, Mindanao, to Pres Roosevelt, 18 Mar 35 (FDR). The letter was written in Arabic and translated; signed in all cases with thumbprints, in most cases with Arabic characters as well, and in a few cases in English.

did in fact contribute to its uncoordinated pluralism. Their cultural and religious practices and their economic success distinguished them from the mass of Filipinos. The Chinese rural money lender or city banker, the Japanese plantation laborer or urban retailer, all tended by their clannishness, foreign ways, and remittances abroad to draw critical attention toward themselves. Industrious and successful, protected and encouraged by Americans, they aroused Filipino envy, social discrimination, and attempts to curb by law their economic power.

The Chinese had been in the islands since early Spanish days. They were more numerous than the Japanese, outnumbering them five or six to one (80,000 or 100,000 to 16,000) in 1931. They had always intermarried readily; Filipinos visibly part-Chinese were estimated at three-quarters of a million, and many others had less Chinese blood.[3]

There had been very few Japanese until American officials invited their labor on the Benguet Road in 1905. By 1931, however, the 16,000 Japanese in the Philippines were only slightly fewer than those in Japan's Pacific mandates, twice as many as those in all British Malaya, and three times as many as those in the Netherlands East Indies.[4] The size of Japanese investments in the Philippines was only a small fraction of the investments of Chinese, but they dominated the abaca industry and nearly controlled the whole province of Davao. On a wall map of Japanese trade zones in the office of the Consul in Davao, the island of Mindanao was marked "Domestic," just like Korea and Formosa.[5]

Japanese power was growing on Luzon too, in fishing, timber, and general merchandising. Regulations against Chinese went back deep into the Spanish period. In the same spirit a long history of regulations by the Philippine legislature began under Harrison to try to control the "Japanese problem," either by closing off separately all avenues of enterprise, or by shutting down Japanese immigration altogether. American officials, however, concurred only in forbidding

3. I estimate the number of alien Chinese from several official and semi-official sources for 1931; the estimate of Chinese mestizos is from Joseph Ralston Hayden, *The Philippines: A Study in National Development* (New York, Macmillan, 1942), p. 695.
4. "Emigration from Japan to the Philippine Islands," by Leo D. Sturgeon, American Consul, Tokyo, 2 Apr 31, Box 89, MSS of Gen Frank R. McCoy, Library of Congress.
5. Naval intelligence report relayed by Director, Naval WPD to CNO, 20 Oct 31, JB 305 ser 499.

aliens to own land. Otherwise they discouraged or vetoed anti-
Japanese legislation, either to promote economic development or to
avoid offending the Japanese government. Moreover, for every Filipino who wanted to restrict the Japanese there was another who
was willing to assist; private citizens for a share of the profits served
as dummy owners; officials, well bribed, abetted Japanese enterprise despite inhibitory regulations. Such was the "Japanese problem," chronic, latent, popularly exaggerated, but actually none too
serious until the military expansion of Japan in the 1930s.[6]

Besides native minorities and those created by Oriental immigration, there were of course the Occidental communities, of which the
8700 Americans and the 4600 Spanish were the largest.[7] Although
their economic power was probably greater than that of the Orientals, years of imperialism made them more the pinnacle of the social structure than an alien enclave. They had ruled so long that
the average Filipino felt that government belonged to them rather
than to him. In a corollary way, he felt "society" belonged to them,
too. In India, the caste system tended to prescribe a man's way of
life, regardless of who ruled. But many Filipinos, despite themselves,
looked for both tradition and fashion in the manners of the Westerner. They might loathe his sahib attitude but to them he represented the Greater World. While Christian Filipinos treated their
own religious minorities with contempt and discriminated against
Oriental immigrants, they usually treated the Westerner with deference.

The major class difference in the Philippines, however, was simply
between the wealthy and the poor. The wealthy, whether urbanites
or members of the landed gentry, or both, were usually cosmopolitan
in blood. The poor, usually rural, were almost all of unmixed Filipino
blood. The imperial presence of the United States tended to accentuate the color distinctions between the two classes, to diminish educational distinctions between them, and to leave economic distinctions largely unaffected.

Color-conscious Americans tended to emphasize color discrimina-

6. A running account of Japanese-Philippine relations, and a general picture of the
"Japanese problem" is available in the correspondence, 1926–41, between the Japanese
consuls in Manila and Davao with the Ministry of Foreign Affairs in Tokyo
(Gaimushō, S 10.1.1.0–18 and S 10.1.1.0–19).
7. 1939 Census.

tion. The Spaniards had been willing to intermarry and had accordingly helped produce a range of skin colors all the way from "near white" to dark mahogany, a range at least partly correlated with wealth and education. But the American colonist, repeating the pattern of the British in America rather than the French or Spanish, seldom intermarried. The Philippine mestizo, whether his blood was partially Spanish, partially Chinese, or both, when he felt greater color discrimination from above, was more apt to pass it on down below. The better society, as many mestizos unconsciously envisioned it, was one infused with more white blood, but the American kept his blood to himself while trying to pass on his politics. Sometimes the American seemed hypocritical to the Filipino, as when he attempted to uplift the pagans and Moros (both rather dark, for the most part) and to protect the Chinese and Japanese against discriminatory legislation. How could the American criticize the divisions in Philippine society when he held himself aloof from it? How serious was the pluralism represented by Chinese and Japanese, pagan and Moro, how grave the split between upper and lower class Filipino, compared to the basic division in colonialism itself: Americans ruling, Filipinos ruled?

In a major way, however, Americans did provide a means of social mobility that had not existed in scope before. Between rural and urban areas, lower and upper classes, the United States spun the connective web of a public education system. It served to foster a small middle class and to provide Filipinos with the means of bettering self and family. Public education also helped, of course, to spread ideals of social and political democracy, but the basically authoritarian patterns of teaching, and of family and religious life, inhibited their growth.[8] The American style of education became a Philippine passion, but that passion did not necessarily extend to the American style of democracy.

After the new rulers had separated church and state, the church remained dominated by foreigners, although disestablishment indirectly assisted the growth of native Philippine churches. The secularization of the state and its Filipinization went hand in hand, and the overt power of the Spanish and predominantly Spanish mestizos declined in civil administration, as elsewhere. In sum,

8. See especially Rex Drilon et al., "Philippine Democracy Reexamined," pamphlet based on Philippine *Historical Bulletin,* 6 (Dec 1962).

American rule, intentionally and unintentionally, directly and indirectly, increased the opportunities for native Filipino talent to express itself in government and the school system, in business and even the church. Through free, popular, and secular education, the United States partially satisfied and further stimulated the great Filipino appetite for learning, and more and more Filipinos achieved the levels of competence needed to run their country.

The policies of the United States, however, contributed very little to relief of poverty, the most serious problem of all. An attack on poverty, through a program of economic development, could also have revolutionized the society. While repeatedly pointing to the inequitable distribution of Philippine income, American officials lacked a philosophy of radical improvement until the New Deal, in 1933. By then, however, the legislative power had been in the hands of Filipinos for seventeen years, and most of the legislators were medieval in philosophy: peasants were merely the perennial poor. Even had governors general or high commissioners tried to apply the distributist ideas of the New Deal, they would have been either caught short by New Deal anti-imperialism, which encouraged further diluting of what remained of American executive power in the Philippines, or frustrated by resistance from Filipino legislators, who regarded the cleavage between rich and poor as traditional and inevitable. In the late 1930s, Quezon was impressed by the land reforms of Cárdenas in Mexico, and Philippine peasants in Central Luzon began to awaken to the need for social change; but the Philippines would achieve sovereignty in 1946 without significant progress in that direction.

Partly excusing and partly compensating for this general Filipino apathy to socioeconomic reform was a social organization so strong and flexible as to insure a measure of emotional and material security for even the most badly used agricultural laborer. This social organization was common to the eight major cultural-linguistic groups in the Philippines, which comprised nine-tenths of the population.[9] Regional and linguistic differences meant a great deal to the indi-

9. Descriptive matter and statistics here and following, chiefly from *Area Handbook on the Philippines,* University of Chicago for the Human Relations Area Files; Fred Eggan, Evett D. Hester, and Norton S. Ginsburg, supervisors; preliminary edition, 1956 (hereafter, *Philippine Handbook*).

vidual, but Tagalog, Ilokano, Cebuano in common held similar ideas about land tenure, religion, and family.

More than 65 per cent of working Filipinos ten years old and over were employed in agriculture during the 1930s. Many of them owned their own land—usually small plots—and those who owned none hoped someday to do so. Land was and is the major source of wealth; it was and is a major source of social status; it was and is family-sacrosanct, passed on from generation to generation, frequently without title or probate. Parents held it in trust for their children, and only dire and exigent circumstances could persuade them to interrupt the transmission of the "patrimony." Even wealthy and citified Manilans tended to retain provincial land holdings as the source of family origin and identity, and in a partially modernized economy, investment and speculation in land continued more attractive to many of them than investment in corporations and speculation in stocks.

Nearly 80 per cent of Filipinos were Roman Catholic, despite the inroads of Protestant missionaries and nationalist schismatics of the Aglipayan and later churches. As a result of Spain's long centuries in the Philippines, Catholicism had been crucial in the formation of the Filipino's conscience and temper. Even when his understanding was shallow and his performance lax, the Filipino hungered for the periodic sense of personal renewal, the ritual life, and the community solidarity which the Church offered.

Even that mighty sinner, Manuel Quezon, came back to the Church after years as a Mason. Some scoffed that he did so for political reasons. More likely his devout and devoted wife, Doña Aurora, a prominent churchwoman, persuaded him to return, but that is no more susceptible to documentation than the other subtle influences brought to bear by women on the private and public lives of Philippine leaders. Not until the women of the Philippines campaigned for, and won, the right of suffrage, 1935–37, did their activities become in part a matter of public record. It is certain only that Quezon, ill again with tuberculosis in 1931, became a practicing Catholic after a lapse of more than twenty years.

If Quezon's was the manner of the sophisticate, it was very unlike the manner of the *tao:* to the peasant, deity was neither an abstract principle nor a useful assumption; it was personal and real. He thought of God as a wise and tolerant father and of the Virgin as a kind and loving mother. Christ he thought of above all as a sufferer, and with "the beaten, scourged, humiliated and defeated Christ" he readily identified himself.[10] The Son accompanied him in misery, the Mother comforted him in trouble, the Father understood his inner failings.

The intimacy the Filipino felt with the Holy Family was partly an expression of the supreme importance in his life of his own family.[11] He reckoned his relatives through both his father's side and his mother's. When he married and produced a child, that birth, as much as the marriage itself, united the families of father and mother. They would have several children, and that, the "nuclear family," would be the core of their life. Growing out beyond that, their relatives on both sides would constitute the "extended family," even to third and fourth cousins in faraway provinces.

This so-called "bilateral family system" of the Filipino contrasted with both the Japanese and the American. In Japan, relatives were reckoned "unilaterally," through the male line only. Thus the Japanese sense of family narrowed into loyalty to clan. Counting relatives patrilineally in time as the Japanese did, rather than bilaterally in space, may also have helped account for their sense of history, greater than the Filipinos', and for their lesser adaptability to democracy.

At another remove, the Filipino family system contrasted with the American, which was also bilateral, but greatly affected by industrialization, urbanization, geographical mobility, and high standard of living. Corporate demands and community activities washed out the extended American family; the same pressures, plus self-reliant individualism, weakened even the nuclear American family. The Filipino family, stronger to begin with, had far less to contend against and remained the basic institution in almost every area of Philippine life.

Small wonder, then, that both Japanese and American overlords should have chafed, during their separate periods of dominion and in their separate ways, at the conservative localism of the Filipino,

10. *Philippine Handbook*, pp. 663–64.
11. The ensuing analysis of the family system is based chiefly on Carl Landé, "Politics in the Philippines," doctoral dissertation, Harvard, 1958, Ch. 4; and *Philippine Handbook*, pp. 415 ff. My own researches and observations account for differing emphasis and expression.

and his corresponding lack of a sense of nation. His sense of family spread out and stopped with kin; it did not reach up to a symbolic national father in a divine emperor. His sense of community tended to be coterminous with his sense of family; it did not reach out to an organization which afforded him a living or to a state which supplied him protection. For most Filipinos the family itself was his fraternity, sorority, and social security; it was Rotary Club, and Old Folks' Home; it was sometimes a closed-shop union, frequently a business, and always in part a government. Land was a family trust, wealth was family-shared, and religion family-centered. The family provided for all members the most intimate satisfactions and the ultimate protections.

Nevertheless, the designs of the more ambitious men and the pleasures of the less ambitious could not be satisfied through blood kin alone. The Filipinos had accordingly developed ritual and affinitive means of expanding the family to include friends, partners, employers, and those with whom one engaged or might someday engage in vital business. An institution that assisted this expansion was the Catholic practice of godparenthood. At the great ritual occasions of youth—baptism and confirmation—the parents were canonically required to select an adult sponsor of the same sex as the child. In actual practice, many Filipinos made marriage another occasion for choosing sponsors. At each of these occasions, furthermore, they chose not one or two but several functionaries, submerging the religious purpose in the family purpose—to expand one's kin.

The closest relationship which thus developed was not a tutorial one between child and godparent but a fraternal one between parent and godparent. The familial structure of Philippine emotions caused the Filipino to feel—and the feeling was reciprocal—a tie not only with the sponsors he selected—his *compadres* and *comadres*, co-fathers and co-mothers of his children—but with their brothers, sisters, and spouses, as well as his own brothers' and sisters' spouses. The possibilities of multiplying his kin were extraordinary. If he had five children and on each of the three ritual occasions he chose four sponsors, each of whom was one of a separate family of four, and each married, he had theoretically added to his kin by ritual bond a total of four hundred and eighty people of his own generation. Such a giant proliferation was unlikely for several reasons: choosing sponsors among existing blood kin, repetition of selections, overlapping of relatives, and so forth. But it is in any event clear that the extended Filipino family was by *compadrazgo* further extended.

The family also grew in less formal ways. Friendship among Filipinos was tentative and uncertain unless ritualized. If it were not ritualized in church, then it was by secular familiarities. Pet nicknames, references to a common town of origin, to a school mutually attended, or to an important event shared were all part of daily reintroduction to acquaintances. The same might be true in the West, but without the special urgency felt by the Filipino to establish a quasi-kin bond. By blood, by rite, by ritualized affinity, the Filipino knew his kin; they made up his "we"; and those outside of it were "they"—enemies, neutrals, and persons of no significance.

Philippine social psychology was in large part family psychology. Probably the most important idea in the Filipino's dealings with others was the idea of self-esteem—his own, his family's; that of the other man and his family. Reciprocal concern for "face" was characteristic not only of Chinese and Japanese; all major Philippine languages contain words expressing the same idea. Even where the words are absent, in some of the minor languages, the people tend to express by other means the same feelings. The emotional set and the vocabulary of the average Filipino required him to feel and to say, in particular situations and to particular people, "I am ashamed *to you*." Although he might feel it, he did not say, "I am ashamed *of myself*."

Both sensitivity and shame were expressed in the Tagalog word *hiya*. A person who had none (*walang hiya*) was one with "a thick face" (*makapal ang mukha*) and was much despised. Much admired, contrariwise, was the person who exhibited both sensitivity on his part and delicacy in respect to all whose reputations were touched by his actions. The creditor reluctant to collect an overdue debt from a friend, the supervisor unwilling to discharge an incompetent employee, the tenant embarrassed at too many presents from his landlord, even the child who was shy with an adult stranger—all showed proper *hiya*. Concern for the self-esteem of friends, respect for the standing of inferiors, keeping up appearances with superiors, and tentativeness with non-kin—all were examples of virtue mixed with wisdom—virtue in that one demonstrated *hiya* appropriate to one's family, and wisdom in that one forebore wittingly or unwittingly to trespass upon, or in any way diminish, the *hiya* of another family.

Another crucial concept was *utang na loob,* or "debt of honor." One who accepted from another a significant unsolicited gift or service was understood not only to be under obligation to return the favor, but also to have entered into a running reciprocal relationship in which each party had reasonable call upon the time, energies, and worldly goods of the other. To maintain *hiya,* one had to live up to the expectations incurred through *utang na loob.* These feelings accounted for some of the special intensity of personal relationships among Filipinos, and for some of the peculiar quality of the Filipino-American colonial relationship as well. Did the United States deeply affect the Filipinos with generous policies of schooling their young? Then the Filipinos owed a debt of gratitude, and would help Americans resist the invading Japanese. Did the Filipinos not fulfill their role in the contract of honor by fighting with General MacArthur on Bataan? Then why did the United States not reinforce them with ships and planes and men? And why did it not insist, after the war, in obtaining for the Philippines a large reparations settlement from their common enemy, Japan? Thus the ideas of *utang na loob* and *hiya* conflicted with the Benthamic calculus or the Hamiltonian analysis that the United States customarily practiced in domestic and foreign policy, and tried also to apply in colonial affairs.

For the rural and small-town Filipino, and even for the modern Manilan, social status and moral stature were always in the balance together. The seat of judgment was not in heaven but in society. To be held in shame was condemnation, and to be held in honor was acquittal. Such was the social context in which American colonial officials tried to encourage a responsible two-party system and to develop a government with a progressive sense of the public interest. Such was the context in which Japanese officials would later try to erase political factionalism and establish a Japanese style of social efficiency.

2

Division and Coherence in Philippine Politics

SINCE THE DAYS of Rizal, perceptive Filipinos had been worried that their people lacked a sense of national community. They would continue to worry long after achieving independence, but at least they could point to the emergence, long before independence, of a national political life which expressed native values while still meeting some American norms.

The Philippine political party was unideological and only loosely institutionalized, tending to form around charismatic persons rather than special programs. Like the family, it was open and flexible, construed by each individual as his kin ties and personal proclivities suggested. The process by which a man became a party leader was similar to that by which he became a family patriarch. A man of relative wealth and wisdom, through concern for and submission to the needs of his relatives, might earn himself a kind of distinction as "acting patriarch," but as the power was earned, it might be lost, to someone who promised more for the family welfare.

A politician, likewise, built a personal following in which popularity, patronage, and pork barrel were important and, no less, the wealth in his own hands, or the hands of helpful friends. He carried the vote by rearing a pyramid of personal affection and kinship security, and debts of gratitude, from a broad base upward to himself.[1]

1. Carl Landé, "Politics in the Philippines," Ch. 5; Willis Sibley, "Leadership in a Philippine Barrio," *Philippine Journal of Public Administration, 1* (1957), 154–59. These tendencies have become more pronounced since 1946.

Other politicians, however, might try to erect their own pyramids by the same means, out of some of the same families and groups; hence the constant subliminal courtship between the politician and his public.

If in these ways the party resembled the extended Filipino family, at its core there was always a "nuclear family." This inner circle of leaders might be torn between two sentiments: *tayo-tayo*, and its nemesis, *amor propio*. The first—"just among us"—was an intimate and fraternal feeling of cohesion. The second, the self-love of one or another among the group, might often threaten the first. One bound all together in an artificial family; the other, just because the family was artificial, might split any one person apart from any other, or several others.[2]

On a given crucial issue before the public, there usually existed two extended political "families," interlocking and overlapping. The very need for a decision brought out old antagonisms and new affections which could split and change even the "nuclear families" at the cores of the parties. The question was not resolved until one family had grown strong enough to overbear the other. In the meantime, interminable maneuvering, parrying, declaring, and denouncing surrounded and submerged the question, while the principals seemed to delay or even avoid its solution and the public enjoyed the agitation. Courtship of key people and bidding for pivotal affections are commonplaces of democratic politics the world over—but the Philippine family system brought them out with unusual intensity.

In manner as in structure, Philippine politics resembled family life. Winning friends, absorbing them as kin, was like winning neutrals and opponents, absorbing them in party. A complex diplomacy, the use of go-betweens and emissaries, an elaborate politeness and generous hospitality were as much part of wooing political allies as of wooing personal friends. Because it was hard to separate the familial from the personal, it was difficult to separate the political from either. To work with a friend was pleasant and reassuring; one

2. For these observations, developed out of many conversations with him, I am indebted to Jose Lansang. I distinguish between *hiya*, a complex of sentiments of collective as well as personal self-esteem, and *amor propio*, a far more individual sentiment. The latter, a Spanish term, is more pronounced in the Hispanic mestizo, with his highly developed personal ambition and stage presence.

could not work at all with "one of them" until he had been made "one of us."

No case illustrates the point better than that of the proud and gifted Claro Recto. His amor propio caused him generally to prefer leading a hopeless minority to following a strong majority. In a three-way split in 1922, his Democratas held the balance of power, but they allied neither with the Osmeña nor the Quezon factions of the Nacionalistas and were eventually squeezed out of prominence. Recto was close to Quezon but not to his followers; he was close to Osmeña's men while estranged from their leader. He therefore went his own way with the Democrata party until it almost faded from sight. When he recalled the crisis years later, no factors of imperial or domestic politics appeared to him as vivid or as moving as his emotional affinities.[3]

Later, in 1931, Recto ran against Jose Laurel, a Nacionalista, for the Senate seat in the Batangas-Tayabas district. He needed, he felt, to modify the implicit challenge his candidacy presented to Quezon, the other senator from the same district; he thought he might even win with Quezon's secret support. Recto therefore wrote Quezon, trying to insert a wedge into the Nacionalista triumvirate. Everyone grants, he said, that if the election were held now, "I would hold a substantial majority over Laurel. Roxas and Osmeña hope to change this climate of opinion with your moral influence. I firmly hope you will send letters and cables presenting to your friends the question of trust." Whom could Quezon trust more—the charming Recto, whom he affectionately called "paysano," or the austere Juris Doctor from Yale whom he called only "Dr. Laurel"? Recto reminded Quezon of their mutual friends and their personal friendship. "The stars and the asteroids," he declared, "live in the perfect harmony of the Universe. I believe, therefore, that in my case, you will give to friendship and the party of the opposition what is due them, and to your political colleague (*correligionario politico*) what is due him." Was Quezon sick? Might he forbear for reasons of health from influencing the contest? "The Cid won battles even after death, and you are only ill."[4]

Quezon was not persuaded to undercut Laurel and the principle

3. Interview with Don Claro Recto, 7 Nov 58.
4. Recto (Manila) to Quezon (Monrovia, Calif.), 24 Mar 31 (Q).

of party regularity.[5] Even so, Recto won all but a few towns and the haciendas of the Zobel and Roxas families, which delivered the vote as Quezon asked. Quezon consoled Laurel: "Even I could not have beaten Recto in this campaign." In the great showdown of 1933 Quezon went to great lengths to deal Recto over to his side. Laurel, emotionally more attuned to Osmeña's style than Quezon's, moved away from Quezon to Osmeña's side, where he ever after remained. As for Recto, the one brief period in his life in which he enthusiastically dropped the role of Olympian oppositionist began when Quezon made him majority leader of the Senate in 1933. At the conclusion of the maneuvering, Recto composed a prose poem in praise of the only man he ever truly acknowledged as his leader.[6]

As Recto's career shows, and Laurel's, the Filipino politician cherished in his friends not their principles but their proximity; he valued them less for their convictions than for their affections. The company he found himself among meant more than the side of an issue they took. The absorption or adoption of new members into the tayo-tayo group was accompanied less by logical persuasion than by emotional persuasion; if it was successful and everyone's self-esteem was satisfied at having brought off a matter of delicacy and importance, then bursts of laughter, ebullient chatter, back-slapping, and arm-taking followed. Tayo-tayo meant conviviality. It also meant enhanced family sense and party strength, with tighter controls of the power apparatus.

On the other hand, to criticize opponents publicly was a serious matter, for the job or role of that person was not separated from his personal, his familial, and even broader considerations of face. If political necessity required it, the critic readied for all the reverberations such an assault implied. He "regretted the necessity," but once begun he was unrestrained, for the point of compromise was already past. Winning or losing mattered terribly in such instances, and how one played the game mattered much less. A frontal clash usually ended with a crowing victor and a sulking loser, for one's prestige

5. "Sa Lahat ng Manghahalal ng Ika-Limang Purok Senatorial" (To All Voters of the Fifth Senate District), a Laurel campaign pamphlet, containing a letter from Quezon to Laurel, 14 Apr 31, endorsing the latter's candidacy. The Quezon MSS also contain a large file of messages from Quezon to local and national party leaders and to key business figures, asking them to back Laurel.

6. *Philippine Magazine*, 30 (Sept 1933), 139; Recto interview, 26 Nov 58.

was enhanced, the other's face lost. Because of these dire consequences, ordinary political intercourse was inclined against decision
and for equilibrium.

In conversation, the Filipino aimed to blandish and not to shame.
He tolerated American bluntness only as a foreign idiosyncrasy, far
preferring men who could match his native *delicadeza*. For the sake
of delicacy he interspersed his talk with euphemisms, circumlocu-
tions, and protective white lies.[7] If the occasion demanded, however,
he would rise to the warm recollection, to the broad compliment,
the earnest pledge. More tactful than the American at one extreme,
he could be more reckless at the other, in *palabas*, or self-interested
exaggeration. Both tendencies are evident in a letter to Quezon from
Senator Juan Nolasco, whose impassioned and grandiose use of religious references nearly obscured the fact that he was referring to a
political showdown with Osmeña. "In the eleventh hour of the
Filipino people," he declared, "we must have a decision based on
the faith of a Moses in God, in himself, and in his people, in order
to cross the desert and the Red Sea to reach the Promised Land.
. . . The people await the Chief's decision, and desire the voice of
command, for all are ready to follow. The difficulties and dangers
of the journey matter not, for all will be saved when there is faith
in God, oneself, the people, and the sanctity of the enterprise." [8]

In American eyes, Philippine politics seemed to elevate personality
above public interest, to concentrate on the temporary and tangential
instead of the enduring and substantial. American eyes, however,
may not have been perfectly focused on the scene. Perhaps the
Filipino had a different sense of substance than the American, and
above all desired two things in a leader: charisma and consanguinity
—if not a literal blood relationship then a figurative one. If it appeared that the Filipino did not know where his interests lay, perhaps
the Westerner did not understand whence Filipino interest sprang
—from family prestige and security.

Philippine democracy, in both manner and structure, was thus a
compromise between two very different cultures, a compromise
partly planned, partly accidental, and partly inevitable. American
policy achieved very early a great change in the manner of Philip-

7. *Philippine Handbook*, pp. 350–53, 435–36.
8. Nolasco to Quezon, 21 May 33, aboard the SS *Conte Rosso* (Q).

pine nationalism, turning it from militancy to moderation, from revolutionary to constitutional means of achieving independence. The sovereign power extended its confidence to the colonized people that they could learn democracy, and the democratic aspects of Philippine society, some latent, some already potent, emerged with an answering confidence.

To this cooperation, however, there were some important limits. Leonard Wood found it necessary, for reasons not clear, always to have a white witness present when he spoke with Filipino leaders on substantive matters. His mistrust stirred a Filipino senator to remark, "I much prefer a government of compadres to a government of suspicion." [9] Wood's offense against Philippine pride at the same time stifled the sense of intimacy Filipinos needed to work well with non-kin, especially American Protestant whites, who were alien, imperial, and transient. Fortunately, Wood's successors did not perpetuate his error. Henry Stimson, a patrician, took a trusting attitude on principle and found it successful. Theodore Roosevelt, Jr., and Frank Murphy, political extroverts, took it intuitively and felt no regrets. What Dwight Davis said of Quezon was true of nearly every Filipino, in dealings with nearly any American—he was "absolutely trustworthy as long as he feels that he himself is being trusted." [10]

But how long could anyone happily struggle to cross a cultural gap in one's own country in order to win the trust of an invader? Filipinos certainly preferred a government of compadres to a government of suspicion; they even preferred it to a government of compromise with trusting foreigners. While learning the American administrative ethic, they could only look forward to the day when they need not repress or apologize for the Philippine family ethic. While learning American democratic practice, they promoted Philippine nationalist sentiment.

In political structure as in political manners, American achievements had their limits. Although colonial administrators strove to develop a viable two-party system in the Philippines, no such thing appeared until after America's withdrawal, when two national parties emerged (and once as many as four) with frequently shifting personnel. During American sovereignty, however, the very presence

9. Quoted by Acting Gov Gen Eugene Gilmore (Manila) to Henry Stimson (Washington), 3 Sept 27 (HLS).
10. Davis to Sec War, 26 Mar 31 (BIA, Quezon-P).

and pressure of imperial power inhibited the fissiparous, familial tendencies of Philippine politics. There was only one national purpose —to achieve independence; only one major political issue—diminishing the imperial restraint against achieving the national purpose. Until 1934 the paramount question debated in Philippine national politics was that of imperial restraint, most sharply symbolized by the veto power of the governor general, backed by the veto power of the President of the United States. Whether it be called the independence issue or, more accurately, the autonomy issue, national discussion boiled down to the question: Who shall head the government?

The single issue, furthermore, was almost always in the hands of a single party, the Nacionalistas, who dominated the country from the first municipal elections in 1905 until the Japanese dissolved all political parties in 1942. The Nacionalistas made it appear that to be against them was to be against independence and for imperialism. With such tactics they beat off the challenge of the Democratas in the early 1920s, the major threat from a second party.

Factionalism and internal feuding were more dangerous to the Nacionalistas. As would any two contending patriarchs in the same family, Osmeña and Quezon quarreled. Twice, in 1922 and 1933, they broke their followers into quite separate organizations. Each time, however, they reunited in coalitions—1923 and 1935. The threat of the Democratas in the first instance and the completeness of Quezon's victory in the second both suggested coalition, especially to Osmeña's less secure minority. In any case, when their own feuds were calmed, the Filipinos felt that the imperial presence of the United States required them to unite. United States officials regretted the one-party system but never took advantage of the Philippine factionalism to "divide and rule" or interfered with coalitions determined to end American rule.

The triumph of fusion over fission in Philippine politics owed a great deal to Quezon and Osmeña, whose leadership was unmatched in length and stability in any colonized country. The circumstances they were given to act upon were equally remarkable, however— the independence issue alive and useful for three dozen years, and the freedom and means to exploit the issue. The United States gave the Philippines the promise of ultimate independence and a usable version of democratic process; withholding final independence, she allowed the Filipinos to mature their own familial democracy over a full generation's time. Although Filipinos might find a two-party system impracticable until they achieved independence, and a genuine sense of national community impossible for generations to come, they rapidly developed their capacities for democracy during the American colonial period. The democracy which evolved was a complex result of native tradition and aspiration, of imperial suffrance and restraint.

3

Nationalism and Its Limits

TWENTIETH-CENTURY NATIONALISM in Southeast Asia has typically had cultural and economic beginnings. The Young Men's Buddhist Associations, in Burma, and Sarekat Islam, in Indonesia, are illustrative cases. The Filipinos, however, directed their cultural and economic nationalism more against Oriental minorities than against Occidental rulers: against Chinese and Japanese rather than Spanish and American.

Having absorbed Christianity from one conqueror, the Filipinos accepted it in the next; and they were also eager to make the most of the opportunities Americans provided for secular education. Some Filipinos doubted American good faith concerning the economy—one journalist attacked a colonial official who prospected for gold with an editorial entitled "Birds of Prey," and a prominent playwright dwelt upon the symbolic shooting of an eagle. But these publicists, and political orators like them, did not capture the imagination of the majority.[1] Instead, conservative leaders of the middle and upper classes seized hold of nationalism early in the century, won the confidence of the masses, and never surrendered the issue or their following. "By carrying out a successful fight for independ-

1. The playwright, Tolentino, *Yesterday, Today, and Tomorrow;* the editor, Fidel Reyes, "Birds of Prey," in *El Renacimiento,* concerning Commissioner Dean C. Worcester; the orators, Dominador Gomez and Crisanto Evangelista.

ence they deprived the radicals of the opportunity to associate capitalism with colonialism, and socialism with patriotism in the minds of the people." [2]

Only in the 1950s, after independence, would the prime expression of Philippine nationalism become cultural and economic. Before that, during the decades of American rule, as in the last years of the Spanish, Philippine nationalism was chiefly social and political. [3]

In the early years of American rule, many prominent Filipinos, some of whom had once wished to become a province of Spain, like Morocco, desired statehood in the American union. The American Commission discouraged them, however, and when they took their plea to Washington, Elihu Root with a few words turned most of them into nationalists: "Gentlemen, [he said] I don't wish to suggest an invidious comparison, but statehood for Filipinos would add another serious race problem to the one we have already. The Negroes are a cancer in our body politic, a source of constant difficulty, and we wish to avoid developing another such problem." [4]

So confronted, the Philippine Federalista party and its successor, the Progresista, had little chance against Nacionalistas by faith or by party affiliation. The Philippines was not acceptable as a constitutional equal of American states because Filipinos were not acceptable as the social equals of white Americans.

The act of conquering the Philippines had, in fact, signified a new high, or low, in American racism. Theories of Anglo-Saxon superiority, then in use to rationalize imperialism, were essentially similar to the racial theories used to justify white supremacy in the South. Northerners could hardly criticize a rush of Jim Crow legislation below the Mason-Dixon line when across the Pacific they were extinguishing the infant Philippine republic. As Senator Ben Tillman of Georgia declared, "The North has a bloody shirt of its own. Many thousands of them have been made into shrouds for murdered

2. Oscar Lopez, quoted by Carl Landé, "Politics in the Philippines," p. 369.
3. I am grateful to Hernando Abaya for pointing out the changing character of Philippine nationalism, and to Jose Lansang for improving my understanding of its early economic aspects.
4. Felipe Buencamino, Sr, a member of the group who confronted Root, told this story many times in the hearing of his son, Felipe, Jr, who repeated it to me in conversations of 27–28 June 58. He emphasized that the words "invidious" and "cancer" were assuredly verbatim.

Filipinos, done to death because they were fighting for liberty." [5]
Thus America, at the turn of the century: imperialism helped to fix
discrimination upon the Negro, while the Negro's status made impossible the assimilation of the Filipino.

One ex-governor general advised another, about to be inaugurated,
that in the Philippines "social recognition was more valued than
political concession." As chief executive, he should interest himself
in names, families, personal welfare; give little gifts and issue many
invitations.[6] The advice was excellent, not just because of the familial
psychology of the Filipino but because of his racial sensitivity.
Strong signs of the latter had appeared in the war against Spain,
when Tagalog revolutionaries smashed the noses of Western figures
in church and public statuary.[7] If they found the racial arrogance of
the Spaniard objectionable, they found that of the American more so.

Cameron Forbes thought that American social recognition of the
Filipinos "distinguished our administration from those of European
countries in the Orient and makes our experiment more successful," [8]
but the American period was in some ways a regression from Spanish
times. Intermarriage had once been free and frequent, but color
prejudice arrived with the first American families—teachers, missionaries, and wives of officials and businessmen. Taking a mistress was
accepted practice, but very few prominent Americans married Filipinos. Those who did, mostly footloose soldiers who stayed on after
the campaigns, were called "squawmen." [9]

Americans institutionalized their prejudices by setting up their
own clubs, schools, and even churches. The Army and Navy prac-

5. Quoted in C. Vann Woodward, *The Strange Career of Jim Crow* (2nd ed. New
York, Oxford, 1957), pp. 55–56. Hubert Howe Bancroft, historian of the Spanish-
American West, added his voice to the racism of the day, exulting in America's con-
quest of Spain, while warning against assimilation of the Filipinos. "Have we not
already absorbed enough of the base blood of Europe and the black blood of Africa?
Now we are bringing upon ourselves a horde of that hybrid population found in all
the old Spanish colonies, made up of endless intermixtures of Indians, Negroes, and
Spaniards, together with the Kanakas of Hawaii, and the Mongolians of the Asiatic
isles, with all their still lower and more degrading race intermixtures." *The New
Pacific* (New York, The Bancroft Company, 1900), p. 602.
6. W. Cameron Forbes to Theodore Roosevelt, Jr, 18 Feb 32, Journals, *4*, 237–38
(WCF).
7. Examples among wood carvings in the collection of Don Luis Araneta, Manila.
8. Forbes to T. Roosevelt, Jr, 18 Feb 32 (WCF).
9. These observations I owe to certain long-time American residents of the Philippines.

ticed discrimination, and Filipino officers found themselves better treated in the United States than in their native land. Even Forbes admitted that "sundry Americans dislike the Filipinos and yet want to do business with them. If they are rude and damn them up and down, they'll lose their business; hence they have to be polite or get out." [10] A Filipino lawyer described the cordiality of the American as ending "after business hours"; then "he makes no effort to conceal his contempt for any social intercourse. . . . To the Filipinos the real American resident is a perfect reproduction of Dr. Jekyll and Mr. Hyde." [11]

Discriminatory treatment was especially galling to prominent native politicians, businessmen, and professional men. Leaders of their own people, they found it intolerable to be slighted by overseas Americans, many of quite ordinary caliber, whose status and egos were inflated by colonial circumstances. Some Filipinos reacted by admiring the Japanese, heritors of an ancient culture and the leading Oriental power. Some even studied the Japanese chivalric code: Jorge Bocobo and Maximo Kalaw, both of whom had been *pensionados*, or fellowship students, in the United States, and Jose Laurel, who studied law at Yale and Oxford and received an honorary degree from Tokyo Imperial University in 1938. A less distinguished but more fervent example of Japanophilia was Pio Duran. Rather than be treated like Negroes by the Americans, he argued, Filipinos should consider being assimilated by Japan. "Our children's children will become citizens of the mightiest Empire or Republic in the Orient, if not the world." To those reluctant to believe him, Duran quoted Kipling about the twain never meeting.[12]

Most educated Filipinos, however, preferred to believe the contrary—that in their country East and West had met and were being reconciled. They tended to seek a social life integrated with those whose Occidental culture they shared. They had their own clubs, where they could discriminate for or against whomever they chose

---

10. Maj Vicente Lim, "The Philippine Islands—a Military Asset," Memorandum to the Commandant, The Army War College, 29 Apr 29, McCoy MSS, Box 41; Forbes Journals, 3, 307 (WCF).

11. Pio Duran, *Philippine Independence and the Far Eastern Question* (Manila, Community Publishers, 1935), pp. 148–49.

12. Ibid., pp. 152, 164. Duran was then a professor of law at the University of the Philippines; before, during, and after the war he was a lawyer for important Japanese firms. During the war he was a collaborator; after the war, a congressman.

(the famous Club Filipino, in fact, was established in order to prac- tice counter-snobbery against Westerners), but they still aspired to company in which Westerners were a majority.

From this situation grew some of the more vivid insults of the colonial era. A gentleman's agreement existed among the Westerners of the Baguio Country Club, the Manila Polo Club, and the Army- Navy Club to exclude Filipinos. As a test case, a group of responsible young Filipinos, led by Conrado Benitez, a college dean and news- paper editor, presented themselves at the Baguio clubhouse and were turned away. When they reported to Quezon, he called for pressure upon the owner of the land to cancel the club's lease unless Filipinos were admitted; and soon they were.[13]

The Polo Club was more difficult. Founded in 1909 by Cameron Forbes and men of all racial backgrounds who were interested in the imperial sport, its membership had soared over the years as it became popular for swimming and tennis, bridge and bar. British and Amer- icans dominated the board of directors, outnumbering Philippine- born Spanish, like the aristocratic Elizaldes, who found the others "very mediocre people, certainly not of the better type of Americans here." The majority of the board tended to discriminate against any not of their own ilk. Strong support from the Elizalde brothers saved the president of the Spanish Chamber of Commerce, Tirso Lizarraga, from being blackballed, but could not save Adrian Got, general man- ager of the Tabacalera Company. They proposed for membership Enrique Razon, chief pilot of the Port of Manila, but he was turned down because he was part Filipino, and Major Manuel Nieto, who was refused because he was a side-kick of Quezon's. Fed up, the Elizaldes quit the club. They invested three or four hundred thou- sand pesos in land, "borrowed" a prefabricated building from the Philippine Carnival, and in a few days had formed a new club, Los Tamaraos.[14] There the Elizaldes played polo until the war, their team of four brothers one of the best in the world.

Social affronts, personally wounding, were remembered long after abstract causes had lost their glow. "Whenever the subject of Amer-

13. Carlos P. Romulo, I Walked with Heroes (New York, Holt, Rinehart and Winston, 1961), p. 117–18.
14. In composing this account I have relied, in descending degree, upon: Joaquin Elizalde (Manila) to Cameron Forbes (Boston) 31 Mar 36 (copy Q); Elizalde inter- view, 30 July 63; Romulo, pp. 118–19; Florence Horn, Orphans of the Pacific (New York, Reynal and Hitchcock, 1941), pp. 132–33; Forbes Journals, 3, 301 (WCF).

ican colonization comes up in the Philippines," wrote a daughter of a prominent revolutionary family, years later, "someone is certain to bring up the fact that before independence Filipinos were not allowed inside the Manila Army-Navy Club. . . . Who knows how much longer we would have remained unaroused if the white men had understood that Asians hold personal dignity above economic or political development." [15]

Although incidents persisted and Joaquin ("Mike") Elizalde complained to Cameron Forbes in 1936 that it was rather late in the day for American discrimination against Filipinos, the inauguration of the Commonwealth did relax certain American attitudes. Filipinos were then in nearly all positions of power and prestige and on their way to national sovereignty. For good relations and their own prosperity Americans had to be cordial not only during business hours but afterwards. The situation confirmed what the nationalists had long contended: the best way to obtain equal treatment socially was to acquire equal status politically.

Philippine nationalism had more than social causes. Some of its origins, perhaps the strongest, were political. Seen in the historical perspective of the Spanish Empire, the Philippine and Cuban revolutions of 1896 were merely delayed explosions of the same powder that blew up in Latin America in 1809–25. Twentieth-century Philippine nationalism was an inexorable postlude to the anti-imperial wars of 1896–1901. During the wars the plans of a constitutional republic had been drawn in the Philippines, although military exigency never let it grow beyond a dictatorship by Aguinaldo.[16] Now America had promised by constitutional development to evolve another republic in the Philippines. Filipinos cooperated, and moderate constitutionalists replaced military nationalists as her leaders.

The leaders were never content with the pace at which domestic powers were turned over to them. In the early years, the upper house of the legislature, the majority of the cabinet, the major executive powers and many minor administrative posts were all in American hands. Young Philippine *pensionados* in the civil service, who

15. Carmen Guerrero-Nakpil, Manila *Chronicle*, 9 Dec 57.
16. Cesar Majul examines this subject at length in *The Political and Constitutional Ideas of the Philippine Revolution* (Quezon City, University of the Philippines, 1957); so does Teodoro Agoncillo in *Malolos, the Crisis of the Republic* (Quezon City, University of the Philippines, 1960).

had been trained in America at American expense, resented the low colonial ceiling over their ambitions. They formed, not long after the opening session of the first Philippine Assembly, a nationalistic group called the Philippine Columbian Association.[17] Most of their grievances over salary, rank, and promotion were eased or dissolved during the Harrison administration, and their more abstract appetites for power were temporarily satisfied by the manner in which Harrison encouraged Osmeña to arrogate executive power to himself.

Post-Harrisonian investigations led to new checks. Cameron Forbes was overheard to mutter, concerning Filipino ambitions, "Those whom the gods would destroy they first make mad." [18] When Wood became governor general he put restraints upon Filipino power which meant to be protective, but they carried the intended implication that Filipinos were unready for self-government and the unintended one of natural white superiority. Their political ambitions thwarted and social sensitivities aroused, Filipinos remembered ever after a Quezonian shot directed at Wood, "I would prefer a government run like hell by Filipinos to one run like heaven by Americans." [19]

For every cautionary injunction of the Republican era, the Filipinos had a brave rejoinder. They met the orthodox warnings—"Economic stability must precede political freedom"—with heretical replies—"Give us the freedom and we will develop ourselves." "Remember," Jose Laurel reminisced thirty years later, "we didn't have fiscal powers of any kind. Banking, monetary, tax legislation, that was all in American hands. We wanted that, to learn how to use it. That was our answer." [20]

17. At the time of the Fiftieth Anniversary Celebration of the Columbian Association, 29 Jan 58, a great deal of material on its history appeared in the Manila press.
18. Jose Sanvictores, who overheard Forbes, recalled this in a speech, Philippine Columbian Association, 29 Jan 58.
19. The context of this famous remark is usually forgotten by those who quote it, Filipino or American. Quezon in 1926 went on a provincial speaking tour to publicize his National Supreme Council, a coalition which he had formed against Wood. The crux of his remarks, as recorded by Teodoro Kalaw, was: "I would rather have the legislature abolished and have the Governor General govern alone. There has been no party in power since he assumed his post because he is the power, the only power. . . . I would prefer a government run like hell by Filipinos to one run like heaven by Americans, because no matter how bad, a Filipino government might be . . . improved" (MS autobiography, pp. 259–60). No other American official gave Quezon occasion to make the same charge.
20. "Do you believe," Laurel was asked, "that it was the wisest answer?" He thought a second, and shrugged: "Well, it was our answer." Interview, 11 Aug 58.

Laurel exaggerated, but forgivably. The very process of supervised development, the existence of tutelary restraints, the occasions for pedagogical compliment and criticism, were all essentially galling to men of his caliber. Native intellect and earned degrees gave them unusual competence and a confidence that they would learn faster by making their own mistakes than by being shielded from the opportunity to err. To the degree that America's "colonial experiment" was then and is still an occasion of self-congratulation for the colonizer, and of patronizing praise for the colonized, Filipinos were and are resentful. One Filipino businessman has expressed the reaction of his countrymen:

> In a more arrogant form, this Kipling mentality appears in the British, the Dutch, and the French. If the little native has learned to walk erect and make the little noises of democracy, it is all due to the painstaking upbringing he has received— oh how it warms the heart to see one's creatures so precocious! . . . When the guinea pig can nozzle all the appropriate slots and does not shed hair or go blind, all credit goes to the experimenter. But if it crouches in a corner, alternately snarling and whimpering, half-dead from too big a dose of innocent tyranny and astute benevolence, then, of course, it is its own miserable fault.[21]

If a prospective colonial administrator showed even a trace of this mentality, he touched off a Filipino campaign against him. Republican presidents more than once considered General Frank McCoy for the governor generalship, but Filipino leaders, suspicious of his service with Leonard Wood, always rubbed out his chances. In July 1930, Hoover nominated as Vice Governor General and Secretary of Public Instruction the journalist Nicholas Roosevelt, who was eager for the job. In Roosevelt's recent book, however, the Filipinos had found what they considered slighting references to their capacities for self-government. Quezon led so strong an attack on the nomination that Roosevelt's friends, especially General James G. Harbord, Chairman of the Board of RCA, finally persuaded him to withdraw.[22]

21. Hilarion G. Henares, Jr, Eisenhower Exchange Fellow from the Philippines, "An Informal Essay Report," 1958, as paraphrased from a column by Carmen Guerrero-Nakpil in the Manila *Chronicle*.
22. On McCoy: Quezon to Guevara, 27 Feb 29, to Roxas, Osmeña, 13, 16 Apr (Q); Forbes Journals, 3, 12, 13 (WCF); Stimson diary, 29 Oct 31 (HLS). On Roosevelt:

From the Filipino point of view, Roosevelt was guilty of the capital sin of the colonizer, later defined as "not cupidity . . . or predatoriness, but vanity—that arrogant self-esteem which assumes that one nation is wiser and superior . . . bringer-up of another people." [23] Vanity calls up vanity, and pride evokes pride. Philippine nationalism, social and political, expressed itself mildly when accommodated, but vigorously when challenged or insulted.

Philippine nationalism, nonetheless, was far from absolute. By European standards it was far even from being mature, for it was not coterminous with a sense of nationality. Linguistic and regional differences prevented the Philippines from forming cohesive and positive nationalistic sentiments. Unity, such as it was, derived from a loose tesselation of anti-imperial feelings. Even then, among the mass of the people, there was much pro-American, if not pro-imperial, spirit. In a familial sense, America was mother, father, or older brother to the Philippines, a protector in the international community. A debt of honor (utang na loob) existed between the two peoples; it could be paid only by continued reciprocal giving and could not be severed. Clearly the connection between the two peoples must continue even if "independence" should arrive. Many people certainly did not understand the meaning of "independence," and one earnest provinciano even wrote the Bureau of Insular Affairs asking to be sent a sample.[24]

Beyond these general limitations to nationalism were the special ones enjoined by a sense of practicality among men in power. In 1929, certain American congressmen proposed tariffs and import quotas on Philippine products. Quezon told Henry Stimson that if the United States held the islands by force while depriving them of their market, "It will destroy me in my faith in the American people and your government. . . . I will quit politics and go home and teach my boy to be a rebel." [25] When it became clear, however, that

Nicholas Roosevelt, The Philippines: A Treasure and a Problem (New York, J. H. Sears, 1926); New York Herald Tribune, 22 July 1930, Box 38, McCoy MSS; Horace B. Pond to Gen James G. Harbord and John M. Switzer, 25 July 30, and Harbord and Switzer to Pond, 31 July, both incorporated in Pond to Quezon, 30 Jan 33 (Q).
23. Henares, "Essay Report."
24. Told the author by Richard Maxwell, Interior Section, National Archives, 1956.
25. Stimson diary, 6 Jan 29 (HLS).

independence could not be had without import quotas and tariffs, many Filipino businessmen, especially in the sugar industry, became very lukewarm nationalists indeed. Quezon himself adopted a less heroic stance and tried as hard to save sugar as he did to win independence.[26]

Some men, deeply concerned for the cultural integrity and economic development of the Philippines and for the social equality of Filipinos, were nonetheless opposed to separation from the United States. Don Cayetano Arellano, Chief Justice of the Supreme Court, told his friend Miguel Ossorio, pointing to the dugout canoes on the Pasig River, that "if there is no ship to take me to Hong Kong when independence comes, I will go and risk my life in one of those bancas." Ossorio himself, a modern entrepreneur of the most imaginative and energetic kind, later chose to become an American citizen. To a lawyer who warned him that he could save a great deal of money by not doing so, Ossorio replied that he would prefer, if necessary, "to live in one room in this country rather than in a palace in the Philippines." [27]

Others felt differently. Mike Elizalde, whose parents, like Ossorio's, were both Spanish, was educated in Spain, England, and Switzerland, and had served a year in the Spanish Army. He gave up his overseas citizenship just as Ossorio was acquiring his and became instead a naturalized Filipino, saying that the wisest course was to accept gracefully an independence which he considered inevitable. Most of the Spanish and American communities in Manila thought he was "crazy," and even his brothers doubted him, although they too became Philippine citizens.[28] Some critics thought that Mike Elizalde envisioned a kind of Latin American republic dominated by Spanish mestizos. Whatever his motives, during the Commonwealth era he would enjoy both the abuses and rewards of intimate friendship with President Quezon.

For those whose blood or whose heritage was less cosmopolitan, the question of choice did not even exist. For them, whose fathers had signed the Malolos Constitution and had fought with Aguinaldo

26. Theodore Friend, "The Philippine Sugar Industry and the Politics of Independence, 1929–1935," *Journal of Asian Studies*, 22 (1963), 179–92.
27. M. J. Ossorio to the author, 1 May 63.
28. Joaquin Elizalde, "P," BIA: Elizalde interview, 30 July 63.

or on their own, the issue was much simpler. How long must one compromise one's own character in one's own country? How long must one accept an alien order, however modern, efficient, and benevolent, when one would prefer a native chaos—not because it was chaotic but because it was native?

4

Leadership and Its Problems

ALTHOUGH NATIONALISM was surely the leading political phenomenon in all colonial Asia by 1931, Patrick Hurley, Hoover's Secretary of War, reported at length on a trip to the Philippines in that year without even mentioning the word.[1] Like many Americans in official position, he thought of it as negligible or artificial, forgetting that the Filipino leaders of his time had all lived through the most militant period of nationalism in the history of their country. The era of glory and terror at the turn of the century had profoundly affected each of them, although their own views might have become more moderate since then.

One of the elder figures, Rafael Palma, had been a revolutionary journalist, as had Osmeña; Quezon, a guerrilla, had not surrendered to the Americans until 1901; Roxas, somewhat younger, had been born in 1894, eight months after Spanish guards had shot his father in the back. The children growing up at the turn of the century learned at first to hate and fear the new conquerors as they had the old. Americans in 1901 tortured Jose Laurel's father in a Batangas concentration camp. Carlos Romulo, three years old, saw a beloved neighbor hanged by the Americans in the village square. Later he, like Roxas, would learn his ABCs from an American soldier, and the

1. Unpublished report to the President, 1931, special file, BIA.

fear would turn to affection.[2] But even American kindliness would not erase the recollected thrill of fighting to be free, or submerge the anticipated pride of leading an independent nation. If, in the early 1930s, there was not yet a strong or clear idea of nationalism in the mass of the people, that was beside the point: the vision existed in the leaders, and should they tend to forget, the people would remind the leaders of their slogans.

Who led the Filipinos? In the nineteenth century, the Spanish priest-figure, uniting in himself both church and state, had helped bring on the revolution. Filipino intellectuals drummed up resentment against clerical and bureaucratic abuses and, in the fighting which followed, native soldier-statesmen came to the fore.

In the American era, however, the lawyer-politician took over. State and church were separated, and nationalism learned to express itself by moderate and constitutional means. The only prominent priest-politicians left were leaders of the Philippine Independent Church: Gregorio Aglipay, personally popular in the Iloko regions, and Isabelo de los Reyes. Few soldier-politicians remained either, and they were veterans of the revolution: Teodoro Sandiko, Jose Alejandrino, and above all, Aguinaldo, chief of the Veterans Association.

Where imperial arms prevail, native warriors do not prosper. Despite his reputation in America, Aguinaldo's Philippine following was mainly provincial and sentimental; his veterans, like Aglipay's church, provided the core of his following. As for businessmen or engineers, few were prominent in politics, probably because of the dominance of American and Chinese capital and the technologically undeveloped state of the country.[3]

The chief requirement of a would-be leader was ability to plead the rights of a subjugated people to the imperial sovereign and to

2. Rafael Palma, My Autobiography, Alicia Palma Bautista, trans. (Manila, Capitol, 1953), pp. 27–44; Teodoro Locsin, "Sergio Osmeña," Philippines Free Press, 28 Oct 61, pp. 2 ff; Quezon, The Good Fight (New York, D. Appleton-Century, 1946), pp. 75–80; Carlos Quirino, serialized life of Roxas, Philippines Free Press, 1 Feb 58, pp. 26–28; Jose Lansang to the author, 24 Mar 62; Romulo, I Walked with Heroes, pp. 29–30.

3. I have followed and elaborated upon the analysis of Takeuchi Tatsuji, in Report of the Research Commission on the Philippines, Rōyama Masamichi, et al., for the Japanese Military Administration (4 vols. Manila, 1943), 2, 118–24. This and subsequent references are to Prof Takeuchi's unpublished English translation of Vol. 2, which he has kindly made available to me.

demand progress toward independence. Democracy breeds and encourages advocates; native government was composed mainly of lawyers, and the priests and soldiers mentioned above were all in opposition to it.

The most eloquent and significant minority leader, Don Juan Sumulong, was also a lawyer, who criticized the inattentiveness of the Nacionalistas to the economic ills of the Philippines. Disputatious and courageous, Sumulong made a career of pointing to the less popular, more difficult, and essential problem—the well-being of the common people.

Meanwhile, majority leaders—Quezon, Osmeña, Roxas, and others —lived on the endless emotional capital of the independence issue. All lawyers by training, they rose because of their genuine eloquence, putting voice to the nationalism which American conquest had frustrated. Sometimes they used the issue insincerely, for their own advancement. To the latter temptation Manuel Roxas in his youth frequently succumbed.

Roxas had burst on the national scene in 1922, the year of the first Osmeña-Quezon struggle. Osmeña had made what he later admitted to be his "greatest error in politics" [4] by leaving his position as speaker of the House to run for the Senate, in hopes of winning control there. Quezon emerged from the fray as president of the Senate and Roxas with his sponsorship became speaker of the House. After initial difficulties he began to rise in stature to join his two elders in the Philippine ruling triumvirate. But Roxas could never quite capitalize upon his position as he hoped. Always the two others, as president and vice president, loomed over him, and his own fortunes depended on relations between the two.

While Quezon was in California convalescing from tuberculosis, Roxas organized, with Osmeña's support, a nationalistic society called *Ang Bagong Katipunan,* The New Association. Although its namesake, the original Katipunan, was the secret society which had fomented and organized rebellion against Spain, the A.B.K. was neither secret nor truly rebellious. With a moralistic oath of membership it tried, somewhat fatuously, to capture the spirit of the 1890s from Aguinaldo, and with various pledges toward economic nationalism tried to steal from Sumulong his modern following. It collected a

4. Osmeña made this lament to Evett D. Hester during his wartime exile in Washington. I have it from an interview with the latter, 21 Mar 58.

hundred thousand members, a treasury of fifty thousand pesos; it held open mass meetings.[5]

Quezon assured Governor General Davis that the A.B.K. was not incendiary, but he had his own unspoken reasons for anxiety. Although not "subversive" of American sovereignty, the A.B.K. could be very dangerous, in the elections of June 1931 and after, to Quezon's own political supremacy.[6] He could not help worrying about an alliance between an old enemy and a one-time ally. Roxas had turned against him. Ambitious, frustrated, and badgered by a termagant wife, the young Speaker struggled to master his ragged nerves and build his career by sheer vigor and determination. In his face, thick-lipped, fat-cheeked, with a black cowlick falling on the forehead, were signs of more brute stamina than had either Quezon, who seemed to exist on power of will, or Osmeña, who subsisted on wisdom alone.

Ordinarily, Roxas' aggressiveness was ill-matched with Osmeña's aloofness, but the two men, out of mutual weakness, were now allied. Both came from the Visayas, the central islands, whereas Quezon came from Luzon, to the north. Divided, Roxas and Osmeña defeated each other but united they might conquer Quezon. For his part, Roxas needed Osmeña's prestige and organization, perhaps even realized what he could learn from Osmeña's mellow techniques, his caution, and soothing touch. Osmeña, in turn, wanted the additional support of Roxas' following, and in order to have a determined ally he was willing to put up with a rash one.

By 1931 the center of gravity in Philippine politics had for some time been shifting from the older, Spanish-speaking men who were attracted by Osmeña to the younger, Americanized men. Osmeña was extremely proficient in Spanish, but a decreasing number of people spoke it (2.6 per cent in 1939); even his appeal to the Hispanicized elite was limited by his strongly Chinese ancestry. He learned the law and history of the United States but never really mastered English idiom and never became intimate with many

5. "Ang Bagong Katipunan" (The New Association or Gang), memorandum compiled from reports by Army Intelligence, Philippine Dept, 15 Nov 30 to 31 Mar 31, Box 40, McCoy MSS.
6. Quezon to Davis, 13 Jan 31 (Q). Jake Rosenthal, a poker-playing, joke-cracking friend, kept Quezon up on the activities of the A.B.K. in letters of 4, 27 Jan, 2 Feb, 6 Apr, 4 June 31 (Q).

Americans as Quezon did. Eight years in America had taught Quezon much about that nation's character and even won him the affectionate nickname of "Casey," [7] but Osmeña had never been out of the Philippines for any length of time.

In the early days he was much too powerful, too busy, to bother with travel. Those who knew Osmeña as an old man, beaten by Quezon in 1922 and 1933 and, after Quezon's death, beaten by Roxas in 1946, could barely imagine him as a young man, an autocrat as demanding as Quezon at his worst and a parliamentarian far more exacting than Roxas at his best. As speaker, Osmeña had mastered American constitutional procedure, and by example set a standard in the early assemblies which at once educated the Filipinos and impressed the Americans. He demanded probity, attention to the rules, and plenty of homework. He came to refer to the Legislature as "an instrument of liberty"; it was a tool he had fashioned himself. As for political rivals, he knocked them down with such ease that even Quezon used to say, "It is useless to [try to] defeat Osmeña; he is in alliance with God." [8]

Finally Osmeña was beaten, and would be beaten again and again. Having enjoyed unrivaled power from the age of twenty-nine to forty-four, he would live thirty-nine more years in subordinate positions and in retirement. Few men have suffered a longer time the disappointment of a has-been, but Osmeña never allowed his losses to embitter him. His face in age retained the same firm line of mouth, the same steady-eyed look of the young man with the gavel posing for photographs in 1907. The wrinkles spread in even rows up the high brow and in angles down from the wide, flat nose; he looked and acted more and more the mandarin. His associate and admirer, Jose Laurel, chose a Chinese proverb with which to honor his declining years: "The best of men are like water; water benefits all things and does not compete with them." [9] Osmeña weathered age as he would meet a friend. He died in 1961, having survived Quezon

7. While Resident Commissioner in Washington, Quezon spoke at Tammany Hall. Boss Murphy fancifully introduced him as the descendant of an Irishman who had fled in trouble to Spain, where his name "Casey" had been Hispanicized to Quezon. Most of Congress, many other Americans, and a few close Filipino friends called him "Casey" after that. Felipe Buencamino, Jr, to the author, 28 June 61.
8. Teodoro M. Kalaw, MS autobiography, p. 338.
9. Jose P. Laurel, "Peerless Filipino Statesman," Philippine *Historical Bulletin*, 3, No. 3, 39–44.

by seventeen years, Roxas by thirteen. He had lived eighty-three
years and left fourteen children.

If Osmeña, even in youth, had the look of the centuries upon him,
Quezon showed the mood of the moment. His eyes would flash, his
nostrils flare with excitement; and when he was angry even his ears
and eyebrows wiggled. He could not stand without pacing or sit
without shifting, and when he spoke he gesticulated.[10] If Osmeña
tried to simplify his complex self and express only the essential,
Quezon tried to give vent to his many selves, lest, pent up, they tire
with their thrashing the sick body which housed them.

For every man, for every situation, Quezon had a special tone and
special touch. A Philippine writer has captured his lordly informality
on a visit to a provincial town in the Bicol region. The townspeople
had swept the road, whitewashed the boulders on either side, built
triumphal arches of bamboo and palm leaves, erected a platform
bedecked with flags. Quezon arrived and dropped unceremoniously
into the chair reserved for him. "I saw a reddish skinned man, [the
young provinciano wrote] with lines furrowed on his face and tired
restless eyes beneath a native-made sun helmet. He was dressed in
khaki." When he spoke it was without heat; he pleaded mildly for
cooperation, honesty, less politicking. Some loved, some hated him
but all "the crowd, forgetful of the time and the sun, listened on,
hanging on every word as if they understood English, then listening
again as the diminutive interpreter repeated his statements in the
vernacular, clapping their hands and whispering among themselves
now and then: 'He looks like his pictures.' 'He is not thin.' 'He is very
red. Why! Why!' " An open conference followed the speech, in which
Quezon listened attentively to all.[11]

In Manila, among the cosmopolitan rich and the mestizo powerful,
several of whom were his compadres, Quezon had other manners.
Young protégés, companionable roués, and lifelong friends surrounded him. Imperious with enemies, affectionate with comrades,
he made himself immediately and intimately felt with strangers.
Although he was shorter even than Osmeña and Roxas, his physical

10. All descriptions of Quezon agree on his extraordinary mobility of feature, body,
and mood. Vicente Bunuan and Felipe Buencamino, Jr, have most graphically described him to me.
11. Bienvenido N. Santos, "President Quezon Visits Our Town," *Philippine Magazine*,
33 (1936), 235–36.

nearness was incomparably commanding, an attractive energy to which scores of women succumbed. Even the most level-headed and skeptical felt his magnetism. An American woman married to a Filipino recalled dancing with Quezon: "He had a way of holding you in the lower back, and, with a touch of the spine, making you do just what he wanted." A prominent Filipina observed: "They always say that women couldn't resist Quezon. But neither could men. He was irresistible to them. He would say 'Ah, tu, Pepe' or 'Ah, tu, Manolo,' and they'd turn to mush." [12]

Quezon's own emotions were high strung and sharply tuned, and he played upon others' feelings with an instinctive virtuosity. He often wept; he could make crowds weep. He could turn a hostile audience quickly in his favor. With "misty allusions to his misunderstood and misconstrued 'position'" he frequently united people and leaders with poignant pleas for cooperation in "'this most crucial period of our history.'"[13] Nor was Quezon afraid to show tears with American governors: the steely-eyed Stimson, who impressed one Filipino as having "iced tea in his veins," noted it at least twice; and the gentle Christian, Francis Sayre, drew tears to Quezon's eyes on All Souls' Night by presenting him with flowers at his dead son's grave.[14]

One who knew both Quezon and Osmeña well insists that Quezon, although a more demonstrative sentimentalist, was actually less sensitive than Osmeña. More genuinely than Quezon, he claimed, Osmeña recognized and repaid his friends. On the other hand, he remembered his enemies too well. "Once a friend has defaulted, he can no more hope to belong to the inner circle." Osmeña found it too hard to "forgive and forget, not the [consequences] of disloyalty, but the pain of loss." Against this emotive obstinacy in Osmeña, Quezon himself reacted. Their mutual friend, wondering why Quezon in later years treated Osmeña stiffly, thought he had the answer: Quezon was unable "to forgive Osmeña's inability to forget his political imprudences. 'I mean well *this* time,' [Quezon] must think. 'I was misled that *other* time. Why must he harp on that?'"

Their attack on problems was so different as to have brought about

12. Interviews with the author, Aug and Oct 58.
13. Kalaw MS, p. 353.
14. Stimson diary, 9 Aug 26, 6 Jan 29 (HLS); Francis B. Sayre, *Glad Adventure* (New York, Macmillan, 1957), p. 190. The incident recounted by Sayre took place in 1939.

clashes even had not ambition made them rivals. Quezon had a quick eye for flaws in a plan, but otherwise no care for details. Osmeña, the scholar, loved to approach a situation with wide-angle vision and microscopic precision. "I also come to the same decisions," Quezon would say, "only it takes me less time."

"But I never make your mistakes," Osmeña would answer.

"When I do make mistakes," Quezon would counter, "I use the time you waste making studies in rectifying them."

Osmeña could only shrug his shoulders. Quezon, like a housewife, must always have the last word.

For his own greater political success Quezon had an explanation in keeping with his character. "The trouble with you," he told Osmeña, "is that you take the game of politics too seriously. You look too far behind you and too far ahead of you. Our people do not understand that. . . . All they want is to have the present problem solved, and solved with the least pain. That is all." [15]

Quezon's approach to politics struck the judicious Teodoro Kalaw as being "either clowning or opportunism." [16] But for the mass of Filipinos it was leadership of the charismatic kind they desired, leadership with an ardor and a flair that kindled their hearts. The sound and thorough Osmeña, if more learned and more sincere, nevertheless appeared both less earnest and less exciting. The people wanted a thaumaturge, not a philosopher. Osmeña pondered too long, hesitated and vacillated too much for them. Quezon vacillated too, but so swiftly that he appeared to be inspired.

Surely the national style and the national taste would have been different had China ruled the Philippines for three centuries rather than Spain. But insofar as the Filipinos liked autocrats for rulers, they preferred the fire and pride of the "Kastila," as Quezon was called, to the calculation and mellowness of "El Chino," Osmeña; they desired a warrior cavalier before a scholar bureaucrat. Surely, too, American rule, as well as Spanish, had affected the national character, but here again Quezon had the advantage. Insofar as Filipinos liked democrats for rulers, Quezon appealed to them with his arm-in-arm, eye-to-eye, heart-to-heart manner, his anecdotes of guerrilla days, his boyish escapades. Osmeña was an admirable gentleman, but too proud to make capital of his own flaws, too reserved

15. Kalaw MS, pp. 352–55.
16. Ibid., p. 351.

to reveal his own weakness and say, as Quezon might, "Follow me, because I am like you."

Most Filipinos felt singularly blessed to have both the Castilian and the Confucian as leaders, but others dissented. A prominent Japanese political scientist regarded Quezon at best as "an ideal politician for a country still under alien sovereignty." He thought Osmeña "only a cautious and scrupulous lawyer, trying desperately to present before a judge, called the United States, evidence as favorable to his client as possible, without . . . displeasure to the judge." In neither man did he find evidence of "principles of government applicable to an independent state." [17] The Japanese would some day try to supply such principles, under the heading of "moral justice." In the meantime, the sharpest critic of Philippine leadership was a Filipino—Don Juan Sumulong, who, long before Quezon adopted the slogan of "social justice," stood staunchly for the reality. The existing system of government was not representative, he said, and would lead to revolutionary opposition.[18]

The Nacionalista leaders, however, would not behave like sovereign statesmen until they received sovereign authority. Nor would they reach deeply into socioeconomic problems until they felt sovereign responsibility. In the meantime they occupied themselves with the contest for power inside the Nacionalista family. In 1931, with the independence question reopened, Quezon and Osmeña began circling each other like tigers, expecting another major clash. Quezon had beaten Osmeña once, in a three-way fight when Sumulong and the Democratas had been a strong third force. Now the Democratas were impotent; the third force was the personal following of Manuel Roxas; and Roxas was working with Osmeña.

17. Rōyama, *Philippines Research Report,* 2, 207–09.
18. Hayden, *The Philippines,* pp. 370–71.

Part 2: The Crises of the Great Depression

"Let . . . the wide arch
Of the rang'd empire fall!"

SHAKESPEARE
Antony and Cleopatra

5

Dominion Plans

AFTER SEVERAL YEARS of quiescence, international conditions, not insular ones, revived in Washington the question of the eventual status of the Philippines. First the Great Depression in 1929, then the Manchurian Incident in 1931, made Congress take thought and made the Filipinos in turn confront their own future. What shape should that future assume? Between the conceits of the most avid imperialism and the fancies of the most rabid nationalism, there lay, in 1931, a broad range of discussable questions. Should American sovereignty continue in the Philippines indefinitely and without modification? Only a very few so contended. Should the Philippines have full sovereignty immediately and without qualification? Not even Quezon and Osmeña privately believed so. Philippine missions to Washington had periodically been requesting full and instant independence since 1919, but the top Filipino leaders had been warming up to the idea of a dominion relationship. India, for example, was slowly moving toward such status through the Round Table Conferences in London, in 1930–32.

When William Howard Taft had proposed, in 1908, an American-Philippine tie like that between England and Australia, no self-respecting Nacionalista would lend himself officially to the idea. Much later, however, Henry Stimson successfully nurtured the idea in Osmeña, who in 1929 publicly discussed Canada as an example of a people gaining increasing autonomy without damage to existing ties of law and government.

The same idea was growing in Quezon, too: in 1925 or 1926 Roy Howard, chairman of the Scripps-Howard newspapers, had tried out the notion of a "partnership" on Quezon. "Getting more experience, and growing more conservative," a close associate of Quezon's recalled, "we thought: 'Independence? Wait a minute.'" By 1928 Quezon would say to Stimson, "Give us certainty and we will take dominion status." But, he warned, "like your President T. R.—if you quote me on this, I will say you lie." [1]

The next few years reopened the independence question and the rivalry between Osmeña and Quezon; neither man dared talk too openly of dominion status for fear of leaving the independence platform to his opponent. The more daring was Quezon; where once he had played the radical, now he essayed the bold conservative.

During several months in the United States in 1931, Quezon had discussed dominion at length with the War Department[2] and had explored a "Free State" plan devised by businessmen concerned with the Philippines.[3] He made no promises either to American military-diplomatic interests or to financial-commercial interests, but prolonged exposure to them both lowered the pitch of his rhetoric. Furthermore, the deepening depression in America probably promoted realism in his appraisal of the Philippine situation, and his third prolonged convalescence in as many years may have been conducive to an objective frame of mind.[4] In any case, Quezon now

1. Special Report of the Sec War, 23 Jan 08, Sen Doc 200, 60:1; Stimson to Wood, 11 Oct 26, and Manila *Tribune*, 6 Sept 29 (HLS); Quezon to Howard, 19 Dec 30 (Q); Felipe Buencamino, Jr, conversation with the author, 28 June 58; Elting Morison, *Turmoil and Tradition* (Boston, Houghton Mifflin, 1960), p. 297.
2. See Ch. 6, p. 74.
3. Free State Plan, revised 6 Oct 31, BIA 364–841. Scattered clues suggest that the Spreckels sugar and shipping interests were chief sponsors of the plan. Oscar Sutro, prominent San Francisco lawyer-financier, drafted it, and many New York business figures with Philippine interests or experience supported it, such as Gen James G. Harbord. The contact men in Washington were John M. Switzer, former president of the Pacific Commercial Co., and W. Edward Bruce, a friend of Franklin Roosevelt and Robert Frost, who had gone broke with business ventures in the Philippines.
4. To alleviate his tuberculosis, Quezon spent three periods at the Pottenger Sanitorium, Monrovia, Calif.; Dec 1927–Aug 1928; Oct 1930–Mar 1931; Aug–Sept 1931. He was never completely cured, and his death at Saranac Lake, N. Y., Aug 1944, is largely attributable to the disease.

assumed the most conservative stance taken in Philippine politics since the Progresista and Federalista parties, fifteen and twenty years before.

Arriving in Manila, October 1931, Quezon undertook a long report on the results of his recent months in America and, while composing it, issued a trial statement of his conclusions. As his first solution of the Philippine question, Quezon advocated immediate independence with free trade for five years, with limitations on immigration and on imports of sugar and coconut oil from the Philippines. If the first were not acceptable, he suggested immediate establishment of an autonomous government, trade and immigration restriction as above, with a plebiscite on independence after ten years. If neither of the other two plans were acceptable, he said that the Philippines would welcome an independence bill in any form.[5]

A close look at the proposals suggests that Quezon was really in favor of the second one. He knew that the first solution was entirely contradictory to American trade policy and totally unacceptable on other grounds to Hoover's administration. As for the third solution, Quezon admitted that the Republicans still had enough strength in Congress to uphold a veto of any independence bill the administration disliked.

The second solution was in keeping with his discussions on the West Coast and in the War Department, except that it provided for independence if ultimately desired. It would allay some of the criticism from economic competitors of the Philippines; complete autonomy would go a long way to satisfy Philippine nationalism; the "partnership" with America would continue for ten years at least and, depending on the plebiscite, that partnership might be prolonged indefinitely. Quezon's first and third statements appear devised to rally his following; he hoped to lead them in the direction of the second statement. He had conceived and expressed his report in its essentials half a day before the Japanese unexpectedly marched on Mukden. As they overran Manchuria in the following weeks, he must have felt confirmed in the line he had chosen.

5. Gov Gen Davis to Sec War, 28 Oct 31, BIA 364–811. Quezon's final conclusions were the same as those he announced in the preliminary release.

But Quezon found very little support in Manila. Even as he labored on a series of drafts of his final report,[6] Sumulong and Aguinaldo attacked his preliminary statement, the latter charging him with "manifest treachery." When he presented his finished version to the Legislature, the Democratas jumped on him with profuse objections focused on his second formula—autonomy with plebiscite. The reaction of the press against him and the lack of support accorded him by the Nacionalistas both dismayed Quezon.[7] He had explained himself fully to Osmeña and Roxas and had even drawn the latter into the drafting of the report. Osmeña, however, had already moved to block him with a resolution for "immediate, absolute, and complete independence," which passed both houses unanimously.

Quezon had accompanied his report with resignations both as leader of the party and president of the Senate.[8] Not true retirements—they never were with Quezon—these documents were rather invitations to both bodies to renew his mandate to lead. Midway through his six-year term of office he was asking for a "vote of confidence" both upon the issue involved and upon his own leadership. By submitting his resignations along with the report, he wished, as he later said, "to force the legislature and my party to adopt a clear and conclusive attitude"[9]—in other words, to win acceptance for the unusual departure represented by his second formula by staking his leadership and personal dignity upon it. The legislature did not oblige. It neither approved nor disapproved the report,[10] and adjourned in some confusion after creating a new mission to strive for "the earliest concession of independence."[11] To save his face,

6. Repeatedly redrafted, 27 Oct–7 Nov 31, with Roxas, Jorge Bocobo, and others assisting (Q); presented to party caucus, 8 Nov, and legislature, 9 Nov; cabled by Gov Gen Davis to Sec War, 13 Nov et seq. (BIA); entered by Sen Hawes, 22 Dec, in *Cong Rec* 72:1, 1069, 1151–54.

7. Gov Gen Davis to Sec War, 6 Nov 31, BIA 364–820; New York *Times*, 6 Nov 31, BIA 364-a-w-873, part 4; "Statement de La Minoria Sobre El Report Sometido Por El Presidente Quezon A La Legislatura, Noviembre 9, 1931," incomplete copy; and Quezon to Gen James G. Harbord, 31 Dec 31 (Q).

8. Typescript drafts with holograph revisions by Quezon, and incomplete final copies survive (Q).

9. Undated fragment, 1931, pp. 4, 5, 7 surviving (Q).

10. The New York *Herald Tribune*, 10 Nov 31, erroneously stated that after an unsuccessful move to block the Quezon report by adjourning sine die, the legislature finally *passed* it (BIA 364–825a).

11. 9th Phil Legis, 1st sess., Conc Res (Concurrent Resolution) 12, 9 Nov 31.

however, both party and Senate rejected Quezon's resignations. While shunning his program they acclaimed his person.

Now the Filipino leader stood in an unusually ambiguous position. The mass of the people did not accept his views, while an educated minority did. Over a period of time the minority could persuade the majority, but only a minority of the minority, mostly businessmen and sugar-millers, were immediately willing to come out behind Quezon. Osmeña and Roxas privately believed in the long-range wisdom of Quezon's proposals, but they contradicted them in public.[12] Even Quezon's personal following was no longer strong enough to pass his report without the assistance of Osmeña men or Roxas men, and those factions, working together, could not be split apart. In short, during Quezon's short time abroad, Osmeña and Roxas had seriously undercut his following at home.

Quezon's response to his predicament is a study in political ambition and skill. He was genuinely intent at one point upon resigning for good, and he drafted a statement which thanked God for giving him the ability "to avoid one of the greatest dangers of democracy, which is the fondness for power and the anxiety to preserve it at all cost." [13] Attacks on his proposals, however, aroused in Quezon that very fondness, that very anxiety. He based his resignation finally on "increasingly precarious health," while promising that the party could still count on him as far as diminished physical strength would permit.[14] The party accordingly renewed its confidence in him as president.

Having held on to the party leadership, Quezon proceeded to explain his position to the public in such a way as to refresh his reputation as a nationalist. To a sympathetic reporter he gave a bedside interview. He attacked the existing system as "offensive to the dignity of the Filipino people," especially the veto power of the governor general, who "is made so infallible that he can with a stroke of the pen and without any responsibility except to his personal judgment . . . negate the product of the best minds of our country."

12. Manila newspapers show reactions from all quarters, Nov 1931, passim (BIA); Quezon summarized public response to Gen James G. Harbord, 31 Dec 31 (Q).
13. "1ᵃ formula, Al Comite Executivo del Partido Nacionalista-Consolidado" (Q). Quezon not only convinced himself but Gov Gen Davis of his sincerity; Gov Gen to Sec War, 6 Nov 31, BIA 364–821.
14. This, apparently the third version of his resignation, was sent to the party Executive Committee, 7 Nov 31 (Q).

To the criticism that Quezon had deviated from his party's platform, he answered that his duty was to interpret it to fit the people's present needs. "Conditions alter cases," he said. When he had been resident commissioner in Washington fifteen years before, the Philippines were only slightly dependent on the American sugar market; the people demanded less in the way of expenditures for health, education, and public works; and the international situation was less threatening.

Now, if the sugar market was suddenly withdrawn, many men would be thrown out of work, and the insular administration, its revenues reduced, would be unable to sustain its ordinary projects, let alone meet emergencies such as epidemics and typhoons. With financial failures the world over and Manchuria invaded, it was no time to court disorder and danger. "Would it be consistent with the best interests of the people," Quezon asked, "to demand immediate, absolute, and complete independence from America, only to fall into the hands of a power which might, conceivably, treat us more despotically than America ever thought of treating us?" The interview ended when Quezon's young son entered the room. "Daddy," he ventured, "Mother says it's time for prayer"; and he led his father off.[15]

Quezon's chief concern in the next two weeks was to keep Osmeña and Roxas from getting strategic advantages over him. They would soon leave for lobbying in Washington; he would remain in the Philippines. They had strengthened their political organizations while he was away; turnabout was fair play. Even so, the pressure for an independence bill was mounting in America; suppose Osmeña and Roxas should cash in on it and come home with that incomparable prize, in whatever shape? Quezon needed to curtail that possibility, even, if possible, to eliminate it.

Unknown to his colleagues, he cabled Hurley, trying to extract an agreement to which he could bind their mission before it left. Restriction of imports and immigration, he told the Secretary of War, would only be acceptable as part of a bill setting a definite date for independence, or allowing the people at a definite time to

15. Draft of Manila *Tribune* interview with Quezon, [11?] Nov 31, revisions in blue and black pencil (Q); access to Quezon and intimacy of style suggest Carlos Romulo as the author.

decide their own fate by plebiscite. Hurley balked at such a plan, and even when Quezon stepped up his tone—"I am crying in a desert"—Hurley held back. Still unconvinced that there existed a nationalist sentiment, he required that the "Filipino leaders should present public and authoritative evidence" of support of their program before the War Department could approve it.[16]

The acting Governor General, George Butte,[17] and his advisor, Colonel Louis Van Schaick, then got behind Quezon, and praised his efforts to the Secretary. Quezon complained that Hurley was making his political sacrifice futile; the administration's attitude would leave the Osmeña-Roxas mission "no alternative but to swing back regardless of consequences to the demand for complete, absolute, and immediate independence."[18] Despairing of success and deciding to resign, Quezon sent Felipe Buencamino after Van Schaick to retrieve the cablegram before it was sent; but Van Schaick said that the cable was already transmitted. He discovered later that it did not go out until two hours after Buencamino called,[19] but go it did, and finally changed Hurley's mind.

Next morning Van Schaick found Quezon, in dressing gown, delighted with an answering cable: "I want you to win your fight," Hurley said, expressing willingness to conform as far as possible to Quezon's program.[20] That evening Van Schaick returned to ask if Hurley's change of attitude had persuaded Quezon to cut out the

16. Davis' relay of Quezon's message to Sec War, 7 Nov 31, BIA 364-821½; Van Schaick's relay of Quezon's message to Gen MacArthur for Sec War, 24 Nov, and draft thereof; Hurley to Quezon, 2 Dec. These latter messages are from a dittoed collection of cablegrams in code exchanged between Manila and Washington, 28 Oct 31–May 32 (Q). The collection consists of precoded versions of cables sent from Manila and decoded versions of cables received from Washington. I refer to it hereafter as "Cablegrams, Series I." Because of differences in time, Manila's dates appear one day later than Washington's. Many of the cables originating in Manila also exist separately in draft form, but my references, unless otherwise designated, are to the final versions. The same is true of scattered cablegrams for the period May 32–May 33, assembled by the author and referred to as "Cablegrams, Series II."
17. George C. Butte was Acting Gov Gen from the time Dwight Davis departed in late Nov 1931 until the arrival of Davis' successor, Theodore Roosevelt, Jr, in Feb 1932.
18. Butte to Sec War, 1 Dec 31, Cablegrams, Series I, and BIA 364-834.
19. Journal of Col Louis J. Van Schaick, 1 Dec 31, BIA 364-838½. Van Schaick in 1937 deposited with the BIA a typed copy of his diary for 1–7 Dec 31. I have been unable to locate a complete original.
20. Guevara, Osias (Resident Commissioners) to Quezon, 1 Dec 31; Quezon to Guevara, Osias for Sec War, 2 Dec, Cablegrams, Series I.

"immediate" slogan to which he had reverted. "Cut it out, hell!" Quezon snapped. "I propose to suppress the whole statement. . . . I have Osmeña and Roxas in here helping me write a letter to you. Come on in."

Quezon's rivals were seated at a littered table, drafting and re-drafting replies to Hurley. Quezon sat down and ran his hand through his long grey-streaked hair. Periodically he parried Roxas' attempts to insert the word "independence" in the letter. Worn out from the phraseological fencing match, Osmeña and Roxas finally withdrew for a rest.

When they were out of earshot, Quezon leaned forward to Van Schaick: "You see those two fellows do not dare try to oust the old man yet, sick as he is. . . . They fear the Administration will side with me . . . and that, if they break with me, they will be on the losing side. . . . So they are using me to further their own political interests." He ground out his words harshly. "I told them . . . not . . . to think I was such a fool as not to know what they were do-ing. I warned them not to provoke me . . . because . . . as near death as I am, they know Manuel Quezon will fight, and they are not ready to face it."

In a milder manner, he reflected: "When I was young, I had a desire to help my people, but coupled with it there was . . . a tre-mendous desire to help Manuel Quezon too. I was a Bohemian, a high liver, impetuous, and my past is not spotless, but"—he spoke more softly—"in spite of it all Rizal never lived to know the affection of his people as I have, . . . little as I deserve it. Now that I am older . . . I just want to do for my people all that I can before I go."

Now he must prevent Roxas from indiscriminately talking inde-pendence, yet he must insist upon a voice for the Filipinos in their future. Quezon recalled the establishment of American rule—"I keep remembering it was done by force of arms"—and his voice shifted back to its public tone. "I cannot go out and fight at the head of my people, and . . . I cannot just sit and submit to the present situation. But you let independence be left to our option, and I am convinced that the best interests of both nations will be served if the link is not completely severed. Let America rule us ever so lightly against our will," Quezon concluded, with a familiar threat, "and I want to rebel. That is why I resigned yesterday."

At the sound of footsteps in the corridor, Quezon imparted a last confidence to Van Schaick: "When I told Osmeña and Roxas not to provoke me . . . Roxas regretted that I did not trust them, and Osmeña professed deep sorrow. . . . But I know them." [21]

The other two entered and the drafting resumed. Late at night they concluded, submitting the original Fairfield Bill of 1924 as a basis for negotiation, with immigration and trade provisions brought up to date. As before, the provisions of most concern to Filipinos were for an elective governor general and for twenty years of autonomy followed by a plebiscite on independence. [22]

The next morning Quezon, in bed, received Van Schaick by reaching under the pillow and producing the latest message from Hurley. As the Colonel read it, the thought rose in his mind that this was the "high point in Philippine-American relations." Hurley proposed (1) an elective governor general for the Filipinos, (2) an American high commissioner with veto power on financial affairs, and American control of defense and health, (3) immigration and trade limitations to be reciprocal if the Filipinos desired, (4) the Filipinos to set up a state or dominion form of government, as they preferred, and (5) the question of independence to be set aside for the time being. [23]

"This is a tremendous concession," said Van Schaick when he took leave of Quezon. "The first thing to do is accept. Then if you can get them to change it, so much the better." Although the omission of ultimate independence bothered him, Quezon's first reaction was nearly as enthusiastic. [24] He thought Hurley's recognition of Filipino capacities "splendid." If the Secretary would only give them the right to dissolve the partnership in fifteen or twenty years, he would "cause to disappear all resentment now obtaining over former assumption of race superiority, all resentment against dependence imposed by superior force, and leave only the feeling that the races are different, not superior or inferior." A permanent link might then

---

21. Van Schaick Journal, 2 Dec 31.
22. Quezon letter to Butte, 2 Dec 31, original two drafts addressed to Van Schaick (Q); Butte cable Sec War, 3 Dec 31, BIA 364–835. The latter cable is oddly missing from the Series I Collection.
23. Hurley through Guevara to Quezon, 3 Dec 31. Hurley was not responding to the Butte cable of 3 Dec, which had not yet reached him, but to a brief cable from Quezon to Guevara, Osias, 2 Dec; Cablegrams, Series I.
24. Van Schaick Journal, 3 Dec 31.

be possible. Change or not, Quezon concluded, he would do everything possible for the Secretary and his proposal. "If the program is going through I'll come back to Washington . . . all the way on a stretcher to help him and to thank him." [25] So Quezon wrote in the flush of success.

Quezon, however, was given to second thoughts, and third. The mission was leaving in two days; suppose they should get from Congress an independence bill, leaving Quezon stuck supporting the dominion proposal? Quezon could not persuade Osmeña and Roxas, on the eve of their sailing, to pledge support of Hurley; in the end, therefore, he did not pledge himself. He waited eight days before replying fully and directly to Hurley's proposal. In the meantime he conveyed to Butte his hope that ultimate independence would be conceded to the Philippines, a concession that would leave the door open for either alternative, total separation or permanent connection.[26] For the public, Quezon took on a tone of lament. In a letter of farewell to the mission published in a Manila newspaper, he revealed that the administration had not accepted even his most conservative formula.[27]

The mission thus departed with no more binding instructions than the legislative resolution to seek the "earliest" independence possible. Quezon had tempered the Osmeña-Roxas tone of early November, but it was too late to confine them within the administration's solution; in their dealings with the American Congress they would be essentially beyond his control. But equally so was he beyond theirs, when it came to the Philippine scene.

Osmeña made a short last-minute call upon Van Schaick, asking him "in great confidence" to keep a restraining hand on Quezon. "You have great influence with him. Please use it. He is impetuous, impatient and apt to go to extremes. . . . Please keep thinking of our situation there [in Washington] and influence him not to do things that will make our part more difficult." Van Schaick agreed

25. Quezon holograph to Guevara, Osias, undated and unsent (Q). Although some of its wording appears in the Quezon cable of 11 Dec 31, I ascribe the date of 3 Dec to this piece because of its impulsive enthusiasm, a Quezonian characteristic on first reaction. He took a more guarded tone the very next day. See notes 26–27, below.
26. Butte to Sec War, 4 Dec 31, BIA 364–836.
27. Quezon to Osmeña, 4 Dec 31, published in *La Opinion*, 5 Dec, translated BIA 364–918B.

to try, insisting that Osmeña on his side make allowances for the situation in Manila.[28] Van Schaick's importance to Quezon, however, was chiefly as a channel to Hurley. In a future domestic political fight he would have no influence.

On December 6, 1931, the mission sailed. A few days later Quezon sent off a full-bodied answer to Hurley's proposal, complimenting it handsomely, but stating that he could give no assurance either that the mission felt the same way or that he himself would not endorse legislation which followed more closely the lines he had suggested. Did he mean, the Resident Commissioners inquired, for Hurley's clarification and their own, that "no solution or program is satisfactory without independence?" That is what he meant, Quezon replied.[29]

So ended the idea of a Philippines permanently attached to the United States in "partnership" or "dominion"—ended but for two brief flurries. Hurley momentarily considered an immediate independence proposal, excepting Mindanao, Sulu, and the Mountain Province, but President Hoover killed the idea of split-level development.[30]

Meanwhile San Francisco and New York interests were circulating their "Free State" bill for the Philippines, with the word that Quezon helped prepare and now supported it. Senator Harry Hawes, sponsor of an independence bill, summoned the Resident Commissioners to his office, flourished a copy of the Free State plan, and said that if the story were true "he would quit and denounce us [the Filipino leaders] and consider himself deceived." [31]

Quezon satisfied Hawes with a declaration that he had not pre-

28. Van Schaick Journal, 5 Dec 31.
29. Quezon had cabled his initial thanks to Guevara, for Sec War, 5 Dec 31, his full reply to MacArthur for Guevara, Osias, 11 Dec. The exchange on clarification consisted of Guevara, Osias to Quezon, 11 Dec, and Quezon to Guevara, Osias, 17, 18 Dec, Cablegrams, Series I.
30. Guevara, Osias to Quezon, 24 Dec 31; Quezon to Guevara, Osias, 26 Dec. Other messages bearing out the Hoover administration's unwillingness to go further are: Quezon to Guevara, Osias, 1, 15, 16, 18 Jan 32; Osmeña, Roxas to Quezon, Aquino, Alas, 15 Jan; Guevara, Osias to Quezon, 18 Jan; Osmeña, Roxas to Quezon, 18 Jan, Cablegrams, Series I; also, Stimson diary, 8 Jan 32 (HLS). The two Resident Commissioners, Guevara and Osias, had prepared Osmeña and Roxas as chief Philippine agents in Washington with a 12-page brief of the situation in America, addressed to them in Honolulu, 23 Dec 31 (Eduardo de la Rosa MSS).
31. Guevara, Osias to Quezon, 19 Dec 31, Cablegrams, Series I.

pared and had not seen any such proposal.[32] Then he quickly cabled John M. Switzer, contact man for the free-state group, that the radical attitude of the Legislature made any plan impossible unless it included ultimate independence. The free-staters replied with a warning and an appeal. The choices as they saw them were absolute independence (with Japanese imperialism threatening), nothing at all (with Philippine nationalism frustrated), or their own moderate compromise on a dominion relationship. Would not Quezon please lead his people down the middle of the road? Quezon told them that he doubted whether he could, at that moment, lead his people anywhere.[33]

32. Quezon to Guevara, Osias, 20 Dec 31, Cablegrams, Series I; Hawes to Quezon, 27 Dec (Q).
33. Quezon to John M. Switzer, 21 Dec 31; Switzer and J. R. Pardee to Quezon, 28 Dec; Gen Harbord to Quezon, 28 Dec, Quezon to Harbord, 31 Dec, Cablegrams, Series I; Brig Gen Frank L. Parker, Chief BIA, memo to Sec War, 23 Dec 31, reporting phone calls of 22–23 Dec from W. Edward Bruce, BIA 364–841.

6

American Exposure and Japanese Expansion

IN DISCUSSING the dominion plan in Philippine domestic politics we have run ahead of the international story. Three great blows shook the structure of Western imperialism in the twentieth century—the two world wars and the Great Depression in between. The United States differed from European powers in depending far less, economically and emotionally, upon holding colonies. In adversity, therefore, it gave them up more readily. The stock market crash of October 1929 and the Japanese invasion of Manchuria, September 1931, brought out latent American anti-imperialism, which ultimately outweighed the determination of the Hoover administration and various private interests to hold on to the Philippines.

Even before the crash, depression had hit American farmers in 1921 and again after 1926. The world sugar market had been slumping since 1925. Heavy Filipino immigration after 1926 had created job and wage competition on the West Coast. Secretary of State Henry Stimson testified, fresh from a year in Manila as governor general, against ensuing proposals to apply American tariff and coastwise shipping laws against the Philippines. "We have gotten beyond the caveman age in regard to colonial development," he said. "We do not and cannot now hold colonies by force." Neither should the United States discriminate against them economically while they were under the flag.[1]

Stimson helped kill the legislation in committee, but Senator William King provided him with a new problem. King later declared to Quezon that he was animated by "abhorrence of tyranny in any form," but this conviction fit nicely with his representing the state of Utah, which depended heavily on sugar beets, and with his habitual opposition to large naval construction. Now, as an amendment to the tariff bill, he offered a resolution for immediate Philippine independence. If America could not apply duties on territory under her flag, then lower the flag first and raise the tariff afterwards. Stimson later told King that a tariff would make the Filipinos "hate us as long as history lasts." The Senate, less dubious, barely defeated King's amendment, 45 to 36.[2]

On October 28, 1929, not long afterwards, stocks listed on the New York Exchange took a 12.3 per cent loss in value, and the next day another 10 per cent, with a record volume of sixteen million shares traded. Simultaneously, the Philippine Legislature, while all three leaders were out of the country, appointed them and others as a new mission to seek "immediate, absolute, and complete independence." [3] By the time the mission arrived in Washington the whole of the United States was in financial crisis, and the special sectors already touched by Philippine competition were supporting King's solution for ending Philippine competition. Unable to grapple with the major causes of depression, they were hysterically eager to attack a minor cause of their own distress.

Senate hearings opened on January 20, 1930, the day that the first Filipino died from racial violence in California. Osmeña and Roxas represented their country, Quezon remaining home, as he would again in 1931–32, partly because of his tuberculosis. A member of the Senate Committee on Territories, Harry Hawes, privately invited the Philippine delegation to his office and offered his help. As

---

1. House Ways and Means Committee, Hearings, 70th Cong., 2nd sess., 10638 ff.; subcommittee, House Committee on Commerce, Hearings, 70:2, 685 ff. (quotation, p. 685), in appendix of Sen Terr, *Hearings on Philippine Independence* 71:2. Also, Stimson diary, 28 Aug 30 (HLS); Roxas, Osmeña to Quezon, 17, 19, 26 Apr 30 (Q).
2. *Cong Rec* 71:1, 3567–68, 4063–66, 4369–4426; "Memorandum of Conference, June 18, 1931" (Q); Stimson diary, 16 Mar 31 (HLS).
3. Consul General, Shanghai, to Sec State, 24 Oct 29, BIA Quezon-P; 8th Phil Legis, 2nd sess., Conc Res 29.

a young man he had represented the Republic of Hawaii when it was annexed in 1898. After years as a railroad lawyer in Missouri he had come up through state politics to serve three terms as a congressman from a St. Louis district, and he had won election to the Senate in 1926. "Before I retire from public life I should like to feel that I have contributed something towards the happiness of a large section of mankind." He asked, "Do you and your people honestly and truly want independence?"

Roxas and the others "almost stumbled over each other" in affirming that the leaders and the people genuinely wanted it;[4] Hawes declared he would help them get it. *Time* magazine later named him "Beets"; the Manila *Bulletin* associated him with Cuban sugar, and Secretary of Agriculture Arthur Hyde said in cabinet that Hawes was accepting retainers from Missouri interests for his work on the Philippine bill, but there is no documentary record of such connections.[5] The Filipino leaders' continued trust in Hawes implicitly sustains his declarations of sincerity, as does his voting record of opposition to premature tariff and immigration laws against the Philippines. As mentor to the independence mission, he encouraged it to cultivate sympathetic legislators, farm and labor lobbies, and journalists who could represent their cause.[6]

While Roxas and most of the mission worked in Washington, Osmeña and others were in London at the Naval Conference. Stimson had been against any independence mission, but at least in London the Filipinos might learn the realities of world power. The Secretary of State sometimes doubted that his own President understood those realities. "How long must we keep the Islands," Hoover had impatiently asked Stimson, "in order to do our duty to them?" Stimson argued that the United States had great unfulfilled responsibilities in the Philippines, requiring an indefinite period of

4. Marcial P. Lichauco, then Secretary to the Philippine Mission, in his biography of *Roxas* (Manila, 1952), pp. 61–62. Son of a member of Aguinaldo's Revolutionary Committee at Hong Kong, and himself a Harvard lawyer, Lichauco had collaborated with Moorfield Storey in an anti-imperialist tract, *The Conquest of the Philippines by the United States, 1898–1925* (New York, G. P. Putnam's Sons, 1926). He later became Roxas' law partner and personal confidant.
5. *Time*, 14 Sept 31, New York *Herald Tribune*, 27 June 33 (BIA); Stimson diary, 11 Oct 31 (HLS).
6. Lichauco, *Roxas*, pp. 63–66.

time to be acquitted.[7] Stimson's reasoning only really struck home when Hoover learned in 1930 that if the United States were to "withdraw from the Philippines, Great Britain would insist on a wholly different ratio in the matter of warships." Cameron Forbes noted that "apparently the success of the whole disarmament program, on which the President has set his heart, depended on our staying in the Philippines." Retention of the islands meant a relatively large American navy, which Hoover disliked; but the alternative, independence, "would upset the whole disarmament conference apple cart." Great Britain, in that case, would not be satisfied with a navy at parity with the American.[8]

The Filipinos in London apparently tried to clear the way for independence plus security by asking for a neutralization treaty, but the idea never rose beyond the level of unofficial shop talk.[9] A member of the World Court, Sir Cecil Hurst, at a dinner party in The Hague, expressed a popular British attitude: Philippine independence "would set the whole East ablaze." At another dinner, in the Netherlands East Indies, a high Dutch official said that if America left the island, "it will be necessary for the Dutch and British immediately to take control," and the British in Singapore were "reliably reported" to agree.[10]

The Japanese had their own reasons for rejecting the Philippine formula; neutralization would not lessen their own defense needs.[11] Even when the United States and Great Britain conceded Japan parity in submarines and 70 per cent of parity in cruisers and destroyers, the "big navy" and restless nationalist elements in Japan found the settlement demeaning. Premier Hamaguchi, who defended it vigorously, was shot by a young fanatic and died nine months

7. Stimson to Quezon, Osmeña, through Gov Gen Dwight Davis, 12 Nov 29, BIA Confidential File 26480–110; Stimson to Quezon, 30 Dec 29 (HLS); Forbes Journals, 3, 2–3 (WCF); "Memorandum of Events Since Taking Office as Secretary of State," Stimson diary, 28 Aug 30 (HLS).

8. Quotations from Forbes Journals, 3, 13, 68 (WCF); on associated matters, *Cong Rec* 72:1, 7513; Washington *News*, 24 Feb 30, BIA 364-a-w-873, pt. 2.

9. The topic is not mentioned in London Naval Conference documents published in *For Rel* 1930, *1*, 1–131, but several papers carried pertinent articles and dispatches: *The Economist* (London), 25 Jan 30, Washington *Post*, 12 Feb, New York *Herald Tribune*, 9 Mar, BIA 364-a-w-873, pt. 2.

10. Hague Legation dispatch 204, 28 Nov 31, SD 793.94/3149; Naval intelligence report, relayed by Director, Naval WPD to CNO, 20 Oct 31, JB 305 ser 499.

11. Ambassador to Japan (Castle) to Sec State, 25 Jan, 14 Feb 30, *For Rel* 1930, *1*, 9–10, 24–25.

later from the effects of the wound.[12] The United States, by contrast, was so economy-minded and inclined to isolation that it did not even build up to treaty limits.

When Stimson came home from London, the Philippine mission went to see him, presumably to obtain his help in safeguarding their American market. His appearance before the Senate committee to oppose independence was a "hopeless fight," he admitted, because they were "already committed by a large majority to Philippine independence." Tired from traveling, five times interrupted by a belligerent Hawes, Stimson suggested, defensively, that he was appearing at the request of the Philippine mission itself. Roxas in embarrassment denied it, and the whole mission backed him up in a declaration overzealously dated the day *before* Stimson testified. Pedro Gil said that Stimson had declared, without invitation, his willingness to testify. Later Stimson complained to Quezon that Roxas had not backed him up. Quezon replied that Roxas "had gone to the devil," [13] and Mrs. Quezon added privately to Stimson that she had always told her husband Roxas would do this.

This incident, however, involved less duplicity than misunderstanding. Stimson had been accustomed to representing Filipino economic interests with their endorsement. Politically, however, he was now their antagonist, and they had miscalculated in thinking that they could bring into play only that half of Stimson which was useful to them. They did not try again. Pedro Gil declared in Manila that the worst enemy of Philippine independence was Henry L. Stimson.[14]

The independence cause, however, had many friends in the farm and labor lobbies; and the midterm elections of 1930 returned a Democratic majority in the House, with an even split in the Senate. Hoover grimly remarked, "We certainly have become a minority

12. Robert A. Scalapino, *Democracy and the Party Movement in Prewar Japan: The Failure of the First Attempt* (Berkeley, University of California Press, 1953), pp. 238–40; Delmer Brown, *Nationalism in Japan* (Berkeley, University of California Press, 1955), p. 189; Richard Storry, *The Double Patriots* (Boston, Houghton Mifflin, 1957), pp. 52–53; Robert J. C. Butow, *Tojo and the Coming of the War* (Princeton, Princeton Univ. Press, 1961), pp. 48–49.
13. Sen Terr 71:2, 657–82, esp. 672, 680–81; Sen Report 71:2, No. 781; Stimson diary, 28 Aug 30, 10 May 31 (HLS).
14. Preliminary Report of the Independence Mission of 1929–30, 25 Aug 30, BIA 26480–120; Manila *Bulletin*, 18 Sept 30, BIA, Stimson-P.

government." [15] In the spring Stimson welcomed Quezon to Washington in the hope of working out an administration solution to the Philippine question, thus forestalling congressional action. He was willing, Quezon said, to accept an immigration quota (with laborers prohibited) and import quotas on sugar and coconut oil (though no tariff). Quezon's reasonableness spurred Stimson to set up for him a series of conversations in the War Department.

Over a period of six weeks, Quezon talked with Secretary Patrick Hurley, Major General Frank McCoy, Brigadier General Frank MacIntyre (who had just completed seventeen years as Chief of the BIA), and others, entertaining various plans for more autonomy.[16] Then Senator King, concerned over rumors of a Filipino "change of front," called him into private conference.

"I would like to tell you now," Quezon said, "as plainly as language can make it, that we have not changed front and would take independence now in any form." Quezon told McCoy roughly the same. The round-robin conversations in the War Department ended inconclusively in late July, Quezon and Hurley agreeing simply to go to the Philippines together, without preconceived plan.[17]

Harry Hawes, however, preceded them, campaigning in the Philippines, making shirt-sleeve speeches. Privately he suggested that the Filipinos imitate Sam Adams' Bostonians and throw a tea party of their own. Before a joint session of the Philippine Legislature he warned against plans to delay independence fifteen years or more—"graveyard settlements," he called them.[18]

The ship which carried Hawes home crossed in mid-Pacific the one bringing out Patrick Hurley, the first Secretary of War in twenty

15. Stimson diary, 30 Mar 31 (HLS).
16. Stimson diary, 10, 19, 20, 21, 25 May, 3 June 31 (HLS); "Memorandum for the Secretary of War, Secret," and "Subject: Concerning certain proposed changes in the relations between the United States and the Philippine Islands (Conversations between Secretary of War and Mr. Quezon)," both unsigned and undated, probably by McCoy; Sen Arthur Vandenberg to Hurley, 15 June 31, Hurley to McCoy, 22 June, McCoy to Hurley, 3 July, McCoy MSS, Box 41.
17. Quezon, "Summary of the views submitted by Mr. Quezon to the Secretary of War regarding the situation, [late June] 1931," and "Memorandum of Conference [with Senator King], June 18, 1931" (Q); Quezon to Hoover, 15 June 31, and Hoover to Quezon, 16 June, BIA 364–786½; John Martyn, admin ass't to Sec War, memo for confidential file, 29 July, BIA 364–816½.
18. Philippines Herald, 23 June 31, Manila Bulletin, 24 June, New York Herald Tribune, 14 July, Boston Transcript, 8 Aug, BIA Hawes-P; re "tea party," Stimson diary, 10 Nov 31 (HLS).

years to visit the Philippines. Quezon, his would-be traveling companion, had remained behind, once again weakened by tuberculosis.[19] He might also have been leery of entering, in such conservative company, the radical atmosphere left by Hawes.

Immediately before Hurley landed in Manila, urban labor unions staged a "humiliation day" in sympathy for victims of California race riots. The Secretary nevertheless managed a theatrical triumph shortly after arrival, by climbing on a truck inside the grounds of Malacañan as an independence parade marched by. The crowd swirled toward the gates to see the living symbol of American authority. There stood the self-made man from Oklahoma, erect and proud, with a moustache as thick as Leonard Wood's. Sight of him broke up the parade. Manuel Roxas tried to get the crowd moving again, but failed until the police came to help.

Hurley and Roxas were more than symbolically at cross-purposes. When Hurley observed that less than a quarter of the population understood the meaning of independence, and those opposed to it were not permitted free speech, Roxas criticized him for coming with a closed mind, pursuing a prejudiced inquiry, and having "lazy recourse" to stock questions. Before the Secretary departed on September 26, the Legislature, instead of inviting him to speak, presented him with a resolution for "immediate political separation" from the United States.[20]

The world depression after 1929 had struck Japan full force. The farm and fishing communities were especially hard hit, and from them the Japanese army drew its best recruits. Misery spread the Marxist heresy in Japan, tending to evoke traditionalistic nationalism as a counter force. Among the most extreme nationalists were certain officers of the Kwantung Army, contending abroad against China's attempts to regain the upper hand in developing Manchuria and at home against the Japanese liberals who wanted to cut military expenses.

While Western powers, economically stricken, were unwilling to

19. BIA, Quezon-P. Before Quezon decided to stay on the West Coast, Moscow *Pravda* cynically and erroneously reported, 17 Aug, that his sailing together with Hurley proved that the question was settled in advance; SD 811B.01/146.
20. New York *Herald Tribune*, 21 Aug, 10, 15 Sept 31, New York *Times*, 11, 15, 18–20 Sept, Philippines *Herald*, 22, 26, 28 Sept, Washington *Star*, 24 Sept, *Time* magazine, 14 Sept, BIA Hurley-P; text of resolution, BIA 364–837.

undertake military action abroad, the Kwantung Army planned and executed a coup in Manchuria, beginning September 18, 1931. In succeeding years the Japanese military was able to penetrate China and to ignore the West. Stealing first the initiative from the moderates in Tokyo, and finally the government itself, they began to conceive of a Greater East Asia upon the model of Manchukuo—satellite to Japan.

Among the Japanese people, the Army won glory and respect for techniques of "direct action." The internationalism of the 1920s began to wane. In its stead there began to rise the most classic form of Japanese nationalism, guided from above, fearful of foreign powers, touchy about equal treatment. With a new and sharper accent the Japanese spoke of their "mission" in East Asia.[21]

The portents for the Philippines were unpleasant. Almost no Japanese had lived there in 1900; by 1931 there were 16,000. Japanese-Philippine trade had been negligible in the Spanish era; now it was worth $17,000,000 per year.[22] The Japanese were leaders in developing hemp, and prominent in lumber, fishing, and retail trade. Two energetic entrepreneurs, Ohta Kyosaburo and Furukawa Yoshizo, with the help of their government and with homeland *zaibatsu* (economic combines), had led in the building of a Japanese commercial and cultural enclave in the province of Davao.[23] The trade map on the wall of the Japanese consul there labeled the island of Mindanao, along with Korea and Formosa, as "Domestic." [24]

Should the Japanese ever decide to move southward and succeed, the Filipinos could expect no better treatment than Formosa. In Japan's colonial laboratory there were some achievements of which the Japanese might be proud, but others were alien to the phi-

21. On the Manchurian incident and sequela: Brown, pp. 198–99; Storry, pp. 54–93; Butow, pp. 30–41; Yoshihashi Takehiko, *Conspiracy at Mukden: The Rise of the Japanese Military* (New Haven, Yale University Press, 1963), pp. 151–218.
22. "Emigration from Japan to the Philippine Islands," Leo D. Sturgeon, American Consul, Tokyo, 2 Apr 31, McCoy MSS, Box 89; "A Symposium on the Philippine-Japanese Trade," Filemon Perez, Sec Commerce and Communications, 1 Nov 33, BIA 6144–181.
23. Shibata Ken'ichi, *Dabao kaitakuki* (History of the Colonization of Davao) (Tokyo, Kōa Nihonsha, 1941) pp. 43–58, 67–72; Furukawa Yoshizō, *Dabao kaitakuki* (History of the Colonization of Davao) (Tokyo, 1956); Florence Horn, *Orphans of the Pacific* (New York, Reynal and Hitchcock, 1941), pp. 273–78; Cecil E. Cody, "The Japanese in Davao," *Comment*, No. 7 (Manila, 1958), pp. 23–26.
24. Naval intelligence report, relayed by Director, Naval WPD to CNO, 20 Oct 31, JB 305 ser 499.

losophy of Filipino-American cooperation. Cameron Forbes found only 70 per cent of provincial and municipal administration in Formosan hands, and virtually none of the general administration. Instead of the Japanese ruling for the benefit of the Formosans, "a portion of the skimmed milk is left . . . and the cream is all taken to Japan." [25]

The Japanese conquest of Manchuria was considerably advanced when, on his way home from Manila, Patrick Hurley cabled a series of brisk questions to Washington. Of the Army and the Navy, of the Department of Commerce and of State, he asked: Are the Philippines, from your point of view, currently a liability or an asset to the United States? [26] The replies reflected no special anxiety about the meaning of Japanese expansion for America's position in East Asia and the West Pacific. All found the Philippines an asset, none a liability.

That the Army should think so was the most surprising. The last estimate of situation ORANGE in 1928 regarded Japan as being able to put 300,000 men in the Philippines within 30 days. The United States would have been able to meet that force with 11,000 regular troops (of which 7,000 were Philippine Scouts), plus the Philippine Constabulary of 6,000, and an air component of only nine bombers and eleven pursuit planes. The schedule of reinforcement from Hawaii would be highly uncertain.[27] The Army members of the Joint Board, led by Chief of Staff Douglas MacArthur, nonetheless found the Philippines "a military asset" and concurred with the Navy that it ought to be retained.[28]

In MacArthur's case, Hurley's question called up a personal attachment to the colony. His father had served there in the Spanish-American war; he himself had done so, fresh out of West Point, as a second lieutenant of engineers in 1903–04; and again in 1922–25, as a brigadier general, commanding the Philippine Division. During MacArthur's most recent service, as Major General and Com-

25. Forbes Journals, 3, 343 (WCF).
26. The cables were dispatched 2 Oct 31. The replies are collected in no single place; the answer from Commerce is quoted in Hurley's own draft report to the President, preserved in a special BIA file; location of other replies is given in subsequent notes.
27. Louis Morton, "War Plan ORANGE: Evolution of a Strategy," World Politics, 11 (1959), 233–34.
28. Joint Board to Sec War, 23 Oct 31, JB 305 ser 499.

manding Officer of the Philippine Department, 1928–30, his acquaintance with Manuel and Aurora Quezon ripened into friendship. Quezon in turn was impressed with MacArthur, not least because, unlike the run of Army men, he treated Filipinos as social equals. When the question of replacing Stimson as governor general came up, Quezon suggested MacArthur, having found his proposed policies as acceptable as his manners were agreeable.[29]

The governorship eventually went to Dwight Davis, but MacArthur had his sights set higher anyway. When Hurley issued a rather bland pronouncement in 1930 about retaining the Philippines, MacArthur wrote him that it was "the most comprehensive and statesmanlike paper that has ever been presented with reference to this complex and perplexing problem. . . . If nothing else had ever been written upon the subject your treatise would be complete and absolute. It leaves nothing to be said and has brought confidence and hope out of the morass of chaos and confusion which has existed in the minds of millions of people."

MacArthur was writing already as if his were the voice of both the American people and the Filipino people. His policies would never fail to recognize their affiliation, nor would his rhetoric lack the thrill and the presumption of seeing the interests of the two peoples as one, safe in his own keeping. Less than two months after his letter to Hurley, MacArthur was appointed Chief of Staff, with the Secretary's vigorous recommendation.[30]

The Navy was more emphatic than the Army in its assessment of the Philippines: even though no first class naval base had ever been built there, and the Washington treaties forbade its construction, naval thinking remained enough suffused with Mahanian theory to find the islands "a *distinct* naval asset to the United States."

The two services bridged over the differences in their appraisals with a compromise, declaring the Philippines "a *positive* asset . . . from the standpoint of combined military and naval operations and strategy." Admittedly the colony was "inadequately defended and beyond quick supporting distance of our nearest base, Oahu," but in peacetime it was "a powerful stabilizing factor in Far Eastern af-

---

29. On the governor-generalship: Quezon to Roxas, Osmeña, 13, 16 Apr 29 (Q).
30. MacArthur to Hurley, 21 May 30, BIA 364–725A; also quoted in full by Hurley to the author, 30 Mar 61. In his *Reminiscences* (New York, McGraw-Hill, 1964), p. 89, MacArthur wrote that he accepted the appointment chiefly because his mother wanted him to.

fairs," and in wartime it would be "indispensable." The Philippines in American possession were, all told, "an asset to the world generally, with the exception of Japan." [31]

The Department of Commerce was the least enthusiastic of those consulted, merely granting that it was a "fair conclusion" that the Philippines was more an asset than a liability. The Department of State had no such hesitations, for the answering pen was Henry Stimson's. Possession of the Philippines was "an enormous asset," he declared. It had become "a physical base for American influence —political, economic, and social—in the Far East," a place to demonstrate before Orientals as well as Europeans "American ideas, ideals, and methods" of promoting individual and general welfare.

Progress in the Philippines depended upon American guidance and the material assistance of free access to the American market. If these were removed, economic chaos and sociopolitical anarchy would ensue, followed with domination by a foreign power, probably China or Japan. "To every foreign eye it would be a demonstration of selfish cowardice and futility on our part." The presence of the United States in the Philippines had already developed a new political equilibrium throughout the West Pacific and East Asia. Withdrawal of sovereignty would unsettle relations among all nations there; it would disturb colonial governments and "would render more difficult the safeguarding of American interests both in the Far East and throughout the world." [32]

On the second anniversary of the Wall Street crash, Stimson and Hurley spent a "Philippine evening" together. Stimson, more sympathetic to the Filipinos, tried to disabuse Hurley of an antipathy "based . . . largely upon his contact with the white collar leaders of the independence movement." Hurley was founding his policy largely on concern for the pagans and Moros, who generally distrusted Christian Filipinos and desired maintenance of American rule. Stimson's advice and Quezon's pleading over the next several weeks somewhat softened Hurley's attitude about increased autonomy, but he tended still to think of the destiny of thirteen million

31. Joint Board to Sec War, 23 Oct 31, JB 305 ser 499; italics mine.
32. Stimson to Hurley, 29 Oct 31 (SD 811B.01/149A; also HLS 3F–0919); partially anticipated by memos of Dr Stanley Hornbeck, Chief, Division of Far Eastern Affairs: 13 May 30, SD 811B.01/133¾; 10 June 31, McCoy MSS, Box 41; 16 Oct 31, SD 811 B.01/148½.

Filipinos in terms of minorities totaling 8 per cent.[33] Stimson's own policy, tying Philippine destiny to the status quo for hundreds of millions all over Asia, was in effect only slightly more liberal.

In succeeding months Stimson felt the full impact of Japanese conquest in Manchuria and reacted against it. He privately warned Admiral Pratt, Chief of Naval Operations, to be on guard against surprise attack.[34] He wrote public letters to Senator Hiram Bingham, advising urgently against Philippine independence, lest it encourage in "the Orient . . . one of those historic developments which will disturb the whole earth," [35] and to Senator William Borah, iterating in full his policy of nonrecognition of Manchukuo.[36]

Japanese critics professed to find a contrast between the "imperialistic tone" of Stimson's first letter and the pacifistic pretensions of the second.[37] To Stimson, however, saving the Philippines from would-be liberators was an inseparable corollary of saving China from its invaders. Although he complained to reporters that Congress' attitude on the Philippines was making his notes to Japan useless,[38] he persisted in the two courses of trying to preserve Manchuria for China and the Philippines for America. To both causes he brought the mind of a skilled advocate, refreshing old arguments of Hay, Mahan, and Roosevelt, and others of Root, Taft, and Wood. Inspired by fin-de-siècle expansionism and empowered with his own experience and conviction, Stimson's arguments were the last, most generous eloquence of American empire.

33. Stimson diary, 29 Oct 31 (HLS); Hurley report to the President, several drafts, never published, BIA Special File. For Quezon-Hurley correspondence, see Ch. 5, pp. 62–67.
34. Stimson diary, 2 Mar 32 (HLS).
35. The letter was later published, Cong Rec, 4 Apr 32. Hoover had seen and approved it, but said also that because of disagreement "on certain fundamentals . . . I do not want . . . to be tied from expressing my own views." Hoover to Stimson, 13 Feb 32 (HLS, IF–2137).
36. Richard Current, Secretary Stimson (New Brunswick, Rutgers University Press, 1954), pp. 97–102, and Robert H. Ferrell, American Diplomacy in the Great Depression (New Haven, Yale University Press, 1957), pp. 183–88. Both analyze the Borah letter without mention of the Bingham letter which was its underpinning.
37. New York Herald Tribune, 6 Apr 32, BIA 364-a-w-873, pt. 5; Tokyo Asahi, 6 Apr, Tokyo Nichi Nichi, 7 Apr, SD 811B.01/169.
38. Stimson diary, 18 Feb 32 (HLS).

7

Lobbies, Interests, and Illusions

WHY DID legislation scheduling independence for the Philippines pass Congress in the 1930s, a dozen years before European powers began to relinquish their colonies on a worldwide scale? Clearly no bill would have succeeded without both a strong independence movement in the Philippines and strong anti-imperial sentiment in the United States. Other American possessions—Hawaii, Puerto Rico —did not want independence; other Western powers—France, Holland, Portugal—did not wish to give independence.

Historical discussion of the Philippine independence acts has centered obsessively on American economic interests. These, however, could not have pushed the matter through alone, or even aided by various social and military considerations. The anti-imperial principle was necessary to consummation of the independence movement in the United States.

In 1932 the Democratic party, traditionally pro-independence, dominated Congress. Americans with interests in the Philippines were anti-independence, but they now mostly confined themselves to working for as long a transition period as possible. This group fell roughly into four classes: (1) Americans with overseas investments in the Philippines, such as RCA, Standard Oil, and California Packing Company, (2) importers and processors of tax-free Philippine products, (3) manufacturers and exporters of products to the tax-free Philippine market, and (4) "Manila Americans"—American residents who lived in the Philippines and carried on business there. Of these the most active against independence were the second and third groups, together represented by the Philippine-American Chamber of Commerce in New York, which had eighty member firms and individuals. A Democratic congressman from Missouri accused them of "spilling . . . poison in the minds of the American people," [1] although their propaganda campaign in the national press was actually rational and honest.

On the pro-independence side was a truly irrational lobby, aimed against agricultural imports from the Philippines: sugar, coconut oil, and cordage. These were only miniscule causes of American agricultural distress, but farm representatives lunged at them as if they were the farmers' only vulnerable enemy. [2] Lobbyists for Midwestern dairymen and Southern farmers arrayed themselves against coconut oil, in defense of butter and cottonseed oil. The National Dairy Union and the National Cooperative Milk Producers Association, the major lobbyists, used reprehensibly fallacious arguments. They alleged falsely that American farmers could improve their competitive position against coconut oil by a two-cent per pound tariff. [3] Moreover, when tariffs became reciprocal the farmers would suffer further, because the Philippines was one of the United States' best customers for exported flour and dairy products.

Logic, however, had little sway in the Great Depression. Nineteen beet-growing states west of Ohio and eight cane-growing states in the South were working against Philippine sugar, through the American Farm Bureau Federation, the National Grange, and the National Beet Growers' Association. [4] In fact, 90 per cent of Philippine sugar competed, not with the American-grown product, but with sugar from Cuba. Lobbyists for continental sugar could neither have expanded their market nor raised their prices by shutting out the Philippine product, for the price was established by the world

1. House Ins, 72:1, 201–31, 239–69 (quotation, p. 269), 329–339; Sen Terr, 72:1, 77–105, 443–45, 567–70; American Chamber of Commerce *Journal* (Manila), 12 Mar 32, and passim; BIA 27685 and 364–989.
2. Grayson Kirk, *Philippine Independence: Motives, Problems, and Prospects* (New York, Farrar and Rinehart, 1936), pp. 73–80.
3. House Ins, 72:1, 170–84, 188–99; Kirk, pp. 80–88.
4. House Ins, 72:1, 149–70, 185–88, 425–30; Sen Terr, 72:1, 67–104.

market rate plus the preferential tariff on Cuban sugar, which would still come in.[5]

Those who had the most to gain from tariffs on Philippine sugar were those who had promoted the overrapid growth of Cuban sugar in the 1920s, such as the Chase National Bank, the Royal Bank of Canada, certain Boston banks, and the National City Bank of New York. Now, in the midst of revolution in Cuba and depression in the United States, they were trying to save their investments. Quezon accused the National City Bank of "paying millions to propagate in the United States the idea that the competition of [our] sugar was destructive to American beet sugar."[6]

Quezon, as usual, exaggerated, but sounder critics also singled out the National City Bank as the leader of the lobby—Arthur Krock, who picked up his news in Washington, and Cameron Forbes, who deduced from conversation with financiers and friends in New York that the bank was "conniving at the independence movement of the Philippines and endeavoring to get them chucked away to save some of their pennies in Cuba." More than pennies were involved; National City officers later estimated that they lost about sixty million dollars in Cuba at this time.[7] With no less selfish anxiety than the dairy, cotton, and beet farmers, they tried to save themselves by getting rid of the Philippines. It was a year of desperate measures, on Wall Street, on Main Street, and on the Great Plains.

Another strong force for Philippine independence consisted of groups opposed to Filipino immigration, for economic or social reasons, or both. Only in the late 1920s had Filipinos begun to come to the United States in great numbers, some directly, and some after working in Hawaii. By 1931 about 60,000 had arrived, nine-tenths of them males. Most of them were under thirty and engaged in agricultural work or domestic service; four-fifths of them were on the

5. Kirk, pp. 89–93.
6. *Diario de Sesiones de la Legislatura Filipina*, 12 Oct 33, p. 748; also Quezon to OsRox, 2 Jan 33 (Q). OsRox was the abbreviation used in cables and adopted by the newspapers to designate the Philippine Legislative Mission for Independence, led by Osmeña and Roxas. The answering abbreviation, Quaqual, stood for the legislative leaders in Manila, Quezon, Benigno Aquino, and Antonio de las Alas.
7. New York *Times*, 5 Apr 32; Forbes Journals, 3, 494; 4, 269–71, quotation p. 269 (WCF); author's conversation with National City Bank officers, 29 July 60. I was unable to obtain permission to consult bank records.

Pacific Coast.[8] They were willing to work for wages considerably below the American standard. The California State Federation of Labor, with similar bodies in Washington and Oregon, began agitating in 1928 to have Filipino laborers thenceforth excluded.

When exclusion efforts failed in Congress, the American Federation of Labor joined the independence bandwagon. They were against "imperialism," but even more against wage competition. Although the depression slowed Filipino immigration from 10,500 in 1929 to 2,500 in 1931, the AFL yielded to racial as well as economic passions and argued against the Filipino as a "non-assimilable Asiatic," like other Orientals excluded before him.[9]

The Filipino, in short, had fallen heir to two conflicting American traditions: reliance upon immigrant hands to do the least remunerative labor and hostility to alien encroachment upon ethnic homogeneity.[10] Now the second tradition was fully roused. "We have enough race problems now in the United States," declared Senator Shortridge of California: "the Negro problem; the Chinese problem; the Japanese problem. . . . It is [my] purpose to prevent the growth of the Philippine problem." "I have no racial prejudices," declared Representative Welch of the same state, but "God gave the non-assimilable Asiatics a place in the sun, and that place is the Orient." [11] Several Southern senators equally "free" from racial prejudice supported the Filipino exclusion movement and, when that foundered, the movement for Philippine independence.

Powerful nativistic societies joined the movement. The American Coalition, representing forty-six different patriotic organizations, and the American Legion had both backed the discriminatory Immigration Act of 1924. The argument for "racial purity," which had almost led to a rupture in diplomatic relations with Japan, they now used in order to break off the colonial relationship with the Philippines.

Actually, the Filipino who came to America was likely to speak English, to have been schooled in love of American customs, to be anxious to acquire American skills and knowledge. The problem he

8. "Filipino Immigration into the Continental United States," special BIA report, 14 Jan 32; Bruno Lasker, *Filipino Immigration to Continental United States and to Hawaii* (Chicago, University of Chicago Press, 1931), p. 324.
9. House Ins 72:1, 122–26, 233–38, 271–74, 378–84; Sen Terr 72:1, 113–18; Yakima (Washington) *Herald*, 5 Aug 31.
10. Lasker, *Filipino Immigration*, p. 328.
11. *Cong Rec* 72:1, 8069; House Ins, 72:1, 379.

posed was "not that of the stranger who cannot be Americanized, but rather that of the would-be American who refuses to remain a stranger." [12] American nativists, however, were not susceptible to common-sense reasoning, and no countervailing lobbies fought on behalf of liberal immigration laws.

The debate on Philippine independence was not only economic and social. Despite the efforts of some sponsors of the bill to exclude argument on strategic questions, it flowed in. The Joint Planning Committee of the Army and Navy, cabinet officers Stimson and Hurley, and President Hoover himself, all argued strongly against Philippine independence. Hiram Bingham in the Senate and the journalist Nicholas Roosevelt both carried forth administration arguments against eroding the American position in the Orient, undermining European interests there, and encouraging Japanese imperialism.[13]

Ranged on the other side, however, were the many who wishfully desired noninvolvement in all foreign broils and the few who drew unsparing conclusions from the actual state of American armament. In the first category was the general public and most of Congress, disillusioned by the sequel to the World War, apathetic or opposed to American naval and military spending, and to the exercise of American influence abroad. Until 1931, such persons dismissed strategic arguments against Philippine independence as "the Japanese bugaboo." Japan, they declared, had no interest in the islands; her people would not like the climate. Even after the Manchurian incident, Harry Hawes presumed to say that "the greatest strength the Philippines have is their . . . weakness." [14]

Other congressmen took the Manchurian incident more realistically, and saw Japanese expansion as clinching evidence for an American retreat to Hawaii.[15] The United States had twice already ransomed Philippine security, for recognition of Japanese special in-

12. Lasker, pp. 33–38, 298–304; quotation, p. 331.
13. Adm Mark Bristow to Sec Nav, 2 Feb 32, GB 405 ser 1564; Bingham, *Cong Rec* 72:1, 14700, 14818–19, 72:2, 386–87, 446–50, 574; Roosevelt, New York *Herald Tribune*, editorials and articles, passim, 1929–33; for administration arguments, see pp. 77–80.
14. Various senators and representatives, *Cong Rec* 71:1, 3567–68, 4065–66, 4370–90, 4412–26; 71:2, 5539–46, 8745–49; Hawes quotation, House Ins 72:1, 12 Feb 32.
15. House Ins 72:1, 298–99, 340.

terests in Korea, in 1905, and Manchuria, in 1908. Congress had foregone fortification of the Philippines in 1921, partly in order to persuade Japan to accept the lesser end of a 3:5 ratio in capital ships. Since then, the American navy had fallen under treaty strength while Japan's had kept up to the mark; and while Chief of Staff MacArthur complained without effect about his puny standing army,[16] the Kwantung Army was trying to swing Japanese national policy by the tail. Though the dignity of the forum forbade saying so, many in Congress were willing to complete a series of awkward accommodations to Japan by a graceful and final withdrawal from the West Pacific.

As American interests expressed themselves more openly and forcefully, Philippine interests began to clarify themselves in response. Other factors complicated the simple desire of the nationalist to run his own country in his own way. An element of propertied Filipinos favored an extended transition to independence, or even permanent attachment to the United States. They had made their stand known to Osmeña over the Jones Bill in 1916, to Stimson ten years later, and to Hurley on his visit in 1931.[17] If publicly committed to independence, they were privately more concerned with economic adjustment.

Now that seven-eighths of the Philippines' expanding export trade went to the United States, men with land and capital devoted to export produce and businessmen anticipating a general setback to the economy stepped in to defend the status quo. Because American farm lobbies were insisting on immediate quota limits if they could not have immediate duties, all exports were threatened, especially sugar, which provided two-thirds of Philippine export income and 30 per cent of the total income of the islands.

Filipino millers and planters responded jointly by lobbying for as large a national quota as possible and separately by increasing production to the limit, so as to obtain the largest possible personal share of the quota when it should be decided.[18] The independence

16. Annual Reports of the Chief of Staff, in Annual Reports of the Secretary of War, 1931–34, esp. 1933.
17. Osmeña to Quezon, 1916, passim (Quezon and de la Rosa MSS); Stimson diary, 9 Aug 26 (HLS); House Ins 72:1, 393, 420–22.
18. Full details in Theodore Friend, "The Philippine Sugar Industry and the Politics of Independence, 1929–1935," *Journal of Asian Studies,* 22 (1963), 179–92.

mission in Washington, however, warned the Philippine Sugar Association, as well as the coconut oil and cordage interests, that they must expect compromises, for over fifty lawyers, publicity agents, and other parties were in Washington trying to influence the independence bill.[19]

Where limits upon imports might hurt the Filipino's pocketbook, limiting or excluding immigrants hurt his pride. Why be shut out as Orientals when Spanish-speaking Mexicans crossed the borders of the United States in greater numbers annually than the accumulated total of Filipinos? Roxas showed that Spain had never excluded Filipinos, nor did the Dutch their Javanese subjects, nor the Japanese the Koreans. "Not even the crudest mercantilists," Quezon said, had held colonies by force while keeping their inhabitants at arm's length.[20]

After considerable thought, however, Quezon accepted restriction as a price of independence, because the national interest required that "our labor remain at home." Many Philippine businessmen and provincial governors agreed. They were unwilling to sponsor unpopular limits on emigration, but would be pleased to let the United States take the blame on the other end. Certain labor leaders concurred, in order to diminish the likelihood of importing manpower from China or Japan. Thus the Osmeña-Roxas mission, despite the insult and injustice involved, cooperated with the AFL in the passage of the act which carried a minimal limit on Filipino immigration.[21]

Engrossed in the political aspects of the independence question and increasingly disturbed about the economic aspects, most Filipinos were insensitive to the strategic factors. Claro Recto had publicly discussed the international position of the Philippines with the political scientist Maximo Kalaw, who was then advocating Asian solidarity under Japanese leadership, or a Monroe Doctrine for Asia. "American Monroeism," Recto said, "has saved the Republics of Central and South America from European interference; but . . . not from interference by the United States. Asiatic Monroeism will be a mere substitution of white rule in Asia by the Japanese, or

19. OsRox to Quaqual, 28 Jan 32 (Q).
20. Lasker, *Filipino Immigration,* pp. 278–80; Lichauco, *Roxas,* pp. 67–68; undated, incomplete MS in Spanish (Q).
21. Quezon to John M. Switzer, 2 Oct 31 (Q); Lasker, pp. 282–83; Lichauco, pp. 63–70.

perhaps the Chinese, or possibly the Soviets." To Kalaw's implicit critique of his racial pride and explicit doubts about his nationalism, Recto replied that he wished to see an end to the "secular domination, the insulting arrogance, and the false caste privileges" of the white. But Occidental culture and commerce would still be needed, and should be accorded equal rights and opportunities "to preserve the necessary equilibrium between those two great agencies of civilization, the East and the West." [22]

Despite Recto's fear of Japanese conquest and his hard Darwinistic picture of the world, most Filipinos subscribed to Kalaw's easy familial theory of international relations. Without sharing Kalaw's enthusiasm for the Japanese, they believed that the nation was an agglomeration of families and the world at large was a family of nations. Was not the League of Nations itself a kind of family council for disputes among contentious kin? Was not the peace of the Pacific insured by the Washington treaties and the world at large committed to peace by the Kellogg-Briand Pact? The Philippines was surely safe.

Since defense and foreign relations had been in imperial hands for centuries most Filipino leaders did not trouble themselves with such considerations. American taxpayers spent fifteen million dollars a year on the internal defense of the Philippines, but insular taxpayers spent nothing at all. Patrick Hurley asked a prominent Filipino where the funds—equal to three-eighths of the whole insular budget for 1931—would come from when the Philippines was sovereign. "Almighty God will take care of us," was the reply. "I can't debate the question with God and you," Hurley said.[23]

Many Filipinos welcomed the idea of the United States retaining bases, which suggested protection even after independence. Others gave in reluctantly, as Quezon did: "If the American people say that they will not grant us independence unless we . . . let them retain a military and naval station here, we cannot do anything." Quezon glibly pacified the objections of a compadre who foresaw socially "unpleasant incidents" as a result of American retention of bases.[24]

22. Claro M. Recto, *Asiatic Monroeism and Other Essays* (Manila, General Printing Press, 1930), quotations from pp. 32, 48.
23. Transcript of press conference, 18 Jan 32, BIA 364–897.
24. Philippines *Herald*, 26 Mar 32, BIA 364-a-w-873, pt. 5; Quezon to Ramon Fernandez, 6 Apr 32, Fernandez to Quezon, 16 Apr (Q).

Juan Sumulong immediately spotted a worse danger than barroom brawls with American sailors. Foreign bases might involve the Philippines in a war not of her making, yet American military experts agreed that at the start of a war they might have to abandon the islands. The United States might attract its enemies to the Philippines but could not repel them. For Sumulong the answer was "no bases." [25]

For Major Vicente Lim, later Brigadier General, the answer was a rough division of labor: the United States could provide naval power in a magnitude comparable to Japan's; and the Philippines could provide military strength where the United States was unable and unwilling. One hundred thousand soldiers, Lim believed, would be necessary to defend the Philippines adequately; since the whole American standing army was only 115,000, native manpower was obviously necessary. Lim recommended inauguration of an ROTC program, enlargement of the enlisted reserve, coordination with the Constabulary, training in aircraft and anti-aircraft, and complete reorganization of existing forces to suit climate, terrain, and expected mode of warfare.[26]

The critiques by Sumulong and Lim were both responsible and realistic beyond the measure of the ruling politicos, and beyond the understanding of most of their complacent, pacific countrymen.

Discussion of independence had forced Philippine politics into new alignments. Quezon had once written: "The Democratas are so darn fools [sic], and Aguinaldo three times more, that they can never hope to . . . constitute a strong opposition party, even when we give them the chance." [27] In February 1932, after years of ineffective opposition, the Democrata party dissolved itself, leaving its members free to seek new affiliations.[28] The former Democrata leader, Juan Sumulong, joined forces with Aguinaldo and a number of others in the Federation of Independent Citizens. They stood for immediate and complete independence and directed a running fire at objec-

25. Philippines *Herald,* 11 June 32, BIA 364–918.
26. "The Philippine Islands—A Military Asset," Memorandum to the Commandant, The Army War College, 29 Apr 29, McCoy MSS, Box 41.
27. Quezon to Brig Gen Frank McIntyre, 11 June 28, BIA Quezon-P.
28. New York *Times,* 20 Jan 32, Philippines *Herald,* 1 Feb, BIA 3427-a-w-46; Manila *Tribune,* 2 Feb, BIA 364–918E.

tionable provisions of the developing legislation, especially against military bases.[29]

Most prominent people, however, were content to see how matters turned out before they criticized. Quezon set up a finance committee of private citizens to collect money from various sources for independence and to assure the public that it was properly handled.[30] The Philippine Sugar Association, presumably the largest contributor, donated through this body after initially sending funds directly to Washington, an act which had embarrassed Osmeña and Roxas.[31] When independence legislation cleared its first hurdle, few were satisfied.

In April 1932, the Hare Bill came to the floor of the House, providing low import and immigration quotas and full tariff after an eight-year transition to independence.[32] Only by bringing up the bill with rules suspended—forty minutes debate, two-thirds vote necessary for passage—did Speaker Garner prevent the farm bloc from inserting in the bill amendments providing immediate independence and immediate tariffs. The vote was 306–47 for passage. All the nay votes were Republican, twenty of them from New England and Middle Atlantic states and nine more from Midwestern industrial cities. "What a travesty, what a tragedy! Forty minutes to found a nation!" said Representative Charles Underhill of Massachusetts, ". . .'God, forgive them, they know not what they do.'" The Philippine mission reported, however, that only Garner's stratagem had saved the bill from mutilation.[33]

Will Rogers summed up adverse American editorial comment: "The freedom of a race of people never entered into it. . . . The only reason why we ever held 'em this long is because the Japanese didn't use sugar in their tea. But they are liable to start using it any day." The Japanese government itself was unofficially pleased,

29. Quezon to Ramon Fernandez, 26 Jan 32, Quezon to OsRox, 17 Feb, OsRox to Quezon, 17 Feb (Q).
30. Memorandum by Miguel Unson, Chairman of the Finance Committee, 9 Feb 32 (Q).
31. Quezon to OsRox, 2 Mar 32; Osmeña, Roxas to Quezon, 2 Mar; Quezon to Osmeña, Roxas, 3 Mar (Q).
32. House Report 72:1, No. 806.
33. *Cong Rec* 72:1, 7622–32, quotation p. 7628; New York *Times, Herald Tribune,* 3, 5 Apr 32, Washington *Star,* 4 Apr, BIA 364-a-w-873, pt. 5; Report of the Philippine Legislative Mission, Manila *Sunday Tribune,* 30 July 33 (hereafter, "OsRox Report").

but the European colonial powers and Americans with investments in the Orient were naturally disgruntled. Even the Filipino reaction was lame. Newspaper editorials sought awkwardly to praise the bill, and the Legislature, although it congratulated the OsRox mission, did not endorse its achievement.[34]

More ominous still for the mission was a press statement issued by Quezon. If given the freedom to act voluntarily, the Philippines might consider some kind of permanent relationship with America: "The Filipino's position, with his definite, dignified civil status, could be as satisfactory as a Canadian's is under England." [35]

In the Senate, emergency legislation for the depression and a filibuster organized by Arthur Vandenberg stalled the independence bill. In July, with twenty-eight Democrats already in Chicago for the convention, Harry Hawes admitted temporary defeat, while extracting from the floor leaders an agreement to take up this bill as unfinished business during a lame duck session scheduled for December.[36]

The half-year breathing spell offered the Filipino leaders a chance to repair their united front, but led to more tension instead. Quezon, who had felt the situation getting out of his control, requested the mission to come home and report to the Legislature. The mission declined. Quezon suggested that Osmeña and Roxas appear at a party convention to revise the platform, now that "immediate, absolute, and complete independence" was clearly impossible. Osmeña and Roxas replied that a party convention was unnecessary because Philippine elections were two years away, and changing the platform now would weaken their case in America. Quezon declared that the government was in a financial crisis; further remittance of the mission's allowance might be difficult. The mission replied that they would take a further cut in their per diems rather than run up the additional expense of a round trip, home and back.[37] Dubious about

34. New York *Times*, 5 Apr 32. Other reactions: Washington *Post*, Richmond *News Leader*, Manila *Bulletin*, 5 Apr, *La Opinion*, 6, 9 Apr, *The China Press*, 6 Apr, New York *Herald Tribune*, 6, 12 Apr, BIA 364-a-w-873, pt. 5.
35. Quaqual to OsRox, 5 Apr 32, Cablegrams, Series I; Washington *Star*, 3 Apr, BIA 364-a-w-873, pt. 5.
36. OsRox to Quaqual, 1 July 32 (Q); *Cong Rec* 72:1, 13254–66, 14697–706, 14709–21, 14795–99, 14811–14, 14816–22, 14862–69; OsRox Report.
37. Guevara, Osias, "Memorandum Concerning the Philippine Mission," 2 July 32 (de la Rosa MSS); Quezon to OsRox, 6 July, OsRox to Quaqual, 6 July, OsRox to Quezon, 6 July, Quaqual to OsRox, 9 July, OsRox to Quaqual, 9 July, Quezon to

the independence bill and anxious that Osmeña and Roxas not achieve their goal, Quezon tried for two weeks, unsuccessfully, to cajole and threaten them back to Manila and within the ambit of his power.

Osmeña and Roxas clearly had a personal stake in staying in Washington—the possibility of upsetting the man who had lorded it over them for ten years. They also, however, had objective reasons. To return might mean losing "a reasonable certainty of achieving the enactment of an independence bill . . . in exchange for what, at best, would seem mere possibilities." To rouse interest in Congress over Philippine independence all over again would be especially difficult because Hawes and Hare, fervent advocates of the Philippine position, were retiring from Congress, and many new members unfamiliar with the problem would be coming in. The mounting American economic crisis might crowd the Philippine question out of consideration.[38] Harry Hawes helped prompt the mission's decision by repeating a remark he had heard a "high official" make of the Filipinos: "They are a 'soft' people, given to exciting and impressionable conduct, but lacking in earnestness and perseverance." Leaving now, Hawes said, would put the Filipinos in danger of losing ground.[39]

The mission stayed, and as an afterthought requested Quezon to come join them, to manage the bill through its final stages. Quezon did not answer.[40] While the various American interests for Philippine independence were growing more consolidated, all Philippine interests were in danger of being subordinated to rivalry among the foremost leaders.

OsRox, 11 July, OsRox to Quezon, 13 July (two messages), OsRox to Quaqual, 14 July, Quaqual to OsRox, 20 July, Cablegrams, Series I. The dittoed collection of Washington-Manila cables ends with one of 10 Apr, but inasmuch as a title page indicates that all cables for the period 28 Oct 31–10 Sept 32 were once collected in a single volume, I have also included under the designation "Series I" all the loose cablegrams I discovered in the Quezon collection for the period 10 Apr–10 Sept 32.
38. OsRox Report.
39. Hawes to Osmeña, Roxas, 9 July 32 (de la Rosa MSS).
40. OsRox to Quezon, 10 Sept 32, Cablegrams, Series I.

Part 3: The Debates on Independence

"The arts of statesmanship . . . are still amazingly primitive. Prejudice, guess-work, special interests, and phantom fears still threaten for long to usurp the place properly belonging to reason in so-cial affairs."

IRWIN EDMAN
Arts and the Man

8

The First Philippine Independence Act

THE CAUSE OF INDEPENDENCE advanced in 1932 with a rattle of ominous statistics concerning the American economy. In August of that year, Frank McIntyre wrote Quezon about conditions in the United States: foreign trade at its lowest level in twenty-five years, aliens departed outnumbering aliens arrived for the first time in memory, and bonus marchers camping at Anacostia Flats (until at the command of Secretary of War Hurley, General Douglas MacArthur, assisted by Major Dwight D. Eisenhower, drove them out with bayonets and tear gas). Economic factors, McIntyre said, "unless radically improved before December, will insure the quick passage by Congress of pending Philippine legislation."

Until March 1933, conditions worsened considerably. Between Hoover's electoral defeat and Roosevelt's inauguration, the index of industrial production dropped to an all-time low of 56, and twenty-three states suspended or drastically reduced banking operations. The wholesale price index of farm products had reached its lowest point since 1899, and farm wages were the lowest in thirty years. In January 1933, it was calculated that the farm sales dollar was worth only half the buying dollar. In this atmosphere, the last lame duck President fought with the last lame duck Congress, and the Philippine independence question came to a head.[1]

1. McIntyre (now Philippine Trade Commissioner) to Quezon, 20 Aug 32 (Q); *Wall Street Journal*, 2 Jan 33; Richard Morris, ed., *Encyclopedia of American History* (1st ed. New York, Harper & Bros., 1953), pp. 341, 482.

By December 1932, discussion had narrowed chiefly to the Hare Bill from the House and the Hawes-Cutting Bill in the Senate, both of which provided for a constitutional convention to be held immediately, and a plebiscite on independence to be held at the end of a transition period. The major difference in the bills was the length of the transition; the House bill provided for eight years, but the Senate version asked for seventeen to nineteen.

Senator Arthur Vandenberg, whose following was too weak and too wholly Republican to succeed, proposed his own alternate bill. The United States, Vandenberg said, could sensibly do either of two things: grant the Philippines an unequivocal independence at the earliest possible date, or create an effective period of economic preparation for independence. The first "would mean immediate and absolute collapse." The Hawes-Cutting Bill tried to approach the second, but the bill suffered from having "reached out too assiduously for [a] meeting of minds," thereby losing "some of its own logic and continuity." Vandenberg's own bill pursued the second alternative uncompromisingly—a twenty-year period of trade adjustment followed by, rather than preceded by, a constitutional convention. Only then could the Filipinos realistically draft themselves a charter for independence. Meanwhile the United States should retain the power to guide Philippine foreign relations, for it would certainly be held responsible in any case for steering a wise course in Far Eastern affairs.[2]

The Senate, however, ignored Vandenberg and worked on the Hawes-Cutting Bill, while lobbyists for the farm organizations worked on the Senate. They could not wait nineteen years for full tariff protection, "not . . . even four years," some lobbies claimed, "and remain solvent." Their consensus was for annual tariff step-ups of 20 per cent, beginning at once and reaching 100 per cent after five years, simultaneous with complete independence. The plebiscite, which left a final option to the Filipinos, should be stricken.[3]

The farm bloc in the Senate responded by slicing down the duty-free quotas on Philippine agricultural products, and then cutting

2. *Cong Rec* 72:1, 13258–66; 72:2, 320–23.
3. Eight farm and dairy organizations to Sen Arthur Capper of Kansas, 9 Dec 32; twelve national farm and dairy organizations, several state branches, and four national farm newspapers to Sen Joseph Dickinson of Iowa, 14 Dec; letter from various dairy, livestock, and newspaper interests to Sen Reed Smoot of Utah, 14 Dec; *Cong Rec* 72:2, 397–98, 445, 572.

down the transition period. The sponsors of the bill—Hawes, Bronson Cutting of New Mexico, and Key Pittman of Nevada—had set the period at nineteen years, compared with the Hare Bill's eight years, partly to strengthen their bargaining position in conference. But a motion by Dickinson of Iowa for a five-year transition barely lost, 38 to 37. Before the managers could shape and introduce a twelve-year compromise, Senator Edwin Broussard of Louisiana obtained a vote on an eight-year transition with no plebiscite. The amendment passed, 40 to 38.[4]

Amid a babble of parliamentary inquiries, Hawes exclaimed that "the entire philosophy of the Senate bill is destroyed." Bargaining with Huey Long, the managers found that the farm bloc would swallow a twelve-year bill, but not a plebiscite which might permit the Filipinos to prolong their dependency and protect themselves against an eventual agricultural tariff. The managers' compromise would not go through, Long intimated, unless things were done his way, the farmers' way. He was ready to talk for sixty days, he said, as he took the floor and launched out upon a mock history of the Louisiana Purchase. He lampooned Hoover and declaimed against the "Wall Street imperialists" and the "god of greed." America today, Long continued, was worse than the Cannibal Islands, where hungry men ate the flesh of others: "We allow . . . a million people to starve because one or two men . . . enjoy the starvation and thirst of a million." "God help the poor Filipinos," Long said; "I will help to keep them from . . . the hands of the imperialists of America."

Long was doubtless closer to victory than to God. By agreement with the Committee on Territories, James Byrnes of South Carolina contrived an amendment which made ratification of the Philippine constitution "an expression of the will of the people . . . in favor of independence." His motion passed, 44 to 29. Thus the Senate encouraged the Filipino electorate to confuse the validity of a frame of government with the viability of a form of government. The now-mangled bill required a popular decision on both frame and form before the premonitory burdens of nationhood could be truly felt, and ten years before independence could be achieved.

In face of this confusion Arthur Vandenberg made a last stand: recommit the bill, he asked, and rewrite it, placing adoption of the

4. *Cong Rec* 72:2, 326–35 (general debate); 405, 455 (Dickinson motion and vote); 319, 338, 455–56 (Broussard amendment and vote).

constitution at the end of the transition period instead of at the beginning. "Keep our flag up or take it down. But do not half mast it." His motion lost, 54 to 19. Huey Long had not needed sixty days in which to achieve his purpose, but only one, in which he had unbottled all the evil genies of the Great Depression. They still suffused the Senate chamber when the much-amended Hawes-Cutting Bill passed, without a record vote.[5]

Before New Year's Day of 1933, the final bill, further compromised in conference, passed the Senate again without a record vote, and the House without even a quorum, 171 to 16. Representative Charles Underhill, who in April had misquoted Christ, now misquoted Madame Roland. "O Liberty!" he mourned, "how many crimes are committed in thy name!"[6] In its final form, the bill was highly flawed but hardly criminal. Despite the greatest domestic crisis since the Civil War, the conferees had granted the Philippine mission most of what they asked.[7] Of the provisions, political, economic, and military, which would most affect future Philippine-American relations, the mission achieved notable success in the first two categories, and left the third category unchallenged.

First, political provisions:[8] the Filipinos had asked for the lesser of the two transition periods (eight, rather than twelve, years). The conference split the difference and made it ten. The House bill had in it provision for a plebiscite, but Quezon, Osmeña, and Roxas all were opposed,[9] arguing that it would be a superfluous gesture for an obviously nationalistic people, and also feeling, perhaps, that it was too flammable a matter upon which to have the first national vote in the Philippines. They were gratified when the conference accepted the Senate's no-plebiscite version.

In May, Harry Hawes, hoping to soften opposition from the Hoover cabinet and other articulate internationalists, had brought

5. Ibid., 72:2, 457 (Hawes quote); 459–60, 464–65 (Long's bargaining and threat of filibuster); 577–87 (Long's speech); 634–39 (Byrnes amendment and vote); 644–46 (Vandenberg speech, motion, and vote); 658 (vote on passage of the bill).

6. Ibid., 72:2, 926 (Senate); 1148 (House); 1135 (quotation).

7. Sen Benigno Aquino to members of Congress, 21 Dec 32, Cong Rec 72:2, 1160–61; OsRox Report; Forbes to Ellery Sedgwick, 6 Jan 33, Journals, 4, 352 (WCF).

8. Conference Report, Cong Rec 72:2, 917–20, 1071–76; Conference Committee Print No. 21, 22 Dec 32, HR 7233 (IF–2789, HLS).

9. Quezon to Osias, 15 Feb 32 (Q); OsRox Report.

Cameron Forbes, a Hoover supporter, former governor general of the Philippines, and ex-ambassador to Japan, into the drafting of the bill. Hawes overplayed his hand, for Forbes later required him to repudiate a statement that his, Forbes', support proved that the Philippines was in no danger from Japan. Forbes intended only to strengthen the powers obtained by America during the transition period, along lines previously contemplated by insular officials.

The question at issue was the relative power of the Philippine president and of the American high commissioner. To weaken the former and strengthen the latter, the "Forbes amendments" made more explicit the right of American presidential intervention through the high commissioner, and designated a financial expert on the staff of the high commissioner to hear appeals from the decisions of the insular auditor. These the mission succeeded in softening, having previously persuaded Forbes to withdraw a third amendment.[10]

The mission, through Hawes, had already obtained an amendment symbolically elevating the president of the Commonwealth above the high commissioner. The Senate, by hurried voice vote, awarded Malacañan Palace, the executive mansion, to the former, and relegated the latter to what had been the headquarters of the commanding general of the Philippine Department. Whatever the constitutional limitations upon him, the Philippine president would be the supreme figure of the islands in his own and in his people's eyes.[11]

The second major category of provisions was economic. To protect what Forbes frequently referred to as the "200-million-dollar-a-year-trade" between the United States and the Philippines, he had cooperated with Ned Bruce, the lobbyist for the West Coast Chambers of Commerce.[12] American manufacturers and exporters were gratified to be spared limits and tariffs on American products entering the Philippines until independence. The Philippine mission complained about the lack of reciprocity involved. Their own agricultural exports were to undergo five years of 5 per cent annual step-ups in duty, followed by full tariff upon independence. Quota limits were to go

10. Forbes to Sen Walcott, 7, 31 May 32, to Bruce, 9 May, to Hawes, 27 May, 6 June, to Theodore Roosevelt, Jr, 3 June, Hawes to Forbes, 2 June, Journals, 4, 261–63, 273–74, 276 (WCF); Cong Rec 72:1, 11274–75, 11492; OsRox to Quaqual, 26, 28 May, and Quaqual to OsRox, 28 May (Q); OsRox Report; Teodoro M. Kalaw, MS autobiography, p. 324; "Outline History of Forbes Amendments," BIA 364-a-936.
11. Cong Rec 72:2, 169; OsRox Report.
12. Forbes diary, 15 Jan 33, Bruce to Forbes, 15, 20 Jan, Journals, 4, 361–64 (WCF).

into effect immediately but, in these at least, the higher figures of the House bill, 850,000 tons of sugar and 200,000 tons of coconut oil, prevailed over the lower figures adopted by the Senate. Both quotas were considerably under current Philippine production, which was reaching its peak, but considerably above the figures demanded by the American farm bloc.

In the end, furthermore, Hiram Johnson of California relented and rewrote the clause excluding Filipino immigration during the Commonwealth period; the final bill permitted a token entrance quota of fifty Filipinos annually until independence.[13] Thus the Filipinos were spared the indignity of being treated like other unwelcome Orientals while still under the American flag.

Concerning military and diplomatic provisions, the Filipinos took a passive attitude, and no changes were made. "Two-thirds, if not more," of the Senate Committee on Territories, one of its members later recalled, were at all times in favor of surrendering on the date of independence all American military and naval reservations in the Philippines. Neither the Army nor the Navy recommended keeping bases after independence, but the managers inserted such a provision in order to allay administration and congressional Republicans' criticism of the bill on grounds of "balance of power." [14]

Shortly before passage, one of the senators in favor of retaining the bases, David Reed of Pennsylvania, inserted a contradictory provision in the bill, requesting the President, when independence was achieved, to enter negotiations with foreign powers to conclude a treaty of perpetual neutralization of the Philippines. Either Congress or the State Department had rejected the idea every time since it first appeared in the 60th Congress, but now it passed in the confusion.[15] Either of the two policies might be consistent, but not both. The United States might withdraw military power, in which event international paper was all that could protect the Philippines, or it might remain. If it remained, no international agreement was feasible; as one pundit said, "You cannot neutralize a fort." [16]

13. OsRox Report. *Cong Rec* 72:2, 258–59 (Johnson amendment abolishing quota of 100); 919 (compromise result of quota of 50).
14. *Cong Rec* 72:2, 1080, quotation from ibid., 73:2, 5118; Memo, CofS, MacArthur, to Asst CofS, WPD, Kilbourne, 26 Feb 34, WPD 3389–6.
15. *Cong Rec* 72:2, 258. Previous history: Stimson to Hornbeck, 21 Jan 32, SD 811B.01/159; *Cong Rec* 71:1, 4426 *et prec.*; Historical Memo, BIA 364–740 K.
16. Raymond Leslie Buell, quoted, New York *Times,* 15 Apr 32.

The Filipino leaders did not try sharply to define the strategic possibilities. They accepted the idea of neutralization as potentially protective and tolerated the provisions for bases as not necessarily obnoxious. When Quezon, in November, had conveyed some criticism from the Legislature, Osmeña and Roxas replied that it would be difficult to begin questioning bases now, in view of the Legislature's failure to oppose them since the beginning of the independence movement. Quezon himself had spoken in favor of bases in the past.[17] He now dropped the subject, not to raise it again until circumstances required him to look for issues with which to fight Osmeña and Roxas.

"It is no principle with sensible men . . . to do always what is abstractedly best." So McIntyre had written Osmeña in July, quoting Cardinal Newman. "We may be obliged to do, as being best under circumstances, what we murmur and rise against. . . . We see that to attempt more is to effect less; that we must accept so much or gain nothing." McIntyre thought there was much surplusage in the independence bill and some "obvious evil," but "the part of wisdom of those seeking this legislation is . . . to eliminate what of evil may be eliminated without delay or risk, and to accept, with its infirmities on it, the best Bill that can be secured." [18]

If Osmeña was not by exhortation persuaded, he was by temperament inclined to exactly that course of action; and by ambition as well. But other temperaments, and other Filipino interests involved in the same legislation, had been growing less and less enthusiastic about the mission's work as it approached closer and closer to the only kind of success open to it—a success of discriminating compromise. The Nacionalista party had refrained from endorsing either the Hare Bill or the Hawes-Cutting Bill. When Hawes in May had inserted the Forbes amendments in the Senate bill, Quezon had broken out in vigorous opposition to them, until the mission said that senatorial "friends of the Filipinos" counselled waiting until conference to change details.[19]

17. Quaqual to OsRox, 2 Nov 32, OsRox to Quaqual, 5 Nov, Cablegrams, Series II; Maximo Kalaw quoted Quezon in favor of bases in 1919 and 1922, Philippines *Sunday Herald*, [25?] Aug 33.
18. McIntyre to Osmeña, 8 July 32 (de la Rosa MSS).
19. Manila *Bulletin*, 5 Mar 32, BIA 364-a-w-873, part 5; OsRox to Quaqual, 23, 26 May, 1, 3 June, OsRox to Quezon, 28 May, Quezon to de las Alas, 25 May, Quezon to OsRox, 25, 30 May, 2, 7 June, Quaqual to OsRox, 6 June, Cablegrams, Series I.

In July a legislative joint committee had refused to express confidence in the mission or to authorize it to remain in Washington. The mission was not obliged to return home, but it was aware of a diminishing mandate for its activities. Quezon had tried to give the mission the free hand it requested by preventing the Legislature from passing specific resolutions on the pending bills,[20] but in doing so he had had both to master rambunctious party regulars and to control his own rising disquiet.

Near the end of the Philippine legislative session in November, Quezon and his lieutenants cabled the mission "an expression of the sense of the Legislature." The requisites for an acceptable bill were that it fix a definite date for independence, eliminate the Forbes amendments, allow a minimum sugar quota of 1.2 million tons, and except the principal Philippine ports from use as naval stations. There was also a "general feeling" against a plebiscite. Under the circumstances, what chance had the King Bill, for immediate and complete independence?

The King Bill had no chance now, Osmeña and Roxas replied, although it might have under a Democratic administration. They pointed out that the theory of all the bills was to curtail the special Philippine position in American trade, and that a harmony among many interests was necessary to pass any bill now.[21]

After Roosevelt's overwhelming victory a few days later, Quezon was unwilling to heed counsel of moderation from Osmeña and Roxas. Hoover and the Republicans would go out of office in March, and, Quezon hoped, a new Wilson would come in, willing in principle and detail to accommodate the Democratic party and himself to Philippine interests. Quezon decided to send a personal envoy and delegate of the Legislature to Washington in order to bring the mission in line with Filipino sentiments, especially his own. He chose Senator Benigno Aquino, an Osmeña man, and instructed him to have the mission work for the King Bill. If such proved impossible, they should accept no other bill unless it (1) provided for a time of preparation not exceeding ten years, (2) restricted the power of

20. Parker to Sec War, 21 July 32, BIA 26480-a-139; New York *Herald Tribune*, 30 Aug, BIA 364-a-913; New York *Times*, 5 Oct, BIA 364–915.
21. Quaqual to OsRox, 2 Nov 32, OsRox to Quaqual, 5 Nov, Cablegrams, Series II.

American presidential intervention, and (3) provided a sugar quota of at least 1.2 million tons.[22]

Even before Aquino reached Washington, almost a month later, Quezon had in effect denied him any discretion at all. Upon hearing of Long's amendment cutting the sugar quota to half of the Philippine aim and of Johnson's immigration exclusion amendment, Quezon had cabled the mission to work for immediate independence: "if this is impossible in this session let there be no bill." [23]

Quezon may have chosen Aquino in the hope that he would influence his leader, but the very opposite occurred. Osmeña convinced his follower that only by seeing the Hawes-Cutting Bill through, and using the opportunity of the conference to make changes, could they obtain an independence bill at all. Aquino, a proud combination of egoist, nationalist, and anti-white, was not one to let the opportunity slip, or to stay inactive for reasons of protocol. A day after his arrival he cabled Quezon, urging him to settle for the best bill possible. "Acceptable legislation or nothing," Quezon cabled back. He proceeded to have the Independence Commission in Manila approve unanimously his original points of instruction to Aquino and all subsequent cables following them up. Aquino, undeterred, retorted on December 22 that the conference bill was the best possible solution and that no better could be expected in the future. Quezon then flatly reprimanded him for ignoring his instructions.[24]

Now Quezon's imagination seized on means not of improving but of defeating the Hare-Hawes-Cutting Bill. He attempted to extract from his Legislature a request that President Hoover veto the merged House and Senate versions. But, as in November 1931, he had reached the limits of his power and persuasion. The Filipino legislators, seeing independence at last realizable in some form, underwent a change of mood. Called together as the Independence Commission, they saved Quezon's face by again ratifying his already once-ratified series of instructions to Aquino. Yet they wanted the

22. Quezon to Aquino, 14 Nov 32. Quezon based his letter chiefly on a general agreement adopted in majority caucus, 5 Nov, presumably the same that appears as "Resolucion Concurrente No. 19, Adoptada 9 de Noviembre de 1932" (Q).
23. Quezon to OsRox, 10 Dec 32, Cablegrams, Series II.
24. Aquino to Quezon, 13, 17, 19, 22 Dec 32, Quezon to Aquino, 15, 18 (twice), 23 Dec, Quaqual to OsRox, 17 Dec, Cablegrams, Series II; Osmeña to the author, 10 Oct 58.

power to act upon the bill themselves. They did not wish Herbert Hoover to end the game with a veto before they themselves had played. Hence they agreed to the OsRox plea, and asked the President to sign the bill. Despite Quezon, perhaps partly because of him and his autocratic tendencies, the Legislature desired "full liberty of action to accept or refuse" the independence act.[25]

President Hoover found himself bombarded with pressure, advice, and inquiry as the independence bill moved through Congress and came to his desk. Many besought him to sign it, including William Green, president of the AFL, who found it "reasonably satisfactory," and Cameron Forbes, who thought that it removed the irritants to Philippine-American trade without impairing the trade itself. Elihu Root, the great architect of Republican Philippine policy, thought it time for democracy to dissociate itself from imperialism. The Philippine mission, in an interview of January 11, sought Hoover's signature as the culmination of its work.[26]

Hoover, whose memory was often faulty, later declared that the Philippine mission had asked him for a veto, but Osmeña and Roxas reported the opposite to the Philippine Legislature. Internal inconsistencies mar Hoover's account, an eyewitness testifies against him, and other evidence suggests the consistency of the mission,[27] which had no clear motive for reversing itself.

Perhaps Hoover's confusion arose from the mission's reporting Quezon's attitude to him. On January 2, in the longest cable of a long exchange, Quezon had derided the bill "as the work of the National City Bank" and as "a joke that is unfair and harmful to us, but profitable to American manufacturers and exporters, [and] to Cuban sugar and beet sugar interests." Quezon would "not . . . be sorry if the President vetoes the bill," but even if he did not, the

25. Quezon to Aquino, 18 Dec 32, Quaqual to OsRox, 29, 30 Dec, Cablegrams, Series II; New York *Herald Tribune*, 30 Dec, BIA 364-a-924.
26. Theodore Joslin, *Hoover off the Record* (Garden City, Doubleday, 1934), pp. 338–39; Forbes Journals, 4, 504–06, 5, 115–16 (WCF); Philip Jessup, *Elihu Root* (2 vols., New York, Dodd, Mead, 1938), *1*, 369–70
27. Supporting the President's version: *The Memoirs of Herbert Hoover, 2, The Cabinet and the Presidency 1920–1933* (New York, Macmillan, 1952), p. 361; Forbes Journals, 5, 115–16 (WCF); Hoover to the author, 23 Dec 60; Hurley to the author, 30 Mar 61. Supporting the mission's version: Aquino to Quirino, 6 Jan 33, OsRox to Quaqual (two messages), 11 Jan, Cablegrams, Series II; Lichauco, *Roxas*, pp. 93–95, 98.

Philippines would reject the bill "in order to get a better one from the Democrats." [28] The American Farm Bureau Federation, perhaps the most active of the farm lobbies, also switched sides at the end and, like Quezon, requested Hoover to veto. The Federation believed that the bill did not protect the American farmer.[29]

These defectors to his side did not, however, speak Hoover's language as Winston Churchill did. Arguing for retention of the Philippines, as Kipling once had pleaded for annexation, Churchill thought the question above "the bookkeeping considerations of profit and loss," an issue which "can only be decided upon considerations of national duty, dignity and honor, and upon its international repercussions." [30]

Despite Churchill, Hoover might have let the bill pass. He was against colonies in principle. He was opposed to a large navy and to the navalists' using the Philippines as an argument for an expanded fleet. While campaigning in beet country, he had suggested a smaller quota for Philippine sugar than even Congress would consent to. His feelings about Filipino immigration are implicit in his regret that "Nordics of all kinds" were being excluded from the United States while Puerto Ricans—"undersized Latins"—were being admitted.[31] Yet he had decided before Christmas to veto the bill. Why?

As an inarticulate motive, Hoover may have wanted to fight for the sake of a fight. He had taken hard his defeat at the polls; he was "dangerously suspicious" of Roosevelt;[32] Congress had repeatedly and increasingly frustrated his programs; he was in a mood to use the veto—the last power left him. His articulate motives, however, were in part Churchillian. He gathered up the arguments of four cabinet secretaries and from them fused a state paper of some eloquence. "We are dealing here," he wrote, "with one of the most precious rights of man—national independence interpreted as separate nationality." Independence, he said, was "not to be reached by yielding to selfish interests, to resentments, or to abstractions," but to be carefully achieved over a period of at least fifteen years, with increasing autonomy followed by a plebiscite. "Neither our successors

28. Quezon to OsRox, 2 Jan 33, Cablegrams, Series II.
29. OsRox Report.
30. Winston Churchill, "Defense in the Pacific," *Colliers,* 17 Dec 32 (H).
31. Hoover, *Memoirs, 2,* 359; Stimson diary, 28 Aug 30, 30 Mar 31 (HLS).
32. Stimson diary, 3 Jan 33; Arthur M. Schlesinger, Jr, *The Crisis of the Old Order, 1919–1933* (Boston, Houghton Mifflin, 1957), pp. 443–46.

nor history will discharge us of responsibility for actions which diminish the liberty we seek to confer, nor for dangers we create for ourselves as a consequence of our acts."[33]

Secretary Stimson, even more Churchillian, was discouraged because Hoover said "he differed with me radically on . . . the Philippines" and because he ruled out a permanent colonial relationship. Nevertheless, Stimson felt that the veto was basically constructed on correct strategic grounds; he warned Japanese Ambassador Debuchi that whatever happened to the bill, American policy in the Far East would not be changed.[34]

"This legislation puts both our people and the Philippine people . . . on the path leading to new and enlarged dangers to . . . freedom itself." The clerk had barely finished reading the concluding sentence of Hoover's veto message when the House acted upon it, and voted 274 to 94, almost three to one, to override it.[35]

Hoover, upon hearing the news, laughed "the mirthless laugh that meant fight." Farm lobbyists joined the administration entreating Senate leaders to uphold the veto. William Randolph Hearst jumped in and personally called more than twenty key senators to ask their support of the President. Hawes and the other managers brought up the issue quickly in the Senate to avoid a swelling cry in the national press.[36]

Of the senatorial debaters, Arthur Vandenberg supported Hoover's message with a special enthusiasm, inasmuch as it closely resembled his own plan. William Borah of Idaho typified the opposition. There would always be storm clouds over the Orient, he said; and as for Stimson's argument about a base of American influence, he was "not sure . . . that it is well for the Filipinos, or well for the United States, to have an island of western culture in the midst of an oriental ocean, unless we are prepared in some way to transform the nature of that oriental ocean."

Although the beet sugar growers of Idaho wanted him to uphold the veto, Borah would not. "Whatever may be the virtues of a

33. *Cong Rec* 72:2, 1820; letters of Hoover's secretaries, ibid., 1925–29; drafts and notes of Hurley and Stimson letters, BIA 364-w-925, 929; McCoy MSS, Box 89; Stimson MSS, IF–2790, IF–1128, 3F–1292.
34. Stimson diary, 12 Jan 33 (HLS).
35. *Cong Rec* 72:2, 1820, 1827–28.
36. OsRox Report; Joslin, *Hoover off the Record*, p. 338.

democracy," he concluded, "one of them is not the capacity to govern or rule another people." After Borah had raised the pennant of anti-imperialism, Robert LaFollette, Jr., saluted it in the name of the Declaration of Independence. Bronson Cutting declared that "the ultimate force behind this legislation" is the force which had been behind it ever since "the first protests against the imperialistic adventure" of 1898.[37]

In somber meeting the cabinet heard news of the Senate roll call: 66 to 26 to override. "Pitiful . . . ," Hoover said. "Whatever the subject, there are not thirty senators we can depend upon. It's a rout." A switch of five votes would have upheld the veto, but, Stimson commented, "All the weak-kneed veterans went back on us at the last moment, including old Borah, who apparently made a pretty bad speech. He had been counted as on our side." [38] So ended the Republican policy of Philippine retention.

What accounts for the United States Congress passing an independence bill for the Philippines a dozen years before the effects of World War II brought other imperial powers around to the same policy? Analysts have always stressed the economic factors, especially the sugar and dairy interests. These, to be sure, were responsible for the immediate momentum for the bill, but they did not dominate its actual construction. When Senator Dickinson asked for immediate tariff step-ups, and full tariff in seven years, the Senate voted him down, 48 to 20. Although the farm lobbies favored Dickinson's amendment, senators from beet and cane states voted 25 to 10 against it.[39] More conclusive still, when the farm lobbies in the end asked to uphold the veto of the whole bill, the Senate voted to override it, the senators from sugar states even more strongly (38 to 8) than the rest.

Senators of the Deep South and Far West (25 to 1 for overriding) may have been reflecting social alarm against immigrants of another color and culture, but such a motive can be demonstrated only in one quarter of the Senate, and even then clearly in the Far West only. If economic motives were more dilute than assumed and social motives too diffuse to be crucial, the factors which provided the

---

37. *Cong Rec* 72:2, 1852–57 (Vandenberg); 2004–07 (Borah); 2003–04 (Cutting).
38. Joslin, p. 339; Stimson diary, 17 Jan 33 (HLS).
39. *Cong Rec* 72:2, 649–53.

margin to override Hoover's veto were strategic and political. The seventeen beet sugar states, excepting California and Washington, were identical with the strongholds of isolationism. Butler Hare of the House may have expressed their point of view: "Why should we hesitate because of a little international instability in the Orient?" [40]

Hesitate at what?—at making good on the promise of independence extended seventeen years before in the Jones Act. Even then the Clarke amendment, which would have made the Philippines independent by 1920, had passed the Senate, and only failed in the House by a small margin for which Roman Catholic influence was responsible. If the objections of dignitaries of the Church were the last barrier to Philippine independence, politically and strategically desirable in 1916, then surely the motives behind the independence act of 1933 need not have been merely, or even mostly, selfish economic ones. Nor, surely, did 20 out of 45 Republican senators and 81 of 174 representatives bolt against their party leader on grounds of special interest. More likely, in many cases, the traditional Republican policy no longer gripped their consciences, and they felt, on principle, that it was time for America to relinquish its sovereignty to the Filipino people. Allowing economic selfishness and social prejudice all their weight, still no independence act could have passed, even in the dismal lame duck session of 1933, without a desire for disentanglement from the Orient and without the cumulative impact of the anti-imperial tradition.

40. Ibid., 72:2, 1825.

9

The Anti-Pro Fight: (1) Alignment of Forces

EARLY IN 1933 Hoover and his cabinet looked first to Albany, then to Manila, for help in defeating the independence bill. At one point they expected assistance from Franklin Roosevelt in sustaining the veto. Stimson spent a day at Hyde Park and left with the strong impression that he had convinced the President-elect of the evils of the Philippine bill. But Roosevelt never spoke out; he seemed to wish the whole matter consummated before he took office. After the bill passed, he told Joseph Tumulty, who was acting for Quezon, that the next step was up to the Filipinos. Stimson was not optimistic: "Poor little Quezon now has the entire burden thrown on him of stopping it. I'm afraid he can't do it." [1]

"Poor little Quezon" was meanwhile in a dither of indecision. Once again he tried to get the mission to come home, by suggesting a convention in April to consider the Hare-Hawes-Cutting Act. But the mission wanted Quezon to join them in Washington, to satisfy himself that they could do nothing more there at present. [2] Osmeña wrote Quezon pledging his loyalty: "Our independence cause is facing a more grave situation than it has faced during the last twenty-five years." Together they had "tasted the bitter fight" from the begin-

1. Joslin, *Hoover off the Record*, p. 339; Stimson diary, 9, 17 Jan 33 (HLS); Quezon to Tumulty, 20 Jan (Q).
2. The most important messages in a long series are: OsRox to Quezon, 20 Jan 33 and Quezon to OsRox, 20 Jan, Cablegrams, Series II; also Teodoro M. Kalaw, MS autobiography, pp. 324–25.

ning. "In these last decisive moments" they should let "the people see us united . . . giving all . . . our best efforts for their liberty and happiness." [3]

With a mutual friend, Don Alejandro Roces, mediating, Quezon agreed to cooperate with Osmeña.[4] The latter temporarily held the upper hand, and Quezon did not dare lead a movement for rejection of an independence law without exploring other possibilities. Before sailing for the United States in March, however, Quezon did his best to draw popular support behind him. In a radio broadcast overseas he chided Americans for proffering an exclusion and tariff act in the guise of independence. In a broadcast to his own people, he declared that, under the act, "the Philippines would remain a conquered province of the United States, just as we are now, but she would be under no moral or legal obligation to look after our interest and to protect us from foreign invasion." [5] Quezon left, accompanied by a "mixed mission" of no official status but of sufficient numbers and breadth to give him strong moral support in dealing with the OsRox mission.[6]

Quezon had his handpicked mission formulate a statement of the split opinion in the Philippines. Some were for acceptance (because the act was a step forward and "certainly not to be gambled away" for unlikely improvements) and some were for rejection (because Philippine trade and commerce would be "crippled," and America, through military bases, "would be in a position to exercise practical suzerainty . . . without corresponding obligation"). The memorandum ended with the question: "Is it possible to work out a program for a common action on the part of the Legislative Mission and the Mixed Mission?" [7]

Osmeña met Quezon's group in Paris and attempted to win them over with a convenient interpretation of the H-H-C Act, saying, for instance, that American "reservations" referred only to a future em-

3. Osmeña to Quezon, 28 Jan 33, Cablegrams, Series II.
4. Luciano de la Rosa (transmitting messages from Roces, who was talking with Quezon) to Osmeña, 3, 13, 18, 20 Feb 33 (Q).
5. "A Message to the American People: Speech Delivered by Senate President Quezon over the Columbia Broadcasting Station, transmitted from Station KZRM, Jan. 30, 1933"; "Address of Senate President Manuel L. Quezon over Station KZRM at 9:00 P.M., March 16, 1933" (Q).
6. Manila *Tribune*, 18 Mar 33; further information in BIA 364–948, 949 and BIA 26480–156A, 162.
7. Memo of 1 Apr 33, signed aboard the SS *Conte Verde* (Q).

bassy. This explanation aroused suspicion from a group that had just "seen with their own eyes what kind of independence Egypt was enjoying, or rather not enjoying, with the presence of English army and navy reservations." [8]

In Washington the mixed mission found, as Osmeña had told them, that Roosevelt was too busy with domestic affairs even to discuss the H-H-C Act. Failing also to impress the Secretary of War, Quezon retreated into negotiations with Osmeña and Roxas. After lengthy discussion Quezon yielded to an agreement, signed on April 25, at the Willard Hotel.[9] Both missions would recommend to the Philippine Legislature acceptance of the law with two interpretative insertions: (1) that the provision concerning reservations be construed as excluding military or naval bases adjoining Manila and other important ports and (2) that the Legislature be empowered either to modify the trade provisions in the transition period, or to reduce that period from ten years to five.

"I know American psychology," Quezon boasted to a Filipino reporter. "I know how to get along with them." [10] He overplayed his role, however, at a conference with several senators in Key Pittman's office. Pittman himself defined "reservations" as meaning military bases, a provision necessary to get the vote of "the imperialists." Quezon, excited and gesturing, pictured the ignominious position of a future Philippine president, surrounded by American flags and American bases at Cavite and Fort McKinley. Majority Leader Joseph Robinson interrupted him: "Why don't you come clean and be frank? We believe you don't want independence. If so, why don't you say so?" Leaning forward and pointing a finger at the speechless Quezon, Robinson told him to "go ahead . . . and do what you want with the bill in the Philippines. We will do our duty here as we see it." [11]

8. Undated draft of a subsequent speech by Quezon to the Legislature, probably July 1933 (Q).

9. Untitled document, 25 Apr 33, Willard Hotel, Washington D.C., MS copy in Quezon papers, printed version in *Diario de Sesiones, Senada de Filipinas.*

10. James Wingo, "The Independence Merry-Go-Round," Philippines *Free Press,* 10 June 33.

11. In addition to this version of the story (Wingo, *Free Press,* 10 June 33), Romulo, Quezon, and Osmeña each had their own story. Romulo, who was not present, had Quezon telling Robinson to "go to hell" (*Free Press,* 17 June), which was so unlikely that even Quezon, in versions increasingly kindly to himself, never said so, either in his draft report to the Legislature, July 1933 (Q), or in his speech before

Leaving Capitol Hill, Quezon told Osmeña and Roxas that their agreement was off. Later, on the fifty-first of the famous Hundred Days, President Roosevelt, busy with emergency measures, saw Quezon and the OsRox mission. He finally convinced Quezon of what Tumulty had told him in January: that the Filipinos had to act first. Both missions made plans to return home immediately.[12]

"Manoling, you are brilliant," Quezon had said to Roxas in Washington, "but your interpretation does not convince me."[13] For the next six weeks, across the Atlantic to Paris, overland to Venice, then to Hong Kong by way of Suez, Osmeña and Roxas tried to entreat Quezon to go back to their Willard Hotel agreement. Eventually Quezon gave them to know that he would abide by the agreement; and once more, before the last leg to Manila, he repeated his assurances.[14] Meanwhile, however, Jose Clarin and Quintin Paredes, Quezon's legislative leaders in Manila, were complaining that news reports of his capitulation to Osmeña and Roxas had "disoriented" and "demoralized" Quezon's followers. Quezon replied that he was unchangingly opposed to the act.[15] At the same time, while members of the OsRox mission played cards and dominoes with Quezon, and Osmeña chatted pleasantly with him in the tearoom, their followers in Manila had organized the League for Acceptance of the Hare-Hawes-Cutting Law, whose published prospectus attacked Quezon's leadership.

Aboard ship, classic Filipino tact prevailed in a rapidly degenerat-

the Senate of 13 Oct 33 (*Diario de Sesiones*, pp. 753–54). Osmeña appeared to draw a curtain of discretion over the affair (*Diario de Sesiones*, 25 July 33, p. 90); he could afford to, having been, with Roxas, Wingo's source for the original story (Author's interview with Wingo, 30 Mar 57). I have accepted Wingo's version as the nearest approximation of the truth, for he checked it with Robinson and could assess the probabilities fairly.

12. Osmeña account in *Diario de Sesiones*, 25 July 33, p. 90; Quezon, ibid., 13 Oct, pp. 753–54; Hawes to Quezon, 2 May 33, Quezon to Hawes, 6 May (Q); Wingo, *Free Press*, 10 June 33.

13. Philippines *Free Press*, 17 June 33, p. 42.

14. Osmeña, *Diario de Sesiones*, 25 July 33, pp. 90–91. For other light on the trip: Quezon to Jose de Jesus, 22 May (Q); Gov Vicente Formoso, "Mes Impresiones Personales" (Q).

15. Quezon to Alunan, 16 Apr 33; Quezon's cable to Clarin, Paredes ("sent by Senator Osmeña"), 29 Apr, spoke of a "common program," but Quezon's later cables, presumably not submitted to Osmeña, contained enough aggressive matter for Clarin and Paredes to publish excerpts from them. Of these, several, damaged and undated, survive (Q).

ing situation. In Manila the two camps prepared or sought separate receptions for the two delegations, but the leaders required the partisan celebrations to be merged into one. As long as they were in each other's physical presence, Quezon, Osmeña, and Roxas preserved their diplomatic unity and immunity to spite. They landed June 11, 1933, as a triumvirate.[16] Within days, however, they were bitterly split.

Osmeña needed a roomy battleground. Quezon would win if the question were decided in the narrow confines of the legislature he controlled. While verbal skirmishes among their followers mounted, Osmeña challenged Quezon to let the whole people decide on the H-H-C Act, by plebiscite, although the act specifically provided that such decision be taken either "by concurrent resolution of the Philippine Legislature or by a convention called for the purpose."[17] Quezon could not balk at Osmeña's suggestion without appearing antidemocratic. On June 18, he signed with Osmeña and Roxas an agreement to a plebiscite.[18] To cut down Quezon's popular image and material advantage further, Osmeña, Roxas, and their followers toured the provinces to present their case to the people.

They found, Osmeña declared, a "reign of terror" in which no government officials, nor any of their dependents, dared speak out against the bill.[19] To reduce Quezon's power as chief dispenser of patronage Osmeña challenged him to resign as president of the Senate; he himself would resign as president *pro tem*, and they two would battle the question as common men, in the manner of "Juan de la Cruz." To this second challenge Quezon reacted with an exaggerated show of injury. He returned the fire—against Osmeña personally—and promised to "carry on the fight . . . whatever its consequences."[20] The dual resignation proposal offered him the opportunity to spring a trap which he had been months preparing. When the Legislature convened he would resign; but would the Senate accept his resignation?

16. Romulo dispatch to Manila *Tribune*, late May 1933, with revisions in Quezon's hand (Q); Romulo, *I Walked with Heroes*, p. 192; Lichauco, *Roxas*, p. 105; South China *Morning Post*, 7, 9 June 33, Manila *Tribune* 7–11 June, Philippines *Herald*, 11 June, Philippines *Free Press*, 17 June, p. 42.
17. Section 17, Public Law No. 127, 73d Congress.
18. Philippines *Herald*, 19 June 33; Philippines *Free Press*, 24 June.
19. Osmeña, *Diario de Sesiones*, 25 July 33, p. 92.
20. Philippines *Herald*, Manila *Tribune*, 28–29 June 33.

Quezon intended to launch a major reorganization of both houses without a general election, a move which certainly had no precedent in Philippine parliamentary history, as Quezon later admitted.[21] His object was clearly to remove opponents from key positions in both houses: Osmeña as president *pro tem* of the Senate, Roxas as speaker of the House, Pedro Sabido and Benigno Aquino as "majority" floor leaders in House and Senate. The first showdown, then, would neither be on the independence question nor at the polls; it would be on party leadership and in the Legislature.

Aside from the popular appeal of having obtained an independence act, Osmeña's and Roxas' other major assets in a fight with Quezon were their support from the administration of the University of the Philippines, the backing of the T-V-T (*Tribune-Vanguardia-Taliba*) newspaper chain, and the loyalty of a number of key men in all branches of government. Just as Osmeña and Roxas had made political capital of his absence in 1931, however, Quezon had been at work to counter or to undermine his antagonists' influence while they were in Washington.

First he contended with Rafael Palma, the distinguished president of the University of the Philippines. An old-style nationalist who had faced both Spanish might and the Clarke amendment without fear, Palma broke his political silence to speak out and write articles in favor of accepting the H-H-C Act. Quezon charged him with abusing what should be a neutral office. Palma replied that on questions of national import, the president of the state university had not only a right but a duty to declare himself.

The question at issue, which deserved to be resolved on its merits, was instead decided by application of political thumbscrews. Quezon cut back the budget for the university by a full third. Palma, fearing to jeopardize by his presence the welfare of an institution he had loved and served well, resigned the presidency.[22] Another leading "pro," Dean Maximo Kalaw of the College of Liberal Arts, also resigned. Quezon appointed a political follower as the new president—Jorge Bocobo, previously dean of the Law School.

21. Philippines *Free Press*, 5 Aug 33.
22. *El Debate*, 28 Dec 32, *La Vanguardia*, 28 Jan 33; Quezon to Palma, 8, 16 Feb 33, Palma to Quezon, 9, 17 Feb; various materials in file entitled "University of the Philippines" (Q).

Quezon was even more concerned that one major newspaper chain was against him and the other not clearly for him. Don Alejandro Roces was a friend of Quezon, but an imperious and independent one: his T-V-T chain supported Osmeña and the independence act. The other major publisher, Don Vicente Madrigal, was a compadre of Quezon but a friend of Osmeña's also, and too absorbed in his other business enterprises to be able or willing to dispose his D-M-H-M chain (*El Debate-Mabuhay-Herald-Monday Mail*), behind one man or the other. Quezon solved his problem by rounding up a group of backers to purchase the chain from Madrigal.

Quezon whittled the purchase price from ₱400,000 down to ₱300,000 (equal then to $150,000) and found in Dr. Baldomero Roxas a man "whose name will give to the newspapers the prestige of being completely independent in policy." Protracted and secret negotiations brought a number of prominent subscribers into the deal, including Don Andres Soriano, president of the San Miguel Brewery and of Soriano-Roxas y Cia., a company widely active in trading, investment, and insurance. Horace Pond, president of the Pacific Commercial Company, also joined. Quezon obtained an option to buy majority interest within ten years, with an option for the rest going to Carlos Romulo, formerly of the T-V-T chain.[23] Quezon not only acquired a chain of newspapers but had stolen from Roces the most brilliant journalist in the country, Romulo, to run them, and through them to convey Quezon's political point of view.[24]

23. Quezon to Benito Razon, 20 Mar 33, Razon to Quezon 22 Apr, 10 May, Soriano to Quezon, 4 May, Soriano to Soriano-Roxas y Cia., 8 May (Q). After meeting the down payment and operating expenses, the syndicate for which Dr Roxas was the front withdrew when Quezon's faction won the 1934 election. They left the paper to Madrigal, forfeiting the original investment and expenses as a "contribution" to Quezon's cause; author's interview with Modesto Farolan, 27 Aug 58.
24. In his memoirs (*I Walked with Heroes*, p. 192), Romulo asserts that he "was carrying on a steady barrage of criticism against Quezon" even *after* "the Hare-Hawes-Cutting Act was submitted to the electorate, and Quezon . . . won the election." In fact, however, the H-H-C Act was not voted on by the Legislature until October 1933, and the next election was not until June 1934. Romulo had resigned *before* either event (New York *Times*, 16 Aug 33), and one may infer from Quezon's correspondence with Razon that he had agreed to do so as early as March or April. He had, in fact, switched sides in the middle of the fight. Torn between his idol, Quezon, and his benefactor, Don Alejandro Roces, Romulo with much trepidation chose the former (*Heroes*, pp. 193–96). After a subsequent reorganization of Quezon's *Herald*, Romulo became publisher-editor in 1937, with a large share of stock. In 1941 he won a Pulitzer prize for a series of articles on the international situation in the Orient prior to Pearl Harbor.

Quezon also practiced his wit on Governor General Theodore Roosevelt, Jr., whom an aide once described as "an inexplicable mixture of sincerity, decency, quick-wittedness, carelessness and bravado." Roosevelt privately disliked the Hare-Hawes-Cutting Act but refrained from expressing his views publicly.[25] Quezon nevertheless maneuvered him into working against it, by proposing a reorganization of the executive and judicial branches of government. Because the Great Depression was then having its delayed effect upon the Philippines, Roosevelt agreed, expecting that reorganization would save money. By letting Quezon mastermind changes of personnel, however, Roosevelt permitted frequent displacement of pros by antis.[26] Osmeña's followers and American civil servants were both distressed. Jose Laurel thought Roosevelt a "laughing-stock," and an American bureau chief thought him "a fawning, maudlin, puerile, native-kissing publicity hound." [27] Roosevelt himself thought he had been balancing the budget, but inadvertently he had been serving the political fortunes of Manuel Quezon.

In addition to his own political skill, Quezon needed cash to win. The Philippine Legislature at one time had annually authorized appropriations of ₱1,000,000, or $500,000, for an independence fund, from 1918 until the Insular Auditor declared the practice illegal in 1924. Subsequent campaigns for voluntary contributions in the 1920s raised around ₱40,000 at first and then flagged.[28] The OsRox group, as a legislative mission, received a legal appropriation of $42,050 in 1932, but spent in fact more than twice that much. The insular government made up the difference by graduated cuts in the salaries of Filipino employees from 2 to 10 per cent. In the first two months of 1933 the mission had already spent 60 per cent of their new annual appropriation.[29]

The leaders had planned a campaign in 1933 for an additional

25. Evett D. Hester to Joseph Ralston Hayden, 1 July 33 (H); Theodore Roosevelt, Jr, to Sec War (Hurley), 28 Dec 32, Theodore Roosevelt, Jr, MSS, Box 6.
26. Teodoro M. Kalaw, MS autobiography, p. 328; Forbes Journals, 4, 369 (WCF).
27. Author's interview with Jose P. Laurel, 4 Aug 58; Arthur Fischer, Director of the Bureau of Forestry, to Clinton Riggs, forwarded by Riggs to Forbes, 8 May 33 (WCF).
28. D. R. Williams, *The United States and the Philippines* (Garden City, Doubleday, Page, 1924), p. 195; M. J. Ossorio to the author, 1 May 63; Bunuan to Quezon, Roxas, 13 Feb 29, Quezon to Roxas, 11 Jan 31 (Q).
29. BIA 364–946; 26480–146C, 149, 152, 161.

$100,000 of voluntary contributions from government employees and "the merchants and all the persons of good will." [30] Quezon, however, no longer wanted money to support the H-H-C Act. In mid-March, for putative reasons of economy, he ordered the mission members who were still in Washington to come home, and he cut off their per diems, save those of Osmeña and Roxas. To preserve its unity the mission remained, and spread the allowances for two among them all.[31]

About this time, Quezon launched a drive for funds *against* the H-H-C Act. Private subscriptions for "independence" forked into two streams, the smaller for Osmeña and Roxas, the larger for Quezon.[32] Miguel Unson, chairman of the year-old Finance Committee, was on Quezon's side, and so were most of its members, prominent private citizens.[33] Quezon's own private accounts for 1933, in contrast to those of 1931–32, show periodic disbursements for "gifts" of ₱9495.80 to twenty-six individuals, presumably for publicity and persuasion. The disbursements fluctuated with the political crisis, heaviest in July, ending after October.[34]

Quezon's own financial contribution was miniscule compared to what was necessary. He could rely on the Elizaldes and Soriano; they appear already to have been in a long-term financial relationship with him, giving monies over a period of several years, which he ostensibly was loaning back to them at 8–9 per cent interest: Mike Elizalde at least ₱45,000, Soriano at least ₱65,000.[35] The latter,

30. "Memorandum for the Honorable Speaker Manuel Roxas: Funds for Publicity in Favor of Independence," unsigned, undated, 1933 (Q).

31. Quezon, Paredes to OsRox, 18 Mar 33, OsRox to Quezon, 29 Mar (Q); Quezon to Sec War, 19 Mar, BIA 26480–143.

32. For two instances: Rafael Alunan, for the Philippine Sugar Association, apparently sent a check in April to Vicente Singson Encarnacion, which Quezon deposited in his own name at the Chase National Bank in New York City. When that was exhausted, Alunan deposited $9758.05 on June 6 for Quezon to draw on. (Quezon to Alunan, 29 Apr 33, and Chase National Bank statement in Quezon's name, June 33.) The first check may be the one for ₱3,997.50, or about $2,000, mentioned in a letter from Benito Razon to Alunan, 22 Apr 33 (Q).

33. Unson to Quezon, 8 July 33, Quezon to Unson, 10 July (Q).

34. "Journal," noting personal deposits and disbursements of Sen and Mrs Quezon, Nov 31–Dec 33 (Q).

35. "True Deed Accounts," 1933 (Q). Shown this document, 30 July 63, Ambassador Elizalde neither confirmed nor denied knowledge of it, and said that the amounts involved were too small to recollect. Mailed this document for comment, Col Soriano did not reply.

through a business associate, also kicked in another ₱200 per month to the new anti-H-H-C fund.[36]

These and other wealthy Hispanic cosmopolites preferred Quezon as a friend for his magical persuasiveness, and trusted his *duende*— the devilish muse which inspired his politics. Osmeña, on the other hand, struck Mike Elizalde as a "conservative Chinese burgher," and he contemptuously referred to him as "El Chino." With Americans too, Quezon inspired more affinity: "Casey," the poker player, one of the boys. He had the Spreckels family with him, Alfred Ehrman, Horace Pond, and others, who found Osmeña by contrast an unsatisfactory leader.

Quezon's efforts to protect Philippine sugar added to his camp a majority of sugar centralistas. One of Osmeña's arguments, splendidly designed for the masses, told against him here. If this act is defeated, he said, the United States will not pass another, and the Philippines will have let slip its opportunity for independence. Many sugar-millers, even those of Osmeña's territory in the Visayas, saw the H-H-C as primarily a sugar limitation act and could imagine nothing better than its defeat.[37] One of the largest sugar entrepreneurs, M. J. Ossorio, was against independence on principle and through his centrals supported Quezon in the crisis.[38]

Hidden transactions bred suspicion. Senator Jose Clarin charged that Senator Ruperto Montinola, a member of the OsRox mission, had accepted a large retainer from the National City Bank. Montinola countercharged that Quezon had accepted money from Philippine centrals. A senatorial investigating committee found no evidence in subpoenaed books to support Montinola's case. They found him guilty of "moral turpitude" in impugning Quezon's integrity; the Senate fined him six months' salary and warned that repetition

36. Benito Razon, a business associate of Soriano, took note that Alunan had agreed personally with the latter "on the quantity of ₱200 monthly as his contributions towards the expenses of the campaign in the Philippines *against* the H-C [sic] bill." Razon to Alunan, 22 Apr 33 (Q).
37. Fuller details in Theodore Friend, "The Philippine Sugar Industry and the Politics of Independence, 1929–1935," *Journal of Asian Studies*, 22 (1963), 179–92.
38. Ossorio, who became an American citizen at about that time, did not recall financially assisting Quezon in this instance (interview with the author, 29 July 63). Don Felipe Buencamino, Jr, an intimate of Quezon, was present and active in the campaign, however, and remembered the Ossorio centrals as contributing to Quezon's cause (interview, 28 June 58).

would mean expulsion.[39] Quezon men, of course, dominated the committee.

Sugar mill account books did not tell the story of Philippine politics. Senator Claro Recto revealed years later that the Quezon side had raised a million pesos "to get a new independence bill." The heaviest contributors were the Elizaldes: "They had to save Quezon's face. They were very close friends of his." [40]

Before he could get a new independence bill, Quezon had to defeat the first one. Those who wanted a longer transition, or no independence at all, gave him funds, but Quezon also needed popular enthusiasm and therefore sought the support of those who wanted independence immediately: General Aguinaldo, Bishop Aglipay, and Judge Sumulong. The general and the bishop spoke in hollow echoes of fin-de-siècle nationalism, but still had large personal followings. Sumulong, more intelligent than either, cared less than they for power and preferred the pleasure of criticizing popular cant and autocratic leadership. All three had at various times opposed Quezon, and all three would again in the future oppose him. While the independence question was sundering old alignments, however, Quezon hoped to bring these irregulars onto his side.

The lure was an even more uncompromising and independent nationalist, General Artemio Ricarte. One of the members of the original Katipunan, Ricarte had refused to take an oath of allegiance to the United States. He had chosen exile in Japan until, he said, he could see his native flag fly alone. In Yokohama, aging and impecunious, he ran a coffee shop, where he reminisced with Filipino visitors, and accepted gifts to keep himself solvent. Quezon thought of him early in 1933, while he was still testing "immediate independence" as a grounds of opposition to the H-H-C Act. He asked Jose P. Santos, son of a well-known Filipino scholar and a friend of Ricarte, to send him a copy of the act, asking his opinion of it without mentioning Quezon's name. Santos did so. The act, Ricarte wrote back, in rich Tagalog rhetoric, was like a pill that seems

39. Quezon to Jose de Jesus, 22 May 33; committee hearings and other materials in various files (Q); Philippines *Free Press* 19 Aug 33; *Philippine Magazine*, 30 (1933), 273.
40. Author's interview with Sen Recto, 4 Sept 58.

"to be sweet and tasty, but its core has a poison that kills." Quezon's early opposition to it showed that he was a true leader of his people, Ricarte concluded, signing himself as ever with his revolutionary name—"Vibora" (the viper).[41]

Now, Quezon asked, would Santos show this letter to General Aguinaldo, Bishop Aglipay, and Judge Sumulong, none of whom, for respect of Santos' father, would withhold an honest opinion? The replies were all in favor of Ricarte's stand; Aguinaldo gratuitously observed that it was the first time he had ever agreed with Ricarte about anything. Next Quezon employed Santos to publicize Ricarte's position through the columns of the Tagalog daily, *Mabuhay*.[42] From the others came forthright opinions too: Aglipay, an article entitled "Famine, and Before Independence, Death"; from Aguinaldo, a series of speeches;[43] and from Sumulong, continued vocal opposition to the act.

The two generals, the Bishop, and the Judge all represented valuable radical support for Quezon. The most radical element of all, the Communist party, was with Quezon only accidentally; it was opposed to the independence act but still more to the ruling class. The party leader, Crisanto Evangelista, had written Quezon in 1931, apropos his report to the Legislature, that "your . . . reactionary reasoning and demagogy . . . will precipitate the social upheaval, and consequently you are digging the grave of your capitalist-imperialist regime."

Evangelista and many others were in jail, but remaining party leaders distributed instructions to members on the issue of the day: they should organize meetings which appeared to be "held by committees against the Hare-Hawes-Cutting Law, and not . . . by communists." They should make the people realize, in any case, that Quezon and Osmeña were both deceiving the people, wishing "to

41. Ricarte to Santos, 23 Jan 33, published in *Mabuhay*, 19 Feb (Q). Dr Jose P. Bantug described Santos' role in an article in the Philippines *Free Press*, 16 Aug 47.
42. Bantug, ibid.; Ricarte to Santos, 29 Jan 33, Ricarte to Quezon, 15 July; *Mabuhay* clippings, 26 Mar, and others undated (Q).
43. Aglipay in *La Opinion*, 30 Jan 33, typewritten copy (Q). Aguinaldo wanted independence within five years, new markets, and a native army; speech of 21 Apr 33 (Q). In an interview with the author, 25 Oct 58, Carlos Quirino translating from Spanish, Gen Aguinaldo said Quezon promised him to work for independence within three years,

defend or perpetuate in the islands the sovereignty of America and to keep alive aggression [against] the poor." [44]

Few politicos of the day made labor the field of their political careers. Of these, fewer still were *illustrados,* or members of the educated gentry. The most prominent of these, in turn, was the socialist Pedro Abad Santos, an ascetic who won no political office but who was an inspiring teacher; his best peasant pupil, Luis Taruc, later led the Hukbalahap guerrilla army and the postwar rebellion. Both teacher and pupil distrusted the Nacionalista leaders, but other illustrados in labor politics played the conventional game: Ramon Torres, from the sugar province of Negros Occidental, and Francisco Varona, of Tondo, the poorest district of Manila.

Once co-editors of *El Debate,* last example of the romantic style of political journalism, Torres and Varona were now split apart by politics. Varona came out strongly for the H-H-C Act. Torres, traditionally an Osmeña man, might have been expected to do the same, but instead he joined Quezon. The Filipinos, Torres wrote Quezon, had only obtained better treatment from the United States than Central American countries by having a single strong party. Now that the Americans, "spurred by economic crisis," are "knocking down everybody" they needed unity more than ever. Because many people were not eating in Bicol and Leyte and because "suffering is nearly a general thing, . . . there exists the same psychological situation that caused the fall of Hoover in America." Torres implied that his popularity with the masses could help prevent Quezon suffering the same kind of fall; he was ready to join battle, "if we do not fear inspiring the imperialist vultures with new hope." [45]

Quezon expressed pride that an Osmeña man took his side and put his "seal of approval on my labor policy." A year later he would reward Torres by making him the first to hold cabinet rank as Secretary of Labor. Now he explained why schism was forced upon him: Roxas, in his first speech after landing, had "insidiously" questioned

44. Evangelista to Quezon, 14 Dec 31; "READ DEEP AND ACCOMPLISH: Orders to all members of the Communist Party in the Philippines," flysheet in Tagalog, circulated in Manila and environs, 1933 (Q).
45. Torres to Quezon, 4 July 33 (Q).

Quezon's Filipinism "of face and heart" [46] and Osmeña had accused him of disloyalty to the revolution in "being afraid of independence." He had tried, Quezon said, to limit himself to refutations, but Osmeña had grown more aggressive and appealed to regionalism to win the Visayas. Quezon told Torres that Osmeña was a passionate egotist: "Obsessed by hatred of the enemy or by the longing for victory, he will avail himself of any weapon whatever to obtain his objective. Leadership of a people is dangerous in the hands of such men, and if they have to govern, they will govern without me." [47]

The bare facts Quezon's letter presented were essentially true: Osmeña and Roxas had taken an aggressive initiative, questioned his patriotism, and appealed to regionalism. But had Quezon not forced them to do so? By purchasing the Madrigal newspapers, by taming his academic critics with a cut in the university's budget, by reorganizing the government to promote his own men, by tightening his grip on the Legislature, he left no area for Osmeña and Roxas to fight in but the public one. When they opened the fight, desperate to recapture the ground lost in an absence of a year and a half, they permitted Quezon to adopt a stance he loved well: injured innocence defending slandered patriotism.

Although desire to beat Osmeña and Roxas was certainly foremost in Quezon's thoughts, an old friend forced him to reflect on the international implications of the H-H-C Act. Roy Howard, fresh from a visit to Japan, found it astonishingly jingoistic. He could visualize granting independence to the Philippines "as a possible great boon to the United States, but a great disaster to the Philippines." He wrote to Quezon, appealed to him to depart from the independence program: "Your entire public record justifies the belief that you would not hesitate at a course which you believed to be the proper one, even though it involved your political elimination." [48]

The last, of course, was too much to expect of Quezon now that

46. "De cara y corazon." The reference was, first, to Quezon's markedly Castilian features (one observer saw "the short arched nose of the conquistador") and, second, to his supposed affection for, and affectations of, things foreign. Racial allusions, although sometimes made in private conversation, were rarely made in public—hence Quezon's furious reaction. In the mid and late 30s the Sakdalistas tried to inject race into domestic politics, but they were not noticeably successful.
47. Quezon to Torres, 8 July 33 (Q).
48. Howard to Quezon, 12 June 33 (Q).

he had so fiercely joined battle with Osmeña. Howard's letter never-theless moved Quezon to make his foreign policy consistent with his domestic politics. "I am going to oppose the Hare-Hawes-Cutting Act," said Quezon, "not upon the ground that it gives independence to the Philippines . . . but upon the ground that it does not give complete independence."

The clause reserving military bases both qualified Philippine inde-pendence with respect to America and jeopardized independence with respect to Japan. "If America," he continued, "is to retain these naval and military stations without adequate fortifications and garri-sons, and a superior navy, it would only serve as an invitation to war with Japan." The lesser danger for the Philippines was for the United States to get "entirely out . . . because Japan would then have one excuse less in attacking, that of protecting herself against the menace of your military presence in the islands."

What relationship, then, did Quezon envision with the United States? "It is our ordained fate to have to depend upon some big nation, not necessarily as a colony, but as a sort of planet." Al-though he eschewed the unpleasant word "satellite," Quezon im-agined something like it: "a sort of alliance, or as you call it, partner-ship in commerce and defense." [49] The United States would natu-rally be the leading partner, but Quezon did not mind as long as the Philippines had complete *political* independence.

Howard had exacted of Quezon an analysis which, even with its shortcomings and ambiguities, went further than anything his coun-trymen were then asking of him, or anything which he supplied them. Quezon's public campaign against the H-H-C Act focused on the indignities and economic difficulties it contained and on the personalities of his opponents. It is even doubtful whether he would have supported a better act, as long as Osmeña and Roxas were its sponsors. And they, sincere enough in believing that the H-H-C Act was a usable compromise of all interests involved, might very well still have supported a worse bill, as long as it could have served as a platform for opposing Quezon and possibly beating him.

49. The preceding quotations are from Quezon to Howard, 26 June 33, and from a subsequent draft elaboration of the same thoughts, 11 July (Q).

10

The Anti-Pro Fight: (2) Quezon Wins

IN MID-1933, the fate of the independence act lay with the Partido Nacionalista. Manuel Roxas, who understood the party well, once described some of its distinctive characteristics, as the commanding institution in Philippine politics. Between conventions, the executive committee was the repository of all powers in the party; the last convention had been in 1926. There were no national party funds, except what the leaders spent personally; there was no national campaign except speech-making tours by groups of leaders; there was no national party office, save that of the president of the party, and no other staff than his staff.[1] Party structure focused on the party leader. Quezon, the party leader, eleven years before had employed his power to install Manuel Roxas as speaker of the House; now, on July 20, 1933, he employed it to displace him.

Earlier in the week Roxas and Osmeña had met for two hours with Quezon without settling the differences between them. At a caucus of Nacionalista representatives crowded into Speaker Roxas' office, the party whip, Felipe Buencamino, Jr., now offered a motion: since his distinguished friend, impervious to suggestion, declined to resign, the speaker's chair should be declared vacant. The galleries outside were filling up, mostly with student admirers of Roxas. Buencamino's motion passed by a twenty-vote margin, and

1. Joseph Ralston Hayden, notes of conversation with Roxas, 27 July 31 (H).

the members filed out to join the minority and present the motion on the floor.[2]

After three hours of speeches for and against Roxas, the sweltering crowd grew disorderly. When a defender of Roxas spoke, they broke into applause and cries of "Mabuhay!"[3] Down on the floor a Quezon man asked that the rules of the House be invoked. "Gritos en las galerias," reads the record at this point; "Gritos de 'fuera' en las galerias." "Throw him out," the spectators were calling at their monitor. The temporary chairman pounded his gavel and briefly suspended the session, but when he reopened it, the noise sprang up again. "El aborto," the record reads, "el aborto en las galerias y pasillos, invadidos par el publico." Police entered to break up scuffles in the galleries and aisles.

As confusion rose, Roxas strode to the chair, took it over for the last time, and called for order. "My friends who are in the gallery," he said, "any pain that I would feel because of any action that the House may take . . . I assure you, has been erased by your sympathy." As the demonstrators and the members themselves came to order, Roxas dismissed the policemen from the chamber. "I want you," he addressed the galleries again, "to show that you respect discipline, and, for that reason . . . have the right to exact discipline from the members of this House."[4]

Decorum restored, the debate proceeded. The twentieth speaker, and the last, was Roxas himself, who characteristically wiped his perspiring face with his bare hand as he spoke. He pleaded for a plebiscite, asking that "you, gentlemen of the House, not . . . deny our people their right . . . to decide themselves this question which affects their happiness: the acceptance or rejection of the Independence Law." The House then proceeded to vote Roxas, its speaker for eleven years, out of office, 50 to 29.[5] The students rushed down from the galleries, hoisted Roxas on their shoulders, and carried him from the hall. Outside on the steps of the Legislature he made an

2. Philippines *Free Press,* 29 July 33.
3. Literally "long life," an idiomatic expression Theodore Roosevelt, Jr, had learned, adopted, and used like his father's "Bully!"
4. *Diario de Sesiones,* 20 July 33, p. 46; Philippines *Free Press,* 29 July. I have used Roxas' words as printed in the *Diario* rather than the slightly freer language attributed him by the press.
5. *Diario de Sesiones,* 20 July 33, p. 48.

impromptu speech—his greatest, he later considered, but the words were unrecorded.[6]

"I fell from the speaker's chair into the arms of the people," Roxas said later. Jealous of Roxas' popularity and generally infuriated, Quezon sat down to write. Seven pages flowed out, oscillating between epistle, referring to Roxas in the second person, and speech, referring to him in the third. "You and your followers and supporters," Quezon scribbled, "tried to thwart the will of the majority on the floor of the House by staging a demonstration that was a disgrace to the House of Representatives and a blot upon your good name and that of your supporters, a discredit to our claims of capacity to establish and maintain a democratic government, and a most dangerous seed for future mob rule of our country."[7]

Five months later Quezon told an American official that public discussion of the act in the Philippines convinced him "that the Filipino is much more orderly and much less explosive than any of the Latin-Americans in the Western Hemisphere."[8] In the heat of the moment, however, he warned Roxas that "the comedy which you . . . staged . . . in any other country . . . [might] have ended in a tragedy."

Quezon had his own drama to enact in the Senate. He submitted his resignation, as Osmeña had challenged him to do, but covered it with three consecutive days of speeches explaining his position. He allowed that the OsRox mission had acted in good faith for what they conceived to be the best interests of the country. But the mission, the creature of the Legislature, had disobeyed its instructions. Quezon told his own version of his trip to Washington and defended himself against the charge of using, in the provinces, pernicious and irregular influence against the independence act. Now that the Legislature was undertaking to reorganize, he said, he could not help being pained at the necessity of removing certain officers.

6. Philippines *Free Press,* 29 July 33; interview, Rep Gerardo Roxas, son of Manuel Roxas, 25 July 58.
7. Undated holograph, [July?, 1933] (Q).
8. Memorandum, 20 Dec 33, "Conversation between Mr. Quezon and General [Creed F.] Cox, this date" (FDR). Cox had succeeded Gen Frank Parker as Chief of the BIA.

"We are all before the bar of history," Quezon concluded on the third day, nostrils flaring with excitement. "Let him who dares shirk his duty. As for me, never, never, never." [9]

Osmeña replied in one day, with a forty-eight page speech read in Spanish, the tongue he preferred. He defended the mission's action in accepting a compromise independence act. He read into the record the Willard Hotel agreement on that act, and described Quezon's intricate vacillations afterwards. He pictured the OsRox campaign in the provinces, where, he declared, fear of Quezon was suffocating free speech. "In our youth," he concluded, speaking of Quezon, "we were always together; we always loved and treated each other as brothers." But brotherly affection has its limits: "I have followed Mr. Quezon as far as I can: but I can no longer follow him without betraying my duties to our country." He must vote *yes*, "with all the pain in my soul," upon Quezon's resignation from the presidency of the Senate. He must vote his protest against "a personal leadership gained through intrigue and machinations," against the "corrupt influence of the patronage of a *cacique*," and against a policy of "contradictions" in relation to the "independence law . . . which in the hour of sacrifice, the heroes and martyrs of our history dreamed of." [10]

Thus Osmeña's protest against Quezon's leadership took the same tone as Quezon's against Osmeña had eleven years before. "Personal leadership" was the charge, and the rhetoric of democracy was employed against the tradition of *caciquism*. But only four men joined Osmeña in his protest; Quezon's resignation was refused, 16 to 5, and a subsequent vote of confidence for him passed by the same margin. The Senate then accepted Osmeña's resignation, 15 to 2.

These votes were not upon the issue of democracy versus boss rule, but upon a choice between two styles of semidemocratic caciquism. Quezon, the Castilian, the affinitive genius of Philippine politics, won over Osmeña, the Confucian, the scholar-bureaucrat. Stripped of high office for the first time in twenty-six years, Osmeña left the Senate chamber. "His party has repudiated him," Quezon

9. Quezon's speeches appear in the *Diario de Sesiones*, 20–22 July 33, pp. 12–14, 51–54, 56–59; they are also covered in the Philippines *Free Press*, 29 July.
10. *Diario de Sesiones*, 25 July 33, pp. 84–95. I have used the Philippines *Free Press*, 29 July, p. 38, for its translation of Osmeña's concluding remarks.

declared from his home in Pasay. "Let him and his followers leave the party and form a new one." [11]

Quezon proceeded to install his own men, Clarin and Paredes, in the places of Osmeña and Roxas, and to appoint new floor leaders and committee chairmen. Controlling both houses in key personnel as well as total numbers, he could have raised the Hare-Hawes-Cutting Act for consideration at once and rejected it on the spot, but instead he waited ten weeks.

Two considerations moved Quezon to caution: one foreign, one domestic. First, the Roosevelt administration had called a trade agreement conference on sugar, to settle by industry-wide negotiation a situation which had become anarchically competitive. The year 1933, one expert said, might be "conservatively characterized as the most chaotic in American agricultural history." [12] Of American agriculture that year perhaps the most chaotic sector was sugar.

One of several competing suppliers, the Philippine Sugar Association, hoped to get a larger quota through round-table bargaining than they had by congressional lobbying, and to that end employed ex-Senator Harry Hawes as their representative in Washington. Through the summer Hawes struggled at the trade agreement conference to improve the Philippine position against continental and other insular producers. He asked for 1.2 million long tons, 40 per cent more than the H-H-C Act provided. [13] The Legislature in Manila hesitated to reject the H-H-C Act while the discussions were going on, lest they appear too sugar-hungry. When the Washington *Post* leveled the charge against them anyway, they enacted the traditional resolution for immediate, absolute, and complete independence. [14] Finally the War Department persuaded Hawes to settle for 1.1 million long tons, and the trade agreement was signed.

If the Legislature now rejected the H-H-C Act, its sugar quota

11. *Diario de Sesiones*, 31 July 33, pp. 188–90; Philippines *Free Press*, 5 Aug, p. 39. A résumé of the ten-day battle in the Senate appears in BIA 3427-a-w-46, and a summary of the legislative crisis from June through September in BIA 364–961.

12. John E. Dalton, *Sugar, A Case Study of Government Control* (New York, Macmillan, 1937), p. 65.

13. The course of these negotiations may be traced in detail through BIA 4122-a-133 and BIA 4122-w-464, through correspondence and cables among Hawes, Alunan, and the Philippine Sugar Association, July–Sept 1933 (Q), and through various material indexed under "sugar," "Philippines," and "Hawes" (FDR).

14. New York *Times*, 1 Aug 33, BIA 364-a-w-873, part 7; Philippines *Free Press*, 5 Aug, p. 39.

would be inoperative, and the Philippines could hope to obtain a larger quota by 30 per cent if the trade agreement went into effect. An even more delicate matter, however, delayed them further. Quezon had twice publicly agreed—in June and again in July—to holding a plebiscite on the independence question. He could not slip out of the commitment without seeming to prove all Osmeña's charges about his caciquism. Yet he was reluctant to go through with the commitment because of the volatility of the issue: the populace might boil over on the OsRox side.

The struggle—Quezon to avoid a plebiscite, Osmeña to obtain one—veered in favor of Osmeña when, on September 21, the House passed a plebiscite bill presenting the electorate with a simple choice on the independence act: yes or no; accept or reject.[15] Quezon first agreed to this straightforward form of ballot, then refused it. Osmeña could not help smiling; "Every time President Quezon sees a crowd, he changes his mind." Quezon's majority amended the House bill so that a man who voted no was also permitted to express a preference, either for immediate independence or for the existing act with more free trade and no more bases.[16] "Do you want this act?" Quezon's ballot asked in effect, "or do you want something better?" Quezon was confident he could persuade the people to want something better.

The Senate minority fought Quezon's biased wording, and on October 6 presented a ballot equally loaded. It prefaced the yes or no choice with the information that an affirmative vote did not close the possibility of amendment by the American Congress, while a negative vote meant that the law was killed "as if it had never been enacted." With ballots as their battlements, the antis and pros closed for another fight, Quezon ruling that the session of October 6 would be continued until the whole issue was decided.

The loaded minority ballot was immediately put to voice vote and defeated.[17] Osmeña was now faced with the choice of accepting the loaded majority ballot, or, by voting against it, seeming inconsistently to deny the public an exercise of choice. Quezon, for his part, still feared that an objective ballot might go against him; and

15. *Diario de Sesiones*, 22 Sept 33, pp. 486–87. A caucus of the Senate majority had previously agreed in principle to a plebiscite; New York *Times*, 16 Aug, BIA 364-a-w-873, part 7.
16. Philippines *Free Press*, 30 Sept 33, p. 34; *Diario de Sesiones*, 6 Oct, pp. 678–80.
17. *Diario de Sesiones*, 6 Oct 33, pp. 680–82.

he did not really want to bother with a loaded referendum on an act which he intended to supplant, in any case, with one of his own making. Maneuvering on both sides continued until dawn on the morning of October 7. During party caucuses on the floor of the Senate, Osmeña found a formula for defeat with a minimum loss of face.[18]

"What would be the attitude of the majority," Osmeña asked Quezon, "if I presented a motion for the acceptance of the Hare-Hawes-Cutting Act and such a motion is turned down? Would the majority still go ahead with the plebiscite?"

Quezon answered directly: "We are willing to assume the entire responsibility for rejecting the Hare-Hawes-Cutting law, but not for killing the plebiscite. On this last, you share the responsibility with us. We do not want to appear as refusing to give the people an opportunity to accept the law if that is what they want to do." [19] Since there was no hope of obtaining a neutral ballot, Osmeña gave in. After consulting their followers again, the two men signed an agreement abandoning the plebiscite because of disagreement as to its form, "and in order to avoid . . . unnecessary expenses."

One last exercise remained. Osmeña, smiling enigmatically, presented a resolution for the acceptance of the independence act. Four voted in favor of it, and fifteen against.[20] At 5:12 A.M., ending an eighteen-hour session, the Philippine Senate turned down the terms of independence offered by the United States of America.

A quarter century later, Osmeña thought that a plebiscite on the H-H-C Act "would have been preceded by a bitter campaign in

18. Ibid., pp. 696–97, with unrecorded details explained by Quezon, 12 Oct 33, p. 741.

19. Ibid., 6 Oct 33, p. 697; I have adopted the translation of this exchange appearing in the Philippines *Free Press*, 14 Oct 33, after checking it against the Spanish of the *Diario de Sesiones*. The session in question was technically that of 6 Oct, although it actually continued into the morning of the 7th.

20. Ibid., pp. 698–99; Philippines *Free Press*, 14 Oct 33; Gov Gen to Sec War, 11 Oct, BIA 364–963. After considerable word play, both houses of the Legislature agreed that instead of "rejecting" they merely "declined to accept the act," and created a new mission to seek an act providing "conditions . . . that will not imperil the political, social, and economic stability of their country." Sen Con Res 29, 30, *Diario de Sesiones*, pp. 708–09; House Con Res 61, *Diario*, pp. 736–37; Con Res 45, 46, 9th Phil Leg, 3d sess, *Diario*, pp. 746–47; BIA 963, 965, 972, 984; Philippines *Free Press*, 21 Oct 33; *Philippine Magazine*, Nov 33, p. 235. The wording of the final resolution may have been affected by Stimson to Quezon, 14 June 33 (HLS).

which the issues would have been twisted and tortured. It would have divided the people, perhaps beyond bridging, taken a longer time, and cost a lot of money." But if a true plebiscite had been held, and "the people voted with reasonable knowledge of the facts, the Hare-Hawes-Cutting Act would have been overwhelmingly approved." [21]

The statistics available suggest only that a referendum would have been close; they do not clearly indicate a winner. The editorially independent *Free Press* conducted a straw vote in April 1933, mailing out 10,000 ballots with stamped return envelopes to selected subscribers, allotting them by province in rough proportion to the total population. The ballots returned would seem to refute Osmeña: 44 per cent ran in favor of the bill and 56 per cent against it.[22]

The poll, however, was subject to the same kinds of criticism as the *Literary Digest* polls which in 1936 predicted that Landon would beat Roosevelt: it sampled those wealthy enough and interested enough to purchase a magazine subscription, a small percentage of the technically literate. Even then, a change in slightly more than 6 per cent of the votes would have yielded a pro answer instead of anti. A pro result was the more likely in the general electorate, which was far less inclined than readers of the *Free Press* to analyze the law closely, to have investments affected adversely by it, or to imagine national debility as a result of it. The electorate was composed of literate males over 21, roughly half of all adult men. Many of these were at best feebly literate, and less than a third were regular readers of newspapers or magazines.[23]

Had a plebiscite been held, could Quezon's machine, his wealthy friends, and his personal popularity have overcome two dozen years of propaganda for independence, toward which he himself had been a major contributor? Quezon had a number of provincial governors working for him, and most of the provincial treasurers. Of 126 petitions he received from municipalities, 110 were on his side, expressing economic anxieties about the act, or confidence in Quezon's leadership.[24]

21. Osmeña to the author, 10 Oct 58.
22. Philippines *Free Press*, 1 Apr 33.
23. *Census of the Philippines: 1939*, p. 288.
24. Memo of Quezon meeting with governors, 11 July 33; Leon Guinto (Undersecretary of Interior and Labor) to Quezon, 26 June; petitions surviving from the period Dec 32–Feb 33 (Q).

The psychology of Philippine politics, however, does not lend itself to asking a leader to do something he finds repugnant. Perhaps Quezon feared the number of opposite petitions that might be going to Osmeña, or perhaps he was dissatisfied with the number which came to himself. Perhaps he feared a result in his favor as much as one against him: a national no on the H-H-C Act could be used by Congress as an excuse for taking no further action. In any event, Quezon forestalled a national ballot until he knew he had a safer product to sell: his own popularity—running for President in 1935.

After the failure of the plebiscite plan and the subsequent rejection of the law, Osmeña had one more stratagem left: an effort to call a special convention on the question of the independence act. Article 17 of the H-H-C Act provided an option—either a special convention or the ordinary Legislature might decide the question. On this matter the results of the *Free Press* poll were unmistakable: 82 per cent were in favor of a special convention.[25] Thinking people apparently doubted the representativeness of their Legislature.

For Osmeña to suggest a convention, after all that had transpired, was nevertheless a futile gesture, except as an occasion for remarks on how the people had been ignored. He managed at least to irritate Quezon into a display of autocratic behavior. On October 23, while Osmeña held the floor for his cause, Quezon tangled him in weary dispute on the meaning of Article 17. After answering a series of questions from Quezon, Osmeña raised his hand for silence and the privileges of the floor. Quezon angrily complained that he expected the same courtesies he extended: "I waive the interpellation," he said and stalked out of the Senate.

After a momentary hush Osmeña spoke in an even voice: there were certain established rules for debate in the Senate, certain procedures recognized all over the world. "This Senate," he declared, "does not belong to President Quezon. This Senate belongs to the Filipino people." [26]

As true as Osmeña's statement should have been, concrete political facts belied it. The Senate did belong to Mr. Quezon, and so did the

25. Philippines *Free Press*, 1 Apr 33.
26. *Diario de Sesiones*, 23 Oct 33, pp. 797–808; Philippines *Free Press*, 28 Oct, pp. 4 ff.

House; important votes in each proclaimed as much. An analysis of the voting upon the acceptance question in October, together with the reorganization vote in July, plus still earlier party and press surveys of legislative opinion, indicated that the Legislature did not vote on the acceptance question as a matter of substantive high policy, but as a trial of leadership. The merits of Quezon and Osmeña were almost solely at issue, and not the merits of the H-H-C Act. From January to October 1933, the same men pronounced themselves, or voted, in the same ways (see table).

From the data one might conceivably argue that the Senate and House voted Osmeña and Roxas out of office in July because of their policies, which were subsequently rejected in October. But in Philippine politics that would be putting the cart of policy before the horse of personality. Only three out of seventy-eight members of the House, for instance, took a position on Roxas' ouster that was clearly contradictory to their position on the independence act. The Legislature demoted Roxas and Osmeña because they had forced a trial of power with Quezon; the same majority then voted to reject the H-H-C Act because it was the OsRox policy, and finally to accept, much later, virtually the same act because it had become Quezon's policy. Policy and personality were inseparable, and the determining of the two was personality.

Roxas in October claimed that 14 senators and 54 representatives, that is, a majority of both houses, would vote, if permitted, for *conditional* acceptance of the act. The only poll which considered that possibility shows that the Senate might have voted so, but not the House. In the latter, Roxas would have had to have *gained* several votes between July and October, whereas he was clearly losing ground during that time. Even had both houses voted for conditional acceptance, such action would have had little effect, legal or moral, upon the American Congress, whose attitude was "take it or leave it." Practically speaking, conditional acceptance would have been the same as rejection, except to save face for Osmeña and Roxas.

A shrewd observer of Philippine life summed up the events of 1933 thus: "After maneuvering like a drunken sailor all over the deck of Filipino politics . . . Don Manuel finally gathered behind him all the radicals (he led them to believe that he is in favor of a

POLLS AND ROLL CALLS OF THE PHILIPPINE LEGISLATURE, JANUARY–OCTOBER, 1933

	House			Senate		
	Anti	Pro	Misc.	Anti	Pro	Misc.
January: newspaper poll[a]	Paredes-Alas followers 44	Roxas followers 26	Others 26	No Survey		
April: Nacionalista party assessment[b]	Anti-H-H-C 58	Pro-H-H-C 24	Unknown 12	Anti-H-H-C 17	Pro-H-H-C 7	Unknown 0
July: Free Press poll[c]	51	accept without reservations 31	accept with reservations, or in favor of plebiscite 14	10	accept without reservations 8	accept with reservations 6
July: reorganization of legislature[d]	to oust Roxas 49	to retain Roxas 29	Not voting 18	for vote of confidence in Quezon 16	against vote of confidence 5	not voting 3
October: on motion to "decline to accept" H-H-C Act[e]	for motion 54	against 21	21	for motion 15	against 4	5

a. Philippines *Herald*, 5 Jan 33, BIA 3427-a-w-46.
b. Jose Clarin to Hilario Dugenio, Sub-Chairman, Executive Committee, Anti-Hare-Hawes-Cutting League, 29 Apr (Q).
c. Philippines *Free Press*, 15 July.
d. Ibid., 29 July, 5 Aug,
e. Ibid., 14 Oct.

more immediate, more complete and more absolute independence than that provided in the H-H-C) and all the conservatives, sugar barons and other propertied gentlemen (because he led them to believe that he is in favor of a less immediate, less complete and less absolute independence than . . . the H-H-C). Gathering both ends he left Osmeña only a narrow middle ground and he won in the Legislature hands down." [27]

In rejecting the terms of independence offered by the United States, Quezon displayed a freedom and a power without comparison in the colonial world. Gandhi and Nehru, for instance, had just been released from jail. The fortunes of their Congress party were at the lowest point in a decade, and independence for India was nowhere in sight. While Indian leaders rested and bided their time against the British, Quezon was planning a trip to the United States to obtain an independence act more to his liking.

27. Evett D. Hester to Theodore Roosevelt, Jr, 11 Jan 34, T.R. Jr MSS, vol. 7.

11

The Second Independence Act

DEPOSED AS SPEAKER of the House, his independence act defeated, Manuel Roxas found it aggravating to be asked by Quezon to accompany him on a trip to the United States for a new law. "There are two Mr. Quezons," Roxas declared. He would have nothing to do with either one: the "astute and slippery politician who babbles immediate, absolute, and complete independence," or "the highbrow, superbly conservative statesman . . . who speaks of a political partnership with America, and is a devotee of free trade with the United States." [1] When Osmeña also declined to accompany Quezon, hoping to leave him stuck with the H-H-C Act,[2] Roxas predicted failure in "Mr. Quezon's well known game of saying one thing in the Philippines and the contrary in America." "If he comes back with a new law," said Roxas, "I shall march at the head of the parade which shall meet him . . . I shall kiss his hand and . . . pledge him my support."

"What chance do I have in the United States?" Quezon asked Vicente Bunuan, a friend who had spent ten years in Washington as a Philippine propagandist. "None, virtually none," Bunuan answered. In Washington, Senator Key Pittman, a drinking partner of

1. Roxas quotations, here and below, from Philippines *Free Press*, 21 Oct 33, pp. 4 ff.
2. Quezon to Osmeña, 15 Oct 33 (not sent), and 19 Oct, three messages to "Mi Querido Senador," "Mi Querido Sergio," and "Chico," signed "Manolo" (Q).

Harry Hawes, avowed that "Mr. Quezon may be political dictator at home but . . . Congress refuses to be dictated to." [3] Quezon set sail nonetheless in November 1933 for the United States by way of Japan, accompanied by Rafael Alunan, President of the Philippine Sugar Association, Senator Elpidio Quirino, a protégé, and Don Isauro Gabaldon, a bearded, cantankerous nationalist.

By charging Quezon with duplicity in his diplomacy, Roxas both struck the truth and missed it. Certainly Quezon did present two different cases in the two different capitals, and so, on some occasions, had both Roxas and Osmeña. Quezon, however, was capable not only of duplex politics, but triplex, and more: he adopted as many attitudes as needed to clear maneuvering room for himself and to obtain desirable conditions for his country. Part troubleshooter, part troubador, he mustered, in each office, each city, the requisite mood—anything from savage anger to courtly charm. "Quezon, the composite person," Roxas had called him: but beneath the political multiplicity there was a redeeming essence, an artistic integrity perhaps, which enabled him to play his many roles without wearying his audience. Tragical, comical, historical, or pastoral, he was always Manuel Quezon, a man saved from his vices not by virtue, but by virtuosity.

> I am going to be a storm—a flame—
> I need to fight whole armies all alone:
> I have ten hearts; I have a hundred arms; I feel
> Too strong to war with mortals—

Joe Tumulty, on retainer as a lobbyist, quoted *Cyrano de Bergerac* to his old friend,[4] who sallied from Manila armed with endless spontaneous arguments. Quezon first wrote Governor General Frank Murphy, imploring his support in securing a new act. He wanted independence in two or three years, accompanied with reciprocal free trade for fifteen or twenty. Japan could not object to such a relationship because it would be similar, Quezon wrote, to hers with Manchuria. Japan could only object to American retention of military and naval bases, which would appear to threaten Japanese se-

3. Vicente G. Bunuan, undated speech, "The Unusual in Quezon"; Philippines *Free Press*, 28 Apr 34, p. 4, quoting Pittman.
4. 16 Feb 34, one of a series of letters, Tumulty to Quezon, in that year (Q).

curity and which might involve the Philippines in a war between the two countries.[5]

Shortly after, Quezon spoke in Tokyo, where he changed his accent to please an official audience. American bases, he declared, would be an infringement of Philippine sovereignty. He emphasized his faith in Japan's good intentions; the Philippines had nothing to fear from the north.[6]

Arriving in America in early December, Quezon changed his tone once more. In a private talk with Henry Stimson, who had returned to law practice in New York City, Quezon predicted that the Japanese would seize the islands within two years after independence, unless economic ruin came sooner. The proposed tariff step-ups meant probable revolution before 1946. "The blood which is sure to be shed would be on my conscience," Quezon said. He appealed for special economic relations to prevent catastrophe.[7]

A week later, in Washington, Quezon saw Secretary of War George Dern. He had already intimated that any bloodshed would be on Dern's conscience. In case of a revolution provoked by economic ruin, the United States Army would have to intervene, and "Americans would have to kill Filipinos again." [8]

Finally Quezon encountered Franklin Roosevelt and there met his match. Stimson had told the President that Quezon's reopening the Philippine question "presented a . . . chance for action which fifty or seventy-five years from now would be deemed more important perhaps than even the work in the depression." [9] Roosevelt, however, was always too absorbed in other matters to give the Philippines much thought. At luncheon in the White House he chatted amiably about how he had once rescued a Manila churchbell— Anno Domini 1748—from an American naval junkyard and had it returned to the Philippines. Switching abruptly to business, he told

5. Quezon to Murphy, 7 Nov 33 (Q); also Quezon to Murphy, memo, 3 Nov, BIA 364–1050.
6. Gov Gen to Chief, BIA, 15 Nov 33, Quezon–P; *Philippine Magazine, 30* (1933), 278; Nolasco to Quezon, 25 Nov, commenting adversely upon Osmeña's criticism of Quezon's speech (Q).
7. Stimson diary, 11 Dec 33 (HLS).
8. Memorandum, 18 Dec 33, "Conversation between Secretary of War and Senator Quezon, this date, Walter Reed Hospital"; Memorandum, 20 Dec, "Conversation between Mr. Quezon and Gen. Cox, this date, BIA" (FDR).
9. Stimson diary, 26 Oct 33 (HLS); Stimson to Franklin D. Roosevelt, 14 Dec 33 (FDR).

Quezon that the sugar, dairy, and labor interests were still power-ful. "If you insist upon better economic considerations, you may get your independence in twenty-four hours."

Quezon's answer was brave enough: "Mr. President, if it is the intention of the United States to no longer have interest in the Philippines in the Far East, now or in the future, we may as well have independence as soon as possible." But Quezon was not in a position to require Roosevelt to define American policy in East Asia. Roosevelt instead asked him to submit a written set of concrete pro-posals on Philippine independence.[10]

Quezon's report, completed in mid-January 1934, was a modified version of his earlier letter to Murphy. He used the *palengke,* or market place, tactic of asking much more than he expected to get. The powers in Washington responded with the perfect counter: they appeared unwilling to give anything at all. Senator Millard Tydings, now Chairman of the Senate Committee on Territories and Insular Affairs, announced that Congress would consider extending the life of the Hare-Hawes-Cutting Act an additional nine months, giving the Filipinos another chance to accept it: nothing more.[11] Quezon said to Stimson, "I see nothing but to go home and teach my son to rebel." [12]

Instead he remained, met once with Tydings, and then went to the White House, where he was informed that the President had not read his report. Instead of Quezon, Roosevelt gave an interview to Camilo Osias, a pro. Immediately afterward Osias sailed for Manila, given to understand that the Philippines would have an election in June with the H-H-C Act as the main issue.[13] Two days later, however, Roosevelt saw Quezon, raised the Philippine prob-lem in cabinet meeting,[14] and apparently decided to let Quezon

10. James Wingo, Philippines *Free Press,* 17 Feb 34.
11. Quezon to Franklin D. Roosevelt, 15 Jan 34, BIA 364–1050; *Cong Rec* 73:2, 639–40, 1217. Osias had asked for the extension, as Osmeña and Roxas desired. Even Aguinaldo and Sumulong supported it, presumably fearing to let the opportunity for independence escape; Teodoro M. Kalaw, MS autobiography, p. 332.
12. Stimson diary, 24 Jan 34 (HLS).
13. Wingo, Philippines *Free Press,* 17 Mar 34.
14. Harold Ickes, *The Secret Diary of Harold L. Ickes, 1, The First Thousand Days, 1933–1936* (New York, Simon and Schuster, 1953), p. 145. President Roosevelt, usually ill-informed and confused about the Philippines, continued to think that the Philippines had an election with the H-H-C Act as the issue; Franklin D. Roosevelt, *On Our Way* (New York, John Day, 1934), p. 241.

explore congressional opinion on changing the H-H-C Act. Thus Roosevelt gave the Filipino antis the upper hand over the pros.

During the first two weeks of February Quezon met several times with Millard Tydings, who proved as staunch as Roosevelt against being drawn into the intricacies, contingencies, and ambiguities in which Quezon preferred to deal. "You want to play draw poker," Tydings said to Quezon, "but I'm playing showdown."

He laid his cards on the table: as the President had said, Congress would only change the economic terms by worsening them. If Quezon wanted improvement of the military terms, there was some hope, considering the deepening isolationism in Congress. Many Army officers were known to fear their exposed position in the Philippines and to prefer contracting the defense perimeter; many Navy officers, however, were still fascinated with the possibilities of being a makeweight in the West Pacific and with expanding the fleet and bases. Tydings therefore committed himself to striking Army bases from the old act and to making naval bases subject to negotiation at the time of independence. In return Quezon was to promise to support the changes at home.[15]

Tydings put his proposal in the form of a memorandum and signed it, but Quezon still hesitated briefly. He was playing draw poker, unknown to Tydings, at different tables. Quezon had sought out Senator King and left the impression that he was committed to King's immediate independence bill. Between negotiations with Tydings, he had gone to Long Island and convinced Theodore Roosevelt, Jr., that he really desired the H-H-C Act to expire quietly, so that a dominion plan could be considered.[16] Quezon liked to breed alternatives in the same way a horticulturist grows roses—in the hope that one would win a prize.

Possibly the statesman in Quezon considered either immediate

15. Undated list of the conditions upon which Tydings would negotiate, with memo attached from Tumulty, who represented the Philippine Sugar Association, 2 Feb 34, Nat Arch, Legis Sec, Sen 73A–F25, 125–26; memorandum of conversations, including final terms, between Tydings and Quezon, signed also by Rep John McDuffie, Chairman, House Committee on Insular Affairs, dated 15 Feb 34, copy in possession of Gen Carlos P. Romulo, given him by Tydings; Tydings to Franklin D. Roosevelt, 26 Feb 34 (FDR); interview, Sen Millard Tydings, 15 Sept 56.
16. Wingo tells of the meeting with King, *Free Press*, 17 Mar 34; Theodore Roosevelt, Jr, to the President, 12 Feb 34 (FDR); Theodore Roosevelt, Jr, *Colonial Policies of the United States* (Garden City, Doubleday, Doran, 1937), p. 181.

1. The first joint session of the Philippine Legislature, 15 Nov 1916, Quezon and Osmeña presiding.

2. Members of the revolutionary congress of 1899, in reunion at their meeting hall, Barasoain Church, Malolos, 8 Dec 1929; General Emilio Aguinaldo, *front center*.

3. Brigadier General Arthur MacArthur (*second from left*) and staff, 1899.

4. Major General Douglas MacArthur, with Manuel Quezon, Sergio Osmeña, and Manuel Roxas, 1928.

5. Chief of Staff Douglas MacArthur relaxes after driving the Bonus Marchers from Anacostia Flats, Washington, D.C., 28 July 1932.

6. "From every mountain side
   Let Freedom ring!"

7. "Will Uncle Sam Now Withdraw His Rook from the Philippines?" The chess pieces are actually set so that Uncle Sam can win the game if he does not remove his rook.

8. Manuel Quezon, during his service as an anti-American guerrilla officer, 1899–1901.

9. President Quezon with Field Marshal Douglas MacArthur, 1936 or
1937.

10. President Quezon enters the grandstand with High Commissioner Frank Murphy for ceremonies inaugurating the Commonwealth, 15 Nov 1935.

11. Secretary of War George Dern and party, Tokyo, en route to inauguration of the Commonwealth, 1935. Among the Japanese entertaining them are present and past Ministers of War, and some staff officers who later planned the Philippine invasion.

12. Meeting at Quezon's home in Mandaluyong, some days before evacuation to Corregidor: Laurel, Vargas, MacArthur, Quezon, Mrs. Quezon, Roxas, and Manuel Nieto, aide to Quezon.

13. Quezon congratulates Jose P. Laurel after swearing him in as Secretary of Justice, 17 Dec 1941; Jorge Vargas looks on.

14. Party in Malacañan, 25 June 1942: Major General Hayashi Yoshihide and Advisor Kihara Jitaro with Vargas and Laurel.

15. The Philippine Executive Commission with Japanese officers, late January or early February 1942. *Front:* Claro Recto, Rafael Alunan, Antonio de las Alas, Jose Yulo, Jorge Vargas, Lieutenant General Maeda Masami, Major General Hayashi Yoshihide, Benigno Aquino, Jose Laurel. *Back:* civilians, Kihara Jitaro and Quintin Paredes; Japanese officers unidentified.

independence or permanent connection a sound solution of the Philippine problem, in view of the growing threat of the Japanese. But Quezon the politician had an election to fight in June; he had to present something superior to the Osmeña-Roxas achievement, at the risk of losing the election, or at least of losing face. In the Philippines he had begun early in 1933 to change his focus from the trade terms of the bill—difficult to explain to his people—to the military terms, with the simple and visible irritants they implied— foreign flags, foreign uniforms. Now he found that he could get satisfaction on the latter score. Perhaps he realized that neither the King bill nor young Teddy's letter to his cousin Franklin had a chance of swaying Congress. After fifteen minutes hesitation over the agreement with Tydings, Quezon added to it his hurried, squiggled signature.

Tydings then cabled Quezon's opponents, his lieutenants, and the leading independents to obtain their consent to the agreement. Osmeña and Roxas hesitated a few days, and then asked that the change in the military clause be presented as confirming their own interpretation of the original clause in the H-H-C Act. Tydings, however, would permit no conditions or qualifications. He enlisted Harry Hawes in the effort to convince the two opposition leaders, and Hawes, with misgivings, complied. By February 24, all the people whose support Quezon deemed necessary to the agreement had swung behind it, Osmeña and Roxas presumably hoping to present it as a vindication of their own work.[17]

On March 2 the President sent a message to Congress asking for the enactment of a new independence bill as agreed upon. His message included the statement, requested by Quezon and drafted by Quezon and Tydings, that "where imperfections or inequalities exist, I am confident that they can be corrected after proper hearing, and in fairness to both peoples." [18]

The Filipino idea of an agreement is far more conditional than the Western: a significant change in conditions may release the

17. Tydings to Osmeña, Roxas, Aguinaldo, Sumulong, Clarin, Paredes, Recto, 16 Feb 34; latter five to Tydings, 22–24 Feb; Osmeña, Roxas to Tydings, 19 Feb; Tydings to Osmeña, Roxas, 22 Feb. Hawes apparently showed Tydings a distressed cable to himself from Osmeña and Roxas, at which point Tydings enlisted a reluctant Hawes in the job of persuasion; Nat Arch, Sen 73A–F25, 125–26.
18. *Cong Rec* 73:2, 3580–81.

party adversely affected from the obligations he has undertaken. Such a change, adverse to Philippine sugar and coconut oil, occurred between the time of Quezon's signing the agreement with Tydings and the debate in Congress upon the new bill.

The Agriculture Department, having rejected the trade agreements on sugar reached in September 1933, had left the sugar industry still in chaos. President Roosevelt explored the possibility of "retiring" all acreage from the inefficient American sugar beet industry, over a thirty- or forty-year period. He entrusted the idea to Secretary of War George Dern, who reported against it;[19] he had less than $600 invested in beet sugar, but as former Governor of Utah, "the original sugar beet state," his imagination was dominated by its great product.

Roosevelt ultimately sent Congress a message which preserved the status of the beet growers while bending to State Department warnings that political stability in Cuba depended on assured access to the American sugar market. Congress, in turn, trimmed insular quotas to build up domestic beet. The end result gave the Philippines slightly more than had the H-H-C Act,[20] but the quota was made retroactive to January 1, 1934. Under such terms the Philippines could expect to lose half a million tons of its largest crop in history. Quezon, Frank Murphy, Harry Hawes, and the Philippine Legislature pleaded and petitioned to Congress against making the quota retroactive, without success.[21]

More surprising and more threatening still, the Senate Finance Committee undertook consideration of a three-cent per pound excise tax on oils used within the United States but produced outside. Quezon was quick enough to see that the measure was actually a protective tariff in disguise, which would hurt the Philippine coconut industry, but he was not strong enough to kill the measure. Despite an eloquent radiogram from Frank Murphy, the protectionists gath-

19. Dern to the President, 21 Mar 34 (FDR).
20. Sumner Welles to the President, 20 Aug 33, 7 Feb 34 (FDR); Dalton, *Sugar, Government Control*, gives tables of quotas at different stages of bargaining, pp. 102, 123.
21. Murphy to Sec War, 13 Mar 34, forwarded to the President, 14 Mar (FDR); Hawes to Sen Pat Harrison, Chairman, Sen Fin Comm, 9 Apr, to Quezon, 12 Apr, to Murphy, 18 Apr (Q); 9th Phil Leg, 3rd Spec Sess, Con Res 50, 2 May 34, BIA 364–1013.

ered speed and passed the measure in early April. President Roosevelt rebuked Congress for a breach of faith in dealing with the Philippines, but the excise remained.[22]

Waiting for the new independence legislation to come up in Congress, Quezon began to have regrets about his agreement with Tydings. If a congressional majority could unilaterally amend Philippine-American trade relations in a manner inimical to the Philippine economy, why should he feel bound to an agreement signed with a single senator, however personally well-intentioned that senator might be?

Quezon prepared an escape hatch. Two weeks after his agreement with Tydings, he affirmed in writing to Senator King that if the latter urged consideration of his bill, "I, as well as the members of my delegation, will support it in preference to the revival, with amendments, of the Hawes-Cutting Bill." [23]

The House on March 19 passed the amended revival, rules suspended, by a voice vote. Quezon's delegation was split concerning what to support in the Senate. The farm lobbies were behind the King bill, because it provided for immediate full tariff.[24] Dickinson of Iowa proposed, as he had in 1932–33, a less abrupt compromise, a five-year bill. Elpidio Quirino urged Quezon and the Filipino delegation formally to support the Dickinson version.[25]

Meanwhile debate had opened in the Senate. "Yesterday's anathema becomes today's jubilee," observed Arthur Vandenberg. "The Hare-Hawes-Cutting atrocity . . . now becomes the Tydings-McDuffie benediction." Vandenberg declined to celebrate an independence which would be a "counterfeit luxury" without economic self-sufficiency. Knowing that his twenty-year bill had no chance, he proposed the opposite: independence in two years, followed by eight years of gradually increasing tariff.[26]

22. Murphy to Sec War, 24 Feb 34, *Philippine Magazine, 31* (1934), 108; Quezon to Harrison, 6 Mar; J. D. Craig to Quezon, 12 Mar, to Cox, 1 June, to Tydings, 2 June; Howard to Quezon, 28 Apr (Q); 9th Phil Leg, 3rd Spec Sess, Con Res 53, 2 May 34, BIA 364–1013.
23. Quezon to Quirino, 16 Feb 34, to King, 20 Feb, reindorsed 28 Feb (Q).
24. Letters of representatives of the several farm organizations to Tydings, 27, 29 Jan 34, Nat Arch, Sen 73A–F25, 125.
25. Quirino to Quezon, 21 Mar 34 (Q).
26. *Cong Rec* 73:2, 4986–92; quotations, pp. 4987, 4989.

Huey Long spoke for Dickinson's bill and summed up the view of isolationists as well as farmers: "Look right underneath the cooking stove and see what is there. . . . These international students are what has ruined this country." [27]

That night the Filipino delegation belatedly reappraised their position and decided to put themselves behind Dickinson and Long. The next morning Quezon drafted a letter to Tydings. Disheartened, he said, by evidence of a strong movement to restrict Philippine-American trade by any means whatever, he and his delegation had decided that independence in five years was preferable to ten. Despite Senator Tydings' objections to rewriting the bill on the floor, Quezon listed the necessary changes that could be made. "I do not want you, my dear Senator," Quezon concluded, "to feel that . . . I am turning my back against our agreement. . . . You have no reason to believe that I am moved by any purpose other than to get the best out of a bad situation." [28]

Before Quezon could send the letter, Tydings got wind of the delegation's intentions. He summoned the mission to his office that morning, March 22, and warned them not to water their stand.[29] Afraid, perhaps, to offend the chairman of the key committee handling Philippine-American affairs, the Philippine delegation curbed its panic and resumed its former ground.

That day Tydings asked the Senate to be considerate of the Filipinos. "We have 10 men to their 1 if it comes to a question of war. . . . We must hold their hand a little . . . until they get used to walking on the international pathway." The Senate voted down King's immediate independence and full tariff bill, 44 to 28; defeated Vandenberg's two-year bill, with eight-year tariff preference, 49 to 24; and killed Dickinson's five-year measure by the biggest margin of all, 49 to 22.[30]

The Philippine delegation had misjudged Dickinson's strength; had ignored Vandenberg's bill, which most closely resembled their January report to the President; and had double-crossed Senator King. The latter devoted some time to a rancorous critique of

27. Ibid., pp. 5096–5105; quotation, p. 5098.
28. Quezon to Tydings, 22 Mar 34, typed but pencilled "not sent" (Q).
29. Wingo, Philippines *Free Press*, 23 June 34.
30. *Cong Rec* 73:2, 5117 (Tydings); 5237, 5282–83 (votes).

Quezon, fixing his eye all the while on Quezon himself, seated in the gallery to the left of the Vice-President's chair.[31]

Had all of the Senators who voted for the three alternatives to Tydings' bill been united on one, they would still have numbered only 36, thirteen short of an absolute majority and a few shy of carrying a roll call diminished by absentees. The Philippine matter was old business; most senators thought it should have been closed business. Their vote to pass the Tydings measure, 68 to 8, was a re-affirmation of the motives which had lain behind passage of the Hare-Hawes-Cutting Act. "Well," said Millard Tydings to Elpidio Quirino, who thanked him in front of the senators' elevator, "you are on your way now." [32] Time marches on, leaving banalities for foot-prints.

"You are going to write big history . . . international history." Harry Hawes had once hoped his own name would be on the inde-pendence act, but now wrote to compliment his friend, "Glad" Tydings. The latter judged his accomplishments more modestly. "It is not the bill I would have written," he said, but "a bill not wholly good was, if they wished it, better for the Filipinos than no bill at all." [33]

Moscow *Pravda* thought the bill almost wholly bad; the sugar lobbies behind the bill gave it sordid motivations, and the American right to retain naval bases left the Philippines "in reality . . . no independence whatever." *La Prensa* of Buenos Aires offset Moscow's shallow cynicism with naïve generosity: "This is the first time that a colonizing country renounces its sovereignty over one of its posses-sions of its own free will . . . and we congratulate ourselves that the author of this noble decision should be an American nation." [34]

31. The *Congressional Record* never carried these remarks; Wingo, Philippines *Free Press*, 23 June 34. Quezon that evening began, but apparently did not finish, a de-fense of himself intended for Tydings to present in the Senate; holograph, 22 Mar 34 (Q).
32. Wingo, Philippines *Free Press*, 23 June 34.
33. Hawes to Tydings, 17 Feb 34, Tydings to Editor, Baltimore *Sun*, 2 Mar, Nat Arch, Sen 73A–F25, 125–26. Years later Hawes said that if he had it to do over again, he would not have introduced independence legislation for the Philippines; author's interview with M. J. Ossorio, 30 July 63.
34. Moscow *Pravda*, 21 Mar 34; Buenos Aires *La Prensa*, 20 Mar. A Russian critic, G. I. Levinson, sees the law, like Roosevelt's Good Neighbor Policy, as merely an-other step toward more effective imperial expansion. Lacking manuscript sources en-

Quezon returned to Manila nine pounds heavier than when he left, sporting a Rooseveltian pince-nez with black string. Roxas was not there to "kiss his hand" as promised, but a demonstrative crowd gave Quezon alone the acclaim he had had to share the year before.[35]

In the triennial election, coming in June, the OsRox side hoped to obtain the popular mandate they believed might have been theirs in a plebiscite. Quezonian maneuver, assisted by Governor General Frank Murphy, diminished their chances. During the anti-pro fight the newly arrived chief executive had maintained a "breathless neutrality," [36] but extended factional differences were conducive neither to the economic and social progress he wished to foster nor to the constitutional stability of a future commonwealth. Murphy therefore assented when Quezon asked him for a special session of the Legislature to consider the Tydings-McDuffie Act before the June elections.[37] Thus he forestalled another vicious debate on the independence issue.

Osmeña and Roxas could soberly do only one thing: participate in a unanimous ratification of the act. In consultation with Quezon, Osmeña drafted a resolution accepting the Tydings-McDuffie Act, "because the Filipino people cannot, consistent with national dignity and love of freedom, decline." They also mentioned Roosevelt's promise to adjust inequalities. Together, on May 1, 1934, Quezon and Osmeña entered the Senate doors arm in arm. The Legislature unanimously ratified their resolution.[38]

Then the two leaders dropped arms and fought the last stage of their extended political battle. The issue bewildered many Filipinos: whose independence bill was it? A rural citizen wrote Millard Tydings: "We who are in the backyard of Philippine culture beseech you who are honest man . . . what is the truth about this bill?" [39] Tydings did not answer directly, but an honest reply would have

---

tirely, he cannot see that the law was a matter of minor business to Roosevelt, but a major and necessary political asset to Quezon; *Filippiny Mezhdu Pervoi i Vtoroi Mirovymi Voinami* (The Philippines Between the First and Second World Wars) (Moscow, Izdatel'stvo Vostochnoi Literatury, 1958), pp. 101–03.

35. Philippines *Free Press*, 5 May 34.

36. Quotation from Evett D. Hester, "Modern History," *Philippine Handbook, 1,* 189; Lichauco, *Roxas,* p. 103.

37. Quezon to Murphy, cable from Pittsburgh, forwarded through BIA, 3 Apr 34; Proclamation of the Gov Gen, No. 680, 12 Apr.

38. 9th Phil Leg, 3rd Spec Sess, Con Res 52, 1 May 34, BIA 364–1013.

39. Arsenio Teves to Tydings, 12 Apr 34, Nat Arch, Sen 73A–F25, 125–26.

described the H-H-C and the Tydings-McDuffie acts as identical in essentials, except for the removal of American Army bases from the latter. Quezon had accepted the OsRox handiwork and presented it in a new wrapping.

Election results proved that most Filipinos preferred things presented with a Quezonian flourish. Of Quezon's severest personal critics, only Osmeña and Roxas and the labor-beloved Varona won seats in Congress; Montinola and Palma, Sabido, Tirona, and Camilo Osias lost.

Quezon's faction, on the other hand, fared less well than its leader. Two financial principals, Mike Elizalde and Vicente Madrigal, had worked hard for Quezon, assisted by two rising young men, Jose Yulo and Carlos Romulo.[40] Quezon followers achieved a three to one margin in the Senate and five to one in governorships, but they won the House much less decisively. There, Nacionalista antis numbered 42, as against 21 Nacionalista pros and 18 antis who called themselves Democratas, even though that party was officially dead.[41] The vote in general seemed to reflect provincial dissatisfaction with Nacionalista leadership and with an enfeebled general welfare.

The campaign apparently exhausted the last of the million pesos gathered by Quezon's backers. Although Joe Tumulty pleaded straitened circumstances to Quezon (he owed $156,000 to the Trustees in Bankruptcy for Insull, Son & Co.), he never received the final payment of the lobby fee Quezon had promised him.[42] The last sacrifice to Quezon's victory was Joe Tumulty's friendship.

Quezon's erratic behavior during the discussion of independence, 1929–34, was consistent only in self-interest. He had advanced three possible courses of action in his report of November, 1931, to the Legislature. He had used the two most contradictory courses, the dominion plan and immediate independence, as bases for criticizing the Hare-Hawes-Cutting Act in 1932–33. The third course—"inde-

40. Madrigal, Elizalde, Yulo, Romulo to Quezon, 26 Feb 34; Madrigal to Quezon, 28 Feb; Elizalde, Yulo to Quezon, 26 Mar; Madrigal, Elizalde, Yulo, Romulo to Quezon, 4 Apr (Q).

41. Philippines *Free Press*, 16, 23 June 34; *Philippine Magazine*, July 34, p. 7; political résumé in BIA 3427-a-w-46; Hayden, *The Philippines*, p. 363, gives a different count.

42. Quezon to Tumulty, 29 Jan 34, Tumulty to Quezon, 29 Jan, 17 May, 16 July, Quezon to Tumulty, 9 July (Q); author's interview with Sen Claro Recto, 4 Sept 58.

pendence bill in any form"—could be used as rationale for accepting the Tydings-McDuffie Act in 1934.

Before he submitted to the last, however, Quezon made and broke the Willard Hotel agreement with Osmeña and Roxas; made and broke a promise to Senator King; made an agreement with Senator Tydings and was on the point of breaking it when Tydings stopped him. He expressed himself to yet other purposes, short of promise, to yet other people, in an attempt to achieve a bill ensuring maximum security and prosperity for the Philippines and unhampered sovereignty for its president. Finally he accepted a compromise that did not comport with his best judgment, in order to win his final test with Osmeña and Roxas. Perhaps he consoled himself, confident in his prowess, that he could later have the Tydings-McDuffie Act amended. Instead he would live the rest of his life with it in discomfort.

"When the historian," Quezon wrote, "passes upon what we have all said and done at this momentous period in our history—a period in which we either build or destroy our nation's well-being—how petty and how small must our dissensions and disputes seem to him! How insignificant to him our cherished slogans by the side of the nation's future safety and welfare!" [43] An historian need not add to Quezon's own judgment.

43. Undated Quezon holograph [1934 or 1935], address to youth group (Q).

Part 4: The Trials of Transition

"It very seldom happens among men to fall out when all have enough; invasions usually travel from north to south, that is to say, from poverty upon plenty."

JONATHAN SWIFT
"THE BATTLE OF THE BOOKS"

12

Development of the Commonwealth

THE MAJOR PROBLEMS of the Philippine Commonwealth were three: maldistribution of political power, slow and uneven economic development, and military insecurity. Manuel Quezon, however, saw only two demands on his government: "If we are prepared to defend our country we are free from foreign molestation; if we are just to our people, we will be free from internal rebellion. That is the whole problem—the club in one hand and the bread in the other." [1] Characteristically, he did not see his own primacy and increasing power as a problem to his people. Neither, for that matter, did many of the Filipinos who met in 1934–35 to draw up a constitution.

Although the Philippine constitution imitated the American model in structure (except for a unicameral legislature) and in formal appearance, through it ran a spirit distinct from, if not contrary to, that of the American. In provisions for compulsory civil or military service and in declarations toward rearing youth to ideals of civil efficiency, there appeared the principle of state supremacy over the individual. It appeared again in two socialistic provisions, one enabling the state to own and operate public utilities and enterprises, the other requiring it to regulate all employment relationships.

Tradition encouraged the Filipinos not only to suppress the individual but also to exalt authority. The delegates vested extraordinary constitutional powers in the president, giving him an item veto over

1. Press conference, 22 Jan 37, Friday, 10 A.M. (Q).

appropriation, revenue, and tariff bills, and permitting the Legislature conditionally to delegate to him its powers over trade and tariff. "In times of war or other national emergency," Congress could authorize the president almost limitless critical powers.[2] Quezon, who intended to be the first president to operate under this document, would inherit accepted ideas of the Spanish *caudillo* and the Filipino *datu,* as well as specific powers sometimes exceeding those of American governors general. Quezon himself interpreted the constitution as "reversing" American philosophy: "the good of the state, not the good of the individual, must prevail." [3]

One observer thought the Philippine constitution flexible enough to accommodate everything from a representative republic to a temporary but renewable dictatorship. Another narrowed the possibilities to one overwhelming probability: "an irresponsible autocracy, with power concentrated in the President, the Speaker, and to a much lesser degree, in a few of their intimate political associates." Neither machinery nor tradition compelled a victorious party to respect the will of the voters, but such a system, supple in its possibilities for the autocrat, was "in harmony with the instincts, traditions, and past practices of the Filipino people . . . the *natural* system . . . in their present state of political development." [4]

In the six prewar years of the Commonwealth this "natural system" of "irresponsible autocracy" grew more pronounced. Quezon overcame the fierce schism of 1932–34 and, through mollification, coalition, and, finally, fusion, reestablished the single ascendant party characteristic of Philippine colonial politics.

The constitutional convention itself might have been an occasion for partisan politics, for the anti Hare-Hawes-Cutting delegates only outnumbered the pros by eighty to sixty. Quezon and Osmeña had wisely stayed clear of the deliberations, and Quezon further stabi-

2. Quotations and condensed description from Hester, "Outline of our Recent Political and Trade Relations with the Philippine Commonwealth," *Annals of the American Academy of Political and Social Science,* 226 (1943), 77–83.
3. Speech at Baguio, quoted by Hester, ibid., p. 81.
4. The first observer was Hester; the second, J. R. Hayden, in a memo sent to Gov Gen Murphy, "Comments upon draft of Constitution of Philippine Commonwealth as requested by His Excellency," 31 Dec 34 (H). In his book, *The Philippines: A Study in National Development,* pp. 32–59, Hayden stepped much more lightly on this subject.

lized them by keeping former opponents happy with preference. Tirona crawled back to favor; Aquino would eventually be made campaign manager of the Nacionalistas.[5] Montinola was made a figurehead vice-president of the convention, Roxas was chairman of the crucial drafting committee, and Laurel a member of the committee. Laurel had the ambition and qualifications to be president of the convention, but Quezon assisted the other leading candidate, the anti Claro Recto, into the chair, and appealed to Laurel on patriotic grounds to accept a lesser job.

Once the convention's work was done, the first truly national elections followed. After considerable maneuvering, with Don Miguel Unson as intermediary, Osmeña had agreed to run for vice-president on a coalition ticket with Quezon.[6] Quezon had two opponents, Aguinaldo and Aglipay, but together they attracted less than a third of the popular vote, the General about 17.5 per cent, and the Bishop about 14 per cent.[7] Anachronistic and bombastic, they represented a far less penetrating criticism of Quezon than did Judge Sumulong, a third former ally during the anti-pro fight. Sumulong was opposed to the very principle of the coalition itself, as strengthening the oligarchy that had already run the Philippines for a quarter of a century, heedless of the "unrepresented minorities."[8]

Sumulong's critique went to the core of the Quezonian system, but it did not deter the oligarchs from going a step further, in 1937, and fusing the two wings of the coalition into a single party. As a result, in the 1938 elections, every single member chosen for the unicameral Assembly styled himself a Nacionalista. Of the 98 elected, 71 were regular party candidates, 21 had run in "free zones" where no regular candidate had been designated, and only 5 were rebels who had beaten machine nominees.[9] "To oppose the government," said Claro Recto, who had by now resumed his preferred

5. Tirona to Quezon, 31 Oct 33; Aquino-Quezon election correspondence, 15 June–16 July 34 (Q); Hayden, *The Philippines*, pp. 441–43.
6. "White Book of the Coalition," pamphlet, 60 pp. (Manila, 1935); Osmeña to Quezon, 21 May 35, reassures of the good faith of the leading pros in the proposed coalition, despite rumors that they would not enthusiastically support Quezon's candidacy (Q).
7. Hayden, pp. 401–35, contains an excellent account of the presidential election.
8. Sumulong is quoted in Hayden, pp. 369–71; the answering spokesman for the coalition was Laurel.
9. Hayden, p. 442.

stance of detachment from the majority, "is simply to play the flute and act the . . . fool." [10]

Rarely did a man like Recto withdraw from a close relationship with Quezon, preferring the grandeur of solitude. Most preferred the security of *tayo-tayo* with the nation's leader. From the moneyed Spaniards and mestizos who had supported him in his fight with Osmeña, Quezon more openly than ever solicited contributions to his party and his person. Sometimes he called up Adrian Got, the General Manager of Tabacalera, to say, "Got, I need some money"; the reply was a blank check, filled in by Quezon as high as ₱10,000. Vicente Madrigal was honored with less direct suggestions. At a birthday party for Manuel, Jr., Quezon asked his compadre, "Don't you have a gift for the education of your godson?" Madrigal quickly sent a blank check to Quezon.[11]

John Gunther reported in a magazine article that Quezon once asked for and obtained from Philippine sugar interests fifty thousand pesos at a crack, but that to assist campaigns and junkets he always turned first to the Elizaldes.[12] Quezon demanded that Gunther rectify both statements; he enclosed affidavits from the Sugar Association to the contrary and directed Mike Elizalde, then Resident Commissioner in Washington, to clear things up. "It is not only a great injustice to me, but also to the Government and people of the Philippines, to give the impression to the public that . . . a man can be elected to the highest position in the gift of the people, who is so utterly devoid of ethical principles that he goes around as a matter of course and asks the rich people or great corporations to give him money whenever he needs it." To avoid trouble, Gunther excluded the statements from *Inside Asia,* but Quezon disliked the book anyway, and threatened to sue for a million dollars.[13] Although Quezon and the Sugar Association were highly embarrassed, Elizalde was not. Blindly, fondly, proudly, he followed and supported Quezon. As another observer wrote, "No one could ever imply that Quezon

10. Manila *Tribune,* 2 May 38, BIA Recto–P.
11. The Got story was told me by a friend of his; the Madrigal story by one who had it directly from a friend of the Quezons.
12. John Gunther, "Manuel Quezon," *Atlantic Monthly, 163* (1939), 66–67.
13. Jorge Vargas to Gunther, 3 Feb 39; Vargas to Elizalde, 3, 11 Feb; Elizalde to Quezon, undated; quotation from Quezon to Elizalde, undated draft with holograph revisions; Gunther to Vargas, 20 Feb (Q); Florence Horn, *Orphans of the Pacific* (New York, Reynal and Hitchcock, 1941), p. 79.

was subservient to the Elizalde millions. If anything, the Elizalde millions were subservient to the President of the Philippines." [14]

Talented politicians were even more subservient to Quezon than wealthy entrepreneurs. They provided work, ideas, and loyalty. If, in Quezon's mind, their ambitions began to exceed their talents, he would chasten them until they repented. He held Roxas at arm's length for several years after the anti-pro fight; sent Paredes off to Washington as resident commissioner; defeated Quirino in 1938 by directing money and influence to his opponent. He said privately[15] that if he were to make either Recto or Laurel his successor, the one would fight the other and retard Philippine development. Once he publicly[16] put his arms around both the forgiven Roxas and the rising Jose Yulo and said, "Here are two future presidents of the Philippines." Osmeña, who was present and ignored, could only try to keep a bland countenance. Chief among those whose devotion to Quezon matched their competence were Jose Abad Santos and Jose Yulo. Quezon made the latter, a young lawyer, speaker of the Assembly.

The Assembly showed its dedication to Quezon by presenting him with a large perfect black pearl. Later it amended the constitution to permit the president two four-year terms in office, instead of one term of six. High Commissioner Francis Sayre recommended a veto of the amendment as an "exceeding danger to democracy," opening the way to indefinite incumbency and dictatorship.[17] President Roosevelt, just then running for a twelve-year tenure, may have felt it inconsistent to limit Quezon to half of that, for he let the amendment go through.

Quezon meanwhile announced a theory of "partyless democracy," which evoked new fears of "dictatorship" in Sayre and made him wonder what forty years of American tutelage had availed.[18] The High Commissioner was too abstractly alarmed. Further economic development was necessary for the Philippines to have democracy in substance as well as form. In the meantime, there were definite

14. David Bernstein, *The Philippine Story* (New York, Farrar, Straus, 1947), p. 186.
15. Informant's name withheld.
16. Several informants agree on this story.
17. Sayre to Roosevelt, 25 July 40, quoted in Francis B. Sayre, *Glad Adventure* (New York, Macmillan, 1957), p. 198.
18. Quezon, "Theory of a Partyless Democracy" (Manila, Bureau of Printing, 1940); Sayre to Roosevelt, 1 Aug 40, and speech at University of the Philippines, 2 Apr, Sayre, ibid., pp. 196–97.

cultural limits upon dictatorship in the Philippines. Political power depended upon building, in a generous and reciprocal spirit, family pyramids; neither the bargaining process nor the popular ethos encouraged the kind of mystical and militaristic Hitlerian dictatorship that worried Sayre. Quezon could ascend to a new summit of political power, but he could not transcend his own culture. "Partyless democracy" was only his theoretical toy, for there would always be a process of appointment, preferment, and entertainment, affected by a complex structure of alliance and affinity, of rite and blood relationships.

After the United States lowered its flag, popular democracy would eventually reach the point where a Filipino commentator could praise his own times in comparison with Quezon's. The masses of the 1960s had begun to realize that the people were sovereign, whereas in the 1930s they had "thought sovereignty resided only in the 'best people,' that is, their masters. They [had] thought of their votes only as something to sell." [19]

The second major problem of the Commonwealth was economic development. Quezon had promised "bread," but in practice he offered far more rhetoric about "social justice" to the people than he did loaves or fishes. Quezon was actually far more concerned with improving trade relations with the United States than with basic internal development.

The Tydings-McDuffie Act provided for progressive 5 per cent export taxes on Philippine products beginning in 1941 and, upon independence in 1946, a "brutal leap" to 100 per cent tariff. During the ten-year transition period, there would be no reciprocal limits or duties on American products entering the Philippines—a "shocking inequality." [20] Meanwhile the Philippines would have to prepare for expenses far exceeding those of colonial dependence, expenses for a diplomatic-consular service, a national defense program, and the promotion of industry, among others.

Both Manila Americans and Filipinos began to predict economic disaster. One prognosis had the Philippines, without the American market, unable to produce an annual government income of more than thirteen million pesos. As a result the Filipino administration

19. Teodoro Locsin, Philippines *Free Press*, 2 Dec 61, p. 2.
20. Quotations from Fischer, *Un Cas de Décolonisation*, p. 217.

would probably curtail public services in reverse order of their present importance: school and health services first, public works next, and after that the governmental superstructure itself. No executive could cut back national defense, because he would have to rely on it to preserve his power. Soon the Philippines would have regressed "to the approximate position of a small Central American country." The constitution would "become quickly nothing more than an episode in the transfer from American to Japanese rule."

How avoid this fate? Businessmen of both nationalities, Americans more strongly and openly than Filipinos, felt that the United States must reverse either its political position, to permit a dominion relationship, or its economic position, to permit reciprocal preference in tariff.[21] In fact, however, Congress faced the Philippines with a hardening philosophy, more radically anti-imperialistic than that of the Filipinos themselves. Congress now desired independence *from* the Philippines, complete and absolute, by a certain date; it was incapable of imagining the process of decolonization as taking more time, or requiring more care, than that which it had already prescribed.

Quezon was able to make Roosevelt attempt to remedy "imperfections and inequalities," as promised, only by separating economic discussion entirely from political variables. Together, in 1937, they appointed a binational host of experts to study the economic question at length. This, the Joint Preparatory Committee on Philippine Affairs, conducted public hearings in Washington, San Francisco, and Manila, spent three months in the Philippines, and visited 34 of its 50 provinces. Their report[22] represented the most skilled and thorough investigation of the Philippine economy up to that time, and their recommendations, incorporated in draft legislation, aimed at softening and stretching the period of economic adjustment.

Upon the date of independence, instead of the "brutal jump" to complete dissociation, there would begin a 15-year period in which regressive duty-free quotas would be substituted for progressive export taxes on most products. For products whose adjustment had

21. "Analysis of the Proposed Constitution of the Philippine Commonwealth," WPD 3389–10, by Lt Robert Aura Smith, Military Intelligence Reserve. Smith was city editor of the Manila *Daily Bulletin* and New York *Times* correspondent in Manila while secretly attached to the office of the Asst CofS, G–2.

22. Joint Preparatory Committee on Philippine Affairs, *Report of May 20, 1938* (4 vols. Washington, U.S.G.P.O., released in Sept 1938).

already begun in the form of quotas, including sugar and cordage, the next step would be a progressive decline in tariff preferences: 25 per cent would be levied the first year, 1946, and 5 per cent each additional year for the next fifteen, up to 100 per cent in 1961. American products entering the Philippines were to be subject to a reciprocal tariff, likewise graduating toward 100 per cent, thus eliminating most of the "shocking inequality" of the earlier arrangement.

The key congressional figure handling the necessary legislation was Senator Millard Tydings, Chairman of the Committee on Territories and Insular Affairs. Despite President Roosevelt's attempts to "purge" him from the party in the elections of 1938, Tydings had won, and now conducted himself with injured pride and increased power. Upon request of a special Philippine mission, led by Osmeña, Tydings introduced a draft bill along the lines of the Preparatory Committee's report, but assumed no responsibility for it. The bill met heavy opposition in committee hearings and looked hopeless.

The Philippine mission and the State Department drastically cut their ambitions and substituted regressive quotas for progressive taxes on a few products in the period 1941–46.[23] This extremely modest proposal still had little chance without Tydings, "in all this laborious affair, an indecipherable enigma." "We don't know," Osmeña wrote Quezon, "whether he is inspired by his animus against President Roosevelt, or if it is against you and all of us." [24] Roosevelt finally softened Tydings by calling him up personally for a White House conference on the Philippine question. Tydings' attitude of hostile indifference changed to one of support.[25] With some amendments the second bill went through both houses quickly.[26]

An isolationist brand of anti-imperialism had required watering

23. *Report of the Special Mission to the United States, 1938–1939* (Manila, Bureau of Printing, 1939).
24. Osmeña to Quezon, 9 May 39 (Q).
25. "Outline of Matters to Be Taken up by Vice-President Osmeña with President Quezon by Long Distance Telephone Tonight, May 12, 1939, 8:00 P.M., Washington Time" (Q).
26. *Cong Rec* 76:1, 10591–601; 10897–900. The Resident Commissioner, Mike Elizalde, complained to Quezon that Osmeña had handled the negotiations with such secrecy and hauteur that he felt, before his friends, like "a man without any influence." He threatened to return to Manila at once, but Quezon cajoled him into staying on the job, which he did until 1944. Then Osmeña, Quezon's successor to the presidency, asked for his resignation and replaced him with Carlos Romulo. Elizalde to Quezon, 30 Oct 39 (Q); Romulo, *I Walked with Heroes*, p. 236.

the Joint Preparatory Committee's recommendations down to almost nothing and disposing of its research as so much academic rubbish. Quezon said so in politer words when he presented the results to the Assembly: "The law . . . does not solve adequately nor completely the larger and more important problem of economic readjustment"; under its terms basic Philippine industries could not hope to survive "our emergence as an independent state."[27] When war broke out in Europe, two weeks later, the Philippines lost the last glimmer of American attention for her economic problems.[28]

If American policy was insensitive to the emerging problem of economic development in the ex-colony,[29] some of the blame for stagnancy in the transition period must rest with Philippine enterprise and with the Commonwealth government.[30] Philippine businessmen tended to emulate the American Chamber of Commerce in seeking trade preferences rather than to change methods of production and marketing, or to diversify their endeavor. Clinging to the artificial sustenance of the American market they did little to face the challenge of economic development. Even the sugar industry, the best organized and most proficient technically, stood still once the quota race of 1929–34 had ended.

Government corporations in the rice and corn industries, in the coconut and fiber industries, did not help much, subject as they were to inefficient expenditures of energy and to corrupt diversion of funds. Quezon, who promised help everywhere, private and public, delivered very little. The coconut oil excise tax turned out to produce almost one-third of Philippine government revenue, and it enabled the Commonwealth to balance its budget at the expense of the American housewife. Quezon was loath to fight the tax and thereby

27. Message to the National Assembly, 15 Aug 39, quoted by Hester, p. 85.
28. Last efforts are summed up in: Hester, p. 83; Roxas (now Secretary of Finance) broadcast to the United States, 17 Nov 39, printed Cong Rec 76:2, 21236–37; praised by Quezon, Manila Daily Bulletin, 19 Nov 40, and by others, Philippine Magazine, 37 (1940), 403.
29. Fischer, pp. 217–23.
30. For the intentions of the Commonwealth, see "Economic Adjustment and Philippine Economy," speech by Osmeña, 23 June 40 (Manila, Bureau of Printing, 1941); for its negligible accomplishments, Charles O. Houston, "Rice in the Philippine Economy, 1934–1950," Journal of East Asian Studies, University of Manila, 3 (1953), 13–85; "The Philippine Coconut Industry, 1934–1950," ibid., pp. 153–81; "The Philippine Abaca Industry, 1934–1950," ibid., pp. 267–86.

aid the local coconut industry at the expense of his own administration.

Meanwhile he spoke frequently on behalf of "social justice"; he inaugurated a minimum wage program for government employees (one peso a day); in 1938 he released several Communist leaders from jail. All these moves served more to enhance his own popularity than to elevate the standard of living among the people. As long as possible, Quezon connected poverty with imperial policy. Growing discontent nevertheless showed that leaders of a fully sovereign Philippines would one day have to answer to their own people for "bread." In 1935, peasants in Central Luzon broke into riotous rebellion. The "Sakdalista" explosion was charismatic and disorganized (the leader, Benigno Ramos, was in exile in Japan); in the mind of Pedro Abad Santos, the Socialist leader, the whole affair was "silly stuff."

Following the Sakdal failure, however, Philippine radicalism moved into an era of more sophisticated protest.[31] A political "united front," led by Sumulong, tried and failed to slow down the Nacionalista steamroller, but in every frustration new men were trained and grew determined, like Abad Santos' disciple, Luis Taruc. With discarded and captured arms they would one day become the "Anti-Japanese Peoples' Army," and later a rebel movement against postwar Philippine government. Picking up Quezon's lost club, they would fight for bread instead of pleading for it.

The Commonwealth of the Philippines from 1935 to 1941 enjoyed one of the earliest genuine possibilities of economic decolonization in modern history, but in those six years one finds little economic development externally stimulated or natively sought.

Failure to meet economic problems was partly a result of military problems. For the military predicament itself, only Douglas MacArthur presumed to have an answer. Quezon, an old friend, had asked him, shortly after passage of the Tydings-McDuffie Act, "General, do you think that the Philippines, once independent, can defend itself?" "I don't *think* that the Philippines can defend themselves," MacArthur replied. "I *know* they can."

After MacArthur explained and expanded his ideas, Quezon asked

31. David R. Sturtevant, "Sakdalism and Philippine Radicalism," *Journal of Asian Studies*, 21 (1962), 199–213.

him if he would be willing to come to the Philippines and put them into practice. "We cannot just turn around and leave you alone," MacArthur said. "All these many years we have helped you in education, sanitation, road-building, and even in the practice of self-government. But we have done nothing in the way of preparing you to defend yourselves against a foreign foe." [32] After a record length of tenure as Chief of Staff, and with the permission of President Roosevelt, MacArthur became Quezon's military advisor. He arrived in Manila in time for the inauguration of the Commonwealth.

Meanwhile, the Joint Board of the Army and Navy was completing an unhappy reexamination of America's position in the Pacific and of War Plan ORANGE, which dealt with the possibility of war with Japan. The United States remained committed to the Open Door Policy in China, and was still basically responsible for the security of the Philippine Commonwealth. Yet the United States Army numbered only 120,000, of which but 10,000 were in the Philippines.[33] The Navy was in general both understrength and overaged. The Asiatic Fleet comprised about one-quarter of American destroyer and submarine strength, but had no battleships or carriers at all.[34]

As long as Philippine independence had been in debate, the two services had continued to agree, despite dissent from commanders in the area, that the islands were a positive military-naval asset.[35] Now that independence was a matter of schedule, their underlying differences of opinion came out. The Army, in the interests of a contracted defense perimeter, for the first time made no provision for reinforce-

32. From Quezon, *The Good Fight* (New York, D. Appleton-Century, 1946), pp. 153–55, and Quezon speech before Filipino ROTC trainees, 18 Jan 37 (FDR); an abbreviated version of the same interview appears in Gunther, *Inside Asia* (New York, Harper and Bros., 1939), p. 290. MacArthur implies that the talk took place late in 1935 (*Reminiscences*, p. 102), but the date was actually late March or early April 1934.

33. Annual Reports of Sec War, 1930–35; Louis Morton, "War Plan ORANGE: Evolution of a Strategy," *World Politics*, 11 (1959), 221–50, esp. 244. The ensuing discussion is based on Morton's article, as well as my own study of the same sources.

34. Samuel Eliot Morison, *History of United States Naval Operations in World War II, 3, The Rising Sun in the Pacific: 1931–April 1942* (Boston, Little, Brown, 1948), p. 28. Morison's figures are for the Navy in 1931, but they had not changed significantly by 1936.

35. CG Phil Dept (Maj Gen E. E. Booth) and Cmdr Corregidor Garrison (Brig Gen S. D. Embick) to CofS, 25 Apr 33, WPD 3251–15; CG Phil Dept (Maj Gen Frank Parker) and CinC Asiatic Fleet (Rear Adm F. B. Upham) to CofS and CNO, 1 Mar 34, JB 325, ser 533; JB studies, from 1930–34, passim.

ments. The existing garrison of 10,000, plus whatever Filipino army MacArthur might raise, must carry the defense against Japan; they could be expected to hold out for six months. The Navy, in the interests of their theory of offensive war, was willing to augment military and naval forces during the commonwealth period. But once hostilities began, the Navy estimated its return with reinforcements through the Japanese mandates as taking two to three years.[36] In the logical gap between "six months" and "two years" was the unexpressed assumption that Japan could conquer the Philippines; that under existing conditions the islands could only be defended for a sharply limited time.

General MacArthur himself, as Chief of Staff, had gone on record as thinking American troop reinforcement unlikely in the foreseeable future and as standing against the United States retaining bases in the Philippines after independence.[37] How then could he answer Quezon so optimistically? He answered, it appears, out of great contempt for War Plan ORANGE and great confidence in himself. He had told President Hoover that "if mobilization became necessary during my tenure of office my first step would be to send two divisions from the Atlantic Coast to defend the Philippines . . . every inch . . . and . . . successfully." ORANGE was useless; the man in command was all important. "A big man" would pay scant attention "to the stereotyped plans that may be filed in the dusty pigeon holes of the War Department." [38] MacArthur never thought of himself as a little man. Although orthodox military opinion despaired of the United States defending the Philippines, MacArthur believed it could. To Quezon he proposed an even more staggering heresy: that the Filipinos themselves could do it.

A former area commander had said that defense of the islands by Filipinos alone was "not within the wildest possibility." [39] In return, MacArthur pointed out the natural advantages of the Philippines:

36. Separate reports, Army members JPC to JB, and Navy members JPC to JB, 5 Mar 36; JB 325, ser 573.

37. CofS memo to Gen Kilbourne, Asst CofS, WPD, 26 Feb 34, WPD 3389–6; CofS to CG Phil Dept, 6 July 34, WPD 3251–17.

38. MacArthur to unidentified Army officer, sometime in 1940, quoted in Frazier Hunt, *The Untold Story of Douglas MacArthur* (New York, Devin-Adair, 1954), p. 138.

39. Maj Gen Johnson Hagood to President Hoover, after tour as CG Phil Dept; quoted in Hayden, pp. 742–43.

it was geographically isolated, mountainous, and densely forested. On Luzon, the major target, the only two coastal regions that would permit a large enemy force to land were both broken by strong defensive positions, "which, if properly manned and prepared would present to any attacking force a practically impossible problem of penetration." Only a prolonged naval bombardment could make invasion possible, and a combination of air and marine defenses could deny Philippine waters to an enemy navy. Even should a landing be successful, narrow mountain passes, as well-defended secondary positions, would be hardly penetrable inland.

To make the most of limited native resources, a Philippine army should consist of small mobile units, free of heavy impediments and trained in simplicity of supply, conservation of ammunition, and maximum use of local means for transport and subsistence. "While giving ground stubbornly and skillfully when forced to do so," they could "by quick local concentration strike back in speedy counterstrokes and with overwhelming fire at every opportunity presented." MacArthur envisioned these land elements as being able to fight "a war of relentless attrition, of resistance from the water's edge to the furthermost retreat left available." Hit-and-run bombers, hit-and-run torpedo boats, and a semi-guerrilla army: these were MacArthur's answer to the problem which many of his contemporaries said was unanswerable.[40]

Specifically, MacArthur asked Quezon for an air force of 250 light bombers and a naval squadron of 50 to 100 torpedo boats. The standing army should number 19,000—very small compared to Thailand's 100,000. The citizen reserve should number 400,000—not too large compared to the Swiss program of universal training. MacArthur proposed to accomplish the entire preparation in the ten years remaining before independence, at a total cost of eighty million dollars, or eight million per year. Five million would provide the offshore patrol, ten million the air component, thirty million the regular force, and thirty-five million the reserves. The reserves would be trained at a rate of forty thousand men a year, each man serving as a civil duty and receiving only five centavos a day as remuneration. From money

40. Discussion based on MacArthur, *Report on National Defense in the Philippines* (Manila, Bureau of Printing, 1936), and in some particulars on Vicente Albano Pacis, *National Defense, A Basic Philippine Problem* (Manila, Philippine Education Company, 1937); quotations from MacArthur.

allotted to the reserves a large amount would thus be left over for military supply and equipment.[41] Given what he asked for and time to complete his program, MacArthur said that "it would take a half million men, ten billion dollars, tremendous casualties and three years time successfully to invade the Philippines."[42]

Before becoming fired with MacArthur's conviction, Quezon had told a Shanghai audience that the Philippines would have to "rely on world good will" until it built a force adequate to prevent invasion, which would take at least fifty years.[43] But during his two tours of duty in the Philippines in the 1920s, Douglas MacArthur had built a firm friendship with Quezon and impressed him as a great military authority. He said ten years, and Quezon believed.

The two men might easily have been antagonists: Quezon, so quick and hot to cut down rivals; MacArthur, aloof, with an almost chilling sense of his own destiny. But perhaps MacArthur's rhetoric and eloquence appealed to Quezon and kindled his own richness of expression, in the same manner that Roy Howard's flashy clothes sent Quezon on sprees of buying shirts. Perhaps Quezon's warmth, his impetuous tenderness, opened up the best in MacArthur, and called out that charming energy so much hidden in solitude, in the study of history, and the service of his country. Now, in his fourth Philippine tour, MacArthur's personal life took on a new shape. His devoted mother died; he took an adoring wife; he fathered his only son. In Quezon he had a friend and more. To Frank Murphy, who was jealous of the intimacy of the two, Aurora Quezon once answered: "But, Frank, you don't seem to understand: Douglas is our brother." More than that: MacArthur made the Quezons godparents of his boy. The General and the President were compadres.[44]

Mutual interest completed a relationship based on fondness and respect. Quezon had solved MacArthur's problem of what to do

41. Ibid. In his *Reminiscences*, p. 104, MacArthur adds: "In the event of crisis, the hope and expectation was that modern weapons would be supplied by the United States."
42. New York *Times*, 29 May 36 (H); MacArthur quoted again to essentially the same effect, *Philippine Magazine, 36* (July 1939), 286–87. Compare Elihu Root's estimate, shortly before he died in 1937, that "Japan could take the Philippines in a week and that it would take five years and twenty-five billion dollars to beat them," quoted by Stanley Washburn to Sec Nav, 28 Nov 41, WPD 4544–19.
43. *Philippine Magazine, 31* (June 1934), 220.
44. Hunt, *Untold Story*, p. 183; MacArthur, *Reminiscences*, p. 140.

after retiring as Chief of Staff at fifty-five. The General now commanded 22 per cent of the Philippine national budget annually, whereas, during his tenure as Chief of Staff, the military expenditures of the War Department had been less than 5 per cent of overall government expenditures. Even if the absolute amount of the Philippine budget was small, the people admired MacArthur and accepted on faith his philosophy of preparedness. Quezon was convinced of MacArthur's dedication to the interests of his "second country"; and that dedication both strengthened his own resolve and expanded his ego as chief executive. Realizing that his own mercurial temper could not defend the country by itself, Quezon was grateful for MacArthur's steel. In June 1936, he appointed him Field Marshal, making MacArthur the only American ever to hold that rank anywhere in the world.

The two men shared the labor of replying to critics of their plan. MacArthur as Chief of Staff had grown used to American resistance: pacifistic college students had picketed him, and he had had several arguments with President Roosevelt over proposed military cutbacks, one of them so strenuous that the general had vomited afterward on the White House lawn.[45]

Now Governor General Frank Murphy, fearing "militarization" of the Philippines, supported the Constabulary's program of making that body the nucleus of the Philippine army until the Scouts were later released from U.S. Army service.[46] Even the Army War Plans Division preferred the South American system of building upon the Constabulary, which they thought less likely to "defy . . . the central government." Chief of Staff Malin Craig and his planners also pointed out that, unlike Switzerland, the Philippines was not a compact land unit; the Japanese Navy could both control its interstitial waters and cut off foreign sources of supply.[47]

Admiral William H. Standley, Chief of Naval Operations, doubted the efficacy of torpedo boat and light bomber forces in protecting Philippine waters, and Major General Basilio Valdez, later Chief of

45. Frederic S. Marquardt, *Before Bataan and After* (New York, Bobbs-Merrill, 1943), p. 258; Hunt, pp. 135–36, 152. MacArthur writes of his struggles as Chief of Staff for preparedness in *Reminiscences*, pp. 90–92, 97–102.
46. Murphy to Sec War, 22 Dec 34, WPD 3251; Gen Vicente Lim to Quezon, 14 Dec (Q).
47. Brig Gen Stanley Embick, "Military System of the Philippine State," Gen Craig and nine others concurring, 3 Jan 35, WPD 3389.

Staff of the Philippine Army, thought it beyond Philippine means to repulse enemy warcraft.[48] MacArthur's Swiss-model plan went through nonetheless, and he obtained used and substandard equipment from the American Army to supply his own.[49] Murphy, as High Commissioner, tried behind the scenes to have MacArthur relieved, but MacArthur retired from the U.S. Army so as not to be subject to transfer from the Philippines.[50]

As MacArthur's prestige helped muffle professional doubts, Quezon's enthusiasm helped counter civilian antagonism. One dubious American was converted by close view of the program; he wrote favorably of Quezon and MacArthur, and unfavorably of the strange combination of imperialists and pacifists who opposed the building of a native Philippine defensive army. American liberal journals, however, continued to charge the program with militarizing and debasing Philippine education, draining the Philippine economy, blurring traditional distinctions between civil and military authority, and needlessly provoking Japan. Quezon replied face to face at a Foreign Policy Association luncheon in New York, in the summer of 1937. In a highly emotional exchange, Oswald Garrison Villard, editor of the *Nation*, asked Quezon if it were not better to teach Filipino youth to live rather than to kill. "If I believed that the Philippines could not defend itself," Quezon said, "I would commit suicide this afternoon." [51]

Back in the Philippines, Quezon had the Madrigal-Romulo chain of newspapers wage an editorial campaign for the defense plan, chiding the readers for defeatist attitudes of mind bred by a history of subjugation. Aguinaldo and Sumulong nevertheless made defense expenditures their major dartboard, and proposed that the Philippines rely on neutralization for its safety. Quezon finally grew so irritated with Aguinaldo that he had his government pension taken

---

48. Standley notes on MacArthur *Defense Report,* A 16–1/EG52 (360523), Nat Arch, Navy Sec; Valdez quoted by Hayden, pp. 949–50.

49. MacArthur-Craig correspondence, 9 July 36 et seq., AGO 093.5, Sec 1; in which objections of Dept of State were overcome, and objections within the Army (Embick to CofS, 7 Jan 36, WPD 3389–18) were concealed.

50. Courtney Whitney, *MacArthur's Rendezvous with History* (New York, Knopf, 1956), p. 5; Hunt, p. 188.

51. Change of mind: Fred Howe to Eleanor Roosevelt, quoted by Hunt, p. 188–89; MacArthur, *Reminiscences* (pp. 105–06), implies that this letter was an official report to the White House. Quezon's exchange with Villard was recalled by Carlos Romulo, Philippines *Herald,* 22 Nov 41.

away, and he used the opportunities Sumulong provided to "refresh some of my sarcasms." [52] Those who believe in neutralization live in a fool's paradise, Quezon said, ignorant of the lessons of contemporary history.[53]

Quezon dreamed that his army would some day resemble China's, which he inspected at Canton. Filipino soldiers avoided looking at him, but in China, "my goodness, every soldier looked at you with stern eyes." At Whampoa Military Academy: "Every time I mentioned the name Chiang Kai-shek they automatically stood at attention." [54]

The discipline of China's elite troops, however, was too much to expect in the Philippines, which had almost no military tradition. Quezon and his military advisors endured a variety of harassments, including difficulty in attracting enough regular army personnel in the ranks; reservists declining active duty; trainee strikes and demonstrations against officers; occasional terrorism by detachments in provincial areas; individuals running amok in uniform; and botched maneuvers. Political difficulties included alleged favoritism in award of Army contracts and continued rivalry between the Scouts and the Constabulary.[55]

His military establishment was more a trial than a tribute to Quezon, but he gladly suffered it so long as it promised security. The Chinese example reassured him, and he speculated in December 1936 that "if China goes as she is going now . . . Japan will be much more than satisfied to hold Manchuria." [56] In July 1937, Japan instead undertook to absorb all of North China. The incident at Marco Polo bridge started full-scale warfare which would last more than eight years. China resisted, but China retreated. Chiang's men fought but they could not win. Into Quezon's mind may then have crept the first doubts about MacArthur's plan.

During the commonwealth era, Manuel Quezon began to experience the rigors and anxieties of the presidency he had long coveted. Americans underestimated the economic dependence into which

52. Re Aguinaldo: Manila *Bulletin,* 9 Dec 35, 6 Feb, 22 Oct 39 (H); re Sumulong: Transcript of Presidential Press Conference, 22 Jan 37 (Q).
53. Quezon speech to ROTC units, University of the Philippines, 18 Jan 37 (FDR).
54. Transcript of President's press conference, 18 Dec 36 (Q).
55. Manila *Bulletin,* Manila *Tribune,* 1937–39, passim (H).
56. Press conference, 18 Dec 36 (Q).

they had led the islands, and Filipinos would not face the inexorability of the political independence for which they had bargained. Both refused to face the true extent of their common military peril. Forces were gathering that would make a mockery of Quezon's policy—"the club in one hand and the bread in the other"—forces that would ultimately leave Quezon without anything in either hand.

13

The Philippines and Japan's Southward Advance

PROBABLY NO OTHER EVENT of the early 1930s pointed up the shifting balance of power in East Asia as much as the Philippine independence acts of 1933–34. The retreat of American imperial power and the advance of American liberal thought touched off reactions everywhere. Japan was pleased to see the withdrawal of a force which might potentially deter her own advance; meanwhile, her own colonies were under such tight control that the example of autonomy could not inflame them.

The Western powers, however, were apprehensive of serious difficulties in dealing both with Japanese imperialism and the nationalism of their own colonies. The Commander-in-Chief of the British Asiatic Fleet declared the "probability" of the British "taking over the Philippines to prevent their falling into the hands of the Japanese." The Australians reacted to each step of American withdrawal with "increasing bitterness." The Dutch, with most to lose in national income. should they lose their colony, generally saw freeing the Filipinos as "folly . . . because they are not fit for it." [1]

The approach of commonwealth status for the Philippines excited Southeast Asian nationalists. The leader of the Indonesian National-

1. Minister to China ((Johnson) to Sec State, 12 June 33; *For Rel 1933, 3,* 360–62; Consul Gen Sydney (Moffat) to Sec State, 11 Feb 36; *For Rel 1936, 4,* 51; Dutch views appear in SD 811B.01/179, 26 Jan 33, and Minister to the Netherlands (Emmet) to the President, 24 Mar 34 (FDR).

ist party, M. H. Thamrin, observed in a Volksraad debate that the Philippines, "which will soon be independent, has been hardly forty years under American sovereignty; we . . . have been stumbling more than three hundred years under Dutch rule and still our fore-heads bear the impress of immaturity." The Dutch Government Delegate for General Affairs replied: "Does Mr. Thamrin not hear in China the cutting of the scissors that divide it into spheres of influ-ence? . . . And . . . is Mr. Thamrin deaf to the voices which are raised everywhere in the Philippines respecting the independence which has fallen as an unripe fruit in the lap of the population and of which they would gladly be rid?" [2]

Indonesian nationalists looked up to Quezon nevertheless and, when he visited Soerabaja in September 1934, they took him to a secluded, darkened, and guarded house to ask, "How should we go about getting independence?" "Open all these windows and shutters, then take away your guards," said Quezon. "Hold your meetings in the open and in front of the Dutch themselves . . . make a hell of a lot of noise! And if you do that long enough, you'll eventually get what you want." [3]

But Dutch officials continued to regard Quezon as "more subver-sive . . . than Marx, Lenin, Trotsky, and Stalin rolled into one." They seldom even allowed news of the Philippine Commonwealth to be published.[4] When Quezon projected a return trip in 1939, with a party of fifty-five, the Department of State talked him out of it.[5] War had broken out in Europe and the State Department did not wish to jeopardize relations with Holland by proclaiming anticoloni-alism in Southeast Asia.

The reaction of the Chinese nationalists to the Commonwealth was mixed: although anti-imperialist in principle, they had in prac-tice relied upon Occidental power, especially American, for protec-tion against the Japanese. Chiang Kai-shek said privately, "While I

2. Quoted in G. G. Van der Kop, "Netherlands India and Philippine Independence," *Philippine Magazine,* 32 (1935), 486 ff.
3. Carlos Quirino, *Quezon, Man of Destiny* (Manila, McCullough, 1935), pp. 35–36; confirmed by R. S. Wirjoprano, Sec of the Indonesian Nationalist Party, *Philippine Magazine,* 32 (1935), 640.
4. Wilbur Burton, "Indonesia and the Philippines," *Philippine Magazine,* 37 (1940), 306 ff.
5. Sec State to Hi Comm (Sayre), 15 Nov 39; Hi Comm to Sec State, 15, 17 Nov, SD 811B.001 Q/137–39.

am completely in sympathy with the Filipinos' understandable desire for complete independence, I am not at all certain but what that independence might not, at this time, be obtained at too heavy a cost."[6]

Certainly the overseas Chinese in the Philippines agreed. Before 1898 they had suffered frequent repression at the hands of Spain, but since then they had prospered under the United States. Americans had nothing to fear from the Chinese, tended to admire their business acumen and to protect them from the passage of discriminatory laws. The Chinese had increased in population and in wealth and now they feared that, when their protectors left, Filipino jealousy would erupt in a fresh and acute discrimination.[7] The President of the Chinese General Chamber of Commerce, Alfonso Sy Cip, observed that conquerors came and went, but the Chinese remained in the Philippines, had a stake in the country, and were valuable partners in its growth.[8] Other Chinese, against growing Filipino discrimination and Japanese competition, looked for assistance from the Kuomintang, of the kind which Japan gave overseas enterprise. Still others, wealthy merchants, less hopeful, began to liquidate and to transfer their holdings to Shanghai.[9]

Another minority, the Spanish community in the Philippines, was also disturbed. They mistrusted the Philippine government and expected it to turn against them. Distressed at the United States' giving up sovereignty, some Spaniards, stirred by Franco's victory, even talked in the late 1930s about reannexation to Spain should the Axis win the European war.

During the civil war the members of Manila's elite Casino Español had torn down the Republican flag and replaced it with Franco's; American Army intelligence estimated that four-fifths of Philippine Spaniards were pro-Franco. Except for the Basque Capuchins, Spanish religious orders in the islands were for the Nationalists and celebrated Te Deums for the fall of cities to the cause. A Nationalist

6. *Central Daily News* (semi-official journal of the Kuomintang), 19 Jan 33, BIA; Chiang quoted, Roy Howard to Quezon, 13 June 33 (Q).
7. Ch'ên Lieh-fu, *Fei-lü-pin yu Chung Fei Kuan hsi* (*On Philippine-Chinese Relations*) (Hong Kong, 1955), Ch 7, pt 4.
8. Speech, copy in Sterling Memorial Library, Yale University, discussed by James Lilley, Dept of State, with the author, 31 July 61.
9. New York *Times*, 24 June 34; Philippines *Herald*, 10 Jan 35, BIA w-370-a-11.

replaced a Loyalist as General Manager of Tabacalera, the largest single employer of Spanish labor. Most of the leading Loyalists in the Philippines were not actually Spanish but Philippine citizens: Aguinaldo, Aglipay, and Pedro Abad Santos.

The leader of the Falange movement was the entrepreneur Andres Soriano. Acting as an agent for Franco without notifying the Department of State, Soriano drew a warning from Sumner Welles, conveyed by Manuel Roxas, a friend and business associate, that he was violating the Espionage Act. When the United States recognized Franco's government, Soriano acted freely and easily. His first collection of funds for Franco obtained about two million pesos, of which his personal contribution, half a million, was the largest. During Soriano's periodic trips to Spain, control of the movement lay in the hands of his uncle, Enrique Zobel, with whom it foundered. Soriano himself, a man of few words, of great balance and authority, always managed to unify it upon his return.[10]

The Elizalde family remained largely neutral because of their Philippine citizenship, their partly Basque origins, their lack of interest, and their jealousy of Soriano. Even so, the mother led a women's group for Franco; the youngest brother, Frederico, fought in Spain, and so did a brother-in-law, Ignacio Jimenez, who organized a Falange unit before he left.

At its most intense, the Falange movement raised questions about the democratic content of the Spanish heritage in the Philippines. The Commonwealth government, however, had nothing to do with the movement. The Dominican fathers of the University of Santo Tomas earned a scathing rebuke from Quezon for playing Franco's national anthem at a dinner in the President's honor.[11]

Others interested in the informal foreign relations of the Commonwealth suggested orientation toward the Latin American republics, or toward "Malaysia Irridenta." Cultural affinities, near or far, were less likely, however, to affect the posture of a small country than the magnetic field of power in which it found itself. Being practical, Quezon had to address himself to safeguarding Philippine interests in the growing tension between Japan and the United States.

10. J. Weldon Jones to Sec State, 10 Aug 39; Report, Military Intelligence Division, Phil Dept, "The Spanish Community in the Philippines," 11 Oct 39; "Notes" and other materials, Soriano file (HC).
11. Marquardt, *Before Bataan*, pp. 224–25.

Roy Howard, on trips through East Asia in 1925 and 1929, had concluded that talk of a Japanese-American war was "mere blather." He returned in 1933, and changed his mind. In Japan, he wrote Quezon, "Liberalism and .... a respect for treaty obligations have not been entirely snuffed out, but . . . are unquestionably in a state of nearly complete eclipse. . . . Reason and hard sense have abdicated in favor of emotionalism tinged with fatalism. . . . [Everyone is] prepared to prove that Japan has been tricked out of her birthright by white race diplomacy, and that the time has come for Japan to strike in an effort to secure the favored place in the sun." [12]

For Howard's observations there was to be a crescendo of supporting evidence. What he loosely called "a Nipponese version of Nietzscheian philosophy" exploded between 1930 and 1936 in a series of assassinations of moderate leaders by ultra-nationalist fanatics. The slogans *kodo* and *hakko-ichiu* gained general currency, expressing a righteous determination to bring a Japanese mode of order into the world, inspired by obligations to an Emperor with divine attributes. Diplomatic frustration gave rise to a systematic criticism of the "static justice" of the West, which emphasized treaty rights and obligations; in its place Japan sought a "dynamic justice," which attached "the greatest importance to equitable distribution of economic forces." [13]

All of these, and other indications, raised the question: in what manner would the Japanese fill the vacuum of power and influence being left by the retraction of the United States? One American alarmist, chief spokesman for the Philippine Sugar Association, likened the American withdrawal to that of Rome from England in 68 A.D., which incurred danger for the English from the "painted savages of the north." With more restrained pessimism, Dr. Hendryk Colijn, the Dutch Prime Minister, said, "Japan is like the Roman Catholic Church—patient and resolute, willing to wait and gain its objective without fighting, feeling pretty sure that in the long run most of what it is after will fall into its lap." [14]

12. Howard to Quezon, 12 June 33 (Q).
13. Quotations from Rōyama Masamichi, *Foreign Policy of Japan, 1914–1939* (Tokyo, Japanese Council, Institute of Pacific Relations, 1941), p. 172.
14. George Fairchild to Sen Millard Tydings, 24 Sept 35 (referring to Conan Doyle's *The Last Galley*), Nat Arch, Leg Sec, Sen 73A–F25, 142; Minister to the Netherlands (Emmet) to Pres, 17 Aug 34 (FDR).

By slow absorption or by forceful strike?—Westerners speculated on the manner of the eventual takeover. Yet the Japanese themselves were unsure of their strategy and hence of their tactics. The ministries of the army, the navy, and foreign affairs were at odds with each other and even split within themselves upon the scope, direction, character, and timing of Japanese expansion. After the first independence act, a Foreign Office spokesman had declared Japan's willingness to sign a treaty neutralizing the Philippines, but a high-ranking naval officer contradicted him on the same point, because of interim, and possibly long term, American retention of naval bases.[15]

Within a month of the second independence act, the Gaimusho's Chief of Information and Intelligence, Amau Eiji, uttered a now-famous declaration of Japan's mission to lead East Asia and of opposition to Western interference. Amau's superiors left the world in doubt as to the official status of the statement, but the American State Department took it as an "indicator" of Japan's China policy, and the Philippine press took it as a harbinger of Japan's future Philippine policy.[16]

By the fall of 1935, field army cliques were controlling Japanese foreign policy more than the Gaimusho, and the navy was trying to catch up in influence. In renewed discussion of naval tonnage ratios, Japanese delegates refused a smaller tonnage than the United States, even should the latter give up its bases in the Philippines. When their efforts "to eliminate the invidious ranking of nations" failed, the Japanese in January 1936 withdrew from the London Naval Conference. The move was popular at home, relieved the navy of a handicap in its disputes with the army over strategic emphasis, and enabled it to expand without limit. Naval strategists began to draft plans for a force strong enough to dominate the Western Pacific.[17] Ultra-nationalist assassins destroyed the existing government in late February, and military-naval personnel clearly dominated the new Hirota government, formed in March.

15. Articles, Tokyo *Yomiuri*, 18 Jan 33, Osaka *Mainichi*, 19 Jan; editorials, Tokyo *Asahi*, 17 Jan, *Jiji*, 19 Jan, *Yomiuri*, 19 Jan, *Hōchi Shimbun*, 20 Jan, enclosed by Amb Grew to Sec State, 26 Jan, SD 811B.01/181.
16. *For Rel, Japan 1931–1941*, 1, 223–39, esp. 224–25 (first unofficial statement, 17 Apr 34), and p. 231 (memo by Hornbeck, 26 Apr 34); BIA 6144–194, 23 Feb 35.
17. *Philippine Magazine*, 31 (1934), 460; *For Rel, Japan 1931–1941*, 1, 249–309; Robert J. C. Butow, *Tojo and the Coming of War* (Princeton, Princeton University Press, 1961), pp. 77–78.

The Japanese Consul General in Manila, Uchiyama Kiyoshi, had meanwhile been asking the Tokyo office for a clarification of policy toward the Philippines. Concerning the "so-called plan to expand toward the south: How determined are we? Has the military already adopted a concrete plan?" Unless policy were clarified, Uchiyama expected behind-the-scenes activity by the military, or a Japanese uprising in Davao. The government of the Commonwealth would adopt a "thoroughly negative and ambiguous" foreign policy "of fighting poison with poison," trying to prevent Japanese encroachment by using America, while trying to absorb such economic establishments of both countries as would be profitable to Filipinos. "In other words, the Japan policy of the Philippine government for the next several years will be like the Japan policy of the Mukden government prior to the Manchurian Incident."

Uchiyama feared that the Japanese might lose both present rights and future opportunities, and "the so-called program to expand to the south will become just an empty dream." He therefore submitted two alternatives, Plans A and B, to cover the possibilities of an obstructionistic Philippine government or a partially cooperative one. In the first case, Japan should meet the situation "decisively, by adopting principles and measures the Japanese government has adopted in North China." They should ask the Filipinos to "reconsider" anti-Japanese policies, at the risk of "unpleasant consequences," while recognizing "the danger of causing a totally unexpected conflict between Japan and America if one false step is taken."

Uchiyama's Plan B assumed the possibility of altering popular Japanophobia and establishing a pro-Japanese government. The major means would be to step up, over a period of time, techniques already in some measure employed: "We can . . . publish a pro-Japanese newspaper, manipulate the representatives, join hands with the opposite faction, stir up anti-American sentiment, arouse public opinion in Japan, and . . . adopt other behind-the-scene measures. We should educate the people of this country . . . that we have no territorial ambitions but only a desire to expand economically." [18]

Although Uchiyama asked his superiors for "a complete understanding with the army and naval authorities," the ministries in

18. Uchiyama, through Chief of the American Bureau, Horiuchi, to Foreign Minister Hirota, 8 Oct 35, carried by Uchiyama's administrative officer, Wajima, in person to Tokyo, Gaimushō S460, pp. 657–73.

question remained at odds for ten months thereafter. After the naval-ists left London, they began a propaganda campaign in the Japanese press, accentuating interservice rivalry. Against the army's "conti-nental school," which stood for advance in China, contended the navy's "blue water school," which argued for emphasis on the insular areas to the south.[19]

The Hirota government finally effected a *modus vivendi* among its struggling ministries in the summer of 1936. From June 30 through August 15, the premier and the ministers of army, navy, foreign affairs, and finance developed a new and coordinated national policy of making Japan a "stabilizing power" in East Asia, including the "South Seas." The navy had won its desired assignment of obtaining command of the West Pacific. Expanding Japanese influence was to affect the Southeast Asian colonies of Western powers, but because of the residual American power in the Philippines, Japan would be prepared to guarantee its neutrality.[20]

Tokyo at last answered Uchiyama's question: southward advance was to be no "empty dream" but a determined peaceful penetration backed by augmented military force. Progress in the Philippines should follow the lines of Uchiyama's Plan B: infiltration, persuasion, subsidization.[21]

Even before the Hirota government's attempt to coordinate policy, Japanese activity in the Philippines had increased from natural causes. The approach of commonwealth status and the waning of the depression increased both political and economic opportunities. Resident Commissioner Pedro Guevara perhaps exaggerated in say-ing that the Japanese had an annual budget of half a million pesos for propaganda in the Philippines; in any case, Governor General Frank Murphy noticed an alarming subsidization of key men.[22]

The Gaimusho meanwhile complained against the tariff policies of the Occidental powers in general, which controlled newspapers and parliaments, "adversely affecting the interests of the natives, the majority of whom desire to purchase cheap goods." Consul General

19. Grew to Sec State, 30 Apr 36; *For Rel, 1936, 4,* 129–34.
20. Butow, pp. 82–84.
21. Because captured Gaimushō files on the Philippines contain very few items originating in Tokyo, there is no direct reply included. However, I take Uchiyama to Arita, 13 July 36 (S461, pp. 1079–80), as indirect evidence that something ap-proximating Uchiyama's Plan B had been agreed upon.
22. Stimson diary, 2 Feb, 5 Mar 35 (HLS).

Kimura Atsushi, in a controversial speech, applied this doctrine to the Philippines, declaiming the advantages of expanded low tariff trade with Japan, and proposing separation of the peso from the dollar, making it "the equivalent of the yen."[23] In 1934 the Japanese for the first time displaced the United States as chief seller of cotton piece goods in the Philippines, and President Roosevelt noted this "avalanche of cotton goods into the Philippines." To prevent the Philippines raising tariffs against Japan, the State Department worked out a compromise. The two exporting nations finally agreed on a rough fifty-fifty split of the Philippine market.[24]

The Japanese also desired an expanding role in the internal economic development of the Philippines. The manager of the Yokohama Specie Bank, who was also head of the Japanese Chamber of Commerce, confidently predicted a flight of American capital, leaving the Orient to the Orientals. He told the Filipinos, "We are like one people";[25] but the Filipinos did not feel brotherly. When the Japanese tried to influence the constitutional convention through friendly delegates, especially Laurel, Lorenzo, and Castillejo, a strong "Filipino first" movement opposed them, and a delegate from Davao exposed the collusive practices of the Japanese in his province.[26]

The draft constitution, as a result, contained restrictions on rights of foreign nationals to develop and exploit the natural resources of the islands. The Japanese ambassador in Washington protested and asked that these provisions be deleted, but in vain.[27] Faced with a law requiring 61 per cent Filipino ownership in extractive and agricultural corporations, the Japanese frequently thereafter resorted to evasion of the law, paying Filipinos to serve as dummy owners of concerns which were actually Japanese.

The Philippine government wished not only to limit the influx of Japanese goods and money, but also Japanese citizens. Because the

23. *Philippine Magazine, 31* (Sept 1934), 385–88; ibid. (Oct 1934), 411.
24. *Philippine Magazine, 31* (Nov, Dec 1934), 482, 550; Stimson diary, 31 Oct 34 (HLS); Roosevelt to Hull, 19 Nov 34 (FDR); *For Rel, 1935, 3*, 952–1048, passim; ibid., *1936, 4,* 806–935, passim; ibid., *1937, 4,* 793–800, 803; ibid., *1938, 4,* 619–26; ibid., *1939, 4,* 462–70; ibid., *1940, 4,* 992–95.
25. *Philippine Magazine, 31* (May 1934), 179.
26. Acting Consul Kaneko to For Min Hirota, 26 July 34, Gaimushō, S459, pp. 455–62.
27. *For Rel, 1935, 3,* 1080–87, including Japanese ambassador to Sec State, 4 Mar 35, pp. 1081–82.

exclusion act of 1924 had poisoned Japanese-American relations, American officials had dissuaded the Filipinos from repeating the insult. By 1939, however, Japanese immigrants exceeded Chinese for the first time in Philippine history. This fact, coupled with increased Japanese political activity, led the Philippine Assembly in 1940 to limit immigrants from Oriental countries. Despite Japanese machinations, the Assembly, by a vote of 28 to 17, set the quota at five hundred, considerably beneath the actual rate of recent years.[28] Again the Japanese both protested and evaded the law, abetted by self-interested Filipinos. Despite the exposure of scandals and a purge of the Immigration Bureau, Japanese and Chinese could still buy their way into the country at three thousand pesos per head.

Limiting laws and movements of various kinds did not seriously hamper the growth of Japanese interests. Chinese boycotts in the early 1930s had only forced Japanese commerce to strengthen its organization, and the great *zaibatsu* in Japan tightened their connections to many local enterprises. Since 1920, the Yokohama Specie Bank had had a branch in Manila, and in 1938 the government-controlled Bank of Taiwan, which did business all over the South Seas, also expanded to the Philippines. The B.B.B. Brewery put up a big plant outside Manila in 1937; *Domei* established a Manila news office in 1939, and the Japanese government railways soon after.

In fields where they had been longer established, Japanese interests continued to grow: they owned a significant share of the lumber business and had nearly squeezed the Filipinos out of deep-sea fishing. Japanese owned shares of several mining corporations, under the 39 per cent permitted by law, but they obtained options on other iron, manganese, and copper through conditional loans to Filipinos by a Japanese credit corporation. Japanese controlled 70 per cent of hemp production in the province of Davao and were expanding into copra.[29]

28. Manila *Bulletin*, 19 Sept 39, 13 Apr 40 (H); Hayden, 724–26; disagreements aired by Sayre and For Min Arita, *For Rel, 1940, 4*, 322, 330.
29. Hayden, 713–14; Bryce Oliver, "Japan Takes Over the Philippines," *American Mercury, 48* (1939), 257–58; "Far East: Philippine Islands: Japanese Economic Penetration of the Philippines," mimeographed paper [Department of Commerce?], 23 Feb 35, BIA 6144–194; A. V. H. Hartendorp, *History of Industry and Trade of the Philippines* (Manila, American Chamber of Commerce of the Philippines, Inc., 1958), p. 60; Catherine Porter, *Crisis in the Philippines* (New York, Knopf, 1942), pp. 101–02.

The most systematic expansion of foreign business was in Davao, and the most alarming to Filipinos because of the political infrastructure that accompanied it. Japanese citizens owned nearly 60,000 hectares, or about two-thirds of the total cultivated area in the province. The 18,000 Japanese there were less than a tenth of the resident Filipino population in 1939, but they paid half of the local and insular taxes collected in the province. They employed 12–14,000 Filipino laborers and indirectly contributed to the livelihood of many more. They had built more than three-quarters of the roads in the province. Their engineers, economists, and agriculturists were constantly improving methods of production and making them freely available to others. They exported for themselves, using no middlemen. Eighty per cent of Davao's imports came from Japan.

The Japanese government encouraged this growth. It cooperated in selecting emigrants, who at one time numbered more annually than to any other area except Manchuria; it subsidized shipping connecting the Philippines to the mandates, thus enabling emigrants to make the trip at ridiculously low fares. The consular service and the Japanese Association provided arrivals with guidance, agricultural services, and a common attack upon local problems. Schools, hospitals, and social organizations gave them a tightly woven community life. Both in economy and in spirit the new arrivals were closely tied to their homeland. In short, the Japanese had developed in Davao "a well-nigh perfect organization for the economic penetration and development of a new country." [30] As a sour joke, Filipinos nicknamed the province "Davao-kuo."

American officials, alarmed at what their early encouragement and later neglect had produced in Davao, looked for a solution before they turned over the chief executive power to the Filipinos. Eulogio Rodriguez, Frank Murphy's Secretary of Agriculture and Commerce, sponsored the most thorough of all investigations of the problem, wrote the most critical of all reports, and proposed the most severe solution in the history of the question—cancellation of all illegal Japanese leases.

The Rodriguez policy, in practical terms, would have driven the Japanese off half the land they were then cultivating. Acting Governor General Hayden, with Murphy's consent, withheld for further

30. Hayden, pp. 712–20, quotation from p. 718; Porter, pp. 99–103; Oliver, pp. 257–63; Willard Price, "Japan in the Philippines," *Harpers, 172* (1936), 609–19.

study the cancellation policy, but put into effect those of Rodriguez'
proposals that would prevent further illegal leasing.[31] All this, half
a year before the inauguration of the Commonwealth, caused the
Japanese fright and anger in Davao, and even in Formosa, their
colonial laboratory.[32]

Consul General Uchiyama sought out Quezon. He found him too
"smooth" to elicit "complete confidence," but nevertheless "aware
of the importance of the international phase of the question, and
. . . concerned about both official and public opinion in Japan."
A week before his inauguration Quezon secretly asked Uchiyama
to let the Gaimusho know that he would kill the cancellation policy
when he took office. In return he asked the Japanese to expel the
Sakdal leader, Benigno Ramos, from Japan, and to understand the
Philippine defense plan as a means of gaining "complete independence . . . free . . . from all American control."

To forestall a Quezon relapse, the Japanese consulate sought to
employ a Filipino prestigious enough for him to listen to; the first
choice was Jose Laurel. When Quezon considered appointing Laurel
his legal advisor or putting him on the Supreme Court, the consulate
urged Laurel to take the former. "I don't want to become a bell boy
at my age," Laurel growled, giving Uchiyama cause to fear that he
was "seeking to run out on us." Laurel eventually got a seat on the
court, which pleased him. He promised to "continue to work for
the solution of the [Davao] problem from behind the scenes," which
relieved Uchiyama.

The Japanese then found a new lobbyist in Pedro Sabido, who
agreed to take the job for 2,000 pesos down, ignorant that the down
payment to Laurel had been 5,000 pesos. When the question was
successfully settled, Sabido was to receive 10,000 pesos more.[33] At
a dinner given by Quezon for leading assemblymen, Sabido declared
that Japan's development of Davao was "not based on territorial or
political ambitions," but "on the spirit of co-existence and co-
prosperity." To relate the Manchurian problem with Davao was

31. Report of six-man investigating committee to Rodriguez, 11 Feb 35; Rodriguez
to Hayden, 19 Feb; Hayden "Memorandum for the Press, May 8, 1935." Some of the
Governor General's staff favored a lenient policy toward the Japanese; Van Schaick
to Hayden, 19 Feb; E. G. Chapman (legal advisor) to Hayden, 16, 27 Feb (H).
32. CofS, Army, in Taiwan, to Dep CofS [Tokyo], 10 Oct 35, Gaimushō S460, p. 676.
33. Uchiyama to Hirota, 20 Sept, 7 Nov 35, 6, 12 Feb 36; Gaimushō S460–61, pp.
619–24, 717–19, 825–32.

"highly irresponsible," Sabido said: "Japan is actively supporting the general will of the people of Manchuria and is making great sacrifices to maintain the independence of that nation. If this policy is a crime, it is the best and most welcome kind of crime." [34]

Laurel, Sabido, and other advocates of alignment with the Japanese influenced Quezon far less than his own interpretation of how the international winds were blowing. He publicly minimized the "Japanese problem" and maximized the Japanese "contribution" to the Philippines. Americans had encouraged the Japanese to go to Davao, he observed, and Filipinos had ensconced them by selling their land and perjuring themselves about the transactions. If the Filipinos would now learn technique and industriousness from the Japanese, their coming would prove a long-run blessing.[35]

Even with Quezon's benign approach, the Japanese consulate could neither negotiate nor purchase a "fundamental settlement" of the Davao question. Quezon, for international reasons, did not want to throw them out; but, for national reasons, he did not wish to legalize or solidify their position. Secret negotiations as late as September 1941 left the situation largely unchanged: existing illegal leases permitted, all further infringements supposedly prohibited.[36]

"The real danger that impends against the Filipino people," Claro Recto had said in 1934, was an "Asiatic Monroeism" which would mean "economic vassalage" and "political extinction." To ward off the danger from Japan he proposed "economic collaboration" with the United States,[37] but, in the years that followed, America showed no desire for such collaboration and left largely to Filipinos the responsibility for protecting themselves.

From the beginning of the 1930s to the end, the overseas population of Japanese in the Philippines nearly doubled, to thirty thousand; exports to the Philippines rose to thirteen million dollars a year, and investments approximately doubled, to over thirty-two million dollars.[38] Against this impressive growth, the laws the Fili-

34. Uchiyama to For Min Arita, 13 May 36, ibid., pp. 1008–11.
35. "Speech delivered by H. E. the President, in Davao on the occasion of the laying of the cornerstone of the barrio obrero, June 28, 1939" (Q).
36. Gaimushō, S461, pp. 1257–59, 1263–76, 1280–83, 1287–88, 1290–92, 1296–99, 1300–14, 1319–25, 1327–29, 1336–39, 1346–48, 1350–52.
37. *Philippine Magazine*, 31 (Oct 1934), 412.
38. Hayden, p. 714; Porter, p. 99; *Census of the Philippines: 1939*, p. 400.

pinos drew were only hindrances, not major deterrents, to Japanese influence, for many citizens and even officials conspired to evade them. If the Philippines had not fallen into economic vassalage, neither had it risen much in native economic development, its best protection against vassalage. Of such development the Commonwealth did not seem capable in the breadth, depth, and pace necessary to minimize Japanese inroads.

"Political extinction" was as yet very far from threatening. A transient American reporter sounded an alarm against an "Oriental Sudetan movement," but he exaggerated grossly.[39] Japanese consular correspondence reveals only one first-rate leader on the payroll—Jose Laurel, who, after becoming a Supreme Court justice, withdrew from all but informal help to the Japanese, and begged that his name be kept out of diplomatic dispatches. Sabido, who succeeded him, was a man of the second rank. The ubiquitous Duran was of the third: he spent an estimated $30,000 and a vast quantity of Japanese beer in a vain effort to enter Congress. In Davao, in 1941, two opponents for Congress sought Japanese support; the consulate in turn asked the Foreign Ministry for five thousand pesos to "support and guide both candidates" and to deal with the winner.[40] Small potatoes.

Some skilled newspapermen accepted consular subsidies, notably Modesto Farolan; some Filipino businessmen, hedging their bets, cultivated relations with the Japanese. The Philippine-Japan society, founded in 1935 in Tokyo, fostered cultural relations. But, among Filipinos, the number of true Japanophiles was few: some anti-white, anti-Western intellectuals, like Aurelio Alvero, and some disaffected fanatics following Benigno Ramos. The total Japanese infiltration was modest indeed. The politically minded Filipino, as he stood between two empires, remained sentimentally attached to the familiar one which was rejecting him and suspicious of the unfamiliar one which wished to befriend him.

Some critics have implied that Quezon himself was in Japanese pay, but they cannot point out any Japanese close enough to him to dare make an offer. Even had Quezon accepted a gift, he would have rejected, as dishonoring the presidency, the notion of doing

39. Oliver, pp. 258–59.
40. Concerning Duran: Horn, *Orphans of the Pacific*, p. 264. Concerning Davao: Cons Kihara Jitarō to For Min Matsuoka, 7 July 41; Gaimushō S461, pp. 1317–18.

favors in return. He had elicited funds for independence junkets from American businessmen, but certainly had not bestowed corresponding benefits. He had warned his rich Manila backers, after the election of 1935, not to expect special privileges.[41] He had accepted, even asked for, money from Catholic, Francoesque ultraconservatives like Adrian Got, while at the same time declaring his admiration for the anticlerical, semisocialist government of Cárdenas in Mexico, which refused even to recognize Franco's regime. Whatever gifts were proffered to Quezon he received in the spirit of the Aga Khan, accustomed to being paid his weight in diamonds.

Toward the Japanese, as Uchiyama predicted, Quezon was "thoroughly ambiguous," playing what a later generation would call the neutralist game. While he built an army with American help, he accepted Japanese help in developing the economy; and he hoped that he and his country would not get caught in between.

41. Horn, pp. 78, 85; Gunther, "Manuel Quezon," *Atlantic Monthly,* Jan 1939, p. 61.

14

Dilemmas of Semi-Sovereignty

SUPERFICIALLY the commonwealth era, from 1935 to 1941, was one of culture, sport, and grandeur. Manila had a fine ballet group and the best symphony orchestra in the Orient, for whose weekly concerts fifteen hundred people came, formally dressed. In the Elizalde brothers, Manila had one of the world's better polo teams. In Manuel Quezon the Philippines had the only native chief executive in colonial South and Southeast Asia. He responded to the position with increasingly individualistic elegance: sometimes he dressed in riding breeches, sun helmet, riding crop; sometimes adopted the barong tagalog, all-purpose native shirt; sometimes received visitors dressed like an Edwardian dandy—green suit, purple handkerchief, purple boutonniere. But no one dared to smile, for the Philippine flag flew, or dangled, at the same level as the American.

Equal but separate, the two flags symbolized a question that vexed Quezon: how much sovereignty did the Philippines have, and to what extent was he a "chief of state"? Common sense might suggest that sovereignty, like pregnancy, could not be partial; that one either was or was not sovereign. The United States, however, had taken an uncommon step in requiring adoption of a constitution ten years before independence. "Sovereignty shall reside in the people," it said, and the people elected Quezon President. On the other hand, the Tydings-McDuffie Act reserved to the United States powers over finance, defense, and foreign relations; the American high commissioner had supervisory powers on these and advisory power on other matters. The boundaries of these powers were vaguely defined, a failure which put a strain on American tact [1] and Quezonian temper at the very christening of the Commonwealth.

How many guns should be used to salute President Quezon at the inauguration ceremony? General MacArthur had originally prevailed upon President Roosevelt to agree to full honors for Quezon, twenty-one guns. Those who would be, unlike MacArthur, serving America first and the Philippines second, disagreed. Nineteen guns, they said—no more than was due a state governor, or American authority would be at least symbolically compromised. When, after much discussion, Roosevelt reversed himself, Quezon declared that he would not attend the ceremonies; he would take the oath of office at home the night before. Murphian cajolery and a cablegram from Roosevelt finally brought Quezon around, and the ceremonies went off pleasantly.[2] But that was just the beginning.

In 1936–37, Quezon made a trip around the world, forcing questions of precedence thick and fast upon the State Department. Roosevelt approved a joint suggestion of the Secretaries of War and State, that because the President of the Philippines had no recognized international status, he should receive no salutes outside Philippine national waters. A number of nations, however, were eager to give Quezon full honors: in Canton, the Chinese displayed the Philippine flag and their own, but not the American. In Europe, Quezon accepted decorations from foreign states without prior congressional consent. Mexico gave him twenty-one guns; and the Japanese ambassador there gave dinners for Quezon on two successive evenings with no Americans invited.

"I am the son of a farmer," Quezon had told a State Department official, insisting that he did not care about formalities. He nevertheless showed an obsessive rancor over the American conduct in the matter and extreme gratification over foreign salutes, medals, flags, and feasts. Quezon was moved not just by ego in the Western sense but by face in the Philippine sense. As a son of the revolution and elected president of his people, his own dignity meant the dignity of his country.

1. Murphy to Hayden, 5 Dec 35 (H).
2. Dern to Roosevelt, 9 Nov 35, Roosevelt to Dern, 9 Nov (draft), Dern to Roosevelt, 12 Nov, referring to Quezon to Dern, 11 Nov (FDR); "Protocol and Philippine Affairs," historical memo, 2 Mar 37, SD 811B.001, Q/84.

Quezon sought direct invitation to the coronation of King George VI, but the State Department informed him that he could only attend under the auspices of the American ambassador to the Court of St. James. Did he have to "climb a tree" to see the thing? Complaining to a British businessman, Quezon shouted, "Colonel, all that stuff of your Kipling about the white man's burden is pure nonsense!" [3]

In Manila the Japanese raised questions of precedence by their eagerness to cultivate Quezon. They toasted him as an equal of the Emperor of Japan and the President of the United States, and took only casual notice of the High Commissioner. Paul McNutt, after he assumed that office in February 1937, suppressed these social slights and corrected the habit of foreign consulates of bypassing the High Commissioner's office on matters of business which concerned it. [4] To these American definitions of political etiquette and administrative procedure, Quezon charmingly acquiesced upon his return home in August. Perhaps he was fatigued with petty disputes; perhaps he wanted to start off on the right foot with the new High Commissioner; perhaps he distrusted the excessive deference of the Japanese, who had recently gone on the march in North China.

At a public banquet in Rizal Stadium, after the President of the United States had been toasted, Quezon toasted McNutt, who returned the gesture. Then Quezon spoke. "There can be no possible conflict between the High Commissioner and myself," he said. "The government of the Commonwealth is not an independent government. . . . Every official of this country from the President . . . down to the last . . . messenger, in fact every Filipino citizen, owes allegiance to the United States. We render America that allegiance without mental reservation, not only because it is our duty. . . but also because we are bound to America by . . . the deepest ties of gratitude."

Referring obliquely to Japan, Quezon concluded with the hope that after independence "every rising sun . . . will set on a happier and greater America and Philippines, bound closely together by everlasting ties." [5] In finally minimizing the precedence question,

3. SD 811B.001, Q/17, 37, 55, 62, 83, 102, 111–12, 130½; Q/84; Q/123. The Englishman who reported the last remark very probably cleaned up its language.
4. Manila *Tribune*, 15, 18, 19 May 37; New York *Times*, 22, 25 May; Manila *Bulletin*, 18, 19, 25, 27 May, 24, 29 July (H).
5. Manila *Tribune*, 21 Aug 37 (H).

American discretion matched Quezonian prudence. McNutt's successor, Francis Sayre, declined invitations to certain functions in order to permit the Philippine President to take unrivaled prominence.[6]

The flaws of the Tydings-McDuffie Act made some Filipinos want to advance independence before 1946, others to delay it. Quezon felt both ways at different times. Ego and nationalism, one and inseparable, were the foundation of his political instinct, and he spontaneously sought for himself conditions of unhampered leadership and for his country accelerated independence. When he reflected more carefully, he stressed the value of continued economic relations with the United States.

Playing upon this latter mood, two men were able to convince Quezon, briefly, of the superior value of postponing the day of independence. Roy Howard and Paul McNutt both had the special confidence and gusto required to contradict an autocrat. Jovial executives, good drinking companions, shrewd gamblers at poker, they supplied Quezon that aura of manly braggadocio in which big events were discussed as casually as tossing off a shot of scotch and reversals of policy undertaken as colloquially as raising a stake at cards.

Roy Howard had stimulated Quezon to his concept of the "small planet–great planet" relationship in 1933, with his correspondence about the Japanese. Quezon had acted on his healthy fear in hiring MacArthur, but nothing further came of the idea of a "satellite" relationship until Howard visited Quezon just after the inauguration of the Commonwealth. They sailed together, incommunicado, on Quezon's yacht. On December 11, 1935, Manila papers and the Scripps-Howard chain in America simultaneously published an article by Howard declaring that the dream of independence was already fading from Filipino minds because of Japan and predicting that the Filipinos might turn to Great Britain for protection if the United States refused them dominion status.

Quezon had privately read the article two or three times before it was released, and thought it good education for his people. All powers concerned about the Japanese hailed it, and T. V. Soong, Chiang Kai-shek's brother-in-law, called it "eminently realistic." Two

6. Sayre, *Glad Adventure*, p. 209.

former Philippine resident commissioners favored it, and so did Filipino businessmen, who saw in it a way to "survive Oriental competition." A radical labor leader emphasized the common man's reaction to higher taxes and compulsory military training: "If independence means only happiness for Quezon, Osmeña, Roxas and the rich . . . to hell with such independence."

The opposition, however, was stronger. As Howard later recalled it, anti-Quezon editors "ripped open my gullet and smeared Quezon with the blood." The crucial attitudes were those of the two legislatures: Philippine assemblymen muttered about "conspiracy" and "bamboozlement," and in the United States Senator Tydings conceded the validity of Howard's observations, but felt them nonetheless contrary to the temper of Congress and his personal feelings. The National Grange rose up against fundamental revision of the independence law, and Senator Borah supported them.[7]

Paul McNutt's presence in Manila later had the same political effect upon Quezon that correspondence and friendship with Roy Howard had had. McNutt was a most persuasive man: with his black eyebrows and wavy silver hair, he looked like a younger, firmer Warren Harding, someone to be relied on. McNutt aimed to be the Democratic nominee for President in 1940; perhaps sensing that, Roosevelt had shunted him off to the Philippines, as, earlier, Harding had done to an already defeated rival, Leonard Wood. McNutt, however, kept himself before the American people with a return trip in March 1938 and a series of provocative statements on the Philippines, climaxed by a formal radio broadcast.

Quezon had recently said it would take "fifty years to bring the American people around" to understanding a dominion arrangement,[8] but he secretly agreed to a reexamination of the problem if McNutt took the initiative.[9] The existing policy, McNutt said, was "scuttle and run." From the Philippine viewpoint it meant the "threat of racial extinction" by heavy Asiatic immigration, a questionable defensive capacity, and "economic disaster" from the sud-

7. *Philippine Magazine*, 33 (1936), 5–6; Stimson diary, 20 Mar 35 (HLS); Tydings to Geo. H. Fairchild, 16 May 35, Nat Arch, Leg Sec, Sen 73A–F25, 142; author's interview with Roy Howard, 7 May 62.
8. Quotation from Quezon conversation with Sayre and Joseph Jacobs, Chief, Off of Phil Aff, 2 Mar 37, SD 811B.000, Q/84; Amb William C. Bullitt reported from Paris a conversation to the same effect, to Sec State, 5 May 37, SD 811B.001, Q/114.
9. Paredes, Romero, Roxas, Razon (from Washington) to Quezon, 4 Mar 38 (Q).

den loss of the American market. The United States would lose its Open Door Policy, freedom of the seas, freedom of the air, and its voice in Oriental diplomacy, while its "monument . . . to a new benign colonialism" would perish. Therefore, McNutt suggested allowing "to the Philippines every ounce of domestic autonomy they can absorb—holding in our own hands foreign affairs, tariffs, immigration, currency, and public debt—scarcely more than marks of the necessary reservations of a dominion." [10]

Manila heard all this clearly; American businessmen sent McNutt congratulatory cables. Quezon declared to the press that McNutt's presentation of the facts concerning economic relations was "unassailable"; disquieting world events also made reexamination necessary.[11] Certain American army circles were aghast at McNutt's proposal: if carried through, one wrote, it "would give the Filipino leaders a blank check upon American life and American resources." [12] Certain Filipino politicians were upset for different reasons: accepting the proposal would give a blank check to their political opponents. When several of Quezon's lieutenants gave out press statements against it, Quezon summoned them to his office that same evening. Felipe Buencamino, Jr., arrived first and found Quezon in a fury, eyes flashing, nostrils quivering, ears wiggling. Buencamino thought, "This is the end of me."

"Goddammit," Quezon said, "Do you think you're powerful enough? . . . What is this, your coming out with a policy contradictory to mine?"

Buencamino began gently, soothing his compadre. He and the others were actually *in favor* of postponing independence, but, with Assembly elections coming up, to say so might endanger Nacionalista candidates. "A lot of maneuvering" would be necessary before taking up any such position. By the time Recto, Osias, and the others arrived, Buencamino had worked up enough steam to put his own disturbed question to Quezon: "Who's the leader of this country, anyway, you or McNutt?"

10. Excerpts from New York *Herald Tribune,* 15 Mar 38 (H); McNutt reproduced in full his own speech in SD 811B.00, 23 June 38. He believed that he expressed the sentiments of responsible business elements in the Philippines; ibid., 21 July, 8 Oct 37.
11. Quezon quoted by Chicago *Daily Tribune,* 16 Mar 38 (H); American business reactions described in SD 811B.00, 23 June.
12. Brig Gen Stanley Embick, Dep CofS, War Plans Div, memo of 2 Mar 38, AGO 093.5.

Face. Encircled by his own subordinates, Quezon argued further, then gave in: "By Jesus, you're right." [13] He called in reporters and foreign correspondents and reversed himself, saying that he had not heard on the air McNutt's paragraph about American retention of certain powers in the Philippines, and now that he had read it he could not agree with it.[14] So ended McNutt's reexamination proposal, one day old.

Quezon was satisfied to let others talk of postponing independence so that he could assess the reactions, but occasionally he spoke out for advancing independence so that he could gather the credit. In March 1937 he began to propose independence by July 4, 1939; and in March 1939 he proposed it for 1940. In each case he wanted an extended period of privileged trade relations, fifteen years or twenty, a policy Roy Howard had criticized years before as "wanting to have your cake and eat it too." [15]

In 1937 Quezon showered the State Department with petty grievances concerning the High Commissioner, "bull-headed generals," and congressional tinkering with the Tydings-McDuffie Act. He obtained an interview with the President, whom he then trusted deeply. He wished Roosevelt to stabilize Philippine-American relations before the end of his second term: as father America, to introduce daughter Philippines to the society of nations. Roosevelt would not commit himself to an accelerated debut, but he did set in motion events that produced the Joint Preparatory Committee.[16]

Quezon went home and warmed himself into a rhetorical glow over immediate independence, but failed to bring his audiences to their feet. By Christmas of 1937, MacArthur and others had per-

13. All quotations are from Felipe Buencamino, Jr, who vividly recalled the incident in conversation with the author, 29 June 58.
14. Grunder and Livezey, *Philippines and U.S.*, p. 229, citing New York *Times,* 16, 17 Mar 38. E. D. Hester, in an interview with the author, 16 Jan 58, certified that several people, including Richard Ely, chief clerk and passport officer of the High Comm's office, were with Quezon at the time of the broadcast and found every word of it clearly audible. Roxas, who was in America at the time, sent congratulations to McNutt on his speech and never retracted them.
15. Howard to Buencamino, 24 Oct 32 (Q).
16. Memo of conversation, Quezon with Sayre and Jacobs, 3 Mar 37, SD 811B.000, Q/84; High Comm's report, "General Conditions in the Philippines," 21 July 37, pp. 47–55, SD 811B.00; speech, Rizal Stadium, Manila *Tribune,* 21 Aug 37 (H); Quezon to Jorge Vargas, sec to the Pres, 8 Apr 37, en route to Mexico City (Q).

suaded Quezon to drop his campaign, which disappointed only Aguinaldo and Sumulong, the last lonely immediatists. Most Filipinos had become moderately accustomed to the terms of the Tydings-McDuffie Act, especially businessmen, who preferred "to stake their immediate future on Congress rather than on a prematurely independent government." [17]

Quezon flared up again in 1939, with the idea that he might bargain with Congress for a prolonged economic adjustment by proposing to expedite political separation.[18] The Joint Preparatory Committee's recommendations, however, stood against him: advanced independence would of itself reduce the funds available for economic adjustment and liquidation of Philippine bonded indebtedness, and an accelerated defense program would only worsen the difficulty. Even if Quezon's proposal passed, Sayre warned him that the State Department for separate and sufficient reasons concerning "world conditions" would recommend a veto.[19]

Sayre instead explored with Senator Millard Tydings the likelihood of an opposite movement in Congress—to retard independence. If it came, Tydings said, he "would move an amendment to the amendment making clear that the United States, in postponing independence, undertook to defend the Philippines, and to build sufficient defenses and fortifications to protect them." Tydings, who had proposed giving nearby Puerto Rico its independence, was even more anxious to get out of the West Pacific than out of the Caribbean. His colleagues would be eager, too, if they realized the price of defending the Philippines. "After two days' debate as to the cost and consequences of such an amendment," Tydings said, "it would be voted down quickly." [20]

Since the executive branch of American government opposed the hastening of independence day, and the legislative branch opposed delaying it, only a strong and unambiguous petition from the Philippines itself might have changed the policy formalized in 1933. The initiative for such a petition came from Jose Romero, a prominent assemblyman from the sugar island of Negros, in September 1939.

17. Hunt, *Untold Story*, p. 191; SD 811B.00, 21 July 37, 1 Feb 38.
18. Quezon (Manila) to Osmeña (Washington), 30 Mar 39 (Q).
19. *Joint Preparatory Committee on Philippine Affairs, Report of May 20, 1938, 1,* p. 157; Osmeña, "Outline of Matters to Be Taken up by Vice-President Osmeña with President Quezon in Long Distance Phone Conversation Tonight, April 12, 1939" (Q).
20. Sayre, memo of conversation, 10 Nov 38, SD 611.11B3/343.

General war had just broken out over Poland. Romero, adapting the rhetoric of William Jennings Bryan, asked his countrymen to "pause before . . . we crucify our nation upon the cross of an untimely independence." He attacked Benigno Aquino, who shortly before had warned that colonial status meant racial "slavery" and that relaxing the struggle for independence would mean loss of face before the world. Romero replied, "We can lose not only face but body and soul . . . by another foreign conquest; but no nation in the world will despise us for pausing to reexamine our national problem in this era of international anarchy and in the face of danger of economic chaos." [21]

If Quezon had really wished to explore the idea of postponement with his people, without involving his own reputation, this was the opportunity. Labor leaders, except for the Communists, were open to persuasion or already active in the retention cause, mainly out of fear of falling into alien hands. A poll of middle-class and professional elements showed three-fifths in favor of continuing commonwealth status indefinitely. But Quezon's legislative lieutenants barely let the idea take shape before forcing a vote on it. Romero, who claimed to have won the support of twelve or fifteen assemblymen, found several of them scared into absence or abstention when the vote was taken. The Assembly expressed itself against reexamination and postponement of independence, 53 to 6. [22]

Quezon's military opinions were meanwhile changing fast. Austria, Czechoslovakia, and Albania had all recently lost their independence, and Poland's invaders had conquered that country in a month. Although Quezon had once believed MacArthur—that Ethiopia need never have fallen to Mussolini had she been properly prepared [23] —now the evidence seemed overwhelming that determined industrial-military powers could absorb any small state, no matter how valiant. He began to lose faith in his military advisor.

To seek reassurance from the Japanese, Quezon visited Tokyo and there received soothing and ceremonious treatment. When he returned he spoke in a new tone, shocking to MacArthur, and surprising even to those who had grown blasé over Quezon's reversals

21. Manila *Bulletin,* 24 Sept 39 (H); *Philippine Magazine, 36* (Nov 1939), 437, 443.
22. Manila *Bulletin,* 31 Aug, 25 Sept, 1, 2, 3 Oct 39 (H); Sayre, p. 193.
23. Manila *Tribune,* 20 June, 4 Aug 36 (H).

of himself. The Philippines, he said, could not be defended successfully even if every last Filipino were armed. His people should acquire the moral strength to endure, if necessary, another three hundred years of subjugation.[24]

To his legislative leaders and cabinet Quezon said that "developments in the European war have convinced me of the futility of
spending money to carry on our program of defending the Philippines from foreign aggression, and this objective cannot be attained
with the limited resources of the country for many years to come."
Accordingly he established the Department of Defense, which reduced the importance of MacArthur's office.

Without explicit orders from Quezon himself, no Army buildings
could be constructed or further trainees called up. The Commissioner
of the Budget would have to approve any further acquisition of
arms, ammunition, and equipment. Quezon deemphasized ROTC
units, told the Army to remove itself from public school training
in discipline and citizenship, and directed to the school system
savings from curtailed military expenses. His orders cut the Army
budget by three million pesos, cut the annual number of reserve
trainees in half, and canceled the mobilization previously ordered
for 1940.[25]

Secretary of Defense Teofilo Sison gave the public a rationale for
the new policy: "Until the Philippine relationship with the United
States is completely severed, the defense of the Philippines against
external aggression is the full responsibility of America." [26] Quezon
meanwhile called on President Roosevelt to carry out the neutralization provision of the Tydings-McDuffie Act. In a few months Quezon
had thrown out all the assumptions with which he had lived for the
last five years and had adopted instead the educational policy preferred by the American liberal press, the diplomatic policy of Aguinaldo and Sumulong, and the defense policy of MacArthur's military critics.

So sharp was Quezon's disillusionment with MacArthur that he
asked High Commissioner Sayre to have him relieved. When Sayre
asked him to put the request in writing, Quezon decided instead to
require MacArthur to deal with him through his personal secretary,

24. Marquardt, *Before Bataan,* p. 241.
25. Manila *Bulletin,* 2 Nov 39; Quezon to Sison, undated draft [late 1939] (Q).
26. Manila *Bulletin,* 9 Mar 40 (H).

Jorge Vargas. Once, when denied access to Quezon, MacArthur said,
"Jorge, some day your boss is going to want to see me more than I
want to see him." [27] The two compadres were estranged.

Retired from the American Army and nearly abandoned by
Quezon, MacArthur now lost his staff assistant of the last six years,
Col. Dwight D. Eisenhower. An argument over the size of the regular
Filipino Army had destroyed their intimacy two years before; now
Eisenhower wanted to join maneuvers in Louisiana and catch up on
weapons developments. "I can't afford to go on teaching schoolboys
any longer," he told his friends. He requested and received a trans-
fer.[28]

By the time Eisenhower left, the Philippine defense plan had
produced 100,000 trained reservists, about one-third of MacArthur's
own reduced goal, and only 75 to 100 "really good" flyers. There
were only 40 or so planes on hand, most of them for training, as
against a goal of 250 combat planes; there were only two motor
torpedo boats, as against a minimum goal of 50, and no more would
be delivered, since the British suppliers were at war.[29]

MacArthur was still optimistic, but upon new premises. He was
encouraged as much as ever by the enormous tactical difficulties of
overseas invasion and also by "the lack of a plausible reason for
attack." The Philippines, he said, "may achieve a respectable defense and enjoy a reasonable safety if it is prepared and determined
to repel attacks classed as adventurous, both in strength and purpose." For the first time he stressed the "ultimate responsibility" of
the United States for defense of the Philippines and classed the
Philippine Army merely as "a practical reserve for the small con-
tingent of American forces stationed in this outpost." [30]

Roy Howard wrote Quezon late in 1939 that "the American public
is badly balled up as to just what your ideas are." Quezon, in fact,
could clearly formulate the dilemma of his administration; he simply
could not resolve it. "America cannot . . . concede more govern-

27. Author's interview with E. D. Hester, 1 Mar 58. Hester, who was attached to
the High Comm's office as economic advisor, heard this from a colleague at the time.
MacArthur mentions neither the estrangement nor Quezon's change of policy in his
Reminiscences.
28. Hunt, pp. 191–93; informant's name withheld.
29. Manila *Bulletin*, 27 Jan, 15 Mar 40 (H); Eisenhower, "Memorandum to President
Quezon," 22 June 42 (Q).
30. Philippines *Herald*, 26 Jan 40 (H).

mental powers . . . without endangering her own interest and security, nor . . . can the Filipino people assume responsibility . . .
with . . . such limited powers as have been vested in the Commonwealth." [31]

He had tested two ways out of the dilemma: immediate independence, to which Roosevelt and the State Department would not agree,
and prolonged dependence, to which Congress would not agree.
Similar self-canceling counterpressures existed in the Philippines:
politicians against delay for fear of losing votes, and businessmen
against advance for fear of dislocating the economy. Worse still: in
the haphazard tesselation of American Far Eastern policy there was
no clear design for the Philippines. The executive branch was mildly
internationalist and would denounce Japan; the legislative branch,
stoutly isolationist, would appease her. The Navy was asking for a
stronger offensive capacity; the Army for a contracted defense
perimeter.

To have followed either of two policies consistently might have
saved the Philippines great destruction: to give rapid independence, withdrawing all American bases, or to expand at once,
and hugely, American air, sea, and land forces in the Philippines
specifically and the Pacific generally. Instead the United States
mixed its policies: the administration continued a rhetorical and
diplomatic harassment of Japanese expansion in East Asia, while
Congress voted down, so as not to offend Japan, an appropriation
bill designed to turn Guam into a first class naval base.[32] Quezon's
own statesmanship could not transcend the confused circumstances
to which American policy limited him. His own political conduct,
never calm and classic, became desperate and baroque.

Imperialism in retreat confers few benefits. Capitalists, frightened
by nationalism, reduce investments. Government, pulling out, cannot
make the reforms or ask the sacrifices which will release hidden
native energies. In the case of the Philippine Commonwealth, extraordinary danger compounded the ordinary stagnancy of transition.
Unable himself to confer security, unwilling to require sacrifices of
those able to make them, Manuel Quezon could do little more with
his semi-presidency than to suffer it and enjoy it; to radiate charisma
and restrain his own anxiety.

31. Howard to Quezon, 15 Sept 39; speech to the National Assembly, 18 Oct 37 (Q).
32. Concerning Guam: Morison, *Rising Sun,* pp. 32–34.

Part 5: The Great Ordeal

"Un peuple invainçu se croit invincible."

RENÉ JOUGLET
Au Japon

15

Invasion

THE PHILIPPINES since 1896 had lain vulnerable at the intersection of new lines of power in Asia, vulnerable even under American rule, because the United States did not take its imperial commitment seriously enough to cover the strategic exposure that it involved. From 1905 on, after the Japanese had beaten the Russians, Theodore Roosevelt worried about American weakness in the Philippines and tried unsuccessfully to get remedial appropriations from Congress. Later on, two popular military experts, Hector Bywater and Homer Lea, even forecast the manner of the Japanese offensive with its key landing at Lingayen. Only Baron Shidehara, as Foreign Minister in 1930, said that a Japanese "attack was impossible, since even if it were immediately successful with regard to the Philippines, it would only be the beginning of a war in which Japan would in the long run be completely ruined."

The events of 1941–42 were to prove everyone right except Shidehara, who stood for a rational and liberal Japanese foreign policy. If he was inaccurate, time would at least prove his wisdom. In the press of circumstance, however, Shidehara's friend Henry Stimson, now Roosevelt's Secretary of War as he had once been Taft's, remembered Homer Lea from thirty years before, "a little humpback man," who had even predicted invasion of the continental United States. The once "fantastic" now seemed "quite possible." [1]

Conceivably, the Philippines could have been spared invasion. In 1941 it was important to neither imperial power, but stood between them. The United States was far more concerned with Europe and the North Atlantic. Japan had no special desire to absorb a self-governing democracy into its New Order, and was interested in areas other than the Philippines for vital resources. Her diplomats proposed, as part of a general understanding with the United States, a joint guarantee of Philippine independence. To pay for this promise not to invade, the United States must insure nondiscriminatory treatment of Japanese in matters of immigration and business. American negotiators, who were silent about economic discrimination, pointed out that the immigration law was technically not discriminatory and observed that neutralization would become appropriate only when the Philippines were independent in 1946. This arid exchange was typical of the talks as a whole. Secretary of State Cordell Hull, as early as May, told Stimson that "everything was going hellward." Chances of avoiding war, he said, were one in ten. [2]

The chances soon lessened still further. Japan moved troops into French Indo-China, and the United States responded in late July by freezing Japanese assets, putting an embargo on oil to Japan, and placing Douglas MacArthur in command of rapidly enlarged American forces in the Philippines. The Japanese already thought of the Philippines as a "pistol aimed at Japan's heart," and now the United States was conspicuously loading the pistol.

What each side did out of defensive psychology looked to the other like aggression. MacArthur had said years before: "Armies and navies, in being efficient, give weight to the peaceful words of statesmen, but a feverish effort to create them when once a crisis is imminent simply provokes attack." [3] Now he was in command of just such a feverish effort.

1. Homer Lea, *The Valor of Ignorance* (New York, Harpers, 1942, 1st ed., 1909), pp. 173–77; Hector Bywater, *The Great Pacific War: A History of the American-Japanese Campaign of 1931–33* (Boston, Houghton Mifflin, 1925) pp. 46–58; Shidehara quoted in Amb to Japan (Castle) to Sec State, 14 Feb 30, *For Rel 1930, 1,* 24–25; Stimson diary 10 Feb 42 (HLS).
2. Morison, *Rising Sun*, p. 165; Stimson diary, 13 May 41, 27 May (quote) (HLS); *For Rel, Japan, 1931–41, 2,* 325 ff., esp. 398–402, 451–54, 458–64, 486–92.
3. Quoted by Amb Joseph Grew, 27 Dec 34, *For Rel 1935, 3,* 822.

MacArthur had been trying to be recalled to active service since early in the year and at the same time to get his grand concept of Philippine defense accepted in Washington. When Roosevelt finally appointed him Commanding General, United States Armed Forces in the Far East (USAFFE), he ended not only MacArthur's retirement but also his ostracism by Quezon. The Philippine leader's attitude abruptly switched from aloofness to deference.[4]

The War Department itself began in midsummer to heed Mac-Arthur's counsel. His optimistic requests for a rapid build-up in the Philippines coincided with news of the excellent performance of Flying Fortresses operating from the British Isles. Perhaps if enough men and planes were shipped to the Philippines, defensive forces there would deter invasion, just as the English had dissuaded Hitler from crossing the Channel. This MacArthur had once hoped to do for an independent Philippines by 1946. But the country's resources, or perhaps its will, had been falling short. Now he aimed to achieve the same goal, with the aid of American will and resources, by 1942. In his strategic concept the War Department concurred, and Henry Stimson became a strong proponent of maximum delay before any showdown with the Japanese.

As reinforcement continued, MacArthur seized an opportunity to force revision of the mission of his forces. War Plan RAINBOW 5, which reached him in September, contained the combined planning of the allies for a global war, but reflected the old ORANGE mission for the Philippines: defense of Manila Bay alone, with loss of the Philippines implicitly assumed long before the fleet could arrive with aid. MacArthur objected that RAINBOW 5 failed to recognize either the creation of USAFFE under his command or the mobilization of the Philippine Army, which he had been six years in raising and training. The old "citadel" type of defense was outmoded. He sought in October and won in November the expansion of his mission "to include offensive air operations in the furtherance of the strategic defensive, combined with the *defense of the [whole] Philippine Islands as an air and naval base.*"[5]

Meanwhile the Commander-in-Chief of the Asiatic Fleet, Admiral

4. Stimson diary, 21 May 41 (HLS); Hunt, *Untold Story,* pp. 203–10; Sayre, *Glad Adventure,* p. 217.
5. Gen William Bryden, Acting CofS, to MacArthur, 21 Nov 41, WPD 4402–112 (italics mine). MacArthur gives a full account of his strength by Dec 1941 in *Reminiscences,* p. 110.

Thomas C. Hart, had sought out MacArthur to discuss the cooperation of their forces. The initial interview went badly. Hart's long-
standing mission called for him to withdraw at the outbreak of war
and operate in the Indian Ocean until the westward advance of the
Pacific Fleet made more aggressive tactics possible. On his own initiative Hart had decided to flee only as far as friendly British or Dutch
ports, to deploy his submarines around Luzon and enemy areas, to
return his surface craft to the north when the situation permitted.
Although Hart was approaching the more confident warfare Mac-
Arthur advocated, the General seemed impassive and unimpressed.
"The Navy has its plans," he finally replied, "the Army has its plans,
and we each have our own fields." [6]

Despite this rebuff, Hart was so encouraged by the air build-up
that he came to share MacArthur's strategic concept for the Philippines. Against the advice of his immediate associates, including his
chief of staff, he proposed to Washington a radical change in his own
fleet's mission: instead of retiring behind the Malay Barrier, he fight
the coming war from Manila Bay and employ all its potential in
defense of the Philippines. In effect, he wished to parallel Mac-
Arthur's order to the Army—no withdrawal from beach positions—
with a similar order to the Navy: no withdrawal from Philippine
waters. [7]

After some delay, however, the Navy explicitly refused Hart's proposal to concentrate in Manila Bay, and held him to the existing
mission of saving the surface fleet through flight. [8] Since the ORANGE
debates of the late 1930s, the attitudes of the two services had completely reversed. The Navy, formerly dauntless, was now in Stimson's
mind "defeatist." Hart's superiors warned him that "these accretions
of Army strength . . . will by no means positively insure the Philippines or your bases against determined attack." The Army, formerly
without hope for the Philippines, was now bold: MacArthur thought
the islands would be impervious to invasion by April 1942; Stimson

6. Adm T. C. Hart, "Narrative" (1942), p. 22; quotation from "Supplementary of
Narrative" (1946–47) (Off of Naval Hist, Navy Dept Service Center, Arlington, Va.),
pp. 6–7.
7. Louis Morton, *The United States Army in World War II; The War in the Pacific,*
4; *The Fall of the Philippines* (Washington, Off of Chief of Mil Hist, 1953), p. 69;
Hart, "Narrative," p. 25; "Supplementary," p. 6.
8. Hart, "Supplementary," p. 6. MacArthur, who later was rather critical of Hart
(*Reminiscences,* p. 128), apparently never knew of Hart's attempt to have his orders
changed.

asked only until early January 1942 "to secure our position." [9]

The Anglo-American freezing of assets in July 1941 and the refusal of Dutch colonial authorities to supply oil had shocked the Japanese. Their political maneuvers up to this point had been based only on a vague war strategy, but now they debated specific war plans in case they had to seize by force the rich natural resources of the "southern area."

The Japanese Army favored a counterclockwise advance from land to sea beginning with Malaya and leaving the Philippines to last, in order to delay American participation in the war. The Navy wished to go clockwise, from sea toward land, beginning with the Philippines lest it "become impregnable." They feared American naval and air forces might become strong enough to disrupt and reverse Japanese progress. By mid-August, "continental" and "blue-water" schools had reached a compromise: simultaneous initial operations in the Philippines and Malaya, the centers of American and British strength, followed by swift advance southward from both points to the Dutch oil fields. [10]

As Japanese-American relations deteriorated, a series of liaison conferences in Tokyo met late in October to study the optimum time for commencing war, should it be necessary. Great Britain would be weaker in March 1942, and Soviet Russia would be less likely to enter against Japan. But data on the build-up in the Philippines and other areas indicated that the United States would be so much stronger then as to "make aggressive operations absolutely impossible." During the night of November 1–2, the climactic conference concluded that unless negotiations had succeeded by midnight November 30, hostilities would begin—a month, incidentally, before Stimson's goal for preparation, and five months before MacArthur's. [11]

While diplomatic efforts continued, the Japanese went ahead with preparations for military and naval strikes. Sugiyama, Chief of the

9. CNO to CinCAF, 7 Nov 41, copy WPD 4402–112; Stimson diary, 6 Oct 41, and passim (HLS).
10. Off of Chief of Mil Hist, Japanese Monog No. 150, pp. 3–11.
11. Ibid., pp. 10–11, 87–89; Robert J. C. Butow, *Tojo and the Coming of War* (Princeton, Princeton University Press, 1961), pp. 314–24. From postwar uncovering of Japanese records MacArthur correctly understood that the major Japanese motive for attacking the Philippines was to prevent completion of his defense plan and to cut off the American build-up of late 1941 (*Reminiscences,* pp. 111–12).

Army General Staff, estimated that they could conquer the Philippines in fifty days. The whole southern area, including the oil fields, should be Japanese in five months, unless Soviet Russia or the American fleet intervened in significant force.[12] To prevent the latter contingency, Japan planned to surprise and paralyze the main American fleet at Pearl Harbor. On November 13–15, Army, Navy, and Air commanders met in southern Honshu to complete plans for invading the Philippines.[13]

In Manila, Manuel Quezon was harried and frustrated. He feared a war coming, a war which he had not made and could not avoid. He sought to have applied to purposes of defense the accumulated revenue from the processing tax on Philippine sugar, an estimated fifty-two million dollars. High Commissioner Francis Sayre balked. As a Christian optimist, Sayre was slow to recognize the increasing probability of war; he thought Quezon had previously misused the coconut oil excise fund, and as a democratic pedagogue he intended to teach Quezon a lesson.

Quezon boiled over: if Roosevelt could get seven billion dollars from Congress to help England, Greece, and China, why not some for defense of the Philippines? He threatened to bypass Sayre and beg the money directly from Roosevelt, or even, lest "my people die like rats . . . to steal it. . . . My God, Mr. Commissioner, I want you to help me get that money. . . . That is your duty." Sayre gave in, but Congress did not take the necessary action until it was too late.[14]

Quezon and Sayre also quarreled over responsibility for civil defense and the protection of noncombatants. Sayre in April had resisted the creation of the Civilian Emergency Administration as "dictatorial," but Roosevelt supported Quezon.[15] From July onward, according to Admiral Hart, Sayre grew more alert to the emergency.[16] In the end Sayre was complaining that his own office lacked sufficient funds, personnel, and jurisdiction for the job of civil de-

12. Japanese Monog No. 150, p. 30.
13. Morton, *Fall of the Philippines,* p. 57.
14. Quezon, undated draft of letter to Sayre, 1941 (Q); Sayre, *Glad Adventure,* p. 216–17; Grunder and Livezey, *Philippines and U.S.,* pp. 237–38.
15. Quezon to Sayre, 7 Apr 41, Sayre to Ickes, 9 Apr, Franklin D. Roosevelt to Sayre, 12 Apr, Sayre "Memo of Interview [with Quezon]," 16 Apr (HC).
16. Hart, "Narrative," pp. 16–17.

fense, and he blamed Quezon and the government of the Commonwealth for not doing enough.[17] Quezon in turn blamed Philippine
civil liberties groups and "American imperialists in the Philippines
as represented by the *Bulletin*" for hamstringing him, causing "the
greatest defeat and humiliation that I have received in my public
life." On November 28, he admitted that his country was unprepared
for war, lacking sufficient fuel, food and air raid shelters: "if . . .
our people die here, unprotected, by the bombs, those men who have
stopped me from doing what I should have done ought to be hanged
—every one of them on the lamp post." [18]

The armed forces were better coordinated than the civilian juris-
dictions, but still were rent by differences of strategic emphasis and
expectation. On November 26, Sayre called a meeting with Mac-
Arthur and Hart. The Hull-Nomura conversation in Washington had
reached a critical impasse; the War Department had sent a "final
alert," and the Navy a "war warning" to their commands in Hawaii
and the Philippines. The three top American authorities in the Philippines studied the messages together.

"One of the three," Hart recalled later, "expressed greater optimism than did the other two." That one was MacArthur, whom
Sayre remembered as pacing "back and forth, . . . smoking a black
cigar and assuring Admiral Hart and myself . . . that the existing
alignment and movement of Japanese troops convinced him that
there would be no Japanese attack before the spring. Admiral Hart
felt otherwise." [19] The day before, in fact, a conference of flag officers
had met aboard Vice Admiral Takahashi's flagship *Ashigara*, off
Formosa. They discussed the invasion of the Philippines, for which
all was prepared. And on the same day as the meeting of Sayre, Mac-
Arthur, and Hart, November 26, a task force put out from Japan.
Its mission, unless recalled, was to disable the American fleet at Pearl
Harbor.[20]

17. Sayre to Franklin D. Roosevelt, 1 Dec 41 (HC). MacArthur contributes further
information on the controversy over civil defense in his *Reminiscences*, pp. 110–11.
18. "Speech of His Excellency the President at the University of the Philippines on
the Occasion of the Celebration of National Heroes Day," 28 Nov 41 (HC). Quezon
later summarized his differences with Sayre over this issue, going back to the summer
of 1940, in a letter to Frederic S. Marquardt, draft with revisions, 13 May 43 (Q).
19. Morison, p. 155; Stimson diary, 27 Nov 41 (HLS); Hart, "Narrative," p. 30;
Sayre, p. 221.
20. Morison, p. 156; Butow, p. 340.

The Philippine public, until mid-November of 1941, was worked up over the national elections, and their democratic ferment pleased Carlos Romulo. Returning to Manila after covering East and Southeast Asia, the ace reporter felt like "the man in the legend who traveled the wide earth in search of the golden egg only to find it in his garden." Nationalist movements elsewhere were "cowed" and the people "crushed" by European colonialism; in Indo-China, the very word nationalism was taboo. The Filipinos might be unduly concerned with domestic politics on the eve of war (as Admiral Hart thought), but elsewhere in that region of the world undue restraints upon political expression had bred a far worse atmosphere. British policemen in Hong Kong clubbed their way through a crowd of Chinese at an inaugural ceremony. "Mellican not like Blitess," a rickshaw boy told Romulo. "Mellican give! Damn Blitess!"

Although he warned them of Japanese harshness and atrocities, Romulo found many Burmese and Javanese leaders looking forward to an invasion and expecting to collaborate. Both Queen Wilhelmina and Prime Minister Churchill had declared that the Atlantic Charter did not apply to them. "With the exception of America," an Indonesian said, "all the [Western] nations in the Far East are here to exploit us. That exploitation will not end until one of our own colored peoples assumes leadership. It is suicide for us to oppose the leadership of Japan."

Only in Thailand did Romulo find some of the lineaments of freedom "more boldly etched" than at home, yet Thailand was so thoroughly infiltrated, subverted, and intimidated by the Japanese that Romulo predicted, correctly, mere token resistance when an invasion should come. The Japanese were already in control of Indo-China. In Chungking, Chiang Kai-shek warned Romulo, "You had better prepare in the Philippines. You are going to be the next victims." [21]

"The Japanese Empire," Premier Tojo told the imperial conference of December 1, "is now on the threshold of progress or collapse." The conference sanctioned with ceremony decisions already taken: the striking forces and invasion fleets were not to be recalled, but were to proceed with their several missions. To weaken the Filipino

21. Romulo articles in Philippines *Herald*, 1, 7, 8, 10, 11, 17, 20, 30 Oct, 11 Nov 41; Romulo, *I Saw the Fall of the Philippines* (Garden City, Doubleday, 1943), pp. 6, 11, 12, 20–22. The last two words of the Chinese coolie are censored in Romulo's book; I have supplied them from the implication of the text.

will to fight, and also to give the United States less cause to fight for the Philippines, the Quezon regime was to be kept in power.

Quezon was meanwhile expecting the Japanese consul, Kihara Jitaro, back in Manila from his month-long visit to Tokyo. The Foreign Office cabled a message for Quezon: "Kihara has . . . caught a cold . . . and is resting . . . unlikely to return . . . as scheduled." [22] Before Kihara the Air Force came.

"I could not hold back the tears of joy I felt," a Japanese pilot told a reporter shortly after the first landing in the Philippines. "We had gone through intensive training for a long period of time in preparation for this battle, and now we have dealt a spectacular blow." [23]

At Pearl on December 7, Japanese pilots had crippled the Pacific Fleet. Even with the Philippines thus warned, the Japanese succeeded in destroying most of the American air power in the Philippines on the ground at Clark Field. On December 11, they badly damaged the naval base at Cavite, and Hart, exposed from the air, decided to withdraw his surface fleet. He left twenty-nine submarines behind to assist MacArthur, who was determined to meet the enemy "at the beaches, where they are most vulnerable."

Neither Hart's subs nor MacArthur's troops met the enemy effectively. On December 22, eighty-five Japanese transports, without air cover, landed 43,000 men at Lingayen. In seventeen days they carried out nine successful amphibious operations in the Philippines, and in this, the biggest landing, they lost only one ship. At one place on the Lingayen coast the Philippine Army stoutly resisted the invader, but almost everywhere else the Filipino reservists broke and fled.[24] A day and a half after the landing, MacArthur notified all force commanders that "WPO-3 is in effect" [25]—the ancient ORANGE plan he had once described as "stereotyped" and "defeatist."

22. Japanese Monog No. 152, p. 41; Butow, pp. 343–48, 359–63; For Min Togo to Cons Gen Niirō, 2 Dec 41, Gaimushō, S461, p. 1355.
23. International Military Tribunal Far East, prosecution exhibit 809, Sec II, pt 26.
24. Morison, pp. 164–83; Morton, pp. 122–44. MacArthur treats Clark Field briefly (*Reminiscences,* pp. 117, 120). He apparently always believed that the Japanese had landed "approximately 80,000 combat troops" and had followed them up with "nearly 100,000 replacements" (pp. 123–24, 132). Morton's careful study (p. 216), however, puts the total Japanese strength on Luzon at about one-third the combined figure suggested by MacArthur; many of these were later withdrawn to fight in Java; no Japanese reinforcements arrived in the Philippines until late February and even they eventually totaled only about 22,000.
25. Morton, p. 163.

On December 24, MacArthur had Quezon and Sayre transported to Corregidor with their personal and official families. He ordered his air commander, General Lewis Brereton, to Australia, leaving behind a small number of fighting planes and many airmen, who later became infantrymen. On the same day Hart decided to join his surface forces in the Indies, leaving behind three gunboats and six PTs with the subs and a number of shipless sailors, who, like the planeless airmen, joined the infantry.

On Christmas Day, MacArthur declared Manila an open city. By New Year's Day he had carried off a successful sideslip into Bataan Peninsula, there to delay the Japanese amid the jungles.[26] The "war of relentless attrition," of which he had spoken in 1936, would be attrition of the defender instead of the invader, unless men, planes, and ships reached him in massive quantity.

MacArthur pleaded to Washington strenuously and repeatedly for an Asia-first strategy and for sending the entire air production and resources of the United States to his command. Japan, he said, was isolated from her allies and "completely susceptible to concentrated action." For the whole American war effort, "the Philippine theatre . . . is the locus of victory or defeat."

Despite MacArthur's warning that it was a "fatal mistake," President Roosevelt, Secretary of War Stimson, Chief of Staff Marshall, and General Eisenhower, Chief of the War Plans Division, nevertheless remained Europe-firsters. Concerning reinforcements, however, MacArthur had the sympathetic ear of all of them, especially Stimson. The Secretary and General Marshall influenced the Joint Board to reverse a decision which had rerouted the large *Pensacola* convoy and abandoned the Philippines.[27] Nevertheless, when *Pensacola* reached Australia on December 22, Japanese domination of sea and air made it impossible to move northward to the Philippines.[28]

Winston Churchill, in Washington for the Arcadia Conference, asked Stimson and Eisenhower for a briefing on the Philippines,

26. Morison, pp. 195–98; Morton, pp. 164–238; John Toland, *But Not in Shame: The Six Months after Pearl Harbor* (New York, Random House, 1961), pp. 137–51; MacArthur, *Reminiscences,* pp. 124–26.
27. MacArthur to Marshall, 10 Dec 41, WPD 4544–26; 13 Dec, OPD ExecO; 27 Dec, AGO 381; Stimson diary, 10, 14, 17, 22 Dec 41, 2 Jan 42 (HLS); Morton, p. 153.
28. Morton, p. 154.

which he received in "zipper pajama suit and slippers." Next day, Christmas, Stimson was warned of an apparent decision "to discuss the turning over to the British of our proposed reinforcements for MacArthur"—sacrificing the Philippines to save Singapore. "This astonishing paper" made Stimson "extremely angry"; he called Harry Hopkins to let him know that if such a course were persisted in, "the President would have to take my resignation." Roosevelt immediately called a conference with Stimson, Marshall, Arnold, Knox, King, Stark, and Hopkins present, to repudiate any such intention.[29] Conferences with the British nevertheless clarified the priority of holding Australia and Burma.

Stimson was trying to strike a reasonable course between those not interested in reinforcing the Philippines at all—Churchill, the British staff, and the American Navy—and Douglas MacArthur, who was not interested in forces and supplies going anywhere else. By January 2, even Stimson admitted that while "every possible line is being tried out . . . we shall probably all have to go through the agonizing experience of seeing the doomed garrison gradually pulled down while our preparations are not yet completed." [30]

The very next day, the War Plans Division completed a study of the steps required to relieve the Philippines: to gain naval and air superiority south of the line Malaya–Borneo–Celebes, to extend it northward to Indonesia and finally Mindanao; covered and supported by air and naval forces, to land on Mindanao and secure a base; operating therefrom, to reopen communications and drive north. To accomplish this would call for 750 more planes than were presently available. It would require the transfer to the Pacific of seven to nine capital ships, five to seven carriers, about fifty destroyers, about sixty submarines, and the necessary auxiliary vessels, for all of which the only tenable base would be the wreckage of Pearl Harbor. "Several hundred thousand" additional troops would be necessary, of which America had only 4,600 in Australia and 18,000 in the States ready for early transfer to the Far East. Thus the planners, of whom Eisenhower was chief, concluded that the forces necessary for relief *could not* be delivered on time, and *should not* be diverted from the Atlantic Theater.

Stimson thought the study "very gloomy," worked out "with ruth-

29. Stimson diary, 24, 25 Dec 41, 16 Jan 42 (HLS).
30. Ibid., 2 Jan 42.

less severity and some overstatement," "a bad kind of paper to be lying around the War Department at this time." Neither he nor Marshall countersigned it. "Everybody knows the chances are against our getting relief to him," Stimson said of MacArthur, "but there is no use saying so beforehand." [31] Stimson and Marshall continued to try, and so did many others. Small amounts of food and fuel, ammunition and medicine, filtered through the Japanese blockade, but no warship, no fighter plane, no fighting man, ever reached Luzon.[32]

31. "Relief of the Philippines," 3 Jan 42, WPD 4639–3; Stimson diary, 5 Jan (HLS).
32. Morton, pp. 396–404.

16

Filipino Collaboration with the Japanese

THE WAR was not going to be quick; MacArthur's defense plan had already been discarded; reinforcements had not appeared. Quezon was forced to reckon with a brief period of absentee presidency. He could not know, although he may have feared, that absence would turn into exile, prolonged until his death. Before evacuating to Corregidor, he held cabinet meetings twice a day. He resisted the idea of leaving and even drafted a letter of refusal to MacArthur, which his Secretary of Justice, Jose Laurel, went over. Quezon read it to his cabinet, then gathered reactions, including Laurel's: "What do you think, Secretary? I do not want to go to Corregidor because our people will think I am abandoning them." "I don't think so; they will understand," Laurel answered, and all but one of the many present agreed. Quezon drew Laurel aside afterwards, put an arm about his waist, and asked him to go with him to "The Rock."

The next day, at the final cabinet meeting, Quezon's voice was choked. Only a few could go with him—obviously Osmeña, the Vice-President, and Roxas, who was an aide to MacArthur. Overnight, however, Quezon had changed his mind about Laurel and decided to take Jose Abad Santos, the Chief Justice, instead. He knew of Laurel's friendship with the Japanese and thought he could thereby help protect the Filipinos. Another who must stay was Jorge Vargas, who knew the daily mechanics of government most intimately; Quezon designated him "Mayor of Greater Manila."

Quezon then made all present promise not to reveal what he was next going to say. Pointing out Laurel and Vargas, he ordered, "You two will . . . deal with the Japanese."

Laurel burst into tears: Corregidor, please; if not, then permission to retire with his family to Batangas province. Quezon did not relent. Laurel came to his lawyerly senses: what were they to do then, and what should they not do? Quezon asked Vargas to ask MacArthur for an opinion on that question, which opinion Quezon reported to Laurel later, in the presence of several others. "Do what you think necessary," the General had said, except one thing—take no oath of allegiance to the Japanese. "If you do, when we come back, we'll shoot you."

Quezon then left for the bay, and while his launch was being loaded, spoke eloquently to those on the dock of his hatred of going, his duty to go. He walked slowly with Vargas to the float and the two shook hands. Quezon's boat speeded him away and Vargas, watching, said a little bitterly, "Well, some of us have to stay. I've got more to do now than I know how." [1]

On January 1, 1942, Japanese forces moved into Manila. General Homma's Chief of Staff, Maeda Masami, and his officers began to get in touch with Filipino leaders so that the New Order might begin at once. On January 5, Jose Yulo called together several men, at his home on Peñafrancia Street, to exchange impressions about the invaders. They pondered what might be "the most dignified and patriotic attitude" to adopt under the circumstances and, although they adjourned inconclusively, it was not without "emphatic, repeated and vehement protestations of loyalty and attachment to the President of the Commonwealth, Hon. Manuel L. Quezon." [2]

1. Author's interview with Laurel, 21 Oct 58; Jose P. Laurel, *War Memoirs of Dr. Jose P. Laurel* (Manila, Laurel Foundation, 1962), pp. 3–6; John Toland, based on an interview with Osmeña, in *But Not in Shame* (New York, Random House, 1961), pp. 137–38, and Toland to author, 25 July 64; Royal Arch Gunnison. "The Filipinos Fight On," *Colliers*, 1 July 44, pp. 46, 54–55, based on reportorial coverage of Quezon and conversation with Vargas; Manuel Roxas, "Brief Summary of the Activities of Manuel Roxas, Brigadier General, Philippine Army Reserve, and Presently President of the Philippine Senate," 29 Sept 45 (Mauro Garcia Collection, Manila). Gen Basilio Valdez, in an interview with the author, 29 Aug 64, confirmed the account of the cabinet meeting essentially as above, but said he had no knowledge of any consultation with Gen MacArthur.
2. "Actas de las Reuniones de Prominentes Filipinos Celebradas en la Residencia

Maeda continued, meanwhile, to sound out individual politicians in the hope of finding some who would cooperate with him. During the first several days he had important conversations with Paredes, Recto, Vargas, Aquino, and Laurel. In each case he opened with the request for help in reestablishing peace and order in greater Manila, in the curbing of looting, in bringing in harvests of rice, and in all manner of measures encouraging and facilitating a return to normality.

To that much no one objected; but Maeda wanted more. To Paredes, for instance, he suggested that the Filipino leaders persuade their people to "abandon military resistance to the Japanese, since nearly all the Philippines had been taken by them and could not be recovered by the Americans." Furthermore, "the Filipinos ought to form part of the co-prosperity of the New Order proclaimed by the Japanese Empire, and ought to form a committee charged with organization of a National Government in cooperation with the Military Government."

There Paredes balked. As to peace and order, rice and normality, he and the others "were disposed to cooperate in all that was possible." But, Paredes said, President Quezon was chief of the nation: "All the Filipino leaders followed him, and what he said was what was done: it would be better to deal with him." General Maeda answered, "I am not interested in President Quezon, for he has fled from Manila." He alleged that Americans had treated the Filipinos like slaves and now were tying the legs of Filipino soldiers to prevent them from retreating from the line of fire.[3]

In the days that followed, the initial six who met at Yulo's house added a subsequent seven, and then more, until they numbered thirty men. Mindful of Quezon's advice, and of his presence across the bay on The Rock, most of them preferred if possible to persuade the Japanese to recognize the Commonwealth government. They did not wish to take an oath of loyalty to the invaders; neither did they wish responsibility for pacifying the provinces. Only on one condition, Paredes implied, might he be willing to do the latter: if the Japanese would give them a republic, then they might go into the

---

del Ex-Speaker Jose Yulo en la Calle Peñafrancia No. 353, Distrito de Paco, Ciudad de Manila, Filipinas," 5 Jan 42 (Mauro Garcia Collection), hereafter cited as Peñafrancia Conferences.

3. Peñafrancia Conferences, 6 Jan 42.

field and persuade their countrymen, "who would put down their arms only in order to have their own government."

Aquino seconded the idea, but Jorge Bocobo thought it unwise to play into the Japanese hands for propaganda purposes and to "notify the whole world that the Filipinos had abandoned their loyalty to the United States of America." Rafael Alunan backed up Bocobo, criticizing the idea of a puppet republic in the style of Nanking; better to leave the whole thing in Japanese hands, "so as not to be marked as traitors." Bocobo's idea was to "limit our collaboration to works of an Emergency Civil Administration."

Between the Paredes-Aquino idea and that of Bocobo-Alunan, Jose Yulo fashioned a compromise: to request Japanese recognition of the Commonwealth government, with elections of Provisional President and Vice-President in the absence of the regular officers and their incapacity to carry out their duties. Despite Laurel's legal objections, the meeting expressed itself as behind Yulo's suggestion, bearing in mind that the Japanese might use force against them, or the population, if they did not take some course of submission.[4]

Maeda, however, would have nothing to do with the Commonwealth, in fact or name. Quezon remained a rallying point for fighting the Japanese forces; many fine young Japanese had died at Filipino hands as a result. The Commonwealth, which owed its creation to American sovereignty, vanished, so far as he was concerned, with the disappearance of American sovereignty in the Philippines.[5] To Jose Laurel and others, Maeda made it clear that there remained only two genuine alternatives: "a government of iron backed by military force" and a "gobierno-muñeco"—puppet government. The subject of a republic might be raised in future conversations, but now the Japanese would prefer some "initiative" from the Filipinos toward a limited government, rather than "obliging" them to form a government "according to the whims" of the military administration.[6]

A group of strongly pro-Japanese Filipinos, including Aquino and Leon Guinto, had already met separately to plan civilian leadership under the occupation. The Japanese Army, unknown to General Ricarte, had a long-standing plan to make him president and had

4. Ibid., 7 Jan 42.
5. Ibid., 8 Jan 42.
6. Ibid., 9 Jan 42.

flown him to Manila for that purpose. Benigno Aquino wanted the job, however, and the meeting split between the two candidates.[7]

The Peñafrancia group meanwhile tried to get in touch with Quezon on Corregidor and failed. If they continued to resist creation of a puppet government, the Japanese might give the opportunity to persons inclined to be "mercenary, irresponsible and unscrupulous." Thus intimidated, they moved down a twisting path of legalistic debate toward collaboration. While the Japanese Army was too busy fighting to care, a group of its civilian advisers chose Jorge Vargas over both Ricarte and Aquino as the key puppet.[8]

On Bataan, the combined Filipino-American forces actually outnumbered the Japanese attackers, but were already suffering grave shortages of food and clothing, medicine and shelter. General Homma still hoped for victory on his fifty-day schedule, although his superiors transferred a full division of his forces to fight in Java. Controlling the sea and the air, the Japanese bombed and blockaded the defenders and pressed them with infantry. On January 23, MacArthur reported to Marshall his impending retreat from the first line of defense to his second and last: "All maneuvering possibilities will cease. I intend to fight it out to complete destruction."

That very day, Filipino politicians officially constituted themselves as the provisional Council of State to carry out the orders of the Japanese Military Administration. Gathered together in the former residence of the high commissioner, they drank, with the Japanese, toasts to the cooperation of their two peoples.[9] With the morning's ink and the afternoon's champagne, the leaders in Manila limited their own possibilities of maneuver and moved a step closer to complete submission.

The members of the newly established Executive Commission of the Council of State could tell themselves that Tojo's government had promised "the honor of independence" as an eventual reward for

7. Author's interview with Col Ōta Kaneshirō, aide to Gen Ricarte, 20 Sept 58. Ōta says the meeting took place on Jan 6 or 7.
8. Quezon, *The Good Fight*, pp. 290–92; Peñafrancia Conferences, 10, 12 Jan 42; Ōta interview.
9. MacArthur to Marshall, 23 Jan 42, AG381 (11–27–41 Sec 1); Peñafrancia Conferences, 23 Jan 42.

cooperation.[10] Vargas, their chairman, broadcast the more sensible justification that "our crops have to be harvested and our fields cultivated, our roads and bridges reconstructed, . . . gainful occupations . . . resumed and . . . industry rehabilitated. These we cannot accomplish under a reign of terrorism and lawlessness. . . . The sooner we repair the ravages of war . . . the less injury we will suffer in the end." [11]

Many Philippine citizens were glad that old Commonwealth officials were taking over, rather than letting the Japanese tender power to others who might wield it for profit and political vengeance.[12] To MacArthur, Quezon defended his old associates. They were neither quislings nor traitors but "virtually prisoners of the enemy. . . . They are victims of the adverse fortunes of war, and I am sure they had no choice." Of MacArthur Quezon then asked "whether any government has the right to demand loyalty from its citizens beyond its willingness or ability to render actual protection." [13]

On Corregidor, as rations waned and casualties mounted, everyone developed his own means of keeping up the appearance of normality. Sergio Osmeña saved the wisp of napkin provided at meals and used it to shine his shoes. Mrs. Quezon set up an oratory with candles in a corner of the tunnel. Five-year-old Arthur MacArthur marched about singing "The Battle Hymn of the Republic," his Chinese nurse following behind. Arthur's father surveyed the situation outside with heroic detachment; when bombs fell or shells came over, he remained calmly standing, while others dropped flat.[14]

MacArthur had once said of Marshal Petain that he "should have cut off his hand" rather than sign a surrender to the Germans. Washington was now considering how to evacuate him from the Philippine rout in order to lead a Pacific rally, but his old friend

10. For Min, speech to Diet, 20 Jan 42, reported by Grew, at sea, undated, *For Rel, 1942, 1,* 787.
11. "Address by Sec. Jorge B. Vargas over Station KZRH, Manila, 1–31–42, as Chairman of the Philippine Executive Commission" (Q).
12. Marcial P. Lichauco, *Dear Mother Putnam* (Manila), p. 19.
13. MacArthur to Adj Gen, 28 Jan 42, *For Rel, 1942, 1,* 888–89; also quoted in part, with President Roosevelt's reply, in MacArthur, *Reminiscences,* pp. 136–37.
14. Romulo, *I See the Philippines Rise* (Garden City, Doubleday, 1946), p. 23; Sayre, *Glad Adventure,* pp. 232, 239; MacArthur, *Reminiscences,* pp. 131–32.

Pat Hurley warned that it must be arranged so as not to compromise "his honor and his record as a soldier." [15]

When Marshall first cautiously raised the question with him, Mac-Arthur only repeated, more urgently, his earlier requests for a basic revision of combined strategy. His advice was for the United States to take advantage of the fact that the Japanese forces were spread out over 2,000 miles of ocean, by launching a great sea thrust. There was no need to fear enemy bomber strength, practically all of which was engaged on the southern front. If his advice were not followed, MacArthur "unhesitatingly predicted" that "the war will be indefinitely prolonged and its final outcome will be jeopardized." Having requested that his views be presented to the "highest authority," MacArthur concluded that "from my present point of vantage I can see the whole strategy of the Pacific perhaps clearer than anyone else."

In his reply Marshall offered some considerations which Mac-Arthur had perhaps not clearly seen. By the seizure of Guam and Wake, and by building up heavy air protective forces there and in the Marshalls and Gilberts, the Japanese had provided themselves with naval flank security. By their success at Pearl, the Japanese had eliminated "virtually the entire heavy striking elements of the Pacific Fleet"; "unannounced losses in aircraft carriers" made it impossible to launch a general westward offensive from Hawaii, or to oppose Japanese aggression other than from air bases remaining in Allied possession in northern Australia and the Netherlands East Indies.

Marshall concluded with courteous echoes to certain MacArthur themes—building all strength possible in the Pacific, and hoping that Russia would enter the fight against Japan—but his message stripped away the rhetoric of valor to emphasize the grave fact: given a Europe-first strategy and early disabilities in the Pacific, MacArthur could expect no imminent and massive assistance of the kind he sought.[16]

Japanese forces in the Philippines were meanwhile weakening. On February 8, Homma and his staff, although they had already used up the fifty days allotted for conquest, decided to discontinue

15. Marquardt, *Before Bataan*, p. 243; Morton, *The Fall of the Philippines*, p. 353.
16. MacArthur to Marshall, 4 Feb 42, Marshall to MacArthur, 8 Feb, CofS Phil Situation File.

operations and to ask Imperial General Headquarters, in Tokyo, for reinforcements. Before they could launch a major attack against MacArthur's forces on Bataan, they must rest, reorganize, tighten their blockade, and accrue vastly more men and arms.[17]

Such news, had he any way of learning it, might have given Quezon some grim hope. Instead he was hearing "Europe-first" broadcasts from the United States, by President Roosevelt, Secretary of the Navy Frank Knox, and others. One mentioned thousands of aircraft destined for Europe; Quezon blew up. "Where are the planes this *sinverguenza* is boasting of? *Que demonio*—how typically American to writhe in anguish at the fate of a distant cousin while a daughter is being raped in the back room!"[18]

Quezon's morale sagged when, on February 6, General Aguinaldo broadcast an appeal to MacArthur to yield to greatly superior force. Quezon longed to return to Manila and to affect the situation there by any means. He dictated a sharp complaint to President Roosevelt at being "abandoned" and proclaimed it "my duty as well as my right to cease fighting." General MacArthur warned Quezon, in effect, that the Japanese would like to have him as a puppet, and talked him out of sending the message.[19] But the mood flared up two days later, stronger still.[20]

Anxious and restless, Quezon plunged again into his plan for returning to Manila. He called in his "war cabinet." He wanted to ask Roosevelt's permission to issue a manifesto requesting immediate,

17. Morton, p. 347. MacArthur came wishfully to believe that Homma "was on the point of giving up the effort to overwhelm us and substitute a plan to bypass the islands" and that "if only help could have reached the Philippines, even in small form . . . the end could not have failed to be a success" (*Reminiscences*, p. 133).
18. Charles A. Willoughby and John Chamberlain, *MacArthur: 1941–1951* (New York, McGraw-Hill, 1954), pp. 55–56; see also, ibid., p. 37, and MacArthur, *Reminiscences*, p. 130.
19. Quezon to Franklin D. Roosevelt, 6 Feb 42 (not sent) (Q); Quezon, *The Good Fight*, pp. 265–68. MacArthur, *Reminiscences*, pp. 134–35, discusses Aguinaldo's broadcast, but not its effect on Quezon.
20. Toland (*But Not in Shame*, pp. 210–12) pictures as the cause of Quezon's flare-up the arrival on Corregidor of Benigno Aquino's son, Antonio. Young Aquino had swum from Bataan to report antagonism at the front between Filipinos and Americans, and the fact that the former were receiving much less rations. Aquino indeed made that brave swim, and his report indeed disturbed Quezon. But in an interview with the author, 29 Aug 64, Aquino could not establish the exact date of his swim, except that it was early February. Aquino's written notes (which Toland generously lent the author) contain internal evidence suggesting that the swim might have taken place *after* Quezon's neutralization proposal.

absolute, and complete independence, with the entire demobiliza-
tion, evacuation, and neutralization of the Philippines to follow. Both
Roxas and Osmeña opposed the idea: Americans would misunder-
stand it, Japanese would not take it seriously, and the Filipino people
themselves might not sanction it. Quezon tried to answer back, and
was racked with coughing. His "cabinet" finally approved the proposal unanimously so as not to weaken him.[21]

Roxas afterward told Carlos Romulo about the meeting. Both
agreed that it was an understandable decision for Quezon, "with his
frail body hungering for the food and physical comforts of Malacañan
Palace just across the bay," but Roxas thought it wrong to cease
fighting and deal with the Japanese. Osmeña was even more upset;
he told Romulo to be ready to leave with him by submarine for the
United States to set up a government in exile. "Quezon thinks the
patriotic thing to do is to give up," he said, ". . . but I think the
opposite."

Romulo, in a "Voice of Freedom" broadcast to Bataan, implicitly
expressed his own reaction to the idea with a particularly fervent
message. Quezon, annoyed, sent for him. Coughing, nervous, "a sick
man ridden with guilt" over Filipino deaths, he cross-examined
Romulo in an effort to hear support for his idea. "I tell you our
. . . country is being destroyed. Do you expect me to continue this
sacrifice? The fight between the United States and Japan is not our
fight. I want to go back . . . and try to protect . . . our own
people, Romulo, not America."

"But this is against everything you said before the war."

"Of course it is." Quezon's cheeks were red with high spots of
fever and his voice occasionally broke. "We are dying . . . because
we are not getting protection from those who promised us protection.
. . . We must try to save ourselves and to hell with America." Abad
Santos was helping him write a telegram: "I want President Roosevelt to know how I feel, as the leader of boys without arms or defenses." [22]

Quezon's telegram to Roosevelt asked him to make public Quezon's
plea for an immediate armistice. There should follow consultations
in Manila—Japanese and Americans, with Quezon—upon a series of

21. Osmeña to the author, 10 Oct 58; Lichauco, *Dear Mother Putnam*, p. 46, concerning Roxas; Romulo, *I Walked with Heroes*, p. 218; Toland, p. 213. Gen Basilio
Valdez, MS speech, 18 Aug 64, differs in details but agrees in essentials.
22. Romulo, *Heroes*, pp. 219–22.

further proposals: that the United States should immediately grant, and the Japanese recognize, the complete and absolute independence of the Philippines; that the Philippines be at once neutralized and given tariff autonomy and as soon as possible be demilitarized.

High Commissioner Sayre conditionally supported the message, if reinforcements were not forthcoming in time to avail. General MacArthur took the military grounds that it was a "temporizing plan": if the Japanese accepted it, America would secure a delay "at least equal" to a continued battle effort which "at any time" faced "complete destruction." If the Japanese rejected it, "it would psychologically strengthen our hold because of their Prime Minister's public statement offering independence."

In forwarding the plan, MacArthur reported among the Filipinos a "temper . . . of almost violent resentment against the United States" and a belief that "they have been betrayed in favor of others." [23] Very possibly he shared some of that temper against Washington. Quezon's plan, with a covering message from himself, may have seemed to General MacArthur like an opportunity to shock Roosevelt's administration into action on the Philippines. The two messages were so anguished that no American official could fail to be moved. And if Washington could not or would not reinforce the Philippines, Quezon's plan may also have seemed to offer a means

23. Quezon to Roosevelt, contained in MacArthur to Marshall, 8 Feb 42, Stimson diary, interleaf (HLS); also appearing in For Rel, 1942, 1, 894–96, and in CofS Phil Sit File. MacArthur says that he "remonstrated with Quezon as best I could against the proposals involved, and said bluntly that I would not endorse them, that there was not the slightest chance of approval by either the United States or Japan. Quezon listened patiently and then revealed his true purpose in sending the message. He said he fully realized that his plan would not be accepted by either country and that it was entirely impractical. But that he felt that only something of an explosive nature could shock Washington into a realization of the importance of the Far East. . . . He explained that he did not expect me to approve his suggestions, but asked that I present the military situation in a purely professional light. This I did, and asked Washington to instruct me" (Reminiscences, pp. 138–39). MacArthur's account of Quezon's reasoning is extremely improbable in view of Quezon's own admission in his autobiography that he was quite earnest in his willingness to negotiate. Three other Filipinos testify to the same point, and to the depth of Quezon's anxiety. Romulo (in his autobiography), Roxas (to Lichauco), and Osmeña (to Eyre; see note 27 below). MacArthur's account of his own reasoning may, in the large, be accepted. But his message to Marshall that accompanied Quezon's to Roosevelt was in no wise the "blunt refusal to endorse" that MacArthur alleges was his stand in conversation with Quezon. If it did not go "more than half way" in support of Quezon, as Stimson felt upon reading, it went a long way at least.

of saving MacArthur's reputation as a soldier. Surrender was a politician's job, not a general's, and here was a politician offering to cease fighting. MacArthur was willing to battle, if necessary, to "complete destruction," including his own; but it was worth exploring a plan which might still salvage his army, his family, and his sacred honor.

As he read the first part of Quezon's decoded message, Henry Stimson thought, "I don't blame him, although his telegram brought forward a number of alleged instances of failure to help on our part which were not true." He spent an hour and a half with Marshall discussing the "ghastly" situation, and then went back to his estate and "had a sharp rattling game of deck tennis." [24]

The next day, Stimson found the completely decoded message "most disappointing, . . . wholly unreal, . . . taking no account of what the war was for or what the well known characteristics of Japan towards conquered people were." "Worse than that" was MacArthur's "very somber picture of the Army's situation" and his going "more than half way towards supporting Quezon's position."

Marshall and Eisenhower had begun drafting a reply, which they put on a different plane after hearing Stimson's opinions. When they took Quezon's message to the White House that morning, Roosevelt asked Marshall what they proposed to do about it. Marshall, who had fully adopted Stimson's reasoning, yielded to the Secretary. Stimson rose from his seat and gave his views, "standing as if before the court." The President listened very attentively and said that he agreed. That afternoon at the White House, Admirals King and Stark joined them. "The President was very quick and helpful in his suggestions"; by four o'clock all was ironed out, and Stimson, after having a massage, went home to dinner.[25]

The reply went to MacArthur in two parts. The first, written by Eisenhower and Marshall, was for MacArthur's own eyes; the second, written by Stimson, was to be passed on to Quezon; both were signed "Franklin D. Roosevelt." The first emphatically refused Quezon's proposal and, in complete understanding of MacArthur's military predicament, requested him to make his "resistance as effective as circumstances will permit and as prolonged as humanly possible."

The second message, to Quezon, seized upon the latter's reference

24. Stimson diary, 8 Feb 42 (HLS).
25. Ibid., 9 Feb 42.

to Tojo's promise of independence: "I have only to refer you to the present condition of Korea, Manchukuo, North China, Indo-China, and . . . other countries . . . to point out the hollow duplicity of such an announcement. The present sufferings of the Filipino people, cruel as they may be, are infinitely less than the sufferings and permanent enslavement which will inevitably follow acceptance of Japanese promises."

As for the American promise of independence to the Filipinos, implicit in forty years' conduct and explicit in the Tydings-McDuffie Act, "the honor of the United States is pledged to its fulfillment . . . regardless of its cost." "So long as the flag of the United States flies on Filipino soil as a pledge of our duty to your people, it will be defended by our own men to the death. Whatever happens to the present American garrison, we shall not relax our efforts until the forces which we are now marshaling outside the Philippine Islands return . . . and drive the last remnant of the invaders from your soil."

Stimson felt that a message "consigning . . . a brave garrison to a fight to the finish" might have been easy for "noble Romans" to send, but for "ordinary Americans" it was extremely difficult. Later he would say: "To give the order was a matter of duty, but it was in its loyal execution that the true glory would be found." [26]

At first the reply from Washington infuriated Quezon. He rose from his wheelchair and demanded of an invisible audience: "Who is in better position, Roosevelt or myself, to judge what is best for my people?" Then he dictated his resignation. In cabinet meeting Osmeña failed to persuade Quezon to reconsider. But as Osmeña was on his way to the latrine early the next morning, Quezon awoke with a coughing spell and called him in. They reminisced. Osmeña then argued that Quezon should beware making a mistake that might brand him in history as a coward and traitor. He also referred to the safety of Quezon's family and alluded to the many instances of rape reported of Japanese soldiers. Quezon replied, "Compadre, perhaps you are right. I shall think it over." [27]

26. Roosevelt to MacArthur, and Roosevelt to Quezon, 9 Feb 42, Stimson diary, interleaf (HLS); also appearing in *For Rel, 1942, 1,* 897–98, in CofS Phil Sit File, and in Stimson and Bundy, *On Active Service,* p. 404.

27. James K. Eyre, Jr, *The Roosevelt-MacArthur Conflict* (Chambersburg, Pa., The Craft Press, 1950), pp. 39–42; see also pp. 79–85. Eyre's book is marred by errors in detail and by extravagant deductions, but the factual account of this incident rings true. Eyre served on Osmeña's personal staff at the end of the war.

When Quezon thought about it, he saw Roosevelt's message in a different light. Much later he wrote that "when I realized [Roosevelt] was big enough to '. . . place the burden of the defense of my country upon the sacrifice and heroism of his own people alone, I swore to myself and to the God of my ancestors that as long as I lived I would stand by America regardless of the consequences to my people and to myself. We could not in decency be less generous or less determined than President Roosevelt."' At the time, Romulo learned that the crisis was over when he met Osmeña sniffing the air —the salt and cordite—on top of The Rock. Osmeña said gravely, "I believe our President has changed his mind." Quezon, indeed, replied firmly to Washington and never thereafter considered surrender.[28]

MacArthur, anxious to repair any suspicion that his own resolve was faltering, wired that he had not "the slightest intention in the world of surrendering the Filipino elements of my command." His plans consisted in "fighting my present battle position in Bataan to destruction and then holding Corregidor in a similar manner." He and his family would "share the fate of the garrison." Soon he resumed his pleas for a reversal of strategy, for a massive American effort to destroy Japan's "sensitive" lines of communication, and to bring Russia into the Pacific war.[29]

Washington ignored MacArthur's rash global strategy just as MacArthur refused the rash local strategy of some of his officers who wished now to counterattack and break out of Bataan. Homma thought that in late February, Philippine-American troops could have "walked" to Manila "without encountering much resistance on our part." The Japanese were reduced to about 3,000 effectives, while MacArthur's effectives were still probably at least five times that number. The recapture of Manila, however, would have been followed by another retreat to Bataan, with depleted human and material resources. The whole effort would have endangered MacArthur's primary mission, which was to defend Manila Bay as long as possible from his position on Bataan.[30]

28. Quezon, *The Good Fight*, pp. 275–76; Romulo, *Heroes*, p. 223; Quezon to Roosevelt contained in MacArthur to Marshall, *For Rel, 1942, 1*, 900.
29. MacArthur to Adj Gen, for Roosevelt, 11 Feb 42; Stimson diary, interleaf (HLS); MacArthur to Marshall, 16 Feb, CofS Phil Sit File.
30. Morton, pp. 350–52. Morton gives no exact figure on American effectives at this time; I have made a conservative estimate from various indications in his text.

On February 25, the first Japanese reinforcements reached Homma. In the lull before their arrival, in temporary but considerable military jeopardy, the Japanese High Command resumed its pressure on the political leaders in Manila. They posed a problem which the small Executive Commission thought too serious to handle by itself. It decided to put the matter before the thirty or so members of the Council of State, a larger, looser body which was convoked less to make decisions than to share responsibility for them. In Malacañan on February 18, Chairman Vargas read to the Council a telegram that the Commander-in-Chief of the Japanese forces wished the Executive Commission to send. The telegram asked President Roosevelt, on behalf of the Filipino people, to call a halt to hostilities and thus avoid the further sacrifice of Filipino lives in a useless and unequal battle, in which they could not expect reinforcement. "Such being the proposition," Vargas said, "ought any telegram be sent?" [31]

If the American forces across the bay fought on, they nevertheless lived bitterly with the feeling of being abandoned. The Filipino politicians, like other informed countrymen, not only felt abandoned but felt that they had been dragged into a fight not of their own making. Why continue the battle? What had the brown man to gain by fighting for the white man, who was rapidly losing prestige in the Orient? Manila had fallen six weeks past, and Singapore three days before.

Some were in favor of sending the telegram, tempted by the fatalism of the subjugated; Manila, after all, had seen a series of conquerors. New ambitions tempted others: Since formation of the puppet government, a number of men had begun to envision power inaccessible to them under the Quezon regime and to anticipate influence through Japanese sponsorship which they had never had under the Americans.

Whatever the inner circle of the Executive Commission might feel, the psychology of compliance had not yet pervaded the outer circle of the Council of State. The eighteen members of the council who expressed opinions broke roughly into four groups: three ambiguously cooperative, three with special opinions, five cautiously op-

31. "Acta de la Sesion del Consejo de Estado Filipino Celebrado el Dia Miercoles, Diez y Ocho de Fevrero de Mil Novecientos Cuarenta y Dos en el Salon del Consejo de Estado, Malacañan, Ciudad de Manila, Filipinas" (Mauro Garcia Collection). Hereafter referred to as "Minutes of the Council of State."

posed, and seven strongly opposed. No one came out clearly in favor of the idea.

Amando Avanceña went so far as to suggest a telegram "mentioning the issues of the war, and appealing to the heart of President Roosevelt in order to stop the war here," and two followed him. But the largest group came out against it for various reasons: "I doubt if sending the telegram at this time would produce any effect" (Osias); "It is outside the jurisdiction of the Executive Commission" (Melicio Arranz); "I don't like the idea" (Quirino). Dominador Tan put forth a common view: "Already our people call us traitors, and if we don't keep the confidence of the people, we will presently be of use to nobody."

Between those who shared the opposite opinions of Avanceña and Tan were several who followed the artful mediator, Jose Yulo: "I believe that we ought to be more practical in this question. Our people will feel us to be traitors and if we send the telegram it is possible that they'll kill us. If, however, in sending the telegram we follow a positive design, or we can influence President Roosevelt toward reestablishing peace, then we could send it; but if it is not going to affect the general plan of war in the Pacific, it would be useless." Another who was cautiously opposed, but for different reasons, was the Japanophile Pio Duran, who thought that the American reactions would only be: "Which side are we fighting for anyway?" and "To hell with the Filipinos."

Such meager power as the Filipinos now had lay not with the Council of State but with the Executive Commission. The discussion showed that members of the latter were about evenly split in their opinions. Recto, Alunan, and Paredes associated themselves with Yulo's "go-slow" practicality, whereas Aquino, Laurel, and de las Alas were for signing.

Recto called for further study while continuing the struggle in Bataan and the unoccupied provinces. Alunan thought there was no point in sending a message that would influence neither Roosevelt, nor the progress of the war, nor its result. "Furthermore," he said, "our brothers are still fighting for our liberty in the field of battle and we ought not to be the first to give up. Reinforcements might yet come from America and American Government might return; and we ought still (in any case) to preserve our loyalty to the Commonwealth and our chiefs." As for the telegram, they ought not to go along with it, but if required to sign it, he seemed to suggest, they should resign. When Aquino challenged Alunan on that point, Paredes came to the latter's rescue: "To send such a telegram will lose the public's confidence in us, and we will cease to be useful to the Administration and to our people. . . . It is advisable to explain to the Military Chiefs the contradictory effects of sending the telegram in question."

Those in favor of the telegram spoke strongly, but without swaying the opinion of the meeting. Benigno Aquino declaimed on the principles of the Greater East Asia Co-Prosperity Sphere, on America's failure to prepare the Philippines sufficiently to defend itself, on the certainty that America would never return, and on the wisdom of ceasing to fight. Jose Laurel expressed his legal opinion that "the sovereignty of America in the Philippines has ceased, as well as that of the Commonwealth Government." The telegram "ought to be sent in order to stop the slaughter of our brothers who are fighting on Bataan." Antonio de la Alas also wanted to "avoid the carnage of our brothers"; "I believe," he said, "that the struggle is now useless. America has promised to send us reinforcements and help, and up till now there's been nothing. . . . We have been compelled to go to war and we have been abandoned." [32]

The entire excited discussion was, in a sense, futile. When Quirino at one point asked Vargas for the Commission's opinion, he said, "We are going to sign the telegram." Jose Laurel later observed that the telegram to Roosevelt, as well as an appeal to the Filipinos on Bataan to surrender, "had to be sent by the Executive Commission with or without concurrence or approval of the entire Council of State." [33]

In another sense, however, the discussion was far from futile. It recorded for history the disinclination of most Filipino leaders, even under pressure, to express disloyalty to the Commonwealth government or to show disdain for American constructiveness in the previous forty years. The Executive Commission must, against the better judgment of half its members, send the surrender telegram. But a large majority of the Council of State presented the commission with sentiments abroad among the people and reminded them that

32. Minutes of the Council of State, 18 Feb 42.
33. Ibid; Laurel, narrative fragment, "The Reunion of Prominent Filipinos in the House of Jose Yulo in Peñafrancia, Paco, Manila," 23 Oct 44 (JPL).

they trespassed upon the peoples' basic loyalties at the cost of popular confidence in themselves. Even in 1944, when habit had made more congenial and practice more perfect the collaboration of a few Filipinos, certain Japanese admitted that the overwhelming majority of the people were against Japan and sympathetic to the United States.

The Philippines could not by negotiation escape being caught between two military adversaries. The armistice and independence which Quezon on Corregidor sought by telegram was, as Roxas and Osmeña rightly anticipated, unacceptable not only to the Americans but to the Japanese, who, in their dealings with the remnant leaders in Manila, made it clear that there was no alternative to absorption in the Greater East Asia Co-Prosperity Sphere. The surrender which Aquino and Laurel in Manila wanted to seek by telegram was also, as Yulo, Alunan, and Paredes rightly anticipated, unacceptable to the United States, whose policy Roosevelt's reply to Quezon laid down: independence only on American terms, and a fight to the end.

Eventually the end came. Quezon and Osmeña escaped to Australia. Just before he left, Quezon slipped the signet ring from his finger to MacArthur's and said, brokenly, "When they find your body, I want them to know you fought for my country." [34] Washington, however, did not wish the General to share the fate of his garrison, but commanded him in mid-March to Australia.

On April 3 Homma resumed attack with about 22,000 additional infantry, sixty more twin-engined bombers, and new artillery and air units. For the sake of American morale, Henry Stimson wanted an inspiring fight to complete destruction—the Alamo massacre re-enacted, but with seventy thousand men instead of seventy. He was a little disappointed when a white flag on Bataan, April 9, took the decision out of Washington's control. [35]

Corregidor lasted another month, but the point Stimson wished to make had already been established: valiant American resistance in the face of great odds would inspire the whole war effort; the United States had avoided a French debacle, wherein too early collapse had led to schism and despair. Furthermore, the Filipinos had fought with the Americans on the whole willingly, and after some

34. MacArthur, *Reminiscences,* p. 140.
35. Morton, pp. 413–14, 454–67; Stimson diary, 8, 9 Apr 42 (HLS).

trials, well. The United States was spared the mortification of the Dutch, watching Indonesian nationalists welcome the Japanese as liberators.

For the Filipinos, however, there were few such satisfactions. They had lost many lives, much of their liberty, and considerable property. Their government was split, not merely in two, but in three: collaboration, Commonwealth, and Communist.

Japanese power had drawn many into unhappy durance working with the conquerors. Others went different ways. Manuel Roxas, to whom Quezon had delegated practically all his powers as president, had barely escaped execution in Mindanao. When he returned to Manila under military surveillance, he exaggerated and even intensified his poor health, so as to have an excuse not to collaborate. Jose Abad Santos, also loyal to the exiled Commonwealth leaders, was less lucky. When captured, he flatly refused to collaborate, and the Japanese shot him. His brother, Pedro Abad Santos, the radical leader, had sought arms from General MacArthur for a people's guerrilla army, without success. Before he died, from ill health worsened in a Japanese prison, he had a last meeting with his student Luis Taruc, who, with the brilliant Lava brothers, had organized a peasant army for the defeat of the Japanese and for the creation of a Marxist social order in the Philippines.[36]

A war which the Philippines had not caused was already tearing at both the political and the social fabric of the country. The contest between imperial powers would aggravate all the inherited handicaps to Philippine national unity and would stimulate open class warfare.

36. Roxas, "Wartime Activities"; Lichauco, *Roxas*, pp. 167 ff; Quezon, *The Good Fight*, pp. 301, 312; Luis Taruc, *Born of the People* (New York, International Publishers, 1953), pp. 53–54; interview with Luis Taruc, 11 Nov 58.

17

The Wartime Republic: Beginning and End

"I HAVE COME THROUGH, and I shall return." MacArthur reached Australia by PT boat on March 17, 1942. Quezon and Osmeña had left earlier, but, retreating slowly south by submarine, plane, and PT boat, arrived a week later. They found American forces there only one-third the number they had left behind on Bataan and Corregidor. Quezon burst out with fresh curses upon Roosevelt. In time, however, Osmeña persuaded him that there was nothing to do but proceed to Washington and organize a government, while MacArthur fought the war in the Pacific on a shoestring.[1]

The new government-in-exile included Mike Elizalde, who in Washington had initiated plans to evacuate Quezon, and Colonel Andres Soriano, who had helped the escape by going on air reconnaissance himself.[2] Together they made a curious cabinet: the two politicos, Quezon and Osmeña, never quite trusting each other; the two proud entrepreneurs, Soriano and Elizalde, with conflicting personalities. Osmeña and Elizalde, as usual, kept a cool distance apart. Soriano laid private plans for the postwar development of the Philip-

1. Hunt, *Untold Story*, pp. 271–72; Eyre, *The Roosevelt-MacArthur Conflict*, pp. 93–96.
2. Evacuation and sequel are covered in Morton, *Fall of the Philippines*, pp. 356–60; Sayre, *Glad Adventure*, pp. 240–49; Quezon, *Good Fight*, pp. 279–328; Lichauco, *Roxas*, pp. 144–57; and Romulo, *I Saw the Fall of the Philippines*, pp. 280–322. Elizalde's role is documented by the Stimson diary, 31 Dec 41, 17 Jan 42, and interview with the author, 30 July 63; Soriano's role by Quezon, pp. 221–22, 303–04.

pines and intrigued successfully for an assignment at MacArthur's headquarters, so as to be in the vanguard returning.[3] Quezon needed a cabinet for window-dressing only; his main job was to publicize the Philippine role in the war and to remind Washington of the separate national interest of his people.

For the first time since 1916, Quezon had daily resident experience of the anomalous position of Filipinos in the United States. They were welcomed as soldiers—by May 1942, 20,000 of them were in American armed forces—but they meanwhile remained aliens. Carlos Bulosan expressed the predicament of Filipino civilians best. While he turned out poetry celebrating Filipino-American affinity, he privately exclaimed that "to a Filipino here, democracy is a toilet behind which he hides with fear. . . . I have grown tired struggling to live." He was unable to get a white-collar job because of his race.[4]

At a statesman's level, Quezon experienced a similar frustration. Harold Ickes, Secretary of the Interior, had jurisdiction over the Philippines, and treated the Commonwealth President as a subordinate. Quezon, infuriated, tried to deal directly with the White House whenever possible. Roosevelt accommodated his dignity by making the Philippine Commonwealth a member of the wartime United Nations and by inviting Quezon to meetings of the Pacific War Council. He did nothing, however, to amend the Europe-first strategy that Quezon criticized.

Quezon felt, and said, that the United States was fighting an imperialistic war to save the British empire and its interests in the Mediterranean; the prime theater should be the Pacific, and the American public had been badly duped into thinking otherwise.[5] Roosevelt did not agree, nor did anyone else of importance in Washington. Quezon could only wait for MacArthur to mount a return to the Philippines, while his own tubercular body weakened. The

3. Large "Soriano" file, especially Soriano to Quezon, 15 May 43, enclosing report on projected "Industrial Expansion in the Philippines," in which Soriano was associated with American interests on the West Coast (Q). Of several Soriano letters of resignation from the cabinet, that of 6 Oct 43 is the most explicit. Quezon to Soriano, 14 July 44, finally accepted the resignation.
4. Carlos Bulosan, *Voice of Bataan* (New York, Coward, McCann, 1943); Bulosan to Charles D. Abbott, 15 May 42 (Poetry Room, Lockwood Memorial Library, State University of New York at Buffalo).
5. "Memorandum for Mr. Welles," undated, probably early 1943, "Attempt to Estimate the Situation," 6, 24 July 43, "Notes on the Situation," 19 Aug (Q).

Philippine capital would be in Japanese hands for more than three years. Allied forces would recapture Paris, even Warsaw, first; and only Warsaw, of the world's great cities, would suffer as much as Manila.

When it could transcend purely military considerations, the Japanese Military Administration of the Philippines interested itself in the cultural and economic reorientation of the country. Major General Hayashi Yoshihide, the first Director General of the JMA, celebrated the fall of Bataan with a lecture to the Filipino leaders on the American policy of "deceit and misguidance." The United States, he said, had sapped Filipino strength with luxury goods, scattered their energies by excessive encouragement of individual rights, and handicapped their future by not building enough vocational schools. Vargas replied as expected. He was "grateful" for the Japanese victory, which had "vindicated all Asiatic peoples whose rights and genius have been denied due recognition by occidental civilization." He admitted the spiritual defects of his people and pledged them to a program of "rehabilitation." [6]

As the chief goal of rehabilitation, the Japanese expected the Philippines to take its place in a self-sufficient economic sphere. Japan would be the industrial center for which the "Southern Area" would be a market and a supplier of raw materials. While the Philippines was increasing its rice crop, Indochina could make up any deficiency; it would make its own flour, which it had been buying from the United States; cultivate more tobacco, and eventually export cigarettes to the whole sphere instead of importing them from America; continue sales of abaca to Japan and Europe; use its copra for soap throughout the sphere and for cattlefeed in certain parts; become a supply area (along with Taiwan and Java) for sugar, alcohol, and butanol; and furnish the entire lumber needs of the area. Resettlement of the farming population, rotation of crops, and fixed cash-rent instead of share-rent tenancy would all increase Philippine productivity.

A basic re-education must accompany all these improvements; a new economic consciousness must displace the concerns with family, religion, and politics which as yet possessed the Filipino

6. *Official Journal of the Japanese Military Administration, 4* (Apr 1942), v–xii, esp. vi, x.

mind. Spain had prepared the Filipinos for heaven; America for white-collar jobs. Japan would help instead to prepare the Philippines for economic development; would produce fewer lawyers and politicians, more experts in agriculture and forestry, more technicians in light industry, and more students of business administration.[7]

Japan might succeed in diverting the Philippine economy to her own ends, but in developing it constructively she totally failed.[8] Her program of promoting new cultural attitudes also failed. The Filipinos were suspicious of talk of Asian brotherhood. They thought their Christian morality superior to the Japanese and dismissed the invader's glorification of Spartan virtues as hypocritical, for the JMA smiled on jai alai, horse-racing, gambling of all kinds, and licensed prostitution.[9]

For the Japanese, time was short, methods crude; and the conquered were uncooperative. General Hayashi left for another assignment, convinced that the Filipinos were the "laziest" of all the peoples with whom he had had army experience, including Chinese, Mongolians, Siberians, Koreans, Burmese, and Thai. Murata Shozo, the chief civilian adviser to the JMA, declared that Filipinos did "nothing but stand on their rights"; they would have to cultivate other qualities to satisfy the Japanese that they deserved independence. Unlike Hayashi, Murata was not surprised at what he found, because, he said, the Filipinos "have no culture of their own. How could a people, culturally bankrupt, be independent spiritually?"[10]

Whether or not the Filipinos learned the proper "sincerity" or acted with the proper sense of "duty," whether or not they even wanted a Japanese style of independence, they were going to get it. Both Roxas and Laurel separately advised Hayashi's successor, General Wachi Takagi, against bestowing independence, because they

7. Rōyama Masamichi et al., *Philippines Research Report, 4* (Manila, JMA, 1943), esp. Ch 3, pt 1, and Ch 6, pt 1.
8. A. V. H. Hartendorp, *History of Industry and Trade of the Philippines* (Manila, Amer Chamb Comm Phils, 1958), pp. 73–84, 92–95.
9. Undated, unidentified account of early occupation in Manila; by internal evidence attributable to Claude Buss, Exec Asst to the High Comm (HC). Sayre left Buss in charge when he went to Corregidor.
10. Author's interview with Hayashi, 2 Oct 57; Murata, *Japan Times and Advertiser,* 5 June 42, quoted in *For Rel, 1942, 1,* 788.

expected it to be precarious and incomplete.[11] But with the tides of war turning against Japan, Premier Tojo visited Manila in May 1943 and, in a public address, announced that Japan would soon confer the "honor of independence" upon the Filipinos as he had promised. Vargas led the crowd in forced cheers of "Banzai!" [12]

By August the Allies were "leap-frogging" instead of merely "island-hopping" across the Pacific, and by October, when the Philippine Republic was inaugurated, Japan had clearly lost the strategic initiative.[13] General Tojo may or may not have been anticipating these developments and trying to free his military personnel from political duties. The motives of the local JMA, however, are a matter of record.

Independence should be accepted as a "rigid policy" because, among Filipinos, it would "promote . . . trust in Japan and defeat reliance upon America." It would favorably influence opinion in China, India, and Southeast Asia. By showing that Japan was engaged in a defensive, and not an aggressive, war, it would undercut the American and British will to fight. Philippine independence would show Japan's "sincerity" to the world at large.

The Japanese were concerned with the practical effects of their policy as well as with appearing "sincere." They had hoped to reduce their own manpower in the Philippines; they expected the Filipino people to support their own leaders more readily under a "republic." Acquisition of resources for national defense might become more difficult, but in view of the general deterioration of the economy, it would be better to install Filipino administrators than to have the people blame the JMA for their misery. Since the Japanese had promised eventual independence, they would be wise to give it now, while the power of occupation could insure economic and financial policies beneficial to Japan, and favorable disposition of alien property to the Japanese. The JMA realized that the American promise of independence for 1946 required them to do something sooner. Some Japanese held to the "narrow prejudice of Japanizing everywhere," but the more enlightened administrators be-

11. Roxas, "Wartime Activities"; Laurel, *War Memoirs*, p. 11.
12. Hartendorp, pp. 95–96.
13. Samuel Eliot Morison, *The Two-Ocean War* (Boston, Little, Brown, 1963), pp. 282–85.

lieved this only to increase Filipino resistance. Independence would reduce resistance.[14]

Who, then, would be president of the "republic"? Ricarte had proved to be too old and out of touch with the people; when he grew troublesome, the JMA flew him to Tokyo and kept him a virtual prisoner in the Imperial Hotel for four months.[15] Aguinaldo was ridiculously eager for the presidency; although he had no chance for it, he requested a constitutional amendment making the minimum age for a president sixty-five, which provision would have excluded nearly all but himself.[16] Tojo wanted Vargas, in gratitude for his services up to that point, but Japanese authorities familiar with the Filipinos thought him too much a puppet to convince the people and recommended against a "yes man." [17] The JMA thought highly of Don Ramon Avanceña, but higher still of Roxas.[18] When Colonel Utsunomiya Naonori put the proposal to him, Roxas declined it, as he would again when General Wachi pressed the question.

The two leading candidates left were Laurel and Aquino. Utsunomiya asked Roxas' advice; Roxas said Laurel was a great scholar and lawyer, but Aquino was the better politician.[19] Possibly he was trying to spare Laurel, his compadre, an embarrassing involvement, but later, in a private discussion with General Wachi, he supported Laurel's candidacy.[20]

Aquino was a formidable rival; as Minister of the Interior, in touch with all provincial governors and mayors, he was convinced he could beat Laurel in an election. But the last thing the JMA

14. "An Observation Concerning the Time and Form of Philippine Independence," 6 May 43, and "Concerning the Solution of the Philippine Independence Problem," undated; Gaimushō SP 1.7.0–47, pp. 1–30, 31–42.

15. Author's interview with Col Ōta Kaneshirō, 20 Sept 58.

16. Author's interview, 27 Aug 58, with Alfonso Ponce Enrile, who heard the story from Vicente Madrigal. Aguinaldo's letter to Laurel, "Isang Mungkahi Sa Komisong Paghahanda Sa Kasarinlan ng Pilipinas," 5 July 43 (JPL), gives ample indication of pro-Japanese attitudes.

17. Author's interview with Col Utsunomiya Naonori, 29 Sept 58. The latter was Asst CofS, from Sept 1942 until surrender, under Gens Tanaka, Kuroda, and Yamashita. Before the period of the republic he was chief of the General Affairs Dept of the JMA; during the republic he remained the Army's chief liaison officer to the Philippine leaders.

18. "Concerning the Solution, etc.," note 14, supra.

19. Utsunomiya interview.

20. Author's interview with Gen Wachi Takagi, 25 Sept 58; Lichauco, p. 175.

wanted was an election. Utsunomiya, in a two-hour conversation with Aquino, convinced him that he could be the *next* president; meanwhile, Oriental custom suggested that the place belonged to Laurel, who was the older of the two. Aquino acquiesced; Laurel accepted. Vargas was indignant at being pushed aside, and was soothed only by becoming Ambassador to Japan, where he could enjoy the proximity and good opinion of General Tojo.[21]

While these maneuvers were going on, the Japanese made Laurel Chairman of the Preparatory Committee for Philippine Independence. As a lawyer he knew the statutes under which he could be tried when the Americans came back; he said that he would be the first man shot.[22] Nevertheless, he accepted the job, believing that the United States would not return for at least five years, if ever. As a Filipino he felt that he could not reject great responsibility in a crisis.

To make his intentions clear, Laurel repeatedly said that he acted for the Philippines first, and only secondly for Greater Asia. The Japanese found that they could not treat him as their own creature. When a Japanese officer grew hilarious and over-familiar, at a celebration in Malacañan, and poured champagne on Laurel, he picked up a dish of ice cream and threw it in the officer's face.[23]

The people, however, could not be sure of Laurel's motives, and the anti-Japanese guerrillas sharply doubted them. On June 4, 1945, someone lay in wait for Laurel at the seventh tee of Wack Wack Golf Course and, when he appeared, shot him three times in the back.[24] The Japanese sent doctors from Tokyo to save Laurel, but his own tough constitution pulled him through.

In Washington, Manuel Quezon's second term of four years was expiring. Rather than give in to the constitutional limits and yield

21. Author's interviews with Wachi and Utsunomiya; where the two differ in detail, I rely on the latter as having worked more intimately with the problem. Vargas, in interview with the author, 12 Nov 58, denied that he wanted the presidency.

22. Author's interview with Hamamoto Masakatsu, President Laurel's wartime interpreter, 1 Oct 58.

23. Author's interview with Laurel, 21 Oct 58; Laurel, *War Memoirs*, esp. pp. 60–67; biographical and philosophical fragments, 1944–45 (JPL); Hernando Abaya, *Betrayal in the Philippines* (New York, Wyn, 1946), pp. 36–38 (concerning the time of American return); author's interview with Modesto Farolan, 27 Aug 58 (concerning ice cream incident).

24. Laurel, *War Memoirs*, pp. 14–15; Hartendorp, p. 97.

to the patient Osmeña, he sought a rationale to continue himself in office. The people, he said, awaited the return of "Quezon, the leader"; how could he lead if he were not president? [25] Looking around his cabinet for approval, Quezon's eye fell on Elizalde: "You're my appointee, I can't ask you"; on Soriano: "I can't ask you either"; and finally on Jaime Hernandez: "Mr. Auditor General, what do you think?" Hernandez said nervously that it would require thoughtful study. Quezon, furious, told his wife, "Aurora, pack our bags, we're leaving Washington." Afterwards Osmeña came to him and said, "If you wanted help, I was the one to ask." [26]

Quezon wanted Roosevelt to prolong his term by executive order, but Osmeña, always procedurally correct, insisted it be done by act of Congress. Roosevelt himself was ready to let Osmeña take over, lest by perpetuating Quezon in power, he give ammunition to those American critics who charged Roosevelt himself with dictatorship; Secretary Stimson worked to silence the critics and to keep Quezon. Osmeña briefly sounded out members of the press on the wild idea of broadcasting the problem to the Filipino people for their reaction; then he generously gave way, as he had so often done in the past twenty years. The vote in the House, 181 to 107, showed strong doubts, but Congress continued Quezon in office. When a Filipino journalist told Osmeña that history would remember him for placing his country before himself, tears sprang to Osmeña's eyes.[27]

Quezon meanwhile continued his critique of the "British war," asked for a shift of weight to the Pacific, and reminded Roosevelt that his public silence did not mean his heart was quiet; his people had "been too long suffering the atrocities and the iron rule of the

25. Quezon to Franklin D. Roosevelt, 9 May 43; also, handwritten comments on undated syllabus, answering "Question: Can the President of the United States under the Present Circumstances, Legally Suspend the Operation of the Tydings-McDuffie Law and the Constitution of the Philippines?" (Q).
26. Author's interviews, 21 July 58 with Sotero H. Laurel, and 29 Aug 64 with Gen Basilio Valdez. The stories differ in detail, Valdez asserting that Soriano was not present. Young Laurel was a clerk researcher for Osmeña, who, when his father became President of the occupation Republic, resigned to spare the government-in-exile any embarrassment.
27. Osmeña to the author, 10 Oct 58; interview with James Wingo, 29 Mar 57; Stimson diary, 7 Sept, 22, 23, 26, 27, 29 Oct 43 (HLS); Grunder and Livezey, *Philippines and U.S.*, pp. 243–44.

Japanese." [28] Early in 1943, he had considered asking for an immediate grant of independence, so that the United States would not be subject to Axis propaganda about "plagiarizing the magnificent gesture of the Japanese." Later, after Tojo's visit to Manila, Quezon made the request just to beat the Japanese to it, despite the appearance of plagiarism.[29]

Mike Elizalde brought the matter up with his friend Millard Tydings, who, casual as ever, tossed a bill in the hopper for immediate independence. Stimson learned, "most appalling blow of all," that Roosevelt, "all mixed up" about the Philippines, had given Tydings permission. The Secretary of War spent several days slowing down congressional momentum, aided by others in the executive branch, and by anxious Filipinos, especially Soriano. To declare the Philippines independent in the middle of the war would be tantamount to recognizing the puppet government. Stimson convinced Quezon, who "was very grieved and broken up . . . sick, coughing . . . not himself," finally to give up the idea.[30]

Quezon would not live to see his country free or fully sovereign. As he grew weaker he grew more irrational and critical, especially of Osmeña. "Look at that man. Why did God give him such a body when I am here struggling for my life? I am Manuel L. Quezon— I am the Filipino people—I am the Philippines." In August 1944, Manuel Quezon died. When Romulo brought the news, Osmeña burst into tears.[31]

To the end, Quezon had judged leniently those who served in the puppet government: they were acting under duress, in obedience to his instructions to protect the people, and in accord with their conception of the people's best interests.[32] Quezon's opinion of these men may have been the softer for hoping to lead them once again. Some were working under the Japanese with greater enthusiasm

28. Quezon to Franklin D. Roosevelt, 23 Feb 44 (Q).
29. Quezon to Franklin D. Roosevelt, 25 Jan (not sent), 8 Sept 43 (Q).
30. Author's interview with Amb J. M. Elizalde, 30 July 63; Quezon to Franklin D. Roosevelt, 7 Oct 43, to Elizalde, 11 Jan 44 (Q); Stimson diary, 27 Sept, 4 Oct 43 (HLS); Grunder and Livezey, pp. 242–44.
31. Eyre, pp. 131, 133.
32. Quezon to Mrs Vicente Lim, 30 Apr 43 (Q); Quezon to Sotero H. Laurel, 30 Sept, Laurel, *War Memoirs*, Appendix A.

than Quezon's parting words called for. In the main, however, they bargained as sharply with their conquerors as the circumstances permitted, and earned regard among the Japanese as the most recalcitrant government in the Southern Area.

The Japanese did their best, as in other areas, to smother old political institutions with new ones. Late in 1942 they dissolved all political parties and civic bodies into the Kalibapi, a "nonpolitical" service organization. The leaders of the Kalibapi were members of the original and continuing Executive Commission and Council of State. Subsequently the Japanese made a number of them the Preparatory Committee for Philippine Independence.

On July 2, 1943, Colonel Utsunomiya gave the leaders of the new committee instructions for drafting a constitution. Work quickly. Emphasize the moral principle of contribution to the Greater East Asia Co-Prosperity Sphere. Make room for the elastic exercise of state sovereignty; do not let popular participation in government impede efficient administration. He picked up another page of instructions and through an interpreter went on. Laurel listened, sitting up in his hospital bed.

The very idea of Philippine independence, Utsunomiya said, derived from "hakko ichiu," the principle of universal concord. Japan was taking still another step in the liberation of Asian peoples and hoped that the Filipinos would "shake yourselves free from American mental and material influence." Utsunomiya did not forbid study and inclusion of some articles from the old American-influenced constitution, but hoped that the new one would both reflect Filipino ideas and fit the new situation. To these instructions Premier Tojo later added his "particular wish that you refrain from wasting time . . . in fruitless discussions . . . over . . . academic theories and technicalities." [33]

Three days after the meeting with Utsunomiya, Laurel convoked his committee in the hospital. They had "numerous and well-nigh appalling" problems to face, of finance and currency and taxation;

33. "Instructions Given to the Preparatory Committee on Philippine Independence by the Japanese Occupation Authorities," 2 July 43, Gaimushō S 1.7.0.0–47, pp. 54–65 (English versions of special paper A and B from the above, in Laurel Collection; of special paper A only, in salvaged papers of Camilo Osias, collection of Prof H. Otley Beyer); "Resume of Premier Tozyo's [Tojo's] Message to the Members of the Preparatory Commission for Philippine Independence," Manila, 9 July 43 (JPL).

of relations among central, provincial, and municipal governments; of revitalizing agriculture, commerce, and industry. They had to look into domestic labor relations, and foreign trade relations, into public welfare and the judicial system; to improve transportation and communication, and health and sanitation; to provide for national defense and work for cultural reorientation. They must awaken and reshape the entire national life to make independence real and enduring.[34] In the face of these demands, Laurel did not see why they could not, if pressed, knock a constitution together "in forty-eight hours."

He had in mind a temporary constitution, to last for the duration of the war—"five, six, or ten years." The judicial branch should remain as under the Commonwealth. Since the Japanese had abolished all parties and prohibited public meetings, the legislature would have to be a temporary expedient, consisting of the Kalibapi, a semi-representative organ. The executive, Laurel said, ought to be a "constitutional dictatorship."

Two other leading matters remained: civil rights and natural resources. Laurel himself had drafted the Bill of Rights for the Commonwealth constitution, but now he preferred to "transfer all the rights of an accused person to the Code of Criminal Procedure, where they are repeated anyway." In the constitution itself he would prefer a generalized statement of the *obligations* of citizens.

To protect their natural resources they would have to take a definite stand: "The Filipino, I am sorry to have to say it, is weak; his moral fibre lacks firmness; his education and training are disastrously faulty; he cannot enter into economic competition with more mature races, and if he does, he perishes." Laurel implied that the Commonwealth's provisions against alien ownership should be preserved, lest independence "not be worth having" and Filipinos become "beggars in our own homes." [35]

With Utsunomiya's instructions and Tojo's, and with Laurel's ample suggestions, several committees went off to work on various parts of the constitution. General Wachi made ten million pesos available to the Preparatory Committee, monies earlier confiscated

34. "Memoranda," 23 June 43, PCPI folder, Osias materials, Beyer Collection.
35. "Transcript . . . Taken at the Meeting of the Preparatory Commission for Philippine Independence, Held in Room No. 20 of the Philippine General Hospital on July 5, 1943," Osias materials, Beyer Collection; also JPL.

from Philippine banks. Laurel took it and distributed it, keeping careful accounts. Of the twenty members, only Roxas and Avanceña refused the money. Laurel himself accepted some money, the only occasion on which he gave in to Wachi's numerous offers of financial assistance.[36]

The committees shaped the wartime constitution from the prewar version, ignoring almost completely the Japanese organic law. They did, however, accede to instructions on the matter of the "constitutional dictatorship," stripping away most of the legislative and judicial checks to the chief executive and furnishing him with several special powers. Laurel, with numerous revisions, enhanced the presidency still more and sent the document back to the so-called "drafting committee," [37] of which Manuel Roxas was the most influential member.

After remaining aloof from the government for a year and a half, Roxas had felt constrained to insure a more liberal constitution than the other leaders were producing. He suggested a final "drafting committee" be formed; other members insisted that he join it; he insisted that it meet at his house. The committee managed to insert something akin to the old Bill of Rights and delete most of the substitute, which amounted to a bill of obligations. They struck from the preamble reverent references to the Greater East Asia Co-Prosperity Sphere and inserted the declaration that "sovereignty resides in the people and all government authority emanates from them." [38]

Laurel, however, had a last crack at the draft. He left in the Bill of Rights. He struck out references to the sovereignty of the people and pasted on instead a bland label: "The Philippines is a Republican State." He compromised between the drafting committee, which wanted the word "justice" in the preamble, and the Japanese, who wanted the word "morality." If "moral justice" sounded more Japanese than Filipino, Laurel was not pained at making the concession. He had successfully insisted that the constitution define itself as

36. Wachi interview; in this connection see Abaya, p. 28.
37. Sison (Chairman, Judicial Comm) to Laurel, 27 July 43; Alunan (Chairman, Legislative Comm) to Laurel, undated; Laurel, untitled memo revising recommendations by Executive Comm (JPL).
38. "Suggestions from General Roxas," and drafting committee, untitled memo on changes in final draft (JPL); Roxas, "Wartime Activities"; Lichauco, *Roxas,* pp. 173–74.

temporary; the Filipinos could call a new convention a year after the war.[39]

The final result was certainly not a Japanese constitution; nor did it express an indigenous Filipino spirit. Roxas had done what he could to make it an American constitution, with some limited success, but Laurel had had a greater influence than he. Perhaps one defines the product best by calling it an emergency constitution. The Filipino leaders drafted it for the emergency, and the JMA accepted it for the emergency. When Roxas tried to get out of signing it, the Japanese said that he had amended the draft too much to have an excuse for not putting his name on it. Under pressure, Manuel Roxas, on September 4, 1943, joined nineteen others as signers of the Constitution of the Republic of the Philippines.

Now that they were turning over more authority to the Filipinos, the Japanese were concerned about disposition of natural resources and use of public utilities and government companies. They were willing that the Filipinos continue old constitutional injunctions against foreigners, in order that public opinion against Japanese exploitation be appeased. Nonetheless, they wanted the goods. The drafting committee repeated Commonwealth restrictions in favor of Philippine nationals, while enabling foreign use, prohibitions notwithstanding, should the President of the Republic so provide *"by treaty."* Laurel blue-penciled the references to contraindicative language and the words *by treaty.*

From the files of Malacañan there emerged, after the war, a "confidential agreement" between the Philippines and Japan for the use of such resources and utilities. Claro Recto, Minister of Foreign Affairs of the wartime republic, said that he knew nothing about it.[40] Very likely Laurel, using his exceptional powers, negotiated it, although he did not mention it in his memoirs. Who could prevent the Japanese commandeering what materials they needed? Laurel saved his opposition for more crucial issues in which there might lie some chance of success.

39. Draft as received from drafting committee, subsequently revised in red, blue, and ordinary pencil; official copy, Constitution of the Republic of the Philippines, adopted 4 Sept 43 (JPL); concerning "morality," Gaimushō S 1.7.0–47, p. 156.
40. Gaimushō S 1.7.0.0–47, p. 222; "Memorandum on Questions between Japan and the Philippines Arising from the Philippine Independence," and "Basic Principles and Policies," published in full, American Chamber of Commerce *Journal*, Aug 49; interview with A. V. H. Hartendorp, 20 Nov 58.

The most crucial issue pounced with the most surprise. The Japanese brought Laurel, Aquino, and Vargas to Tokyo, in late September 1943, for pre-independence banquets and ceremonies. The climax was a private conference with Premier Tojo; Shigemitsu (Foreign Minister) and Aoki (Minister for Greater East Asia) were also present. Tojo rose and read instructions asking for a Philippine declaration of war against the United States and Great Britain.

Laurel silently prayed and said the Pater Noster. After the translation, he stood and politely said that Quezon, Osmeña, and Roxas were the popular leaders in the Philippines, and not himself; that he could not carry the people, or even maintain a following, with such an unpopular measure; and that it would not be "decent" for the Filipinos to declare war against a benefactor. Freedom or extermination was the ultimate choice, Tojo said, leaving Laurel with the feeling that a declaration of war would eventually be asked as a price of independence.[41]

Although Burma and Thailand cooperated with Japan and declared war against the Allies, Tojo did not force the matter with Laurel until an American invasion of the Philippines was imminent. When pressed again in September 1944, Laurel intended to stick by his refusal to Tojo. He gave his aides confidential instructions to prepare his escape from Manila. Roxas was opposed. Privately he advised Laurel " 'not to make the mistake' of defying Japan 'to become a hero' at the expense of the lives of so many people." Reconsidering, Laurel put the alternatives to his cabinet: (1) to resist the pressure, (2) flee to the mountains, (3) commit suicide, (4) find a compromise. Japanese pressure was too strong to admit resistance; flight might bring serious reprisals; suicide was good Bushido but not a Christian act. The cabinet recommended a compromise, and Roxas was particularly insistent upon it. If the JMA, representing the orders of the Supreme War Council of Japan, demanded a declaration of war, then the Filipinos should formally consent. But they should refuse to raise an army.[42]

The cabinet chose to share responsibility by submitting the question to the Council of State. Only three members of the council showed up for the joint meeting—Miguel Unson, Ramon Fernandez,

41. Laurel, *War Memoirs*, pp. 16–18.
42. Ibid., pp. 23–24, 33–34, 56–57, 61, 64; Roxas, "Wartime Activities"; Wachi interview.

and Rafael Corpus, all distinguished citizens with business and political experience. To cabinet and council, Laurel, in a low, preoccupied voice, read the proposed declaration and proceeded immediately to a discussion of amendments.

Claro Recto moved elimination of a "whereas" which declared that the United States is "intent upon a reconquest of the Philippines and an invasion of our soil made sacred and hallowed by the blood of our forefathers." Arsenio Luz moved elimination of a passage asking Filipinos to "be ready and willing to pledge our fortunes, our lives and our sacred honor"; such exhortation might be misinterpreted as calling back Laurel's promise not to conscript Filipino soldiers.

The declaration thus softened, Laurel asked the opinion of the members of the Council of State. Then and later they reiterated the unanimous opinion of their body, already expressed to the cabinet, that approval of two-thirds of the National Assembly was necessary. Recto replied for his fellow cabinet members that they shared Paredes' opinion, as Minister of Justice: approval of the National Assembly was not necessary.

Someone asked for Roxas. Laurel said that he had declined to attend, having already said that if the Japanese demanded a proclamation of the existence of a state of war, or even a direct declaration of war, the Filipinos should accede. Ramon Fernandez, a compadre of Roxas, verified the same as Roxas' opinion. Unson then asked if the Japanese really demanded a declaration.

"Yes," Laurel said.

"If that is so," Unson replied, "it is a matter of obedience, and I lay emphasis on the word 'obey.' " Fernandez agreed.

After a short silence, Laurel said, "We need not give in to what they ask." He added: "If you advise me NOT to give in to what they ask, I am willing to be sacrificed with you, and not to accede."

Another pause of seconds followed, until Laurel looked at Corpus, who spoke: "Mr. President, I am agreeable . . . because I believe that we will thus save our people from great and heavy sacrifices and the destruction of property."

Apparently satisfied, Laurel summoned other absent members of the cabinet and council for lunch. Before the President left the table for a meeting with the Japanese, Unson asked him a question originating from Fernandez: "Would the sufferings of the people be greater if the Americans or [if] the Japanese considered us hostile?" Laurel rapidly replied, "I prefer that the Japanese do not consider us hostile." [43]

Thus the Filipinos declared a war they intended not to wage. Laurel might deal raw materials across to Japan, but he successfully withheld Filipino youth. Frustrated, the Japanese, over Laurel's protest, formed a volunteer militia of opportunists and Japanophiles, called the Makapili. Ramos, Ricarte, and Duran, all distant in affections and policies from Laurel's government, led the new unit, which General Yamashita hoped would do the work of the uncooperative republic.[44]

So ambitious was Ramos that late in 1944 he proposed a coup d'état displacing all the government except Laurel himself, now indispensable. General Muto, Yamashita's Chief of Staff, liked the idea. Overthrow might bring in persons more concerned for the Japanese Army and civilians, increasingly endangered by the American advance from Leyte. Others on the staff and in the diplomatic corps objected. They were already thinking of good postwar relations rather than immediate cooperation. Furthermore: Ramos might be loyal to the Japanese, but how many Filipinos were loyal to Ramos? Murata, now Ambassador to the Philippines, and General Wachi together talked Muto out of Ramos' scheme.[45]

No one overthrew Laurel's government; it simply disintegrated as American troops advanced. The cabinet evacuated first to Baguio, in December 1944. The winds of war thereafter dispersed them everywhere. Laurel himself went into exile with his imperial protectors, as Quezon had before him—first to Formosa and then Japan. After Japan surrendered, Laurel finally and formally decreed his government at an end.

Some Japanese had shared, in their way, Laurel's dream of the Philippines as a rising Oriental republic. The Marquis Tokugawa Yorisada had lived two years in the Manila Hotel, trying to encourage Filipino-Japanese cultural relations. A commission of scholars led by Dr. Royama Masamichi had produced a careful, thoughtful

43. Memo in Spanish by Don Miguel Unson on meeting of cabinet and Council of State, 22 Sept 44, trans. and publ., *Philippine Press*, 15 July 45, conveyed by Manila Off of High Comm to Washington Off, 17 July (HC).
44. Laurel, *War Memoirs*, pp. 25, 61; Claro Recto, *Three Years of Enemy Occupation* (Manila, People's Publishers, 1946), pp. 56–59.
45. Wachi interview.

research report, aiming as had the Taft Commission, forty years before, to plan the healthy growth of the nation. Even some of the Japanese military had the same generous disposition to help as had John Hersey's fictional Major Victor Joppolo. Colonel Utsunomiya, as a prisoner of war, read *A Bell for Adano,* with sympathy for the problems of military government in Italy and envy for a victory which allowed the Americans to be constructive.[46]

Japanese dreaming, however, had led the Philippines to even more destruction and indignity than American dreaming. Laurel, in the debris of his administration, conjured up a new vision. "The Filipinos," he wrote, "can be happy only by being left alone, however irregular and however stupid it may seem from the point of view of other peoples. That is just like building a house adapted to our own climatic conditions and idiosyncrasies." In order not to suffer in the future from China or Russia as in the present from Japan, the Philippines would have to develop its own resources, even have munitions and airplane factories. The alternative was "our present position of mere 'muñeca' "—of puppetry.

To march toward a point of "national safety," Laurel would call a national assembly after the war; not the present one "whose members are good only in speeching and pork barrelling," but "the intellectual cream of the people." They would draw long-range plans of overall development, to be executed by a "dictatorial government" which would permit freedom of religious thought, of property, and family rights, while absorbing all essential powers to carry out the assembly's plans. The leader of this government must be of a kind that the Philippines had not yet had: "one who would . . . obliterate himself and forget . . . material advantages, power, glory . . . one who would completely dedicate himself to the welfare of the people." The nation would follow his example, even against its will, "because I believe in some occult, some mysterious charm that will compel your people to follow. . . . I am a believer in God and in His Power and in His Reward." [47]

Not long after so writing, the student of Plato and Confucius had to pack and evacuate the palace. Laurel's presidential vision would never have material to practice on other than the cruelly constrained circumstances of wartime occupation.

46. Author's interviews: Prof H. Otley Beyer, 6 Nov 58; Dr Rōyama Masamichi, 19 Sept 58; Col Utsunomiya Naonori, 29 Sept 58.
47. Laurel, fragmentary essays entitled "Political" and "Moral" [Dec 44?] (JPL).

18

The Peacetime Republic: Beginning

"I HAVE RETURNED." On October 20, 1944, General MacArthur waded ashore at Leyte, with President Osmeña a few steps behind. Mac-Arthur's name, MacArthur's promise, MacArthur's strategy and drive bound together the Philippines of 1942 with that of 1944, supplying continuity and hope. "I shall return" had become a watchword and a victory sign scrawled by Filipinos on public walls. For a while MacArthur's return was in jeopardy; the Navy argued at the Honolulu Conference in July 1944 that the Philippines be bypassed in order to attack Formosa. MacArthur insisted, however, that it was psychologically and strategically preferable to retake the Philippines. Moreover, he had said, the United States had a moral obligation to liberate the Philippines, and of this he convinced President Roosevelt, the Commander-in-Chief.[1]

Now the island-hopping and leap-frogging had culminated in the pounce on Leyte, and a series of grim campaigns against the Japanese had begun. There would follow a leap to Mindoro, a landing at Lingayen, the fierce liberation of Manila, and the relentless tracking and crushing of the remnant Japanese, who chose to retreat into the mountains of Northern Luzon, instead of Bataan peninsula as MacArthur had done. Filipino guerrillas, who had harried the

1. MacArthur, *Reminiscences*, pp. 197–98; John Gunther, *The Riddle of MacArthur: Japan, Korea and the Far East* (New York, Harper & Bros., 1951), pp. 9–10; Samuel Eliot Morison, *Leyte* (Boston, Little, Brown, 1958), pp. 3–11.

Japanese with increasing severity, now rose up in strength against them.[2] The guerrillas were merely the most active of a people who largely rejected their Oriental conquerors and who overwhelmingly welcomed the Occidentals' return. Elsewhere in Southeast Asia, 1944–45 was known as the reoccupation; the Filipinos alone called it the liberation.

President Osmeña had numerous problems to handle as he followed the American forces. Harold Ickes had warned him that it would be unwise to return beside MacArthur. "The country will be entirely under military command, and you as a civilian leader will be powerless. Your people will expect many things from you that you will be unable to give them."

Osmeña said he was aware of that, but "in view of MacArthur's request I believe my place is in the invasion. Otherwise the Filipinos would say, 'Where is our government? Where is our President?' They might even think I was afraid."

"Very well," Ickes said, "but don't blame me later on."[3]

When Ickes, as an afterthought, suggested that an American high commissioner accompany Osmeña, he again demurred. Stimson supported Osmeña and interceded with Ickes "to be fair and not to gum the game up by his hostility to MacArthur."[4]

MacArthur, not unnaturally, was critical of Ickes, who, he said, "seemed to think of the islands as another one of his national parks." Contrary to Ickes' warning about military command, Osmeña found that MacArthur was quick to insist upon resumption of civil authority. At Tacloban, the provincial capital of Leyte, he turned over the liberated area to the Commonwealth government, and Osmeña inherited an increasing acreage of victory all the way to Manila,

2. MacArthur, pp. 202–54. The standard military histories are M. Hamlin Cannon, *Leyte: The Return to the Philippines,* and Robert Ross Smith, *Triumph in the Philippines* (Washington, Off Chief Mil Hist, 1954, 1963). Smith, in an excellent account of strategy discussions, pp. 3–17, shows that a Formosa–Amoy invasion was debated against a Luzon invasion until the JCS, in a directive of 3 Oct 44, gave MacArthur permission to undertake the latter, as he had intended since 1942.
3. Carlos P. Romulo, *I See the Philippines Rise* (Garden City, Doubleday, 1946), pp. 51–52; see also Eyre, *The Roosevelt-MacArthur Conflict,* pp. 144–46.
4. Osmeña to Stimson, 4 Oct 44, Osmeña to Franklin D. Roosevelt, 10 Apr 45 (O/Q); Stimson diary, 20 Sept 44 (HLS); Ickes' animus against MacArthur can be traced back to 1936 in his *Secret Diaries, 2, The Inside Struggle, 1936–1939* (New York, Simon and Schuster, 1954), p. 62.

where, in a climactic ceremony on February 27, 1945, MacArthur restored full constitutional government to the Filipinos.[5]

Osmeña and his staff nonetheless felt estranged from MacArthur and his staff. As early as Hollandia, New Guinea, Osmeña had considered turning back, for he sensed a feeling against him. As a scholarly constitutionalist he did not mix well with military officers, and as a critic of MacArthur's defense plan of 1936 he was hardly welcome company among a cadre of veterans of Corregidor intensely loyal to the General.[6] When they reached the Philippines, Osmeña found at least the second of Ickes' warnings true: his people did expect many things of him, and Osmeña could only give them what he got from the American Army. Here lay, perhaps, his sense of presidential frustration, which increased as time went on.

Although the Army was perfectly correct in its attitude toward Osmeña, he did not find it confident in him or generous with him. The official attitude was that thrusting responsibility on Filipinos was the only way to "draw them out of their war-induced trauma."[7] But there was probably as much pure punctiliousness as wisdom in the army's yielding civil authority, and certainly more expediency than either: the Philippines was to be the staging area for a massive invasion of Japan, and it had to be recaptured first. An army in fierce battle, preparing for another expected to be still fiercer, could not be bothered with civil administration.

In Osmeña's hands was left the treatment of collaborators. MacArthur understood Ickes to want "to shoot or hang any Filipino who had anything to do with the puppet government, no matter what reasons they may have had for cooperating." The General stood strongly for the Commonwealth government having jurisdiction in the matter, and Roosevelt and Stimson upheld this policy over that of Ickes.[8] The Secretary of the Interior then suggested to Osmeña that everyone who had held civil office under the Japanese above the level of school teacher be at least deprived of the rights to vote and hold office, until after the election of a new president and legislature.

5. MacArthur, pp. 234–36, 250–51; quotation p. 236.
6. Bernstein, pp. 198–99; Eyre, pp. 168–71.
7. The phrase is from Maj Gen Courtney Whitney to the author, 30 June 64. In his letter and in a subsequent interview, 20 July, Gen Whitney stressed the Army's scrupulousness in staying out of civil affairs and in providing liaison to Pres Osmeña.
8. MacArthur, pp. 235–36.

Any leader of the returning Commonwealth government knew that he would have to contest an election with a resistance figure or a partial collaborator, and Quezon, under the circumstances, would almost certainly have used Ickes' minimum formula. He would then have practiced politically selective absolution in his own interest.

But Quezon was dead. Osmeña, always more constitutionally correct and usually less politically realistic, chose not to apply Ickes' formula. He intended instead to give each man charged with collaboration a hearing as soon as possible. Soon the whole question was tangled up in proceedings too heavy and complicated for the returning government to handle.[9]

Perhaps the greatest confusion in trying collaborators, however, flowed from a peremptory act by General MacArthur, who practiced his own selective absolution. As the Commonwealth government returned with the American Army, the occupation republic had departed Manila with the Japanese. In December 1944, the Japanese military had taken the whole cabinet with them to Baguio, intending to carry them along to Northern Luzon if necessary. Accompanying Japanese diplomats, however, persuaded the Army not to endanger the Filipino leaders, but to leave most of them behind, for the postwar Philippines would need talent, and postwar Japan would need friends. Late in March 1945, Laurel and a few others were flown to Formosa and afterwards to Japan, but the majority were finally allowed to slip away from Baguio without restraint.[10]

In April, two of these, Manuel Roxas and Jose Yulo, made free and struggled eagerly toward the American lines. When they reached their goal, General MacArthur asked to have Roxas flown to him in a special plane, and soon greeted him with an enthusiastic bear hug. Yulo he jailed, like other leading collaborators, to await trial.

What difference was there between the two? Roxas had been Mac-

9. Letter from informant, name withheld. Also, Osmeña to the author, 10 Oct 58: "My thought on the so-called collaboration question was embodied in a statement I made upon landing in Leyte; not the mere act of occupying an office under the Japanese but *the motive in doing so and the record in office* would be the measure of one's loyalty. I still believe in this criterion." (Italics mine.)
10. Author's interviews with Fukushima Shintaro, 4 Oct 57, 17 Sept 58. Fukushima persuaded his immediate superior, Amb Murata, of the wisdom of the policy, and Murata in turn persuaded the Army. Laurel, in his *War Memoirs,* pp. 37–40, accentuates the fact that he argued in behalf of as many of his colleagues staying in the Philippines as possible, but that neither Murata nor the Army gave himself any option but to go to Japan.

Arthur's aide early in the war, and as leader of the Manila Intelligence Group had kept in touch with MacArthur's forces. Quezon had asked MacArthur to rescue him from the Philippines, both out of express fear for Roxas' safety and unexpressed fear of Roxas' growing popularity with the people. When first contacted, early in 1943, Roxas declined to leave. Early in 1944, however, he was willing to go in order to escape his deepening involvement with the Japanese-sponsored republic. A Filipino spy for the Japanese foiled the scheme, and the Japanese executed most of the leaders of the Manila Intelligence Group, including Juan Elizalde. Roxas' life was spared, partly because the Japanese misidentified General Vicente Lim as the "high-ranking officer" to be rescued, partly because Laurel intervened, as on other occasions, for Roxas' safety, and partly because some Japanese believed that executing Roxas would only promote popular rebellion.[11]

Now, in MacArthur's eyes, Roxas' counter-Japanese activities fully excused his participation in the puppet republic. Similar extenuations might have been found for Yulo and others, but MacArthur was either ignorant of or indifferent to them. He and his staff had found a Filipino who spoke their language, and they made the most of it.

When Senator Millard Tydings arrived with a presidential survey mission soon afterwards, MacArthur invited two of the members to lunch, E. D. Hester and J. Weldon Jones. The General discoursed on the principle of the precedence of civil government and made it clear that he had not planned and would not establish a military government in the Philippines. In the present confused and disorderly situation, however, he needed the utmost in efficient and decisive cooperation from the civil government; the Philippines was his staging area for a difficult advance to the north, and ultimately to Japan. He recalled an occasion in 1941 when he had said that Quezon deserved to be President of the Philippines for life. Now that that great man was gone, the nearest thing to him was Roxas, a fine

11. Roxas, "Wartime Activities"; undated memo by C. L. Parsons [1945], "Recital of the Participation of the Philippine Resistance Movement Especially with Relation to General Manuel Roxas" (Roxas MSS); author's interviews with Lt Col Richard Galang, 1 Sept 58, and with Maj Gen Courtney Whitney, 20 July 64; Lichauco, Roxas, pp. 186–92. All of these sources refute the article by Dale Pontius, which doubts that Roxas helped the guerrillas, "MacArthur and the Filipinos, Part I," Asia and the Americas, 46 (1946), 437–40. On Quezon's fear of postwar political rivalry from Roxas: author's interview with James G. Wingo, 30 Mar 57.

executive on good working terms with himself, and of great support before and during the war. MacArthur praised Osmeña as a splendid gentleman, with a traditionally important influence on the Filipino people, but he did not seem to make up his mind fast enough to cope with the existing situation. "I can't work with Osmeña," MacArthur said. The next day Tydings reported that the General had made the same position clear to him at dinner, and he thoroughly agreed: Roxas should be in a position to be useful to MacArthur and the United States in the final phase of the war, and a general election should be held as soon as possible to clear up the confusion in the executive and legislative branches.[12]

That same week, Roxas gave his political followers permission informally to launch his candidacy for the office of president.[13] The sudden appearance of political rivalry probably hindered Osmeña's cabinet in considering objectively a question conveyed from Senator Tydings. Should the Philippines accept independence on schedule, in 1946, or ask for postponement? Invasion, occupation, and reoccupation had so ravaged the islands that many Filipinos thought themselves less ready for independence, economically, than they had been in 1898. After the landings at Leyte, Osmeña had said, "If we don't take it now, we'll never get it," [14] but he might still have deferred to a majority of his cabinet. The cabinet, however, feared that Roxas' camp would charge them with deficient patriotism. None of the cabinet would dare delay, except Tomas Cabili, from Mindanao. There the Moros anticipated more rehabilitation from the United States than from an impoverished Filipino government in which they would have no real influence. Cabili seemed to be indirectly in favor of postponement, saying that his constituents would reelect him on such a platform. But the cabinet as a whole, without great enthusiasm, would take independence on schedule.[15] The manner of Philippine reconstruction was still an open question.

12. Interview, E. D. Hester, 4 Apr 58, and letter, Hester to the author, 30 Dec 63. Courtney Whitney conveyed MacArthur's luncheon invitation to Hester and to Jones, former High Commissioner. Hester later checked his impressions with Tydings, whom he learned to have had a similar experience at dinner that evening.
13. Hernando J. Abaya, *Betrayal in the Philippines* (New York, A. A. Wyn, 1946), pp. 75–76.
14. Informant's name withheld.
15. Hester interview, 4 Apr 58, and letter, Hester to author, 30 Dec 63. Minutes of cabinet meetings were apparently kept only in Osmeña's absence, and do not record this discussion (O/Q).

Before his return to the Philippines, Osmeña had tried to get action in Washington on problems of rebuilding the economy. "Stimson and Hull were friendly and vague; Ickes pontifical and vague; Tydings mildly interested and vague." The White House would not arrange an appointment with President Roosevelt, and Osmeña did not see him until April 1945.[16] Together they had a long, thorough talk which heartened Osmeña in his search for a "complete understanding," not only with the President "but also between the liberating forces and ourselves." [17] Roosevelt, at last informed concerning the Philippines, died a few days later.

Truman came into office ignorant. Ickes tried vigorously to persuade him against following through on independence and even against seeing Osmeña. The new President, however, was a Wilsonian on colonial matters and, like Roosevelt, wanted to inspire liberal Far Eastern policies in the British, French, and Dutch. He decided that he would expedite independence and that "Ickes was to have no part in this procedure." He saw Osmeña three times in April and May and promised help with rehabilitation.[18]

After serving his anti-imperial conscience, however, Truman seemed to lose interest in Philippine problems as greater ones pressed him. Ickes wrote him in July that Osmeña's moderate position was deteriorating. The recently convened Philippine Legislature was merely a forum for bitter recrimination between collaborators and those purporting to have led anti-Japanese guerrillas. If elections were held in November, there was a "danger that Roxas will be elected."

The latter's faction was using two weapons against Osmeña: he had brought back with him neither a rehabilitation program nor a trade formula. Ickes felt that Osmeña's "own lack of vigor and decisiveness had contributed to the failure . . . to form a program"; so had fragmentation of civilian responsibilities, strict Army censorship, and "the resistance of General MacArthur to effective action by the civilian agencies." "But the principal responsibility," Ickes admitted, "lies upon our own shoulders." He recommended the establishment of a survey commission like the earlier Taft and Wood-

16. Eyre, pp. 141–46; quotation, p. 141.
17. Osmeña to Franklin D. Roosevelt, 10 Apr 45 (O/Q).
18. Harry S. Truman, *Memoirs, 1, Year of Decisions* (Garden City, Doubleday, 1955), pp. 65–66, 275–77.

Forbes missions, and the immediate appointment of a high commissioner.[19]

Where rehabilitation is necessary, reform is possible. The Philippines in its suffering, presented an opportunity not only for a kind hand to relieve its suffering, but a strong hand to restructure its economy and its society. The American civilian agencies, however, were too weak and diffuse to act, and that left only the military. The Filipinos on MacArthur's staff, of whom Colonel Andres Soriano was the most prominent, were certainly not reformers. Some, in fact, were connected to the more conservative circles in Manila, and to former Francoites. Courtney Whitney, chief of political affairs, and General MacArthur himself, both held the social philosophy of conservative Republicanism. But even had MacArthur the will to change the Philippines, he had not the time, engaged as he was in fighting and in planning the expected invasion of the Japanese homeland.

Later, as Commander in occupied Japan, MacArthur would initiate, and Whitney guide, far-reaching political reforms, and occupation personnel would supervise the land reform, labor laws, and breaking up of *zaibatsu* that Washington required. Thus the initial American years in conquered Japan conferred more benefits than did the final stages of the American presence in the Philippines—an irony not lost on the more progressive Filipinos.

A high commissioner of broad and liberal views might have been able both to expedite rehabilitation and to inject reform in the Philippine situation, but MacArthur "vigorously opposed" appointing anyone while military operations continued, and Osmeña gently opposed restoring anyone to the job at all, as appearing to prolong Philippine dependency.[20] After V-J Day, however, Truman named Paul McNutt to the office. For some reason the anti-colonialist had chosen a man well known for favoring a dominion plan. A number of Filipinos approached McNutt and asked him, as others had asked Roy Howard, to take the lead for postponement of independence. Howard used his newspapers to warm up the idea, but McNutt watched his ground carefully. The initiative, he said, "must come from the Filipinos"; only if there were "a spontaneous and uninspired request" would the United States be likely to grant it. Such a request did not come, any more than it had from Quezon's government in

19. Ickes to Truman, 17 July 45 (HC).
20. Osmeña to Franklin D. Roosevelt, 10 Apr 45 (O/Q).

the prewar years. In Tokyo, McNutt predicted to Douglas Mac-
Arthur that an independent Philippines would not hold honest elections, because its politics was too corrupt. "Paul, you're absolutely
right," MacArthur said, "but . . . the Filipinos will hold as honest
an election as you ever had in the state of Indiana!" [21]

Harold Ickes meanwhile had delivered his valedictory on the
Philippines. He sent Osmeña a telegram in early September, intended to stiffen the latter's posture against the collaborators and to
strengthen his hand against all political opponents. Ickes asked for
effective prosecution of the "timid, craven, opportunistic helots who
basely collaborated with the cruel enemy who sought to enslave their
people." Until such prosecution was effectively in progress, Ickes
implied that the United States would extend no economic assistance
and permit no elections. [22]

McNutt's first report to President Truman, in late September,
shared Ickes' point of view, although in less evangelistic language:
"By inattention to civil affairs we have allowed the enemy collaborators to come into control of the legislative branch . . . and to
force Osmeña, who is weak and aging, to compromise with them.
For our part, we do not wish to be placed in the position of granting
independence to a Philippine government composed of enemy-
collaborators." [23]

Ickes' telegram gave Osmeña a break: it killed in the Philippine
Senate a bill for November elections. Osmeña wanted no voting until
May 1946, by which time, he hoped, rehabilitation and trade legislation from the United States would have strengthened his waning
popularity.

With McNutt's initial good will, Osmeña returned to the United
States to get the goods he desired: twenty years of free trade and
multiform technical and economic assistance. In October he saw
Truman, and the President signed a directive prepared in the High
Commissioner's office, initiating reconstruction through eleven secre-

21. Hester to the author, 30 Dec 63, gives a more objective account of McNutt's
position than does Abaya, pp. 175–79. The anecdote involving MacArthur appears in
Edgar Snow, *Journey to the Beginning* (New York, Random House, 1958), p. 389.
22. Text of telegram in Abaya, pp. 116–17, Bernstein, pp. 210–11.
23. McNutt, Fortas, "Memorandum for the President Relative to Enemy Collaborators
in the Philippine Government," 29 Sept 45 (HC).

taries of departments and heads of federal agencies.[24] Basic trade and relief legislation, however, was bottled up in Congress and would remain, it seemed, interminably delayed.

All Osmeña could bring back to Manila "was a few dollars and some promises."[25] When Cameron Forbes arrived for a visit at Malacañan, he found Osmeña, his host, "sick and tired and very much inclined to withdraw from the contest." MacArthur, Osmeña complained, had made things very difficult by singling out Roxas, of all the collaboration cabinet, for release; as President of the Senate, Roxas was now obstructing him. MacArthur had also authorized Osmeña to say that Filipino soldiers would get fifty pesos per month back pay; Washington had allowed only eight pesos, and the soldiers blamed Osmeña. Furthermore, because of the exasperating delay in relief, Osmeña still had to go to the Army for practically everything he wanted—supplies, transportation, technical assistance.[26]

At the end of Forbes' visit, Osmeña held a reception for him. The two tired old men received the guests together. Among them were some wealthy Hispanic families and former Falangists who were financing Osmeña's opponent. Various Zobels and Roxases passed by, but Forbes' old polo-playing friends were missing—"none of the Elizaldes came near me." Forbes thought that the Zobels and Roxases "expect to get material advantages if they succeed [in electing Manuel Roxas]"; and because Osmeña had fired Mike Elizalde and replaced him with Romulo, Forbes thought that he was "fairly angry and wants to get the Resident Commissionership back."[27] Elizalde did in fact become the first Philippine ambassador to the United States. Years later he recalled having spent "three or four hundred thousand pesos" supporting Roxas.[28] Only Soriano, it was said, contributed more.[29]

Osmeña meanwhile "had an idea that McNutt was turning against

24. Osmeña to Truman, 12 Oct, 8 Nov 45; Truman to High Comm et al., 26 Oct (O/Q).
25. Forbes Journals, 5, 511–12 (WCF).
26. Ibid., pp. 511–12, 563–64.
27. Ibid., pp. 516, 563. The Roxas-Ayala family of Manila was distantly related to Manuel Roxas, whose family was from Panay (Carlos Quirino, *Philippines Free Press*, 1 Feb 58).
28. Author's interview with J. M. Elizalde, 30 July 63.
29. Abaya, p. 267 n.

him." [30] The High Commissioner had at first been genuinely uncommitted, but felt that in December 1945 and January 1946 the Osmeña crowd several times double-crossed him. Osmeña himself had promised to support a fiat currency valuation bill recommended by the High Commissioner's office, but his men redrafted it in the Legislature so as to win crucial support and more votes for Osmeña.[31] McNutt, however, recommended against the changed version in principle, and Truman vetoed it. Later on, Osmeña's men opposed the trade and rehabilitation acts McNutt obtained. The High Commissioner came down more and more often on Roxas' side, doing nothing overt in his favor, but lending an intangible influence to him.[32]

At one point Osmeña was willing to take Roxas on his ticket as vice-presidential nominee and then resign the presidency to him shortly after the inauguration of the republic. Roxas, however, declined this arrangement. Later, Osmeña briefly agreed to let the Nacionalistas nominate him by acclamation; he would then decline, leaving the honor to Roxas. That arrangement failed also. Osmeña wanted to preserve national unity, but all the members of his cabinet and many party leaders urged him to run separately.[33] So did his wife. Mrs. Osmeña told Forbes "how she was keeping at him to go on with the fight. Fight, fight, fight! She got very intense and took my hand in hers and finally wept." [34]

Osmeña's own high concept of duty was against him. His strength

30. Forbes Journals, 5, 563 (WCF).

31. The original purpose of the bill was to assist creditors who had been paid in Japanese scrip at one-to-one with the genuine peso, against their will or during internment, imprisonment, or absence. The bill assisted them to recover deficiencies based on a time-scale of market value of the scrip. (For the schedule of values, see A. V. H. Hartendorp, *History of Industry and Trade in the Philippines*, American Chamber of Commerce of the Philippines, 1958, pp. 163–64.) The Congress talked about how peasants would be adversely affected, having cleared their indebtedness to landlords and usurers by payment in Japanese "Mickey Mouse money." An expert, however, declares that he never heard of a single such specific case, and that the process worked the other way around: landlords bought land from small farmers who were desperately in need of "Mickey Mouse" to buy food (Hester to the author, 31 Dec 63). A number of congressmen were also among the class that had profited during the war by paying contracts in scrip at one-to-one.

32. Hester interview, 4 Apr 58; Romulo to Osmeña (conveying summary of meeting with Truman), 11 Feb 46, Osmeña to Truman, 11 Mar (O/Q); Bernstein, p. 242.

33. Osmeña to the author, 10 Oct 58; author's interview with Rep Gerardo Roxas, 25 July 58; Lichauco, *Roxas*, pp. 207–12.

34. Forbes Journals, 5, 564 (WCF).

would not permit both administration and campaigning (one correspondent noted that he shook when guns went off in peaceful salute).[35] He therefore concentrated on reconstruction and gave only one speech at the end of the campaign. In his favor were his long service to the country and his return with MacArthur as a symbol of redemption. Upon old political and familial ties his followers could build anew, and his incumbency as President of the Commonwealth served him well: patronage had always been crucial to his power. Two weeks before the election, one of McNutt's advisors noted that "Osmeña has replaced practically all Roxas men in controlling positions in provinces and cities, and insofar as possible in municipalities." [36]

Besides his own home territory in the Visayas, Osmeña was strongest in central Luzon, where the Hukbalahap had replaced the landlords as political bosses. Denied social justice before the war and denied arms by MacArthur at its beginning, disgruntled peasants under Luis Taruc had gathered weapons anyway, from Americans before they surrendered, from deserters, and the dead of both armies. Now they were seeking social justice on their own terms. Their cadre of leaders was, with various degrees of sophistication, communistic. In 1946 they were still waging a parliamentary battle for power, but were ready, if frustrated, to resort to civil war.

Huk forces of 70,000 men controlled the vote in four provinces. Voter registration, in Pampanga especially, was "absurdly high." McNutt's advisor reported, "There is little doubt that the election will be replete with fraud and that circumstantially most of the fraud will be committed by the party in power." [37] Upon a complaint from Roxas, McNutt broke his policy of nonintervention to caution Osmeña against the terroristic practices of his followers in Central Luzon.[38]

Whatever edge Osmeña had over Roxas in Washington, with Truman, Ickes, and the bureaucracy, was useless unless the necessary trade and relief legislation came through in time. It did not come. Roxas meanwhile had the advantage of being favored in the Philippines by the United States Army, which controlled radio and other

35. Interview, James Wingo, 30 Mar 57.
36. Hester to McNutt, 12 Apr 46 (HC).
37. Ibid; also Forbes Journals, 5, 552–55 (WCF).
38. McNutt to Hester for Osmeña, 10 Apr 46 (HC).

crucial media of communication.[39] Roxas' own newspapers attacked
every foreign element except the Spanish, and called Osmeña "the
Chinese puppet leader in the Philippines."[40] Roxas had inherited
from Quezon the support of most of the great financial principals,
and a large majority of the influential collaborators were on his side.

In their inner hearts, perhaps, both Roxas and Osmeña regretted
support from the shadow polities behind them: Roxas, the remnants of the Japanese puppet government; Osmeña, the forces of a
would-be communist government. Both regretted, presumably, the
more vicious tactics of their followers—intimidation and falsification,
slander and terror. Both sought, obviously, American support: Osmeña, relief and trade bills in time to help him; Roxas, a continuation
of the Army support which MacArthur had begun. Each relied on
his specialty in the standard weaponry of politics—Osmeña, patronage; Roxas, wealth.

They differed chiefly in Osmeña's attending to the duties of his
office, while Roxas concentrated on the business of taking that office
from him. A significant alteration in any of the major factors might
have changed the results of the election. Of the two and a half
million votes cast Roxas won 54 per cent, and so became the first
President of the postwar Republic.

Thus the Philippines enjoyed, or endured, its first genuine national
two-party election. So small was the margin of victory that, in many
Latin American countries, it might have provoked a revolution by
the defeated. Osmeña, however, gave his people, in this first instance
of Nacionalista defeat, in this first electoral change of presidents, a
perfect example of dignified, cooperative transfer of power.

Although Congress had authorized creation of the Philippine Rehabilitation Commission in June 1944, that body emerged weak and
unwieldy and met only twice. The Philippines still lacked a trade
formula and relief monies when Paul McNutt returned to Washington from Manila, early in 1946. He expedited both the Bell Trade
Act and the Tydings Rehabilitation Act through a sluggish Congress
and, in doing so, managed to have them amended to resemble more
closely his own vision of Philippine-American relations.

The trade act, as passed, provided for eight years of free trade

39. Author's interview with A. V. H. Hartendorp, 15 Nov 57; Abaya, pp. 266–67.
40. Bernstein, p. 240; Hartendorp interview.

followed by twenty years of tariff step-ups, reaching 100 per cent in 1974. It tied the peso to the dollar and included a controversial provision giving American citizens much the same economic rights in the Philippines that they had enjoyed during the colonial period. The rehabilitation act provided the Philippines with $620 million compensation: $100 million in surplus American property, $120 million to restore public property and services, and $400 million for distribution among persons and firms who could satisfactorily prove that they had suffered war damage.

The trade formula represented a compromise between the desire of Philippine producers and the Philippine government for twenty years more of free trade and the desire of American competition, represented by Senator Tydings, that the Tydings-McDuffie Act simply resume as if interrupted, and thus seal off trade preferences in five years.[41]

McNutt's most important contributions were the parity provision in the first act and the "lynch-pin" provision in the second that tied it to the first. To give Americans the same rights as Filipinos in business and economic development contradicted the Commonwealth constitution and therefore required that it be amended. To insure passage of his amendment, McNutt had the rehabilitation act changed so that no claims in excess of $500 would be paid before the Philippines accepted the trade act, and therefore its parity provision, in full.[42]

These two shrewd devices, in effect, made the rebuilding of the Philippines dependent upon Americans receiving nearly the same business rights under the Republic that they had enjoyed under the Commonwealth.[43] Because of McNutt's lynch-pin, moreover, Congressman Jasper Bell could offer the strange argument for the rehabilitation bill that it would "recreate our sixth best customer in

41. Hester interview, 21 Mar 58, M. J. Ossorio to D. F. Webster, Pres, Phil-Amer Chamb Com, 21 Dec 44 (O/Q); Grunder and Livezey, pp. 259–61.
42. McNutt, "Suggested Amendments to S.1610," 11 Feb 46, revised 25 Feb (Legis Branch, Nat Arch); Grunder and Livezey, pp. 261–62, 264, 267–68.
43. Among the hundreds of individuals and corporations who benefited were Andres Soriano and Paul McNutt. Soriano, as a Filipino soldier, took advantage of "mass naturalization" to become an American citizen in October 1945. The choice of a third different nationality in four years cost him great losses in personal income tax. McNutt's benefits, of course, only came after his term as High Commissioner. His friend, C. V. Starr, who had built up the Philippine-American Life Insurance Company since the end of the war, then made him Chairman of the Board.

world commerce"; that the South could recapture its foremost foreign market in cotton products, New England its best market for textiles, dairy lands their best market for dairy products, and the Midwest an excellent market for flour and other products.[44] Bell's argument makes congressional motives sound more greedy than perhaps they were. Acting in quizzical haste, Congress was nonetheless expressing a belated gratitude for Filipino loyalty during the war; it probably had Philippine interests more genuinely in mind than at any time since before the Great Depression.

In behalf of Congress and McNutt, one might note that the trade preferences and quotas were basically the same as those offered by the Joint Preparatory Committee in 1939, then rejected on Capitol Hill but now, in a friendlier atmosphere, accepted. One might see the Philippines, appreciative of the special benefits of trade preference, conferring a benefit in return—the parity clause. Congress partly designed the latter to assure that American companies, such as Manila Electric, would assist in the rebuilding of the islands. The currency clause, likewise, was inserted to encourage the return of American capital and the attraction of new capital which might otherwise be "fearful of devaluation and impounding." [45]

One must ask, however, if Congress was really more affected by a spirit of gratitude or by an atmosphere of American business growth and strategic expansion in the Pacific. Was it more interested in conferring benefits or in obtaining privileges? Filipino leaders thought the latter. The Legislature resisted the parity amendment until it could do so no longer; then the electorate approved it by plebiscite, apathetically. Jose Laurel, who had reluctantly ceded the same rights to invading Japanese businessmen, thought the parity clause the least forgivable imposition in the history of American colonial policy.[46]

Some of the sharpest criticism of the trade act came from the American Departments of State and Commerce. Absolute quotas were "one of the most vicious of trade restrictions" and were in-

44. *Cong Rec* 79:2, 3506.
45. Richard R. Ely, "The Bell Trade Act," American Chamber of Commerce *Journal*, 29 (1953), 268–73, reprinted from Manila *Daily Bulletin*, 30 Mar 53. Ely, a prewar colonial administrator, was serving as attaché, American Embassy, when he wrote the article.
46. Laurel interview, 4 Aug 58.

compatible with American policy. Allocation provisions would give prewar Philippine producers a virtual monopoly in the leading exports and would throttle new competition. Other sections of the act were without reciprocity and mutuality and were inconsistent with giving the Philippines independence: for example, tying the peso to the dollar and obtaining special privileges for United States citizens.[47]

The American executive branch, which during the Great Depression had favored continuing imperial relationships, now favored ending them. The legislative branch, which had previously been determined to end all imperial ties, was disposed to restore some. In 1946, as in 1933, Congress was the winner. On April 30, the day after Osmeña conceded the election to Roxas, President Truman signed the Philippine trade and rehabilitation acts.

In a little over a year since the recapture of Manila and Corregidor, General MacArthur had indirectly helped to choose a new Philippine President, and High Commissioner McNutt had partly refashioned the prewar Philippine Commonwealth. Congressional policy, through delay and ignorance and confusion, had reinforced the policies of both MacArthur and McNutt. Congress, once too anxious to be rid of the Philippines, was now reluctant to let it go.

Manila celebrated Independence Day, July 4, 1946, with a ceremony on a temporary structure before the Rizal Monument. The Legislative Building, scene of the inauguration of the Commonwealth in 1935, was now an "obscene pyramid of brownish dust." Most of the city had suffered destruction, especially the old Spanish buildings of Intramuros, where the Japanese had dug in for a last suicidal resistance.

Manila was a quagmire in the rainy season; and in the hot season the red dust above the city, thrown up by heavy army traffic, made it look, from a distance, afire. The city was full of jerry-built shelters, and its hasty bazaars were full of gimcrack goods. Soldiers, sailors, and peddlers jammed its sidewalks; whores and pimps and pickpockets, confidence men and influence mongers; ex-guerrillas still in

47. Acting Sec State Dean Acheson to Sen Walter George, Chairman Sen Fin Comm, 2 Apr 46; Arthur Paul, Asst to Sec Commerce, to George, 2 Apr (Legis Branch, Nat Arch).

jungle uniform, and throngs of common men and women, tired and unemployed. To one observer who had loved the old city, the new Manila looked like a carnival in hell.

Rehabilitation funds could help reconstruct homes, business and public buildings, but what could they do for the nonassessable damage: "high death rates and incidence of disease, the general lawlessness and contempt of government, the violence and criminality, marked by a barbaric disregard of human life, the general blunting of the moral sense and abandonment of ethical standards, and the cancerous corruption in both public and private spheres?"

An American resident, freed from a concentration camp, reckoned that "for every tortured man there was a tortured family; with every broken home a dream died; with the death of every one of the hundreds of thousands of those slain in battle, murdered by the secret police or massacred in the final frenzy, the nation died a little." The people had suffered not only from fear and hatred, but humiliation and shame; they were not only naked and hungry, but sick and confused. For a few weeks after the Americans returned, they had responded with delirious joy, but then succumbed again to bitterness, or the apathy of irreparable loss.[48]

Against the grim surroundings, the Independence Day speakers strove to convey a sense of triumph. General MacArthur spoke of the two peoples, who, "despite racial, cultural and language differences and great distances of geographical separation . . . forged an affinity of understanding which survived both the vagaries of peace and the shock of war. . . . Let history record this event . . . as foretelling the end of mastery over peoples by force alone,—the end of empire as the political chain which binds the unwilling weak to the unyielding strong."

A heavy rain began to fall as High Commissioner McNutt spoke, referring to the atomic tests at Bikini a few days before and to the present occasion, "one action an expression of limitless power, the other a manifestation of infinite understanding." At 9:15 A.M. McNutt lowered the American flag. On the same white cord, President Roxas slowly raised the Philippine flag, symbol, he said, of a sovereignty now possessed in full measure. In the hearts of eighteen million Filipinos, he said, the American flag now flew more triumphantly than ever. His people looked back in gratitude and forward

48. Hartendorp, *History of Industry and Trade*, pp. 154, 167–68.

in harmony with the United States: "We are a staging area of democracy in this part of the world." [49]

When the ceremony was over, MacArthur turned to Romulo and said, "Carlos, America buried imperialism here today!" [50] As with his Philippine defense plan, the General spoke more in noble hope than sober truth.

On July 27, 1946, the *U.S.S. Princeton* put into Manila harbor, returning the remains of President Quezon to his native land. As the casket was brought ashore, the ship's guns boomed twenty-one times. The United States had at last given Manuel Quezon the salute of his heart's desire.

A few days before, Laurel and others of the occupation government had flown back, under guard, from Japan. Laurel, who had held a secret mass in Malacañan when Quezon died, obtained permission to pay his respects before the bier.[51] The two presidential exiles had returned from the imperial capitals of their refuge. One awaited burial; the other awaited trial for treason.

49. Ibid., pp. 230–33.
50. Carlos P. Romulo, *Crusade in Asia: Philippine Victory* (New York, John Day, 1955), p. 5.
51. Hartendorp, pp. 233–34.

Epilogue

IF AMERICAN OCCUPATION of the Philippines had ended in 1901 with
military rule, the United States would be remembered more for
cruelty than for generosity, even though Arthur MacArthur had begun the work of reconstruction. But the civil government that followed, designed for "the happiness, peace, and prosperity of the
people," and lasting for over forty years, erased cruel memories and
won the friendship of most Filipinos. Elihu Root had directed that
the government conform as far as practical "to their customs, their
habits, and even their prejudices," and so it was done.

The policy of permissiveness, with few exceptions, won over the
most ardent Filipino nationalists. One who from exile in Hong Kong
had written Theodore Roosevelt asking Americans to leave the Philippines lived to say, fifty-six years later, that the Americans should
come back.[1] Root's policy won Filipino loyalty and more: the envy
of nationalists elsewhere in Southeast Asia and in the wide colonial
world.

Nevertheless, reconciling Philippine customs with American requisites had not been simple or easy. Between the Filipino concept of
the familial polity and the American idea of effective government
there was tension enough to provide, over the years, a handsome
number of misunderstandings, scandals, humiliations, and recrimina-
tions. Nor had all the effects of the American presence and the Root
policy been beneficial, as perhaps the Japanese saw most clearly. Out
of their own remarkable history of modernization and economic de-

1. Celestino Rodriguez, et al. to Theodore Roosevelt, 10 Oct 01 (Central Library,
National Taiwan University); author's interview with Rodriguez, Dec 57.

velopment the Japanese could say that the Filipinos suffered from too much legalism, egotism, and epicureanism; the United States had permitted them to overindulge appetites for personal liberty, white-collar learning, and consumer goods. As General Homma observed, "A nation which indulges in pretty dresses, nice food, physical enjoyment and expensive fashions can never succeed in establishing a strong nation." If the Filipinos needed more vocational education, more social efficiency, more sense of duty and obligation,[2] the Japanese might have provided these correctives. But they lacked both the power to remain in the Philippines and the persuasiveness to change it.

Homma and other Japanese exhorted the Philippines to cease being "a captive of the capitalism and industrialism of the United States" and "to liquidate the unnatural culture borrowed from a far away country."[3] They did not recognize that state capitalism associated with Oriental imperialism might be just as unwelcome as private capitalism associated with Occidental imperialism. They were also slow to see how deeply absorbed from Spain—not just "borrowed"—was Christian culture in the Philippines.

Although American social prejudice had been inexpressibly galling to the Filipinos, they found no antidote in the idea of Oriental brotherhood, especially when it appeared as conquest by yellow non-Christians. Was anything in Western dominance as insulting as the face-slappings administered by Japanese soldiers? The notion of white superiority was never that blatant, and somehow the shared faith of Christianity had made injury less baffling. American colonial discipline, furthermore, usually had not been wanting in tact. In return for tact, the Filipino would forgive a great deal.

The Japanese might have made a "strong nation" out of the Philippines, but only if they had taken it in 1898. Even then, the subsequent histories of Korea and Formosa were not reassuring. By 1941, the Filipinos were already too well developed under American rule, or too spoiled as the Japanese saw it, for the invaders to accomplish much, especially when the higher ideals of the Japanese so frequently had to be sacrificed to military necessities. The Japanese provided no bell for Adano; they melted the bells down to guns.

2. Rōyama, et al., *Report of the Research Commission on the Philippines* (1943), passim.
3. Quotations from *Journal of the Japanese Military Administration*, 2 (1942), v–vi.

For all the sacrifices of 1942–45, there was little constructive good to compensate.

A Japanese diplomat, stirred by Douglas MacArthur's great speech at the surrender ceremonies, wrote afterwards that "we were not beaten on the battlefield by dint of superior arms. We were defeated in the spiritual contest by virtue of a nobler ideal. The real issue was moral—beyond the powers of algebra to compute." [4] If this were true of the war in general, it was most particularly and sharply true in the Philippines, where one tutelary concept had fought against another, and the more permissive and generous had won.

When Carlos Romulo returned to Leyte, he saw a new light in the eyes of his people, a new pride and self-reliance won through suffering and victory.[5] But the light he saw was in the eyes of the guerrillas. The majority of the people had not been enhanced in spirit by war, but had suffered spiritual erosion; they were prey to cynicism, corruption, and a philosophy of *agaw-buhay:* "snatch-life." This damage to the moral fiber of the Philippines, as well as material destruction there, is in part traceable to American military unpreparedness. Any account of the American years in the Philippines must include this vast debit item. And an historian must ask if the damage could have been avoided.

In resolving the colonial crisis of the Great Depression, two courses were open to the United States, other than that actually followed. One was to keep the Philippines indefinitely under American sovereignty, increasing its autonomy preliminary to a dominion plan; Senator Vandenberg's bill proposed something of this kind. The other was to make an early and absolute exit from the Philippines, as Senator King's bill provided.

The former course might have satisfied Winston Churchill. In predicting the descent of "chaos and old night" upon a people unfit to rule themselves, Churchill grossly underestimated the Filipinos, as he did peoples subject to the British. In another prediction, however, Churchill was absolutely correct: that the withdrawal of the United States from the Philippines would contribute to an upset of the balance of power in Asia, and increase the chances of war.[6]

4. Toshikazu Kase, *Journey to the "Missouri"* (New Haven, Yale University Press, 1950), p. 14.
5. Romulo, *Philippines Rise,* pp. 132–34, 140.
6. Winston Churchill, "Defense in the Pacific," *Colliers,* 17 Dec 32.

The corollary of any retention policy (even the ten-plus years of the Tydings-McDuffie Act) should have been a build-up of naval and air forces in the Philippines, begun early and maintained large enough to deter a Japanese invasion. Instead, a feverish effort, too late and too little, actually helped to incite attack. In all American history their is perhaps no such striking example of commitment exceeding armament. Instead of leaving the Philippines with dignity, the United States was driven out in disgrace. By the time the return was complete—to win the war, to restore face, to complete the tutelary job—at least 40,000 Americans, 300,000 Japanese, and 500,000 Filipinos had died on Philippine soil.[7]

As long as depression, traditional isolation, and naïveté about power left Americans unequal to the Churchillian policy of arming to prevent war across the Atlantic or the Pacific, Vandenberg's bill would have led to disaster just as surely as Tydings'. In any event, American diffidence about being an imperial power and the Filipino appetite for sovereignty left no escape, in the 1932–33 lame duck session of Congress, from a bill fixing the date for Philippine independence.

Looking backward, one asks whether the United States could have executed a quick and complete withdrawal from the Philippines, sparing it devastation comparable with that of Poland? War could have come anyway, although possibly later, over the massive snare in China and Japan's southward advance on the European colonies. King's bill, however, would have made the Philippines independent well before December 1941. If Quezon had then refused to permit American bases, the Philippines might have been spared its terrible scourging.

The Japanese would have arrived anyway and eventually departed, but less destructively on each occasion. The Filipinos, like the Thai, would have put up only token military resistance. Because of their cultural attachment to the West and their newly won independence, they would still have been the least cooperative of the peoples in Japan's Co-Prosperity Sphere. National interest, nonetheless, would more readily have justified collaboration; and collaboration would have smelled far less of disloyalty to the United States and ingratitude for her years of help than it actually did.

7. I am now preparing an article in which I will explain and perhaps amend these estimates.

To continue the hypothesis, General Douglas MacArthur would have experienced neither the pain of initial defeat in the Philippines nor the glory of final victory there. Naval views on strategy would have prevailed, and a direct thrust toward Japan would have spared the Philippines' being made a major battleground. All told, the dozen years, 1941–53, would have been easier for the Philippines: little or no destruction from battle, probably less economic raiding by the Japanese, far less opportunity and incentive for a guerrilla army like the Hukbalahap to gather arms and momentum and destroy the peace with a civil war. Corruption would have had far less moral weakening to feed on, and communism less misery by which to profit. Where this escalator of subjunctives might have carried the Philippines in the next dozen years after 1953—without American trade preferences, with far less American financial and technical assistance—is impossible to say.

To return to things as they happened instead: the raising of the Philippine flag in 1946 coincided with a new wave of American expansionism. General MacArthur had returned, and so in a sense had Admiral Mahan and President Taft. To serve national security through strategic expansion, the United States obtained ninety-nine year leases on a number of bases in the Philippines, part of a worldwide system to contain, or encircle, communism. By such means the major Filipino leaders felt their security insured as well. All of them were eager for postwar bases—Quezon before he died, Osmeña after him, and Roxas as President during the subsequent negotiations.[8]

To serve its national interest through economic expansion, the United States reestablished special trade relations with the Philippines and extracted the same business privileges for American nationals that were enjoyed by native Filipinos. The United States, in "recreating our sixth best customer," was talking the language of the turn of the century instead of the depression, when the Philippines appeared mainly to be an agricultural competitor.

In requiring a Philippine constitutional amendment to provide

8. Concerning Quezon: Stimson diary, 12 Aug to 5 Sept 43 (HLS); three memos, Quezon to Sumner Welles, 5 May 43, and two earlier, undated, plus Quezon to Franklin D. Roosevelt, 26 Oct 43 (Q). Concerning Osmeña: Grunder and Livezey, *Philippines and U.S.*, p. 245; Truman, *Year of Decisions*, p. 277. Concerning Roxas: Grunder and Livezey, p. 273, and Roxas MSS, passim.

"business citizenship" for Americans, the United States was taking a step not unlike the Japanese, who required the Filipinos to accord them similar privileges in secret agreements following the 1943 constitution. The methods differed—peacetime plebiscite as against wartime fiat—and so did the response: those Filipinos who voted stood eight to one in favor of the American measure. The Filipinos called the Co-Prosperity Sphere "prosperity-*ko*" or "me-first prosperity"; but most of them were willing to tolerate the United States' recreating some economic conditions of the prewar Commonwealth.

If elements of Mahan's "large policy" and Taft's "dollar diplomacy" returned to the Philippines in 1946, there were major differences in the situation. The Philippines now had political sovereignty, with its inevitable, irreversible effects for change. The Commonwealth era had been stagnant; the postwar years of the Republic were the true years of transition to independence. A two-party system replaced the old Nacionalista machine, a product of Quezon's personality and colonial conditions. A burgeoning entrepreneurial class emerged, probably the largest and liveliest of any Southeast Asian country. If it were not always equal to the demands of a mushrooming economy, it proved that Catholic respect for private property and American methods of private enterprise were deep in the Filipino grain.

The influence of whites and mestizos waned, and against the Elizaldes and Sorianos appeared new political power, new business competence and competition. Because politicians out of power courted the peasants and urban poor, administrations in power had more and more to concern themselves, at least rhetorically, with the long-neglected masses. Thus the day of social reckoning, postponed under American rule and accelerated by war, came steadily closer.

Since the Filipinos had acquired full legislative power in 1916, the social and economic problems had been their own, as well as their colonial governors'. The legislators had been too concerned, however, with independence, as well as too power-minded and too medieval to do much about the poor. Quezon as President of the Commonwealth had sloganeered about "social justice," but accomplished little. Americans to the end meant well but achieved little in this field. MacArthur's occupation of Japan after the war liberalized that country, but his liberation of the Philippines only returned conservatives to power. Then the Huk revolt, symptom of social and economic inequities, rent the Philippines in civil war from 1946 to 1953. American military assistance helped put it down, just as American unpreparedness had led to the war from which it rose.

Symptoms treated, the causes remained. Filipino leadership, having absorbed more about private enterprise from Americans than about social conscience, had not, twenty years after Quezon's death, brought the country much closer to social justice. The established order continued: new faces, new names, guaranteed by the presence of a large domestic army and by the presence of the United States' Seventh Fleet. As for the symbols of Quezon's policy—the club was ready, but bread was still wanting.

A dozen years after the American flag came down, the Filipinos were still talking about independence: not "immediate, absolute, and complete," as the old slogan had it, but economic, cultural, and moral, as new needs required.[9] The Laurel-Langley agreement of 1955 inserted in the Bell Act the reciprocity missing in 1946.[10] New agreements on military bases in the late 1950s helped the Philippines reach another plateau of decolonization. Still the Filipinos struggled against confusion toward a national personality, and strove, surrounded with hazards, toward what Laurel called the "point of national safety."

The Philippines' orientation in foreign affairs was in some ways clearing up and in other ways clouding. When Khrushchev in the United Nations described the Philippines as a colony, the Filipinos proudly defended their affinity with Western culture, their alignment with Western power, their alliance with the United States. Carlos Romulo had written of "Mother America," and if many Filipinos were shy of the phrase, most were nonetheless comfortable with the feeling.

Spain, meanwhile, had lost most of its grandmotherly hold on the Philippines. The "Kastilas" were waning in prominence, and no one any longer seriously considered making the Philippines an eastern branch office of Franco's Falange. At the same time Filipinos were rediscovering their Malay and pre-Hispanic background, and began

9. For sharply articulate samples of a very large literature, see the articles by Teodoro Locsin, Philippines *Free Press,* 7 July 62, 13 July 63.
10. Frank Golay, "The Revised United States–Philippine Trade Agreements of 1955" (Cornell University, Southeast Asia Program, Data Paper No. 23, 1956).

to examine schemes of regional association. Laurel, Romulo, and others had publicized such ideas in the mid-1930s, and Quezon had toyed with them during his wartime exile.[11] Malay federation, however, remained a visionary idea as long as Southeast Asian countries relied on various Western powers, or Russia, for arms or for defense.

A new enemy had appeared, and an old one had not yet won back the trust of Greater East Asia. In 1927 Claro Recto had scoffed at Malay federation as a deterrent to Japanese expansion. Thirty years later, he remained a realist and a pessimist. If the West obtained the upper hand in the Asian cold war, Recto predicted before he died, the United States would let Japan "police" Asia, and the Filipinos would let themselves become dummies for Japanese enterprise. If Communist China obtained the upper hand, the Philippines would become one of her provinces. Overseas Chinese were already strongly entrenched in the Philippine economy, and 90 per cent of them, Recto said, would turn Red if it meant better business. Chinese hegemony was a greater likelihood and a greater danger than ever Japanese had been.[12]

Recto's analysis, as it had a generation before, left the safety of a Christian, democratic, self-governing Philippines to the continued presence of American military power. Once that power had failed. Now the development of Malay-Hispanic-American culture was again in danger from a species of Oriental expansionism. The Philippines, as in Quezon's era, could have complete independence only at the cost of extreme insecurity, and optimum security only at the cost of incomplete independence. But skeptical as he was of American power, sensitive as he was for Philippine dignity, Recto in 1958 no more desired an American military withdrawal than he had in 1927.

The revolution of 1896 had left the Philippines between two civilizations and two empires: feudal Catholic Spain and industrial Protestant America. An emotional commitment developed toward the latter, without displacing most of the habits absorbed from the former. After the colonial crisis of 1929–33, the retreat of the United States from empire and the advance of Japan put the Philippines in

---

11. Quijano de Manila (Nick Joaquin), "The Malay Confederation," *Philippines Free Press,* 22 June 63; Eyre, *Roosevelt-MacArthur Conflict,* pp. 190–91; Bernstein, *Philippine Story,* pp. 102–03.
12. Author's interviews with Recto, 4 Sept, 26 Nov 58.

jeopardy of conquest and then at the mercy of a new invader's reforms. If a few of these were sublimely conceived, all were crudely executed. When, in 1945, other colonial peoples in Southeast Asia spoke of European "reoccupation," the Filipinos welcomed back Americans as "liberators."

Soon, however, the young nation found itself in a new phase of a characteristic Philippine predicament: standing in danger between two empires. The United States, in contrast to its interwar isolation, assumed military commitments all over the world. It contributed to quelling the Huk rebellion and the threat of communist arms in the Philippines; it promoted and led the Southeast Asia Treaty Organization in opposition to communism throughout the region. While no longer an empire in the Kiplingesque sense, the United States had become an empire in a strategic sense, shouldering the "free world's burden" in far-flung places. In Southeast Asia this meant confrontation with a new Chinese empire, ambitious and powerful as China had not been since the eighteenth century. This was an empire in the older sense, eager, just as Japan had been, to "liberate" fellow Asians from the remnants of Western influence. But expansionistic Chinese nationalism and evangelistic Chinese communism posed a challenge to Southeast Asia potentially greater than Japan's had ever been.

In this new threat to national independence, the Philippines was not further jeopardized by military unreadiness, her own or American, as it had been in the 1930s. Security, however, was costly, and the time, money, and emotion spent on it had to be taken away from the socioeconomic development and cultural integration of the nation. An unbalanced economy, a plural society, a fragmented culture were her inheritance from colonial times. Could the Philippines accomplish the work of economic diversification and social and cultural unification, necessary to make a national community out of an ex-colony? How long would the Philippines remain in confusion between two civilizations, inherent and emergent, as well as in peril between two empires, Chinese and American?

Appendix

CHRONOLOGY, 1896–1946

1896		Philippine Revolution against Spain
1898		The United States declares war against Spain
1899	Jan	Constitutional convention at Malolos; Aguinaldo proclaims Philippine Republic
	Feb	The United States annexes the Philippines; Philippine-American War begins
1901	Apr	Americans capture Aguinaldo
	July 4	Civil government commences under Taft (Civil Governor, 1901–04) and appointed Philippine Commission.
1902		Congress passes first Philippine Organic Act
1905		Japanese defeat Russians in war; Taft-Katsura memorandum guarantees safety of the Philippines
1907		First Philippine national election; Osmeña elected Speaker of the Philippine Assembly; Quezon later becomes Resident Commissioner in Washington (1909–16)
1913		Francis Burton Harrison becomes Governor General (1913–21); Underwood Tariff prescribes complete free trade between the United States and the Philippines
1915		Japan, having taken German colonies in the Pacific and Shantung, presses the Twenty-One Demands on China
1916	May	Clarke Amendment, giving Philippines immediate independence, barely fails in House
	Aug	Jones Act passes (second Philippine Organic Act); elective Philippine Senate replaces appointive Commission
1919		First Philippine Independence Mission to Washington
1921		Wood-Forbes Report; Leonard Wood Governor General (1921–27)
1921–22		Washington treaties limit naval building and fortifications in the Pacific
1922		Quezon defeats Osmeña, becomes President of the Senate; Manuel Roxas, Speaker of the House

1923		Philippine cabinet crisis; Wood's departmental secretaries resign, including Jose P. Laurel
1924		Fairfield Bill, scheduling independence in twenty years, dies in Congress
1929		Crash on Wall Street; beginning of Great Depression
1930		Senate hearings on Philippine independence lead to report of Hawes-Cutting Bill
1931	Sept 18	Japan invades Manchuria
	Dec	Osmeña-Roxas Legislative Mission departs Manila for Washington
1932	Feb	Secretary of State Stimson's letters to Senators Bingham and Borah define American policy in the Philippines and Manchuria
	Mar	House hearings on Philippine independence conclude
	Apr	Hare Bill passes House
	Nov	Franklin D. Roosevelt elected President of the United States
	Dec	Hawes-Cutting Bill passes Senate
1933	Jan	Hoover vetoes Hare-Hawes-Cutting Bill; Congress repasses it over veto
	July	Quezon's faction reorganizes Philippine Legislature; removes Osmeña as Vice-President of the Senate and Roxas as Speaker of the House
	Oct	Philippine Legislature "declines to accept" the Hare-Hawes-Cutting Act
	Nov	Quezon leads new mission to Washington
1934	Mar	Congress passes Tydings-McDuffie Act
	May	Philippine Legislature accepts Tydings-McDuffie Act
	June	Quezon faction defeats Osmeña-Roxas faction in triennial elections
		Japanese accelerate economic and cultural penetration of the Philippines
1935	Nov	Inauguration of the Philippine Commonwealth; Quezon its President
1936	Mar	Split report on the Philippines and War Plan ORANGE-3 by Army members and Navy members of the Joint Planning Committee, Joint Board of the Army and Navy
	June	Gen MacArthur's "Report on National Defense in the Philippines"
1937	July	Beginning of full-scale war between Japan and China
1938	Mar	High Commissioner McNutt publicly proposes reexamination of Philippine independence; Quezon repudiates the idea

May   Report of Joint Preparatory Committee on Philippine Affairs (JPCPA)

Nov   Overwhelming victory of the Nacionalista fusion party in national elections

1939 Aug   Congress passes Tydings-Kocialkowski Act, embodying a minimum of the recommendations of the JPCPA

Sept-   Quezon breaks with MacArthur on defense policy; begins cutbacks in defense program
Nov

1941 July   The United States places embargo on shipments of oil and scrap iron to Japan; freezes Japanese assets in the United States. Roosevelt appoints MacArthur Commander, United States Armed Forces Far East

Nov 21 MacArthur's request granted to incorporate his Philippine defense plan into War Plan RAINBOW-5

Dec 7   Japanese bombing of Pearl Harbor, and ten hours later, Clark Field (Dec 8, Philippine time)

Dec 22 Japanese land main forces at Lingayen Gulf

Dec 23 MacArthur forced to abandon his Philippine defense plan, reverts to War Plan ORANGE-3

Dec 24 Quezon, MacArthur, and others evacuate to Corregidor

1942 Jan 2 Japanese forces enter Manila

Jan 23 Japanese sponsor formation of Philippine Executive Commission, Jorge Vargas, Chairman

Feb 8–9 Quezon proposes surrender and neutralization of the Philippines; Roosevelt rejects proposal

Mar 17 MacArthur arrives in Australia; Filipino leaders, who had left Corregidor earlier, arrive several days later

May 6   Gen Wainwright surrenders Corregidor

1943 June Japanese sponsor a Preparatory Commission for Philippine Independence, Jose Laurel, Chairman

Sept   Twenty Filipino leaders sign Constitution for Japanese-sponsored Republic; Jose Laurel, President

1944 Aug   Death of Quezon in Saranac Lake, N.Y.

Oct   First American landings in Leyte

1945 Feb   Last stand of the Japanese in Manila

Aug 15 Japan surrenders

1946 Apr   Roxas defeats Osmeña in presidential elections; Congress passes Bell Trade Act and Tydings Rehabilitation Act

July 4   American flag lowered, Philippine flag raised, in ceremonies of Philippine independence

The Sources

THE SOURCES for this work have been of many kinds, from many places. I mention here only the most pertinent, useful, and novel. For lack of space I have cut out a particularly large category of books covering the period 1896–1929. I have included several articles and books published in the last two years, although I have been unable to use all of them because they appeared after my writing was essentially complete.

BIBLIOGRAPHICAL AIDS

Special bibliographic work on the Philippines is still in its infancy. Charles O. Houston has produced *Philippine Bibliography, I. An Annotated Preliminary Bibliography of Philippine Bibliographies (Since 1900)* (Manila, the University of Manila, 1960). Fred Eggan and Evett D. Hester, of the University of Chicago Philippine Studies Program, have published a serviceable guide, *Selected Bibliography of the Philippines: Topically Arranged and Annotated* (New Haven, Human Relations Area Files, 1956).

Garel A. Grunder and William E. Livezey, *The Philippines and the United States* (Norman, Okla., Oklahoma University Press, 1951), contains a list of United States Government publications, 1898–1951, an invaluable time-saver for researchers on Philippine-American relations. A supplementary potpourri, covering the years 1934–50, is Houston's "Bibliographical Note and Bibliography," *The Journal of East Asiatic Studies, 4* (University of Manila, 1955), 173–244. James I. Irikura's *Bibliography of Japanese Writings on Southeast Asia* (New Haven, HRAF, 1956), the sole guide of its kind in English, contains 110 items on the Philippines.

Three pamphlets during the 1930s kept up with writings on the independence question when it was most frantic: Anne L. Baden, *Philippine Islands, with Special Reference to the Question of Independence* (Washington, Library of Congress, 1931); Anne Duncan Brown, *A Selected List of References on the Philippine Islands* (Washington, Library of Congress, 1935); M. Alice Matthews, *Carnegie Endowment for International Peace, Select Bibliography No. 9* (New York, 1939).

The Journal of Asian Studies publishes an annual bibliographic issue, the best of its kind. Other works which include Philippine categories are: William Langer and Hamilton Fish Armstrong, eds., *Foreign Affairs Bibliography* (New York, Council on Foreign Relations, 1933); R. G. Woolbert, ed., *Foreign Affairs Bibliography* (New York, Council on Foreign Relations, 1945); Stephen N. Hay and Margaret H. Case, *Southeast Asian History: A Bibliographic Guide* (New York, Praeger, 1962).

GENERAL WORKS

Reinhold Niebuhr's *The Structure of Nations and Empires* (New York, Scribner's, 1959), discusses the moral problems of imperial power from ancient Rome to modern Russia. Philosophical, focusing on newly emergent states, is Rupert Emerson's *From Empire to Nation, the Rise to Self-Assertion of Asian and African Peoples* (Cambridge, Harvard University Press, 1960). From quite another angle, K. M. Panikkar reviews the same questions in *Asia and Western Dominance, a Survey of the Vasco Da Gama Epoch of Asian History, 1498–1945* (London, George Allen & Unwin, 1953; rev. ed., 1959). J. S. Furnivall, *Colonial Policy and Practice* (Cambridge University Press, 1948; American ed., New York University Press, 1956) is a comparative study of Burma and Netherlands India, done with great skill and high style. No one has yet woven the Philippines tightly into a Southeast Asian context for comparative study, although John F. Cady has recently published a useful textbook, *Southeast Asia: Its Historical Development* (New York, McGraw-Hill, 1964). Some of the best American scholarship on the Philippines has been limited by lack of indigenous sources and broader regional context. Julius Pratt tells judiciously and concisely the story promised in his subtitle: "How the United States Gained, Governed, and in Part Gave Away a Colonial Empire," in *America's Colonial Experiment* (New York, Prentice-Hall, 1950). Grunder and Livezey, *The Philippines and the United States,* suffers from a paucity of Philippine sources and apparently from faint knowledge of native politics. To *The Philippines, a Study in National Development* (New York, Macmillan, 1942), Joseph Ralston Hayden brought his experience as political scientist and colonial administrator. His book is often too arduously theoretical, but it is very well documented with Philippine newspapers and pamphlets.

The most significant studies of American colonial policy in other languages are G. I. Levinson, *Filippiny Mezhdu Pervoy i Vtoroy Mirovymi Voynami* (The Philippines between the First and Second World Wars) (Moscow, Izdatel'stvo Vostochnoy Literatury Akademii Nauk USSR, 1958), and Georges Fischer, *Un Cas de Décolonisation: Les États-Unis et les Philippines* (Paris, Pichon & Durand-Auzias, 1960). I have criticized both, the former adversely, in a review article: "Decolonization of the Philippines: A Russian and a French View," *Journal of Asian Studies,* 22 (1962), 89–94.

Two recently published works are Whitney T. Perkins, *Denial of Empire: The United States and Its Dependencies* (Lyden, A. W. Sythoff, 1962), and George E. Taylor, *The Philippines and the United States: Problems of Partnership* (New York, Frederick A. Praeger, 1964). The latter is a well-balanced analysis of both the American colonial period and the years since independence, slightly weighted toward the latter.

Philippine history is largely an uncleared jungle. The best approach to the Spanish period is through Horacio de la Costa, S.J., *The Jesuits in the Philippines, 1581–1768* (Cambridge, Harvard University Press, 1961). Until Father de la Costa publishes a modern synthesis, the best short summary of the whole Spanish era remains Edward Gaylord Bourne's "Historical Introduction" (pp. 19–88) to the documentary collection by Helen Blair and James A. Robertson, *The Philippine Islands* (55 vols. Cleveland, 1903–09). James Leddy Phelan has contributed a suggestive, if disputable, interpretation of *The Hispanization of the Philippines* (Madison, University of Wisconsin, 1959). In lieu of a general history one may approach the Philippines through the discussions of family, land, religion, and other subjects in the massively useful *Area Handbook on the Philippines* (Fred R. Eggan, ed., 4 vols., New Haven, HRAF, preliminary edition, 1956). Gregorio F. Zaide's *Philippine Political and Cultural History* (2 vols., Manila, Philippine Education Co., 1949) is a standard textbook.

Carl Landé's unpublished doctoral dissertation, Harvard, 1958, "Politics in the Philippines," contains a great amount of original research and insight upon the subject. Charles Kaut's "Utang na Loob" (*Southwestern Journal of Anthropology, 17,* 1961, 256–72), along with Landé, is indispensable to an understanding of Philippine folkways and political manners. Likewise illuminating is Jaime C. Bulatao's "Hiyâ," *Philippine Studies, 12* (1964), 424–38.

Systematic Japanese scholarship on the Philippines is found in Rōyama Masamichi, et al., *Report of the Research Commission on the Philippines* (4 vols. Japanese Military Administration in the Philippines, 1943).

Special Works

Assorted Monographs

In addition to the American journals which customarily publish articles on American, East Asian, and Southeast Asian history, one may frequently find provocative articles in Philippine journals, notably *Philippine Studies* (sponsored by the Ateneo de Manila); the *Philippine Social Science and Humanities Review;* the *Buletin ng Samahang Pangka Saysayan ng Pilipinas* (Bulletin of the Philippine Historical Association); the *Journal of East Asiatic Studies* (sponsored by the University of Manila); and *Comment* (affiliated with the Congress for Cultural Freedom and Official Correspondent for Philippine Center, International P.E.N.).

Upon the colonial crisis brought about by the Great Depression, Grayson V. Kirk's *Philippine Independence* (New York, Farrar & Rinehart, 1936) remains a work of great merit, although lacking entirely in foreign source materials and a comparative context. The crisis attracted study from some European scholars, notably J. A. E. Buiskool, *De Verkrijging van de Onafhankelijkheid der Philippijnen* (Amsterdam, H. J. Paris, 1935) and André Labrouquère,

L'Indépendence des Philippines (Paris, Domat-Mont Chrétien, 1936). The Dutchman's is chiefly a legalistic study; the Frenchman's more generally penetrating because of his expertise on Indochina. As a timely work of propaganda, Senator Harry Hawes' *Philippine Uncertainty* (New York, Century, 1932), still bears reading. I am presently publishing in *Philippine Studies* a series of detailed articles on the Hare-Hawes-Cutting Act, of which three have thus far appeared: "American Interests and Philippine Independence, 1929–1933," *11* (1963), 505–23; "Philippine Interests and the Mission for Independence, 1929–1932," *12* (1964), 63–82; and "Philippine Independence and the Last Lame-Duck Congress," *12* (1964) 260–76. A fourth is still to appear, "Veto and Repassage of the Hare-Hawes-Cutting Act: A Catalogue of Motives."

In *The Commonwealth of the Philippines* (New York, Appleton-Century, 1936), George A. Malcolm undertook a Cook's tour of its problems and prospects. Both are very readably discussed by Florence Horn, a correspondent for *Time-Life-Fortune*, in *Orphans of the Pacific* (New York, Reynal and Hitchcock, 1941). In a series of articles in the *Journal of East Asiatic Studies, 3* (Oct 1953–Apr 1954), Charles O. Houston, Jr., undertook a close analysis of the defects in Commonwealth government policies, chiefly economic. Catherine Porter's *Crisis in the Philippines* (New York, Knopf, 1942) is a brief but excellent obituary of the Commonwealth; her bibliography is a fine aid in hunting down transient articles. John Gunther looked at the era through its most luminous figure in "Manuel Quezon," *Atlantic Monthly, 163* (Jan 1939), 59–70. J. Woodford Howard has just published "Frank Murphy and the Philippine Commonwealth," *Pacific Historical Review, 33* (1964), 45–68. More tendentious works on the period are two by Filipinos—Jose Lopez del Castillo, *Orientaciones Diplomaticas* (Manila, 1939), and Manuel Gallego, *The Price of Philippine Independence under the Tydings-McDuffie Act* (Manila, Barristers' Book Co. Inc., 1939); one by a Spaniard—Ramon Muniz Lavalle, *Filipinos y la Guerra del Pacifico* (Madrid, 1936); and one by an American—William H. Anderson, who employed Filipino ghost-writer James Wingo, *The Philippine Problem* (New York, G. P. Putnam's Sons, 1939).

At the time he wrote, the demographer-sociologist Bruno Lasker covered broadly and accurately the question of *Filipino Immigration to Continental United States and to Hawaii* (Chicago, University of Chicago Press, 1931). Shirley Jenkins, *American Economic Policy Toward the Philippines* (Stanford, Stanford University Press, 1955), deals mostly with the postwar era. Pedro E. Abelarde, *American Tariff Policy Toward the Philippines, 1898–1946* (New York, King's Crown Press, 1947), is a helpful, if uneven, survey. Lippert S. Ellis, *The Tariff on Sugar* (Freeport, Ill., The Rawleigh Foundation, 1933), and John E. Dalton, *Sugar, A Case Study of Government Control* (New York, Macmillan Co., 1937), treat the Philippines' main export in wider contexts. The latter is an exceptionally lucid and well-organized study, by the former chief of the Sugar Section, Agricultural Adjustment Administration.

E. D. Hester's article on the trade revisions of the Tydings-McDuffie Act is a fine summary: "Outline of Our Recent Political and Trade Relations with the Philippine Commonwealth," *Annals of the American Academy of Political and Social Science, 226* (1943), 78–83. Amado A. Castro has put the 30s and 40s in perspective with his skillful Ph.D. dissertation, "The Philippines: A Study in Economic Dependence," Harvard, 1954. Frank Golay has summarized his careful thought on "The Nature of Philippine Economic Nationalism," in *Asia, 1* (1964), 13–30.

Concerning economic development in the Philippines one may find abundant data in the chronicles of A. V. H. Hartendorp, beginning with his *Short History of Industry and Trade of the Philippines* (Manila, Philippine Education Co., 1953), and continuing further into the period of the Republic with subsequent volumes. The major themes of economic growth may be traced through Lyman P. Hammond, "Report on Economic Conditions of the Philippines" (Manila, Bureau of Printing, 1928); Abraham A. Greenberg, "Economic Aspects of the Philippine Question" (unpublished Ph.D. dissertation, Yale University, 1939); Thomas R. McHale, "An Econoecological Approach to Economic Development: The Philippines" (unpublished Ph.D. dissertation, Harvard University, 1960); Marvin E. Goodstein, "The Pace and Pattern of Philippine Economic Growth, 1938–1948 and 1956" (Cornell University, Southeast Asia Program, Data Paper No. 48, 1962).

Public policy concerning corporations is treated in Jose M. Apostol, *The Economic Policy of the Philippine Government: Ownership and Operation of Business* (Manila, University of the Philippines, 1927), and Juan D. Collas, Jr., "The Philippine Law of Corporate Combination" (unpublished Ph.D. dissertation, Yale University, 1959).

Agrarian unrest is treated in two books, two dissertations, an article, and an unpublished manuscript: Luis M. Taruc, *Born of the People* (New York, International Publishers, 1953); Alvin H. Scaff, *The Philippine Answer to Communism* (Stanford, Stanford University Press, 1955); Roy M. Stubbs, "Philippine Radicalism: The Central Luzon Uprisings, 1925–1935" (unpublished Ph.D. dissertation, University of California at Berkeley, 1951); Renze L. Hoeksema, "Communists in the Philippines: A Historical and Analytical Study of Communism and the Communist Party in the Philippines, and Its Relations to Communist Movements Abroad" (unpublished Ph.D. dissertation, Harvard University, 1956); David R. Sturdevant, "Sakdalism and Philippine Radicalism," *Journal of Asian Studies, 21* (1962) 199–213; Jose Lava, "Milestones in the History of the Communist Party of the Philippines." Taruc's book is an eloquent work of propaganda, partly written by William Pomeroy, an American who joined the Huk movement. Lava's manuscript, used in Communist indoctrination, is an interesting but tortuous version of twentieth century Philippine history. Scaff's book is a slim volume mostly concerned with the relocation and rehabilitation of Huks. The other three sources cited provide a broader and clearer picture of peasant radicalism.

There is a small but useful literature on Oriental minorities in the Philippines. Works by Japanese include Watanabe Kaoru, *Hirippin zairyū-hōjin shōgyō hattatsu shi* (History of Commercial Development by Japanese in the Philippines) (Tokyo, Nan'yō Kyōkai, 2nd ed. 1937); Kamabara Hiroji, *Dabao hōjin kaitaku shi* (History of the Japanese Colonization of Davao) (Davao, Nippi

Shimbunsha, 1938); and Shibata Ken'ichi, *Dabao kaitakuki* (The Colonization of Davao) (Tokyo, Kōa Nihonsha, 1942). Since these appeared, Furukawa Yoshizō has published *Dabao kaitakuki* (The Colonization of Davao) (Tokyo, 1956). *Japan and the Philippines, 1868–1898* (Quezon City, University of the Philippines, 1963) is a useful exploration of an elusive subject by Josefa Saniel.

The Chinese appear to have written little about their relations with, or their relatives in, the Philippines, but one competent survey is by Ch'ên Lieh-fu, *Fei-lü-pin yü Chung Fei Kuan hsi* (On Philippine–Chinese Relations) (Hong Kong, 1955).

American dissertations are beginning to penetrate the subject: on the late Spanish period, Edgar B. Wickberg, "The Chinese in Philippine Economy and Society" (Berkeley, 1961, to be published by Yale University Press); on the American period, Khin K. M. Jensen, "The Chinese in the Philippines during the American Regime: 1898–1946" (Wisconsin, 1956); and George H. Weightmann, "The Philippine Chinese: A Cultural History of a Marginal Trading Community" (Cornell, 1959).

To Japanese history the best introduction is *Japan, Past and Present* (3rd ed. New York, Knopf, 1964), a brief and well-balanced survey by Edwin O. Reischauer. Delmer Brown's *Nationalism in Japan: An Introductory Historical Analysis* (Berkeley, University of California Press, 1955) examines the subject from earliest times to the postwar phase. Motives and machinery in high policy are the subject of Takeuchi Tatsuji's still useful *War and Diplomacy in the Japanese Empire* (New York, Doubleday Doran, 1935). Hyman Kublin has percolated a great deal of scattered information into a well-brewed article on "The Evolution of Japanese Colonialism," *Comparative Studies in Society and History*, 2 (1959), 67–84.

Japan's former colonial laboratory, Taiwan, is the subject of a study by Andrew J. Grajdanzev, *Formosa Today: An Analysis of the Economic Development and Strategic Importance of Japan's Tropical Colony* (New York, IPR, 1942). Norton S. Ginsburg's *The Economic Resources and Development of Formosa* (New York, IPR, 1953) has an interesting section on economic development under the Japanese. George B. Barclay looks at the same question from a demographic and sociological point of view in *Colonial Development and Population in Taiwan* (Princeton, Princeton University Press, 1954).

Hilary Conroy shows how the modern expansionistic mood of Japan sprang from forces in Japanese society, in *The Japanese Seizure of Korea, 1868–1910: A Study of Realism in International Relations* (Philadelphia, University of Pennsylvania Press, 1960). A number of fresh studies have recently reexamined the rise of Japanese ultranationalism and militarism in the prewar decade and a half. They include: Robert J. C. Butow, *Tojo and the Coming of the War* (Princeton, Princeton University Press, 1961); David J. Lu, *From the Marco Polo Bridge to Pearl Harbor* (Washington, Public Affairs Press, 1961); Yoshihashi Takehiko, *Conspiracy at Mukden: The Rise of the Japanese Military* (New Haven, Yale University Press, 1963); James B. Crowley, "Japanese Army Factionalism in the Early 1930's," and "A Reconsideration of the Marco Polo Bridge Incident," *Journal of Asian Studies*, 21 (1962), 309–26; 22 (1963),

277–91. Iriye Akira, in "Japanese Imperialism and Aggression: Reconsiderations," ibid., *23* (1963), 103–13, summarizes with interpretive comment a seven-volume project by Japanese historians, *Taiheiyō Sensō e no michi* (The Road to the Pacific War) (Tokyo, Nihon Kokusai Seiji Gakkai [Japan Society of International Politics], 1962–64), which covers in detail Japanese foreign policies from the late 20s to Pearl Harbor. Several splendid analyses of Japanese ultranationalism appear in Maruyama Masao's *Thought and Behavior in Modern Japanese Politics*, Ivan Morris, ed. (New York and London, Oxford University Press, 1963).

Other useful works include F. C. Jones, *Japan's New Order in East Asia: Its Rise and Fall, 1937–1945* (New York and London, Oxford University Press, 1954); Yale C. Maxon, *Control of Japanese Foreign Policy: A Study of Civil-Military Rivalry, 1930–1945* (Berkeley, University of California Press, 1957); Richard Storry, *The Double Patriots: A Study of Japanese Nationalism* (Boston, Houghton Mifflin, 1957).

A short unanalytical chronicle of the subject is Eufronio Alip's *Philippine-Japanese Relations, Historical, Political, Social, Economic* (Manila, Alip and Sons, 1959). The most articulate prewar presentation of pro-Japanese views came from Pio Duran, whose *Philippine Independence and the Far Eastern Question* (Manila, Community Publishers, 1935) still makes fascinating reading. Don Claro Recto's cogent warnings about Japanese expansion are reprinted in his *Asiatic Monroeism and Other Essays* (Manila, General Printing Press, 1930).

Diplomatic and strategic problems between the United States and Japan from 1929–33 are treated in Robert H. Ferrell, *American Diplomacy in the Great Depression* (New Haven, Yale University Press, 1957), for the years 1929–33; Dorothy Borg, *The United States and the Far Eastern Crisis of 1933–1938* (Cambridge, Harvard University Press, 1964), for the title years; and Herbert Feis, *The Road to Pearl Harbor* (Princeton, Princeton University Press, 1950), for the years 1937–41.

American prewar planning is the subject of two excellent articles: Fred Greene, "The Military View of American National Policy, 1904–1940," *American Historical Review, 66* (1961), 354–77, and Louis Morton, "War Plan ORANGE: Evolution of a Strategy," *World Politics, 11* (1959), 221–50. Morton has covered the Pacific theater in general with *Strategy and Command: The First Two Years* (Washington, Department of the Army, 1962). Samuel Eliot Morison's *The Rising Sun in the Pacific, 1931–April 1942* (Boston, Little Brown, 1948) contains a splendid summary going back to the 1920s; it concentrates thereafter on the initial months of the war. Gerald E. Wheeler has written on the *Prelude to Pearl Harbor: The United States Navy and the Far East, 1921–1931* (Columbia, University of Missouri Press, 1963). Wheeler is proceeding now to a study of the Commonwealth period in the Philippines. Roberta Wohlstetter, *Pearl Harbor: Warning and Decision* (Stanford, Stanford University Press, 1962), combines analysis of diplomacy, military policy, and strategic intelligence.

The period from the invasion to the surrender of Bataan and Corregidor is brilliantly covered by Louis Morton in *The Fall of the Philippines;* companion volumes are M. Hamlin Cannon's *Leyte: The Return to the Philippines* and Robert Ross Smith's *Triumph in the Philippines.* All three belong to the series *United States Army in World War II: The War in the Pacific* (Washington, Department of the Army, 1953, 1954, 1963). John Toland's *But Not in Shame: The Six Months after Pearl Harbor* (New York, Random House, 1961) amplifies Morton's account with journalistic detail.

Henry L. Stimson and McGeorge Bundy, *On Active Service in Peace and War* (New York, Harper & Bros., 1947), provides a view from Washington of early wartime strategy. Members of MacArthur's staff saw the strategy very differently: Charles A. Willoughby and John Chamberlain, *MacArthur, 1941–1951* (New York, McGraw-Hill, 1954), and Courtney Whitney, *MacArthur, His Rendezvous with History* (New York, Knopf, 1956).

Frederic S. Marquardt's *Before Bataan and After* (Indianapolis, Bobbs-Merrill, 1943) is an excellent personalized narrative by a former Manila journalist. Three autobiographies touch conditions on Corregidor and political considerations there: Manuel Quezon, *The Good Fight* (New York, Appleton-Century, 1946); Francis Sayre, *Glad Adventure* (New York, Macmillan, 1957); and Carlos Romulo, *I Walked with Heroes* (New York, Holt, Rinehart, and Winston, 1961). Sayre is too cautious to be informative, and Romulo too inventive to be always entirely credible. Quezon's book, although composed during wartime, is generally frank and concrete.

Scholars are beginning to assess the impact of Japan before and during wartime occupation. Grant Goodman has done careful work in "Davaokuo? Japan in Philippine Politics, 1931–1941" (paper read at the Annual Midwest Conference on Asian Affairs, St. Louis, 1962). He has also attempted to prove that "The Japanese Occupation of the Philippines Was a Success" (paper read before the Association for Asian Studies, Philadelphia, 1963). Elmer Lear has studied in detail "The Japanese Occupation of the Philippines, Leyte, 1941–1945" (Cornell Southeast Asia Program, Data Paper No. 42, 1961). David J. Steinberg has just completed a dissertation on "The Japanese Occupation and Philippine Nationalism," Harvard, 1964. Donn V. Hart's article "Filipino Resistance on Negros, 1942–1945," *Journal of Southeast Asian History,* 5 (1964), 101–25, contains useful bibliographic footnotes for the whole period of the war. Teodoro Agoncillo is preparing a history of the occupation that should prove informative and provocative.

Two eloquent apologia by prominent Filipino leaders are *Three Years of Enemy Occupation* (Manila, Peoples Publishers, 1946), by Claro M. Recto, and *War Memoirs of Dr. Jose P. Laurel,* Jose Lansang, ed. (Manila, Laurel Foundation, 1962).

Biographies and Autobiographies

AMERICAN. Hoover's cabinet is served by only one outstanding biography: Elting E. Morison, *Turmoil and Tradition: A Study of the Life and Times of Henry L. Stimson* (Boston, Houghton Mifflin, 1960). Herbert Hoover's *Memoirs*

(3 vols. New York, Macmillan, 1951) are marred by faulty memory. Two biographies of Patrick Hurley have appeared thus far, both of them eulogistic.

Douglas MacArthur awaits a biographer of talent and breadth of view. In the meantime there are insights upon his character in John Gunther, *The Riddle of MacArthur: Japan, Korea, and the Far East* (New York, Harper & Bros., 1950), and useful clues concerning his Philippine service in Frazier Hunt, *The Untold Story of Douglas MacArthur* (New York, Deven-Adair, 1954). MacArthur's own *Reminiscences* (New York, McGraw-Hill, 1964) are fascinating and stirring, although frequently erroneous in detail and magniloquent in tone.

Joseph Grew's *Ten Years in Japan* (New York, Simon and Schuster, 1944) contains the diary entries of a perspicacious ambassador during the decade leading to Pearl Harbor. *The Secret Diaries of Harold L. Ickes* (3 vols. New York, Simon and Schuster, 1953–54) presently covering through 1939, contain some Philippine material, as does Harry Truman's first volume of memoirs, *Year of Decisions* (Garden City, Doubleday, 1955).

PHILIPPINE. Biographical information leading Filipinos is scattered but not impossible to obtain. The inauguration of the Commonwealth produced a spate of sources. Among them are Zoilo M. Galang, ed., *Encyclopedia of the Philippines* (10 vols. Manila, Philippine Education Co., 1936; 3d ed. Manila, E. Floro, 1950–58), of which Vol. 9 treats "Builders of the New Philippines"; Franz J. Weissblatt, ed., *Who's Who in the Philippines* (Manila, McCullough Printing Co., 1937); and an unpublished volume compiled by the Bureau of Insular Affairs, "Who's Who in the Philippines" (BIA 4666–7, 1937—), which refers to published sources and adds fresh information. Since the war, other reference aids have appeared, notably E. Arsenio Manuel, ed., *Dictionary of Philippine Biography* (Quezon City, Filipiniana Publications, 1955), and Isidro L. Retizos and D. H. Soriano, *Philippines Who's Who* (Quezon City, Capital Publishing, 1957).

Biography is an underdeveloped art in the Philippines; autobiography still less developed. Quezon's life, which was all passion and commitment, has received only glancing treatment from Isabelo P. Caballero and M. de Gracia Concepcion, *Quezon* (Manila, International Publishers, 1935), and Sol H. Gwekoh, *Manuel L. Quezon* (Manila, University Publishing Co., 1944). Carlos Quirino, *Quezon, Man of Destiny* (Manila, McCullough, 1935) is much better but still casual. Enozawa Tsune's *Keson den* (The Life of Quezon) (Tokyo, Japan Publishing, 1939) was conceived both by author and subject as an exercise in improving Japanese-Philippine relations. Manuel Roxas' friend and former law partner, Marcial Lichauco, has assembled memories and stenographic notes of after-dinner conversations in *Roxas* (Manila, 1952). Sergio Osmeña does not yet have a biographer.

A Second Look at America (New York, Speller, 1958) purports to be the autobiography of Emilio Aguinaldo, assisted in the writing by Vicente Albano Pacis; the phraseology, however, is almost entirely Pacis', and many of the thoughts are his and not Aguinaldo's. *Religious Revolution in the Philippines* by Pedro S. de Achutegui, S.J., and Miguel A. Bernard, S.J., concerns the life of Gregorio Aglipay (1860–1940) and the church he founded; it is objective so far as Jesuits can be about an unrepentant heretic and schismatic. Rafael Palma wrote briefly and factually of his career in *My Autobiography,* Alicia Palma Bautista, trans. (Manila, Capital Publishing, 1953).

Of the younger leaders of the Quezon era, only Romulo, a brilliant, cherubic egotist, has put his full life on paper. Jose Laurel's memoirs are only fragmentary. (For both, see under Special Works, Assorted Monographs.)

NEWSPAPERS AND PERIODICALS

Newspapers were an indispensable source for this study, even though American reporting was often erroneous and Philippine reporting was highly emotional on colonial problems. The Bureau of Insular Affairs kept clippings on various Philippine topics from the major New York papers, the Washington *Post,* the Baltimore *Sun,* and other papers as far afield as the Yakima (Wash.) *Herald.* The files of the State Department also contain a number of clippings and translations from the world press especially valuable for Japanese and other foreign reactions to American policy in the Philippines and East Asia. On the issue of independence itself, Ten Eyck Associates ran two large surveys of American editorial opinion in 1932 and 1933. Where none of these conveniences have sufficed, I have done my own spot research in American newspapers.

Philippine newspapers are an unusually sensitive and colorful source for political news, with a freedom of expression exceeding that of most Asian papers. *A History of Journalism in the Philippine Islands,* by Jesus Z. Valenzuela (Manila, 1933), sketches a story of rises and falls, amalgamations and bankruptcies.

During the 1930s the two major newspaper chains in Manila were known as the T-V-T (*Tribune-Vanguardia-Taliba*) and the D-M-H-M (*Debate-Mabuhay-Herald-Monday Mail*). The first, owned by Alejandro Roces, supported Osmeña during the anti-pro crisis. The afternoon editions, *La Vanguardia* (Spanish) and *Taliba* (Tagalog), translated and used the morning articles of the English-language *Tribune,* with check-ups and follow-ups. Henry Stimson once complained about the differing editorial tone of the three: most sympathetic to the United States in English, most nationalistic in Tagalog, and midway between in Spanish.

The competing chain also had three editions, *El Debate, Mabuhay,* and the *Herald.* Its ownership changed frequently, but always consisted of Quezon supporters. After Carlos Romulo became editor, he occasionally inflamed Quezon by criticizing some of his vagaries. The other leading Manila papers were the *Daily Bulletin,* which spoke in the interests of the American community, and *La Opinion.*

Several weeklies and monthlies are valuable for historical research. For the 1930s, the *Philippine Magazine,* a politico-literary monthly under the discriminating editorship of A. V. H. Hartendorp, and the *Commonwealth Advocate,* which was under Filipino editorship, contain a number of provocative articles.

The weekly Philippines *Free Press* enables one to sift out the daily chaff and also provides an independent editorial opinion with no axe to grind except "good government." The American Chamber of Commerce *Journal* is packed with useful financial and economic data. Its articles plead for continuation of American sovereignty or special trade relations.

PUBLISHED OFFICIAL SOURCES

Official American Sources

The Congressional Record was a major legislative source for this study, as were hearings and reports of various House and Senate committees and various documents of both houses.

In the executive branch, I have consulted the Annual Reports of the Secretary of War, 1929–35, in which are contained the Annual Reports of the Chief of Staff, United States Army; of the Chief, Bureau of Insular Affairs; and of the Governor General, Philippine Islands. The successors to the latter office issued Annual Reports of the High Commissioner to the Philippine Commonwealth, from 1936 to 1942, and in 1946.

The Reports of the United States Tariff Commission, Second Series, Nos. 18 (1931) and 118 (1937), are especially valuable analyses of economic relations with the Philippines. *The Report of May 20, 1938,* of the Joint Preparatory Committee on Philippine Affairs, contains four volumes of briefs, expositions, exhibitions, colloquies, and recommendations, revealing the state of economic development and dependence in the islands.

International problems posed by the Philippines appear in the printed series of the Department of State, *Foreign Relations of the United States,* with increasing frequency toward the latter part of the period 1929–42. They appear intensively in the special two-volume supplement, *Japan, 1931–1941* (Washington, 1943).

Concerning Japanese expansion, foreign policy, and war plans, I have used printed sources familiar to anyone working on the origins and outbreak of the war in the Pacific. Previously, however, no one has chosen to read these materials with the interests of a minor power as firmly in mind as those of the two major ones. The International Military Tribunal for the Far East, *Tokyo War Crimes Trials,* contains in its transcript of proceedings, exhibits, and judgments, occasional illumination of events in the Philippines. The leading guides to this mass of material are listed in the "Bibliographical Essay" of Robert Ferrell's *American Diplomacy in the Great Depression.*

Further information is available in the two volumes of *Interrogations of Japanese Officials* conducted by the United States Strategic Bombing Survey, selected and published by Rear Admiral R. A. Oftsie. Also illuminating, despite frequent vagueness and occasional inaccuracy, are several of the research monographs prepared by the Office of the Chief of Military History, Department of the Army, and listed in their "Guide to Japanese Monographs and Japanese Studies on Manchuria, 1945–60." Those which deal significantly with the Philippines are Nos. 147, 150, 152 (political strategy before the outbreak of war), 1, 2, and 11 (planning, preparing, carrying out the invasion), and 103 (policies concerning the government under occupation).

Official Philippine Sources

The official publications of the Philippines, published by the Bureau of Printing in Manila, like nearly everything else, were dominated by Quezon. Under the title *Messages of the President* (1935–41) were published both executive orders and proclamations, as well as acts of the Legislature. *The Annual Report of the President of the Philippine Commonwealth* appeared both as a Philippine and an American publication until Quezon went into exile, when it became American only. Annual reports from members of the Commonwealth cabinet were generally innocuous, but two official documents are especially important: *Report on National Defense in the Philippines,* by Maj. Gen. Douglas MacArthur, Military Advisor to the President of the Philippines (1936), and *Report of the Special Mission to the United States, 1938–1939* (1939). The Bureau of Printing also published occasional addresses by Filipino leaders that were intended as indicators of new or revised national policy.

The *Diario de Sesiones de la Legislatura Filipina* was the colonial equivalent of the Congressional Record. Members conducted debate, if possible, in the preferred tongue of the man holding the floor, and as a result about half the proceedings are in Spanish, half in English. There are frequent unannotated ellipses in the published versions, which I have filled in with newspaper accounts by Filipino journalists.

The *Proceedings of the First Independence Congress* (Manila, 1930) consists chiefly of exhortations to the first OsRox mission. *The Philippine Charter of Liberty* (Baltimore, French-Bray, 1933), by Camilo Osias and Mauro Baraudi, is a collection of documents concerning the second OsRox mission and its achievements. For information on population, immigration, literacy, and other topics, the *Census of the Philippines* for 1918 and 1939 provides significant data, generally more accurate in the latter year.

Official Japanese Sources

Irikura's bibliography contains valuable notes on a number of official or quasi-official Japanese publications on the Philippines. The following comments bear on those few which he omits or reports incompletely. The *Official Journal of the Japanese Military Administration,* ed. Bureau of Publicity, Department of General Affairs (13 vols. Manila, Manila *Nichi Nichi Shimbunsha,* Inc., 1942–43) consists almost entirely of proclamations, addresses, letters, etc., and is thus more a published source than a periodical. The Japanese Military Administration also published, far less frequently, an *Official Gazette,* containing budgetary and other administrative data.

In 1943, the Hon. Murata Shōzō, chief civilian advisor to the occupation government, brought to Manila a team of scholars to prepare a report for the guidance of the JMA. This, the Research Commission on the Philippines under the chairmanship of Dr. Rōyama Masamichi, ultimately produced a report in four volumes: "Peoples," vol. 1, was by Rōyama; "Politics and Administration," vol. 2, by Rōyama and Takeuchi Tatsuji; "Religion and Education," vol. 3, by Ōshima Masanori; "Economics," vol. 4, by Tobata Sei'ichi, Itō Choiji, and Sujimura Hirozō.

Murata and Rōyama intended the report to be a Japanese equivalent of the Taft Commission reports, although its recommendations, highly influenced by Japanese experience in Formosa, of course differed greatly. The report had little impact on the Japanese Army, which was preoccupied with military exigencies, and it was ignored by the Filipino leaders, who were permitted a "republic" by the time the report was complete. The authors, who expected official neglect, wrote for a scholarly audience, and the report as a result has considerable academic value.

MANUSCRIPT SOURCES

Official American Manuscripts

The National Archives contain a mass of materials bearing upon every aspect of Philippine policy. I have gone through the Army Section (files of the Adjutant General's Office), Navy Section (combined files of Secretary of the Navy and Chief of Naval Operations), Foreign Affairs Section (Department of State open files), and Legislative Section (Senate Finance Committee and Committee on Territories and Insular Affairs). The last of these was most rewarding, as it contained some of Senator Millard Tydings' correspondence concerning Philippine legislation.

By far the richest Philippine records in the Archives are those of the Bureau of Insular Affairs. To these files there are two introductory guides: Richard S. Maxwell, *Records of the Bureau of Insular Affairs* (Washington, The National Archives, Preliminary Inventories, No. 130, 1960), and Kenneth Munden, *Records of the Bureau of Insular Affairs Relating to the Philippine Islands, 1898–1935: A List of Selected Files* (Washington, The National Archives, Oct 1942). As a policy-making office, the BIA in the 20s and 30s was an old lady plagiarizing the needlework of William Howard Taft. But as a collector, recorder, and cataloguer, the office did invaluable work, to which the Maxwell and Munden guides serve as an abstract index for researchers.

The functions of the BIA were transferred to the Interior Department, Division of Territories and Island Possessions, in 1939, but the key files for the commonwealth period are the High Commissioner's. The relevant guides are Richard Maxwell, *Records of the Office of the U.S. High Commissioner to the Philippine Islands*, and Maxwell, with Evans Walker, *Records of the Office of Territories* (Washington, The National Archives, Preliminary Inventories, Nos. 151 and 154, 1963).

Colonial policy as such always impinged on, and was sometimes defined by, a complex of policies arrived at by the Departments of State, War, and Navy.

State Department material, not published in the *Foreign Relations* series at the time of my investigations, was accessible for the period 1929–42, subject to the review of notes.

War Department records for the crucial periods of the prewar build-up and the invasion of the Philippines are in the World War II Division of the National Archives and Records Service, Alexandria, Va. Morton has splendidly assembled and analyzed this material in *The Fall of the Philippines,* but in order to highlight certain themes, I re-examined large segments of it. Personal clearance was necessary, followed by review of some notes and pertinent portions of the ensuing manuscript, before publication.

At the Naval Department Service Center, in Arlington, Va., I examined records parallel to the Army records. Materials from the General Board and War Plans Division were accessible only through 1935, but the crisis of 1941–42 is amply discussed in the narratives of the Commander in Chief, Asiatic Fleet, Admiral Thomas C. Hart. His original narrative (1942) together with the supplementary narrative of 1946 supplies a candid, critical, and detailed account of naval action. Much of it has gone into Morison's *Rising Sun,* but none has previously been assessed along with a variety of non-naval materials concerning the Philippines.

Personal American Manuscripts

At the high policy level, the most stimulating materials in any American collection are those of Henry L. Stimson, in the Sterling Memorial Library, Yale University. Stimson served as Governor General of the Philippines (1928–29), Secretary of State (1929–33), and twice as Secretary of War (1911–13, 1940–45). During his career he amassed over 5,000 items on the Philippines, including considerable correspondence, official documents of the war period, and an ample and tough-minded diary.

The papers of Joseph Ralston Hayden, in the Michigan Historical Collections, University of Michigan, contain documents and correspondence of a far less privileged nature pertaining to the career of a vice-governor general (1933–35). Hayden was nevertheless the most accomplished scholar of his day on Philippine national development, and the voluminous raw materials he collected toward his book still survive. At the time of my inquiry they were not entirely sorted or at all catalogued, but were nonetheless usable.

The third major manuscript collection for Philippine affairs is that of the Franklin D. Roosevelt Memorial Library at Hyde Park. Roosevelt himself had no special interest in, and was often confused about, the Philippines, but all the leading personalities concerned with the islands and all the major disputes involving them have left their mark in files of the Chief Executive and in ancillary collections.

The collections of Theodore Roosevelt, Jr., Philippine Governor General in 1932–33, and of General Frank R. McCoy are both in the Library of Congress. Roosevelt went to the Philippines from the governor-generalship of Puerto Rico, the only American ever to hold both posts, and his considerable knowledge of colonial affairs is reflected in his manuscripts as well as in his *Colonial Policies of the United States* (Garden City, Doubleday, Doran, 1937). McCoy served as a member of the Wood-Forbes mission in 1921–22, later as an aide to Wood, and occasionally as a consultant on Philippine policy between 1929 and 1932. His many scattered Philippine documents amount as a whole to a blueprint for a dominion plan.

Three other men, each once in the center of Philippine affairs but all of secondary importance for the 1930s, have willed their papers to the Library of Congress. They are Elihu Root, Francis Burton Harrison, and W. Cameron Forbes. Forbes kept a highly literate and informative journal all his life, in which Philippine matters were his foremost concern.

Two collections that would have been most revealing on Philippine affairs have been substantially destroyed. Except for selected Philippine materials (see above, The National Archives, Legislative Section) Senator Millard Tydings, when he retired from the Senate in 1950, burned 128 boxes of records in his backyard. And Senator Harry Hawes, who wanted so much to be remembered in history, made a full assessment difficult by obliterating his files. Only scattered Hawes items on local politics survive, in the Western Historical Manuscripts Collection, at the University of Missouri.

The papers of Frank Murphy, Governor General from 1933 to 1935, were inaccessible in 1962 because of legal complications, but should eventually be opened by the Michigan Historical Collections, University of Michigan. An auxiliary and accessible body of material, the Norman Hill Collection, contains eleven volumes of clippings on Murphy's years as Governor General.

A. V. H. Hartendorp permitted me to make a microfilm copy of his typescript "History of the Japanese Occupation and of the Santo Tomas Internment Camp," which he secretly compiled and composed in Santo Tomas at risk of his life. Some of the material has appeared in his own *History of Industry and Trade in the Philippines,* and more, on camp life, edited by Frank Golay, will be published by McGraw-Hill. Even then, much of the 1,200 pages of data and narrative will remain unpublished.

Official Philippine Manuscripts

Public archives in the Philippines, such as they are, remain for the most part unorganized. Since my research trip in 1957–58, however, the erection of The National Library and the celebration of the Rizal Centennial have given focus and impetus to the preservation and collection of historical records. There are, in any case, rich resources available to the patient researcher.

Many valuable public records of the American period were casualties of war. The Legislative Building burned with all that it contained. The executive offices in Malacañan held the leading records of the Governor Generals and of the Commonwealth. After Quezon left for Corregidor in December 1941, the records were in Vargas' charge. On a Sunday when the Japanese were reported just outside Manila, Vargas went to the office, and finding no assistants there to help him select sensitive papers, ordered the janitors to burn everything. When the staff arrived Monday morning there was not a scrap of paper in sight or in hiding.* Fortunately, some of the destroyed material was reflected in BIA files, or those of its successor offices.

Personal Philippine Manuscripts

Private collections are scattered and unpublicized. By far the richest source for the American period is the collection of Manuel Quezon, willed to the public early in 1942 while escaping the Japanese via Mindanao. After the war the documents of exile, which Osmeña had screened following Quezon's death, were added to the main corpus, making it a full and fascinating record of Philippine public affairs for the whole period 1907–44. When I examined it in 1957–58, in the Bureau of Public Libraries, it consisted of 36 four-drawer filing cabinets and 6 seven-foot bookcases that contained cables, memos, transcripts of press conferences, press clippings, public documents, and letters and speeches in various stages of draft. About 40 per cent of the material was in Spanish, a small amount in Tagalog and other indigenous languages, and the rest in English. These treasures, however, were in furious disorder. The only catalogue extant was a seven-volume one for Quezon's years as Resident Commissioner, 1907–16. The papers to which the catalogue refers were well ordered at the time of compilation in 1939–40, as were the uncatalogued papers, but the collection subsequently suffered two floods (1943 and 1947, when the river Pasig invaded the basement of Malacañan) and two transshipments (to the new Legislative Building, 1950, and to the Bureau of Public Libraries, 1955).

Many papers have been destroyed or lost in transfer. Many of those which survive were blackened, compressed in lumps, partially eaten by white ants, or were simply degenerating as poor paper will in tropical conditions. Some, as a curator wrote, "have penetrating and a suffocating odor which pierces the nose."

Enough remains intact to supply excellent evidence of the involvement of a first-rate mind with his country's destiny. Quezon planning, Quezon plotting; Quezon fiery, Quezon icy; Quezon composing an address in seven drafts; Quezon jotting down ideas fresh and loose on a finished typescript. All the public Quezons and many of the private ones lurk in this collection, which is now well housed and well arranged in the new National Library.

Although the Quezon collection survived flood, other valuable collections did not survive the fires of 1944–45. The battle of liberation destroyed many of Sergio Osmeña's papers in his Manila residence, the pre-1937 papers of Manuel Roxas, the collections of Rafael Alunan, the Kalaw brothers, and numerous others. Some important Osmeña papers survive, including valuable documents of his brief presidency (Aug 1944–May 1946) as part of the Quezoniana collection. Eduardo de la Rosa, his private secretary for many years, kept copies of some important business correspondence, and there are excellent exchanges over the Jones Law and Hare-Hawes-Cutting Act.

Manuel Roxas, like Quezon, willed his papers to the people. From the time

* Author's interview with E. D. Hester, 17 Jan 58; with Constantino Tirona, 29 Jan 58.

he entered the cabinet in 1937 through his death in office as President in 1948, they are largely intact.

Jose P. Laurel raised up a vast collection on the Constitutional Convention (17 volumes of proceedings, 2 of ancillary materials, 10 of interpretive comment by himself, and still other volumes), plus numerous files concerning his legislative and executive roles at various times. These, which I consulted in his office and home, have largely been transferred, since Dr. Laurel's death, to a Laurel Memorial Museum at the Lyceum of the Philippines.

Among other valuable collections, perhaps the largest is that of Jorge Vargas, secretary to Quezon and the "little president" of the Commonwealth, later Chairman of the Executive Commission sponsored by the Japanese, and finally Ambassador to Japan, 1943–45. Vargas amassed enormous quantities of newspaper clippings and preserved some leading documents.

Two scholar-bibliophiles, Arsenio Manuel and Mauro Garcia, have collected various fugitive materials. Professor Manuel's trove consists mostly of pamphlets and published matter; Mr. Garcia's contains some valuable and elusive documents.

Doña Maria Kalaw Katigbak, now Senator Katigbak, kindly lent me the manuscript autobiography of her father, Teodoro M. Kalaw, which covers the late Spanish period through the independence acts. Of the three versions of the manuscript, I quote from Senator Katigbak's own translation from the Spanish, in condensed and corrected copy. Another English version contains many more documents, quoted at greater length.

Official Japanese Manuscripts

Many of the Japanese diplomatic documents captured in Tokyo by American forces in 1945 deal with Philippine affairs. Certain of these can be identified and obtained through the use of Cecil H. Uyehara's *Checklist of Archives in the Japanese Ministry of Foreign Affairs, Tokyo, Japan, 1868–1945, Microfilmed for the Library of Congress, 1949–1951* (Washington, Library of Congress, Photoduplication Service, 1954). The most useful reels are those on Davao, the prewar anti-Japanese movement, and Japanese policy during the occupation. Most of the documents originate in the Philippines, very few in Tokyo. They are an excellent source for local policy-making, but the connection to imperial policy is not always clear.

Through another guide one may approach Japanese military documents for the same period: John Young, *Checklist of Microfilm Reproductions of Selected Archives of the Japanese Army, Navy, and Other Government Agencies, 1868–1945* (Washington, Georgetown University Press, 1959). These microfilms are disappointing on the prewar period, but contain useful Philippine materials for wartime itself.

Personal Japanese Manuscripts

Professor Takeuchi Tatsuji, of the School of Law, Kwansei Gakuin University, Nishinomiya, very kindly had prepared for me a copy of his own unpublished English translation of Vol. 2 of the Japanese Research Commission Report (see above, Published Official Japanese Sources), entitled "Politics and Administration: History and Analysis." This work, 234 pages in typescript, is the joint work of Professors Takeuchi and Rōyama Masamichi. Although based chiefly on prewar publications of Filipino and American scholars, the whole has been filtered through very different minds, reorganized, and freshly analyzed. The result is a distinguished and interesting contribution to the study of the Philippines.

INTERVIEWS AND CORRESPONDENCE

Each of the persons listed below has assisted my work, through formal interview, informal conversation, or correspondence. All were involved in the events of the period as actors or prominent observers, or as relatives or critics of the actors. They are in no wise responsible for any flaws in what I have done. Their opinions in most cases differ from my own and in some cases are sharply contrary to mine. But without them, and a great many not listed here, I could not have written this book, and I am profoundly grateful for the help of all.

Filipinos

Hernando Abaya
Gen. Emilio Aguinaldo
Antonio Aquino
Hon. Jorge Bocobo
Don Felipe Buencamino, Jr.
Vicente Bunuan
Amb. J. M. Elizalde
Don Alfonso Ponce-Enrile
Modesto Farolan
Col. Richard Galang
Jose Lansang
Dr. Jose P. Laurel
Amb. Marcial P. Lichauco
Don Sergio Osmeña, Sr.
Sen. Quintin Paredes
Don Manuel Quezon, Jr.
Carlos Quirino
Amb. Narciso Ramos
Sen. Claro M. Recto
Rep. Gerardo Roxas
Luis Taruc
Gen. Basilio Valdez
Hon. Jorge Vargas
James Wingo

Americans

Prof. H. Otley Beyer
A. V. H. Hartendorp
Evett D. Hester
Hon. Herbert C. Hoover
Roy W. Howard
Gen. Patrick J. Hurley
Gov. Luis Muñoz-Marín
M. J. Ossorio
Gen. Matthew Ridgway
Hon. Francis B. Sayre
Earl B. Schwulst
Sen. Millard W. Tydings

Japanese

Fukushima Shintarō
Hamamoto Masakatsu
Gen. Hayashi Yoshihide
Kihara Jitarō
Nakamura Kōji
Adm. Nomura Kichisaburō
Col. Ōta Kaneshirō
Dr. Rōyama Masamichi
Dr. Takeuchi Tatsuji
Col. Utsunomiya Naonori
Gen. Wachi Takagi

Index

Abaca, 231

Aga Khan, 183

Agaw-buhay, 262, 266

Aglipay, Gregorio, 46, 119–20, 153, 172

Aglipayan Church. *See* Philippine Independent Church

Agriculture, Department of (United States), 142

Aguinaldo, Emilio: criticizes Quezon policy, 60, 166; forms coalition, 89; against H-H-C Act, 119–20, 120 n.; agrees to new bill, 141; desires presidency (1935), 153, (1943), 234; anti-Franco, 172; for immediate independence, 191; Quezon adopts policy of, 193; appeals for surrender, 218; mentioned, 15, 39, 43–44, 46

Air Force, Japanese, 207. *See also* Army, Japanese

Air Force, United States. *See* Army, United States

Alas, de las, Antonio, 225, 226

Albania, 192

Alejandrino, Jose, 46

Alunan, Rafael, 117 n., 118 n., 137, 214, 225 ff.

Alvero, Aurelio, 182

Amau Eiji, 174

American Chamber of Commerce of the Philippines, 159

American Coalition, 84

American Farm Bureau Federation, 82, 105

American Federation of Labor, 84, 87, 104

American Legion, 84

American minority in the Philippines, 6–7, 18; postwar business privileges, 259,

259 n., 268–69. *See also* Manila Americans

Americanization of Philippine government and education, 2 and passim

Amor propio, 27

Ang Bagong Katipunan. *See* Katipunan, Ang Bagong

Anti-imperialism: in United States, 5, 69, 81, 106–07, 108; effect on United States policy, 1, 157

Anti-pro fight, 114 ff.

Antis, in constitutional convention, 152

Aquino, Antonio, 218 n.

Aquino, Benigno, 102–03, 114, 153, 192, 213–14, 215, 218 n., 225 ff., 234–35, 242

Aoki, Japanese Minister for Greater East Asia, 242

Arcadia Conference, 208–09

Arellano, Cayetano, 43

Army, Japanese: expansionism of, 75–76, 174–76; invasion plans, 202–04; and collaborators, 214–15, 244; in retreat, 246–47; and Laurel government, 249, 249 n.; last stand, Intramuros, 261. *See also* Japan, expansion of; Japanese Military Administration; Kwantung Army

Army, Philippine: as reserve, 89, 194; planned, 163–68, passim; cutback, 193–94; absorbed in USAFFE, 200; postwar, 270; mentioned, 183. *See also* Army, United States; United States Armed Forces Far East

Army, United States: racial discrimination in, 36–37; assesses Philippines (1931), 77; Philippine Department, 99;

DATE DUE